THE WAR DIARY
OF A
DESPATCH RIDER'S WIFE

Harold and Vera Heard
1939 to 1945

WILL HEARD

THE CHOIR PRESS

First published in the United Kingdom in 2017 by
The Choir Press

ISBN 978-1-911589-23-5

'The war over, fainted at night drinking, bored.'
Vera Heard, May 8th 1945

Vera, aged 20

Contents

Preface

Icame to write this book out of a deep sense of sadness that I had seen my parents pass away without asking them about the greatest adventure of their lives. Maybe they did not see it that way, but the more that I read about living conditions in the war, about the monumental disaster known as 'Dunkirk' and the supreme struggle for freedom we know as 'D-Day', the more I appreciated that I had failed them and myself. After all, had it not been for the need to support a wife and young family in the disastrous economic conditions of the early 1970s, I would have completed my Economic History postgraduate thesis and become an academic immersed in historical research for the rest of my life. Yet my own parents' history just passed me by.

Nevertheless, they must shoulder some of the blame. Neither of them spoke much about their lives in the war years, even though my father must have gone through many harrowing experiences and, as I now know, my mother had a story to tell which was best kept from her husband.

Perhaps I should not have meddled with the past, but, in her early eighties, my mother gave me some diaries that I had never seen before. They covered the war years and clearly formed an intimate record of her life at that time. They did not chronicle war events but the minutiae of a life lived by a war bride in her early twenties. They were kept for nobody but herself, yet she gave them to me at the end of her life. Why? I cannot answer that, but it is a valid question. I think that the answer is in the diaries themselves and time may yet tell on that one.

Possession of the diaries gave me the impetus that was lacking in earlier years. Here before me was my mother's life in those five crucial years of war. I already had some photographs of my father in Royal Signals uniform. Surely, it was going to be an easy task to chronicle his life at the same time and to contrast their respective experiences. Here was my chance to make amends for two lives once lived that were no more.

The task was not easy. Harold, my father, did not pilot a Spitfire or drive a Churchill tank. He rode a 500cc BSA motorbike and a Willys jeep. He was one four-millionth of the greatest army that ever bore arms. He was a simple squaddie whose life was always a millionth of an inch away from a bullet or a shard of shrapnel, but he was not even a footnote to a footnote in a war history, so it proved impossible to glean much information about his life in the British army. Moreover, he was attached to I (British) Corps from D-Day onwards, a military force without a first-hand written history of any consequence, which meant that I have had to rely on the work of many military historians for my military source material. I am truly grateful to them all.

With thanks to my parents for life, and to my wife, Sandra, for everything else.

CHAPTER ONE

Early Married Life

Vera Alice Blacknell and Harold Arthur Heard were married at Attenborough Church in Nottinghamshire, near Chilwell, on December 16th 1939. Vera was twenty-one years old and Harold was twenty-two.

The couple had to apply for a special marriage licence from the diocesan bishop. The date on the letter accompanying the licence was December 8th 1939.

The marriage had to take place without the normal formalities such as the reading of the banns because Harold had volunteered for duty as a despatch rider in the Royal Corps of Signals.

SOUTHWELL DIOCESAN REGISTRY.

REGISTRAR & BISHOP'S SECRETARY.
W. NOËL PARR.

TELEPHONE 3565-6.

FRIARY CHAMBERS.
FRIAR LANE.
NOTTINGHAM.

8th December 1939

Dear Madam,

By desire of the Rev. G. Hansford, I herewith enclose a Licence for your marriage in Attenborough Church.

Yours faithfully,

W. Noël Parr

Miss V. A. Blacknell,
38 Chetwynd Road,
Chilwell, Notts.

The licence to get married

ii Advertisements   MOTOR CYCLE   NOVEMBER 30TH, 1939

MOTOR CYCLE
REGISTER OF MOTOR CYCLIST VOLUNTEERS

SURNAME............................CHRISTIAN NAMES....................................

DATE OF BIRTH...NATIONALITY.....................

PERMANENT ADDRESS..

PRESENT EMPLOYMENT..

MEMBERSHIP OF MOTOR CYCLE CLUBS (if any)....................................

RIDING AND OTHER MOTOR CYCLE
    EXPERIENCE   ...   *This should be given on a separate sheet, signed, and pinned to this form.*

I wish to have my name registered with a view to enlistment as a volunteer motor cyclist Despatch Rider in His Majesty's Army and, if called upon, undertake to report as directed, immediately. I undertake to inform *The Motor Cycle* of any change in my address and to advise them should my name, through my joining the Forces or otherwise, have to be removed from this Register. I understand that registration can give no guarantee of enlistment. I have not registered my name as a volunteer to enlist as a motor cyclist on any other register.

SIGNATURE...   DATE....................

ON COMPLETION, THIS FORM SHOULD BE POSTED TO THE EDITOR, "THE MOTOR CYCLE," DORSET HOUSE, STAMFORD ST., LONDON. S.E.1. A STAMPED ADDRESSED ENVELOPE SHOULD BE ENCLOSED FOR ACKNOWLEDGMENT OF SAFE RECEIPT.

Motorcycle magazine advert

He had seen an advertisement in *Motorcycle* magazine asking motorcyclists to register with the magazine as available for service as despatch riders should the army call. Harold was a keen motorcyclist. He probably thought that volunteering for motorcycle duties now was preferable to general enlistment with no control over his fate later on.

He enlisted on November 15th 1939. He was posted to 44th Division Royal Signals in Crewkerne on the same day.

By then, the war was barely three months old.

Enlisting as a despatch rider was a good decision insofar as he survived the war without serious injury, even though he lived through the horrors of the Dunkirk evacuation and participated in the fighting following D-Day in France, Belgium, the Netherlands and Germany before demobilisation on January 14th 1946.

Whilst the marriage was arranged in haste, even to the point that there appears to have been no official photographer at the wedding (and no photographs are known to exist), this was not a love match made in haste. They had known one another at least from the time that Vera was sixteen years old.

According to a poem that Harold wrote on March 15th 1940 and Vera kept, that same day in 1934 was the day that they met and, maybe, fell in love. It is surely no coincidence that this was the same day that Harold was born in 1917, so we can reasonably assume that they met during Harold's seventeenth birthday celebrations.

Written to me on our sixth anniversary.

> *If my memory serves me right,*
> *it is just six years tonight,*
> *six years of laughter, fun and tears,*
> *six lovely and delightful years*
> *since we met, light of my life,*
> *and now you are my darling wife.*
> March 15th 1940

Harold's parents were well off compared with the Blacknells. Harold's father had a plumbing business,* but he had also built some houses in Grasmere Road, Beeston, of which the family home at number 3 was one. Harold's occupation at the time of his enlistment was described as 'plumber (general hand)'. He resumed this occupation after the war, getting his qualifications as a 'master plumber' some years later.

Vera kept diaries throughout most of the war. Although they are small in size, with three to four days per page, they are packed with information about the minutiae of her life. Most of this information would not excite attention but for the fact of the war and that her husband was a serving soldier, so her experience of life during this period is of historical interest.

Vera's diary records that she was in work at the start of 1940, though what that work was is unknown. An important element to this story is that she lived with her parents on Chetwynd Road, Chilwell – number 38, to be precise – in a house sited almost shoulder-to-shoulder with one of the main gates into Chetwynd Royal Army Ordnance Corps Depot. This key army installation was built for the RAOC shortly after the First World War on the former site of the National Shell Filling Factory, Chilwell, which had been completely devastated by an explosion in July 1918.[1] More than 130 souls perished in that explosion, and many of the unidentified remains are buried in Attenborough Churchyard. At its peak in the Second World War the ordnance depot was served by nearly 5,000 military personnel as well as 7,000 civilians.[2]

---

*As did his father before him – see http://www.beeston-notts.co.uk/high_road1.shtml for details about the Heard family at 5 Church Street, Beeston.

MAY, 1940

MAY—JUNE, 1940

27 MONDAY

28 TUESDAY

29 WEDNESDAY   ☾ Last Quarter, 1.40 a.m.

30 THURSDAY

31 FRIDAY   Union Day, South Africa, 19

1 SATURDAY

2 SUNDAY   2nd Sunday after Trinity

Sunset 9.2 p.m. at Greenwich. (See below for approximate Provincial Time).
Light Lamps 1 hour after Sunset.
Birmingham, add 10 m.   Manchester, add 16 m.   Glasgow, add 33 m.   Dublin, add 32 m.

76

77

Vera's diary, 1940

The civilian support staff included Vera's father, Fred Blacknell. He had served with 1st Battalion The Sherwood Foresters at Secunderabad, India, before the First World War and with 16th Battalion of the King's Own Yorkshire Light Infantry during that war. He was now employed as a civilian clerk in Chetwynd Depot. Vera was destined to join him in due course.

Moreover, as the Second World War gathered pace, civilian employees at Chetwynd Depot as well as service personnel came to loom large in Vera's life, sometimes through the building of friendships that lasted a lifetime.

Harold and Vera aged nineteen and eighteen

CHAPTER TWO

A Despatch Rider at Dunkirk

War veterans often prefer not to talk about their war experiences and many a son has regretted the passing of a father, having failed to ask his father about something that must have coloured the whole of his father's post-war life both physically and mentally. Harold Heard was no exception to this rule. Much of what follows has had to be gleaned from the few artefacts that Harold and Vera left and from the many written accounts of Dunkirk and the battles following D-Day.

To emphasise this point, let us take what at first appears to be a mundane example. For much of his post-war life Harold wore open-toed sandals even when doing plumbing jobs that had the potential to cause serious accident to his feet. For example, when I helped my dad during the school holidays I saw him carrying a cast-iron bath on his back up a

Under training at Doncaster

narrow staircase in Long Eaton. Quite apart from the sheer strength that he required to haul this bath up the stairs, a slip caused by inadequate footwear could have spelt disaster for him.

The reason for this apparently strange footwear almost certainly sprang from wartime experience.

Harold had suffered badly from trench foot during the war years. This is a medical condition that can cause numbness, swelling, tissue death, blisters and sores in the feet; if left untreated, it can lead to gangrene. It is caused by damp and cold conditions, and it afflicted many soldiers in the trenches of the First World War, hence the name 'trench foot'.

But why should a Second World War despatch rider suffer from a condition that was mainly prevalent in the trenches of the First World War? There is a simple answer. Substandard riding boots, combined with intense periods of work riding a motorcycle in wet and muddy conditions when boots might not come off for several days, left the feet sodden and prone to such afflictions.

Be that as it may, on the face of it the job of a despatch rider – universally known by the acronym 'DR' (and sometimes 'Don R') – might be viewed as a cushy number compared with conventional combative roles in the army. After all, one of the main duties of that part of the Royal Signals dealing with written communications was the setting up of a postal system whenever extensive postal communication was required, so DRs might be regarded as glorified postmen. This was far from the true position.

Douglas Chisholm, a despatch rider attached to III Corps HQ section during the Dunkirk campaign, described his main postal duties thus:

... the theory was that there were two sorts of message deliveries, Despatch Rider Letter Service in which routine non urgent messages were delivered on a regular basis, much as the Post Office did, and the routes were determined purely by the location of the units. This was fine while things were static, but failed when units were not where they were supposed to be. The other service (Special Despatch Rider) meant a D.R. was permanently in place by a wireless truck, teleprinter room or telephone exchange. Messages that were given Emergency Ops status were sent out immediately on receipt, this meant that there ought to be a permanent back-up to fill the gap left when a D.R. was sent out. We worked on a rota system, DRLS normally operated during 'Office Hours' but SDR was a 24 Hour Service, which was covered by two shifts: 08.00 Hrs until 20.00 Hrs,

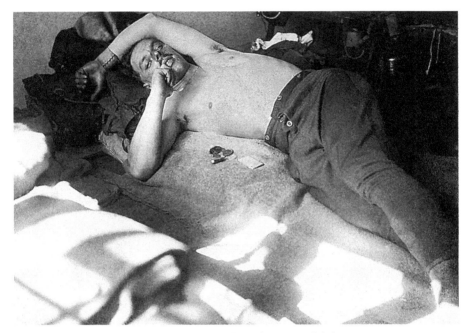

Waiting for the order to 'get on yer bike'

and 20.00 Hrs to 08.00 Hrs. Needless to say the second shift was very unpopular, it often meant trying to find units not on our normal routes, in the dark, a long way away from base, which meant that we often ended this shift feeling dog-tired.[3]

Another job was accompanying convoys of vehicles and armour in a sort of 'husbanding' role, rather like a shepherd guiding his flock from A to B. A posse of DRs would head up and flank a convoy, fetching help when a vehicle broke down, finding roads around obstacles such as massive craters left by bombing action and generally keeping a line of vehicles, sometimes miles long, from getting lost or grinding to a halt.

It is easy to underestimate the danger of such a role and the strategic importance of the last line of communication with troops in the field when other forms of communication have broken down or are non-existent. By definition, despatch riders carried messages that could be of great interest to the enemy, so they were an obvious target for destruction or capture. This risk was particularly great 'in conditions of mobile warfare and open fronts'.[4]

DRs on motorcycles were easy prey to snipers needing target practice as they sped along isolated roads and dirt tracks in unfamiliar terrain, not to mention the simple booby trap set by stringing wire across a road from tree to tree.

Bombs and mortar fire were as much a hazard to DRs as to any other poor squaddie – perhaps more so if the experience of Raymond Mitchell, a DR attached to a commando unit, is anything to go by. Having delivered messages to a forward unit near the River Orne, Mitchell set off on the return trip:

I had passed the glider fields and was rounding the bend towards the Orne bridges when a shell exploded in the field directly ahead, barely fifty yards away, quickly followed by another and another and another. Instinctively I 'rode to ground' – a technique learned for precisely any such self-preservation situation – and landed in a shallow depression against the hedge, with my bike lying alongside.

Lying there, hugging Mother Earth, I realised that here was another 'minus' of a Despatch Rider's life – the noise of a motor cycle engine drowns the whine of approaching shells . . . After a while there was a lull as if both sides were pausing for breath, so I hauled the bike upright and raced off down the hill, kicking the engine into life on the move. Bike and I shot back over the bridges to the relative peace of the beachhead as if the bats of hell were close behind.[5]

Douglas Chisholm had a similar story to tell.

Riding through places that had been bombed was hairy, there was broken glass, wooden door frames with large nails sticking out, roof tiles, bricks, etc., all very unstable and liable to cause punctures. One day riding through a small town with all the debris scattered over the road I thought that the sun had suddenly gone in, I looked up straight into the underside of a twin-engined bomber flying just above roof top height, so it was up the kerb over the pavement and into a shop via the blown-out doorway. I stayed inside for a few minutes, so as not to attract unwelcome attention. I soon realised that being on a bike was not the best way of knowing what was going on all around, it was difficult to hear any but the very loudest and closest noises and impossible to see what was happening behind me, so I began to stop occasionally and have a listen, especially if there was no-one around, I also watched carefully the actions and reactions of

ON ROADS THAT ARE TORN BY SHOT + SHELL
A 'DON R' RIDES, WITH SPEED OF HELL.
THROUGH ROWS + ROWS OF SHATTERED HOUSES
AS IF OLD NICK WERE AT HIS TROUSERS.

Cartoon by 'Ken'

anyone, especially if they were paying close attention to the area behind me. If there was any sign of unwelcome activity I got off the road as soon as possible, parked the bike, and if what I saw looked like trouble moved swiftly off the road at right angles to the direction of approach of the problem, and stayed there until it was safe to resume my journey.[6]

Even convoy duty was a hazardous occupation according to Raymond Mitchell. He recounted the experience of accompanying a convoy of fifty lorries from Dunkirk to Ostend in 1944 thus:

A Despatch Rider rode down the line giving the 'Start Up!' signal and the long string of vehicles rumbled off into the night. The DRs rode behind the 'Pathfinder' jeep until a doubtful part of the route required one of them to remain behind to ensure that all vehicles kept to the planned route. Then came the hair-raising job of regaining position at the head of the convoy.

The truck drivers, travelling without lights along unfamiliar roads made slippery by drizzle, tended to hog the crown of the carriageway; therefore, for DRs needing to get past, with only a few feet between a swaying 3-tonner and a muddy ditch, it was a leap in the dark every time. A few trucks slithered off the carriageway, then one DR would stand by while another went for assistance, but, surprisingly, no Despatch Rider came to grief that night.[7]

It is impossible to overstate the vital role that a DR had in connecting Command HQ units with front line units when all other forms of communication (telephone and radio) were unavailable because lines of communication had not yet been set up or due to enemy action, destroying radio sets and severing landlines. It was precisely in times of extreme emergency that DRs came into their own when highly important messages (and sometimes ammunition) had to be got to units whose precise position in a shell-torn and cratered landscape might not be known.

Raymond Mitchell summed up a DR's lot in this passage:

This almost continuous enemy activity made the life of a DR, moving around in the open, far from a snug hole, particularly hairy. In daylight the drawback of the approach of shells masked by the motorbike's engine was disturbing enough but riders after dark added other problems. Being on duty at night meant remaining fully clothed ready to go at a moment's notice. Curled up in a blanket behind the duty signaller, ears were always attuned to the cranking of the [telephone] call-up handle. A few turns meant that all was well but when it went on and on, it was time to steel yourself for the Signaller's 'Sorry sir, I can't raise them, the line must be cut'. The inevitable consequence would be, 'Better send the DR then,' and you would squirm into your riding coat. Then, shoulders hunched against the cold, a half mile stumble through the trees, kick the engine into life and off on a lonely ride.[8]

That was the start of a DR's problems. The anticipation of a ride in the pitch dark with virtually no headlamp light to guide the way, on roads full of shell holes and debris or down unmarked country lanes dangerously near the front line, occasionally straying into enemy territory, must have had a particular horror for all but the suicidal. Worse still, the noise of the bike's engine advertised a DR's presence to all and sundry, including German snipers.

Ben Kite in his book *Stout Hearts: The British and Canadians in Normandy 1944* is particularly eloquent on the subject of a DR's lonely task.

If the night was noisy with shell fire the DR's mind would be fully occupied trying to sort out what was happening around him. If the night was quiet and particularly when he turned his engine off to consult his map, or search for a gap in a hedge on foot, then he would experience the unnerving sensation of

Cartoon by 'Ken'

imagining every German around was listening and waiting for his approach. Either way his arrival at a front line unit would typically be greeted with an un-welcoming cry to 'Shut that bloody thing off!' [9]

Dunkirk: a very close shave

So, with only four months' training, Harold was about to embark on an adventure that was to lead the British and French armies into ignominious defeat at Dunkirk. This was made only just palatable by the fact that a high percentage of British servicemen got back to British shores, although more than 11,000 lost their lives and over 41,000 were taken prisoner.[10]

44th (Home Counties) Infantry Division (known as 44 Div) was a division of the Territorial Army. It was mobilised on September 3rd 1939, joining the British Expeditionary Force (BEF) on April 1st 1940. It was assigned to III Corps. At the end of May 1940 what remained of 44 Div was evacuated from Dunkirk after the German army threatened to cut off and destroy the entire BEF during the battles of France and Belgium.[11]

44th Division consisted of 131st, 132nd and 133rd Infantry Brigades, five regiments of Royal Artillery, five companies of Royal Engineers, a machine gun battalion, a reconnaissance corps and 44th Divisional Signals – Harold's placement.[12]

Where Harold's troop of DRs fitted into this organisation is not clear. Each infantry brigade in 44 Div had a Royal Signals section, for example, as did 44 Div headquarters. However, 44th Division's role in the BEF is better known.

This is not the place to recount the events of May 1940 in detail. Suffice it to say that, despite the superior firepower and manpower possessed by the combined forces of the BEF, France and Belgium, these forces were overwhelmed by the Germans to the point where Belgium had to surrender and the British and French were completely routed. The Blitzkrieg tactics employed by the German army and air force, together with some questionable leadership under the French Supreme Command, resulted in a disaster but for the rescue of troops from Dunkirk and nearby beaches.

Whilst Harold's experience of war at this time is not known in detail it can be assumed that, as part of 44 Div, he would have shared this formation's fate.

What follows has been culled mainly from Major General Julian Thompson's book *Dunkirk: Retreat to Victory*, and *The War in France and Flanders* by Major LF Ellis.

By May 21st 1940, a wholesale evacuation via Dunkirk was being planned. 44 Div was deployed on the banks of the River Escaut in Belgium (known as the Scheldt in the Netherlands) near Oudenarde, with both the River Lys and the extensive canal system in this part of Belgium and the French border at its back, but was being driven relentlessly towards the coast. As forces dropped back from the Escaut, 44 Div was to be part of a force charged with defending the Canal Line, being the next line of defence, protecting the general move coastward.

Orders then changed. On the night of May 26th the chief of staff of III Corps arrived at the HQ of the general officer commanding 44 Div, Major General Osborne, and told him that the BEF was to withdraw to Dunkirk but that 44 Div was to continue to act as flank guard to the French First Army. Eventually it was intended for 44 Div to withdraw to Poperinghe – a distance of some thirty miles from Dunkirk – and thence to Dunkirk.

The circumstances that the BEF encountered in these terrible days were just those that would test DRs to the limit. There was no hiding place for a lone motorbike rider under extreme duress in a war-torn and unfamiliar countryside, during fast-moving but confused migrations by thousands of men and tons of materiel.

Thomson says in his book that '*despatch riders were especially vulnerable in a withdrawal, because as they took messages from one part of the battlefield to another they sometimes found that the sub-unit they were looking for had gone, and been replaced by the enemy, or that the route they were using was suddenly thick with enemy vehicles.*'[13]

This sentiment was amplified by Major LF Ellis in his book. Speaking of the situation on May 28th 1940, he states:

> *The wide spread dispersal of the 48th and 44th Divisions and the fact that the enemy's advanced columns had already penetrated between the positions they held made the maintenance of communications very difficult ... Use of wireless was very limited and uncertain. Much had to depend on liaison officers and despatch riders, and as the principal roads were often choked with traffic or cut by the enemy, the delivery of messages was a slow and precarious business. Moreover, Advanced General Headquarters was moving on both the 27th and 28th and had been forced off the line of the buried cable which ran through Cassel.*[14]

Major Ellis's account of the last-ditch actions of 44 Div before the inevitable withdrawal coastward is particularly graphic and underlines the view that despatch riders must have been under severe pressure during this time.

> *The 44th Division, in position on the canal running south-east from Hazebrouck and on the Caestre-Strazeele line, were subjected to heavy and continuous shelling and mortar fire all day, and were repeatedly attacked by infantry and tanks. Rouge Croix, between Caestre and Strazeele, was lost and retaken. Further south, the road was crossed by the enemy, who took Clyte Hill, but that too was retaken. On the canal sector, La Motte was entered, recaptured, and lost again in a prolonged struggle; but though the Canal Line was eventually secured by the enemy, they made no substantial progress beyond it, and in the evening they abandoned the attack.*[15]

By the evening of the 27th, German panzer, motorised and infantry divisions were across the canal line and pushing east to squeeze the BEF and First French Army against (German) Army Group B advancing from the east.

May 28th saw renewed fighting on the whole of the line held by 44 Div, but the whole British/French edifice was crumbling in the face of the German onslaught. 44 Div was attacked by 8th Panzer Division in the north and SS Verfügungs and 3rd Panzer in the south.[16]

By May 29th 1940 what was left of 44 Div had been directed to assemble at Mont des Cats, a hill of about 164 metres topped by a monastery, near the town of Godewaersvelde, in French Flanders. It was about five miles from Poperinghe, which was on the principal route to the Dunkirk area for retreating forces.

Major General Osborne, 44 Div GOC, considered this hill 'tankproof' but, of course, it was a prime target for Stuka dive-bombers and heavy artillery as well as the terrible rain of mortar bombs.

Major General Thompson states that '*Mont des Cats was dangerously isolated and potentially easy to cut off. The Germans had approached the feature the previous day, and tanks had shelled it but inexplicably retired. Had they seized the feature they would have sat astride one of the main withdrawal routes to Dunkirk.*'[17]

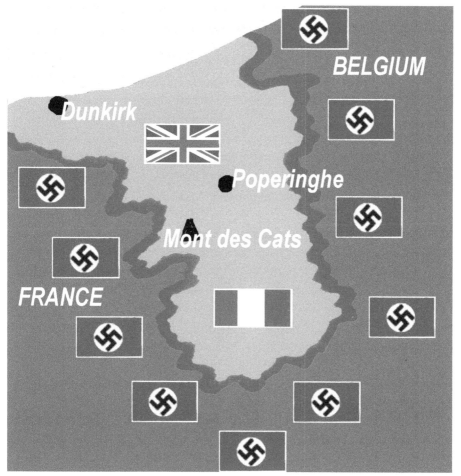

Map of the situation on the evening of May 28th 1940

He goes on to describe the collapse of 44 Div and its inevitable retreat to Dunkirk.

> *... at first light the 44 Division survivors could see motorised infantry and tanks coming over the plain and in a very short time the enemy were engaging Mont des Cats with mortars ... A mass of Stukas arrived overhead and peeling off screamed in ... inflicting about one hundred casualties. Despite a brave effort, the soldiers of 44th Division had had little time to prepare the position, and were in no state to fight off the ground attack that would surely follow this pounding by the Luftwaffe. Although Osborne, the divisional commander, had said that he would stay and fight, he was persuaded by one of the infantry battalion commanding officers to order a withdrawal. He ordered a move in two columns to Poperinghe ... His soldiers did not hang around but streamed off the Mont and trudged northward across country.*[18]

Thompson says that nearly all of 44 Div's vehicles were abandoned on the Mont or on the approaches to Poperinghe.

> *The area was a scene of devastation – guns, vehicles and other equipment lay burning or broken and abandoned. Everywhere, groups of soldiers plodded north, French and British. As they headed for the coast, in the distance they could see a faint streak of smoke, rising from the fires in Dunkirk still over the horizon ... at the tail of the horde of men came the 44th Division.*[19]

Although Harold spoke little about his Dunkirk experience, he did tell of the tortuous evacuation through Poperinghe, which involved the ordered destruction of his motorbike and later his rescue from the Dunkirk beaches.

He told of his desperate attempt to reach a boat some way off shore, swimming for his life. He told how he had nearly given up the fight and just let himself sink in the sea, only to find that the water was shallow at that point, so he did not sink to his death. But that is all he said.

Harold's service papers do yield one interesting fact. Thompson (Appendix C, p. 306) gives details of the numbers of British and Allied personnel evacuated from Dunkirk and nearby beaches between May 27th and June 4th 1940 – June 4th being the last day of the evacuation as a whole. On that last day, 622 men were taken off the beaches and 25,533 from Dunkirk harbour. Since Harold had to swim for his life, maybe he was one of those 622.

His service record states coldly and unemotionally, '*embarked BEF 27.3.40 evacuated ex BEF 4.6.40.*'

Such is life.

Harold's reward for his endeavours was four days' leave with his wife, commencing June 12th.

Vera's diary records that he did not arrive until 8.30 pm on the 12th. On the 13th they went to Harold's sister, Edith, for tea, then on to the Nottingham Hippodrome to see the film 'Notre Dame' (probably *The Hunchback of Notre Dame*, which had been released in 1939). On the 14th they went to Nottingham in the morning, then swimming in the afternoon and then dancing at the Regent (in Nottingham) in the evening.

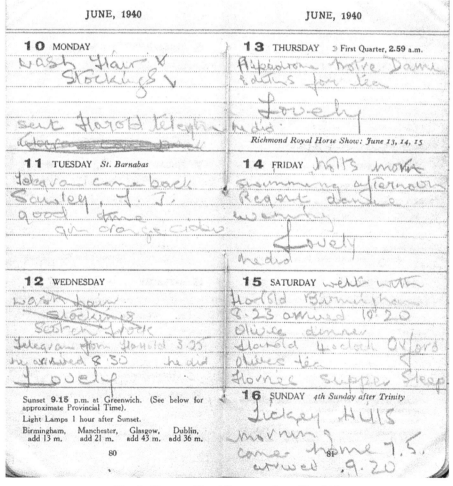

Vera's diary on Harold's return from Dunkirk

Evidently Harold was due to return to his unit in Oxford on the 15th, or at least Oxford was a staging post, because they went to see Vera's Aunt Olive in Birmingham, had dinner with her, and then Harold left Birmingham for Oxford at 4 pm. Vera stayed overnight at another aunt's (Aunt Florrie) and the next day she (most likely accompanied by Birmingham relatives) went into the Lickey Hills near Birmingham (now a country park) before the evening 7.05 train (or bus) home, where she arrived at about 9.20 pm.

Vera also recorded that they made love three times during Harold's leave using the simple but meaningful phrase 'he did'. The diaries do contain such overt references on other occasions, but always with Harold, although I have mentioned the fact here partly to set the context for a major part of Vera's life during the war – namely her life as a gregarious 'single' wife bereft of husband by dint of the war but not of male companionship.

Vera used a number of phrases in her diaries when commenting on her dates with other men, but these are always more covert in nature, such as 'nice', 'very nice' and 'lovely'.

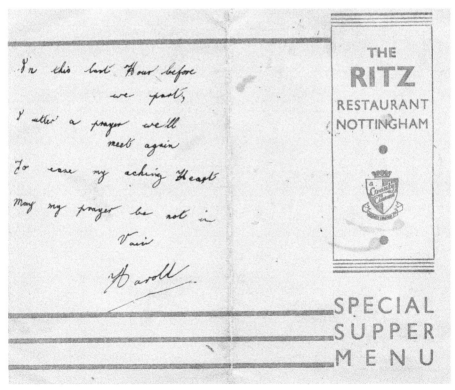

The Ritz menu poem, 1940

CHAPTER THREE

Life at Home

Vera's diary account of Harold's leave following his rescue from Dunkirk underlines that Vera's war is far better documented than Harold's war, although the supply of books and other material about Allied operations in northwest Europe is almost inexhaustible. Harold was a minute cog in a giant war machine, whereas Vera's diaries, commencing on January 1st 1940 and running through to August 1945, quite naturally dwell exclusively on herself and her immediate friends and family.

These were not diaries that dwelled much on her thoughts about the war, or about life in general, for that matter. Indeed the war hardly gets a look in, though its presence clearly affected everyone in some degree, not least a young married woman deprived of her husband for much of the time and living next door to, and working with, a large concentration of servicemen, equally deprived of their wives and girlfriends.

So the fact of war, reduced to a few notes about the occasional air raid and fire watching, is not present in these diaries, but it is ever present in Vera's lifestyle during those difficult years. The war clearly permeated virtually every action by every living person in the UK at that time, often overtly and disastrously for some but also covertly. It seeped through everyone's thoughts and actions as they lived out their lives daily.

These are diaries not about thoughts but about actions, virtually all of which can be related to the exigencies of war, whether in the ever-present need to make do and mend or the need to fill the vacuum created by the deprivation of normal emotional contact when loved ones were far away, possibly never to return.

So, they document activity. Had that activity consisted of sitting by a fireside, reading the odd book and mending socks, waiting for a loved one to come home, then, perhaps, it would not be particularly interesting to the layperson, though it would still be of legitimate historical interest.

These diaries do document darning, washing, ironing, embroidering and knitting, so what makes them stand out as worthy of particular attention?

The answer is that they also document a frenetic social life far in excess of that which any young working-class woman was entitled to expect in peacetime, let alone in the circumstances of total war. They are a historical document in their own right.

Whilst merchant seamen were drowning just to make sure that the nation had enough tea to drink and air raids were pulverising British streets almost daily, Vera seemed to blot out such harsh realities in the smoke haze of darkened cinemas, in the bonhomie of gin and martinis and in the company of men who were not her husband.

For Vera the war years were probably the best time of her life. How else would anyone sum up the end of war with such brevity as this diary entry from May 8th 1945?

The war over, fainted at night drinking, bored.

For Vera, the cessation of hostilities seems to have been an anti-climax – the full stop to chapters in her life that she must have reflected on and mulled over for the rest of her life even though she never spoke about her wartime experiences, just as her husband rarely spoke about his own.

Vera's diary entry, VE Day, May 8th 1945

Perhaps she could not speak about them for fear of upsetting her husband. She certainly kept her diaries out of sight. They did not surface until Harold was long dead and she was in her eighties. This was the first time that I saw these diaries. Again, it is to my discredit not only that I did not ask my father about his experience of war but equally that I did not ask my mother about hers before she died.

This is not to say that reality did not intervene in this life of pleasure. One episode in her life at this time was to haunt Vera for the rest of her life and was probably in her dying thoughts. That was the loss in 1944 of her daughter, Veronica, dead of 'haemorrhagic disease of the new born' and 'prematurity' ten days into her life (according to Veronica's death certificate). Characteristically Vera did not say much about this devastating episode in her 1944 diary, although her diary entries for the week in which her baby died say it all (see chapter five). Later, there is no mention of grief in the diaries, but her grief was there and stayed through to her death. Veronica was buried in Attenborough at the same church where Harold and Vera were married.

So who was Vera Blacknell, who captured Harold's heart and held it for more than fifty years of marriage until he died of bladder cancer on January 1st 1991?

It was not an easy marriage. There were rows that cumulatively might have ended their relationship. On the face of it Harold was a mild-mannered man who preferred a quiet life, but he did have a temper and sometimes it erupted. Notwithstanding his smallness of stature (his service papers show that he was 5'7" and weighed 10 st 6 lbs), he also had a physical strength that was manifest on occasions. Vera was a strong-willed, stubborn and independent woman who could easily have looked after herself if it had come to divorce. The fact that it did not do so must be testament to a love that endured despite it all.

Where did she get that will from? Well, it must have been in her genes, but the war catapulted her into a life that is just not repeatable today. It was a different time and a different age. Had her experience of life in the war not happened then she, like my father, would have been a different person.

That is not to say that pre-war experiences were unimportant, particularly for Vera. She was left-handed and short-sighted. Whilst left-handedness is not a handicap in theory, it certainly can be in practice during the formative years of schooling in a right-handed world, particularly when mixed with a short-sightedness that was not recognised at infant school stage.

Vera always maintained that she would have been a much higher achiever academically had she not had the handicap of short sight, which held her back at school. Judging by pre-war photographs of her as a girl she did not wear spectacles, yet she had astigmatism that was certainly severe enough to warrant them. This condition develops during childhood and gets worse as a person grows through the teenage years. Many photographs taken during the war do not show her wearing spectacles, but this may have been due to her vanity, since her diaries do record the purchase of glasses and their repair.

The development of Vera's left-handed handwriting, as evidenced by entries in her diaries during the war years, shows that she was still struggling to find a style even as late as her mid-twenties. There is an obvious change of style observable in the diaries as time goes by, culminating in the writing style that she made her own throughout the rest of her life.

Vera's physical appearance is also relevant at this stage. Her diaries record such facts as height, weight etc. Her 1940 diary records that she was 5′4″ tall and weighed 8 st 5 lbs. She took a size 5 shoe and her size in gloves, collars and hats was 6¾. There is, however, evidence suggesting that her height was understated in the diary. Vera's War Department pass dated July 6th 1943 records her height as 5′6½″ and her weight as 8 st 6 lbs. Her hair colour was 'fair' and her eye colour 'grey green'.

What the diary could not record was her looks and her personality. Beauty is, of course, in the eye of the beholder, but Vera was good-looking and vivacious with an outgoing personality that was clearly attractive to men. There is no escaping this fact.

She was also someone who seemed to need the company of others almost constantly, whether man or woman, friend or relative. Her diaries are a record of a social life that would be impressive in today's affluent world, let alone a world where total war had apparently stripped the economy of clothing, food and alcohol and replaced them with tattiness and hunger.

Her diaries record no shortage of either food or alcohol, always consumed at the smartest pubs, restaurants and hotels in Beeston, Chilwell and Nottingham. Whilst she did her fair share of mending clothes and stockings, she also had some clothes tailor-made by Harry Hay (husband of her sister-in-law Edith and a tailor by trade) and became the proud owner of a fur coat in 1942 (according to her diaries of October 18th and 25th 1942).

Vera aged twenty-two

Vera was not a socialite. She did not move in such circles. She had neither the background nor the income for high society, although her looks might have carried her through in, say, the 1960s, when many a working-class girl broke through conventional social barriers. On the other hand, war broke down other barriers that would normally have kept a young married woman in the home and out of temptation, and war provided the opportunity for that temptation to be satisfied.

Vera's diaries often record a name or a set of initials of her companion for the evening. Clearly, it is normally easy to identify the sex when a name is present, but a detailed reading of the diaries makes it clear that even when initials are used the person concerned was almost certainly a man.

There are also numerous occasions when Vera went out 'on the town', particularly to the Nottingham Palais dance hall and to parties in Chetwynd Depot, when it is reasonable to assume that she would have met male acquaintances who were not identified by name or initials.

On this basis, it can be said with some certainty, judging by various references in the diaries, that Vera had dates (sometimes on a sustained basis) with British, American, Canadian, French and Polish men, presumably mainly servicemen, and even a Turk (diary entry August 1st 1944).

The most sustained period of social activity took place during the years 1940 to 1943, but she had 'long-term' relationships (i.e. measured in months rather than weeks) with four men, one of whom was a captain in an infantry brigade when she first met him (1942) but had been promoted to Lieutenant Colonel two years later.

It is probably dangerous to judge Vera by the socio-sexual mores of today (2017). After all, contraception was mostly mechanical rather than medical in the 1940s, though that did not render it totally ineffective, and social conventions were much more straitlaced than today despite the relaxation of attitude brought about by war. However, it cannot be denied that a newly married woman would not be expected to socialise with numbers of men within months of getting married, particularly in the absence of her husband on war duty, without the thought that she was something of a 'good time girl'.

It is true to say that Vera's social life did lose pace somewhat as the war went on, particularly during her pregnancy with her first child and subsequent to that child's loss, but its pace during 1940 to 1944 could be described as active, to say the least. During these years, the number of times Vera went out, often in the company of a named man or with someone identified by their initials, was as follows:

	THEATRE		DANCING		CINEMA		RESTAURANT PUB OR CAFÉ	
	in total	with Harold	in total	with Harold	in total	with Harold	in total	with Harold
1940	5	1	16	5	56	19	96	8
1941	10	2	45	13	51	14	57	6
1942	15	5	25	5	47	21	80	12
1943	7	1	9	1	42	10	31	7
1944	5	0	14	0	45	5	57	8
1945	5	0	10	0	17	0	42	0

The data for 1945 covers only January 1st to August 31st. The data does not include times when Vera was visiting, or was visited by, female friends and relatives socially.

Following his evacuation from Dunkirk, Harold was fortunate enough to have been stationed in Britain until his embarkation on D-Day + 5 (June 11th 1944), so he was able to get home on leave on numerous occasions. His service record and pay book list extended official leave periods, but Vera's diaries also note a number of other occasions when Harold was able to get home. Perhaps his duties as a despatch rider enabled him to make a number of unofficial visits home during this period, or else short leaves of absence may not have been recorded in the service papers. There were also occasions when Vera visited Harold at his post, notably when he was training in Doncaster and later on at Maidstone in Kent in the build-up to D-Day.

The number of days when Harold and Vera were together from 1940 to 1945 was as follows:

	1940	1941	1942	1943	1944	1945
Jan	6	3	10	1	0	0
Feb	2	0	1	3	5	0
Mar	3	8	5	7	7	0
Apr	0	4	13	3	1	9
May	0	12	8	3	5	0
Jun	5	1	0	12	7	0
Jul	4	8	10	0	0	0
Aug	7	5	3	3	0	0
Sep	5	0	10	10	0	14
Oct	13	5	0	3	0	0
Nov	6	3	0	0	0	0
Dec	5	0	9	10	0	0
Total	56	49	69	55	25	23

Although entries in Vera's 1945 diary peter out in August of that year, it is reasonable to assume that there were no other leave periods in Britain owing to Harold's duties in the Netherlands and Germany in these months. No other leave periods are recorded in his service papers. He left Germany for home on January 13th 1946.

The total number of days when Harold and Vera were together during the war was 277 – less than one year in six.

Housing and living costs

It sometimes befalls two newly married people to live with the parents of one of them. In this case, the 'marital' home was at the Blacknells' house, 38 Chetwynd Road, Chilwell. This was a three-bedroomed semi-detached house.

Whether the couple could have afforded to buy or rent their own place, had it not been for the war, is unknown. As noted earlier, the Heards were better off and might have subsidised the couple, but this conjecture is not helped by the fact that Harold's father was careful with his money. He died in 1955 leaving an estate worth £12,000, which would be the equivalent of approximately £300,000 in 2017.[20] Apart from minor legacies to his grandchildren, he left equal shares to Harold and Harold's sister, Edith Hay. Harold got the house at 3 Grasmere Road, Beeston, plus cash. Edith got cash.

In the circumstances, however, it probably made sense for Vera to stay in her family home since Harold's enlistment would inevitably result in a posting or postings away from Beeston. This meant that she was living not only with her mother and father but also with her younger brother and sister, Fred and Freda.

The family increased by one on May 6th 1940 (diary entry) with the arrival of Michael, a very late brother to the Blacknell children, but Fred was to join the Royal Navy in November 1941 (diary, November 4th 1941) and so was not at home for most of the war years. As far as is known Freda (born Dorothy Freda in 1920) lived at home throughout the war. The chances are high because no address is recorded for Freda in the diaries, therefore it is safe to assume that she did live at the Blacknells' home.

A number of diary entries indicate that Vera helped her parents in the family home with tasks ranging from shopping duties through to mending, washing and ironing. She also helped in the family allotment on occasions. It is possible that this early gardening experience led to her well-known enthusiasm for gardening in later life.

One duty is possibly tinged with some irony. There are numerous diary entries in which she writes that she is looking after her baby brother, Michael, some twenty years her junior. It is not beyond the bounds of possibility that Michael was mistaken for Vera's child during those occasions when she took him shopping, occasionally also down to the River Trent at Attenborough on a summer's day and even when she was out picnicking with friends (including male acquaintances).

There are no entries in the diaries suggesting that Vera paid a regular rent to her parents or even that she contributed to household finances on a 'one-off' basis during the years that she was living at Chetwynd Road. Whilst she probably did make some financial contribution in one form or another, nevertheless it seems the chances are high that she was not paying rent, which meant that she probably had a reasonable surplus of income over expenditure to fund her very active social life. Not only was it probable that she was living cheaply at home, but she was also in receipt of her own wage and, I believe, her husband's army pay.

Vera did not move out of the family home until October 1944. She had rented a flat at 36 Hampden Street, Nottingham, in September, but she did not sleep there for the first time until October 9th 1944 (diary entry for that day).

This move was probably a watershed in Vera's life. Perhaps it was just time to move out of the family home. She had been in a social whirl for some years during this unprecedented period of total war but inevitably was maturing as the years progressed. By now, she was twenty-seven years of age, so she needed to carve out her own space, and she had had the devastating experience of the death of her daughter, Veronica, on May 3rd 1944. By this time also, Harold was fighting abroad with nothing to reassure her that he would come back alive.

Moreover, on October 28th 1944 Vera got a job at the Guildhall in Nottingham working for Nottingham Council, apparently in the accounts department (diary, October 28th 1944). It seems the move to Nottingham was unconnected with getting a job at the Guildhall since this arose from a visit to the labour exchange in Nottingham on October 28th, i.e. after the move to Nottingham, but it is likely that locating her flat in Nottingham was connected with the view that there would be more jobs available than in Chilwell or Beeston.

By some coincidence, the diary entry for October 28th also shows that Vera had made a date to meet 'Leon' at 3 pm to go to the Ritz (there was both a cinema and a restaurant named 'the Ritz' in Nottingham at the time). She subsequently met Leon on a number of occasions from then until at least August 1945 when the diary entries peter out.

The circumstances of her first meeting with Leon are unknown, but it may well have taken place before October 28th, since the entry on October 28th suggests that the arrangement to meet on that date had been made at an earlier meeting. More of Leon later on.

Clothing and personal appearance

The problem of keeping the nation clothed during the Second World War is a subject in its own right. About a quarter of the British population was entitled to wear one type of uniform or another during the war. This put massive pressure on the clothing industry, but military personnel also needed everyday clothes whilst off duty. The other three quarters required at least as much clothing as before – possibly more so bearing in mind that the proportion of those in work increased compared with the 1930s, creating higher demand for work-based clothing. Everyone had to cope with reduced availability and therefore higher prices.

Clothes rationing started on June 1st 1941 and ended on March 15th 1949. Each person was allotted a ration book with sixty coupons, some of which were snipped out of the book by the retailer when a garment was purchased. The ration book had to be handed to the retailer for snipping before the cash was paid.

The coupon allotment was as follows:

9. Number of coupons needed for the principal articles of adults' and children's clothing

The following table sets out the number of coupons needed for various articles of clothing, other than infants' clothing dealt with on pages vii and viii. The figures in the last column apply to types and sizes which are exempt from Purchase Tax, and depend on the size of the garment—not on the age of the child.

	Man	Woman	*Child
"Woollen" in relation to any rationed goods means containing more than 15 per cent. by weight of wool. "Fur" includes imitation fur.			
Overcoat, Raincoat, etc.			
¶ Mackintosh, raincoat, overcoat, cape, cloak—			
(a) if unlined or saddle-lined, and not woollen, leather, fur or double-texture	9	9	7
(b) if fully-lined and woollen, leather or fur	18	18	11
(c) other than those in (a) and (b)	16	15	10
Overcoat lining (detached)	7	7	4
Jacket, Cardigan, Waistcoat or Pullover			
§ Jacket, blouse-type jacket, long sleeved waistcoat, coat, blazer, woman's cape, woman's bolero—			
(a) if lined and woollen or leather or fur	13	12	8
(b) if unlined and not woollen, leather, fur or double-texture	6	6	4
(c) if unlined, blouse-type and knitted		8	
(d) other than those in (a), (b) or (c)	10	10	6
‡ Bolero, short jacket, short cape—			
(a) if woollen or leather, and with sleeves of not less than elbow length		5	
(b) if not woollen or leather, and with no sleeves or with sleeves of less than elbow length		2	
(c) other than those in (a) or (b)		3	
Cardigan, sweater, jersey, jumper, pullover, bedjacket—woollen and weighing at least 10 ozs. (7 ozs. for children)	8	8	5
Cotton football jersey	4		2
Waistcoat, pullover, jumper, jersey, sweater, cardigan, bedjacket—other than those described above	5	5	3
Trousers, Shorts or Skirt			
Trousers, slacks, over-trousers, breeches, jodhpurs—if woollen; kilt	8	8	6
Trousers, slacks, over-trousers, breeches, jodhpurs—not woollen	5	5	4
Shorts—if woollen	5	5	3
Shorts—not woollen	3	3	3
Skirt, divided skirt—if woollen		6	4
Skirt, divided skirt—not woollen		4	3

* Types and sizes exempt from Purchase Tax, including protective boots, but not children's garments containing silk or fur.
¶ Women's coats and capes fall into one of these categories if over 28 in. long.
§ Women's coats, capes and jackets fall into one of these categories if over 16 in. but not over 28 in. long; also for jackets even if not over 16 in. long.
‡ Not over 16 in. long, and not fur.

Continued from previous page

	Man	Woman	Child
Dress, Gown, Frock or Gym Tunic			
Dress, gown, frock—if woollen and with sleeves of any length		11	8
Dress, gown, frock—not woollen		7	5
Gym tunic, skirt on bodice, sleeveless frock—woollen		8	6
Gym tunic, skirt on bodice—not woollen		6	4
Shirt, Blouse or Shawl			
Shirt†—if woollen	7		6
Shirt†—not woollen	5		4
Blouse, shirt-blouse, shawl, plaid—if woollen		6	4
Blouse, shirt-blouse, shawl, plaid—not woollen		4	3
Blousette		2	1
Miscellaneous Garments			
One-piece shelter suit or like garment	11	11	8
Cassock—if woollen	8		6
Cassock—not woollen	7		5
Overall, Apron or Housecoat			
Apron (with or without bib)	3	3	2
Overall—if woollen	11	11	8
Sleeveless non-woollen overall		6	4
Overall—other than above	7	7	5
Housecoat—if woollen		8	
Housecoat—not woollen		7	
Dressing-Gown, Pyjamas, Nightdress, etc.			
Dressing-gown—if woollen	8	8	6
Dressing-gown—not woollen	7	7	5
Pyjama suit, nightshirt	8	8	6
Nightdress		6	5
Undergarments, etc.			
Combinations, petticoat—if woollen	7	6	4
Combinations, petticoat—not woollen; slip, corselette	5	4	3
Suspender belt (not more than 10 in. in width at widest part), brassiere, bust bodice, modesty vest		1	1
Woollen vest; non-woollen vest with sleeves of any length; woollen pants or trunks; non-woollen pants (long legs)	4	3	2
Body-belt,§ non-woollen briefs (no legs), camisole	2	2	2
Undergarment not elsewhere listed; athlete's vest	3	3	2
Stockings, Socks, Collar, Tie, Handkerchief, etc.			
Pair of non-woollen half-hose, woman's ankle-socks	1	1	1
Pair of other socks, or stockings	3	2	1
Collar, shirt-front,† pair of cuffs, tie—of masculine type	1	1	
4 small handkerchiefs (each of area less than 1 sq. ft.), pair of sleeves	1	1	1
2 large handkerchiefs not more than 2 ft. in length or breadth	1	1	1
Bathing Costume, Bathing Gown, etc.			
Bathing gown—if woollen	8	8	6
Bathing gown—not woollen	7	7	5
Bathing costume	3	3	2
Woollen bathing trunks	3		
Cotton swimming drawers	1		

* Types and sizes exempt from Purchase Tax, including protective boots, but not children's garments containing silk or fur.   † With or without collar attached.   § Knitted or woven body-belt without fastening and without reinforcement by means of elastic, boning or inner lining.

Clothing Coupons
Source: Board of Trade booklet September 1941 pages v. and vi.

Clothing coupon allowance, 1941

Vera's diaries are virtually silent on the subject of ration books or clothing coupons throughout the war. There is only one reference to coupons on the last page of the 1943 diary when she lists the items that she can get for twenty-two coupons, being three for a coat lining, five for a blouse, five for shoes, eight for an underset and one for a brassiere.

However, Vera's clothes expenditure does seem to have been extensive for most of the war. This is not surprising since clothing expenditure would be expected to have a positive correlation with the extent of her socialising, but wartime shortages generally and clothes rationing in particular might be regarded as substantial obstacles to the variety of clothes available of the right fashion for a young woman. Bearing in mind that there were two other women in the Blacknell household – Vera's mother and Vera's younger sister, Freda – perhaps any shortfall of coupons needed to 'finance' Vera's needs may have been made up from transactions with them.

There does seem to have been a flourishing black market, not so much in the clothes themselves but in the coupons required to purchase them.

The rationing system appears to have been full of holes. For example, in 1941/42, the first year of rationing, nearly 27 million additional coupons were issued as replacements to people claiming that they had lost coupons or accidentally destroyed them etc. Officials administering claims for the replacement ration books estimated that as many as 90% were fraudulent.[21]

As with any black market, prices fluctuated. In its infancy the 1941/42 clothing card was easily forgeable, so the cost was about 2/6d per card, but by 1944, when coupons were less easily forgeable, the black market prices were about £5.00 per book of coupons or 2/- per coupon.[22]

There is no suggestion in Vera's diaries that she got involved in such practices, but her clothing consumption does seem to have put her nearer to one extreme of the spectrum than the other. Whether she did need to bend the rules to satisfy her clothing demands must be left open.

The pressure on clothing demand rose as time went by. Prices increased whilst the amount of clothing that individuals could purchase was reduced. The number of coupons allocated to each adult per year was reduced from sixty-six coupons in 1941 to sixty coupons in 1942 and forty-eight coupons in 1943.[23]

The diaries contain a great deal of detail about clothes expenditure, which, in itself, is significant but not surprising. This was a young woman with few commitments and cheap or free housing during a period when she had what was probably a reasonable level of disposable income.

Although the diary for 1940 is the first available for review, Vera was clearly keeping a detailed account of clothing expenditure before this. The diaries contain a complete run of detail from 1938 through to 1944. The data for 1940 to 1944 shows expenditure on clothes each month.

One of the most obvious points of comparison is the one between the pre-war expenditure and expenditure for the two years 1940 to 1941. In the two years 1938 and 1939 Vera spent £7/3/9d and £11/7/10d respectively. This level of expenditure nearly trebled in the next two years. The figure for 1940 is £26/12/7d and for 1941 it is £21/8/11d. The equivalent expenditure in 2017's money for these four years would be approximately £449, £711, £1,663 and £1,340.[24]

The annual analysis of Vera's expenditure is as follows:

	1938	1939	1940	1941	1942	1943	1944
underclothes	1/3/0	1/14/9	2/1/6	4/9/8	2/4/10	19/0	0
stockings	6/6	7/11	1/3/8	2/4/7	8/0	9/3	0
frock	2/0/0	3/15/8	2/2/3	3/17/6	1/17/10	3/0/0	2/13/7
costume	0	0	2/3/6	0	0	6/17/0	0
slacks	0	0	0	0	0	2/19/6	0
blouse	0	0	0	0	6/11	16/5	0
shoes	2/0/0	2/13/9	3/6/6	3/15/9	2/12/5	1/15/3	15/0
hat	8/0	6/11	9/10	6/11	0	0	0
jumper	8/3	5/11	1/11/7	18/6	0	0	0
overall	3/0	14/10	0	0	0	0	0
mac	15/0	0	1/13/9	0	0	0	0
coat/gloves	0	1/8/1	0	0	0	0	0
coat	0	0	9/11/0	3/3/0	2/0/0	0	0
jigger coat	0	0	0	0	0	3/7/2	0
cleaning clothes	0	0	7/11	1/18/4	1/7/3	0	0
gloves	0	0	1/16/2	0	0	11/10	0
scarf	0	0	4/11	2/11	0	4/4	0
shoes repaired	0	0	0	11/9	16/6	0	5/6
nightdress	0	0	0	0	0	0	3/10/0
dressing gown	0	0	0	0	2/2/0	0	0
other	0	0	0	0	0		10/1
TOTAL £	7/3/9	11/7/10	26/12/7	21/8/11	13/15/9	20/19/9	7/14/2

The conversion into today's money is a crude indicator that does not take account of many factors, but it does bring home the massive shift in lifestyle within these four years.

Even so, the absolute level of expenditure in today's terms (for example £32 per week in 1940, using today's money) may not seem high in comparison with the amount that young women can spend on clothes today. However, the comparison of the clothes spending habits of a young woman about town in 2017 with one in 1940 must only be an approximation at best. Women have much greater earning power today and the emphasis on fashion in clothing and footwear these days is intense. Moreover, as noted above, rationing reduced the amount of clothing that one could buy; clothing materials were scarce, therefore the amount available, as well as its variety, was limited. Even if one had the money for fashionable clothing, it was not necessarily the case that one could spend it.

A better comparison, albeit still rather simplistic, would be to relate Vera's expenditure on clothing and footwear to that of the population as a whole during the war years.

Government estimates of personal expenditure on clothing (including footwear) for 1938 to 1943 show that it decreased substantially during these six years. The index of 100 for 1938 dropped to 99 in 1939, then 82, 59, 58 and 55 for the following four years (at 1938 prices).[25]

By contrast, Vera's expenditure trebled between 1938 and 1940 and remained at that high level for the following year before dropping off somewhat in the later years.

Clearly, the most important event driving this increase in clothing expenditure was the complete change in Vera's lifestyle brought about by the war itself and the underlying change brought about by marriage to an 'absentee' husband, but to this mix must be added Vera's motivation and character. As we have seen, she was not a stay-at-home wife waiting for her husband to return from war whilst immersed in the 'make do and mend' ethos that pervaded the whole of wartime life.

However, references in the diaries to the repair of clothing are quite extensive, so to say that Vera did not need to make do and mend would be inaccurate. Darning, washing and mending was the lot of most women during these years. To this could be added recycling worn-out clothes even to the point of completely renewing a shabby coat by '*unpicking the lining, washing it, then taking the entire garment apart, seam by seam, and sewing it back together again inside out, before replacing the lining* [to make the garment] "*almost as good as new*".[26]

Stockings (or the lack thereof) were the bane of most women's lives in wartime. To have a patch on an old coat or maybe a dress where the folds hid the repair might be bearable, but one could not disguise a repair in the lisle stockings worn by most women at that time, and that was simply unacceptable.

Virginia Nicholson put it like this:

*Wearing patched, remodelled skirts, and pilled, frayed sweaters day in,
day out was enough to get anyone down, but self-control faltered when it
came to stockings. It was one thing to look shabby-chic in jerseys made
from unpicked and re-knitted wool, but how could any woman hold her
head up high wearing baggy lisle hosiery the colour of dirty rainwater?
And, like it or not, as skirt lengths rose in proportion to the availability of
fabric, lower legs were now on view.*[27]

Utility stockings were said to be '*shapeless and absolutely to be lacking in
reasonable durability*'[28] and silk stockings were scarce and expensive.

Nylon stockings did not arrive in the country until 1942 and then only
via the instrument of, possibly, rapacious American servicemen intent on
tribute that many girls did not want to give or black marketeers with equal
rapacity, this time for money.

Nicholson again has the last word on this tragedy:

*... with silk in short supply or prohibitively expensive, sickly yellow cotton
lisle seemed like the only alternative ... Less hard wearing than silk, they
needed frequent darning, and when washed, could take up to four days to
dry.*[29]

Vera was not exempt from this problem. Today, it seems most incongruous
that any woman would have to create a diary reminder to wash her
stockings, let alone repair them, but the tender care needed to ensure that
one would have a serviceable, clean pair of stockings available every day
meant that one had to be disciplined. Washing and darning stockings was
mentioned in diary entries nearly seventy times during 1940 alone,
although, judging by later diary entries, this activity tailed off considerably
in later years – or loomed less as a priority in her diary.

There is one matter regarding clothing that must remain a mystery. The
diary entries show that Vera 'ordered' a fur coat on October 18th 1941 and
that she 'fetched' the coat on October 25th. There is even a diary entry
dated March 23rd 1943 to remind her to 'comb fur coat'. Moreover, she was
photographed wearing a fur coat at about the right time for it to have been
the very fur coat mentioned in the diary. There is no date on the
photograph, but she looks the right age for it to be the same coat. Notably,
she was also wearing spectacles for this photograph.

However, there is no information as to the cost of the coat in the 1941
diary even though she lists other clothing expenditure for October 1941 in

minute detail. It must have cost a significant amount had she purchased the coat using her own money, so one would expect her to have recorded the expenditure.

It is possible she was given a second-hand coat (say by a relative or friend), but then why would she use the word 'ordered' in the October 18th entry? Rather than the coat being second-hand, someone else might have paid for it, but who would that be? It is too risky to speculate further about this acquisition, but it is tempting to note that Vera was going out quite regularly with 'George' at this time. There is no certainty about George's identity, but Vera's diaries for a number of years do record the military address of George Marshall – of whom more later.

The fur coat

Two other matters concerned with personal appearance generally should be mentioned: hairdressing and cosmetics.

Although there is virtually nothing in the diaries concerning cosmetics, the diaries record hairdressing appointments at regular intervals. Vera had her hair variously tinted and/or permed on a number of occasions. As one would expect, she would often get her hair done on a Friday in anticipation of social activity at the weekend, and a pattern of sorts emerged in the middle years of the war when she would go to the hairdresser's approximately twice a month.

In the six years from 1940 to 1945 inclusive, the number of hairdressing appointments mentioned in the diaries were eight, nineteen, twenty-three, ten, sixteen and fourteen respectively.

As noted above there is little mention of beauty products such as cosmetics in the diaries. Given the variety of items that Vera does mention purchasing, one would have expected that lipstick and face powder would have been prominent purchases, but there is no mention of lipstick apart from one reference that is actually crossed out and no mention of face powder, although she does mention purchasing powder puffs several times. There are a number of references to purchasing talcum powder.

This absence is somewhat incongruous, as there was no lack of demand for beauty products in the war. According to a wartime social survey two thirds of all women applied cosmetics, with 90% of the under-thirties using them, falling to 37% for those over forty-five.[30]

Cosmetics were not rationed by coupon during the war but the amount that could be supplied was limited by government diktat to only 25% of the pre-war level,[31] so it is little wonder that there was a flourishing black market in such goods. Attempts to curb the black market in beauty products generally resulted in a complex structure of control both of manufacture and supply in the form the Limitations of Supplies (Miscellaneous) Order 1940, the Limitation of Supplies (Toilet Preparations) Order 1941, with an amendment in 1942, and a Number 3 Order in 1943, but the black market persisted.[32]

There is every reason to believe that Vera would have used cosmetics and beauty products to complement her general appearance and ensemble as she did in years after the war, so there is some mystery as to why expenditure on products such as lipstick, face powder etc. is not referenced in the diaries. It is my opinion that to say that Vera did not wear cosmetics because she does not record their purchase in her diaries is just not credible, so how was she acquiring them? Perhaps there is no mention of cosmetics in the diaries because they were being purchased 'under the counter', but this is sheer conjecture. The nearest reference is an entry mentioning talcum powder.

Work

Vera did not enlist in any of the services during the war, notwithstanding that Chilwell Ordnance Depot was home to 4,000 ATS girls by 1945,[33] although she did have a number of clerical roles with the armed forces.

Prior to this, the 1940 diary clearly implies that she had a job but its nature is unclear. A diary entry for January 4th 1940 states 'half of Stephanie's job pushed onto me'. This suggests, albeit only slightly, that she was working in an office environment, although family folklore suggests that she was working as a sales assistant in a draper's shop at some time in her youth. If this was the case then it is possible that she worked at the draper's shop at 5 High Road, Beeston, which was operated by Anne and Sarah Lowe.[34] The Heard family was related to the Lowe family by marriage and Vera possessed a collection of drapery items, such as decorated tablecloths and napkins, which were known to have come from the Lowes' shop when it closed down (date unknown).

Vera's first job connected with the military started in Chilwell RAOC Depot on July 15th 1940. Her pay was £2/5/- per week. This was a clerical job connected with the 'Visidex' system, which is believed to have been a filing system for controlling personnel or stock information. This is unsurprising, since not only was the Chilwell Ordnance Depot home to thousands of military and civilian personnel but it was also a massive store of military goods ranging from humble spares through to tanks and other armoured vehicles. By all accounts, the control of stores passing into, through and out of the depot required a massive clerical input.

One example given in a publication about the depot's work issued after the war is that of the issue of 'stores'. The branch known as 'Storehouse Accounts' had to keep record of every item of store in the depot by means of an account card for each item. At the height of its activity this branch alone had a staff of 360 full-time and 41 part-time workers and it was 'not uncommon' for them to process 100,000 transactions per week.[35]

Vera's work at Chilwell Depot lasted until July 1943 when she started work with a department which was presumably part of the American military establishment. Its official title was 'British Pay and Establishment Office USA Miscellaneous Installations, Western Command'.

Characteristically Vera's time at Chilwell Depot is not well documented in her diaries and neither was her work with the Americans. However, the latter is worthy of some comment because it involved extensive stays away from Chilwell, mainly in Sutton Coldfield and Birmingham, therefore it forms a period of activity outside the norm for the diaries as a whole.

This period also covers a significant event in Vera's life: the conception of her first child, Veronica, and her pregnancy with baby Veronica, which will be considered later.

Vera's pass enabled her to 'pass through War Department property at HQ and USA installations' for the purpose of carrying out 'general financial duties'. The precise nature of these duties is unclear but they took place in and around Birmingham, including Harborne (from where her pass was issued) and Sutton Coldfield. It is possible that she was working for the American pay corps in Britain.

Sutton Coldfield was also home to a major American forces postal sorting centre. It sorted every letter and parcel sent from the USA to troops stationed in the UK and Europe.[36]

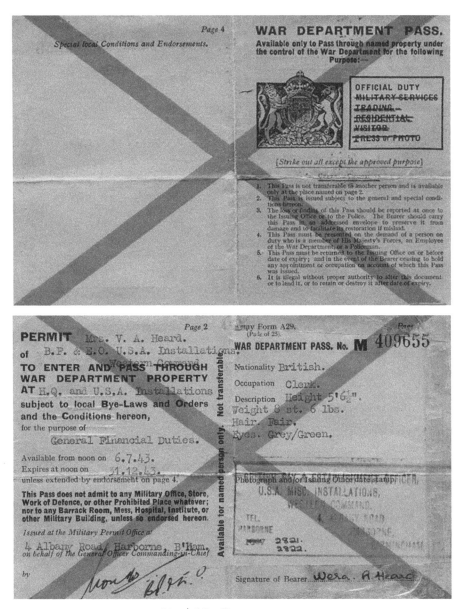

Vera's War Department pass

CHAPTER FOUR

After Dunkirk

Harold's wartime experiences fall into three phases. The first phase started with his enlistment (November 15th 1939), then embarkation to France (March 27th 1940), followed by the disastrous rout of British and French troops that ended on the beaches of Dunkirk and subsequent evacuation (June 4th 1940).

Harold's experiences in the first phase were considered earlier in this book.

The second phase started the day that he reached the English shore after Dunkirk and ended the day that he set off for France once again, on June 11th 1944, just five days after the greatest seaborne invasion of all time, known as D-Day.

So the third phase began on June 11th 1944 and ended with his demobilisation. That process started on January 13th 1946, but it was not until April 1st 1946 that the British army finally gave up its claim to his body and soul (service record).[37]

Fortunately, evacuation from Dunkirk lead to four years' service in England from June 5th 1940 to June 11th 1944, so insulating Harold from direct enemy contact.

Following Dunkirk, Harold spent a further year with 44 Div Signals. He was posted to No. 1 Squadron, Guards Armoured Division Signals on June 21st 1941, then to XII Corps Signals on September 1st 1942 and then, on February 3rd 1944, to I (British) Corps Signals, where he spent the rest of the war (service papers).

After a great deal of research connected with Harold's life in the army it is clear, unfortunately, that there is still a great deal more to do. This is due mainly to two factors that militate against being able to pinpoint Harold's moves and experiences during most of the war.

Firstly, there is little written about the day-to-day operations of either Guards Armoured Division or XII Corps whilst they were based in England.

Secondly, for much of the time that Harold was in northwest Europe, I (British) Corps was assigned to the First Canadian Army. Canadian military historians are understandably more interested in their own military history, with the result that I (British) Corps gets scant attention in their military histories. Moreover, British military historians have also had more interesting events to research and write about than the role of a subsidiary corps in the Canadian army, so the history of I (British) Corps must remain shrouded in some mystery because there are no detailed military histories of this corps available.

Two sketchy histories do exist: *Spearhead: The Story of the First British Corps* by Desmond Bastick, which covers 1901 to 1977, and 'History of I (BR) Corps 1901 to 1967', an internal British army document. They are both slim volumes and cover too many years of history to be of great use concerning operations in northwest Europe.

The fact that I (British) Corp did not play a decisive role in many of the British or Canadian battles is not to deny the fact that many formations, regiments and services that constituted I (British) Corps in 1944–45 distinguished themselves in war with utmost valour. But the role of one lonely DR striving to serve his country, but also trying to stay alive, is understandably not recorded in any military history, nor can we pinpoint his local unit with great accuracy.

That having been said, it must be noted that Harold was attached to I (British) Corps headquarters rather than to some subsidiary army unit, therefore it is possible that a great deal of information resides in Canadian archives and in the National Archives in Kew. However, for the time being, the following account must necessarily rely on supposition to a great extent pending further research, which must concentrate on relevant material in the National Archives and possibly Canada.

44th Division (June 5th 1940 to June 20th 1941)

44th Division insignia

44th Division is discussed at length in chapter two. After returning from Dunkirk the division spent almost two years on home defence in Kent and Sussex in case of invasion. 44th Division would eventually be sent to take part in the North African Campaign, departing the United Kingdom on May 29th 1942, but by this time Harold had been transferred to the Guards Armoured Division.[38]

The Guards Armoured Division (June 21st 1941 to August 30th 1942)

Guards Armoured Division insignia

The Guards Armoured Division commenced operation in the United Kingdom on June 17th 1941. It was made up of elements of the Grenadier Guards, Coldstream Guards, Scots Guards, Irish Guards and Welsh Guards. It remained in the United Kingdom, training, until June 13th 1944, when it departed for France.[39]

Vera's 1941 diary lists Harold's address as 'unit HQ DR the Guards Arm'd Div Sigs Home Forces', but Harold was transferred to XII Corps in September 1942.[40]

XII Corps (September 1st 1942 to February 2nd 1944)

XII Corps insignia

XII Corps was formed in 1940. It was part of the Home Forces at the start of the war and was based at Tunbridge Wells. Notably Lieutenant-General Sir Bernard Montgomery was its commander from April 27th 1941 until August 13th 1942.[40]

Harold's address listed in Vera's 1943 diary is 29th DR Section 12th Corps Signals, Home Forces.

Some idea of Harold's sojourn with XII Corps might be gleaned from the wartime experience of one Alfred Brown who was in the Royal Signals attached to 43rd Wessex Division. This formation was also under the command of Montgomery as part of XII Corps and Alfred Brown spent some time at Cocklington. We know Harold also passed through Cocklington because he sustained an injury there in January 1942 (see below).

Alfred Brown was interviewed by the BBC for the Second World War 'People's War' project.

So all our training was done at Portland and Weymouth, and then we had to move down to Cocklington. That was a mushroom farm, and they'd cleared all the shelves and everything out, where the mushrooms grew, and that was our beds! ... I shall never forget that! And while we were there, we were all given our TB inoculations. Of course that knocked the biggest part of the battalion out for twenty four hours. Some of us were pretty groggy, I know I was. And then after we'd been at Cocklington and done more training down there – it was getting pretty bad in France, the Germans had put in their big attack, they were beating the French and British armies back towards Dunkirk – and they moved us from Cocklington. We were on our way to Tilbury Docks, on trains, and on our way to France. Then I suppose the powers that be, the War Office, knew that France was a dead loss, it wasn't very long after we'd left Cocklington that Dunkirk happened.[41]

Alfred Brown escaped the Dunkirk experience but he was later to feel what real war was like when the 43rd Wessex Division was put on a rigorous training footing. It is probable that Harold shared the same sort of training. Throughout most of 1942 the division was part of XII Corps. Alfred Brown went on to say that:

... we moved from the Cavalry Barracks in May 1941, and from then on – August 1941 we were on Exercise Binge, Exercise Mortmain, Exercise Bumper, Exercise Jason. That was from 3 August to 27 January 1942. In February 1942 we moved from Herne Bay to A Camp in Sandwich, still on the east coast. We were in Kent all the time.

May 1942: more exercises – Exercise Tiger, Exercise Hammer, Hammer 2, Spartan. That was until March 1943 [note: Harold joined XII Corps on September 1st 1942]. *May 1943, we moved to a place called Watershire Park, still in Kent. Then from there we went on Exercise Green Linnet, which was a forced march, non-stop endurance test., June 1943, we moved to Margate, on 4 June we had more exercises: Exercise Thunderbolt, Harlequin. 29th September, we moved to Yorkshire for an exercise: Exercise Blackcock, that was out on the Yorkshire Moors. That was pretty bleak and it was wet. These exercises, they did really toughen us up, because if I hadn't been so fit, I wouldn't have got through what I went through in 1945 ...*

We moved back down from Yorkshire down to Sussex, Topham Wood that was near Bexhill. There we went on more exercises, Exercise Illumination, Falcon ... [42]

Cartoon by 'Ken'

One medical mystery, two 'war wounds', a crash and a cookery course

Harold's home sojourn in the army was not without incident. They were admittedly events that could have happened to anybody at any time, but the fact that they occurred whilst on army duty makes them a little more noteworthy.

Apart from the daily opportunity to hone his skills as a motorcyclist and later learning to drive a jeep, he also learned to cook – or, if he was a competent cook before he enlisted, to cook the army way! This was not simply a recreational course. The composition of DR units in the field meant that they had to have a cook as part of the complement, so Harold was 'it' for his unit.

He passed a cook's course at Longmoor training camp in Hampshire in August 1941, but his newfound culinary skills did not prevent him from sustaining a 'war wound' when, on January 2nd 1942, he was on cookhouse duty at Cocklington Camp (Somerset) and accidentally cut the index finger on his left hand whilst using a 'bread machine'. The verdict of his commanding officer was that the wound was 'not likely to interfere with his future efficiency as a soldier' (service record).

1942 was not a good war year for Harold. Not only did he suffer the ignominy of a bread machine injury, but on April 19th 1942 he was admitted to hospital for eight days in somewhat mysterious circumstances (of which more later). Moreover, on October 12th 1942 he was hit by a GPO car, registration number GLC 147, whilst on motorcycle duty. This collision threw him over the bonnet of the car and into the road. He sustained 'synovitis of the left knee, contusion of the left thigh and abrasion of the right shin' (service record). Again, the verdict was that his injury was 'not likely to interfere with his future efficiency as a soldier' (service record).

A D.R. MUST ALWAYS BE OBSERVANT.

NOT ARF!   KEN

Cartoon by 'Ken'

The time Harold spent in hospital, however, might have interfered with his future efficiency as a soldier, but we will never know whether this was true. There is a complete mystery surrounding these eight days.

The service record states that he was admitted to AMRS Chilwell on April 19th and discharged on April 26th 1942. The precise meaning of 'AMRS' is unknown and open to conjecture, but it was clearly a hospital. There was certainly a hospital in the grounds of Chilwell Depot.[43] With so many service and civilian personnel working in Chilwell Depot it is understandable that a medical facility was necessary, but did it also cater for injured or ill service personnel who were not stationed there?

Vera's diary adds little to the service record but adds even more mystery in saying so little. Harold's pay book shows that he had been given leave for the period from April 18th to April 24th 1942. Vera's diary for April 17th 1942 notes that he was coming ostensibly on normal leave, yet the diary entry for the 18th refers to an 'appointment for Harold with Stear and

Ingle' and the entry for the 19th states, 'Harold ill fetched him in ambulance to Depot hospital.'

Harold's living arrangements whilst on leave are unknown, but if, as is possible, he was staying at Vera's parents' home (i.e. where she was living at the time) then he must have been in a bad way to need an ambulance, since 38 Chetwynd Road is literally a stone's throw from one of Chilwell Depot's main gates. On the other hand, if he was staying at his parents' house at 3 Grasmere Road, Beeston, then he was some miles away from the depot, so an ambulance would make better sense.

Either way, the 'appointment' with Stear and Ingle seems connected to these events.

Although the precise nature of Vera's job at Chilwell Depot is unknown, it is known that she was working for a Major Stear at this time. His exchange and billet number within Chilwell Depot are listed in the 1943 diary and he is mentioned several times in her diaries in a work context. In 1942 she notes that his birthday was August 8th, and her 1943 diary records that she made a pair of gloves for him, starting on April 29th and finishing on May 2nd.

Is it possible that Harold was given leave because of some illness, that Vera pulled strings with Major Stear to get him into the Chilwell Depot hospital, that 'Ingle' was a medical man connected with the hospital and that Harold's conditioned worsened the day after he had seen Stear and Ingle, such that he was rushed to hospital? The truth will never be known, but Harold's condition was clearly serious enough to spend so long in hospital.

Vera records that she visited him on April 20th, 21st, 23rd, 24th and 25th. He came out of hospital on April 26th but did not return to his unit until May 8th 1942, even though no leave period is recorded in his pay book for any time after April 24th.

It is interesting to note that on Saturday May 30th 1942 Vera had a meal (presumably) at 'the County', which was the County Hotel next to the Theatre Royal and the Empire Theatre, with one 'B Ingle' (diary for that date). The County was one of the premier hotels in Nottingham, accommodating many well-known stars appearing at the Theatre Royal and the Empire Theatre, including Laurel and Hardy in 1952.[44]

Vera was to have many dates during the war years in which 'the County' played a part in her very active social life.

CHAPTER FIVE

The High Life?

This is perhaps a cue to divert from Harold's wartime experience in Britain to concentrate on Vera's life in some detail. After all, the next phase of Harold's wartime history encompasses D-Day and the war in northwest Europe through to Germany's defeat. It is fitting, therefore, that this book should culminate in a consideration of that great struggle and Harold's part in it, having already encompassed Vera's seemingly effortless journey through her life at this time, apparently living as a single girl intent on the high life for much of the war.

I admit to pangs of guilt at this point. Can I really understand what it was like for a newly married young woman to live through total war (for that is what it was for the British) without the man she had known at least from the age of sixteen who was now her husband? Can I write her wartime history without applying judgments from my own experience, especially as she was my mother? The reader must judge, but I have tried hard to maintain a modicum of detachment which I hope will be clear to the reader.

Was Vera living the life of a single girl intent on the high life whilst her husband was engaged in a life of enforced servitude to the King? This question (if not the answer) is supported partly by the number of Vera's visits to the County Hotel in Nottingham.

At the end of the preceding chapter, this venue was mentioned as being a premier venue in Nottingham during the war. It was situated next to Nottingham's Theatre Royal and just round the corner from the Empire Theatre.

Vera's diary records that she had drinks or a meal at the County fifty times during the war years, accompanied by a number of different men.

For example, on Wednesday, February 18th 1942 she records a dinner date with 'G'. We have met 'G' before in the context of the acquisition of a fur coat, for it is pretty certain that 'G' was George Marshall. Vera notes that partridge and mushrooms were consumed alongside no fewer than eight whiskies – perhaps 'G' shared this alcoholic cornucopia. It is to be hoped that he did.

The County Hotel, Nottingham (now demolished)

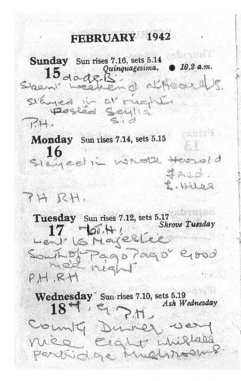

Entertained at the County Hotel

Vera's diary entries for that week in February, in full, read as follows:

Sunday: *Dad's birthday. Spent the weekend at the Heards, stayed in at night. Posted* [letters?] *to Scylla and Sid. Parcel*[?] *to Harold.*

Monday: *Stayed in. Wrote to Harold, Fred and L Hiles. Parcel to Harold. Received letter*[?] *from Harold*

Tuesday: *arranged to meet 'J H' at 7 pm. Overwritten by a 6. Went to the Majestic Cinema* [Beeston] *to see 'South of Pago Pago'. Good film. Nice night. Parcel*[?] *to Harold. Received letter*[?] *from Harold.*

Wednesday: *Meet 'G' at 7 p.m. Went to the County Hotel for dinner. Very nice. Eight whiskies, partridge, mushrooms.*

Thursday: *Went to Club. V*[ery] *Nice. Wrote Sid, Scylla, Darcy, Harold. Received letter*[?] *from Harold. Parcel*[?] *to Harold.*

Friday: *Hair at 5.30 then Charlton* [pub in Chilwell]. *Then a film. Good*

Saturday: *Mans B* [? unintelligible] *Meet G at 7. To County Hotel for dinner. Home in a taxi. Very Nice. Parcel*[?] *to Harold.*

Whilst it may be assumed reasonably that the County Hotel provided food and drinks at the higher end of the scale of sustenance, it should not be forgotten that this was wartime, so this hotel was probably subject to the same restrictions on fare as less well-appointed venues in Britain at that time. According to Cook's Info:

In July 1940, restaurant restrictions started coming into effect. The first regulation was that in one meal you could not have both a meat and fish dish. So a fish starter, and meat main course, was out.

In June 1942, two additional restaurant restrictions came into effect. The first was that no restaurant meal could have more than three courses. The second was that no restaurant could charge more than 5 shillings for a meal (alcohol and coffee excluded). This had the desired effect, of course, of causing restaurants to be more frugal in what they chose to offer, or serve smaller portions of it, so that they could still make a profit on the meal. To ensure that restaurants didn't just try to get around this through 'cover charges', the restriction also stipulated that the highest cover charge that would be allowed was 7/6.[45]

'*You need no ration card for restaurants, although a waiter will serve only one meal to a person at a sitting, and that limited to three courses or five shillings expenditure. Swanky places get around the quality barrier by adding a stiff cover charge, but the three courses are never exceeded. A soup or hors d'oeuvres, an entree and a dessert are regulation. Coffee and drinks are extra. The maitre d'hotel or waiter may 'save' a portion of joint for old customers, but a late diner will inevitably find the menu exhausted and only sausage or mushrooms available.*'[46]

Vera's home life and relatives

However well documented a biography is, no one can know what a person thought at a given point in time unless that person recorded his or her thoughts. Even then, one can only take that record at face value when there may be any number of circumstances in which an individual might not record or might not fully record the truth.

Any interpretation of that record or any assumption about what a person's thoughts or motives were when an action was taken – or not taken – is simply that: an assumption. We can only judge an action using our own experience as a guideline, but within a historical perspective bestowed on us by the passage of time and the interpretation of historians of whatever hue and persuasion.

Therefore, any judgments about Vera's personal life, ranging from her own thoughts through to her relationship with Harold, her male friends, her family and her female friends, must be qualified by those limitations.

So this raises the following questions: why write a diary in the first place and why make the entries that were made in it? The answer to both questions is surely that it was important to Vera to keep a diary and each entry in the diary must have been important enough to her to write it down in the knowledge that no one apart from Vera would be remotely interested in what was being written. These diaries were personal to her, written for her own use and nobody else's, therefore they are an intimate depiction of a life lived in times of monumental importance to the world.

It is only now, seventy years after the war, that, with hindsight and with a historical perspective not available at the time, these diaries and these events, however personal to Vera, take on a sociohistorical perspective generally as well as a perspective perhaps only of interest to Vera's family.

A factor to be taken into account is that, since Vera was writing only for herself, she inevitably had her own way of saying something which meant a lot to her but which the external reader might not understand or might misinterpret. Moreover, there is no need for much in the way of punctuation in a diary written for oneself, but the correct punctuation is vital to correct understanding for the outside reader. Anyone who has read the book *Eats, Shoots and Leaves* (by Lynne Truss) will understand this comment.

Consequently a diary entry which looks almost like a stream of consciousness might be interpreted in a number of ways by the casual reader, but someone who has spent many hours reading and re-reading her diary entries is more likely to interpret the writing correctly. Moreover the handwriting, often in pencil now faded with age and of varying quality, will stump a casual reader, but a reader who has studied the writing has much less difficulty.

With all these caveats in place let us look firstly at Vera's life with herself, so to speak, then at her life with Harold, then her male friends and then her female friends.

Firstly, it may be stating the obvious that Vera was a young woman, in her early twenties, when war broke out. What was important to her, as a young woman, may well have been unimportant to an older married woman with young children or whose children had left the nest to make their own lives.

As noted previously, in the early part of the war there are continual references in her diaries to the need to wash stockings and to mend underwear and other clothes, as well as to making clothes and knitting. Most of these references tend to be concentrated in the 1940 and 1941 diaries, though knitting appears to have been a constant occupation throughout the war. Embroidery took over as a regularly written-of pastime in place of mending clothes as the war progressed.

Were these changes in diary entries indicative of easing conditions in the home as time went on, or were they indicative of changing priorities in diary entries as Vera's life changed? No doubt, she mended clothes throughout the war, but it became less of an event in terms of making entries in her diaries.

Since she lived at her parents' home for much of the war, it is possible that she was doing a lot of this type of housework for her mother as well as for herself.

Her mother, Alice Blacknell, gave birth to Michael at a nursing home on May 6th 1940. She was forty-four years old and Fred Blacknell, her husband, was fifty-seven. Their son, Fred, possibly aged nineteen, and daughter, Freda, aged twenty, also lived at 38 Chetwynd Road as well as Vera.[47]

This was quite a household to introduce a new mouth to in wartime, particularly as Michael's parents were quite old. Michael is said to have been weaned on Carnation milk. Vera helped. Her diary has a fair number of references to bathing the baby, taking him for walks in the pram and so on.

Vera's brother Fred Blacknell joined the Royal Navy in November 1941 (diary entry, November 4th 1941). The 1943 diary notes his ship as HMS *Mansfield*, built in 1918 in the US. It started life as USS *Evans* and appears to have been on loan to the Canadian Navy at the time of Fred's sojourn on it.[48]

Vera's 1944 diary gives Fred's address as HMS *Rowley*. HMS *Rowley* was launched in America in 1943. Presumably, it was supplied to Britain as part of the 'Lend-Lease' programme. Fred may have been aboard when it sank a German U-boat (*U-1208*) in the English Channel southeast of the Isles of Scilly on February 27th 1945.[49]

Vera's sister Freda got a job at 'Parkes' on January 9th 1940. Parkes were probably lace and hosiery manufacturers in Beeston.[50] Apart from the times when Freda accompanied Vera on social outings of one type or another, little is known of her life during these war years.

Interests and pastimes

Whilst Vera's active social life has been mentioned on a number of occasions so far, there also seems to have been a side of her that wanted to better herself through personal attainment, possibly to make up for the shortfall that she felt in terms of her primary education.

This manifested itself in various ways, most notably in the number of French lessons that she took in 1945. The first diary entry recording a French lesson was on July 11th 1945 and the last on October 10th. During this time, she recorded attending French lessons on seven occasions.

Her enthusiasm for the subject may have been sparked by social meetings with French troops or French Canadians, but she records these having taken place much earlier – on August 2nd 1940 when she went out with 'Jack Lois', whom she recorded as having a French accent, and January 28th 1941 when she met a 'French boy' at (or went with him to) the Nottingham Palais.

The 'French boy' of 1941, possibly the same 'Jack Lois' of 1940, clearly followed the Gallic romantic tradition if a scribbled note in one of the 'memoranda' pages in Vera's 1941 diary is anything to go by. There is written the legend '*Toy Jours. A. Tois*', which any red-blooded Frenchman will know as '*toujours à toi*' – 'always yours'. No doubt he whispered it in her ear during a slow waltz at the Palais, and no doubt he was – for a night at least.

Another activity was with a drama club, which Vera joined on February 12th 1942 (diary entry). She records another drama club meeting on February 26th but no further mention is made of this pastime. However, Vera was a founding member of the Beeston Mothers' Club after the war, which had a thriving drama section, and was certainly involved in amateur dramatics for a time.

One short-lived pursuit was Vera's fleeting dalliance with the Communist Party, although she seems to have attended only two meetings with her friend 'Peggy' (on September 16th and November 9th 1942) and it is likely that it was Peggy who suggested attending these, since, as far as is known, Vera never displayed any such political leanings after the war. If anything, she was a natural conservative (small 'c'). But it must be remembered that the Communist Party did not have the stigma attached to it that arose in later times. The USSR was a great ally in the fight against Hitler. British sailors were freezing to death north of Norway supplying war materiel to the Russians in 1942. The Communist Party of Great Britain was larger and better supported at this time than in later years.

Female friends

Vera made female friends who sometimes stayed with her for the rest of her life (or theirs). She was clearly someone who needed to have people around her all of the time. She was continually visiting, or being visited by, friends and relatives. Her later diaries going into the 1960s, '70s and '80s attest to the fact that this was not just a wartime phenomenon.

There was many a time as a seven-, eight- or nine-year-old that I was deputed to make the tea whilst Vera entertained a gaggle of her female friends, all speaking in a strange argot designed to ensure that what they were saying was entirely private to themselves. I can only remember two words of this strange language, namely *haygav yaygoo*, or 'have you', which transpires to be a form of 'gibberish' according to Wikipedia.[51] However, their shared language says much more than that they were playing some form of weird game. It says that they were close, almost intimate friends,

With Syd and Scylla Goffett

and those friendships were borne out of the war years when there was probably much to talk about in private – particularly when it came to friendships with unauthorised males.

Amongst Vera's friends were Scylla Goffett and her husband Syd. In fact Vera and Harold made friends with Syd and Scylla in the 1930s when they went on holiday – this was probably in 1937 when they were holidaying in Anglesey.

Syd was from Knotty Ash in Liverpool; Scylla was his second wife. She was born in Beaumaris (Anglesey). She came to Liverpool when she was five years old. At that time, she only spoke Welsh. She and her husband had many camping holidays in Wales, so they were almost certainly camping when they met Vera and Harold for the first time.

There was clearly a great deal of friendship between them, not least because Syd was as mad keen on motorcycles as was Harold. Apparently, he made a sidecar for his bike himself, and rumour has it that when he was saving to get married he spent his savings on a Harley-Davidson.

Scylla and Vera were special friends, although the precise chemistry between them is unknown. Vera often wrote to her and mentions Scylla more than 140 times in her diaries. She also visited Scylla in Liverpool a number of times, both on short trips and on extended holiday.

Scylla 'and baby' came from Liverpool to visit Vera from August 8th to the 17th 1942 (diary entry), and in the same year Vera and Harold visited Syd and Scylla in Liverpool in late December.

The diary entries for this later visit are interesting from several points of view, not least because this was wartime but it did not seem to stop the normal round of social activities that one would see equally in peacetime. So here is a very short slice of social history – a life lived out over a few days long ago.

The diary entries for this visit read as follows:

Sunday 27th December – *Liverpool train 7.32 Beeston, change Derby, Crewe, arrive 12.10. Went to Scylla's mothers at night, nice time*

Monday 28th December – *Stayed in bed until 2.00, went to film at night with Sid, alright*

Tuesday 29th December – *went into town with Scylla, looked around shops, saw good film. Tyrone Power* [film star]

Wednesday 30th *return from Liverpool, caught 11.45 train from Lime Street, arrived 7.00 hrs very cold here, stayed in at night*

Thursday 31st *start* [period] *sometime (theatre pantomime) pantomime very good Robinson Crusoe. Went to Edith's* [Harold's sister] *for tea. Feb 10 G[?] birth*

Friday 1st January 1943 *Harold returned 15.15 train. Very wet day, don't feel too good. Darned stockings night*

Saturday 2nd January – *12.10 train, raining very heavily when we left. Snow in Derbyshire, found Scylla had a lodger, arrived 19.00 hrs. PH* [it is believed that 'PH' is shorthand for 'posted [to] Harold' or possibly 'parcel Harold']

Sunday 3rd – *went walk in morning, stayed in noon, drink with Sid at night*

Monday 4th – *Scylla's lodger left without paying. Lunch roast goose. Went to town in morning, bought slacks Bon Marche went to docks overhead railway. RH* [it is believed that 'RH' is shorthand for 'rang Harold' and/or 'received (letter from) Harold']

Tuesday 5th – *snowed heavily caught train 12.30 via Manchester arrived at Atten*[borough] *17.00 hrs, good journey, snow at home*

Why Harold and Vera came back to Chilwell on December 30th, only for Vera to return to Liverpool on January 2nd, is unknown, but perhaps the pantomime of *Robinson Crusoe* had been booked long before the Liverpool visit was arranged. We shall never know the identity of Scylla's lodger and why he or she left without paying.

Apart from the visits already mentioned, Vera had stays in Liverpool in July/August 1943, July 1944 and August 1945.

Vera and Harold stayed friends with Syd and Scylla for years after the war, but this friendship was cut short by their friends' untimely deaths. Scylla died of cancer at the age of fifty-two and Syd survived Scylla by five years.

I am indebted to Syd and Scylla's granddaughter Helene Lily Goffett, who was located courtesy of Facebook and provided details of Syd and Scylla's family.

Other friendships made in this era that lasted a lifetime were with Molly Pettinger (née Beeston) and Joan Whitehead (née Davis). Molly and Joan were local to Beeston and were regularly at social gatherings with Vera after the war right through to the inevitable visitation of death.

Another friendship, with Stephanie Jackson (née Burnett), was probably made before the war, since she is first mentioned in January in the 1940 diary. She lived in Farnham, Surrey, after the war. My recollection is that the Jacksons ran a guesthouse that we visited on a number of occasions when I was a young lad.

Several other friends feature in the diaries – Peggy Eddison (married name) and Darcy Clark, for example – but I do not remember their names from the 1950s.

With Joan Davis

With Darcy Clark and Peggy Eddison

Male friends

We now come to part of Vera's life in the war years that must be tackled fearlessly, given that this book is as much a social history as it is a family portrait that I hope will be of interest to my family for many years to come.

Vera was Vera. There is no denying that she was a healthy, outgoing woman with few inhibitions, though her demeanour must have been tempered by the limits of morality and behaviour that existed at that time. What were these mores that limited morals and behaviours in the 1940s?

It has been said many times that wartime had a liberating effect on morals, attitudes and behaviours, not least because of the proximity of thousands of men in the forces, not only from Britain itself but also from all over the world. How was Vera influenced or affected by such social forces?

Many thousands of young women in Britain at that time would have known of America, for example, only from the passions and lives portrayed by Hollywood. Very few would have travelled abroad even the twenty or so miles that separate us from France. Garrison areas of Britain (and the area local to Chilwell was one such area) must have been, frankly, like an unlimited supply of chocolates for local girls whose lives had once revolved around boys of limited horizons and whose only ambition was to meet a boy, marry and have children.

To understand the social processes at work in these times we must briefly look at the work of historians with a better grasp of the lives and attitudes of the women of that age and with better historical resources than the mere diaries of one young woman that are available to me. Yet we must do so in the light of a historical perspective stretching far into the future – much further than the perspective of war.

We know that Vera and Harold married in haste, but not in the sense that they barely knew each other. The adage 'marry in haste, repent at leisure' did not apply. They had known each other and had been together since Vera was sixteen and maybe before that. It was the war that hastened the marriage rather than any other social imperative. Vera was not pregnant, nor did she lack a roof over her head.

Whether they would have married had the war not happened is probably not worth the speculation except to say that, despite the exigencies of the war, they did emerge from it intact unlike many hundreds, if not thousands, of couples whose marriages broke down soon after the reality of peacetime and austerity set in. The course of true love must have run deep, because death was the only thing that parted Vera and Harold in the end.

There were always people who retained the inhibitions of pre-war Britain despite the liberating effect of war, but there were also many people – both men and woman – who were freed suddenly from those inhibitions. Either their natural inclinations led them down a path that was suddenly free of the entanglements of pre-war attitudes to sex or war gave them the opportunity, through geographical distance from their home environment, to sample such freedoms, only for them to revert to the old ways of thought once war was over.

In her book, *Millions Like Us*, Virginia Nicholson considered how war changed attitudes to sex when she wrote:

> At moments of the most terrible bombing, expressing love physically was an act of defiance against the ruptured bones, the crushed guts – the living urgency of sex a kind of triumph over the gory imperatives of war. The available evidence suggests that fear, loss and destruction seem (to some extent) to have precipitated the sexual liberation of both men and women. Compared to the years before the war, in 1939–45 more women were having sex before marriage and with men other than their husbands, more of them were contracting sexually transmitted diseases, more were using contraceptives and women's knowledge of the facts of life increased.[52]

John Costello in his book *Love, Sex and War* observed:

> Inevitably chastity was an early casualty as lovers were forced to abandon the traditional drawn out period of courtship. The 'weekend affair', snatched on a forty-eight hour pass, that preceded many wartime weddings, often substituted for a honeymoon.[53]

John Costello quotes Barbara Cartland, the bestselling romantic novelist, who said of young wives in wartime that the honeymoon:

> … was a happiness overshadowed by the inevitable separation from their husbands, a problematical future, with always the fear that THEY would be widows almost before THEY were wives. Yet they had their happiness; however quick, however fleeting, it was theirs. They were loved and beloved, and by this stage in the war love was about the only thing left unrationed.[54]

Let a wartime bride have the last word before we embark on Vera's personal odyssey through this uncharted, exciting territory. She wrote:

Togetherness in the blackout was the car seat or doorway. We were brought together that way by the pressures of time and shortage of accommodation and a sense of unsettling uncertainty, in fact nothing was positive. Our generation, through sex education in the forces and all the 'free talk', learnt a thing or two about birth control. Few of us lived mentally or physically for tomorrow – or even next week. Many relationships were set for as long as war lasted – or the posting arrived for elsewhere. A free and easy, in some ways a slightly mad style of living took over. Many girls were married or spoken for, but husbands and boyfriends were not there. Company relieved the tension of what was about to happen. In the background a slight fear hid behind the bravado. The then current saying – given with a grin – was 'Don't worry, it may never happen.' It often did! Many girls were left pregnant with no hope of marriage because of death, overseas posting or rejection. Wartime work was plentiful for us and men were there for the taking. Girls were now able to walk into a public house and order their own drinks and buy cigarettes. We paid for our own cinema tickets and the days of sharing costs had begun. No-one would have thought of a date paying her own way before the war. But we didn't feel obliged to allow favours if we didn't fancy the escort in 'that' way.[55]

If we were to pick one sentence from that description that might sum up Vera's life at this time, it would be *'a free and easy, in some ways a slightly mad style of living took over.'* This might be an inaccurate description, because I have no way of knowing what Vera's life was like before she got married, but, however she lived her life in the 1930s, one would have expected her to have led the life of a respectable married woman after her marriage.

Can we see this expected state of grace in her diaries? No. What we see is a 'slightly mad style of living' clearly accommodated by wartime's new liberated environment, when it would appear marriage was just something one had to do to cover only one part of life's demands.

Just look at Vera's social life in her first year as a married woman. It was active, to say the least. The following data has been extracted from the diary entries for 1940.

Date	Event	Venue	Details	With	Vera's comment
02 Jan	cinema	Palladium	Wuthering Heights	L Bradley	no entry
03 Jan	cinema	Palace	The Mikado	S	no entry
09 Jan	cinema	Majestic	Secret ??	S	no entry
17 Jan	cinema	Majestic	Tail Spin	E	no entry
23 Jan	pub	Bluebell	shandy	Stephanie	fun
28 Jan	cinema	Palladium	Jamaica Inn	Harold	no entry
28 Jan	pub	Bluebell	no entry	H[arold]	no entry
31 Jan	pub	Flying Horse, Ritz	gin ginger	Harold	VG [possibly 'very good']
02 Feb	probably café	Kings	lunch	no entry	no entry
06 Feb	cinema	Ritz	Nurse Edith Cavell	no entry	no entry
10 Feb	pub	Rail[way?] H[otel?]	gin ginger	T	no entry
11 Feb	café	Hand's	coffee	T	very nice
12 Feb	theatre	no entry	Arte Ballet	Harold	no entry
13 Feb	cinema	Ritz	Saint in London	no entry	no entry
13 Feb	café	no entry	milk bar	Harry	no entry
18 Feb	café	Hand's café	no entry	no entry	met 6 soldiers, had fun
19 Feb	cinema	Majestic	Beau Geste	T	no entry
21 Feb	no entry	no entry	no entry	with S	met 2 S[oldiers?]
22 Feb	cinema	Astoria	Goodbye Mr Chips	no entry	lovely
23 Feb	pub	Bluebell	whisky	T	no entry
24 Feb	cinema	Ritz	French Leave	T	no entry
24 Feb	pub	no entry	shandy	no entry	no entry
26 Feb	cinema	Majestic	This Man in Paris	no entry	no entry
28 Feb	café	no entry	no entry	T	saw Canadians
02 Mar	cinema	Mechanics	Bachelor Mother	no entry	no entry
02 Mar	café	Ritz	no entry	Freda	no entry
04 Mar	pub	Bluebell	gin g[inger]	T	no entry
06 Mar	pub	Bramcote	shandy	T	T rang up met 8 o'clock
09 Mar	café/pub	Ritz, Bramcote	3 ciders	Tom	VN [possibly 'very nice']

Date	Event	Venue	Details	With	Vera's comment
12 Mar	pub	Bramcote	cheese cider	T	grand time
15 Mar	pub	Bluebell	gin cider	T	no entry
16 Mar	café	Derby	2 cafes	T	very nice
17 Mar	café	Bridgford	milk bar	T	very nice
18 Mar	pub	Bramcote	cider gin ginger	T	good time
19 Mar	cinema	Ritz	Blackmail	Harold	no entry
19 Mar	café	Ritz	no entry	Harold	no entry
20 Mar	cinema	Astoria	no entry	Harold	no entry
23 Mar	pub	Flying Horse	no entry	Steph	met S[oldier?] chap barmy
25 Mar	cinema	Roxy	Second Fiddle	Stephanie	no entry
05 Apr	pub	Bramcote	no entry	T	very nice
06 Apr	cinema	no entry	The Stars Look Down	T	no entry
08 Apr	pub	Bramcote	cider	MW	met two swads [swaddies]
09 Apr	cinema	Palladium	Made For Each Other	no entry	no entry
12 Apr	pub	Bramcote	3 gins cider	met fellow	had darn[?] good time
13 Apr	pub	Bramcote	no entry	Scylla	no entry
16 Apr	pub	Bramcote	no entry	Tom	very nice
20 Apr	dancing	The People's Hall	no entry	L Bradley	no entry
26 Apr	pub	Bramcote	gin	sold[ier]	nice
29 Apr	pub	Bramcote	no entry	sold[ier]s, Steph	no entry
01 May	dancing	Institute	no entry	Mrs Hall	no entry
04 May	pub	Long Eaton	3 gins	Stephanie	darts met nice TH [or JH] had fun VG
07 May	pub	Bramcote	no entry	Tom	very nice
11 May	pub	Trent Lock	5 gins	Tom, Jack	got drunk
13 May	pub	Trent Lock	no entry	Claude	went Derbyshire in car very good
16 May	cinema	Palladium	Old Mother Riley MP	Mr Burnett	no entry
17 May	pub	Trent Lock	no entry	T	OK
21 May	café	Hand's café	no entry	Mr Finely	no entry

Date	Event	Venue	Details	With	Vera's comment
25 May	no entry	Long Eaton	no entry	Stephanie	no entry
27 May	pub	Bluebell, Donnington	gin ginger	no entry	very nice
30 May	cinema	Palladium	The Man Who Knew Too Much	Mr Burnett	no entry
01 Jun	cinema	Savoy	The Rains Came	Mr Burnett	no entry
01 Jun	café	Lyons	coffee	Stephanie	no entry
02 Jun	outing	Dovedale	no entry	Mr B	lovely
04 Jun	cinema	Savoy	French Without Tears	Mr B	no entry
06 Jun	pub	no entry	cider gin lime	Steph	no entry
11 Jun	pub	Sawley	gin orange cider	T	no entry
13 Jun	cinema	Hippodrome	Notre Dame	Harold	no entry
14 Jun	dancing	Regent	no entry	Harold	no entry
20 Jun	cinema	Palace	Love Affair	no entry	no entry
22 Jun	pub	Sawley	2 gins	Tom	alright
23 Jun	no entry	no entry	no entry	Steph, Jeff, Andy	met two swads [swaddies]
24 Jun	pub	Bramcote	2 gins	no entry	very nice
26 Jun	outing	Stephanie's house	no entry	Jeff, Andy	very nice
27 Jun	pub	Donnington	3 gins	BH	very nice
29 Jun	cinema	Hippodrome	Daytime Wife	Andy, Jeff	very nice
29 Jun	pub	Exchange and Kardomah	1 gin and 2 gins	Andy, Jeff	VN [probably 'very nice']
30 Jun	pub/café	Barton, Bluebell	tea Barton	Andy, Jeff	very nice
03 Jul	pub	Blackboy, Exchange	5 gins	Harry	NG [possibly 'no good']
04 Jul	no entry	no entry	'they did not come.'	met two more	nearly drunk OK had fun
05 Jul	no entry	Toton	dinner	Harold	lovely
07 Jul	outing	Doncaster	no entry	Harold [stationed at Doncaster]	no entry
08 Jul	pub	Cad[land], Costock Inn	no entry	no entry	VN [probably 'very nice']
10 Jul	theatre	Empire	J Buchanan E Randolph	no entry	no entry

Date	Event	Venue	Details	With	Vera's comment
10 Jul	pub	Kardomah	1 gin	no entry	no entry
12 Jul	pub	no entry	4 gins	JBS [or FBS]	lovely time
13 Jul	pub	Welbeck	2 martinis	BS	no entry
14 Jul	outing	Doncaster	no entry	Stephanie	[Harold was stationed there]
16 Jul	pub	Cad[land], Bramcotee	3 gins	no entry	very nice
17 Jul	cinema	Ritz	Tower of London	no entry	no entry
17 Jul	pub	the Bell	1 gin supper	no entry	no entry
18 Jul	no entry	no entry	had supper	met Stephanie, Andy, Jeff	alright
19 Jul	pub	the Bell	had supper	Andy, Jeff	no entry
20 Jul	café	Hand's, Mikardo	lunch and tea	S A [or S N]	OK
24 Jul	pubs	Cad[land], Costock	2 gins, martini cocktail	no entry	lovely time
26 Jul	dancing	Palais	no entry	no entry	had fun
26 Jul	pub	no entry	gin French	illegible	VN [probably 'very nice']
28 Jul	outing	Doncaster	no entry	Harold	was ill very sick nice though
31 Jul	dancing	Palais	no entry	no entry	no entry
31 Jul	pub	George Hotel	gin, gin French	Thomas	very nice
02 Aug	no entry	Nottingham	no entry	Jack Lois (French accent)	fun
03 Aug	outing	River Trent	went river	'the boys' [probably Andy and Jeff]	fun
10 Aug	pub	George Hotel	supper drinks	B	no entry
11 Aug	outing	Doncaster	no entry	Mrs Heard, Steph, Harold	44 [Div?] sports lovely
12 Aug	cinema	Palace	Lady of Tropics	no entry	no entry
14 Aug	pub	Park Hotel	2 gins	Harold B, Steph	no entry
19 Aug	cinema	Majestic	Remember The Night	JB	no entry
21 Aug	cinema	Carlton	[We Are Not Alone?]	BA	no entry

Date	Event	Venue	Details	With	Vera's comment
24 Aug	cinema	Elite	no entry	JB	no entry
24 Aug	café	Mikardo	no entry	JB	nice
25 Aug	outing	the Dukeries	no entry	Harold, Peg, Darcy	had fun
28 Aug	no entry	Costock	no entry	BA	v. nice
29 Aug	cinema	Astoria	Ninotchka Greta Garbo	no entry	no entry
31 Aug	restaurant	Flying Horse grill	no entry	JB	no entry
01 Sep	pub	Bluebell	no entry	JB	very nice
02 Sep	cinema	Majestic	[The Great] Victor Herbert	JB	no entry
07 Sep	cinema	Palace	Old Maid	JB	no entry
08 Sep	no entry	Matlock	no entry	JB	very nice
09 Sep	cinema	Palace	Destry Rides Again	JB	no entry
09 Sep	pub	Bluebell	no entry	JB	VG
10 Sep	pub	Bluebell	three drinks	JB	no entry
12 Sep	pub	Bramcote	no entry	JB	very nice
13 Sep	cinema	Majestic	Green Hell	JB	no entry
14 Sep	theatre	Empire	Black Velvet	JB	no entry
14 Sep	pub	Flying Horse	no entry	JB	very good
15 Sep	outing	Edwinstowe	no entry	Steph, JB, JH	lovely
19 Sep	pub	Bramcote	no entry	JB	nice
21 Sep	theatre	no entry	no entry	JB	lovely
21 Sep	café	Hand's café	no entry	JB	lovely
22 Sep	no entry	no entry	no entry	JB	no entry
24 Sep	cinema	Majestic	Mae West film	Darcy	no entry
25 Sep	pub	Bluebell	no entry	JB	had fun
26 Sep	party	no entry	party for soldiers	no entry	terrific fun, lovely
28 Sep	theatre	Empire	A Askey R Murdoch	JB	no entry
28 Sep	pub	Flying Horse	dinner	JB	V N
29 Sep	cinema	Majestic	no entry	JB	no entry
29 Sep	café	Barton	for tea	JB	no entry
30 Sep	pub	Bluebell	no entry	no entry	did not stay long

Date	Event	Venue	Details	With	Vera's comment
04 Oct	no entry	no entry	drink	JB	no entry
05 Oct	party	no entry	Steph's party	met Bill, John came	fun
06 Oct	pub	Ritz, Lyons, County Hotel	tea, drinks	JB	no entry
08 Oct	walk	no entry	no entry	BH	no entry
09 Oct	cinema	Hippodrome	Rebecca	Harold	no entry
10 Oct	walk	no entry	no entry	BH	nice
11 Oct	skating	ice rink	had lesson	Harry	no entry
12 Oct	dancing	Palais	no entry	no entry	no entry
13 Oct	cinema	Ritz	Jones Family	BH	no entry
13 Oct	café	Lyons	tea	BH	no entry
15 Oct	cinema	Palace	Charley's Aunt	Harold	no entry
17 Oct	cinema	Ritz	Johnny Apollo	JB	no entry
17 Oct	pub	Flying Horse	no entry	JB	no entry
18 Oct	pub	Bluebell	no entry	JB	no entry
19 Oct	dancing	Regent	no entry	Harold	no entry
20 Oct	café	Lyons	tea	met Air Force officers	no entry
22 Oct	cinema	Palladium	Leslie Howard film	Harold	no entry
23 Oct	cinema	Astoria	Seven Gables	Harold	no entry
23 Oct	dancing	Palais	no entry	Harold	no entry
24 Oct	cinema	Hippodrome	Pinocchio	Harold	no entry
24 Oct	café	Mikardo	tea	Harold	no entry
25 Oct	cinema	Palladium	'soldier film'	Harold	no entry
25 Oct	pub	no entry	drinks	no entry	no entry
26 Oct	cinema	Ritz	Lillian Russell	Harold	no entry
26 Oct	café	Kardomah	no entry	no entry	no entry
27 Oct	cinema	Hippodrome	White Banners	Harold	no entry
27 Oct	pub	no entry	drinks	Harold	no entry
28 Oct	cinema	Hippodrome	Irene	Harold	no entry
28 Oct	dancing	Palais	no entry	Harold	no entry
28 Oct	dancing/?café	Palais, Mikardo	dancing then tea	no entry	VG
31 Oct	cinema	Palace	The Women	Harold	no entry
03 Nov	café	Barton	tea	Steph, Sold[ier]	very [illegible]
04 Nov	dancing	Institute	no entry	no entry	no entry

Date	Event	Venue	Details	With	Vera's comment
04 Nov	pub	Chequers	drink	Tom	no entry
06 Nov	pub	Bramcote	3 martinis bread and cheese	JB	VN
07 Nov	cinema	Hippodrome	Night Train Munich	Peggy	no entry
09 Nov	cinema	Ritz	Gaslight	no entry	no entry
09 Nov	café/ice rink	Mikardo	tea	no entry	fun
14 Nov	dancing	Institute	no entry	FJ	no entry
17 Nov	Barton	no entry	no entry	Steph and the boys	alright
18 Nov	cinema	Palladium	Contraband	Bill	no entry
19 Nov	cinema	Carlton	It Ended Happily	J	no entry
19 Nov	pub	Flying Horse	no entry	no entry	no entry
22 Nov	cinema	Palace	no entry	Harold	no entry
22 Nov	café	Mikardo	tea	Harold	no entry
23 Nov	dancing	dance	no entry	Harold	no entry
30 Nov	cinema	Astoria	It's a Date	no entry	no entry
05 Dec	dancing	no entry	no entry	Joan	no entry
13 Dec	pub	no entry	no entry	Steph	bottled up
22 Dec	party	Joan's	no entry	Steph, Joan	good
23 Dec	dancing	Palais	no entry	Stephanie	no entry
25 Dec	pub	Bluebell	no entry	Steph, Joan	nearly bottled
26 Dec	dancing	Regent	no entry	Stephanie	no entry
26 Dec	pub	Lion	drinks	Stephanie, met guys	good fun
28 Dec	cinema	Astoria	Typhoon	Harold	no entry
30 Dec	cinema	Hippodrome	Gas Bags	Harold	no entry
31 Dec	dancing	Palais	no entry	Harold	no entry

By anyone's standards this pace of life can only be described as frenetic. 'Burning the candle at both ends' has never been a more apt saying than when used to describe Vera's social activity in 1940.

The following comments concern Vera's social life in 1940 and are based on certain assumptions. We will never know whether these assumptions are correct, therefore readers are entitled to draw their own conclusions based on their interpretation of the data.

My assumptions are as follows:

1. 'T' was male and was probably 'Tom', who is also mentioned by name a number of times.
2. 'Mr B' and 'Mr Burnett' may have been Stephanie Jackson's (née Burnett) brother, but this is irrelevant. What is more relevant is that he was clearly male.
3. 'JB' was probably Mr Burnett, but, again, this is less relevant than that 'JB' was male.
4. 'Jeff and Andy' speak for themselves. It is probable that Vera refers to them when she uses the phrase 'the boys', but they were not boys. She refers to them as 'swaddies'. This is a slang expression for a soldier of the lowest rank. An alternative is 'squaddie'.

Apropos of nothing there is a superb description of a squaddie from *Pattaya Mail* as follows:

As the night wore on the singing got louder and the war stories bolder, mainly from the army contingent, or Squaddies, as they are known. What is a Squaddy? Well, he can be found anywhere: in love, in bars, in trouble and always in debt. Girls love them, towns tolerate them, hotels hide them and governments support them. His interests are girls, females, women and members of the opposite sex. His likes are beer, booze, plonk, alcohol and ale, leave passes and an 'excused-all-duties' chit. No one else could cram into one pocket food for 24 hours, a pack of crushed cigarettes, a box of matches, a picture of his girl, receipts for lost equipment, a deck of cards and an old leave pass.[56]

Jeff and Andy sound like the original 'swaddies'.

A study of her social movements must leave no one in doubt that Vera liked a drink and that she had plenty of male friends willing to buy her one. Again, one may ask why Vera saw the need to keep a diary and why she needed to record minutiae such as how many drinks she had and, possibly, what happened next. Clearly such an active social life meant that a diary was necessary and I believe that, in recording her drinking habits and other comments that are open to interpretation, she was taking delight in 'collecting' her conquests and being reminded of the excitement of her contact with them.

So what conclusions can we draw from this record of 1940, apart from that Vera was having a ball?

Well, firstly, it is interesting to note that she seems to have conducted intense relationships with her male friends. 'T' or 'Tom' seems to have had the best of her in the winter. Spring and early summer saw her testing the water with Mr Burnett and Jeff and Andy, with Harold popping up now and then. Summer and early autumn see 'JB' (presumably he is Mr Burnett) in total command, but what of late autumn and winter?

Further comments about Vera's social life will follow, but, before the later months are considered, what of the earlier months? Vera met 'T' or 'Tom' over twenty times from the first recorded meeting on February 10th at the 'Rail H' (maybe the Railway Hotel – location unknown, but there was, and is, a pub/hotel next to Beeston station called the Victoria), when she had a gin and ginger. The next day (the 11th) she recorded meeting T at Hands Café in Beeston and concluded that the meeting was 'very nice'.

It is worth noting that Harold had telegrammed Vera on February 10th that he was coming home on leave. She wired him £2. He arrived at 6.30 on the morning of the 12th *'when I was in bed. He looked lovely'*. On the evening of the 12th they went to see the Ark (or Arte) Ballet. On the 13th they had tea at the Ritz café (Nottingham). Harold then left for his post at 7.20 pm and *'travelled all through the night'*.

Later on the 13th Vera saw George Sanders as 'the Saint' in a film called *The Saint in London* at the Ritz cinema. At some point she also went to a 'milk bar'. She mentions the name 'Harry' in this context. Whether she had arranged to meet Harry to go to the cinema or whether she met Harry in the milk bar is unclear.

On February 14th she recorded that she stayed in and 'felt miserable'. She had recovered herself by the 18th because on that day she met six soldiers in Hands café and 'had fun'. In the following weeks, she met 'T' regularly. By late May 'T' is no more and 'Mr Burnett' briefly appears, but her time is also taken up by the two 'swaddies', Jeff and Andy.

Then in mid-August 'JB' arrives on the scene – or maybe he was the 'Mr Burnett' she had been out with earlier that year. Whoever he was is probably of no real importance except to note that from mid-August through to mid-October Vera goes out with JB approximately twenty-six times, with their meetings ranging from cinema, restaurant and pub visits to a day out in the Dukeries (a beauty spot north of Nottingham). She recorded that some of these dates were 'very nice' and others 'lovely'. Vera normally kept the description 'lovely' for her meetings with Harold.

The pattern that emerges in 1940 seems quite interesting. What of late autumn and winter? Where are Tom, Mr Burnett, JB, Jeff and Andy, following such enjoyable dates? They hardly get a look in. Harold suddenly takes over for the rest of the year, although there is a 'fallow' period when no one features, presumably because Harold cannot get leave. Virtually all of December up to Christmas seems a period of surprising inactivity.

Why does this change occur? Perhaps Vera realised that she was going off the rails. She had taken advantage of Harold's enforced absence to lead the life of Riley, but she realised she had to slow down, although this 'slowdown' may have been the result of Harold's transfer to Doncaster. Doncaster is only fifty miles from Chilwell, which is nothing on a motorbike. He was constantly on the road in his job and may even have had duties taking him to Chilwell Depot. Moreover, he could probably wangle enough petrol to do the return trip without this arousing suspicion. Consequently, there was a potential for Harold to turn up without notice or with very short notice. Perhaps there was a fear of being found out. The upside was, of course, that Vera was able to see Harold in Doncaster at weekends, which she did on several occasions.

There was also the fact that Vera was rapidly approaching her first wedding anniversary. Her diary entries at this time lend some support to the view that this anniversary was telling on her mind. Harold had seen her often in mid-October through to early November and sporadically in November but clearly could not get leave regularly in November and most of December. As mentioned, Harold's unavailability did not give rise to another round of social activity with other men. Letters and parcels flowed regularly in Harold's direction, though this was not unusual in any year, as we shall see.

On December 15th, the day before their wedding anniversary, Vera recorded that she was 'very miserable'. The war also intruded on her life at this time. She recorded air raids on both December 15th and 16th.

The situation was ameliorated somewhat because Harold was able to get seven days' leave from December 27th, which, of course, extended into the New Year. Vera immediately went to the doctor's and got a seven-day sick note. She signed off on the day that Harold went back to his unit on January 3rd. I doubt whether the doctor was fooled by whatever ailment Vera feigned.

That Vera had to get a sick note so that she could be with Harold for the duration of his leave is one of those minutiae of life at this time that underlines the point that the war was constantly present, even though

Vera's diaries virtually block out the events that were impinging from all sides. She rarely committed her thoughts and feelings about the war to paper.

Clearly, had she not got her own 'leave' for the duration of Harold's leave, she would have been at work. Why else get a doctor's note over the post-Christmas and New Year holidays? If Vera did have some ailment justifying a seven-day note it did not inhibit her from going out with Harold to the cinema, the theatre, several dances at the Nottingham Palais and a party at Stephanie's during this time.

Whilst there was potential for Harold to appear at short notice, this did not happen in his few months at Doncaster in 1941 apart from one occasion in March (the 25th). He was transferred shortly after this to the Maidstone area.

Love letters?

Reviewing Vera's social life during 1940 without the benefit of the diaries might lead the reader to think that she had time for little else during the evenings and no time at all for thinking about her husband, apart from when he was on leave, but this is far from the truth.

Vera was a prolific letter writer during the war and this practice continued throughout her life. Harold was the recipient of most of these letters in wartime. She also sent him a parcel of 'tuck' regularly for most of the war years. Harold wrote back on many occasions.

Indeed the amount of contact between Harold and Vera – daily and twice daily sometimes – makes Vera's social life with other men look somewhat incongruous. Was she leading a double life, or did Harold know all about these other men?

I doubt whether Harold was someone liberal enough to tolerate such goings-on, but equally it is quite possible that he, as a soldier on the continent prior to Dunkirk and stationed at various times in Crewkerne, Doncaster, Tunbridge Wells and Maidstone as well as on the continent after D-Day, also met his fair share of local 'talent'. He was, after all, a handsome man who, in the intimate atmosphere of the blackout, could easily be mistaken for Douglas Fairbanks Junior – one of the greatest film stars of his day. He was a pipe smoker when pipe smoking was considered sexy by many and had steely blue eyes and a winning smile that probably melted the hearts of quite a few young women.

IS THIS 44 DIV SIGNALS ?

Cartoon by 'Ken'

But back to the letter writing, parcels and phone calls. Vera did sometimes record her letter writing using phrases such as 'letter Harold' or 'write Harold', but often she used shorthand such as 'RH' and 'PH'.

From various entries in the diaries, it is clear that the 'H' of 'RH' and 'PH' almost always referred to Harold, although on occasion it might have referred to 'home'. The 'R' of 'RH' appears to be mainly referring to 'received Harold' (i.e. she had received a letter from Harold), but sometimes it may refer to 'rang Harold'. The 'P' of 'PH' referred often to 'parcel Harold' (i.e. she was recording that she had sent a parcel to Harold) but also refers to 'posted Harold'.

A study of the data recorded in the diaries provides a pattern at once predictable and fascinating for its insight into the amount of contact between civilians and military personnel and, of course, between Vera and Harold, whatever they were doing at the time.

The sheer statistics are quite impressive. Vera records sending post to Harold in the form of either a parcel or a letter more than 880 times between January 1940 and December 1945, and records nearly 650 replies from Harold, most of which would be letters rather than parcels. The graph below shows the close correlation between outgoing and incoming post.

The two were in almost constant contact with one another throughout the war. The only period when there appears to have been virtually no postal contact between Harold and Vera begins in the desperate days building up to the Dunkirk evacuation and continues for several months after the evacuation. The lull preceding Dunkirk is understandable, but the lack of postal contact immediately afterwards is unexplainable.

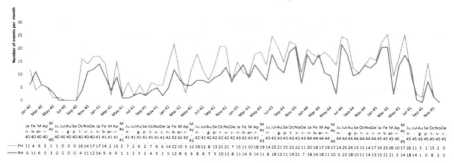

Frequency of postal contact from Vera to Harold and vice versa January 1940 to November 1945

(the blue line is from Vera to Harold
the red line is from Harold to Vera)

Harold Heard

Even during the massive military operation following D-Day, Harold and Vera were in regular contact with one another, which says much for the efficiency of the military postal service which operated throughout this period. 'News from home' was a morale booster for the troops, but how the troops found time to reply and what they were able to say in their letters home given military censorship would be an interesting study in its own right. Knowing what Harold and Vera wrote to one another during these years would be fascinating. Unfortunately, these letters have not survived.

Veronica

Although Vera had suffered the normal tiredness and sickness that accompanies pregnancy, there had been no complications in the pregnancy. Indeed Vera was working up to the hour that her waters broke. Veronica arrived at 7.15 pm on April 23rd 1944, almost one week before Vera's twenty-sixth birthday.

Harold surprised Vera by arriving on April 26th. Veronica was 'getting bigger' and 'feeding well', and on April 29th (Vera's birthday) Vera received a bouquet of orchids from Harold and 'two eggs from Mrs Heard'.

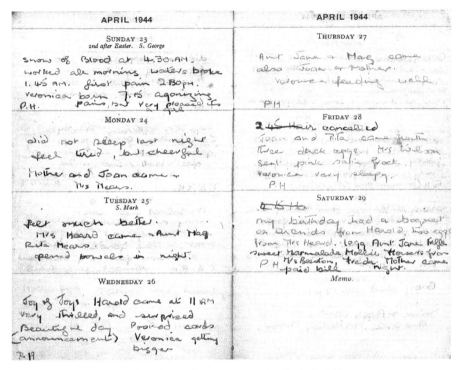

Diary for week commencing April 23rd 1944

Vera must have been overjoyed at her good fortune, but this pleasant state was not to last because on the night of April 30th Veronica had 'convulsions and a heart attack'. Despite blood transfusions, Veronica died at 4 pm on Wednesday May 3rd.

Veronica's loss must have been devastating for Vera. It seems clear that she had been trying for a baby for some time before she fell pregnant. There is a diary entry on July 18th 1943 which now, in the knowledge that she did fall pregnant only to lose her baby shortly after birth, seems poignant.

On this day Vera recorded that she '*worked til 1300 hrs wrote Sunday Pictorial Scylla Joan*'.

At the time that I first read this entry it seemed clear that Vera had read something in the *Sunday Pictorial* (a British Sunday newspaper now long gone) for July 18th that had prompted her to write to the newspaper. I thought that if they had published her letter then this would be a fascinating insight into some part of her life and thoughts.

I went on to the British Newspaper Archive[57] and paid my fee, thinking that there would be something like gold dust at the end of the *Sunday Pictorial* rainbow. I was disappointed. The *Pictorial* did not have a

APRIL—MAY 1944	MAY 1944
SUNDAY 30) *3rd after Easter* Baby taken ill in night with convulsions and heart attack. very unhappy and worried Sent for Harold Pokka, grandma, Aunt Dora, & Jack all came.	**THURSDAY 4** Harold came arrived at 7.30 pm very pleased and relieved. Mrs Heard came at night & Hilda.
MONDAY 1 MAY *SS. Philip and James* *Bank Holiday in Scotland* Harold arrived 4 pm returned on 11 pm train left here 9.pm. Very unhappy. Baby very ill very worried. Mother came night. P. H. (Mrs Hears. Aunt Edith, Mollie)	**FRIDAY 5** Joan, Mother, and Harold came at night. Harold with me all day other beds empty.
TUESDAY 2 Baby suffering from Heomophilia gave Blood Transfusion. feel better now I can do some thing Mrs Heard came. Aunt Mag. Mother. Baby slightly better at P.H night	**SATURDAY 6** Michaels Birthday. Mollie coming came out of Nursing Home at 2 pm very glad. Baby buried proper funeral feel very miserable.
WEDNESDAY 3 Baby died at 4 pm. Mollie & Peggy came, Aunt Edna, Mrs Heard, Mother,	*Memo.*

Diary for week commencing April 30th 1944

letters page, let alone one that had reproduced Vera's letter.

So I scoured the pages of the July 18th edition, asking myself what article could have possibly prompted Vera to write to the paper, then it became obvious. There was an article entitled 'Oh! I Wish He Were Mine', which dealt with the stories of four married women who wanted children but had not managed to conceive. Although the author of the article was not named, this was clearly a regular spot devoted to medical matters.

The following week's edition of the paper gave the answer to Vera's probable response to the earlier article. The follow-up article, written by the same journalist (presumably), was entitled 'Gossip About Babies' and referred to all the letters that the paper had received from women who wanted children.

The journalist wrote, '*Letters have come to me in hundreds, many of them quite heart-rending. And nine out of every ten implore me to help them so they can give their husband a child.*'

With Veronica, her hopes had been answered so quickly, only to be dashed within days of Veronica's birth in such a cruel way.

Other diary entries that followed her *Sunday Pictorial* note certainly support the idea that Vera wanted to get pregnant.

There is one fact that most women cannot escape, and that is the menstrual cycle. It is reasonable to suppose that a woman of the right age will know approximately when her period will be due each month, and many women who keep diaries are likely to keep a note not only of the approximate date for the start of her period but also of the actual date.

Vera was no exception to this rule, therefore it should be possible to pinpoint the event of conception, and hence the probable father, with some accuracy.

Although one missing period does not automatically mean that a conception has taken place, missing a series of periods culminating in the arrival of a baby nine months later gives a clear indication. The first missed period will then normally indicate the identity of the father, so long as there were not a number of potential candidates at the relevant time.

Vera had always made a diary note to remind her when her next period was due by using the phrase 'start sometime'. This note was invariably in pencil and presumably would be made at least a month in advance, at the start of the previous month's period, if not several months in advance.

Vera had recorded that she 'started' on August 22nd 1943. The diary entry for September 25th 1943 contained the phrase 'start sometime' in pencil, but this had been crossed out and the legend 'hope not' had been added in pencil and then crossed out. The full entry for that day reads: '~~start sometime hope not~~ *went to Dr's booked nursing home stayed in night.*'

Therefore Vera must have conceived at some time in late August or early September for her baby to arrive on April 23rd 1944.

Presumably, even at the earliest stage of pregnancy, Vera felt that she was pregnant. Why else would she have seen her doctor, who presumably did not dissuade her from this view, and then booked her place in a nursing home on the same day?

The fact that she booked the nursing home so far in advance might not have been unusual in those days. Maybe it was convention to do this as soon as you felt that you were pregnant. Maybe the pressure on resources in wartime contributed to this decision.

A reasonable question to ask, in the circumstances that have been described in previous passages, is whether Veronica was Harold's baby or whether she might have been illegitimate. After all, Vera had been playing the field in very particular wartime circumstances when close relationships with the opposite sex were common and the rate of illegitimacy in Britain soared.

Illegitimate births increased from an annual pre-war average of 5.5 per thousand births to 10.5 per thousand over the six wartime years, with a 1945 peak of 16.1 per thousand.[58] This wartime phenomenon was not confined to any one section of society. Every age group of mother had babies out of wedlock, concluded one social researcher:

Some were adolescent girls who had drifted away from homes that offered neither guidance nor warmth and security. Still others were women with husbands on war service, who had been unable to bear the loneliness of separation. There were decent and serious, superficial and flighty, irresponsible and incorrigible girls among them. There were some who had formed serious attachments and hoped to marry. There were others who had a single lapse, often under the influence of drink. There were, too, the 'good-time girls' who thrived on the presence of well-paid servicemen from overseas, and semi-prostitutes with little moral restraint. But for the war many of these girls, whatever their type, would never have had illegitimate children.[59]

With these statistics in mind it seems that, if the diary entries are accepted at face value, it is as certain as it can be that Veronica was Harold's child. Vera had visited Harold in Tunbridge Wells in September 1943, arriving on the 11th and leaving on the 13th. It is possible that she added 'hope not' to the September 25th entry because she hoped that she was now pregnant.

Unfortunately, there is a minor doubt about the identity of the father because Vera noted on September 8th 1943 that she had gone 'with North to Stoneleigh'. She was working for the Americans in the Harborne/Sutton Coldfield area at this time and other diary entries suggest that a man named Vic North was her boss.

Vic North had featured earlier in her 1943 diary, and there is a strong indication (by virtue of her use of the initials 'VN' and the name 'North' against entries for various evening dates) that he also featured in earlier diaries.

Stoneleigh is a pretty village in Warwickshire and probably owes its existence to Stoneleigh Abbey and the park and hall. It is possible that this visit was connected with war work at Stoneleigh Hall rather than being a weekend outing for pleasure.

Ironically, she had tea at 'Queens' with her old flame 'George' (presumably George Marshall) on September 18th but recorded that she was 'rather bored'. Moreover, it seems clear that she was pregnant by this time since she visited the doctor's only a week later, apparently to confirm her pregnancy.

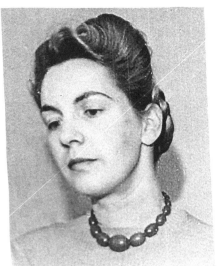

Vera aged 26

George Marshall

George Marshall was but one of a number of officers that Vera seems to have dated during her active social life. Others include Lt Foster (August 30th 1941), Captain Lodge (March 9th 1942), Captain Hendes (February 23rd and May 13th 1943) and Captain Platten (March 12th, March 18th, March 25th, April 1st and May 22nd 1942). Presumably they were all working at Chilwell Ordnance Depot.

However, George Marshall deserves more detailed mention quite apart from his apparent connection with Vera's acquisition of a fur coat. The reason for this is that his address appears in the diaries – an accolade reserved only for a select band of brothers. It seems reasonable to assume that, if Vera recorded the addresses of men that she had been out with, they probably meant more to her than any other casual male acquaintance.

Earlier, mention was made of George Marshall as a possible source for the fur coat that Vera 'acquired' in 1942, and his address appears in every diary from 1942 to 1944. It is also possible that even George's wife's address is recorded because the 1941 diary records a Mrs G Marshall of 27 Grange Road, West Hartlepool.

Taking the diaries all together, we can trace George's promotions through those addresses as the war went on as follows:

1942:   Captain G Marshall, Officers Mess, 75th Infantry Brigade, Home Forces

1943:   Captain G Marshall Officers Mess, 75th Infantry Brigade, Home Forces (first entry then crossed out)

1943:   Major G Marshall 42 Armoured Division Sub Park, Home Forces (second entry then crossed out)

1943   (third entry): Major G Marshall RAOC RSZGH APO 4728

1944   (front of diary): Major G Marshall RSZGH APO 4728

1944   (end of diary): Lieutenant Colonel George Marshall No 5 BOD MEF

Although the acronym 'RSZGH' is a mystery, George's final posting to BOD 5 MEF is quite telling. George probably got his final promotion by agreeing to move to Egypt, since No. 5 Base Ordnance Depot of the Middle Eastern Force was based there.

A trawl of the available material online suggests that George Marshall may have been 'mentioned in despatches' during his time in Egypt. There were three George Marshalls listed as officers in the Royal Army Ordnance Corps, one of whom was a temporary lieutenant colonel numbered 58846 when mentioned in despatches.

Although the first record of George's military address is in the 1942 diary, Vera appears to have first dated him in August 1941. The first date with George did not happen when it was supposed to. The diary entry for August 2nd 1941 reads in pencil '*5.30 Geo*' (being the diary note implying that a date had been arranged), but this is followed by an entry in ink: '*did not go met Steph*[anie] *went dancing R.L. very nice*'. Perhaps Vera had cold feet about this date, but she then proceeded to date George nine times in that August, six times in September and nine times in October. She dated him six times in the whole of 1942, twice in 1943 and then once in 1945.

This seems to follow the same path as Vera's relationship with 'T' or 'Tom' and Mr Burnett (or JB) in 1940. If she really liked someone, it seemed to be a full-on romance for a few months and then virtually nothing thereafter. With George, however, it is possible that his military life got in the way. He was promoted three times during the course of the diaries, including a transfer overseas, so it is possible that he simply was not available in later years.

Leon Kalinowski

Although Vera did go out with other men in later years, her social life did not have the same intensity as with Tom, Mr Burnett and George Marshall in 1940 and 1941. There was just one more 'fling' in 1944 and 1945 that had the hallmarks of the earlier period, and that was with Corporal Leon Kalinowski, whose address is given in the 1944 diary as MQ 29 RAF Station Newton (Nottinghamshire).

Mention is made of Leon here, under a separate heading, because talking of him amongst the rest of Vera's varied male friends would take Vera's relationship with Leon out of context. According to her diaries, Leon was the only man that Vera dated regularly after the death of her newborn daughter, Veronica.

We must not forget that life was changing for many people in Britain after the Americans became our allies and the war started to turn round in our favour. Life was also changing for Vera specifically, who was getting older and maybe a lot wiser.

By the time that Leon came on the scene Vera had left home to live in her own flat in Nottingham and was looking for a job there. This materialised soon after her first meeting with Leon, when she got a job in the accounts department at Nottingham Guildhall. Although she was a married woman for all of the war, she had lived at home by dint of circumstance. Now she was fully independent.

But, surely, the most important event shaping her outlook on life at this time took place in May 1944 with the death of her ten-day-old daughter, Veronica. She must have come down to the ground with a crash when this happened, even though her thoughts and feelings about this event hardly emerge from subsequent diary entries. She certainly thought of Veronica throughout her life and mentioned her birth to me on numerous occasions over the years. This was no unfortunate but transient event in an otherwise enjoyable war.

Therefore, the timing of Leon's emergence in Vera's life is in a completely different context to that of her earlier male friends, so making her relationship with Leon Kalinowski somewhat different from her earlier flings.

RAF Newton was situated seven miles east of Nottingham. Between July 1941 and December 1946 it was used as a training base with No. 16 (Polish) Service Flying Training School providing basic and advanced training for Polish airmen serving with the RAF, using RAF Tollerton as a satellite landing ground.[60] Leon was Polish by birth.

The first mention of Leon in the 1944 diary is an entry for October 25th 1944 as follows:

Leon 3 pm Ritz Freda 7 pm. He could not get. Went to Palais not very good drinking night bored Freda stayed the night bought suite from Griffins

Clearly Vera must have met Leon before October 25th, otherwise there would have been no entry to remind her that she had arranged to see Leon at the Ritz (restaurant). It was to be an afternoon meeting but he could not make it.

There is no entry in the diary prior to that date that could be construed as the day when Vera met Leon, although a pub called the Flying Horse was a favourite haunt of Polish airmen during the war, as was the Palais de Danse, and Vera certainly frequented both venues. A member of the Polish RAF wrote:

On Sundays, when there is no flying, we go by trolleybuses to Nottingham ... and mostly finish in the Palais de Dance. Dances are very popular ... as the females outnumber the males, who are mostly in the forces, we have the field to ourselves. There is a very good canteen in town ... and generally the forces are well looked after.[62]

Presumably they were in contact by phone to arrange the next date, because Vera met Leon at Nottingham Hippodrome three days later on the 28th October. This was also the day that she went to the labour exchange and got the job at Nottingham Guildhall.

November 1st saw another arrangement to meet at the Ritz, but she received 'a wire' from Leon that he could not make the date. November 9th sees another diary entry concerning a proposed date with Leon, but he could not make that date either.

Vera wrote a letter to Leon on November 16th and finally met up with him again on the 18th. They had a meal at the County Hotel in Nottingham, which she described as 'very nice'.

From then on there were regular meetings with Leon, often at the County but also at the cinema and various pubs. She records seeing Leon another nineteen times.

The last meeting recorded in her diary was on October 27th 1945 at the Bentinck Hotel and the County Hotel. Her diary entries virtually ceased from that time forward for the rest of 1945, so there is no telling whether that was her last meeting with Leon. October 28th was the last day when she made any entries in her 1945 diary apart from the most basic of notes such as hair appointments, for example.

There is nothing in the diaries that suggests that Leon spent any of these nights with Vera, notwithstanding that she now had her own flat in Nottingham within easy walking distance of the city centre.

Why did she stop making diary notes at this time? She had made diary entries for every day from January 1st 1940 until now. Admittedly, the war was over, but there is no reason to suppose that she was writing the diaries as a deliberate act connected with the war per se. Moreover, a diary exists for 1958 and many diaries exist for later years.

The 1958 diary does have some significance because it was on December 19th 1957 that Vera's mother was killed in a tragic accident as she attempted to cross a busy road from behind a bus that she had just alighted from. The driver was found to be intoxicated, but Alice Blacknell might also have contributed to the accident when attempting to cross the road.

The 1958 diary pages start from December 22nd 1957. It seems quite clear that Vera retained this diary because it recorded her mother's death and the aftermath. Was this the first diary to be kept since 1945? In my opinion, this is unlikely. It is more likely that Vera kept a diary in earlier years. If this is the case, why did she not retain these diaries and why did the 1945 diary entries peter out in October of that year? Why did she retain the 1940 to 1945 diaries when they contained substantial information about extramarital activity (at whatever level one cares to put that activity)? These are relevant questions even though there are no answers.

Whilst attempting to find out more about Leon Kalinowski I came across a valuable source of information in the form of a site dedicated to Polish airmen.

Leon was a corporal mechanic. His RAF service number was 794854. He was born in Skryhiczyn, Chelm, Poland. He died in Kielce, Poland, on October 13th 1976.[63]

Until Victory

I (British) Corps, February 3rd 1944 to January 14th 1946

Insignia of I (British) Corps

At 7 pm on June 1st 1944, Vera received a 'wire' (telegram) from Harold. The contents of that wire are unknown, but we can guess, because Vera caught a train from Attenborough station at 11.58 that same evening and was in Farnham, Surrey, by 8.30 am the next day (diary entries for June 1st and 2nd 1944). There is little doubt that Harold had informed her that he would not be in England for much longer. Whether Harold had direct information that the D-Day landings would take place within days or whether he guessed so through the rumour mill is unknown. Either way, he was right. The landings took place on June 6th.

Vera wired Harold on her arrival. He was able to meet her at 11 am on June 3rd. They walked around Farnham and had a drink that evening.

It seems that Harold was able to stay with Vera for several days. Her location is unknown, but from various diary entries at this time it seems that Stephanie Jackson (née Burnett) was also in the area and may have been living in Farnham. She certainly was living there after the war.

The diary entries from June 4th to the 8th read as follows:

June 4th *Harold and I went to camp on the bikes nice ride in the morning came back for dinner went to pub at night*

June 5th *Harold went at 7 am. Came back 3 pm went to pub at night*

June 6th *[D-Day] went to the pictures in the afternoon with Harold pub night very nice Mission to Berlin George Sanders invasion France*

June 7th *went to bed afternoon went over to Harold's camp to fetch pass not signed Crookham X Roads Haque Camp Fleet*

June 8th   *Harold came at 2.30 they[?] phoned for him at 5.30 Steph and I went in the lorry with the boys to camp met Pat and had nice night Harold moving off 5 am. 9 June*

So it appears that Harold spent at least the night of June 4th/5th with Vera. The entry for June 7th is intriguing. It appears that Harold had to go back to his camp, which was called Haque (or maybe Hague) Camp, near Crookham crossroads, but that he was unable to get a pass. However, he then saw Vera at 2.30 pm on June 8th but was called back to camp at 5.30 that afternoon in preparation for embarkation to France.

Harold did not embark for France on June 9th. He must have gone into a holding area somewhere near the coast, because his service record shows that he embarked on June 11th.

His initial destination in France is less certain, but there is some indication that Harold landed at the 'Mike' section of Juno Beach just outside Courseulles-sur-Mer. This is conjecture, but Peter Rock, son of Bill Rock, a great wartime and peacetime buddy of Harold's, told me that his father had said that they had to aim for a big 'M' when they landed in France. It is possible that there was a large hoarding, visible from the sea, with the letter 'M' painted on it, and this possibly stood for 'Mike', a subsection of Juno Beach and the main D-Day landing point for Canadian troops. Moreover Courseulles-sur-Mer was an early location of I (British) Corps HQ (see below).

Unfortunately there are severe obstacles in the way of writing an account of Harold's wartime experiences in northwest Europe.

I have already referred to the fact that Harold talked little about the war. Moreover, his job as a despatch rider assigned to I (British) Corps HQ means that he cannot be connected directly with the exploits of any particular army unit such as the Guards Armoured Division, which was the subject of books by illustrious commanders and others, though it can be said that I (British) Corps' commander General Sir John Crocker was one of the most respected of all British commanders in the war.

I (British) Corps itself was too large to be able to pinpoint particular military actions that Harold may or may not have been involved in. Clearly, as a despatch rider servicing I Corps HQ, Harold was likely to have transported many despatches to sub-units of I Corps, but I Corps consisted of many thousands of soldiers being members of many different military units.

Band of Brothers

I (British) Corps' 'Order of Battle' in the northwest Europe campaign from D Day to 1945 was as follows:

GOC: Lieutenant-General John Crocker

Corps troops:
- *Inns of Court Regiment, Royal Armoured Corps (armoured cars)*
- *62nd Anti-Tank Regiment, Royal Artillery (left November 1944 for British Eighth Army)*
- *102nd Light Anti-Aircraft Regiment, RA*
- *9th Survey Regiment, RA*
- *1st Corps Troops, Royal Engineers*
- *1st Corps Signals*

Attached:
- *4th Army Group, Royal Artillery*
- *150th (South Nottinghamshire Hussars Yeomanry) Field Regiment, RA (suspended animation January 1945)*

- *53rd (London) Medium Regiment, RA (209 & 210 (London) Batteries)*
- *65th Medium Regiment, RA (222 (Fraserborough) & 223 (Banffshire) Batteries)*
- *68th Medium Regiment, RA (212 & 233 Batteries)*
- *79th (Scottish Horse Yeomanry) Medium Regiment, Royal Artillery*
- *51st (Lowland) Heavy Regiment, RA*

Assignments of corps to armies, and divisions to corps, changed frequently during the campaign:

As of 6 June 1944
- *British 3rd Infantry Division*
- *3rd Canadian Infantry Division*
- *6th Airborne Division*

As of 7 July 1944
- *British 3rd Infantry Division*
- *3rd Canadian Infantry Division*
- *51st (Highland) Infantry Division*
- *59th (Staffordshire) Infantry Division*
- *6th Airborne Division*

As of 1 August 1944 (now part of First Canadian Army)
- *51st (Highland) Infantry Division*
- *6th Airborne Division (returned to United Kingdom 3 September 1944)*
- *49th (West Riding) Infantry Division*
- *7th Armoured Division*

Harold could have been involved in DR duties that took him to the local HQs of any of the above units during his time in Europe. This is the downward-looking path, but he could also have had duties that took him upwards at least to Montgomery's HQ (I Corps being a sub-unit of Montgomery's 21st Army Group) and the First Canadian Army HQ. His wartime experiences in this sort of detail will never be known.

Even I (British) Corps' detailed wartime history has not been written, so there is no direct source of published material. However, I did do extensive research amongst published material about subject matter that was connected with I Corps, such as various Canadian military histories as well as those of the two principal divisions under I (British) Corps command – namely the 51st (Highland) Infantry Division and the 49th (West Riding) Division.

I have listed my source material at the end of this book, but I wish to make mention here of two military historians who helped me get over a major stumbling block to my research by giving me the key to great sources of primary material in the National Archives at Kew.

I contacted Mark Zuehlke, author of two books (amongst others) about the First Canadian Army (*Terrible Victory*, about the Scheldt Estuary Campaign of September–November 1944, and *Forgotten Victory*, covering the winter of 1944–45), with a plea to help me find primary source material about I Corps on the grounds that he would have come across such material in his research of Canadian military operations. He was most sympathetic to my cause and put me into contact with a Dutch military history researcher named Johan Van Doorn.

Johan sent me details of many War Office files stored at Kew that will help me with further research and, crucially, details of a Canadian archive that contains microfiche of the war diary of I (British) Corps. This made fascinating reading, although military 'text speak' has its own lexicon which makes it difficult to understand at times.

However, the most important information that I was able to glean from this war diary was the precise location of I Corps HQ at any given time.

Because the sources supplied to me by Johan will clearly require extensive and detailed research I have decided to carry on with what material I have from secondary sources to make sure that this book is finished, rather than suspending it as an unfinished work pending that detailed research, which could last for years.

Without the detailed National Archives research, we are left with something of a black hole around the sort of detail that one would dearly love to include in a monograph of this sort. Vera's diaries are no help apart from documenting when Harold was on leave.

Mercifully, there is some detail that can be gleaned from the few artefacts that Vera saved – mainly photographs and a meagre tranche of written material. When coupled with what is known about I Corps operations, this information is sufficient to sketch in Harold's likely movements over the years from D-Day in 1944 to his demob in January 1946.

The crucial information as to Harold's possible location from the Canadian archive is as follows:

Location of I (British) Corps Headquarters, northwest Europe, June–December 1944

Archive ref.	Date	Location
T2541/1	02 June	Southampton
T2541/1	05 June	At sea
T2541/2	06 June	Courseulles-sur-Mer
T2541/4	10 June	Douvres-la-Délivrande
T2543/6	07 August	Biéville
T2543/7	09 August	Giberville
T2543/7	10 August	South of Mondeville
T2543/10	17 August	Quatrepuits
T2543/14	23 August	La Motte (about five miles west of Lisieux)
T2543/17	30 August	Bois Inger
T2544/1	01 October	Zandhoven
T2544/4	05 October	Turnhout
T2544/6	08 October	Zandhoven
T2544/7	13 October	Turnhout
T2544/11	24 October	Camp de Brasschaet (Brasschaart)
T2545/1	01 December	Tilburg
T2545/5	12 December	Breda

Note that the above is not a definitive list due to gaps in the microfiche for various dates

One of the key sources of information directly relating to Harold's movements is in the form of a soup plate he owned, which was painted with various insignia, geographic destinations and a cartoon. It is quite likely that Harold or one of his unit painted this plate, because it clearly relates to key moments in his wartime history. The style of writing on the plate does compare quite well with Harold's handwriting.

The four insignia painted on the plate at positions north, south, east and west clearly relate to Harold's wartime placements. The northern position is taken by the insignia for I (British) Corps and the southern by the Guards Armoured Division. The western position is allocated to Harold's first placement –the 44th Division – and the eastern position to XII Corps.

The spaces in between the insignia list geographic locations that clearly

The painted soup plate

relate to Harold's time with I Corps: the rivers Rhine, Roer and Maas, then the towns of Caen, Falaise and Dieppe in France, followed by Turnhout, Tilburg and Breda in Belgium and the Netherlands. Finally, we reach Germany with Goch, Rhede and Iserlohn as key places on the plate.

Without this plate we would have virtually no information to go on concerning Harold's wartime experiences after D-Day, but with it we can begin to piece together something of the history of his movements and the military operations that he may well have been involved in.

Given that these geographic locations must have been of great significance to Harold and therefore were given pride of place on the plate, we may also conclude that the absence of certain locations might mean that they were of less significance to him, notwithstanding that I (British) Corps was known to have been directly involved in a major military action there. For example, the port of Le Havre was the site of one of I (British) Corps' major battles, under the code name of 'Astonia', yet the plate does not mention it. However, it does mention Falaise. This was the site of one of the most decisive battles of the Second World War, but I (British) Corps appears to have played a supporting part rather than a part at the sharp end.

I think that we must follow the logic of the information on the plate and link it to what is known about I (British) Corps' movements in northwest

Europe in 1944 and 1945. This might then give a flavour at least of what Harold was up to in these crucial years.

However, to understand the history of I Corps in this period, there is another major factor to take into account, and that is the history of the First Canadian Army. Montgomery assigned I Corps to the First Canadian Army with effect from July 23rd 1944, so to say that Harold was a minute cog in a giant war machine is no exaggeration.

Notwithstanding this apparently miniscule role in the war effort, we also have the distinct possibility that, since Harold was part of I (British) Corps HQ signals squadron, he could have been involved in communications not only between I Corps and Montgomery's HQ but also between I Corps and the First Canadian Army HQ. Maybe listing Falaise on the commemorative plate should be seen in this context.

But let us look at the brief period from Harold's arrival on French soil somewhere between June 11th and 12th to late July 1944. At that time, I Corps was under Montgomery's direct control and played a significant role in the battle to take over Caen following D-Day.

Caen was only eight to ten miles from Gold, Juno and Sword beaches, which had landed tens of thousands of British and Canadian troops and equipment on the few days from June 6th to the 11th. Montgomery's express aim was to take Caen on D-Day itself, yet fighting was so intense and the logistical exercise was so great that Caen, by then virtually a heap of rubble, did not finally fall to British and Canadian troops until more than a month later. This was I Corps' first battle and probably more intense, in terms of its direct involvement, than any in the succeeding year.

Thereafter I Corps was subservient to a Canadian master, and a master whose interests were possibly served better by keeping I Corps in a subsidiary role.

Every published source makes mention of the strained relations between the British and Canadian hierarchy in the northwest Europe campaign, but the matter is best illustrated by this extract from Mark Zuehlke's book *Forgotten Victory*.

> *Montgomery tended to meddle in the decision-making process for senior appointments to ensure that they were to men who were part of his inner circle. But he accepted Crocker* [General Officer Commanding I Corps] *without apparent question. In the opening weeks of the invasion, the compact nature of the bridgehead in Normandy was such that Crocker oversaw the British–Canadian operations in the invasion's left*

flank. Not until July 23 did I British Corps come under First Canadian Army and Crerar's command. Although Crocker was noted for his mild temperament, the two clashed immediately. First, Crocker had been highly critical of 3rd Canadian Infantry Division's Major General Rod Keller and actively sought to have him sacked. Second, he refused to implement the first operational directive Crerar gave him. Ever ready to bristle at any sign that British officers considered themselves innately superior to Canadians, Crerar flew into a fury. He told Montgomery that Crocker, either for personal reasons or 'because of the fact that I am a Canadian ... resented being placed under my command ... [and showed] no tact nor desire to understand my views.' He asked Montgomery to swap him for another British corps commander. Montgomery refused ... Thereafter relations between Crerar and Crocker remained strained ... At the same time Crerar consigned Crocker and his corps to the role of supporting II Canadian Corps rather than serving as an equal partner.[65]

Maybe Harold's life as a DR was made less dangerous because of this clash at the top. Is it possible that he experienced a less intensive experience than other DRs at the front of the firing line? Who knows, but suffice it to say that once Caen had been overcome I Corps always seemed to have the support role mentioned by Mark Zuehlke, apart from during the liberation of Le Havre under the operational code name of 'Astonia'.

Although Le Havre does not figure on the commemorative plate it is almost inconceivable that Harold did not play a role in that operation. Perhaps it was just that there was not enough space on the plate to insert this name. Therefore, I will consider it in this monograph, but let us first dwell on Caen, which is the first of the towns mentioned on the plate.

Caen: Operations Charnwood and Goodwood, July 7th to 20th 1944

Charnwood commenced with the aim of attacking and capturing Caen on July 8th 1944, ending the next day. Elements of I (British) Corps (3rd Canadian Division, 59th Division and 3rd British Division) took part, resulting in I Corps occupying a part of the town, so the attack was partially successful, but it had to be followed by further attacks by XII (British) Corps and XXX (British) Corps, then by another major operation known as Goodwood.

Goodwood (July 18th to 20th 1944) involved three British armoured divisions: the 11th, the 7th and the Guards Armoured Division. Again, this only met with partial success, but a simultaneous operation by Canadian troops in the south of Caen was more successful. II Canadian Corps under the codename Operation Atlantic cleared areas south of Caen that would prove valuable in assisting the future operation called Totalise, which aimed to surround and cut off a major portion of the German army in Normandy around the area of Falaise, a small town about nineteen miles south of Caen.

July 23rd saw I (British) Corps being subsumed into the First Canadian Army, its first role being to take control of the eastern end of the Normandy bridgehead.

Falaise: Operations Totalise and Tractable, August 7th to 23rd 1944

The operations known as Totalise and Tractable proved to be among the most decisive of the war.

Operation Totalise ... was an offensive launched by Allied troops of the First Canadian Army during the later stages of Operation Overlord ... The intention was to break through the German defences south of Caen on the eastern flank of the Allied positions in Normandy and exploit success by driving south to capture the high ground north of the city of Falaise. The goal was to precipitate the collapse of the entire German front, and cut off the retreat of German forces fighting American and British armies further west. The battle is considered the inaugural operation of the First Canadian Army, which had been formally activated on 23 July.[66]

I (British) Corps' role as a supporting formation has been mentioned already. This was its part in Totalise. It backed up the First Canadian Army rather than being a spearhead, which is somewhat ironic because I Corps' insignia was a light-coloured spearhead on a red lozenge background. However, once the Falaise operation was drawing to a close I Corps was allowed its head.

I Corps' role in the Falaise operation was to protect the eastern flank of the First Canadian Army, but once this was done it was ordered to strike out northeastwards in the direction of the River Seine and the channel ports of Le Havre and Dieppe.

On 15th August, with General Simonds' Corps [Second Canadian Army] approaching Falaise, the moment had come. On that day, following a conference with General Montgomery, General Crerar instructed General Crocker to capture St Pierre-sur-Dives without delay. On the 16th the Army Commander, conferring with Simonds and Crocker, told the latter that he was required to press on along the axis St Pierre-sur-Dives–Lisieux. To assist him the 7th British Armoured Division ... had been transferred to the First Canadian Army and would be placed under Crocker's command forthwith.

The advance began on a small scale on the 15th; that day, the 49th Division ['The Polar Bears'], in the centre, took Vimont. On the 16th the 51st [Highland] Division, on the right, captured St Pierre-sur-Dives, while the 49th got some troops across the Dives at Mezidon. On the left the 6th Airborne Division's movements began [acting as infantry] early on the 17th. On the same day the 7th Armoured Division joined in the advance. During the next few days the 1st Corps pushed westward against stiffening opposition. Liverot was taken on the 20th August and by the 22nd the 7th Armoured Division was fighting in Lisieux, where the Germans resisted strongly. The town was not cleared until the 24th. In the meantime, the 6th Airborne Division was engaged in a similar contest farther down the River Touques at Pont l'Eveque.[67]

The battle of Falaise was now over and the First Canadian Army was ordered to advance towards the River Seine. These few words are easy to write, but what of the human cost of this military exercise?

The First Canadian Army was only one component of a much larger enterprise involving the US and the Polish armies, not to mention the Germans who died or were wounded and the civilians who were caught up in it.

The cost of lives and injury in the whole of the First Canadian Army alone from August 1st to the morning of August 23rd 1944 amounted to over 12,000 men killed, wounded or missing. Of these 423 officers and 6,992 men were Canadian, 276 officers and 3,594 men were British and 127 officers and 1,247 men were Polish.[68]

The D-Day landings and subsequent operations had finally started to push the German army back from the coast. Defeat of the German army at Falaise marked the end of the Normandy campaign, but the liberation of Normandy was not without the loss of much blood.

The Battle of the Falaise Pocket ended the Battle of Normandy with a decisive German defeat ... More than forty German divisions were destroyed during the Battle of Normandy. No exact figures are available but historians estimate that the battle cost the German forces c. 450,000 men, of whom 240,000 were killed or wounded [Williams, A. (2004). *D-Day to Berlin.* London: Hodder & Stoughton, p. 205]. *The Allies had achieved victory at a cost of 209,672 casualties among the ground forces, including 36,976 killed and 19,221 missing* [Hastings, M. (2006) [1985]. *Overlord: D-Day and the Battle for Normandy* (reprint ed.). New York: Vintage Books USA, p.303]. *The Allied air forces lost 16,714 airmen killed or missing in connection with Operation Overlord* [Tamelander, Michael; Zetterling, Niklas (2003) [1995]. *Avgörandes ögonblick: Invasionen i Normandie 1944.* Stockholm: Norstedts förlag, p. 341]. *The final battle of Operation Overlord, the Liberation of Paris, followed on 25 August and Overlord ended by 30 August, with the retreat of the last German unit across the Seine* [Hastings, p. 319].[69]

We can only imagine Harold's experiences from June to the end of August 1944. There can be no doubt that he, along with many thousands of other ordinary men from all walks of life and from many countries supporting the effort to eradicate the German scourge, lived a life in those few months that none of us have lived since.

We must forever remember these people and be thankful that we have been able to live our own lives free of oppression and tyranny.

DRs need two forms of fuel – the chef is second from the right

Just as an aside, maybe it is pertinent to see what Vera was doing whilst Harold was playing his part in this war. The picture is one, more or less, of domestic bliss. No matter what horrors were happening in northern France, life had to go on at home, and so it did. Her diary entries for August 1944 are as follows:

Aug 1st: *ironed in the morning went to the Victoria Dance Hall with Freda had good time with Turk tea Café de Paris dancing at night*

Aug 2nd: *Ritz 6.30 pm J.P. cleaned bedrooms in morning rather boring night went round* [Nottingham] *castle grounds*

Aug 3rd: *cleared living room in the morning bottled fruit afternoon Mollie* [Beeston] *came night*

Aug 4th: *4 pm. Majestic Turk to late Market early only 1lb of plums shopping in Co-op noon Joan came went Bluebell at night lovely weather*

Aug 5th: *7 pm. County J.P. Eileen Churchs afternoon went to see Harry* [Hay] *he was in pain. Saw J night very boring*

Aug 6th: *sunbathed in garden in afternoon lovely and hot saw J 7.30 rather boring*

Aug 7th: *stayed in all day sunbathed in the garden in the afternoon lovely weather now with Mother*

Aug 8th: *rather cloudy today went Mollies in the morning sunbathed in the afternoon Joan* [Davis] *came night went her house*

Aug 9th: *Mollie 3.30 pm. Meadow Lane went picnic down the Trent with Mollie Michael* [Vera's baby brother] *Beeston in the morning*

Aug 10th: *Eileen for tea not coming bought plums in the morning and bottled them went swimming in river at night with Winnie Oxley*

Aug 11th: *Hair 2.30 pm. Joan Fair* [probably Goose Fair] *5 pm. got plums in the morning had hair done noon had fun in boxing booth at fair with Joan*

Aug 12th: *grandma's bottles Grundy's bottles and plums Long Eaton pan kettle Aunt Jane cakes and parcel for Harold bottle rhubarb for Joan*

Aug 13th: *cleaned bedroom in the morning peeled onions for pickling afternoon went to Bluebell* [pub] *at night with Joan*

Aug 14th: *washed frocks this morning cut privet bushes went to the river for picnic with Michael swimming very nice*

Aug 15th: Joan coming have glasses frames mended photographs taken see shoes down town til 4 pm. most beautiful weather

Aug 16th: Joan came at night went to the Astoria 'Jack London' good film

Aug 17th: went swimming with Geofrey in the [crossed out 'morning'] afternoon very nice bottled fruit

Aug 18th: Mrs Calvert 2 pm. took the baby down to Eileens went to the Astoria at night 'The Uninvited' very good film dull day

Aug 19th: pouring with rain went to Nottingham with Joan went Hippodrome 'Fanny by Gaslight' very good

Aug 20th: wrote insurance, Scylla, Patricia, Peggy rained very bad weather Joan came night Bluebell

Aug 21st: went to see Mollie in the morning, Madge afternoon she is married again wrote army pay office

Aug 22nd: get plums for Madge 6lbs not very good unhappy day Joan came night

Aug 23rd: rained in the morning cleared up in the afternoon Mollie came for tea very pleasant

Aug 24th: went to Heards [father- and mother-in-law] in the morning down the river with Michael in the afternoon preserved fruit at night

Aug 25th: Edith Wright went for tea and to see Harry at night he is very ill Edith came did shopping in the morning joined the co-op

Aug 26th: go to Joans wedding 2.30 Hancocks had a good time nice reception did not get home until 1.30 am.

Aug 27th: stayed in the morning went to Joans for tea Astoria afternoon 'Birth of the Blues' Bing Crosby alright

Aug 28th: letter from Joan this morning me to go with her to the doctors, went was very interesting also went to see Gone with the Wind

Aug 29th: Draw money Go Wrights stamps Plums for Madge Mrs Wright Mollie toothpaste piles doctors Joan night went to Davises in the evening

Aug 30th go David early bottle fruit Harold parcel Madge plums Barbara 6.30 pm Palais Edith Wrights had marvellous time at the Palais

Aug 31st: clean bedroom write letters go Wrights go David Harolds parcel clean shoes washing very busy all the day Harry died today

'Harry', mentioned in the entries for the 5th, 25th and 31st, was Harold's sister's husband. He is believed to have been a tailor by profession but was in the Royal Air Force during the war. He died of injuries (and subsequent complications) as a result of falling off the wing of an aeroplane onto the runway.

First Canadian Army: general strategy

To put Harold's movements into context at a micro level we need to ask what the Canadian army's role was in the North West Europe Campaign. Why did Harold list the rivers Rhine, Roer and Maas on his commemorative plate and why the towns of Dieppe, Turnhout, Tilburg, Breda, Goch, Rhede and Iserlohn?

The answer is to be found in Montgomery's overall strategy for the Canadian armies. They were to fight their way up the left flank of northwest Europe, i.e. the coastal sector.

We have already noted that no sooner had the battle for Falaise entered its final stage than I (British) Corps was ordered northeast to the Seine and beyond.

Montgomery's strategy was to protect the left flank of the First and Second Canadian Armies whilst the Second British Army protected their right flank. Ultimately, the Canadian armies were intended to take Antwerp in order to provide this vital northern port as a supply line to the northern armies as a whole (Canadian, British, Polish and US), given that the supply line stretching from the D-Day landings would get too thin to be of effective use in the north.

This task proved to be one of the hardest fought campaigns of the war in Europe. Taking Antwerp was not the problem. The problem was that the navigable waterway from the North Sea to Antwerp, including Walcheren Island, was heavily defended by German troops who had been ordered by Hitler to fight to the last man.[70]

Moreover, not only were the Germans not going to budge from the low-lying mud flat islands of the Scheldt estuary but the terrain could be easily flooded to provide yet more of a defensive barrier. It was one thing to capture Amsterdam, but it was another to capture the waterways that enabled the ports to operate once again.

Le Havre and Dieppe: September 1st to 12th 1944

I Corps reached the Seine on August 29th 1944. Reconnaissance elements of I Corps crossed the Seine on August 30th at Duclair and

Caudebec-en-Caux. They were able to report that the enemy had withdrawn.[71]

Now we have a mystery which unfortunately cannot be answered without extensive research at the National Archives in Kew and may never be capable of resolution. Why did Harold's commemorative plaque mention Dieppe but not Le Havre?

In a nutshell, Dieppe was given up by the Germans without a fight and without any apparent involvement by I Corps, whereas Le Havre was the subject of a major onslaught by the two main fighting elements of I Corps, namely the 49th and 51st Divisions.

Tantalisingly men on motorcycles actually did feature in the capture of Dieppe, but Harold's involvement is highly unlikely.

The 2nd Division's reconnaissance unit, the 8th Reconnaissance Regiment (14th Canadian Hussars) had arrived at Totes, just half way from Rouen to Dieppe and less than twenty miles from the latter place, in the course of 31 August. They took the village after a sharp little fight; and next morning they pushed on towards their goal.

About ten o'clock in the morning of 1 September, the extreme forward elements of the 'Recce' cautiously approached Dieppe. They reached the wire and the minefields; but no enemy guns spoke out to cover these obstacles; and shortly after ten two men on motorcycles, pushing forward to the edge of the town itself, appeared at the head of the Rue Gambetta, the long straight street which slopes steeply down to the west end of the Dieppe waterfront. The people of Dieppe had watched the German rear parties leave the previous day, and since that moment had been waiting to greet the liberators. Now they threw themselves at the two motorcyclists, and in the words of a local newspaper, 'Ce fut un moment de délire'. When the vanguard of the unit began to arrive a little later, they found the streets jammed with cheering people who covered their vehicles with flowers.[72]

Le Havre was a different kettle of fish. I have decided to include a brief consideration of this action here because, as I said before, I (British) Corps was entirely responsible for the liberation of Le Havre and I am sure that Harold would have been involved since he was a DR attached to I Corps HQ.

The two main fighting units in I Corps, being the 49th (West Riding) Division and the 51st (Highland) Division, were tasked with liberating Le Havre.

The great ocean port, surrounded by water on three sides, was heavily defended by coast artillery batteries, most of which could only fire to seaward. Though the land defences were incomplete, Colonel Eberhard Wildermuth, the fortress commander, had a garrison of more than 11,000 troops supported by 76 field and medium and anti-aircraft guns.

The systematic softening of the enemy's defences began on 5th September with a heavy bomber attack and a bombardment from H M Monitor Erebus. Her 15-inch shells were landing on the German defences when she herself was hit by a 14.8-inch gun of the Grand Clos battery. Her port after-hold flooded and she withdrew to Portsmouth for repairs. She returned to the attack on the 8th, but again was hit and retired. On separate days, Bomber Command struck at three areas of the port's defences dropping some 4,000 tons of bombs. Then on the 10th the naval and air bombardments intensified. Sixty aircraft attacked the Grand Clos battery and later, in two major attacks by nearly 1,000 bombers, the RAF dropped a further 4,900 tons of explosives. Following it, Erebus and the battleship Warspite engaged casemated guns on the perimeter defences of Le Havre. The Grand Clos battery replied but finally was silenced by Warspite's guns.

All day on the 10th 1st Corps' gunners had been working on the destruction of German artillery and mortars. Then, at 5.45 that afternoon, the infantry and armour attacked.

Crocker's plan was to take the fortified areas on the northern and eastern outskirts of the city, then, while the 51st Division cleared the coastal fortifications north of the port, the 49th would take the harbour itself.

On the left the 56th Brigade ... seized the Northern Plateau and crossings over the Fontaine River.

At midnight the 51st Division on the right, aided by 'artificial moonlight' (searchlight beams reflected off low clouds), began clearing the northern edge of the Foret de Montgeon ...

On the 11th, 49 Division took the Southern Plateau, on the eastern outskirts of the city ... They suffered heavy casualties from mines before tanks and Flails were brought to their assistance. By nightfall, the Division reached Fort de Tourneville. Meanwhile the 51st had driven in from the north and taken the high ground at La Hève, overlooking the Channel ...

[On the 12th] the battle continued until late in the day. The 51st Division took Fort Ste Addresse, Octeville and La Hève, the 49th cleared the docks and the Schneider works. The last of the enemy to surrender was a small group on one of the quays.

The battle had taken 48 hours and had cost fewer than 500 casualties;
conversely 11,302 German prisoners were now out of the war.[73]

The First Canadian Army then swept up the Boulogne and Calais ports
before moving towards its main objective, namely the ports of Rotterdam
and Antwerp.

Montgomery's orders were direct and to the point. The following is a
direct quote from those orders:

10. *The whole energies of the Army will be directed towards operations*
    designed to enable full use to be made of the port of Antwerp.
    Airborne troops are available to cooperate. Air operations against the
    island of Walcheren have already commenced . . .
11. *HQ 1st Corps and 49 Div. will be brought up from the Havre area as*
    early as possible, to the Antwerp area. 51 Div. will be grounded
    completely in the Havre peninsula, and its transport used to enable
    the above move to take place; the Division will remain grounded as
    long as transport is required by Canadian Army for maintenance or
    movement purposes.
12. *Canadian Army will take over the Antwerp area from Second Army*
    beginning on 17th September . . .
13. *Having completed the operation for the opening of Antwerp, vide*
    para 10, Canadian Army will operate northwards on the general axis
    Breda–Utrecht–Amsterdam . . . Task: to destroy all enemy west of the
    Army boundary, and open up the port of Rotterdam.[74]

Examination of the map of the Scheldt estuary and the region surrounding
Antwerp will show that Antwerp is approached by sea via the River
Scheldt. Antwerp is not on the coast but sixty miles inland. Any seaborne
transport has to approach via the East Scheldt passage past the two
low-lying islands of Walcheren and Beveland, both of which were heavily
defended by the Germans both seaward and landward.

The operation to clear these islands and the immediate hinterland
proved to be the most formidable task the Canadian armies encountered
in the whole of the war.

This is not the place to give an account of this military operation but
only to see how I (British) Corps dovetailed with the Canadians.

Turnhout, Tilburg and Breda: September 19th to November 8th 1944

These three towns form a triangle with Breda at the northern point, Turnhout at the southern point and Tilburg at the eastern point. According to Google Maps, the total distance between the three towns, around the perimeter of the triangle, is fifty-two miles. Breda is the furthest from Antwerp, being twenty-eight miles away. In other words, this is a compact area some way away from what would become the main zone of fighting around the Scheldt estuary.

However, this area did not escape from the fighting. Indeed, had the commemorative plate been larger Harold may well have also included two other towns, namely Bergen op Zoom, a coastal town overlooking the eastern Scheldt estuary, and Roosendaal, which was situated between Breda and Bergen. Bergen was about twenty miles west of Breda.

An account of military manoeuvres in this area would be quite complex, but at their root was the need for this area to be bottled up so as to prevent the German army based on the Scheldt estuary from escaping the island of Walcheren and the isthmus of Beveland as the Canadians and British mounted intensive operations in this area.

From September 19th I (British) Corps took over the 'Antwerp Sector' from XII Corps, establishing its HQ near Turnhout on September 23rd.

> It was to 'keep its main strength on its left, in order to assist the speedy northward thrust of 2nd Cdn [Canadian] Corps'; on the right it would link up with the 12th British Corps of the Second British Army. When these dispositions had been made the Canadian Army sector would extend from the Channel coast to a boundary, nearly 20 miles east of Antwerp, running through Herenthals, Turnhout and Tilburg...
>
> The 49th [Division] immediately began pushing north through Herenthals and found that the enemy had withdrawn behind the Antwerp–Turnhout Canal. On the 24th British troops crossed the canal and successfully bridged it some six miles west of Turnhout. During the next few days the bridgehead was gradually extended in the face of stiff opposition.[75]

It was at this time that General Crerar had to step down as GOC of the First Canadian Army due to illness. He left officially on September 27th 1944.[76]

He was succeeded by General Guy Simonds, who, until then, had commanded II Canadian Corps.

Crerar's intention had been to seal off South Beveland by pushing two divisions (presumably the 49th and 51st) of I (British) Corps up to Bergen op Zoom and Roosendaal.[77]

On October 2nd General Simonds outlined the mission of I (British) Corps thus:

    a) *Thrust North Eastwards on Hertogenbosch*

    b) *Direct 2 Cdn Inf Div to clear the area North of Antwerp and close the Eastern end of the Zuid Beveland Isthmus until this diversion reverts to operational command 2 Cdn Corps*

    c) *Subsequently develop operations successively towards Breda and Roosendaal to cover the Eastern flank and rear of 2nd Cdn Inf Div directed Westward on Zuid Beveland* [78]

The 2nd Canadian Infantry Division had been placed temporarily under the command of I (British) Corps.

There then followed complex organisational changes to I Corps. At midnight October 6th/7th control of the 2nd Canadian Infantry Division passed from I Corps to II Canadian Corps. At noon on October 7th 51st (Highland) Division re-joined I Corps from Le Havre. I Corps was also joined by the 7th British Armoured Division. I Corps then took over the front through to the River Maas, although the thrust towards Hertogenbosch had faltered somewhat.[79]

To say that the military operations northwest and northeast of Antwerp (Bergen, Roosendaal) were the product of muddled thinking is not quite right, but for a time there was a dichotomy between Eisenhower (the Supreme Allied Commander) and Montgomery of the 21st Army Group, of which the First Canadian Army was a part. Montgomery had long wanted to spearhead a thrust into the Ruhr – Germany's major industrial heartland and direct route to Berlin – whereas Eisenhower wanted a broader-based thrust into Germany as a whole. He needed Antwerp and Rotterdam as the northern supply line.

Following a very pointed interchange of ideas between the two men, Montgomery had to pull back and accept the position. Antwerp became the top priority target, but a lot later than military historians consider was advisable.

This caused a literal change of direction as well as a change in strategy for the First Canadian Army.

What it amounted to was that whereas at the beginning of the Scheldt operations the right wing of First Canadian Army had been directed north-east on an axis divergent from the Scheldt to assist the Second British Army, now the Second British Army was to be directed on a north-westerly axis. General Dempsey [GOC of the Second British Army] *was to take over the right sector of the Canadian Army's line and push westward; while the Canadian Army, with larger forces now available to it, was to clear the country north of the South Beveland isthmus to free the Second Division's flank . . . .*

As soon as the new orders took effect the situation north of Antwerp was transformed . . .

General Crocker's headquarters issued its instruction for the operation designed to 'prevent the enemy interfering with 2 Cdn Inf Div during its ops to capture South Beveland' early on the 17th [of October]. *Subsequently designated 'Suitcase', it was to be carried out by four divisions, each from a different Allied country. On 20th October the 49th (West Riding) Infantry Division would attack on the axis Brecht–Wuestwezel and the 4th Canadian Armoured Division on its left directed on Esschen. The 1st Polish Armoured Division and the 104th Infantry Division would come into action later . . .*

At 7.30 a.m. on the wet and chilly morning of 20th October General Foster [GOC 4th Canadian Armoured Division] *launched his Division towards Esschen, with Bergen op Zoom as a further objective beyond. This advance would clear the flank of the 2nd Division and prepare the way of the Second Army's attack towards the Maas which was to go in shortly afterwards and which, it was hoped, would trap the German Fifteenth Army south of the wide river. It went well. Esschen fell to the 10th Canadian Infantry Brigade on the morning of 22nd October. Thereafter resistance stiffened as the Germans fought to keep open an escape route for their troops around Woensdrecht, and the 4th Canadian Armoured Brigade, pushing north-west from Esschen, was held up at Wouwsche Plantage and captured the place with some assistance from the 10th Brigade, only on the morning of the 26th. The following day the 10th, now advancing on the 4th Division leftward axis, entered Bergen op Zoom after overcoming opposition from the 6th Parachute Regiment. To the east the 49th Division was approaching Roosendaal; and the 104th US Infantry Division, the first American formation to fight under the First Canadian Army, had come in on the 49th's right and taken Zundert. Still farther east, on the extreme right flank of the 1st*

Corps, the Polish Armoured Division captured historic Breda on 29th October.

In the meantime, on 22 October, the Second Army had launched its attack directed on 's-Hertogenbosch and Tilburg, and steady progress was made here too. The 12th Corps entered 's-Hertogenbosch on the 24th and cleared Tilburg . . .

Anticipating relief from embarrassment on its right by the advance of the 1st Corps under Montgomery's new policy, the 2nd Canadian Infantry Division was able, on 23rd October, to begin the final clearing of the Woensdrecht area preparatory to operations against south Beveland.[80]

I have quoted extensively from the official history of the Canadian army because I want you, the reader, to understand the complexity of what was happening north of Antwerp at this time, to aid a visualisation of what a lowly DR might have been involved in.

The image on page 101 shows a page from I (British) Corps' war diary in October 1944. The text reads as follows:

Camp de Brasschaet

October 29th: Breda cleared today by 1 Pol Armd Div when tps entered they found only a few snipers. Enemy held up the advance of 2 Cnd Armd Bde about 3 miles SW of BREDA. 2 Cnd Armd Bde had moved NORTH as quickly as their vehs would carry them and mines and obstacles would allow, and deployed for nights area 937337. 104 US Inf Div cut off BREDA-ROOSENDAAL rd area 8133 and 8233. 49th Inf Div reached outskirts ROOSENDAAL. 4 Cdn Armd Div attempts during day to cut BERGEN-STEENBERGEN rd just failed and 21 Cdn Armd Regt and coy Met Bn reached 6232. Rd BERGEN-ROOSENDAAL firmly held between 65-62 grid line. Enemy fighting very hard on each flank of 1 Corps front. BOBFORCE ceased to exist wef 1800 hrs.

October 30th: 49 Inf Div occupied ROOSENDAAL today and succeeded in getting recce up to X rds 683382. Leading bn area 732376 remainder 49 Inf Div conc area ROOSENDAAL. Polish Recce reported brs 000415, 945409 and 898420 blown. Enemy mortars and MGs very active area 858420. 104 US Inf Div some progress made in attempt to establish br head over canal though this had not been accomplished.

War diary, I (British) Corps, October 29th and 30th 1944

Imagine the amount of communication between I Corps and its various sub-units that would have to take place by radio, by telephone but also by the physical transfer of information. Maps, for instance, could not be communicated over telephone lines and radio waves. Orders had to be written down to ensure proper understanding of what officers required to be done. Communication by telephone and radio could be disrupted by enemy action or might not be set up for days in a fast-moving battle. There was also the sheer physical movement of men and machines, which needed direction and coordination.

How hard must soldiers like Harold have worked in those days, and what dangers must they have faced?

MESSAGE FORM

FROM 43 Div   Date/Time 26 15 45   A
                              For Action

TO 129 Bde 130 Bde 214 Bde 9 Cdn Inf Bde RA RE Sigs 8 Mx
   43 Recce Regt Comd C.1 A/Q Main Camp Phantom G Ops
   30 Corps 51 Div 3 Cdn Div Infm

G.398 . SECRET . ISUM to 261500A . FIRST . own front . HIENEN
cleared after tough resistance incl high proportion MGs two AFVs last
night 058500 . identifications 15 PG div 3 6 8 9 10 coys
and asslt pl 115 PGR 3 coy 33 engr bn . 6 para div oh right
PW 1 6 7 15 coys 16 PJR also 6 para mortar bn stated
thirty six 12cm mortars in area 080577 . ANTROP 072559 cleared in
night identification 12 coy 24 PJR . SECOND . right flank . own
tps 090563 took 221 PW during night incl 1 bn 104 PGR Bn GRAFING
3 coy 33 A tk bn . PW states 104 PGR received no rfts since
VERITABLE . own tps also reported one mile from HINGDEN 2253 and
at 235460 . THIRD . res . both regt 116 Pz div identified SOUTH
of WESEL . comd 60 PGR captured states promised tks but did not turn
up comment air claims yesterday AFVs reported EAST of DINSLAKEN
29 KO more damaged . FOURTH . Tac R . five tks 075053 facing
WEST 0745 hrs . one tiger 113618 0815 hrs . all infm

AS WRITTEN   IN CIPHER   PRIORITY   Time System Op

                                   DRLS   THI
                                                    TOR

SGD   SGD

Example of a DRLS (Despatch Rider Letter Service) message104

The role played by I (British) Corps in the Battle of the Scheldt has not been the subject of separate study by military historians (at least in published works). It has been overshadowed by the desperate battle that took place to free the Scheldt estuary of the German army, which was mainly a Canadian army affair (although British paratroopers were instrumental in capturing the island of Walcheren), and by the fact that it is Canadian military historians who have written the history (quite rightly).

However, a study of the map of military operations in the area of the Scheldt will show that I (British) Corps was in the thick of it and was a vital component of the next phase of the liberation of the Netherlands and the subsequent breakthrough into Germany.

By early November 1944 I Corps had completed the clearing of the country up to the Lower Maas, and:

> ... with the approaches to Antwerp free of the enemy and the country up to the Maas similarly cleared the Battle of the Scheldt was over. It had been a hard and bloody business.
>
> From October 1st to November 8th the First Canadian Army on all its fronts had taken 41,043 prisoners. Its own casualties for the same period were computed as 703 officers and 12,170 other ranks, killed, wounded or missing. Of these, almost precisely half ... were Canadians.[81]

The Maas (Meuse): November 9th 1944 to February 7th 1945

Note that the Dutch name for the river is 'Maas'; the German name is 'Meuse'.

Relatively speaking, the three months that followed intense military activity north of Antwerp proved to be a rest for Harold. There were no major operations involving the First Canadian Army, although the British and Americans were heavily engaged in the forest of the Ardennes.

Plans were being drawn up for the First Canadian Army to undertake offensive operations southwest from the Nijmegen area between the Maas and the Rhine and northwards across the Nederrijn to secure the high ground between Arnhem and Apeldoorn with a bridgehead over the Ijssel River.[82]

Montgomery had already issued orders to the First Canadian Army to hold the line in the area south of the Maas from 's-Hertogenbosch westwards. Once this area had been cleared he anticipated that the First

Canadian Army could hold it with only two divisions, so he stripped the American 104th Division and the 49th (West Riding) Division out of General Crerar's army.

> *Thereafter Sir John Crocker's 1st British Corps would hold the line of the lower Maas as far east as Maren, northeast of 's-Hertogenbosch, with the 'minimum strength necessary, maintaining a reserve of mobile and armoured troops in suitable positions to deal with any enemy attempts to cross the river'.*[83]

This relative calm was not to last. Mid-December 1944 proved to be the time for yet another decisive battle in northwest Europe.

This is not the place to describe the events of the Ardennes offensive, but it must be said that, for once, the Germans took the Americans and British by surprise. Whilst the battle concluded with the German army being pushed back across the Rhine, had there been a German victory then I (British) Corps would have been directly in the firing line.

The Battle of the Bulge commenced on December 16th 1944 and ceased a month later. It was one of the bloodiest battles of the war. Had the Germans broken through American and British lines, the way would have been open for the Germans to retake Antwerp. They would have had to clash with the First Canadian Army to get there, so involving I (British) Corps in a major and perhaps disastrous battle.

In fact, at its nearest point, the German army got within two miles of the River Maas.[84] Von Rundstedt, commander in chief of the German army in the west, had ordered Army Group H to cross the lower Maas once the Ardennes thrust had made sufficient progress. The light defence of the Maas river area under I Corps' watch, ordered by Montgomery a month or so earlier, nearly spelt disaster for it and hence my father.

> *Crerar* [GOC First Canadian Army] *regrouped 1st British Corps on whose front the attack would fall and positioned divisions ready to counterattack. All administrative units were ordered to prepare for their own defence . . .*
>
> *Between Headquarters First Canadian Army in Tilburg and the Maas, 18 kilometres to the north, stood one platoon of infantry and an armoured car troop. For the first time it looked as if the staff might have to defend themselves. Officers, clerks, drivers, cooks and signallers drew extra ammunition and grenades, dug slit trenches and manned guard posts.*[85]

Northern Germany, 1945

This last-ditch defensive posture proved to be unnecessary, but the fact that it was ordered signifies the imminence of a German breakthrough that could have been catastrophic.

The Roer, the Rhine and Goch: Operation Veritable, February 8th to March 11th 1945

The likes of Harold Heard and indeed Montgomery himself were not to know that, for them, the war would be over following the unconditional surrender of the Germans on May 8th 1945. Indeed, no battle had yet been fought on German soil, nor had the Rhine been crossed, so there was no let-up in the main thrust and elements of I (British) Corps were soon destined to join the fray once again.

I use the word 'elements' here because I Corps does not appear to have been directly involved in the next major battle, known as Operation Veritable, but Harold's commemorative plate lists three highly significant benchmarks within Veritable (the Roer, the Rhine and Goch) that lead me to believe that he must have been directly involved. If so, then it is likely that he was in some way connected with the 51st (Highland) Division at this time.

51st (Highland) Division was one of the army formations longest connected with I (British) Corps and certainly played an important role in Operation Veritable. Moreover, its mission involved the capture of Goch, a historic town in North Rhine-Westphalia in northern Germany. Indeed, Goch was the Division's final objective in the battle.

The fact that Harold's plate lists the river Roer is also significant. This is a tributary to the Maas more southerly than the normal 'stomping ground' for I Corps, but it featured greatly in the role played by the US Ninth Army in Veritable. These forces were not part of First Canadian Army but had been assigned to Montgomery's 21st Army Group for the duration of Veritable. Since the First Canadian Army was also part of the 21st Army Group, it is not inconceivable that Harold had duties that took him into the fray around Roer dams.

Operation Veritable (also known as the Battle of the Reichswald) was the northern part of an Allied pincer movement that took place between 8 February and 11 March 1945 during the final stages of the Second World War. The operation was conducted by Field Marshal Bernard Montgomery's Anglo-Canadian 21st Army Group, primarily consisting of the First Canadian Army under Lieutenant-General Harry Crerar and the British XXX Corps under Lieutenant-General Brian Horrocks. The U.S. Ninth Army was incorporated into the 21st Army Group. The objective of the operation was to clear German forces from the area between the Rhine and Maas rivers, east of the German/Dutch frontier, in the Rhineland. It was part of General Dwight D. Eisenhower's 'broad front' strategy to occupy the entire west bank of the Rhine before its crossing. Veritable (originally called Valediction) had been planned for execution in early January, 1945 when the ground had been frozen and thus more advantageous to the Allies. The Allied expectation was that the northern end of the Siegfried Line was less well defended than elsewhere and an outflanking movement around the line was possible and would allow an early assault against the industrial Ruhr region.

The operation had complications. First, the heavily forested terrain, squeezed between the Rhine and Maas rivers, reduced Anglo-Canadian advantages in manpower and armour; the situation was exacerbated by soft ground which had thawed after the winter and also by the deliberate flooding of the adjacent Rhine flood plain. Second, Veritable was the northern arm of a pincer movement. The southern pincer arm, Operation Grenade, by Lieutenant General William Hood Simpson's U.S. Ninth Army, had had to be postponed for two weeks when the Germans released the waters from the Roer dams and river levels rose. No military actions could proceed across the Roer until the water subsided.

Veritable started on schedule, with XXX Corps advancing through the forest and the 3rd Canadian Infantry Division, in amphibious vehicles, clearing enemy positions in the drowned Rhine flood plain. The Allied advance proceeded more slowly than expected and at greater cost. The delay to Grenade had allowed German forces to be concentrated against the Anglo-Canadian advance and the local German commander, Alfred Schlemm acting against the assessments of his superiors, had strengthened the Siegfried Line defences and had fresh, elite troops readily available to him. The fighting was hard, but the Allied advance continued. On 22 February, once clear of the Reichswald (German: Imperial Forest), and with the towns of Kleve and Goch in their control, the offensive was renewed as Operation Blockbuster and linked up with the U.S. Ninth Army near Geldern on 4 March. Fighting continued as the Germans sought to retain a bridgehead on the west bank of the Rhine at Wesel and evacuate as many men and as much equipment as possible. Finally, on 10 March, the German withdrawal ended and the last bridges were destroyed.

After the war, General Dwight D. Eisenhower, the Allied Supreme Commander, commented this 'was some of the fiercest fighting of the whole war' and 'a bitter slugging match in which the enemy had to be forced back yard by yard'. Montgomery, the 21st Army Group commander, wrote 'the enemy parachute troops fought with a fanaticism un-excelled at any time in the war' and 'the volume of fire from enemy weapons was the heaviest which had so far been met by British troops in the campaign'.[86]

For a full description of Operation Veritable refer to Stacey (1966), pp. 560–90.

Again, we have no information on Harold's experiences during Operation Veritable, but it is certain that he did play his part.

I make no apologies for quoting extensively from relevant military histories and take no joy from the fact that the fighting was bloody, but I feel that the following description of the 51st (Highland) Division's actions in taking Goch should be recounted here. Again, I ask the reader to imagine the sort of work that Harold must have undertaken in his support role as a despatch rider with I (British) Corps HQ.

The HD [Highland Division] main objective was Goch but on the way from Kessel were three more defended villages. General Rennie now ordered 152 bde [brigade] *into action after their difficult five-mile advance in the Reichswald forest. 5th Seaforth were directed on Asperden, 5th Camerons on Hervost and 2nd Seaforth on Grafenthal.*

On 16th 'D' Coy [company] *2nd Seaforth started from Kessel and soon captured a crossroads 1500 yards down the Goch road; 'B' Coy then took two woods 500 yards beyond, and finally by 2245 'A' had captured Grafenthal monastery. At the same time, having absorbed 60 new reinforcements 5th Camerons under a powerful barrage crossed the river at Hekkens and advanced on Hervost, taken without much difficulty. Helped by the waddling deadly Crocodiles* [flame-throwing tanks] *six large pillboxes were then seized. 'C' Coy threw 30 phosphorous grenades down their ventilators and 'B' dealt with another trio called 'Shem', 'Ham' and 'Japhet'. In the woods around Hervost on the night of 17th/18th 'A' Coy cleared three more strongpoints called 'Faith', 'Hope' and 'Charity' with a total bag of 230 POW* [prisoners of war].

The obvious route to Goch was through Asperden and Alastair Borthwick. 5th Seaforth watched, 'several mattresses of rockets went over, each weighing ten pounds, equivalent to a medium 5.5 inch shell. They made a sound like rushing water as three mattresses each with 300 rockets passed overhead into Asperden.' Led by Lt Col Sym on 'a midnight steeplechase', the battalion followed the barrage and entered the village almost unopposed.

Alastair Borthwick described the technique of dealing with the 60 foot square enormously thick concrete pill boxes heaped over with earth. 'Infantry and supporting arms dealt with the trenches outside. The casement was the weak point but even 17-pdr [pounder] *anti-tank shells simply bounced off. The AVRE* [Armoured Vehicle Royal Engineers] *Churchill tanks with a 40lb 'Dustbin' bombard, thrown by a petard, would blow the steel shutters out of the casemate. Then a Crocodile would come up; squirt unignited fuel through the casemate for half a minute, then fired one ignited squirt after the rest. The garrison died instantly and horribly. Quite soon the German defenders realise that their supposedly "impregnable" Seigfried line pill boxes had become a death trap.'*

The way was now clear for the main attack on Goch, which was a very strongly fortified town, part of the Seigfried line with many pillboxes with an anti-tank ditch on three sides and a river on the fourth. Five key roads and a rail line Cleve–Weeze ran through it. 43rd Wessex Division had advanced to the escarpment just to the east of Goch by the 16th February; and it was the task for the 15th Scottish to attack from the northeast and

HD from the northwest. 153 bde would make the main attack after 2nd Seaforth (153 bde) had made a crossing over the A/Tank ditch with an AVRE bridge, allowing 5th Black Watch to lead into the town. 275 Field Corps RE [Royal Engineers] *made crossings for two-way traffic. The CRE* [Chief Royal Engineer], *Lt Col Carr wrote home 'Ten long days and nights of incessant battling. However, we are getting on and the other side is in very poor shape. HD have taken over 2000 POW and they seem to be coming in more easily now.'*

The Allied Forces and artillery concentrations had destroyed most of the town. This, of course, hampered the advance! The streets were blocked to tanks and wheeled traffic and the house debris was ideal cover for snipers, Spandau [machine gun] *and bazooka* [handheld rocket launcher] *teams. The enemy were well dug in, in the gardens, behind buildings and most of the cellars were occupied by the defenders.*[87]

There then followed several days of intense fighting within Goch which concluded with defeat for the Germans by March 10th, but at a terrible cost to the British. Total casualties of the First Canadian Army during Operation Veritable from February 8th to March 10th were 1,049 officers and 14,585 other ranks; the majority of these were British soldiers.[88]

The spoils of war

Rhede and Iserlohn: March 12th 1945 to January 14th 1946

Precious cargo

April 2nd 1945 saw the transfer of General Crocker's I (British) Corps from the First Canadian Army to General Dempsey's British Second Army, but its days as part of a frontline army were numbered. Fundamentally, this was a product of its final resting place after the Scheldt operations, which left it isolated from the main fighting in the push by the British, Canadian and US armies to cross the Rhine. This resulted in Dempsey plundering I (British) Corps for troops and materiel.

In spite of his solid fighting record, for a variety of reasons, Crocker fought the rest of the campaign in North West Europe somewhat out of the limelight. During Operation Suitcase (20 October to 8 November [1944]), a push from Antwerp to the Maas River, he commanded four divisions from four different nations – the 4th Canadian Armoured Division, the US 104th Infantry (Timberwolf) Division, the 1st Polish

Armoured Division, and the 49th (West Riding) Division. Large and successful though the operation may have been, it was still only a supporting action to protect the right flank of the First Canadian Army as it struggled to clear the Scheldt Estuary. Later, as the First Canadian Army liberated Holland and the Second [British] Army drove into Germany, he mostly watched whilst his formations were fed into other corps and armies . . .

There was also the issue of geography. When 1st Corps had finished Operation Suitcase, it was positioned east of the Scheldt Estuary and on the south side of the Maas River – facing the German 25th Army, which was still on the north bank and would remain there until the final German surrender in May 1945. Someone still had to defend against enemy action from the north and Crocker's Corps was in position: incidentally it was also further away than any other corps in the 21st Army Group from upcoming operations in the Rhineland. With the passing of the German Ardennes Offensive in December 1944, and with the success of allied operations on the Rhine in February and March of 1945, defending the Maas against enemy attack from the north became more and more an economy-of-force operation, and Crocker's force strength was reduced accordingly.[89]

DR Section Rhede nach Bocholt, VE Day. The Brylcreem Boy is on the left. Bill Rock, Harold's great buddy in and after the war, is in the middle at the back, directly behind the DR with glasses.

So we have reached the last resting place of I (British) Corps. I Corps became I Corps District on May 21st 1945 and became part of BAOR (the British Army of the Rhine). It took over responsibility for the area occupied by the British after the Rhine crossing. It was responsible for the states of Rhineland and Westphalia. Its headquarters were originally based at Rhede, about twenty-five miles northeast of Goch. By mid-June the headquarters had moved to Iserlohn. Harold ended his military career at Mons Barracks in Iserlohn.

Harold and Bill Rock (centre), Mons Barracks, 1945

Tug of war! Harold is in the centre on the jeep

Administration of this region was not plain sailing.

The problem that loomed largest at the end of the war, and the one which occupied the Corps the most, was the repatriation of former prisoners of war and displaced persons. British and US POWs released in the Corps area were soon evacuated. Transit camps were set up to forward westbound DPs and ex-POWs from France, Belgium and the Netherlands. Eastbound ex-POWs and DPs were repatriated in June, and Russians and Poles mostly by train between July and September 1945. The total numbers repatriated were large. By 27th May 175,000 had been repatriated while 705,000 were still held. Many DPs and ex-POWs, however, remained behind in Germany.

Harold was given his papers home on January 11th 1946.

Discharge papers

Back home

By the time Harold got back home Vera's diary was no more. The last full entry in the 1945 diary was on October 28th, when she went home to Chilwell for tea and then out to the Bluebell (pub) with her brother Fred and Joan Davis, so we have no comment from Vera as to her thoughts on his homecoming.

Harold's service papers record that his commanding officer in Iserlohn signed his 'Notification of Impending Release' on January 11th 1946, stating that his military conduct had been 'exemplary' with the additional comment that 'this man can and does work hard. He is willing and can be relied on to carry out his orders.'

Harold disembarked on January 13th. Presumably this was by boat along with many hundreds, if not thousands, of servicemen due back under the 'first in, first out' arrangement for demobilisation, although it is just possible that he flew back to Britain because he is recorded as reaching No. 6 Military Disembarkation Station at Strensall (near York) on Monday January 14th. Assuming that the date stamps are correct, then Harold could have got back home to Beeston on either January 14th or 15th 1946.

I was born on September 20th 1946 and my brother, Nicholas, was born on December 17th 1949.

Harold's discharge papers list his British address as 36 Hampden Street, Nottingham, i.e. the address that Vera had been living at since September 1944. However Harold and Vera must have moved back to Beeston shortly afterwards because my mother told me that I had been evacuated from 19 Redwood Crescent, Beeston, in March 1947 when the River Trent overflowed in the great floods of that time. This was a council house that was Harold and Vera's home until the early 1950s when they moved to 5 Heard Crescent, Beeston (named after Councillor Joe Heard – one of Harold's relations).

Harold's father, William Arthur Heard, had retired from his plumbing business just before the war (he died in 1955), but Harold carried on as a plumber for most of his working life.

When his father died, Harold was fortunate enough to inherit his house at 3 Grasmere Road, Beeston, where Harold and Vera lived for many years.

The Heard family, 1956

Appendix

Sources Consulted in Writing the Book

Allport, Alan. *Demobbed: Coming Home After the World War Two*. Yale University Press, 2010. 978-0-300-16886-0

Bastick, Desmond. *Spearhead: The Story of the First British Corps*. HQ 1(BR) Corps, 1977. No ISBN available

Beevor, Anthony. *Ardennes 1944: Hitler's Last Gamble*. Penguin, 2016. 978-0-241-97515-2

Benamou, JP. *Normandy 1944: An Illustrated Field Guide, 7 June to 22 August 1944*. Heimdal, 1982. No ISBN available

Boscowan, Robert. *Armoured Guardsman*. Pen & Sword, 2008. 0-85052-748-1

Chisholm, Douglas H. *Memories: The Wartime Recollections of a Royal Signals Despatch Rider*. Lulu. Available from http://www.southampton.ac.uk/~mic/Dad/index.htm

Church, Judith. *Beating the Invader: Beeston and Chilwell in World War Two and the Floods*. Chilwell Publishers, 2006. 978-0-9553849-0-5

Copp, Terry. *Fields of Fire: The Canadians in Normandy*. University of Toronto Press, 2004. 978-0-8020-3780-0

Copp, Terry. *Cinderella Army: The Canadians in Northwest Europe 1944–1945*. University of Toronto Press, 2006. 0-8020-3925-1

Costello, John. *Love, Sex & War: Changing Values 1939–1945*. Collins, 1985. 0-00-217444-8

Daglish, Ian. *Goodwood: The British Offensive in Normandy, July 1944*. Stackpole, 2009. 978-0-8117-3538-4

Delaforce, Patrick. *Monty's Highlanders: 51st Highland Division in World War Two*. Chancellor Press, 2000. 0-75370-352-1

Delaforce, Patrick. *The Polar Bears: Monty's Left Flank, from Normandy to the Relief of Holland with the 49th Division*. Alan Sutton, 1995. 0-7509-1062-3

Delaney, Douglas E. *Corps Commanders: Five British and Canadian Generals at War, 1939–45*. UBC Press, 2012. 978-0-7748-2090-5

Ellis, Major LF. *The War in France and Flanders*. Naval & Military Press, 2009. 1-845740-56-4

Godfrey, Simon. *British Army Communications in the Second World War: Lifting the Fog of Battle*. Bloomsbury, 2014. 978-1-4725-9133-3

Harrison Place, Timothy. *Military Training in the British Army, 1940–1944: From Dunkirk to D-Day*. Routledge, 2000. 0-7146-8091-5

Hart, Stephen Ashley. *Colossal Cracks: Montgomery's 21st Army Group in Northwest Europe, 1944–45*. Stackpole, 2007. 978-0-8117-3383-0

Horrocks, Sir Brian. *Corps Commander*. Sidgwick and Jackson, 1977. 0-283-98320-5

Kirby, Norman. *1100 Miles with Monty: Security and Intelligence at TAC HQ*. Sutton, 2004. 0-7509-3428-X

Kite, Ben. *Stout Hearts: The British and Canadians in Normandy 1944*. Helion, 2014. 978-1-909982-55-0

de Lannoy, Francois. *21st Army Group Normandie 1944*. Heimdal, 2004. 2-84048-184-7

Lord, Cliff, and Graham Watson. *The Royal Corps of Signals: Unit Histories of the Corps (1920–2001) and Its Antecedents*. Helion, 2014. 1-874622-92-2

McKee, Alexander. *Caen: Anvil of Victory*. Souvenir Press, 2012. 0-285-63559-X

Mitchell, Raymond. *Commando Despatch Rider: From D-Day to Deutschland, 1944–1945*. Pen & Sword, 2009. 0-85052-797-X

More, Charles. *The Road to Dunkirk: The British Expeditionary Force and the Battle of the Ypres–Comines Canal, 1940*. Frontline Books, 2014. 978-1-84832-733-7

Nalder, Maj-Gen. RHF. *The History of British Army Signals in the Second World War*. Royal Signals Institution. No ISBN available

Nicholson, Virginia. *Millions Like Us: Women's Lives During the Second World War*. Penguin, 2012. 978-0-141-03789-9

North, John. *North-West Europe 1944–5*. HMSO Books, 1977. 011-772197-2

Rooke, Duncan. *My Dad's Army*. Matador, 2015. 978-1-78462-136-0

Rossiter, Mike. *I Fought at Dunkirk: Seven Veterans Remember the German Invasion of France*. Bantam, 2012. 978-0-593-06593-8

Saunders, Wilf. *Dunkirk Diary of a Very Young Soldier*. Brewin Books, 2010. 978-1-85858-461-4

Summers, Julie. *Fashion on the Ration: Style in the Second World War*. Profile Books, 2016. 978-1781253274

Stacey, Col. CP. *The Canadian Army at War: Canada's Battle in Normandy*. Dept of National Defence, 1946. No ISBN available

Stacey, Col. CP. *Official History of the Canadian Army, Vol. III: The Victory Campaign*. Dept of National Defence, 1966. No ISBN available

Thompson, Maj-Gen. Julian. *Dunkirk: Retreat to Victory*. Pan Macmillan, 2009. 978-0-330-43796-7

Wicks, Ben. *Welcome Home*. Past Times, 1991. No ISBN available

Williams, Jeffery. *The Long Left Flank: The Hard Fought Way to the Reich, 1944–45*. Leo Cooper, 1988. 0-85052-880-1

Zuehlke, Mark. *Forgotten Victory: First Canadian Army and the Cruel Winter of 1944–45*. Douglas & McIntyre, 2016. 978-1-77162-105-2

Zuehlke, Mark. *Terrible Victory: First Canadian Army and the Scheldt Estuary Campaign*. Douglas & McIntyre, 2014. 978-1-77162-030-7

Zweiniger-Bargielowska, Ina. *Austerity in Britain: Rationing, Controls and Consumption, 1939–1955*. Oxford University Press, 2000. 0-19-820453-1

Notes

1   Morrison, Kathryn, and Alicky Sussman. *World War One at Home*. BBC, 2015, p.9. http://downloads.bbc.co.uk/england/ww1/bbc-world-war-one-at-home.pdf

2   Thompson, MH et al. 'Chilwell 1939–45' booklet, pp. 62, 72

3   Chisholm, Douglas H. *Memories: The Wartime Recollections of a Royal Signals Despatch Rider*. Lulu. Available from http://www.southampton.ac.uk/~mic/Dad/index.htm, accessed Sept 1st 2017

4   Nalder, Maj-Gen. RHF. *The History of British Army Signals in the Second World War*. Royal Signals Institution, p. 265

5   Mitchell, Raymond. *Commando Despatch Rider: From D-Day to Deutschland, 1944–1945*. Pen & Sword, 2009, pp. 60–61

6   Chisholm

7   Mitchell, p. 124

8   Mitchell, pp. 89–90

9   Kite, Ben. *Stout Hearts: The British and Canadians in Normandy 1944*. Helion, 2014, p 286

10   'British Expeditionary Force'. Wikipedia. https://en.wikipedia.org/wiki/British_Expeditionary_Force_(World_War_II), accessed Sept 1st 2017

11   '44th (Home Counties) Division'. Wikipedia. https://en.wikipedia.org/wiki/44th_(Home_Counties)_Division, accessed Sept 1st 2017

12   For the full Order of Battle see http://www.britishmilitaryhistory.co.uk/webeasycms/hold/uploads/bmh_document_pdf/44-Infantry-Division-1940-_1.pdf

13   Thompson, Maj-Gen. Julian. *Dunkirk: Retreat to Victory*. Pan Macmillan, 2009, p. 44

14   Ellis, Major LF. The War in France and Flanders. Naval & Military Press, 2009, p. 205

15   Ellis, p. 207

16   Thompson, p. 209

17   Thompson, p. 212

18   Thompson, p. 215

19   Thompson, p. 215

20   Browning, Richard. 'Historic inflation calculator: how the value of money has changed since 1900'. This Is Money. http://www.thisismoney.co.uk/money/bills/article-1633409/Historic-inflation-calculator-value-money-changed-1900.html, accessed Sept 1st 2017

21   Zweiniger-Bargielowska, Ina. Austerity in Britain: Rationing, Controls and Consumption, 1939–1955. Oxford University Press, 2000, p. 178

22   Zweiniger-Bargielowska, p. 177

23   Zweiniger-Bargielowska, p. 49

24   Browning, Richard. 'Historic inflation calculator: how the value of money has changed since 1900'. This Is Money.

http://www.thisismoney.co.uk/money/bills/article-1633409/Historic-inflation-calculator-value-money-changed-1900.html, accessed Sept 1st 2017

25   Cmd 6454 Statistics relating to the War Effort of the United Kingdom, published in 1944, reported in Zweiniger-Bargielowska, p. 54

26   Nicholson, Virginia. *Millions Like Us: Women's Lives During the Second World War.* Penguin, 2012, p. 291

27   Nicholson, p. 134

28   Zweiniger-Bargielowska, pp. 94–95

29   Nicholson, p. 135

30   Zweiniger-Bargielowska, p. 91

31   Zweiniger-Bargielowska, p. 185

32   Zweiniger-Bargielowska, p. 186

33   Thompson, MH et al. 'Chilwell 1939–45' booklet, p. 66

34   'The High Road in Beeston'. Exploring Beeston's History. http://www.beeston-notts.co.uk/high_road1.shtml, accessed Sept 1st 2017 – see the account of families living at 5 Church Street, Beeston

35   Thompson, MH et al. 'Chilwell 1939–45' booklet, p. 28

36   Elkes, Neil. 'Historians anger at plans to demolish World War II US forces postal depot in Sutton Coldfield'. *Birmingham Mail*, Mar 10th 2011. http://www.birminghammail.co.uk/news/local-news/historians-anger-at-plans-to-demolish-world-149983, accessed Sept 1st 2017

37   All dates from the section headed 'Military History Sheet' in the service papers

38   '44th (Home Counties) Division'. Wikipedia. https://en.wikipedia.org/wiki/44th_(Home_Counties)_Division, accessed Sept 1st 2017

39   'Guards Armoured Division'. Wikipedia. https://en.wikipedia.org/wiki/Guards_Armoured_Division, accessed Sept 1st 2017

40   'XII Corps (United Kingdom)'. Wikipedia. https://en.wikipedia.org/wiki/XII_Corps_(United_Kingdom), accessed Sept 1st 2017

41   Bridport Museum. 'From Kent to Silesia, private to POW'. WW2 People's War, BBC History. http://www.bbc.co.uk/history/ww2peopleswar/stories/83/a8004683.shtml

42   Bridport Museum. 'From Kent to Silesia, private to POW'. WW2 People's War, BBC History. http://www.bbc.co.uk/history/ww2peopleswar/stories/83/a8004683.shtml

43   Thompson, MH et al. 'Chilwell 1939–45' booklet, p. 72

44   'Laurel and Hardy in Nottingham'. Laurel and Hardy Books. http://www.laurelandhardybooks.com/nottingham.html, accessed Sept 1st 2017

45   'British Wartime Food'. Cook's Info. http://www.cooksinfo.com/british-wartime-food, accessed Sept 1st 2017

46   Johnson, Albin E. 'Where the Cupboard is Almost Bare'. *The Rotarian*, 63(3), September 1943, p. 18. Quoted in 'British Wartime Food'. Cook's Info. http://www.cooksinfo.com/british-wartime-food, accessed Sept 1st 2017

47   1939 Register. Find My Past. http://www.findmypast.co.uk/1939register, accessed Sept 1st 2017

48   'HMS *Mansfield*'. uboat.net. http://uboat.net/allies/warships/ship/5892.html, accessed Sept 1st 2017

49 'HMS *Rowley*'. uboat.net. http://uboat.net/allies/warships/ship/5666.html, accessed Sept 1st 2017

50 Chapman, Prof. Stanley. 'A History of Beeston Lace'. Anglo Scotian Mills. http://www.angloscotianmills.co.uk/history.pdf, accessed Sept 1st 2017

51 'Gibberish (language game)'. Wikipedia. https://en.wikipedia.org/wiki/Gibberish_(language_game), accessed Sept 1st 2017

52 Nicholson, p. 105

53 Costello, John. Love, Sex & War: Changing Values 1939–1945. Collins, 1985, p. 19

54 Costello, p. 19

55 Costello, p. 355

56 Elson, Bert. 'Squaddies and other veterans celebrate at Tropical Bert's'. *Pattaya Mail*, 16(28), July 2008. http://www.pattayamail.com/780/features.shtml, accessed Sept 1st 2017

57 The British Newspaper Archive. http://www.britishnewspaperarchive.co.uk

58 Costello, p. 277

59 Costello, pp. 276–77

60 'RAF Newton'. Wikipedia. https://en.wikipedia.org/wiki/RAF_Newton, accessed Sept 1st 2017

61 Ratuszynski, Wilhelm. 'History of No. 304 (Polish) Squadron'. Polish Squadrons Remembered. http://www.polishsquadronsremembered.com/304/304Story.htm, accessed Sept 1st 2017

62 powerandpassion, quoting father's memoirs. Thread: 'Aviation Memorials in Nottinghamshire – 2014'. The Aviation Forum, 2014. http://forum.keypublishing.com/showthread.php?130040-aviation-memorials-in-nottinghamshire-2014/page2, accessed Sept 1st 2017

63 'Kalinowski Leon'. Personnel of the Polish Air Force in Great Britain 1940–1947. http://listakrzystka.pl/en/?p=109760

64 I Corps (United Kingdom). Wikipedia. https://en.wikipedia.org/wiki/I_Corps_(United_Kingdom), accessed Sept 1st 2017

65 Zuehlke, Mark. *Forgotten Victory: First Canadian Army and the Cruel Winter of 1944–45*. Douglas & McIntyre, 2016, p. 38

66 Operation Totalize. Wikipedia. https://en.wikipedia.org/wiki/Operation_Totalize, accessed Sept 1st 2017

67 Stacey, Col. CP. *Official History of the Canadian Army, Vol. III: The Victory Campaign*. Dept of National Defence, p. 266

68 Stacey. *Official History of the Canadian Army, Vol. III*. p. 271

69 'Falaise Pocket'. Wikipedia. https://en.wikipedia.org/wiki/Falaise_Pocket, accessed Aug 31st 2017

70 Williams, Jeffery. *The Long Left Flank: The Hard Fought Way to the Reich, 1944–45*. Leo Cooper, 1988, p. 42

71 Stacey. *Official History of the Canadian Army, Vol. III*. pp. 293–94

72 Stacey, Col. CP. *The Canadian Army at War: Canada's Battle in Normandy*. Dept of National Defence, 1946. Available at: http://ibiblio.org/hyperwar/UN/Canada/CA/Normandy/Normandy-5.html, p. 152

73 Williams, pp. 57–59

74 Williams, pp. 86–87

75   Stacey. *Official History of the Canadian Army, Vol. III*. pp. 364, 367

76   Williams, p. 96

77   Williams, p. 96

78   Stacey. *Official History of the Canadian Army, Vol. III*. p. 380

79   Stacey. *Official History of the Canadian Army, Vol. III*. p. 381

80   Stacey. *Official History of the Canadian Army, Vol. III*. pp. 389–91

81   Stacey. *Official History of the Canadian Army, Vol. III*. p. 424

82   Stacey. *Official History of the Canadian Army, Vol. III*. pp. 427–28

83   Stacey. *Official History of the Canadian Army, Vol. III*. p. 428

84   Williams, p. 175

85   Williams, p. 176

86   'Operation Veritable'. Wikipedia. https://en.wikipedia.org/wiki/Operation_Veritable, accessed Sept 1st 2017

87   Delaforce, Patrick. *Monty's Highlanders: 51st Highland Division in World War Two*. Chancellor Press, 2000, pp. 212–13

88   Stacey. *Official History of the Canadian Army, Vol. III*. p. 522

89   Delaney, Douglas E. *Corps Commanders: Five British and Canadian Generals at War, 1939–45*. UBC Press, 2012, p. 167

Lightning Source UK Ltd.
Milton Keynes UK
UKHW02f0237090218
317626UK00009B/53/P

The Status and
Recognition of Post-1992
Transnistria

An Investigation of the Case for
de jure Independence

Richard Colbey

UNIVERSITY OF
BUCKINGHAM
PRESS

UNIVERSITY OF BUCKINGHAM PRESS
51 Gower Street
London WC1E 6HJ
United Kingdom
www.hero-press.com

Originally published in 2021 as a thesis submitted for the degree of Doctor of Philosophy to the School of Humanities and Social Sciences at the University of Buckingham

This expanded and revised version first published by University of Buckingham Press in 2022

ISBN: 978-1-91505-452-4

CONTENTS

THE STATUS AND RECOGNITION
OF POST-1992 TRANSNISTRIA

PREFACE

THE UKRAINE WAR AND OTHER RECENT DEVELOPMENTS

This work was largely completed by August 2020 (Colbey p.xiv), though some later developments were incorporated, most significantly the election of a new Moldovan president in December 2020. The ways of the academic and publishing worlds mean that the book was not released until October 2022. This Preface explores what has happened to Transnistria in the intervening time and asks whether the conclusion that it would function well as an independent state (Colbey p.226) but is frustrated by political expediency, particularly Russian interests (Colbey p.227), still applies. The material derives from a visit to Tiraspol on 6 and 7 June 2022, my observations there and interviews with Vladimir Yastrebchak, and Natalia Shchukina, who were as generous with their time as they were when I was preparing the main work, as well as analysis of many media reports.

The south-eastern corner of Europe in which Transnistria lies seems a different place than it did when this work was first completed in 2021. The most obvious development is the war in Ukraine. The ultimate premise of this work is that the longer Transnistria thrives as a *de facto* state the stronger the case for independence becomes (Colbey p.227). That is qualified by a recognition that there are many barriers to independence at the moment, however strong the case for it may be (Colbey p.218), and indeed comparisons are drawn with previous Russian occupations of the Donbass and Crimea (Colbey p.219). These are the factors the Ukraine war may bear on.

The war in Ukraine has had a polarising effect throughout Europe, with nearly all European countries having condemned Russia, which finds only Belarus, virtually a Russian vassal state, supporting it. Moldova, under its already EU-leaning president Maia Sandu, who ousted Igor Dodon, who was far more sympathetic to Russia, in December 2020, unequivocally sides with Ukraine. Even before the Ukraine war, Sandu's government was taking a harder line in opposing Transnistrian independence than did Dodon's, and this may be a factor making the attainment of independence more difficult.

Within Transnistria there have been parliamentary and presidential elections in December 2020 and 2021 respectively, with little changing in consequence. President Krasnoselsky's re-election was with alarmingly little opposition. The territory's highest profile political prisoner, Oleg Horjan, remains in gaol, and at least one other episode of imprisonment for political reasons has been reported. The economy has proved reasonably resilient to the challenges created by the Ukraine war, though inflation and an increase in emigration have been among the consequences.

Rocket and drone strikes took place within the territory in late April and early May. While these drew worldwide attention, and a controversy as to whether they might have been 'false flag' attacks, there has been no sequelae to them, and can confidently be seen as attacks by Ukrainians, probably acting in a freelance capacity, causing relatively little damage and having commensurately little political significance.

Transnistria faced the challenges of the Covid-19 crisis in a way that was not dissimilar to many other European countries, veering to a cautious locking-down position. The territory has been commendably transparent about how it was affected, with a high rate of deaths in comparison with most countries, but a much lower one of cases, partly explained by a number of factors, including its aging population and the thoroughness of its reporting. There was no evidence that the Transnistrian government had handled the crisis worse than most European governments.

Pref. 1 THE UKRAINE WAR

On 24 February 2022 Russian troops, whose numbers had been building up in the vicinity for several months, crossed the border with Ukraine, and there were immediate airstrikes on Kiev*. This invasion was not restricted to those parts, Crimea, Luhansk and Donetsk, that were already under varying degrees of Russian control. These troops entered the country in the face of the clear wishes of a democratic government; were wanted only by a tiny proportion of Ukrainians; and defying condemnation by practically every democracy in the world. One of the Russian justifications, de-Nazifiying' the country, which is led by a Jewish social democrat, was beyond laughable. While Russia may have termed it 'a special military' operation, that is a linguistic absurdity, and to use the simpler and wholly apposite terms 'invasion' and war' is not to depart from a neutral commentary.

No discussion of the nuances of this war can be wholly divorced from its brutality and the unnecessary suffering, within and way beyond Ukraine's borders, it has caused. As I write at the start of October 2022, the latest OHCRH estimate is that 5,827 Ukrainian civilians, including 375 children have died directly from the violence (UNHRO 2022a), with a proviso that the real numbers could be higher: as they will be by the time this book is published. They don't for instance include the 440 corpses found in Izyum on 15 September. Each side likes to talk up the military casualties the other has suffered. Ukrainian president Zelensky claimed that 30,000 Russian military personnel had been killed by 3 June (VOA 2022). This was probably an exaggeration but closer to reality than

---

*   Western media now almost universally uses the transliteration of the Ukrainian language Kyiv, but this Preface will for the sake of consistency retain Kiev, as it will Odessa, which has frequently become Odesa.

the 3,200 deaths the Russian independent news outlet *Mediazona* stated on the same date (Pashaeva 2022). By August the discrepancy was even greater: estimates ranging from 1,351 to 43,000 strongly suggesting that partisanship rather than accuracy, or even plausibility, drives most reports on this subject (Keating 2022). Around 9,000 Ukrainian troops had died by 9 August according to a pronouncement by the head of its armed forces, who is likely to have understated them (Reuters 2022a).

About 6.3 million people have fled Ukraine (UNHCR 2022, BBC 2022) and are leading lives of refugees largely in Poland western Europe. This is about 12% of the country's population, but a vastly disproportionate number are women, as men over 18 are prohibited from leaving. Many, perhaps mainly the youngest and brightest, will be reluctant to return even when it is safe for them to do so, devastating Ukraine's human resources, at a time when it will be necessary to devote huge financial resources to rebuilding the country's infrastructure.

The war has led to rapidly increasing energy prices in western Europe, which has exacerbated a more general inflation which arose from many governments increasing their money supply, euphemistically known as quantitative easing, to fund Covid relief programmes (BBC 2020). Food shortages caused by blockades of Ukraine's ports preventing grain exports, which have begun to cause inconvenience to shoppers in British supermarkets, will have an infinitely more devastating effect on poorer countries. The World Food Programme's suspension of aid to 1.7 million South Sudanese has been one of the first manifestations of this. It may well be deaths in a resulting famine will greatly outnumber those caused directly by the conflict.

Resources that were being directed to refugees fleeing other crises, most notably that in Afghanistan, have been diverted to Ukrainians. International fundraising appeals for Afghans and Yemenis shortly after the war started attracted far less support than had been hoped, despite promotion by the UN, and as the director of the Red Cross pointed out, "The crises in Afghanistan, Yemen and Syria among others have only got worse since the Ukraine war" (BBC 2022b). There is less criticism of oppression by other governments, perhaps out of a desire not to drive such governments closer to Russia, which has little history of doing this. China, which has taken an ostensibly neutral stance, is particularly well placed to exploit this distraction from its own oppression in Hong Kong, Xinjiang Uyghur Autonomous Region and Tibet. The Belorussian leader, Alexander Lukashenko, who could easily have been thrust aside after a disputed election in August 2020 (Colbey p.147) were it not for Russian support, now has to be treated with far more respect by the Kremlin, as his country's support for the war is strategically important*, to the disadvantage of its populace.

In short, the war has been a humanitarian disaster. Opinion among western politicians and media has not surprisingly tended towards bellicose support for Ukraine, which is seen as the victim of Russian aggression. That Russia aggression has distracted

---

*   See Wolff & Bayok (2022) for a discussion of Belarus's position in relation to the war and how it might be drawn into it.

from the nuances of the situation, and multitude of unresolved problems caused by the inept creation of borders on the dissolution of the USSR, which flow back to at least the 1939 Molotov-Ribbentrop Pact (Colbey p.30), of which Transnistria is itself a clear example.

The initial Russian aim appeared to be to capture Kiev, perhaps execute Zelensky and annex the entire country. Russian ambition may have become more constrained during the war. Fighting has largely moved away the areas of Ukraine that remain under Kiev control, and Ukraine has launched attacks in Crimea and the Donbass with a view to recapturing territory that has been under Russian control since 2014, and in September took back around 11,000 square miles mainly in the Kharkiv region. Zelensky's government has shown little sign of making peace a priority, and is persistently asking for western military support (Sabbagh 2022a), which may have the effect of prolonging the war.

In the early stages of the war western opinion showed some division as to whether Zelensky should be encouraged to formally surrender the Donbass or at least make territorial concessions. France's president Emmanuel Macron, who the Russian news agency *TASS* (2022) claims has spent 100 hours on the phone to Putin during the crisis, was the main advocate for this strategy (Sheftalovich 2022). He seems to recognise that humiliating Putin while leaving him in office could be particularly dangerous. The G7 conference in Munich however ended on 28 June with the leaders, including Macron, united in promising to increase the economic and political costs to Russia (Wintour 2022), making a short-term negotiated end to the war unlikely.

The views of the Ukrainian people themselves are not so easy to ascertain. Media prominence naturally enough has been given to those who have bravely fought the Russian invasion directly or indirectly, but they are likely to be far more patriotically motivated than the bulk of the population, and there will be at least a substantial minority who will value having a peaceful life over Kiev's aspirations to preserve territorial integrity.

There are concessions that could be made to Putin that would be unpalatable to those who see standing up to a bully as paramount, but which might end the war and save countless lives within and beyond Ukraine. The reality is that the people of Crimea, annexed by Russia in 2014 but with no international recognition, do want to be part of Russia. Criticism of the referendum where that view was expressed was based largely on the perception that it was illegal (Shirmammadov 2016) rather than that it was not a fair reflection of Crimean opinion (Colbey p.186). The pro-Russian separatists in the Donbass had control of that region before the war (Colbey p.200), and the creation of settled boundaries there would make for a society which could function much more effectively, the necessary erosion of Kiev's sovereignty many might feel would be a price worth paying.

The other area in which concessions might have been made is the composition of NATO. Among Putin's pretexts for the war was the lack of an assurance that Ukraine would not join that organisation. Ever since 1991, when on independence Ukraine joined the North Atlantic Cooperation Council, there has been dialogue and cooperation between it and NATO according to NATO (2022). While the relationship has blown hot and cold, particularly during pro-Russian Viktor Yanukovich's presidency from 2010 to 2014 (Reuters 2022), in September 2020 Zelensky approved a National Security Strategy to develop a "distinctive partnership" with NATO leading ultimately to membership (NATO 2022). This was inevitably a provocation to Russia and may even have inclined Putin to start making war preparations, with troops massing near the border a few months later in 'training exercises' (Reuters 2022).

US Secretary of State Howard Baker's utterances that NATO would not expand eastwards in his meeting with Mikhail Gorbachev in February 1990 have been swept aside or even denied in the course of the war. However, US government archive material disclosed in 2017 (National Security Archive 2017) leaves little doubt that the assurance was given and echoed by French, British and West German leaders. Whether Gorbachev would have been able to prevent the German reunification this was said in consideration of is debatable, but it is not unreasonable for Putin to believe he is able to rely on the promise. Indeed, Russian forbearance on the joining of the Baltic states in March 2004 is surprising (Gidadhubli 2004), and had it seriously objected then, it may well be NATO would have backed down. It would scarcely be a concession now for NATO and Ukraine to adopt Baker's assurance and give Russia comfort on that question. Even President Zelensky has accepted that it is not feasible for Ukraine to join at the moment (BBC 2022a).

It is likely that the impact on energy prices will eventually drive western governments to contend for a compromise. Incumbent governments will realise that a damaged economy will have a much greater adverse impact on their chances of re-election than seeming to be 'weak' on Russia. There are many ways the Ukraine situation could play out. The conflict could freeze without formal resolution in the way that indeed Transnistria's did, something which would save lives but not entirely end Russia's international pariah status. Putin dying, whether naturally or through assassination, or being could open up possibilities for constructive negotiation, and might be face-saving on both sides*. Zelensky could decide to prioritise the saving of Ukrainian lives and negotiate a surrender with Russia.

It may be the relish of the surprisingly frequent failures of the Russian military that has fuelled the continuation of the war. Ukrainian resistance has undoubtedly been brave and more successful than might have been predicted at its start. Ultimately, it is not a war that the Ukrainians can emerge from entirely victorious. Short of a massive and successful escalation of the war by Russia, Ukraine will survive as a country but is unlikely to regain control of the Donbass region. Short-term international recognition of Russian sovereignty there, or even in Crimea, without Ukrainian consent is inconceivable, and Putin's purported annexation of four Ukraine territories on 30 September is almost universally regarded as illegal. It has though led to a rapid application by

---

*   Other than that current prime minister, Mikhail Mishustin, would become acting leader, there is no consensus at all who is likely to be Putin's successor (Ball 2022), a state of affairs Putin may well have orchestrated.

Ukraine for NATO membership, which could disastrously drag that organisation into the war if accepted.

Pref.1.1 THE EFFECT OF THE WAR ON TRANSNISTRIA

Politically and militarily, the Transnistrian cause has not been served well by the Ukraine war. Russia is no longer seen by the EU as a country with which diplomatic business can be done. Where there have to be discussions, they are likely to be restricted to core issues about the Ukrainian war. Russia will not make sacrifices or compromises to help the Transnistrian position.

It is conceivable that if no compromise is reached in the Donbass and on the NATO question, Russia would attempt to create a corridor to Transnistria though the Odessa region. That may be militarily feasible, if one avoids romantically overstating the relative strength of the Ukrainian armed forces* – but would come at a tremendous diplomatic and human cost. Were that to happen, it is likely to follow that Russia would take a more direct control of Transnistria, though the world would be unlikely to recognise an independence or annexation in those circumstances. It is more realistic to look at Transnistria's position on the assumption of a stalemate or compromise which would not bring Russia close to its borders.

Transnistria itself has practised a studied neutrality in relation to the war, a position confirmed to me by Vladimir Yastrebchak and apparent from the official "President" website, which gave more prominence to the long-standing dispute with Chisinau over car number plates than the war. This position is despite its Russophile outlook and the hostile manner it has been treated by Ukraine, particularly since 2017 (Colbey p.200).

The war has meant a complete end for the foreseeable future to any negotiations through the OSCE 5 + 2 mechanism (Colbey p.203). Even before it started the Sandu government had started withdrawing from the process, refusing, so Yastrebchak told me, to take part in proposed talks in the autumn of 2021 in Stockholm. Although the OSCE, then under Swedish chairmanship, did meet in that city in December 2021, no substantive progress was made and only platitudes on the desirability of resolving the situation were contained in its concluding statement (OSCE 2021). Yastrebchak's belief that further talks are unlikely to take place in the present situation is obviously correct. Besides the hostility between Ukraine and Russia making any direct talks between them on the topic impossible, European and US disdain for Russian now is such that they may not even recognise that country has a legitimate role in determining Transnistria's future.

---

* The talk, presumably intended as a serious means of furthering war aims, of crowd-funding weapons for Ukraine (e.g. Braw 2022) is a clear illustration of how desperately under-resourced Ukraine is.

Pref.1.2 ATTACKS WITHIN TRANSNISTRIA

Transnistria has been peripherally drawn into the war by several explosions within its territory, which briefly brought the territory to world attention. Early in the morning of 26 April there was an attack on Transnistria's state security building, which is on the corner of residential streets in the centre of Tiraspol, with a grenade launcher, leaving the lower floors damaged but the structure of the building largely intact*. A couple of hours later two explosions occurred in the village of Mayak, close to the Ukrainian border, seriously damaging two radio antennae which were used for broadcasting Russian state radio (Gibbs 2022). Minor damage was caused in another attack that day on the Tiraspol airstrip (Turp-Balazs 2022).

On 27 April several drones flew over Cobansa, only about a mile from the Ukrainian border. There have been suggestions that shots were fired from them perhaps with the aim of triggering an explosion at the large ammunition depot there (RFE 2022). On 6 May four explosions, probably caused by material dropped from a drone, occurred around 9.40pm at Transnistria's other even more obscure airstrip at Voronkovo (Herrera 2022).

The Ukrainian Euromaidan Press (2022) had in a 'Twitter thread' on 6 April alleged that the Tiraspol airfield was being prepared to receive aircraft. The claims were implausible and unevidenced but may have provided motivation to attackers within Ukraine to assault the airfield**. The airfield has not been used for over thirty years. While Sergey Sidorenko (2022) argued in *European Pravda* that it could not be used for military landings as such aircraft would have to fly over Ukraine, where they would probably be shot down, that overlooks the fact that overflying enemy territory is a frequent incident of modern warfare. Vladimir Yastrebchak told me that it is only now used for car races. He also said that while there are military helicopters in Transnistria, they are not serviceable. An attempt to land one in a 2020 military parade in the centre of Tiraspol resulted in a crash which the pilot was lucky to survive.

Were Russia intent on attacking Ukraine from the west, the airfield would take on a vital strategic importance. That potential significance makes it an unlikely target for a 'false flag' operation of the sort that has been pointed to in parts of the western media. The simple explanation given by the Transnistrians officially *Novosti Pridnestrovya* (2018) and by Yastrebchak, that it was the work of Ukrainians who had crossed the border by cutting a hole in a fence, is far more plausible.

The false flag theory founders on the fact that there has been no subsequent action by Russia which it has been used to justify, as well as the implausibility of Russia orchestrating damage to a place that could be of strategic importance to it. It also seems implausible that if the state security services were involved in the attack, and it is hard to see how it

---

*   A photo of the damage is available at Telegram (2022). My own attempts to photograph it in June 2022 were not successful.

** A photo of a supposed runway at the airport in just about usable condition appears on Wikipedia (2022) and has been lifted by some media outfits. However, close examination shows it is from 2007, and it does not reflect the condition of the airfield now.

could take place within Transnistria without that involvement, they would attack their own building: official security operatives are rarely that magnanimous!

Pref. 2 THE TRANSNISTRIAN ECONOMY

Pref. 2.1 THE ECONOMIC EFFECT OF THE UKRAINIAN WAR ON TRANSNISTRIA

The Transnistrian economy is heavily dependent on Russian support, particularly through the complex system of subsidised gas it is provided with (Colbey p. 93). A substantially weakened Russian economy might bear on its willingness to aid Transnistria through the subsidies or otherwise.

The Russian economy has however proved resilient through the war (*The Economist* 2022), neither the diversion of resources to the war nor the imposition of western sanctions having had a significant impact. The Kremlin's insistence that Russian gas had to be paid for in roubles (Davies & Elliot 2022) was a masterstroke for which it has received predictably little credit in the western press. The resulting strength of the rouble has given it access to foreign currencies to a greater extent than it ever has had before. In the first four months of 2022, Russian had a current account surplus of $96bn, more than treble that for the same period of 2021 (Elliott 2022) which rose to $167 billion by July (Bloomberg UK 2022).

Although Shchukina and Yastrebchak both mentioned rising prices in Transnistria to me and I had a feeling I was paying a little more for food and accommodation than I had before, there was nothing to suggest this was any greater than the inflation being experienced in the UK and most of Europe. The Transnistrian rouble remained at the same 16.3 to the US$ it had been in 2019 (Colbey p. 92).

It is possible that the Transnistrian economy will be hurt in the longer term by Moldovan efforts to secure gas supplies from elsewhere (Necşuţu 2022). When the contract for supply to Moldova expired on 1 May 2022, it was rapidly extended for another month (Chirileasa 2022), perhaps in exchange for Moldova granting an internationally recognised environmental permit for the Rybnitsa steelworks. The deal continued after the end of May, though prices had increased substantially by August: 47% according to former president Dodon (Euractive 2022). Moldova is still looking for alternative sources of energy (Gavin 2022) which, with the pipeline from Iași and Ungheni (Colbey p.94) in Romania now completed though not yet operational, is feasible in all but the very short term.

Moldova's position has until very recently been to see gas supplies in purely commercial terms, with connection to the European grid through that pipeline not being attractive because of the higher prices that would be demanded (Necşuţu, 2021). The outlook of the Sandu government; the EU's greater incentive to subsidise and support Moldova; and the likelihood of Gazprom through Moldovagaz becoming more assertive in demanding payments, may change that position. The view I expressed (Colbey p.121) that in relation to gas, "There appears to be a finely balanced interdependence between Russia, Moldova and Transnistria, which it would be in the interests of none to disturb", may not apply now as clearly as it did in 2020. While this could be damaging for the Transnistrian economy, the increased strategic importance of Transnistria means that Russia would have an incentive to compensate for any deficit this left Transnistria in.

Another adverse economic concern may be that the war, particularly in its early stages, fuelled migration from Transnistria, potentially exacerbating what is already a significant problem for Transnistria (Colbey p87). A fear, perhaps not wholly rational, that the war would spread to Transnistria, did result in migration at the start of it. There is no empirical evidence available of this. However, Natalia Shchukina pointed out to me she had noticed fewer people on the streets of Tiraspol than before the war. A moment's reflection made me realise that was my observation too. The *Dolce Vita* café outside the university had been empty at 9am whereas there had always been a few people in it on my previous visits. Even if there is little fear of being caught up in a war now, many who have left will choose for economic and personal reasons not to return. Elena Bobkova, from the Tiraspol Centre for Analytical Research, was quoted in *Balkan Insight* as believing in April around 5% of Tiraspol's 130,000 inhabitants had left the city (Kumzin 2022). More were reported to have fled after the explosions described above (Erizanu 2022).

Transnistria had also received refugees from Ukraine. UNHRO (2022) estimated on 21 April 2022 that about 8,000 had remained, Yastrebchak thought the figure was down to 2,000 by June, in addition to vastly more who had travelled through. Yastrebchak mentioned but did not dwell on the fact that local agencies had with government encouragement worked with international NGOs, such as the Red Cross to provide assistance to them, something the territory has frequently and damagingly been reluctant to do (Colbey p.117). As most refugees have moved on to Moldova or further west, that influx is unlikely to have a significant effect on Transnistria's depopulation issues. Transnistria did itself provide humanitarian assistance for those who passed through, which came from the very limited government coffers as well as international organisations.

Pref. 2.2 THE SHERIFF GROUP

The Sheriff companies continue to pay a leading role in the commercial and political life of Transnistria. President Krasnoselsky has retained cordial relations with the conglomerate, unlike his two predecessors. *Oblovenie*, which is Sheriff's main political party (Colbey p.79), performed strongly in the 2020 elections, winning 27 out of 33 seats, most of which uncontested (Necsutu 2020). A turnout in those elections of just 27.79% may have been due to Covid fears, as well as disillusionment with the process. Although there were not the same concerning reasons for the lack of candidates as there were in the 2021 presidential election, discussed below, the dominance of Sheriff and the lack of a meaningful parliamentary opposition are hardly healthy manifestations of democracy.

Perhaps of less significance was my disappointment finding in June 2022 that Sheriff stores no longer sell German pepper brie (Colbey p.78 fn40). I was intrigued at being told by two ultra-orthodox rabbis on the flight home from Chisinau that they had been summoned to Tiraspol to perform a *kashrut* inspection for Sheriff's Kvint factory. It is unlikely such certification would be sought for the small and generally nonorthodox Transnistrian market (Colbey 144) and may be indicative of Sheriff's plans to expand internationally.

More striking was the unexpected success of Sheriff Tiraspol FC in the 2021/22 Champions League, where several creditable results were topped by a 2-1 win against Real Madid in the Bernabéu stadium in September 2021, described by the London *Daily Mirror* as the biggest upset in Champions League history (Millar 2021). I was though told wistfully by Vladimir Yastrebchak that many of the players had been sold and the Ukrainian coach had left the club to fight in the Ukraine war, and he rightly predicted such success would not be achieved in the 2022/23 tournament: the club were consigned to the second tier Europa League losing 2-0 to Manchester United on 15 September, a game which UEFA required to be played in Chisinau deeming Tiraspol "unsafe".

Even that triumph was borne upon by the Transnistrian political situation. Yastrebchak told me that the money received for the cup run, whose seven points in the group stages should have netted over 22 million euros (Allen 2021), was not paid to the club but to the Moldovan FA, which is expected to pass it on. After several months of negotiations, the problem was only partially resolved. Such sums though do suggest that dismissing the club as "a vanity project" (Colbey p.84) may not be entirely justified.

Pref. 3 POLITICAL DEVELOPMENTS IN TRANSNISTRIA AND MOLDOVA

Pref. 3.1 THE 2021 TRANSNISTRIAN PRESIDENTIAL ELECTION

President Vadim Krasnoselsky was re-elected on 12 December 2021, his only opponent being an obscure local councillor from Hirtop near Grigoripol (*Infotag* 2021), described by Freedom House (2022) as "a local clerk" Sergey Pynzar, with Krasnoselsky capturing 87.04% of the vote. Pynzar was regarded as a little more than a nominal candidate and did not actively campaign.

Freedom House (2022) gave an account of the election line up:

Notable opposition figures Anatoly Dirun and Nikolai Malyshev were not allowed to register as candidates by the Central Election Commission due to alleged irregularities in the signatures collected for their nominations. Another candidate, Sergei Dechev, withdrew his candidacy without explanation. An electoral-code amendment instituted in June removed the "against all" option from the presidential ballot.

While that organisation may have little credibility in its reports on Transnistria normally (Colbey p.126) and its o/4 for even this election process another manifestation of its bias, its comments were probably justified. They accorded quite precisely with what Vladimir Yastrebchak, who went so far as to say Dechev withdrew partly out of fear, told me about the election.

It is unlikely that Dirun, an academic who is frequently critical of the Sheriff Group and *Obnovlenie* (Negura 2021*), or Malyshev, an economist who had been director of the Association of Transnistrian Banks (Vypritskikh 2021), would have presented a serious challenge to Krasnoselsky. However, Avakov (2021) suggests that had they stood, "Malyshev and Dirun would not have been able to defeat Krasnoselsky, but they would have spoiled his image of the people's choice with their scandalous statements." The same could doubtless have been said of Dechev.

The Central Election Commission, which was responsible for rejecting the candidatures of Dirun and Malyshev, had shown a preference of Krasnoselsky in the 2016 election (Colbey p.230), where there were balancing factors that made that support of less significance. Its repetition in this election to the extent of preventing there being any whole-hearted, let alone convincing, candidate running against the incumbent shows a worrying undermining of the democracy that had manifested itself so convincingly in the 2011 and 2016 elections (Colbey p.109).

Writing for the *de facto* States Research Unit, of which he is a regional co-director, just before the election, Lance Bradley (2021) was particularly scathing of the process, alleging, "Democratic legitimation is being strangled by Sheriff, and the election in Transnistria, both in 2020 [for the Soviet] and upcoming this week, are proof of that." While his and Freedom House's (2022) observations may overstate the case, there is a fear that Transnistria, paradoxically under what it is its least corrupt president, may be slipping backwards in terms of the democratic process.

Pref. 3.2 OTHER POLITICAL DEVELOPMENTS IN TRANSNSITRIA

Many of the senior officers of Krasnoselsky's government remain *in situ*, though not Ruslan Mova, the minister for internal affairs who provided helpful information for the work (Colbey p.81), who was replaced by Vitaly Neagu in July 2021. Vladimir Yastrebchak still acts sometimes as a government adviser but no longer holds his semi-official foreign affairs brief alongside long serving foreign minister Vitaly Ignatiev, who does remain in his post. After some inexplicable political manoeuvrings in May 2022, Aleksandr Rozenberg, a former baker, replaced Aleksandr Martynov in the relatively peripheral post of prime minister (*Tadviser* 2022). The strikingly supine human rights ombudsman Vyacheslav Kosinsky (Colbey p.115) was reappointed for five years on 30 March 2022 (Ombudsman of PMR 2022).

---

*   This is the transcript of a substantial and interesting interview with Dirun.

Oleg Horjan (Colbey p.130) remains in prison, where he continues to write numerous letters calling for his own release and making criticisms of the government. Yastrebchak candidly admitted when I asked him about this that Horjan has made things "personal" in relation to those who decide on whether to release him. I interpreted this as a hint that his behaviour has antagonised President Krasnoselsky, who has not been sensible enough to rise above it*.

A worrying story run by the Chisinau based IPN (2022) press agency in February stated there were proposals by Transnistria to make it an imprisonable offence to petition the European Court of Human Rights (ECHR). There appears to be no other source for this, and the allegation is improbable. Russia was expelled from the Council of Europe in March 2022 and the ECHR will cease to exercise any jurisdiction over it from 16 September 2022 (Speck 2022). If Russia ceases to be subject to the court's jurisdiction, then the only prospective defendant for a disgruntled Transnistrian would be Moldova – only internationally recognised states can be defendants (Colbey p.128) – and there is no reason why the Transnistrian government would wish to restrain such claims.

More plausible is an account given to *Balkan Insight* (2022) by human rights lawyer Stepan Popovski (see Colbey p.113) of a man imprisoned for five days, and not released on the expiry of his sentence, for putting a banner on his balcony saying "Let the MGB** go crap itself". This was described as "administrative detention" suggesting that there was not even a judicial process underpinning the sentence.

It does seem that the Transnistrian regime is doing little to reform itself on the use of state powers to silence its opponents. While it may do not do so in a particularly brutal manner, particularly in comparison with Russia, it is not behaviour which helps it put forward a case that it has a government with sufficient respect of democracy, the rule of law and human rights, which should be a major plank in its claim for independence.

Pref. 3.3 THE CHANGE IN THE MOLDOVAN GOVERNMENT

Maia Sandu became the President of Moldova on 24 December 2020, defeating Igor Dodon by 58% to 42%. She had previously been Prime Minster from June to November 2019. Broadly speaking, Dodon could be characterised as pro-Russian and her as pro-EU. She has been highly critical of the Russian invasion of Ukraine. Her position was strengthened by substantial victories for her pro-Europe party in July 2021 parliamentary elections (*Euractiv* 2021).

She has shown an unwavering opposition to the Transnistria position. She has called for the withdrawal of Russian troops from the territory and their replacement with an OSCE civilian observer mission (RFE 2021). Although she claims to favour a peaceful and diplomatic solution to the problem, she has unequivocally made clear her opposition to

---

*   In early 2021 I wrote to Yastrebchak and Mova, adding my own voice to the few calling for his release but received no response.

**   Ministry of State Security.

recognising Transnistrian independence, even in the face of argument that it is delaying the EU accession she aspires to for Moldova. Yastrebchak told me she has made a point of having no public conversations with President Krasnoselsky, in contrast with her predecessor (Colbey p. 38). There is nothing to suggest covert high-level talks.

Sandu's attitude to Transnistria is far less nuanced than Dodon's. She has stated that she rejects arguments that Chisinau should give up Transnistria should it prove a potential barrier to EU membership, and that she is committed to a peaceful and diplomatic solution (*TASS* 2020). Were she faced with a choice between accession or retaining Transnistria it may well be the former and more expedient option would prevail, but she is less likely to allow herself to be backed into a corner where such a choice had to be made. The EU may be reluctant to admit Moldova, both because of the provocation that it would seem to Russia and because of Moldova's weak economy. The possibility of union between Moldova and Romania (Colbey p. 199), one way in which Transnistria could be cut loose from Chisinau, seems less likely than ever. Sandu, while not intractably opposed to it, believes it could only be justified if a significant majority of Moldovans wanted it, something which is clearly not the present position as only around 44% support it (Sanchez 2022).

Pref. 4 THE IMPACT OF THE COVID-19 CRISIS ON TRANSNISTRIA

The Covid-19 pandemic presented serious challenges to the Transnistrian government, just as it did to that of virtually every country in the world. There is little consensus even now as to what was the best approach to take, save that those with strict prolonged lockdowns, like Taiwan and New Zealand, had fewer direct fatalities (Worldometers 2022), and it is hard to pass judgement on government performance. What though can fairly be said is that Transnistria behaved and was affected like most European countries. Before even any cases had been detected in the country, from 13 March 2020 all public gatherings were banned, four days later schools and universities were closed (President 2022). From 30 March a lockdown was imposed with tight restrictions on movement outside people's homes. The state of emergency ended in June 2020 but many restrictions remained in place (President 2022a).

By the time I visited in June 2022, there was no sign of the crisis and hardly anyone was wearing a mask. According to Transnistrian official figures (MoH(T) 2022) as of 25 August 2022 there had been 120,508 cases with 2,234 deaths. Taking a notional population of 500,000, this is an infection rate of 24.10% and with 0.45% of the population dying, which would make it the 69th and sixth highest in the world had it been a country (Worldometers 2022). Comparable figures for Moldova, which probably include Transnistria, would be 14.17% and 0.29%; the UK's are 34.2%* and 0.27%.

---

*   Like many countries' figures, almost certainly a gross underestimate caused by non-reporting of cases.

The explanation for the high deaths figure is not obvious. It may have been a regional matter: most of the countries with higher rates were also in south-eastern Europe. The relatively high number of older people in the territory (Colbey p.87 and Crivenco 2018) will have created a more vulnerable population, which may have resulted in the very high deaths to cases ratio*. In a small population it may be easier to keep accurate count, and Transnistria's reporting of figures has been meticulous**. Healthcare in Transnistria, particularly away from Transnistria is rudimentary (Colbey p.158) and its international isolation may have made it harder for it to get the outside support less resourced countries needed to respond to the virus.

Lockdown in the territory was though relatively strict. Indeed, that was, according to Vladimir Yastrebchak, a factor that led to Ruslan Mova's removal from office, his hardline approach (see e.g. Colbey p.139) having made him unpopular with some of his governmental colleagues. There may be a low vaccination rate – just 31% were said to have completed immunisation (MoH(T) 2022). This was despite a range of western, Russian and Chinese vaccines being available and government encouragement to take it up (MoH(T) 2022).

Whether the performance on deaths was as comparatively bad as the government's own figure would suggest is debatable, but there is little basis to see it as a failure of the government.

Pref. 5 CONCLUSION: HAS THE CASE FOR TRANSNISTRIAN INDEPENDENCE CHANGED SINCE 2020?

The basic premise of the work, "that the Transnistrian government has succeeded in producing a successful society that supports its claim to independence" (Colbey p.225) has been dented, in the last two years. The way the 2020 presidential election candidates were filtered creates a new concern in an area where Transnistrian governance could otherwise be regarded as strong. The powers of the Central Elections Commission may have been exercised over-officiously rather than corruptly in blocking the candidature of Dirun and Malyshev, but at the very least officials can be said to have lost sight of the bigger picture in excluding opposition candidates for technical reasons.

The limited number of candidates in the 2020 parliament or soviet election may be a matter of less concern, because of the circumstances around that time. The dominance of Sheriff in the Transnistrian soviet is a long-established fact, and its increased control post 2020 may not adversely impact on the territory significantly. The continued deten-tion of Oleg Horjan and the reason Yastrebchak gave for it – that his behaviour had made it personal – as well as other examples of detention for the expressing of views,

---

* The strikingly low figures in many African countries are likely to have been the result of a very young population, partly enhanced by a lack of precise recordkeeping, but despite relatively low levels of healthcare.

** There are detailed and frequently produced statistics on the official President website as well as the cited announcements.

cited here and in the main work (Colbey p.137) undermine any case based on respect of human rights. The only matter in my list of matters the Transnistrian government should try to address (Colbey p.225) that there is evidence of improvement on is the willingness to work with foreign NGOs, mentioned in passing by Yastrebchak in connection with assisting refugees.

Not significantly undermined by recent events is the proposition that Transnistria is economically viable (Colbey p.96). Although the hostility between Russia and the rest of Europe could upset the provision of gas subsidies which have been the lifeblood of its economy, logistic and financial factors will probably trump over political ones to prevent that happening to a damaging effect. Russia will continue to have a vested interest in supporting its economy and probably the means to do so. It may be that the Transnistrian economy will suffer nothing more terminal than being drawn into the Europe-wide inflationary spiral as a result of the war, though there is a fear that the constant problem of migration from the territory will be exacerbated.

The rate of deaths from Covid-19 were higher than might have been expected from a country of Transnistria's size, but there were factors explaining that which did not suggest any failure or incompetence on the part of the government. Indeed, a desire to keep the people safe from the disease was the main reason for the political downfall of the interior minister.

Geopolitical factors arising both out of the Ukraine war and the change of government in Chisinau will though make the realising the claim for Transnistrian independence harder. Krasnoselsky, despite the election shenanigans, appears to be a reasonably efficient and popular president who has not faced any allegations of corruption, and the same can be said of his Moldovan counterpart Maia Sandu. It is unfortunate, but not the fault of Transnistria, that dialogue between these two capable politicians has not taken place. Without it there is unlikely to be any consensual resolution of the situation, particularly as the Ukraine war has ended any 5 + 2 negotiations for the foreseeable future.

As the Ukraine war progresses it seems increasingly unlikely that Russia will fulfil any territorial aspirations outside the Donbass. So long as that proves correct, the war there may have little direct effect on the Transnistria situation. The Moldovan government is unlikely to provoke a crisis by substantially altering the *status quo*, let alone taking any military action. Indirectly the Transnistrian cause will not be helped by the disdain western governments and institutions will feel for Russia for many years. Even if that country moves on from Putin, it may remain a pariah state. As the disintegration of 5 + 2 mechanism has shown, there is less likely to be either a will or a forum for constructive negotiation. President Sandu is even less likely than her predecessor, Dodon, to make any unilateral concession. The only possibility for change might be from EU membership, but just as Cyprus could join the EU despite its divided nature, so too might Moldova.

There remains the remote possibility of Russia trying to create an occupied land corridor as far as the Transnistrian border through Odessa. While the likely loss of troop and civilian life; destruction of the Ukrainian economy; and indefensibility of such an action by Russia, perhaps even to Chinese eyes, makes it unlikely, the consequences should still be considered. To predict whether having wrested complete control of the territory from Chisinau, Russia would then prefer it as a Belorussia type satellite state or to integrate it within Russia itself is impossible to say, particularly as pre-war at least Transnistrian opinion on the matter seemed to be evenly divided (Colbey pp.55,56).

While a case can and should still be made, that the Transnistrian people should have the right to develop wholly separately from the rest of Moldova so long as that is what they want, the territory now faces dual obstacles in doing so. The first is internal and within its government's control, that it has failed to tackle human rights abuses, particularly the silencing of dissidents in a way that it should do and may even be falling back from its previously impressive democratic process. The second is the estrangement between its main supporter, Russia, and any other country or organisation likely to be involved in determining its future, makes a negotiated independence less likely. Unless there is a somewhat improbable attempt by Russia to use military force to take control of it, which could prove a humanitarian disaster, there is little reason to believe the present situation will change significantly in the foreseeable future.

LIST OF PHOTOGRAPHS

NOTES

Photograph 1 is reproduced on condition of providing the weblink: https://regtrends.com/ en/2018/12/26/dodon-reveals-the-details-of-the-meeting-with-krasnoselsky/. Photograph 13 was taken by Vladimir Yastrebchak. All other photographs were taken by the author.

ABBREVIATIONS

ASSR	Autonomous Soviet Socialist Republic
BBC	British Broadcasting Corporation
CEC	(Transnistrian) Central Election Commission
CIA	Central Intelligence Agency
CIS	Commonwealth of Independent States
CoE	Council of Europe
DC	District of Colombia
DCFTA	Deep and Comprehensive Free Trade Agreement
ECHR	European Court of Human Rights
ECJ	European Court of Justice
EU	European Union
FIDH	International Federation for Human Rights
GDP	Gross domestic product
IGO	Intergovernmental organisation
ILO	International Labour Organization
IOM	International Organization for Migration
KGB	*Komitet Gosudarstvennoy Bezopasnosti* (loosely, State Security Services)
MEP	Member of the European Parliament
MFA	(Transnistrian) Ministry of Foreign Affairs
MIA	(Transnistrian) Ministry of Internal Affairs
NATO	North Atlantic Treaty Organization
n.d.	No date
NGO	Non-governmental organisation
OECD	Organisation for Economic Co-operation and Development
OSCE	Organization for Security and Co-operation in Europe
PMR	Pridnestrovian Moldavian Republic
PRB	Pridnestrovian Republican Bank (the Transnistrian Central Bank)
RFE	Radio Free Europe
Sect.	Section (of the thesis)
SubSect.	Subsection (of the thesis)

SSR	Soviet Socialist Republic
UEFA	Union of European Football Associations
UK	United Kingdom
UNESCO	United Nations Educational, Scientific and Cultural Organization
US	United States of America
USSD	United States State Department
USSR	Union of Soviet Socialist Republics
WHO	World Health Organization

TERMINOLOGY, STYLE AND TIME FRAME

Terminology

The territory which forms the subject matter of this thesis is known by many names. I generally use that which is most common, at least in the English language, academia, officialdom and the media, **Transnistria**.* Occasional variations on that, which I have not used, include *Trans-Dniestr* or *Transdniester*. These are Romanian-language terms translating loosely to 'across the **Dniestr River**', although the river itself is sometimes known by other names.

The term that seems to be preferred officially in the territory is *Pridnestrovie*, the *Pridnestrovian Moldavian Republic* or *PMR*.** I particularly noticed this being used directly to me when dealing with government representatives as I observed the 2016 presidential election. My interpreter told me there was a similar term, both full and as initials, used in Russian*** when she spoke to officials. When I interviewed the minister of internal affairs, Ruslan Mova, in December 2018, he said he was equally happy with that or 'Transnistria'. However, the official website reports President Krasnoselsky as saying:

'Transnistria' is absolutely unacceptable and offensive in a historical context marked by dark times of fascist occupation and attempts of physical extermination of the people living in Pridnestrovie. (*Novosti Pridnestrovya* 2019a)

This is a reference to the Romanian occupation and resulting massacres, particularly of Transnistrian Jews. With some hesitation, I decided not to alter the nomenclature in light of that. I hope readers of this thesis, particularly those in the territory, will accept that my use of 'Transnistria' is purely a linguistic expedient and not a specific rejection of Krasnoselsky's argument.

Sometimes the term **Left-Bank Moldova** is used for Transnistria in contradistinction to **Right-Bank Moldova** for the non-Transnistrian part. I occasionally adopt those terms, but they are counterintuitive when looking at a map as Transnistria is on the right. Also Bender, which forms part of Transnistria, is on the 'right' side of the Dniestr River.

---

*   In this section, I embolden terms I prefer and italicise those I don't.

** It would be virtually impossible to convert this to an adjective in English, unlike Transnistrian.

*** I do not think it would be productive to reproduce Cyrillic-lettered terms here or elsewhere in the dissertation.

The reporting position is summarised, not wholly accurately, by Public Radio International:

The *Washington Post* and the *Wall Street Journal* call it by its Romanian name, Transnistria. The Associated Press and the BBC* call it by its Russian name, Trans-Dniester. Reuters opts for a compromise between the two that neither side uses, Transdniestria. (Cox 2014)

The issue is also discussed at the beginning of Bill Bowring's paper on the territory. He decides to call it the PMR (2014:1).

Bender, as the city is now invariably referred to in English, is officially known by the Russian variant *Bendery* and, prior to 1992, was *Tighina*, by which it is still occasionally referred to in Romanian publications and Moldovan signposts. There are minor variations on the other major towns, **Rîbniţa** and **Dubăsari,** as I refer to each (without, largely because it would seem an affectation, reproducing the Romanian accentuation). The capital is uniformly **Tiraspol.** I prefer **Chişinău,** unaccented, to the Russian variant *Kishinev.* The Moldovan city of **Bălţi,** not to be confused with the former Beerserabian capital of Balata, is referred to as such again without the accenting: its Russian variant is *Beltsy.*

I have sometimes used **Moldova** to refer to the non-Transnistrian part, appreciating how that could be seen as politically loaded, as indeed could *Moldova proper.* Sometimes the context lends itself to using **Tiraspol** and **Chisinau** as meaning the respective territories each is administered from, particularly when referring to their governments. *Bessarabia* broadly equates to Chisinau-controlled Moldova,** but it is obscure and slightly pretentious and I have rarely used it. It strictly includes Bender and some areas that are now part of Ukraine. Inhabitants of Moldova are referred to as **Moldovans,** in accordance with intuitive and widespread English usage, although there are arguments that *Moldavians* is strictly correct (Encyclopedia of Ukraine n.d.). Buttin (2007:15) says that the name Moldova was only adopted after independence from the USSR, but I have never seen it referred to as *Moldavia.* I usually call the language spoken there **Moldovan,** as most ethnic Moldovans refer to their language and ethnicity (Chamberlain-Creangă 2011:19), although can be regarded as simply a form of *Romanian.*

I generally refer to Transnistria as a **territory** rather than a *state* or *country.* Its currency is **roubles** not *rubles* or *Roubles.* The Transnistrian legislative body is the **Soviet** or **Supreme Soviet** when necessary to distinguish it from any other soviet. *Parliament* would be equally correct, but does not seem to capture the Transnistrian perception of government so well. I have never seen *duma,* which is used for the Russian legislature, applied to Transnistria's. It is also sometimes referred to as the *Supreme Council.* Occasionally, there are variants on the translation into Latin letters of people's names, for instance, (President) **Krasnoselsky** and the rarer *Krasnoselski.**** I then use the one that seems most common and, in particular, aim for consistency.

---

*   There are many references to 'Transnistria' on the BBC website.

**   Strictly the territory between the Dniester and Prut Rivers; see Çamözü (2016:1).

***   As this is not a linguistic study, there will be no exploration as to why some names, e.g. Shtanski, are anglicised with an 'i' and others with a 'y'.

Ukraine is just that, without the frequently prefixed *The,* and its capital is **Kiev** not *Kyiv*. For the territories of Abkhazia, **Nagorno-Karabakh** (also known as *Artsakh*), **South Ossetia** (officially, but never in reality, *Republic of South Ossetia – the State of Alania* after a 2017 referendum) and Transnistria I collectively use the term **pseudo-states**, despite its slightly pejorative air. *Quasi-* or *putative-states* are just as appropriate but little used.

Style

The style I have tried to engage with is that set out in the Chicago Manual of Style. It expounds an author-date system of referencing that seems logical and economical on space. I am also mindful that it is a series of recommendations, not rigid rules. I hope I will be forgiven for a few departures from those recommendations, for instance, in not repeating the year when giving references in the source list.

I have tried to avoid the turgidity of some academic and legal writing. I hope there is no sentence, other than quotes, of over 50 words – and frankly even that is too long.

Time frame

The project began before the formal study, when I first visited Transnistria in November 2014. I have aimed to state the position as it was in August 2020, though some of the material in Chapters 2 and 4 is taken from earlier statistics. I have inserted a few later developments, such as the election of a new Moldovan president in December 2020. I have worked primarily with academic material available to me at 31 August 2020, again with a few references to later articles.

TRANSNISTRIA: A SUMMARY

The territory of Transnistria has largely escaped Western European consciousness.* Legally part of Moldova, perhaps itself Europe's most obscure country, it is a sliver of land, sandwiched between the remainder of Moldova and Ukraine. It measures about 200 miles north to south and rarely more than 30 miles east to west, meaning it is roughly the area of Somerset,** with under 500,000 inhabitants, predominantly Russian speaking. It gained a *de facto* independence in 1992 in a short but bloody war upon the break-up of the USSR.

Transnistria is one of four 'pseudo-states' to have emerged as a consequence of carelessly drawn borders of Soviet Socialist Republics, which were the units granted independence by Moscow in the early 1990s. Transnistria has most of the features of an independent country, despite its reliance on Russian military and economic support: it has clearly marked and enforced borders; a constitution; wholly autonomous institutions of government; its own currency, including the world's first plastic coins; and a defined citizenship. While it issues those citizens with passports, they are valid only for travel to the other pseudo-states. Nearly all its citizens are also entitled to a Moldovan, Ukrainian or Russian passport.

There is virtually a complete lack of formal international recognition of Transnistria, even by Russia, and it only enjoys half-hearted diplomatic connections with the other pseudo-states. The Chisinau government, despite its universally recognised legal sovereignty over the territory, carries absolutely no sway there. There is, however, free movement between the two territories, and for many inhabitants of Tiraspol, a night out enjoying the – to Western eyes perhaps limited – attractions of Chisinau, an hour's drive away, is a regular occurrence. For some, the right to use Moldova's marginally superior healthcare facilities is a draw. Chisinau's international airport, on the Transnistrian side of the city, is also the main means of international travel for Transnistrians, who have no passenger airport of their own.

That freedom of movement is symbolic of how what is one of the world's most longstanding frozen conflicts has also become one of the least unpleasant. There are occasional proclamations from politicians on both sides about how unreasonable the

---

*   I have kept no records of this, but I would estimate that about 20–25% of people with whom I have discussed this project socially had heard of the territory and about half required some prompting about Moldova's status and location. Among North Americans there has been even less awareness of the area.
**   Rhode Island is the US equivalent.

other is and, more rarely, border skirmishes, but significant confrontation has been avoided for the last 29 years.

External attempts to resolve the situation constantly stall. The OSCE's 5+2 group, set up specifically for the task, meets infrequently and has only been able to deal with peripheral issues. The EU, which supports reunification with Moldova, publishes occasional papers, often authored by the estimable Professor Stefan Wolff of Birmingham University, but does very little. Russia, which maintains a peacekeeping force of around 1,000 troops from its 14th Army on the border and provides significant economic support, is seemingly content with the *status quo*. Surprisingly, the tentacles of the CIA and other US government organisations have not reached Transnistria. There is no overt, and almost certainly no covert, US presence.

Presided over by the corrupt but relatively benign Igor Smirnov until 2011, power changed hands peacefully after elections in that year and again in 2016, when the present incumbent Vadim Krasnoselsky secured a large majority over Yevgeny Shevchuk, who had triumphed against Smirnov and the Russian-backed Anatoliy Kaminski in 2011. There is a parliament, known as the Supreme Soviet, which is sometimes politically opposed to the president. This is decreed by a constitution which provides for most of the rights in the European Convention on Human Rights as well as a clear division of legislative, executive and judicial power.

A visitor to Transnistria, who is unlikely to go further than the capital Tiraspol except perhaps to the second city of Bender on the border with Moldova seven miles away, may be struck by the superficial preservation of much of the Soviet ambience. Statues of Lenin remain outside the Supreme Soviet building in Tiraspol and in central squares in other towns. A large dilapidated KGB headquarters,* with 'no photography' signs outside, remains on a central side street. There are wide, under-used roads into the centre, culminating in a grand convergence overlooked by the state theatre and university, the main political institutions being a kilometre out of the centre beside the main road. Little seems to have changed since Ronald Hill** described it in 1967. Much of the population is housed in uniform *khrushchyovka* flats, as apparent in the centre as the suburbs.

There are few attractions for that visitor, other than the political oddity. The Noul Neamț Monastery, a striking blue domed complex of Orthodox buildings, lies about three miles south of Tiraspol. The medieval fort at Bender is open to the public but little visited. Most people on organised day trips from Chisinau take tours offered by the Kvint brandy factory. Although some of its inhabitants told me Transnistria was "beautiful", that is not an obvious description for its featureless flat countryside and unexceptional cities. There are two high quality hotels in Tiraspol; a newly opened luxury one by Bender Fort; several others that are acceptable, back-packers' hostels, and some attempts on international website to let private accommodation. Even during the 2016 presidential election, when there was a significant influx of foreign observers, these were

---

*   Now the Ministry of State Security.
**   Then an Essex Univeristy student, doing the rough equivalent of a 'gap year'.

far from full. There is virtually no visitor accommodation outside Tiraspol. Whatever the future of Transnistria's economy, tourism is unlikely to play a significant part in it.

The economy is relatively weak, hampered by large-scale migration often of the youngest and brightest inhabitants – a problem that equally affects the rest of Moldova. Russian subsidies probably make up 60% of the territory's income and remittances from émigrés around 20%. Agriculture and textile manufacture are the main earned sources of foreign currency. Although the territory is poor by European, even Eastern European, standards, the population are almost all adequately fed and housed and there is a developed education system, including universities, basic free universal healthcare, and pensions for the elderly and disabled.

While there are garish news reports of Transnistria being a centre of money laundering, gun running and people smuggling, these reports have the common feature of not citing evidence or even examples. However, there is undoubtedly some corruption and a sometimes unhealthily close relationship between the government and the territory's most prominent business and employer, the Sheriff group. Sheriff's empire extends to supermarkets, petrol stations, the Kvint factory, heavy industry and an internationally successful football club, which qualified for the UEFA Champions League for the first time in the week this thesis was submitted, where it will play Real Madrid and Inter Milan.

Transnistria is sometimes referred to as the last bastion of the USSR, perhaps more by travel-blog writers than serious commentators. Based on the appearance of its buildings and roads, the Lenin statues and retention of nomenclature such as 'Supreme Soviet' for its parliament, which do give the impression of a time warp, this may have a superficial justification. However, a large number of economic and personal freedoms, including the unfettered right to travel, a robust electoral system and the power of the judiciary to review legislative and executive decisions, are among the compelling positive features which distinguish it from the USSR and perhaps even modern Russia.

MAP OF REGION*

MAP OF TRANSNISTRIA*

INTRODUCTION AND LITERATURE REVIEW

1. THE THESIS

This thesis asks what the future of Transnistria should be. It does so with the aim of showing why *de jure* independence and statehood is a viable solution. The thesis is divided into five chapters: Chapter 1 considers whether, in the context of its history and attempts at nation-building, Transnistria can be regarded as a nation; Chapter 2 the viability of its economy; Chapter 3 its record on democracy, human rights and the rule of law; and Chapter 4 how it now functions as a society. Finally, Chapter 5 asks how independence can be achieved in the light of the constraints of international law and how little support it has garnered from other countries and international organisations for that course.

The conclusion the thesis reaches is not one that has found favour with most of those who have considered the question before. The starting point for the thesis should be Sect.1.3, which asks what Transnistrians want. The evidence presented there – of referendums, my own discussions and other empirical research – is overwhelmingly that the Transnistrian people want to be separate from Moldova. Many, although probably not a majority, would prefer that eventually the territory became a part of Russia, possibly as a Kaliningrad-style exclave (and there is a possibility that this could follow after independence); however, this is not the subject of this thesis.

Nor does the thesis explore in detail other possible solutions to Transnistria's situation. Of course, there has been much political discussion and writing on that. Formalised self-determination, special status and autonomy have frequently been considered, as has a federal solution with Transnistria, the bulk of Moldova and the country's other perhaps notionally autonomous territory, Gagauzia. The Russian Kozak Memorandum (2003; see SubSect.5.2.2) and the German–Russian Meseburg Memorandum (2010; see SubSect.5.2.3) both made proposals which would have confirmed Transnistrian integration with Moldova, whilst giving it considerable autonomy. These are the nearest to government-backed tangible solutions that have been proposed, but they were not implemented, and there is little to be gained by revisiting them.

1.1 FIELDWORK AND METHODOLOGY

This thesis is based on a mixture of primary material gathered in Transnistria and Moldova and analysis of the copious contemporary media and academic writing on the topic.

The most important primary material is in the five appendices, often referred to in the text, one of which (D) is a verbatim reproduction of a telling response I received from the Moldovan government agency that deals with the Transnistrian situation. I could have produced more there – of interviews with judges and human rights lawyers and semi-structured discussions with groups at the territory's main university – but I have instead placed the fruits of these within the text. By detailed study of the extensive existing literature, this thesis attempts a more comprehensive examination of the territory than has yet been published, and this original research adds insight to the understanding of the issues surrounding this unresolved conflict and its possible resolution.

On nine visits to the territory between 2015 and 2019, I spoke to most of the people I wanted to. Only the human rights ombudsman, Vyacheslav Kosinsky, former Foreign Minister Nina Shtanski and, slightly to my surprise, UN expert Thomas Hammarberg proved completely elusive, the former giving elaborate excuses for not meeting and the latter two, as they were perfectly entitled, simply not answering emails. I did not make great efforts to interview President Krasnoselsky or the long-standing foreign minister, Vitaly Ignatiev. Their views on the questions I am investigating are readily available in published material.

The impressions I have formed of those I talked to have informed how much credence I attach to their assertions. I rely on over thirty years' experience as a litigation lawyer, where evaluating the credibility of a client or witness is an essential skill. I treat answers with caution, looking for contradictions, obvious exaggeration, evasion and rigidity. In the text, I evaluate most of the interviews and discussions along with any reservations I had about them, including about the integrity of the process when I was having group discussions with 'non-elite' people. With those factors in mind, I believe that most interviewees were doing their best to answer my questions honestly.

To a limited extent, the dissertation may be regarded as an ethnographic study. Each chapter contains such discussions, particularly Chapter 3 on democracy, human rights and the rule of law, where the input of judges, lawyers in Tiraspol and Chisinau, politicians and civil servants inform my conclusions on the workings of these aspects of Transnistrian life. Several wide-ranging discussions organised for me by the Shevchenko University enabled me to form my own views of Transnistrian opinions, and these form the subject matter of SubSect.1.3.1, which reinforces the conclusions of other researchers that the Transnistrian people very clearly do not wish to be governed from Chisinau.

Some have found Transnistria difficult to research. Rebecca Chamberlain-Creangă complains of only being given intermittent access to Ribnita factories (2011:44), which led her to conduct most of her research in the Rezina cement plant just across the Dniestr. More alarmingly, Helge Blakkisrud and Pal Kolstø observe:

> Due to the lack of relevant and reliable data, the Eurasian de facto states have been characterized as 'informational black holes'. Carrying out fieldwork has been difficult and in some cases dangerous. (2013:179)

My experience of fieldwork was less daunting. Most Transnistrians, particularly the 'elite', went out of their way to help.* However, there were issues in getting reliable data, and establishing the prison population proved particularly challenging. Economic figures published by the central Pridnestrovian Republican Bank may not be completely accurate, but there is no more reason to doubt them than those emanating from central banks in many countries.

Former Foreign Minister Vladimir Yastrebchak was a particularly useful source of both information and introductions to others and was immensely generous with his time. An ally of former President Smirnov, he has come back into favour since Krasnoselsky's 2016 election, ostensibly as a government adviser, but he is regarded by some as effectively the foreign minister.** A charming, but not smooth, slightly dishevelled man, the idea of him being a member of a corrupt, manipulative and feared elite was fantastical. He was sometimes candid and even unflattering in his views on the Transnistrian hierarchy.

Shevchenko University helped arrange discussions with students and staff, which were usually done in semi-formal groups. These quickly reinforced the referendum and poll findings that very few Transnistrians want to be a part of Moldova. Such discussions also enabled me to ascertain how people conduct their everyday lives and how they feel about the way they are governed.

Most of the interviews I conducted in Transnistria were in Russian, usually through my own interpreter. Informal discussions were more often in English. Yastrebchak speaks excellent English, as have all Transnistrian foreign ministers, but it is not otherwise widely spoken even among the Transnistrian elite.

1.2 THE OVERLAPPING ISSUES IN CONSIDERING TRANSNISTRIA

Each of the four chapters that consider Transnistria itself are ostensibly free standing, but many topics could straddle two or more. The media, for instance, is considered in the context of freedoms in Sect.3.6; however, it may also have a role in the nation-building process discussed in SubSect.1.2.2. There are conflicting views expressed by Beyer and Wolff (2016) and Kudors (2010) as to whether the predominantly Russian-language television service has been instrumental in inclining the population towards identifying with Russia. It may also fairly be said that media is an aspect of Transnistrian society

---

*   My advice to any future researchers would be to get on the phone to them. Transnistrian culture does not extend to prompt answering of emails, even if sent in Russian!

**   I was told this by Ion Manole in an interview in his Chisinau offices on 30 May 2019 before he knew of my association with Yastrebchak.

that could have been considered in Chapter 4 but is more conveniently positioned in an overall analysis of the media and its freedom.

Conversely, while education is considered in Sect.4.1 as an aspect of society, the most striking feature of it, the treatment of schools that teach in Moldovan in the Latin alphabet, has been an instance of the government violating freedoms and thus a part of nation-building that could have featured in Chapters 3 and 1 respectively. The Sheriff group, considered in relation to the economy in Sect.2.3, has had such a prominent role in influencing government that it could also have been considered in relation to democracy in Sect.3.2. Indeed, much of what is written in Chapter 2 about the economy can also be considered as bearing on society. This is particularly true of the territory's demography, discussed in Sect.2.4: a topic sociologists often consider at the forefront of the study of a society (Stoetzel 2006) but which is best looked at in the economic context where it has most practical import.

The state's policing function is considered in Sect.4.5, as part of society, and in relation to economic matters like money laundering in Sect.2.2 rather than Sect.3.3 on the rule of law and justice system or human rights and freedoms in Sect.3.5. So many allegations have been made about lawlessness, and particularly human trafficking, within the territory that these matters could have a tremendous bearing on the freedoms Transnistrians should enjoy. That on examination there is virtually no evidence of these, enables there to be a heading in SubSect.4.5.3 entitled 'A Peaceful Society', to expound one of the successes of the present Transnistrian regime. There is anecdotal evidence of some current low-level police corruption now, discussed in SubSect.4.5.1, and worse in the recent past (SubSect.3.5.2), but not so much as to prevent a largely positive view being taken of how Transnistria is policed.

Of course, what matters for the purpose of the thesis's argument is not where any single bit of evidence sits within it but how it all comes together from whichever section it is placed in to support the argument that Transnistria has reached a stage where independence is not only viable but is the best solution to the present situation.

2. THE LITERATURE RELATING TO TRANSNISTRIAN INDEPENDENCE

On the basis of primary or plebiscitary right theory, discussed in SubSect.5.1.4, as the majority of Transnistrians want to secede from Moldova, they should have a right in international law to do so. This theory, whose most eloquent advocate has been Harry Beran (1998), is considered briefly, as is the more conservative remedial right theory of Allen Buchanan (1995, 2007), which states that the right to such secession should only arise where there has been a large-scale violation of human rights by the dominant state. However, these are theories that have gained no traction in the international courts and therefore have no decisive role in supporting Transnistrian independence claims in practice.

The thesis's argument is therefore more pragmatic than theoretical, though theoretical literature is used to put in context the facets of Transnistria, which are explored in examining whether independence is a viable or the best solution. Before considering those facets, it is desirable to understand the extent of not just opposition to Transnistrian independence but often the refusal to even recognise it as a possibility. The positions of countries and international organisations from whom virtually no support for independence can be garnered is explored in Sect. 5.2.

First, let us consider the positions of those scholars who have already explored the current and future legal status of the territory. The approach closest to mine is that of Helge Blakkisrud and Pal Kolstø in their paper, "From Secessionist Conflict Towards a Functioning State: Process of State-Building and Nation-Building in Transnistria":

So far, most literature on Transnistria has focused on the unresolved conflict: either on its origins or on various formulas for solving it. Less attention has been given to the post-secession development of institutions and society. (2013:179)

They take a more holistic approach than most commentators, arguing that even if motivated by the interests of a small elite, the former "racketeer state" has evolved into a "more fully-fledged state with an identity of its own" (2013:203). They express no view on the actual desirability of independence but consider many of the same issues as this thesis, including nation-building, economic viability (2013:188) and services like health (2013:192), though not democracy or human rights. They conclude: "To the new post-Soviet generations, the option of reuniting with Moldova proper seems increasingly less attractive" (2013:216). This approach, like mine, prioritises the matters that are of importance to the people involved and which affect their lives, rather than attaching so much importance to the theories of foreign politicians, diplomats and lawyers.

The best known work on Transnistria may be the New York City Bar Association's Report (2006), *Thawing a Frozen Conflict: Legal Aspects of the Separatist Crisis in Moldova*. While it grudgingly admits that Transnistria has attained *de facto* independence (2006:65), the report emphatically refutes the legality of the regime and argues that anything done by it, beyond that necessary for the immediate security of the territory's people, has no validity and could be undone by the Chisinau government.

Others opposed to Transnistrian independence have followed the New York (2006) arguments, notably Mélissa Cornet in her 2016 paper, *Pridnestrovian Moldovian Republic: What Legal Framework under International Law for Unrecognized Entities*. She considers some of the same background factors that I do, including the history, human rights and position of external actors. Her argument against Transnistria's right to self-determination – she doesn't even contemplate independence – is essentially:

Transnistrians are not a people;
Their rights are not seriously violated by Moldova; and
There are potentially other legal remedies available.

This thesis refutes this as a valid basis for denying independence.

In his PhD thesis, *Uti Possidetis v Self-Determination: The Lessons of the Post-Soviet Practice*, Farhad Mirzayev focuses on the degree of Russian involvement in Transnistria, having regard to the findings of the European Court of Human Rights in the *Ilascu* (2004) and *Catan* (2012) cases (Mirzayev 2014:113). He says the New York report provides evidence of Russia's "negative" influence on the conflict. From this he appears to draw a premise that it would be wrong to support, or perhaps even debate, granting independence to Transnistria and other pseudo-states. He concludes that there are arguments for granting it independence, but that this should be "upon the settlement and reincorporation of the breakaway region under the Moldovan state roof" (2014:233).

Bill Bowring (2014) addresses the 2007 claim of President Smirnov that "historically Transnistria has a better claim to independence than Kosovo" (2014:1)* in a chapter in *Self-Determination and Secession in International Law*. He is sympathetic to the Transnistrian people being allowed at least self-determination, stating, without demurring from, the argument that after twenty years of separation from Moldova on the basis a 'strongly state-like' entity had been established in the territory (2014:24). He too, though, advocates this right being exercised through autonomy or federalism, and envisages it in the same terms as granted to Moldova's existing autonomous region, Gagauzia. He sees that as the most likely outcome, unless Moldova joins with Romania, which he says is highly unlikely but which, although not expressly stated, could lead to independence (2014:26).

A prolific and widely respected commentator on Transnistria is Professor Stefan Wolff, who has been commissioned to write extensive papers on the subject by the EU and others. He does not explicitly position himself on the question of legal status but appears to favour maintaining the *status quo*. In his 2012 report, paradoxically entitled *The Transnistrian Issue: Moving Beyond the* Status-Quo, he states:

> There is considerable agreement across the existing proposals that the Transnistrian conflict requires some sort of territorial self-government as part of the political-institutional arrangements to be set up by a settlement. (2012:25)

Wolff addresses the realities of the situation, in a way which is overlooked by the New York (2006) report, with which this thesis broadly agrees:

> After two decades of separation and relentless pro-independence (and pro-Russian) propaganda, public opinion in the Transnistrian region is generally oriented eastward and has been almost completely isolated from discussions of any political alternatives to independence. (2012:19)

Where this thesis differs is to acknowledge that the Transnistrian population has not merely being subjected to pro-Russian propaganda but has a growing popular desire for

---

*   He then makes no further explicit reference to Kosovo or its situation.

independence that has developed through discussion of the alternatives. Dov Lynch also considers that Transnistria, like the other pseudo-states, has achieved *de facto* statehood and favours a "coordinated approach, spearheaded by the EU, that balances *de facto* and *de jure* independence and sovereignty" (2004: abstract). This approach is similar to, if less finessed than, Wolff's. Neither Lynch nor Wolff ultimately advocates full independence.

While most existing international writing does not support the Transnistrian case for independence, this is not the case within the territory. That argument is expressed in Transnistria's Foreign Minister Vitaly Ignatiev's compendium work (2018), which includes a chapter by President Vadim Krasnoselsky. Much of it is written by Russian legal experts.* It is theoretical and scholarly, with many references to the flaws in the Molotov-Ribbentrop Pact.

Many writers have tried to explain what motivates Russia in Transnistria. In this context, I explore (in SubSect.5.2.2) the writings of Bobick (2014), Felgenhauer (cited by Schearf 2014), Cornet (2016), Sharifzoda (2017) and Kosienkowski (2019). Kosienkowski, in his chapter in *De Facto States in Eurasia*, is most comprehensive, concluding:

> The fundamental divergence is that the Russian authorities want Transnistria to be reintegrated with its parent state under Russian conditions that would anchor Moldova in Russia's sphere of exclusive influence. (2019:29)

This view is in line with the consensus in the writing that the *status quo* is in Russian interests. As things stand, it retains a toe-hold in Moldova, which prevents that country moving closer to the West, in a way a completely independent Transnistria would not.

3. THE QUESTIONS ABOUT TRANSNISTRIA ITSELF

The main body of the thesis is Chapters 1–4, each of which asks whether Transnistria is or has features that constitute a state; these are considered in outline in this section. It is the conclusions in these chapters that each of these exists that underpins the overall conclusion that statehood is a viable and the best outcome. For those who may know nothing about the territory, there is an unreferenced summary of it within the introductory material above.

3.1 NATIONHOOD

The first chapter considers whether Transnistria has become a nation through its people having acquired a specific Transnistrian identity. This involves an excursion in Sect.1.1 through the history of Transnistria and, to an extent, Moldova. Much of the early

---

* For example, 2014:380 and 2014:414, where the President of Union of Lawyers of the Russian Federation and the President of the Russian Academy of Advocates and Notaries write, respectively.

history is taken from Charles Upson Clark's *Bessarabia* (1927), a chronological and analytical account of the area that encompasses both territories. The later period is dealt with equally efficaciously in Charles King's *The Moldovans: Romania, Russia, and the Politics of Culture* (2000). An understanding of Transnistrian life in Soviet times can be gleaned from Ronald Hill's *Soviet Political Elites: The Case of Tiraspol*, an account of government in Tiraspol in the 1960s arising from his time and Chisinau as the "lone westerner" there in 1967–68. This book, which was recommended to me by Vladimir Yastrebchak, is of course dated, but its opening page contains words which could be applied to the post-Soviet political world:

> There is rather more to political life in the USSR than what goes on within the red brick walls of the Moscow Kremlin and that the picture widely held in the west of 250 million honest citizens being ruled by two-dozen somewhat dishonest communist party bosses is a very inadequate caricature. (1977:vii)

The historical background to the struggle between Moldova and Transnistria is explored by Igor Casu (2018) in his contribution to *Eastern Europe in 2018*. He sees the 1968 Prague Spring as when the views of Russian and Moldovan speakers in Moldova began to diverge, leading to a KGB drive against Moldo-Romanian nationalism, which extended to tighter control over literature and art. He argues there were wider implications, particularly in strengthening Soviet patriotism, but that these have little specific bearing on the Transnistrian situation (2018:295). The argument is interesting and plausible; however, there is little evidence, within or outside the article, to tie the Prague Spring to events at that time in Moldova.

A fascinating, if niche, source, is Alexandru Lesanu's PhD thesis (2015), which follows the Ribnita sugar factory until its closure in 2001. He examines the effect that "Repeated changes of borders and political regimes had on social, economic, and technological conditions" in the factory (2015:295). Coincidentally (I think), another factory, making cement, a few miles away but on the Moldovan side of the Dniestr forms the subject matter of a PhD by Rebecca Chamberlain-Creangă (2011). Her interviews with workers there show the establishment of a Transnistrian identity that may extend to some who live in Moldova.

Much of Moldovan and Transnistrian history is separate, and it is striking that the present link between them derives from the short-lived 1939 Molotov-Ribbentrop Pact. Transnistria's own case for independence (Ignatiev 2018) develops the argument that the renunciation of that pact should have had the effect of removing Transnistria from Chisinau's territory.

A separate identity existed by the time of the 1992 war of independence, considered in SubSect.1.1.2, in which around 1,000 Transnistrians died fighting against Moldova. The war is described and analysed by Erika Dailey, Jeri Laber and Lois Whitman's thoroughly researched *Human Rights in Moldova: The Turbulent Dniester* (1993).

The separate development has continued since the war and is considered in SubSect.1.1.3.

Igor Smirnov led the territory from independence until his electoral defeat in December 2011. A falling out with Russia, illustrative of its substantial though not complete influence over the territory, contributed to that defeat, the reasons for which are considered by Magdalena Dembinska and Julian Iglesias (2013) in their paper for *Eastern European Politics and Societies*. These distil down to Smirnov having become over-rigid in his approach to Chisinau. Smirnov's successors, Yevgeny Shevchuk and even more so Vadim Krasnoselsky, have shown greater willingness to engage with the Moldovan leadership.

A particular feature of the post-independence history of the territory has been a nation-building project through which a Transnistrian identity has been positively fostered, as discussed in Sect.1.2. This is in the context of a consensus, identified in SubSect.1.2.1, that Transnistrians are not an ethnicity and arguments that they are not a distinct people, as advanced in the New York (2006) report and tentatively disputed by Bowring (2014:22). There are suggestions by Joris Wagemakers (2012) and Anastasia Mitrofanova (2015) that the identity of Transnistrians is defined mainly in negative terms: a certainty, as Mitrofanova (2015:192) puts it, that they are different from inhabitants of the Dniestr's Right-Bank.

Much writing points to more than that negative identity. A thorough analysis of how the regime has sought to create the Transnistrian identity is carried out by Ion Marandici for *Nationalities Papers* (2020), who points to several means by which this has been done. *Russkii Mir,* which flows from Moscow, is among these. Blakkisrud and Kolstø (2013:178) also alight on this theme, likening it to the approach of Russia's "Soviet predecessor". Ala Şveţ, writing for *History and Anthropology*, talks of "elite manipulation of public opinion" (2012:1) as part of this process. She gives the example of Soviet holidays being adopted.

Marandici sees the nation-building projects as mainly expressing the elite's aspirations (2020:33). While there is little divergence in the literature from the view that these projects have taken place, Marta Melnykevych – having interviewed 190 Transnistrian students – argues that people have not responded positively to them (2014:82). But hers is something of a lone voice. Even Wim van Meurs, an arch-critic of the Transnistrian regime, recognises, while wondering why, that the regime had "bothered to seek national legitimacy" (2015:205). Conversely, Osipov and Vasilevich (2019:13) expressly state that nation-building has been a "success story". Blakkisrud and Kolstø go a stage further and say it has led to Transnistria developing "something akin to full-fledged statehood (minus official recognition)" (2013:82).

The success of nation-building may better still be judged by consideration of what Transnistrians want and think, the subject of Sect.1.3. A common theme of my own research (SubSect.1.3.1), referendums and other research (SubSect.1.3.2), particularly that of O'Loughlin, Toal and Chamberlain-Creangă (2013) who interviewed 912 people in Transnistria, is that Transnistrians do not wish to be governed from Chisinau.

Further research on Transnistrian life was conducted by Tatiana Cojocari (2019). Her questions, answered by 499 respondents, were directed more at perceptions about everyday matters. Her findings on how individuals identify – 37.3% as Transnistrian and 35.7% as Russian – their intentions to emigrate and the television they watch have been incorporated into this thesis, but much more from that comprehensive work is useful background in understanding Transnistrian attitudes. While Cojocari does not ask about what future respondents wanted for Transnistria, the fact that only 14% identified as Moldovan was revealing in terms of the disassociation between the two territories (2019:48).

What emerges clearly from this is that the disparity in Transnistrian and Moldovan history, both modern and recent, of which the recent nation-building has been a fundamental part, has led to the existence of a Transnistrian people. They have at least the negative identity described by Mitrofanova (2015), but on the face of most investigations into their current aspirations, a strong enough identity to have created a distinct people, from which being a nation flows.

3.2 ECONOMY

Chapter 2 asks whether Transnistria has a viable economy, without which statehood would not be feasible. Economic viability is considered against the backdrop of various definitions, the primary one being Gertrude Schroeder's, "the capability to exist and develop as a separate state in a world of highly economically interdependent states" (1992:549). This, she makes clear (1992:550), is not a requirement for self-sufficiency. Commentators on Transnistria have approached this question with this distinction in mind, most explicitly Daria Isachenko and Klaus Schlichte (2007:23), who state that Transnistria is "not self-sufficient but viable".

The thesis considers this question by looking at both broad and specific aspects of the economy. Sect.2.1 considers how it has developed since independence, particularly its relationship with the Moldovan economy (SubSect.2.1.1). A concise but wide-ranging account of the Transnistrian economy was written in 2013 by Kamil Całus for the Centre for Eastern Studies. He provides helpful background information, argues that Russia provides effectively free gas to Transnistria and touches briefly on the influence of the Sheriff group. He revisits much of this for *New Eastern Europe* (2016), where six months before the presidential election, he foresaw not only Shevchuk's defeat but also that the government machinery might then turn on him, which proved to be the case as Shevchuk and his wife fled the country soon afterwards, accusing the Sheriff group of trying to kill him (Ernst 2017a). Całus is a prolific commentator on the territory, bridging the gap between academic writing and journalism. His over-arching view is that "from the Russian point of view, this [Russian financial backing] makes Transnistria a kind of propaganda bait, intended to show Moldovans the benefits of co-operation and closer integration with Russia" (2013:7).

The current state of the economy, considered in SubSect.2.1.2, is partly a consequence of the selling of state assets in the early 2000s. These are examined by Mihály Borsi

(2007), Rebecca Chamberlain-Creangă (2011) and Igor Munteanu (2018). A common theme to their respective analyses is that the denationalisations were generally popular with the population. Chamberlain-Creangă, who spent considerable time in the territory, has particular insight into this and reflects the views of those she talked to that they were seen as beneficial to the region (2011:74). Margarita Balmaceda takes a different position (2013:450), identifying corruption by the Smirnov family in connection with the sale of the main steelworks. However, even to her, it is the 'elites' for whom this caused resentment.

The areas of the economy where the government has a more direct role are considered in Sect.2.2, though the distinction between the private and governmental functions is not always clear. The most fundamental aspects of this may be taxation and currency. It can be seen that Transnistria has a reasonably sophisticated and fair tax system. The exchange rate has been controlled with a degree of success (considered by Blakkisrud and Kolstø 2013) to produce, particularly in recent years, relatively stable rates against the US dollar. Success in such matters supports the argument that there is a working, and hence viable, economy. A more distinctive feature of the Transnistrian economy, explored in the same section, is a governmental interest in cryptocurrencies. While that interest has not yet advanced, it has potential to damage the Transnistrian economy. The unsuccessful experiences of Abkhazia's experiment with this are examined.

A relatively conventional banking system has developed under a constitutionally ordained central bank, albeit largely outside the international system. My own experiences of this are described in Appendix E. There is extensive legislation to prevent money laundering and, despite occasional allegations that Transnistria is a centre for such activity, including by Moldovan government minsters (*Infotag* 2012), there is little evidence to support it. An important point about the economy is that its present state has been reached in international isolation. The possibilities that would arise on ending that isolation, which are also considered in Sect.2.2, would strengthen it.

Another distinctive feature of the Transnistrian economy is the Sheriff group, subject of Sect.2.3. Its business, of which the most visible manifestation is supermarkets, is explored in SubSect.2.3.1. It was founded during Smirnov's presidency and has had a close relationship with the territory's government. The best English-language analysis of the group is Bobick's 2012 paper, *There's a New "Sheriff" in Town: Corruption and Captive Markets in Transnistria*, which is drawn on in considering the role of that business in not only Transnistria's economy but also its politics (SubSect.2.3.2). He takes a balanced view, arguing that its success was largely based on connections it was able to exploit initially – presumably largely within the Smirnov family, although he does not explicitly allege that – but considers it has become a generally benign force economically, socially and politically.

In a shorter but insightful analysis, Piotr Olesky argues:

The Transnistrian President would like to gain absolute power in this quasi-state, but

> Sheriff is making this dream difficult to implement, as the company controls not only the Supreme Council, but also the economy. (2015:1)

This he attributes – questionably, as there are many competing petrol stations and supermarkets – to the group having a monopoly in many areas. Like Bobick, he regards Sheriff as bringing considerable benefit to Transnistria, particularly through its employment policies.

All three presidents have had close links with Sheriff. Shevchuk and Krasnoselsky rose from its ranks and Smirnov's son was a founder, yet Shevchuk ended up with a toxic relationship with the business, which opposed his re-election. It may benefit from the present situation and has expressed no view on independence. However, that is not to say it could not rise to the opportunities and challenges of operating in an independent and recognised state. Its successful football club may have a role in the nation-building project. The political significance of the club is explored by Melissa McDonald (2014), and Steve Menary (2019) argues that football clubs have been used to promote national identities in former Soviet territories.

The small population of Transnistria has a bearing on its economy (SubSect.2.4.1). Like Moldova, it has been affected by economic emigration (SubSect.2.4.2). Brief consideration is given (SubSect.2.4.3) to the conflicting classic economic theories of John Maynard Keynes (1937) and Alvin Hansen (1939) as to whether a declining population is necessarily damaging, the discussion proceeding largely on the basis of the latter's belief that it is damaging.

Extensive research has been conducted on Transnistrian migration by Costin (2012) and Ostavnaia (2017) and on Moldovan migration by Tejada, Varzari and Porcescu (2013), considered in SubSect.2.4.2. Ostavnaia (2017:139) points to the desirability of encouraging migrants to invest in the territory rather than just send remittances. Remittances themselves play a significant part in the economy. Vladimir Fomenko (2017) examines these, calculating that were Transnistria a country, it would have the world's ninth largest dependency on them. This dependency is considered against the arguments that remittances can be harmful to an economy (Fullenkamp 2015), that they do not create significant employment and that they cannot be a basis for economic recovery overall (UNDP 2008). While remittances do not undermine, and indeed may help, the viability of the Transnistrian economy, a dependence on them cannot be healthy.

The Transnistrian economy is even more dependent on Russia, which may provide 70% of its finances (Puiu 2015). This is considered in works of Calus (2013, 2016), discussed above, and inevitably creates a relationship with Russia which makes the EU and most Western countries wary and inclined towards support for the Chisinau government. Detail of the complex question of gas subsidies (SubSect.2.6.1) is provided by Victor Parlicov, Tudor Șoitu and Sergiu Tofilat in their paper *Energy and Politics: The Price for Impunity in Moldova* (2017). They start from, and do not question, the premise that Russia has used Moldova's Gazprom corporation as "a sponsor of separatism in

Moldova", through which "loyalty would be obtained rather than profits made" (2017:6). A simpler explanation is given by Brian Milakovsky (2019) for the Wilson Center, who sees Russia as presenting a bill to Chisinau for the gas, while the latter faces no action for not paying.

While Russian support is, beyond argument, significant to Transnistria, regard is had to commentators such as Madalin Necsutu (2019a), who sees the relationship with the EU as at least reducing that dependency, and Ruslan Kermach (2017), who argues that it provides other routes for the Transnistrian economy to function (SubSect.2.6.2).

It is against these multiple and not always easily reconciled strands that it is asked whether Transnistria does have a viable economy. The answer, returning to the definitions which make it clear that pure self-sufficiency is not a precondition for that viability, is in line with the view of Isachenko and Schlichte (2007:23) that it is "not self-sufficient but viable".

3.3 DEMOCRACY

The third chapter explores the most contentious of the four questions about Transnistria: whether it is free, democratic and subject to the rule of law. A snappy title is sacrificed to set out the terms of reference fully.

The thesis takes the route of considering democracy (Sect.3.2), rule of law (3.3) and various freedoms separately, and what falls into the freedom category is divided into imprisonment (3.4), human rights (3.5), freedom of expression (3.6) and religious freedoms (3.7). First considered, in Sect.3.1, is the Transnistrian Constitution (2011), which sets out the ideals of the nation, aspiring to accord with these ideals. However, as Massimo Tommasoli (2012) has put it, an "institutional approach", or simply following what laws say should be done, does not assist in evaluating the "actual outcomes of processes and procedures", which is what this chapter is largely concerned with.

There is surprisingly little academic writing on the actuality of these matters in Transnistria. The greatest contribution to the existing literature is the report of UN-appointed expert Thomas Hammarberg (2013). Hammarberg's constructive criticisms are respected internally and externally, and there have been attempts to implement his recommendations, particularly regarding prisons. They were mentioned to me when interviewing members of the Transnistrian elite but were treated with scepticism by the Moldovan Bureau of Reintegration, who regarded Hammarberg as insufficiently critical of Transnistria. To an extent, my own work and investigations follow in his footsteps, and this chapter relies on numerous interviews and observations, often accommodated by the local authorities at short notice, the material of which is one of the original contributions of the thesis.

There are dated criticisms of the Transnistrian electoral process from Nicu Popescu (2006) and Oleh Protsyk (2008), and even these were directed towards the lack of effective opposition rather than direct distortion of elections. By the 2016 presidential election, which I was invited to observe and my observations of which I set out in SubSect.3.2.2. and Appendix A, there was no doubt that the electoral process was genuine. The incumbent was defeated and left quietly. Of the 2015 parliamentary election, openDemocracy, historically critical of Transnistria, said it was "a real election for Parliamentary seats" (Litoy 2015).

In relation to the rule of law, interviews with the two most senior judges (SubSect.3.3.1) were encouraging. The head of the Supreme Court explained a system of judicial appointments and removals likely to ensure independence. The head of the Constitutional Court, which has the power to overturn government decisions, talked of the court exercising that power. Bill Bowring writes of a visit to the territory ten years previously in 2004, saying the Constitutional Court had decided cases against the government, "but not often" (2014:7).

Although the evidence is that at the top of the system an independent judiciary applies the rule of law, there may be issues at lower levels even before cases reach courts. Hammarberg's report alludes to payment of bribes, although not directly to judges (2013:18). In an interview with me, Stepan Popovskiy, who can be regarded as Transnistria's leading 'human rights' lawyer, claimed indirect knowledge of judicial bribery, although he did not know how much it would cost to do so. Brief consideration is given in SubSect.3.3.2 to Popovskiy's arguments for a supra-national supreme court, but this is clearly not acceptable to Tiraspol or Chisinau and unlikely to be a practical solution to any failings in the Transnistrian justice system.

Another fetter on the rule of law is the difficulties placed in the way of lawyers taking on causes unpopular with the government (SubSect.3.3.3). This can take the form of intimidating lawyers who do such work. Popovskiy claimed to have been the victim of security forces' heavy-handed tactics, and former President Shevchuk's lawyer, Vladimir Maimust, claimed an explosive device was attached to his car and to have been beaten up after his client had fallen from political grace (Thoolen 2013). Coupled with this is the virtual exclusion of foreign lawyers, and indeed advocacy NGOs, from the territory, meaning the rule of law is not so easily given a 'clean bill of health' as democracy.

Transnistria does have an exceptionally high rate of imprisonment (considered in Sect.3.4), despite having a racially homogenous population and little evidence of crime, particularly street crime – factors sometimes used to explain high rates (Mauer 2017; Hartney 2006). Concern was expressed about this by Hammarberg (2013), and this may have improved a little as a consequence of his recommendations. My own questions on this brought little explanation, and outside Hammarberg's reports (2013, 2018), the topic has not been considered. My visit to a women's prison, described in Appendix C, suggested conditions may not be as bad as some observers (e.g. FIDH 2012) have alleged.

Sect.3.5 deals with human rights concerns in Transnistria, particularly in the context of arguments that Transnistria has no right to secede from Moldova because the latter does not violate Transnistrians' human rights (SubSect.3.5.1). There is a misconception, advanced by Lina Laurinavičiūtė and Laurynas Biekša (2015), that the Transnistrian case is based on allegations of Moldovan abuses. As the Chisinau government has no control over the Transnistrian territory, it is impossible to see how such allegations could be made against it, let alone sustained.

Considered in SubSect.3.5.2 are concerns about Transnistria's own human rights record. Many critics of Transnistria's record, including the UK Home Office (2017) and Freedom House (2018), can be dismissed as ill-informed and politically motivated. The Moldovan human rights organisation, Promo-LEX, whose director Ion Manole I had extensive discussions with, may have a similar bias, but it makes a far more convincing argument. It cites many cases, including that of Boris Mozer, who was compensated by the ECHR for appalling violations when held in captivity in the final years of the Smirnov regime. Promo-LEX is backed by foreign governments hostile to Transnistria, including the US and probably Romania, but that does not detract from the many violations it has identified in Transnistria.

Most of the abuses occurred when Smirnov was in power. However, it is noteworthy that Shevchuk himself fled the territory fearing arrest, and even assassination, months after his electoral defeat in December 2016. More worrying is the continued imprisonment of Oleg Horjan, a peripheral opposition politician, due to a scuffle in a police station in 2017. The sentence was vastly disproportionate to anything he was alleged to have done and appears politically motivated. This is the worst human rights violation in Transnistria at the moment and appears such a crude injustice as to call into question whether the present Transnistrian regime is ready to govern an independent state. This is all the more pertinent as when Alexandru Coliban was released in 2013 after being sentenced to 30 months' imprisonment for 'defaming' Shevchuk in posters, he was credibly described as having been the last political prisoner in Transnistria (Moldova.org 2013). The Transnistrian case of being a respecter of human rights, which has on many analyses a bearing on its right to independence, would be so much stronger were it not for the regression the imprisonment of Horjan represents.

Related to human rights is control of the media and other speech, considered in Sect.3.6. The tests that can be applied to decide whether the media is free in any country are considered in SubSect.3.6.1 and the reasonably wide-ranging extent of Transnistrian media itself in SubSect.3.6.2. There are few direct restraints on press freedom, considered in SubSect.3.6.3. Luiza Dorosenco (2015), writing in the Moldovan *Media Azi*, articulates the pressures put on Transnistrian journalists not to write things that might offend the leadership, and there are instances of websites being shut down by the authorities. The 2010 imprisonment of Moldovan journalist Ernest Vardanean on flimsy spying charges was a real concern, but he was released by presidential decree after several months, and there has been no similar reported action against a journalist since.

There are, however, recent and worrying reports of imprisonment and other state actions against those who have criticised the government, considered in SubSect.3.6.4.

These include threats of further action against Horjan for things he has said while in prison. One young writer felt she needed to flee the country after creating a website about the conditions of conscripts; an elderly couple were imprisoned for criticising Krasnoselsky in a blog; and a gay woman also fled the territory after putting on an exhibition about the LGBT community in a way which offended the authorities. Information about each of these, except the last, was from uncorroborated sources, but taken as a whole they may suggest that the Transnistrian regime has recently become more restrictive in a way that falls short of the standards expected in modern Europe. Some encouragement can be taken from the willingness of the senior ministers and police officers to interact with protesters against COVID-19 restrictions, recorded on YouTube (2020, 2020a), and the existence of a youth club where dissent is frequently expressed, considered in SubSect.3.6.5.

Religious freedom, like that of the media, proved particularly vulnerable in the USSR, though the now independent components of that union have generally allowed, even encouraged in the case of Russia, a religiosity that was previously officially disapproved of, if not totally banned (SubSect.3.7.1). SubSect.3.7.2 explores the position in Transnistria now, where the Orthodox Church is widely followed. A small Jewish community, a leader of which I interviewed, faces no systematic oppression. The most interesting literature on Transnistrian religion is Emily Baran's work (2011) on the mistreatment of Jehovah's Witnesses, particularly under Petr Aleksandrovich Zalozhkov, Smirnov's commissioner of religious and cultural affairs. Her in-depth study, based largely on interviews, has little corroborating evidence but seems credible.

There clearly are faults with Transnistria's record on many of the matters considered in Chapter 3, though not on democracy itself. The faults are not of the most egregious nature, though, and may, particularly in relation to the media, be a consequence of a lack of an historic free press in Transnistria. Were independence obtained, the leadership might be more secure in its position and hence less concerned by criticisms, and interaction with other states would expose it to greater external pressure to improve matters. It is in respect of the matters raised in Chapter 3, particularly in respect of human rights, that the hardest of the questions raised by each of the first four chapters to answer affirmatively arises.

3.4 SOCIETY

The fourth chapter asks whether Transnistria is a functioning society, looked at largely in the context of how its government has risen to the challenges of meeting the needs of the population. The success or otherwise of the present regime in doing this bears on how viable an independently recognised territory would be. This complements the discussion in Chapter 2 on the economy and parts of Chapter 3 on freedoms. From economic viability there flows a governmental ability to meet the needs of the population. Of such needs, education, healthcare and social security are all prescribed as fundamental rights in the constitution. Hammarberg (2013) explored each of those and made recommendations in respect of them.

There is evidence that the provision of education (SubSect.4.1.1), healthcare (Sect.4.2) and social security (SubSect.4.3.1) is adequate. The most thorough examination of healthcare is the report by health administrators Galina Selari and Elena Bobkova (2013), considered in SubSect.4.2.1. While their evidence points to a lack of funding, they identify the provision of adequate hospitals, in accordance with my own observations, and successful (pre-COVID-19) vaccination programmes.

The Romanian-language schools issue, the subject of SubSect.4.1.2, which was a major blot on the human rights record of the Smirnov government, is comprehensively described in the reports of the ECHR. The fullest academic account is that of Steven Roper (2005) for *Communist and Post-Communist Societies*. That is, of course, dated, but provides excellent analysis of the events up until then and the context leading to them. Roper writes from the, virtually indisputable, premise that the Transnistrian actions concerning the schools abused Romanian speakers' rights. This leads him to the "question of how to protect a national majority that is a territorial (federal) minority" (2005:514). Little has been written on the subject since, perhaps underlining the point that the passing of time and the relative liberalisation of government post-Smirnov mean there is no bar on such schools. This was largely corroborated by my discussions within the territory.

The historical context of housing in Transnistria and the rest of the Soviet Union, considered in Sect.4.4, is often overlooked in the West. After Stalin's death, a massive shortage of accommodation was tackled with tremendous humanitarian aims and efficiency. The lack of aesthetic attraction of the uniform *khrushchyovkas* which abound in Tiraspol, Bender and hundreds of other former-USSR cities is a small price for a population securely and cheaply housed; in a way, many Western societies, including modern Britain, have failed lamentably. In a graphic but academically acknowledged work, *Architecture of Soviet Housing and Main Soviet Urban Planning Concepts*, Ganna Andrianova (2014) sets out the history of these and other Soviet housing developments from an architectural perspective. Owen Hatherley looks at this subject in *Landscapes of Communism: A History Through Buildings* (2016) and pithily summed up his views in a short article for CNN (2015a), which I draw on.

The supposed lawlessness of Transnistria and particularly government involvement in it might have been explored along with the rule of law. However, despite there being a considerable body of literature, popular more than academic, I consider this only in the context of policing (SubSect.4.5.1). The allegations of organised crime are considered in SubSect.4.5.2. This is the main feature of the seven pages devoted to the territory in Misha Glenny's book, *McMafia: Seriously Organised Crime* (2009), the best-known work in Britain that refers to Transnistria, having been made into a popular television series in early 2018. Glenny's view of the territory was not helped by having to pay a US$50 – surely he could have haggled – bribe to enter it (2009:113). It seemed inconceivable on my entries to the territory that the pleasant, efficient and often English-speaking border guards would do that. Had they done so, there was a prominently displayed phone number I could have called to complain. More worrying was Glenny's concern that "74 highly accurate missiles that can bring down a 747" had gone missing there (2009:13). This is perhaps an urban myth, retold by Justin Dodge (2011) in *Conditions Allowing Organized Crime in Transnistria* when he talks about suitcase-sized nuclear bombs.

More academically, the weapons theme is developed by Felix Buttin for the *Human Security Journal*. He points to two explosions on public buses in 2006. Although he describes these as "attacks" (2007:18), they may have been consequences of inept weapons-handlers transporting bombs in remarkably unsuitable ways. Tragic though this was – nine people died – they did not portend the horrors envisaged by Glenny (2009) and Dodge (2011). Dodge considers other forms of organised crime and makes comparisons with Cali drugs cartels, the Sicilian *Cosa Nostra* and even *al Qaeda*. While concluding that there are few parallels with those organisations, he alleges that the Transnistrian government partici-pated in crime. The evidence is flimsy and exaggerated, even as a critique of conditions in Smirnov's era. Similarly, Daniela Peterka-Benton premised her discussion for the *Journal of Applied Security Research* on whether Transnistria represented a security threat on an allegation that "it has become a haven for transnational criminal activities including illegal trade in arms, human trafficking, and money-laundering" (2012:71).

Surprisingly, Stefan Wolff cites that 25,000 people are affected by human trafficking (2012:16). He bases this figure on estimates in a report by the US Embassy in Moldova (2009), which claims to take its figures from an International Labor Organization Report (2008), which in turn was said to draw from those provided by the Moldovan Bureau of Statistics. The report in fact does not provide this or any figure, and the supposed official statistics were as elusive in my searches as they doubtless were to those whose claims fed through to Wolff. In 2005, the OSCE carried out investigations about this and were unable to identify a single instance (Lobjakas 2005). The point, though, is that if someone as well-respected as Wolff can adopt and disseminate highly improbable claims about Transnistria, the likelihood of less diligent commentators doing so and creating a false impression of the territory becomes apparent. This is important as much opposition to the Transnistrian cause stems from the perception of lawlessness, and being able to confidently put that aside may considerably strengthen the case for independence.

On what might be regarded as directly environmental matters, considered in Sect.4.6, there is a 2006 comprehensive report by Ivan Ignatiev, who ran and still runs the Ecospectrum Research and Production Association in Bender. The report, although highlighting issues of concern in this context, shows serious attempts by the often-reviled Smirnov government to introduce responsible environmental laws, in advance of many more developed countries, which in a small way enhances the territory's claim to independence. Certainly, one would question the desirability of giving more powers to a government which had not shown responsibility on environmental issues because the effects could be damaging beyond its own borders. Transport, another area in which Transnistria has been relatively successful, is considered in SubSect.4.6.2.

I conclude that no major failings in Transnistria as a society can readily be identified that might preclude it from becoming independent.

4. THE CONSIDERATION OF BARRIERS TO TRANSNISTRIAN INDEPENDENCE

The fifth chapter asks how Transnistria, which has been evaluated in its own right in the first four chapters, can become an independent state, which depends almost entirely on external factors. Some of the considerations relevant to this were discussed in the first section of this introduction. This would require the overcoming of the barriers currently blocking its route to independence, so this chapter considers what those barriers are and how Transnistria may get around them.

Virtually all commentators accept that Transnistria has attained *de facto* statehood, but it has not achieved recognition from other sovereign nations. The Montevideo Convention (1933) specifies certain conditions for a state: "(a) a permanent population; (b) a defined territory; (c) government; and (d) capacity to enter into relations with the other states." Transnistria is able to meet all of these. There are conflicting schools of thought as to whether the recognition that Transnistria lacks prevents it having legal personality and hence being a state in any sense. On the basis of constitutive theory, recognition would merely be an acknowledgement of existing statehood; however, declaratory theory makes recognition a pre-condition for any sort of statehood. A helpful distinguishing definition is provided by Shruti Venkatraman (2018) in the *Edinburgh Student Law Review*, but the theories need not be considered in detail, as it is clear that only international recognition, ideally endorsed by the gold standard of United Nations membership, would give Transnistria the full statehood it aspires to. This thesis tends towards the line that once the territory has satisfied all the conditions of statehood, it should in accordance with the constitutive theory be entitled to statehood.

While primary right theory, discussed above, may give Transnistria a notional right to secede from Moldova as that is what its people want, that does not represent the position in international law. Ostensibly, respect for the territorial integrity of existing nations prevails. In this category of course is Moldova, whose integrity would be violated were Transnistrian independence imposed on it. This reasoning and the extent to which the requirement for such respect, now enshrined in the United Nations Charter (1945), flows from the 1648 Peace of Westphalia is one of the most widely commented upon topics in international law and relations. A full consideration of the literature is not possible or necessary for the contextual examination the thesis gives the topic. However, an understanding of the obstacles to Transnistrian independence is informed by a commensurate understanding of the development of the main theoretical argument against it.

Westphalian sovereignty is authoritatively considered by Derek Croxton. I mainly draw from the work he wrote with Anuschka Tischer, *The Peace of Westphalia: A*

Historical Dictionary (2001). He also wrote in 2013 *Westphalia: The Last Christian Peace*. Croxton's view, which few would significantly depart from, is that Westphalia represented a "stepping stone" towards the modern concept of a sovereign state, of the sort that Transnistria aspires to be. The works of Stephane Beaulac (2004), Daud Hassan (2006) and Rachel Alberstadt (2012), who each take a slightly different position on the development of the concept, are also considered.

What bears on Transnistrian independence is not so much the development of sovereignty but how it is departed from. It is the willingness of states to do that which may assist Transnistria in its claim for independence. The starting point in considering this is the assertion by Stephen Krasner (1999) that respect for sovereignty and territorial integrity is "organized hypocrisy". Stuart Elden, writing in *Antipode* (2007), examines sovereignty in the context of George W. Bush's 'war on terror'. He argues that "the dominant powers are [now] being explicit about the challenge to internal competence or territorial sovereignty while simultaneously stressing the notion of territorial inviolability" (2007:2098). While he does not use the word "hypocrisy", what he summarises amounts to exactly that.

The recognition of Kosovan independence, by the US and most Western countries, in violation of Serbian sovereignty was a clear example of such hypocrisy. While this may have been based on a United Nations resolution (1999), that resolution itself was inconsistent with hitherto-established norms of sovereignty. That in turn leads to Transnistrian arguments (e.g. Ignatiev 2018) that the UN should pass a similar motion in respect of Transnistria.

An ostensibly different approach to Krasner's is taken by Amitav Acharya, whose paper for *Political Studies*, responsive to Krasner's, is entitled "State Sovereignty after 9/11: Disorganised Hypocrisy". He argues a critical flaw in Krasner's thesis is a failure to distinguish between departures from Westphalian sovereignty to protect human security, which might be regarded as principled or organised, and those who simply further a particular ideology driven policy (2007:9)

While it would be convenient to take organised and disorganised positions as opposing sides in the classic 'conspiracy or cock-up' conundrum, the differences between Krasner and Acharya may be largely illusory. Ultimately, the departures from sovereignty Acharya identifies are done with a specific purpose, even if they protect only one country, and the lack of interest in protecting global human security – rarely the concern of a single government – and their narrow purpose does not make them disorganised, or even random. The point that this argument leads to is that were it in the interests of a superpower to disregard Moldova's sovereignty over Transnistria, it would have little hesitation finding an excuse to do so.

It is in a context of ambiguity in the practical application of international law, even if the law in the form of the UN Charter (1945) is itself quite clear, that Transnistrian independence is considered. Moldova, although ostensibly opposed to the idea, could come to recognise it is in its own economic interests. The arguments advanced to me by its own Bureau of Reintegration were unconvincing (SubSect.5.2.1 and Appendix D), and Moldova's former President Dodon talked of yielding sovereignty over Transnistria to Ukraine (RTA 2018). Diana Dascalu, writing for the *Journal of International Affairs* (2019), points out that a federal solution reintegrating Moldova, or indeed Ukraine, with Transnistria would bring debt, a Russian military presence, pro-Russian voters, and what she regards as "corruption [and] democratic backwardness".

Were Moldova to become close to EU membership or, less plausibly, union with Romania, its hold over Transnistria would be hard to retain. This view was expressed to me by the UK's ambassador to Moldova in April 2016. He said this in the context of the union with Romania, which might have been plausible in the aftermath of Moldova's banking crisis in which 15% of the country's GDP had in essence been stolen. NATO membership would, as Woolf (2012) points out, almost certainly be impossible so long as Transnistria were within Moldova. It may be that in fact Russia is now a bigger obstacle than Moldova to Transnistrian independence, as discussed in Sect.2 above.

Both the OSCE, whose 5+2 group is set up to deal with the Transnistrian question, and the EU are supportive of Moldovan territorial integrity. Samuel Goda writing for the *OSCE Yearbook* (2016), points to the dichotomy between Tiraspol's desire for independence (or integration with Russia) and Chisinau's for reintegration. This he says, with understatement, makes the organisation's task "complicated". Neither organisation, nor indeed NATO or the UN, is likely to have a direct role in determining the outcome of the Transnistrian situation.

Kosovo, which proclaimed its independence in 2008 and is now recognised by around half of UN members, is the precedent Transnistria relies on. This is despite a US secretary of state saying the independence was a consequence of factors arising out of the break-up of Yugoslavia, and thus does not set a precedent for other situations (Fabry 2012:666). Nonetheless, the distinguishing factors between the two situations are merely of degree: mainly the benign treatment of Transnistrians by the Moldovans compared with the brutality of Serbia. Writing for the Cato Institute shortly after the Proclamation of Independence, Ted Gallen Carpenter (2008) describes the assertions that it was not a precedent as "extraordinarily naïve". He did not expressly refer to Transnistria but said that it might be so cited by Russia in:

> …dismembering neighboring Georgia by recognizing the independence of that country's Abkhazian or South Ossetian regions. Or the Kremlin could use it as justification some day to wrench the Russian-speaking Crimea away from neighboring Ukraine.

The observation was insightful and Russia did recognise Abkhazia and South Ossetia later in 2008 and annex Crimea in 2014. In anticipation of the Kosovan proclamation, President Putin pointed out:

If we make the conclusion that the principle of the right to self-determination of a nation is more important than the territorial integration, then we'll have to follow this principle all around the world. (Moldova.org 2007a)

It is doubtful that Russian actions in Crimea were based upon recognition of Kosovo, but the recognition of the Georgian territories probably was (Fabry 2012). This thesis considers whether in due course the Kosovo precedent could come to be of practical importance in resolving the Transnistria situation, recognising that the distinctions between the situations were not as clear as the US secretary of state contended.

Comparisons have been drawn between the division of Cyprus and the existence of the unrecognised Turkish Republic of Northern Cyprus (TRNC) since 1974 and Transnistria (e.g. Kosienkowski 2011; Isachenko 2013; and Çamözü 2016). A similar argument could be made that TRNC has a viable economy, is a free democracy and has a functioning society, as is the case for Transnistria. Whether or not its relationship with Turkey prevents it being a distinct nation is outside the scope of this thesis. Çamözü (2016) distinguishes the two situations on the basis that TRNC actually seeks reintegration with the Republic of Cyprus. Less frequently compared with Transnistria, but having more common features, is Somaliland. Voices for its independence are in a minority but include Bridget Coggins, who points to its stability relative to Somalia (2014), and Peter Pham, who highlights the complete breakdown of democracy in the latter. Although Moldova cannot possibly be compared to Somalia, there are elements in Coggins' and Pham's arguments that could be used to support the Transnistrian case.

As one of the four post-Soviet pseudo-states proclaiming its independence, Transnistria is inevitably compared with the other three. Of those, Nagorno-Karabakh, legally Azerbaijani but Armenian-dominated and ravaged by war between those two countries in late 2020, and South Ossetia, which lacks a viable economy, are very different, but there are similarities between Transnistria and Abkhazia. Fischer *et al*. distinguishes between these states in more abstract terms:

The short- to medium-term goals differ between the individual cases, ranging from preserving the possibilities for interaction (Transnistria) through de-isolation (Abkhazia and South Ossetia) to de-escalation and conflict prevention (Nagorno-Karabakh). (2016:6)

Such distinctions may illustrate that a common solution even for Abkhazia and Transnistria is unlikely, though consideration is given in SubSect.5.3.2 as to whether common cause could be made to any effect.

The final factor, considered in SubSect.5.3.3, is Moldova's other autonomous territory, Gagauzia, which comprises four small non-contiguous areas and whose status, unlike Transnistria's, is formalised in the Moldovan constitution. This is sometimes considered as a possible third participant in a federal Moldova (Wöber 2013:23). With no economic viability, independence or probably genuine autonomy – Wöber describes the present one as merely "symbolic" – it is not a feasible, state and considerations relating to it are unlikely to be significant in determination of Transnistrian statehood.

The last hurdle a putatively independent Transnistria would have to get over is the actual implementation of independence. This is considered in Sect.5.4, which examines recent divisions of countries, including Czechoslovakia and Sudan (SubSect.5.4.1), and legal considerations such as the Vienna Convention on Succession of States (1996; see SubSect.5.4.2).

5. CONCLUSION

The conclusion contends that independence and full *de jure* statehood are viable solutions for the present situation and that existing approaches have produced no better solution. The facets of statehood relied upon in the first four chapters are each made out. There are legitimate concerns about human rights and freedoms and some in relation to the rule of law, but these are not sufficient to deprive Transnistrians of the break from Chisinau that the vast majority want. The obstacles to independence identified in the fifth chapter are likely to mean that this outcome is not realised in the short term, and the territory will have to endure a further period of limbo in its current situation. However, no other likely solution can be identified, and circumstances in which the climate might change and lead to independence can be identified, suggesting that may be the eventual outcome.

CHAPTER ONE

TRANSNISTRIA AS A NATION

This chapter will consider whether a Transnistrian nation has been established. A nation, which in this context must not be confused with a state, is defined by Monserrat Guibernau as:

> A human group conscious of forming a community, sharing a common culture, attached to a clearly demarcated territory, having a common past and a common project for the future and claiming the right to rule itself. (1996:47)

This definition is often referred to by commentators considering nationhood (e.g. Tice and Nelson 2004) and is a helpful test to measure Transnistrian nationhood. The common past or history is examined in Sect.1.1, where a largely separate development from Moldova's can be seen. Sect1.2 looks at the active attempts by the Transnistrian leadership since *de facto* independence to create a national identity, or a common culture, out of the different linguistic and ethnic groups within the territory. Sect.1.3 looks at what Transnistrian people want in the context of nationhood, statehood and independence and whether there is that commitment to a common project for the future. Sect.1.4 argues that a Transnistrian nation has been established.

1.1 THE HISTORY OF TRANSNISTRIA (AND MOLDOVA)

The history of the areas that are now governed from Chisinau and Tiraspol contributes to the perception the people of Transnistria have of themselves as distinct from other Moldovans. Although some critics argue this is an artificial and recent construction (SubSect.1.2.1), the perception has a clear historical underpinning and importance in considering any case for independence. While this section concentrates primarily on Transnistria, it is also necessary to consider the development of Right-Bank Moldova to see where there is an overlap between their histories.

1.1.1 HISTORY UNTIL THE PROCLAMATION OF INDEPENDENCE

The origins of Moldova and Transnistria

Moldova officially traces its statehood back to 1359 (Consulate of Moldova n.d.) when a large swathe of territory, encompassing most of modern-day Moldova but not Transnistria, gained independence from Hungary. Moldovan colonialists then settled on the land east of the Dniestr River in the fifteenth century. Under national hero Stephen* the Great (1457–1504), whose picture adorns Moldovan banknotes, Moldova flourished on both banks of the Dniestr, holding off the territorial aspirations of the Ottomans.

Shortly after Stephen's death, that resistance ended, and Moldova and Transnistria succumbed to rule from Constantinople. Moldova then endured a long period as an Ottoman vassal state, with rulers, referred to as *gospodars*, appointed by the Turks. In the eighteenth century, this territory was often the scene of battles or troop movements during conflicts between the Ottomans, Austrians and Russians (Consulate of Moldova n.d.).

The Russian annexation

Catherine the Great advanced the Russian frontier through Transnistria to the Dniestr in 1792, declaring that the area between that river and the Southern Bug River, in modern Ukraine, was to become a principality named 'New Moldavia', under Russian suzerainty. This state of affairs was formally recognised by the 1812 Treaty of Bucharest (Florescu 2004:1293), in which the territory to about 120 miles west of the Dniestr was ceded to the Russian Empire under the name Bessarabia. The territory was then overwhelmingly Moldovan (Clark 1927: Chapter 8).

The Russian Field Marshal Alexander Suvorov then founded Tiraspol: his statue on horseback is today a distinctive city landmark, and he was considered by a considerable margin the "most famous person in Transnistria" by respondents to Cojocari's research questions (2019:48). The city was named after Tyras, the Greek name for the Dniestr on which it was built, there being evidence of an ancient settlement of that name (Hill: 1977:9).

Kolstø *et al.* (1993:977–978) succinctly identify the process of separate development after the proclamation of an independent Romanian state in 1878. Bessarabia was "almost exclusively an agricultural region with a low degree of urbanisation", in contrast with people on the Left-Bank of the Dniestr, who were "engaged in trade" and where "the density of urban settlements was higher".

There was an influx of different peoples, including Russians, Ukrainians, Jews and Gagauz. Clark identifies a process that continues today and is discussed below:

Bessarabia had also a common experience with the other Russian border countries where language and traditions were non-Russian. Finland, Esthonia, Lithuania,

---

* The apparent anglicisation appears to be universally used.

Lettonia (Latvia), the Ukraine, White Russia, Poland, the Caucasus, all were subjected more or less to a process of Russification. (1927: Chapter 8)

An important manifestation of this process, identified by Alexandru Lesanu (2015:10), was the addition of the Bessarabia region to the Russian railway network in 1894, with a line that reached Ribnita.

In April 1918, Bessarabia and Romania united as a result of a near-unanimous vote in Chisinau's parliament during the chaos of the Russian civil war and turmoil in neighbouring Ukraine (Clark 1927: Chapter 24).* The union was recognised by the UK, France and Italy, though not the US or Russia, in the 1920 Treaty of Paris (Graham 1944:669). The Left-Bank territories that had not become part of Romania were assigned to the Moldovan Autonomous Soviet Socialist Republic (ASSR) in October 1924. This also comprised parts of the Ukrainian regions Odessa and Podolia (King 2000:52). The Moldovan ASSR formed part of the Ukrainian SSR.

In 1929, Tiraspol was declared capital of the Moldovan ASSR, replacing the Ukrainian city of Balta (Hill 1977:11). During this time, there was a significant migration of ethnic Romanians, perhaps 20,000, from Transnistria to Romania, whose government provided them with financial assistance and housing (King 2000:181), furthering Russian predominance in Transnistria.

The Molotov-Ribbentrop Pact

On 23 August 1939, the Molotov-Ribbentrop Pact was signed by the USSR and Germany with the ostensible aim of preventing aggression between the two countries, though with no obligation on either to defend the other if it were attacked. The pact may have been a trigger for World War II, as it enabled Hitler to invade Poland and Czechoslovakia in the knowledge that the USSR would not intervene. 'Secret protocols' to the pact included German agreement to the USSR annexing parts of Romanian Bessarabia (King 2000:91), including Bender. Such annexation occurred after a short war in 1940 (Levin and Lavi 2014:299). This territory was then included in the Moldovan ASSR, which on 2 April 1940, became the Moldovan SSR (King 2000:94) (the SSR paradoxically having more autonomy than the ASSR). This was the creation of Moldova with the internationally recognised boundaries that it has today, including Transnistria. Stalin directed the moving of entire industrial units to the area (Kolstø *et al.* 1993:979), most of which were sited on the Left-Bank of the Dniestr.

The pact was not successful in its ostensible aim, and by June 1941, Germany and the USSR were at war. Even after the end of World War II, the USSR would not admit the existence of the secret protocols, probably because it would undermine its legal claim

---

* This union was implicitly recognised at the Versailles Conference in 1919, where considerably greater territory, including Transylvania, was awarded to Romania. This was probably more out of the victor's desire to create a strong buffer in front of Bolshevik Russia than as a reward for Romania's relatively meagre contribution to the First World War (Ranadive 2015).

for control of parts of its territory, particularly of the Baltic states.* The borders drawn up between the USSR and respectively Poland and Romania were based on those in the protocols and gave full legal effect to the annexation of the Bessarabian territories. The USSR only admitted to the protocols in 1989, and its unsustainability was one of the bases on which Estonia, Latvia and Lithuania successfully argued for their independence. The Transnistrian position is that this effective renunciation of the pact should result in its independence (Ignatiev, 2018:417–420), an argument given short shrift by most foreign observers (e.g. New York 2006).

The Second World War

After the 1940 annexation, the Moldovan SSR was under German occupation from 1941 to 1944, but was brutally controlled by the Romanian dictator Marshall Ion Antonescu, who was executed for war crimes in 1946 by a Romanian People's Tribunal. By July 1941, the Bessarabian part of the Moldovan SSR had been fully integrated into Romania. While Romania did not accord similar status to the Transnistrian part, it took military control of that area (King 2000:93). Antonescu used that control to implement the Holocaust in Transnistria. During the time of the Nazi occupation, some 130,000 Jews – mainly deportees from Romania and to a lesser extent Ukraine – were killed in the territory. A further 50,000 succumbed to a typhoid epidemic. The abysmal living conditions inflicted on the community encouraged the disease and weakened the resistance of those afflicted with it. The concentration camp of Bogdanovka, in the Golta district near the Ukrainian border, was used mainly as a centre for slaughter, sometimes by shooting and sometimes by burning alive those locked in a building (Dumitru 2018).

After the war, the entirety of Moldova was fully integrated into the USSR. This led to the enforced introduction of Russian culture and language, including the Cyrillic alphabet, which until independence was insisted on for all official and educational use of the Moldovan language.

Post-war Soviet Union

Under Stalin, the Russification of Transnistria, and to a lesser extent the rest of Moldova, intensified. Ethnic Russians migrated there, and many Romanians were exiled to Siberia or Kazakhstan, only allowed to return after Stalin's death in 1953. By 1941, Moldova's population was 2,356,000, of which 69% were of Moldovan origin, 11% Ukrainian and 7% Russian (King 2000:96). 1936 figures for Transnistria show a total of 280,000, of which 42% were Moldovan, 29% Ukrainian and 14% Russian (King 2000:185). Moscow developed industry in Transnistria to the extent that by the early 1950s it accounted for 40% of Moldova's GDP (Rudolph 2008:165), despite having much less territory and population. From 1951 to 1952, the secretary-general of the Moldovan Communist

---

*   For a full discussion of this topic, see Sato (2010).

Party, charged with implementing much of this policy, was Leonid Brezhnev, who was partially an ethnic Ukrainian (King 2000:98).

From 1960 to 1981, the effective ruler of Moldova was Ivan Bodiul, the secretary-general of the Moldovan Communist Party, a Russian speaker who never fully mastered Romanian. He was noted for a rigorous pursuit of atheism, destroying many churches, particularly until 1976. Brezhnev, who remained a close ally of Bodiul, appointed him deputy chair of the Council of Ministers of the USSR in 1980 (Casu 2018:281). He was then replaced in Moldova by Semion Grossu, another pro-Russian conservative.

Some divisions came to the fore around the 1968 'Prague Spring', with many Romanian-speaking Moldovan politicians openly declaring support for Ceausescu, who had himself expressed support for the Czechoslovakians. The more outspoken Moldovans were dealt with harshly by the KGB, but the Romanian leader did not go sufficiently far to bring the wrath of Moscow on his country. This episode is identified by Igor Casu as giving rise to "the ethno-national aspect fuelled by Romania's critique of the Soviet-led invasion of Czechoslovakia" (2018: 279); simply put, the positions of Romanian and Russian speakers began to polarise in ways that set the ground for war 25 years later. It was an important manifestation of the separate Transnistrian identity.

The effect of the break-up of the Soviet Union

As the Kremlin's grip on power in the outlying Soviet states weakened in the late 1980s, the Moldovan Supreme Soviet took symbolic steps towards asserting a national identity. In 1989, the Moldovan Popular Front, a right-wing party which was to adopt the name 'Christian Democrat' after three years, emerged (Refworld 2005) and sought to end Soviet 'identity' politics, which had emphasised the ethnic and linguistic differences from Romanians. In April 1989, a national flag was adopted and in August the name changed to the Republic of Moldova, dropping 'Soviet' from the title. Moldovan, effectively Romanian, became the national language and Latin letters replaced Cyrillic, leading to strikes in cities with large Russian-speaking populations, including Tiraspol and Bender (King 2000:129). Riots in Chisinau in November 1989 led to the deposing of most of the Communist Party leaders, including Grossu, who was ousted at the behest of Mikhail Gorbachev. His replacement was Petru Lucinschi, the only ethnic Romanian in the top ranks of the Moldovan Communist Party. On independence, the presidency passed to another communist, Mircea Snegur, who was to remain in office until January 1997, when Lucinschi succeeded him (Dembinska and Iglesias 2013).

The revolution in Romania and summary public execution of its dictator Nicolae Ceausescu and his wife on 25 December 1989 increased speculation, and perhaps hopes, within Moldova that there could be a union with Romania. Before these events, there had been little dissent from Soviet rule in Transnistria, which had benefited from that rule disproportionately to the remainder of Moldova and particularly from the industrialisation under Stalin. There was, however, a rapid realisation by Tiraspol of the prospect of Transnistria being integrated into an independent pro-Romanian Moldova. Several polls took place in Transnistria in 1990, which consistently showed that over 90% of citizens wished to break away from Moldova (Troebst 2003).

On 2 September 1990, the Second Congress of the Peoples' Representatives of Transnistria unilaterally proclaimed the Moldovan Republic of Transnistria a Soviet Republic. Fifteen days later, the Moldovan Front leader, Iuire Rosca, declared that "the fragmentation of the Moldovan territories…is a great impediment to our unification with the mother country" (Kolstø *et al.* 1993:989). This was a clear call to oppose the steps taken by the leaders of Transnistria and Gagauzia* and had a polarising effect that made any peaceful resolution less likely.

In December 1990, Mikhail Gorbachev, still clinging to power in Moscow, explicitly declared the decisions of that congress void (Kolstø *et al.* 1993:990). However, neither Moldova nor the USSR took any practical action to prevent the Tiraspol authorities seizing control over the region. Gorbachev's declaration exemplified the Kremlin's ambivalence to the Moldovan question. Indeed, it coincided with substantial troop movements by the Soviet Union to Transnistria with, many Moldovans allege, the purpose of keeping all of Moldova within Russia's control after the now inevitable break-up of the Soviet Union.** Much of the Soviet 14th Army, primarily based in Ukraine, was to be stationed at the garrison in Bender's historic castle (Kolosto *et al.* 1993:992).

The events before and after independence show how the inhabitants of Transnistria can proclaim a separate history from Moldova. Their last unification was the result of a short-lived pact between two tyrannical regimes. Even in the decades when both territories were controlled from Moscow, and theoretically Chisinau, they developed discretely. When the USSR broke up they, predictably, wanted to develop linguistically, culturally and politically in different ways. That these differences were strong enough to lead to a war with nearly 1,000 Transnistrians dead underlines that urge for separation. Any attempt to force Transnistria back into union with Moldova would be an attempt to reverse a strong pattern of history, particularly modern history.

1.1.2 THE WAR OF INDEPENDENCE

The beginnings of conflict

The first bloodshed was in November 1990, when women operating a roadblock attempting to cut off the bridge linking Dubasari to the Right-Bank were shot at by Moldovan

---

* On 20 August 1990, there had been a proclamation by Gagauzian leaders in respect of five non-contiguous districts of southern Moldova. Immediately the Moldovan parliament declared that decision unconstitutional and outlawed the Gagauz separatist movement (Andersen 2019).

** See, for instance, the somewhat inflammatory speech of Vlad Spânu, President of the Moldova Foundation, in Washington, DC, to the US's Helsinki Commission in October 2014 (Moldova Foundation 2014)

police, killing three and injuring thirteen (Dailey, Laber and Whitman 1993:54). The incident did not immediately spark a wider conflict but was followed by a low-key militarisation of Transnistrian society. In late November, Transnistria held separate parliamentary elections, with Igor Smirnov emerging as leader of the separatist Soviet.

On 27 August 1991, Moldovan independence from the USSR was proclaimed, precipitated by the hard-liners' attempted coup against Gorbachev in Moscow. The coup had been condemned by Chisinau, whereas Igor Smirnov, who had emerged as the leader of the Transnistrian resistance, praised the coup leaders as saviours of the Soviet state (King 2000:191). Smirnov formally became the leader of Transnistria, first from 1 October 1991 as chairman, then from that December as president – an office he was to hold until his defeat by Shevchuk in the 2011 election. The Proclamation of Moldovan Independence's preamble included "underlining the existence of Moldovans in Transnistria, a component part of the historical and ethnic territory of our people" (Soviet History 2008), which had consequent misgivings in Transnistria, which was absorbed into the new state while retaining a degree of effective self-government. On 21 December 1991, Moldova joined the Commonwealth of Independent States, which had been formed on the break-up of the USSR thirteen days earlier. International recognition generally followed, with UN membership being granted on 2 March 1994 (OSCE 1994:1).

In September 1991, the Transnistrian Soviet decreed the formation of an armed national guard, and in Bender the local authority set up a militia to perform police functions. The established police force did not disband, though, and there were many skirmishes between the two organisations. Again, Dubasari proved a centre-point of conflict, with a stand-off between pro-Moldovan police officers and the national guard, several fatalities, and then a prisoner exchange in Tiraspol in March 1992 (Dailey *et al.* 1993:7).

There was a brief lull in the conflict after a demand on 17 March 1992 from Chisinau for an end to all military activity was temporarily respected by Transnistrian forces. This did not, however, lead to the disbanding of the Bender militia, and on 1 April, attempts to disarm them by Moldovan police in armoured cars led to several casualties. There was an announcement that day by officers of the Russian 14th Army, garrisoned in Bender, which had hitherto kept in the background. It had probably been approved, if not drafted, in Moscow and said that the fighting was perceived as being a consequence of the violation of the human rights of the Russian-speaking people. It talked of the 14th Army acting as a peacekeeping force but also said that "the conflicting sides must immediately be pulled out from the borders of the Transnistria region" (Bugajski 2000:99); in other words, it called for a Moldovan withdrawal from Transnistria. In a similar vein, on 5 April 1992, the Russian vice president, Alexander Rutskoy, made a speech to 5,000 people in Tiraspol, saying the Transnistrian people should obtain their independence but in a confederation with Moldova and under the protection of the 14th Army.

There were then several meetings of representatives of the foreign ministries of Moldova, Romania, Russia and Ukraine. They sent military supervisors to the area, whose presence mostly held the peace until June. There were occasions where 14th Army positions were fired on by Moldovan forces. A warning by the 14th Army on 19 May that if this continued it would fire back was taken as a threat of war by the Moldovan parliament. On 9 June, the deputy commander of the 14th Army was shot dead. The Russians blamed the Moldovan police and two days later executed, somewhat arbitrarily, a Major Perzhu (Dailey *et al.* 1993:57). Despite this portentous event, the fragile peace still held. Transnistrian MPs returned to the Chisinau parliament but were criticised for this by many organisations in Bender. A federal treaty was proposed between Moldova and Transnistria, but this could not muster a majority in that parliament.

The outbreak of war

On 19 June 1992, Moldovan police apprehended the 14th Army's Major Yermakov as he visited a printing shop in Bender. As the arrest was being effected, gunmen, almost certainly from Bender militias, opened fire on the police. One policeman was killed and several wounded. Sniping continued at the Bender police station. The chief of the Bender police rejected the advice of the military observers present to release Yermakov, saying he would only do so once the shooting stopped (Dailey *et al.* 1993:60). The 14th Army did not seek to intervene at this stage, though were probably providing some arms to the Transnistrian forces (King 2000:192).

Moldovan soldiers were directed to Bender by President Snegur. The Moldovan military was still in embryonic form and required police reinforcements. It is a matter of speculation whether Snegur believed his forces were superior to those garnered by Transnistria. He may even have been counting on the 14th Army supporting him (Troebst 2004:18). It is difficult to see how, absent that belief, naïve though it would have been, he could have expected a military victory against the determined and relatively well-organised Transnistrians.

The composition of those fighting for Transnistrian independence is a matter of controversy. There is no doubt that southern Russian mercenaries and volunteers, known as Cossacks, arrived in the area (Junker 2014). Less clear is the extent to which the 14th Army participated. General Alexander Lebed (Dailey *et al.* 1993:24) was sent from Moscow to take command in June. There are allegations that its troops, having disguised their uniforms, joined in the fighting on several occasions (e.g. Andersen n.d.). More clearly documented were artillery attacks on Moldovan forces. The Moldovan army received weapons, military vehicles and a force of volunteers and military advisers from Romania, but this was of far less significance than the Russian assistance to Transnistria (King 2000:192).

Several hundred people, largely combatants, died in the war. The precise number is impossible to ascertain, partly because of the local custom of burying the dead in back gardens (Dailey *et al.* 1993:63), which during the war was often done without recourse to the authorities. Kolstø *et al.* (1993:975) quote figures for the June fighting from the Chisinau *Nezavisimaya Gazeta* of 203 dead and around 200 missing in Bender alone.

Bowring (2014:8) says "several hundred" died in clashes at the end of 1991 and beginning of 1992. The total throughout was a probably a little under a thousand.

The fighting continued until 21 July 1992, when a peace treaty, entitled "Principles of the Peaceful Settlement of the Armed Conflict in Transnistria" was signed by Presidents Yeltsin and Snegur. Except for a skirmish on 25 July 1992 in the village of Gisca* near Bender, the treaty marked the end of the war. This treaty provided for a security zone and peacekeeping forces – formally Transnistrian, Moldovan and Russian but dominated by the 14th Army and two battalions of Transnistrian Republican Guards. It did not set out a political solution. The conflict was thus frozen and a *de facto* but not *de jure* independence of Transnistria recognised.

1.1.3 POST DE FACTO INDEPENDENCE

President Smirnov was a relatively recent Russian immigrant, having arrived in the territory in 1987 (King 2000:188) as director of Elektromash electronics plant; he became chairman of Tiraspol City Soviet, effectively the city's mayor, in February 1990. Smirnov's position was an indication of Russian influence within the territory. Under a leader with no connection to the rest of Moldova, it was always more likely that the independent Transnistrian identity would develop.

The Russian influence was also enhanced through the continuing presence of Alexander Lebed, who became a member of the Transnistrian Soviet in 1993 (Refworld 2004), and was the nearest to a credible opposition figure to Smirnov in his early years. Tensions grew between him and Smirnov, who Lebed described along with his associates as "corrupt war profiteers" (King 2000:200). Lebed believed that the bureaucracy was making the state unmanageable (Simonsen 1995:528). It is feasible that if he had not been returned to Russia in 1995, he might have intervened to remove Smirnov politically or even militarily. William Hill, who was involved in the OSCE negotiations over Transnistria then, regarded the replacement of Lebed by Moscow as a conciliatory act (Hill 2013).

Smirnov remained in power until 2011, amending the constitution in 2000 to remove the prohibition on a president standing for more than two terms (Isachenko and Schlichte 2007:86). He won the 2001 election with 82% of the votes (Roper 2003:265) and captured an almost identical amount in 2006 (Blakkisrud and Kolstø 2013:2000).

In a 2006 referendum, 97.3% of those voting, on a turnout of around 80%, favoured independence rather than reunification with Moldova. The then foreign minister, Valeriy Litskai, subsequently proclaimed that integration into Russia would take place within seven years (Sanchez 2013).

It was eventually to be a souring of relations with Russia that led to Smirnov's downfall and defeat by Yevgeny Shevchuk in the 2011 election. Dembinska and Kosienkowski (2013:316–317) identify four reasons for this: he had become an obstacle to discussions

---

*   The Russian 'human rights' group Memorial (2019) reports beatings being administered by Moldovan troops and two cows being killed by gunfire.

with Chisinau that Russia now wanted; as Moldova moved closer to the EU and Romania, his rigidity would lessen Russian influence; there was a fear that there might be a 'colour revolution' if he remained in office; and supporting his regime was having too high a price financially. The first two are more plausible. While it was a pro-Russian identity that Smirnov was constantly promoting, doing that was driving a greater wedge between Tiraspol and Chisinau. At the time, Russia was not supportive of either Transnistrian independence or a union with Russia. Smirnov was increasingly rigid in his position, thus reducing Russian manoeuvrability in the area. However, the removal of Smirnov had little input on the nation-building going on in Transnistria and did not impact on its separate development from Moldova.

Shevchuk, who was born in Transnistria, was of mixed Russian and Ukrainian origin but was registered as Ukrainian (Moldova.org 2012). His career was largely with the Sheriff group (SubSect.2.3.2), which Smirnov's son Oleg had been involved in founding, but with which Smirnov had fallen out towards the end of his presidency (Całus 2016a). Early in his presidency, Shevchuk removed Smirnov's son Vladimir from his position of head of the customs committee, which he had frequently been accused of exploiting for personal gain (Wilson 2012). Russia sought the extradition of Smirnov's other son Oleg in connection with the alleged theft of humanitarian aid (Dembinska and Kosienkowski 2013:315). While Shevchuk indicated a willingness to cooperate with this, including, if necessary, an amendment of Transnistrian statute law to allow it, the extradition did not take place.

Russia remained a powerful force within the territory, but the Sheriff group's influence was becoming increasingly overt. Through its main political party, 'Obnovlenie',* it remained in control of the Soviet after Shevchuk's accession and frequently opposed measures he wished to take, in particular legislating to prevent deputies, some of whom remained employed by Sheriff, in the Soviet from holding outside jobs (Grau 2016). Shevchuk's own position was weakened still further by elections in November 2015. He had hoped that he would be able to take control of the Soviet, but in fact, the number of Sheriff-supporting Obnovlenie delegates increased, to 33 out of the 43 seats (Lesanu 2016).

Shevchuk had fallen out with both Russia and Sheriff by the start of 2016, and with the support of neither had little chance of being re-elected in December that year. Vadim Krasnoselsky, speaker of the Soviet and formerly Sheriff's security chief, emerged as the leading opposition candidate. He was Russian-born but of partly Ukrainian origin. There was in fact little policy difference between the two men. The only television debate featured cross-accusations of dishonesty (Lesanu 2016), perhaps more telling when made against an incumbent president. Russia remained neutral during the campaign, but it was a feature of the campaigns that each candidate claimed closeness to Russia. The fact that from a position of incumbency Shevchuk was able to show little tangible sign of a relationship with Russia may have counted against him.

Particularly telling may have been a Sheriff-owned television station broadcasting a programme accusing Shevchuk of a Gorbachev-style policy of unilateral and unmotivated

---

* Roughly translates as 'Renewal'.

concessions. This, points out Giorgio Comai (2016), "In a context where the demise of the Soviet Union is largely perceived as a great tragedy was meant as an offensive and disquieting characterization." Krasnoselsky won the election on the first round with a substantial majority.

Paradoxically, Krasnoselsky has on occasions distanced himself from identification with the USSR, ordering the removal of some Lenin statues and saying to *Russians Today* (2018), "Unfortunately, in Soviet times, the memory of the defenders of the Fatherland was erased. But we are restoring this memory." Conversely, he is an eloquent, if verbose, advocate of Transnistrian independence, contributing a closely argued chapter to the compendium of essays compiled by his foreign minister in 2018 (Ignatiev 2018:283). In that, he talks of the "geo-political catastrophe associated with the collapse of the USSR" (*Russians Today* 2018:291).

Krasnoselsky has maintained more of a dialogue with Chisinau than his predecessors. He met occasionally with the Moldovan president, Igor Dodon,* and talks were described by Krasnoselsky as friendly, though the official photo may suggest otherwise and evidence an ongoing hostility between the territories which their leaders lack the personal capacity to overcome (RTA 2018).

1: Presidents Dodon (left) and Krasnoselsky after 'friendly' talks in Bender in December 2018**

It is clear that the warmest Transnistrian foreign relations will continue to be with Russia. Krasnoselsky and Dodon may both be pragmatic enough to realise that overt hostility will benefit neither side, but as long as their respective positions on the future of Transnistria remain so polarised, there is likely to be little progress without outside influence (Sect.5.2).

Right-Bank Moldova post-independence

In September 1990, Mircea Snegur, who had been chair of the Moldovan Supreme Soviet but quickly renounced communism, was elected unopposed as Moldovan president (King 2000:148). Snegur's time in office was notable mainly for economic problems, making Moldova by some distance the poorest country in Europe, with living standards below Transnistria's (SubSect.2.1.1). There were occasional meetings with Smirnov in the early years of independence – in restaurants along the Chisinau to Tiraspol highway (King 2000:199) – but by 1995, talks between the territories had ceased (Refworld 2004).

In 2001, Moldova became the first post-Soviet country to elect a communist parliament, which in turn appointed Vladimir Voronin, a strong but divisive figure, as president, the constitution having been amended to allow for such an appointment rather than through direct election. During his time in office, Voronin moved from a pro-Russian stance to seeking closer ties with Europe and adopting a rhetoric of accusing Russia of helping separatists in Transnistria (Solovyov 2009). While his rule saw the country's economic crisis eased somewhat (Wagstyl 2009), he made no progress in re-establishing relations with Transnistria, and his hostility to Russia emphasised the territories' separateness. After the April 2009 election, a stalemate arose, leaving Voronin in power as effectively a caretaker until September of that year (Napieralska 2012:97). There was no permanent president until March 2012, when Nicolae Timofti of the Alliance for European Integration emerged as a supposed consensus candidate (Napieralska 2012:103).

In 2014, it became apparent that Moldovan banks had been defrauded of over US$1 billion, or about 12% of the nation's assets. Many senior politicians were implicated, including Vlad Filat, who was prime minister from September 2009 to April 2014, and for three days in December 2010 was caretaker president. In 2016, he was sentenced to nine years' imprisonment (Tanas 2016). Although such losses have not caused as much damage to the Moldovan economy as might be expected, they inevitably make international companies wary of investing in the country.

On 1 July 2016, the Moldova–EU Association Agreement, with its deep and comprehensive free trade area, came into full force, having been provisionally applied since 1 September 2014 (*EUOJ* 2014).

Igor Dodon was elected president just twelve days after Krasnoselsky's election. Dodon's position on Transnistria has been opaque or at least frequently changing (SubSect.5.2.1). His presidency was hampered by other problems, having had his powers and duties removed by the parliament on several occasions (Călugăreanu 2018).

The divergence between Transnistrian and Moldovan history since independence

While Moldova, like Transnistria, has made a meaningful transition to democracy and established a functional departmentalised government, it clearly has been beset by problems which have hindered its development. Its ability to form ties with, and perhaps in the long term even join, the EU has been a positive feature politically and economically. However, the lack of stable government, the pre-2001 economic problems and the 2014 financial crisis (SubSect.2.1.1) remain the most striking features of its post-independence years. While it has recovered from the worst of the economic crisis which beset its early years, it remains the poorest country in Europe, behind war-torn Ukraine (World Population Review 2020), despite its agreement with the EU and the economic advantages that should have brought.

In contrast, Transnistrians have never been in any doubt who their president is, and its governance has not been significantly hindered by differences between the president and the Soviet. Similarly, although there has been misappropriation of state funds, particularly during the Smirnov presidency, it has not, in absolute or proportionate terms, been on anything like the scale of that in Chisinau. Transnistrians were not exposed to the same degree of poverty as Right-Bank Moldovans in the early years of independence, though the respective economic situations are more similar now (SubSect.2.1.1). The prevalence of Moldova's own problems can only undermine its case for reintegration: even if Transnistrians were otherwise disposed towards that, they would be justifiably concerned about being sucked into those problems.

The years since the 1992 war have continued the theme of how little Transnistrian history has in common with that of Moldova. The seemingly static situation in which the territory now finds itself, compounded sometimes by paralysis in the Chisinau government, does not point to any resolution of the Transnistrian issue. However, the longer Transnistria remains stable as an independent territory, the more artificial demands for it to reintegrate with Moldova, a country with which its people feel little in common except geographical proximity, become. The greater economic problems which Moldova has experienced, particularly in the early years of independence, lessen still the attractions to Transnistrians of any reunification.

1.2 IDENTITY AND NATION-BUILDING SINCE DE FACTO INDEPENDENCE

While the history of Transnistria and Moldova points to a separateness, a distinct Transnistrian nation attains credibility by its inhabitants identifying with it – being shown to share a common culture, in Guibernau's (1996) words. In the lack of an apparent ethnic homogeneity to its people, those who want to create that identity, largely the Transnistrian elite, have an incentive to create the image of a nation with which those people can identify. It is necessary to consider both the extent to which the Transnistrians do naturally comprise a people and the extent to which that has been taken forward by a process of nation-building.

1.2.1 ETHNICITY AND IDENTITY

What are Transnistrians?

One of the reasons relied on by the New York City Bar Association (New York 2006:40), among others, for opposing Transnistrian independence is that Transnistrians do not constitute a 'people'. The New York report (2006) relies on Charles King in setting out the historical position:

> There were [in 1900] far more Ukrainians and Russians west of the Dnestr River than in Transnistria, and in some northern raions and in the cities, the Slavic population were just as concentrated as in the raions east of the Dnestr. In Transnistria as a whole, Moldovans formed nearly 40 percent of the total population of just over 600,000. (2000:187)

The 40% figure had not changed significantly by the 2015 census, when 33% of the Transnistrian population were recorded as Moldovan (Crivenco 2018:10). In contrast, the 2014 census in Moldova showed only 4.1% and 6.6% of the population identified as Russian and Ukrainian, respectively (NBS 2014).

Bill Bowring takes a slightly different position, stating (2014:22), "The New York Bar's starting point, upon which all may agree, is that the population of [Transnistria is] not an ethnicity." He asks, however, whether they could "qualify as a people". He considers the arguments of Cassese (1995:59), Kiwanuka (1988) and Brownlie (1985:107–108) and suggests that "people", in this context, "may well be determined by matters of culture, language, religion and group psychology" (Bowring 2014:23).

The obvious flaw in the New York and even Bowring positions is that there is nothing close to a consensus as to what ethnicity is. Conflicting positions are summarised by Henry Hale (2004:458):

> For some, it is an emotion-laden sense of belonging or attachment to a particular kind of group (Connor, 1993; Horowitz, 1985; Shils, 1957). For others, it is embeddedness in a web of significant symbols (Geertz, 1967, 1973; Smith, 2000). Still others see ethnicity as a social construct, a choice to be made (Anderson, 1991; Barth, 1969; Royce, 1982). One recent view treats it above all as a cognitive process (Brubaker,

2002). Some even call ethnicity a biological survival instinct based on nepotism (Van den Berghe, 1981). A few consider it a mix of these notions (Fearon, 1999; Fearon & Laitin, 2000; Laitin, 1998).

In terms straddling most of the approaches identified by Hale (2004), Peoples and Bailey say an ethnic group is:

> A named social category of people based on perceptions of shared social experience or one's ancestors' experiences. Members of the ethnic group see themselves as sharing cultural traditions and history that distinguish them from other groups. Ethnic group identity has a strong psychological or emotional component that divides the people of the world into opposing categories of 'us' and 'them'. (2010:389)

None of these approaches treats ethnicity as inherent rather than primarily subjective. Despite this, it has been argued by Raj Bhopal (2004:414) that ethnicity may have become a substitute for the "scientifically limited and somewhat discredited term race in the scientific literature". The English judicial House of Lords* held (*Mandla v. Dowell-Lee* 1982) that although Sikhs were not a race for the purposes of the Race Relations Act 1976, they qualified as an ethnic group, "defined by ethnic origins because they constitute a separate and distinct community derived from the racial characteristics".

There thus seem to be three potentially overlapping concepts – race, ethnicity and people – which lead to a nation or nationhood, which is the stepping stone to full statehood of the sort Transnistria aspires to. Most variants on primary right theory accord a greater right to secession to a group which can be identified as a people (SubSect.5.4.1).

Transnistria's population is divided, in its own official figures, into three main and separate groups: Moldovans, Russians and Ukrainians. Whether indeed these three groups are themselves different ethnicities or even 'peoples' would be questionable were it not for the fact that each group does identify as such, at least in responses to censuses. Linguistically, and perhaps thus ethnically, Moldovans are similar to Romanians. As most Ukrainians' first language is Russian, not Ukrainian, it might be argued that they are not a separate people either. A clearer divide might be between Slavic people and those who speak Romance languages, including Romanian, but that would be an over-simplification as well, involving treating, for instance, Romanians, Catalans and Portuguese as a single group.

Peoples and Bailey's (2010) definition has attractions in this situation because of its clear recognition that common identity is a basis for ethnicity, allowing a greater subjectivity than the House of Lords' (1982) approach, which was tied into, though not directly coinciding with, race. To restrict recognition of independence to clearly defined racial groups, which is the corollary of Cornet's position (2016), would become itself

---

* That body is now the Supreme Court.

an arguably racist position, depending on a concept that is both highly controversial and virtually impossible to define. Identity is a more accessible determinant of a people, and consideration of Transnistrians is best done in the context of whether they have a meaningful common identity.

Transnistrian identity

Joris Wagemakers tries to trace the history of Transnistrian identity, arguing (2015:50), "In the early stages of the [1990–92] conflict the Transnistrian movement did not have a classic ethno-nationalist character." Instead, there was a fear of a "Fascist ruled Greater Romania" at that time, which led to a negative identity (Wagemakers 2015:51). Such an argument may have historical credibility, particularly in the light of the Second World War regime of Antonescu (SubSect.1.1.1) and that of Ceausescu, who was head of state from 1967 until his execution in December 1989. After that execution, Romania remained in a state of political flux for several years. However, Wagemakers contends that identity issues no longer flow from that and have been replaced by "narratives about and against western, and more specifically what is seen as American values and practices" (Wagemakers 2015:54).

Wagemakers conducted twenty interviews in spring 2013 with Transnistrians aged 18 to 30 of different "ethnic" backgrounds. Although no figures are given, Wagemakers says those of Moldovan background "were generally more negative and sceptical *vis a vis* the Transnistrian state" (2015:52). A woman aged 20 told him, "Transnistria is an invented people, and not like a country, it's a product of Soviet colonisation and propaganda" (2015:53). Such answers suggest that some Transnistrians, particularly those who regard themselves as Moldovan, are impervious to the nation-building efforts of the regime, as discussed below.

While the non-ethnic label attached to Transnistrian identity may be correct, it does not automatically follow that the national identity could only be imposed through power structures. The historic "negative identity" basis identified by Wagemakers (2015) is credible and may have been more durable than Wagemakers himself believes. Mitrofanova (2015:53) regards the identity in quite similar terms, namely as being little more than a definite distinctiveness from those on the Right-Bank of the Dniestr. That may be a step too far, as there seems little to differentiate between those, particularly Moldovan speakers, living close to the border, regardless of which side of the Dniestr they are on. The imposition of an artificial identity may be a feature of many political systems.*

In her thesis (2011), Rebecca Chamberlain-Creangă reports on her discussions with

---

*   In fact, a strong example of artificial creation of an identity may be modern London boroughs, which rarely follow natural community or geographic boundaries but whose councillors and senior officers promote the concept of the boroughs, particularly Haringey where I live, in an attempt to make their inhabitants feel part of something they are not. No one else in Muswell Hill or Wood Green says they are from Haringey, nearly everyone in Tiraspol or Ribnita says they are from Transnistria.

an older man, Teodor, whose mother-tongue was Moldovan and who lived and worked in Rezina; these contrast interestingly with Wagemakers' interviews. Teodor was proud of now primarily speaking Russian at home and work but enjoyed the privileges that being a Moldovan speaker gave him at the cement plant where he was a senior operative (Chamberlain-Creangă 2011:117). He preferred to shop in Ribnita's Sheriff supermarkets the other side of the Dniestr, which – as his unequivocal assertion, "I am not Romanian" (Chamberlain-Creangă 2011:116), suggests – may be based on identity issues as much as a consumer judgement that the Sheriff stores provide better quality and value. This outlook is said to be shared by many of Teodor's Moldovan colleagues.

Although Chamberlain-Creangă does not go on to draw such an inference herself, it may well be that those discussions point to uncertainty in the Right-Bank Moldovan identity, even among Moldovan speakers. In that context, and with the divisions within Moldovan society, particularly on the desirability of union with Romania (Chamberlain-Creangă 2011:269; see SubSect.5.2.1), the stronger identity would appear to be that of the Left-Bank, notwithstanding the responses noted by Wagemakers (2015) in his interviews with Transnistrian Moldovan speakers.

In an earlier work, Chamberlain-Creangă argues that:

A combination of ethnic, urban-rural and labour-professional identities forms the understanding of citizenship characteristic of this region. It is this combination that determines the state loyalty of the inhabitants of Transnistria. (2006: Abstract)

In simpler terms, this may mean that although there are different identities within Transnistria, these ultimately do not detract from the loyalty of each to the Transnistrian state.

In reality, as virtually every relevant conversation I have had there has witnessed, Transnistrians have a strong identity as such within the territory. Even a Moldovan speaker who expressed doubts about the economic case for independence did so in terms of "we" and "us", expressing herself as a Transnistrian in a group discussion at Tiraspol's Shevchenko University in October 2019. Abroad, when people from Transnistria are asked in casual conversation where they come from, many say "Moldova". My experience of such conversations has been that the motivation for this answer is because they want to provide the listener with a place there is a chance they have heard of, rather have to explain geo-political minutiae when a one-word answer was expected.

Transnistria's internal politics also point towards the existence of a clear identity. The overwhelming vote for independence in the 2006 referendum (SubSect.1.3.2) could not have come entirely from manipulation by an elite. The failure of any political party favouring unity with Moldova to gain traction underlines this. The 30% Moldovan speakers could, if so minded, form a strong political movement within the territory, but they have made virtually no effort to do so. The sole instance in which a separate Moldovan identity has asserted itself has been in respect of the Romanian-language schools (SubSect.4.1.2), and even that has been among a small proportion of Romanians. The Smirnov government's heavy-handed dealings with this issue may have evidenced a desperate desire on the part of the regime to ensure there was an unsullied Transnistrian identity. If so, that reaction was based on a misplaced belief that those who wanted such education were intent on widening the language issue into broader political challenges. Wagemakers' (2015) evidence of the tenuousness of Transnistrian identity may have seemed credible, but was based on far too small a study to be given much weight, and virtually all the objective factors considered in this section suggest Transnistrians strongly identify as such.

Bowring's position is premised on the more credible acceptance that there is at least a Transnistrian identity:

> If the inhabitants of the territory of the PMR have indeed acquired their own identity, their own 'distinct character', distinct from the remainder of Moldova, then they may well have a right of self-determination as a 'people'. (2014:24)

He does not address why this should lead to self-determination rather than the independence which a pure plebiscitary right theorist would contend arises in this situation (SubSect.5.1.4). He predicts that there will be a resolution leading to federation or special status within Moldova (2014:26). Even if the reasoning behind that prediction were sound in 2014, it has not, of course, been borne out by subsequent events. However, Bowring's approach is to be commended for escaping the narrow confines of ethnicity. It should not be necessary to distinguish between an ethnic group and a people in deciding the extent to which self-determination should arise. Even if the negative motive behind the creation of Transnistrian, ascribed by Wagemakers (2015) and Mitrofanova (2015), is justified, it makes no practical difference to the existence and effect of that identity, and that identity can be one of the bases on which not only self-determination but independence can be asserted.

1.2.2 NATION-BUILDING PROJECTS

A frequent observation, particularly by writers fundamentally critical of Transnistria, has been that its leadership has followed a course of 'nation-building' to artificially create a national identity – one going beyond the certainty identified by Mitrofanova that the inhabitants are different from those of the Dniestr's Right-Bank (2015:192). Magdalena Dembinska argues, "To support their claim to legitimacy, Abkhazian and Transnistrian elites foster a collective identity" (2018:313), which is largely the process that manifests itself as nation-building. In Transnistria this is done, of necessity, by promoting a non-ethnic identity, in contrast to Abkhazia's attempts to establish a nation-state status for ethnic Abkhazis.

It is likely such an identity was already present when the war of independence was fought. It is axiomatic that if so many people are prepared to fight for something, and in nearly 1,000 cases die, they must identify with something. Even before the conflict with Chisinau, it was argued that there was "a vague but nevertheless tangible common identity of most of [the Transnistrian] population" (Kolstø and Malgin 1998:104). That is not to say that the post-1992 Transnistrian elite did not have motivation to strengthen that identity. The identity has been closely tied to Russia, despite the territory's claim to be roughly equally divided linguistically between Russian, Ukrainian and Moldovan speakers.

The argument is encapsulated by Ion Marandici (2020:1), who states that the Transnistrian regime "has sought for nearly three decades to forge a supraethnic Transnistrian identity". He argues that this is in contrast with most other "parastates",* such as Abkhazia and South Ossetia, which are "firmly rooted in a specific mono-ethnic identity". A means through which this is done is by:

> The diverse community from which PMR draws its political legitimacy...being gradually reimagined as part of the Russkii Mir, a civilizational space in Eurasia centered on a conservative traditionalist ideology in which the Russian culture and history dominate. (2020:2)

Marandici, with the advantage of hindsight over nearly three decades, conveniently identifies six main planks of Transnistrian identity (2020:6):

Statehood and the 1992 war
Patron-state ideology: *Russkii Mir* and Eurasianism
Politicised ethnicities: Moldovans and Ukrainians
Cohesive nostalgic memory regime
Media language and education policies
Others: Right-Bank Moldovans, Romanians and the West.

The assertion of statehood, in the sense of being internationally recognised, might be considered more the goal, than a feature, of the nation-building. The nation-building is a means to achieving that goal as it cements the inhabitants' identification with a Transnistrian state. The 1992 war itself was an indicator that some identity must already have existed, and as Blakkisrud and Kolstø put it, "the war memory was and remains a major source of inspiration for the collective Transnistrian civic identity" (Marandici 2013:196). Marandici (2020) does not, however, attach so much weight to that argument, pointing to different analyses of the war: that of Fruntasu (2002), as conflict between Russia and Moldova; the 1989 Language Law passed in Chisinau (SubSect.1.1.1); and Roper (2005), who sees it as a civil war. No records were kept of the ethnicity of those who died in the war, but it is clear they were not exclusively Russian. A glance at the war memorial in Tiraspol shows a sprinkling of names ending in the Cyrillic *KY*, which

---

*   Referred to more frequently as 'pseudo-states'.

equates to the most common Romanian name ending -cu, and rather more with the typical Ukrainian suffix *KO*. Kolstø, Edemsky and Kalashnikova say that "members of the same ethnic groups – Moldovans, Ukrainians and Russians – participated on both sides" and that it "is therefore a gross oversimplification to present the conflict as a showdown between the ethnic Moldovan and the 'Russian-speaking' part of the Moldovan population" (1993:975).

The process of nation-building and Russkii Mir

While Marandici (2020:8) adopts Laruelle's (2015:5–6) account of *Russkii Mir,** as emerging in the 1990s in an attempt to formulate a coherent policy toward the 25 million Russians living abroad, this shirks the question of who is Russian and whether it can be defined by anything other than language. Marandici cites Krasnoselsky's own explanation of the *Russkii Mir*, which is not so dependent on Russian ethnicity:

> I hold Transnistrian and Russian passports. In our republic an individual can have an unlimited number of passports…My father is Ukrainian and my mother is Russian. But my nationality is Eastern Slav. In my veins flows Russian, Ukrainian, and Polish blood. How can you divide me into parts? The soul does not have nationality…and as part of the Russkii Mir each citizen preserves their own ethnic identity. We have 35 nationalities here and each of them keeps its own culture and language. We have avoided national conflicts, because the philosophy of the Russkii Mir allows us to coexist peacefully. There is no titular nation here. (2020:1)

The *Russkii Mir* theme is picked up on by Blakkisrud and Kolstø, who, without using the term, point to Transnistrian identity:

> Replicating its Soviet predecessor even to the extent of drawing heavily on Russian history, culture and language to fill the empty frame of the supposedly ethnically neutral civic identity. (2013:178)

The claims that the Transnistrian regime aims to create a genuine multi-cultural or multi-lingual state is questioned in virtually all the writing on this topic. Krasnoselsky's own words would be hard to square with anything other than a very Russian-centric view of the territory. The dichotomy is neatly encapsulated by Alexander Osipov and Hannah Vasilevich:

> The dominant ideological formula includes an element of ethnonationalism since the policy has eponymic ethnicity – Moldovan –, and raison d'être of the statehood is the

---

*   For a fuller discussion of this policy, see Igor Munteanu, who argues: "Since Putin believes that the dissolution of the USSR was a historic accident, almost naturally all former Soviet states are not real states but building blocks for a re-emerging post-Soviet state" (2016:83).

preservation of the 'genuine' Moldovan identity against the expansion of 'Romanian nationalism'. Concurrently, TMR is portrayed as a part of the 'Russian Universe' or as territory where Moldovan and Slavonic cultures live in symbiosis. (2017:25)

On this analysis, the Transnistrian perception of the entire Moldovan identity is taken over from the largely Romanian-leaning identity of the Chisinau regime. Osipov and Vasilevich (2017), like most commentators, are sceptical about the genuineness of Transnistrian attempts to promote a multi-cultural and multi-lingual society. The human rights ombudsman* is specifically pointed out as not dealing with language policies and usage, nor cultural rights, and there is no other official body charged with dealing with such issues (Osipov and Vasilevich 2017:12). Laws requiring official engagement in languages other than Russian are often disregarded (Osipov and Vasilevich 2017:13). Most higher education institutions teach entirely in Russian (Osipov and Vasilevich 2017:14). This is summed up as follows:

The local diversity policies are affected by the phobias toward Moldovan nationalism allegedly backed with Romanian involvement, praise to the Soviet 'internationalism' and 'people's friendship' and loyalty to a combination of selected historic myths, which include the 'genuine' Moldovan identity, the Soviet victory in World War II and the Russia/Soviet 'civilizing' mission in the region. (2017:19)

It is against this plausible argument, that multi-culturalism has not developed, that it can be seen how a distinctive, but very much Russian-leaning, Transnistrian nation has been created. That Russian-ness does become part of the national identity. Whether it is part of a perhaps Moscow-led *Russkii Mir* or its creation is locally led is largely outside the scope of this thesis, though Rick Lof (2016:10) points to the increasing absorption into Russian government of most of the institutions for "diaspora communication". The reality is that the Transnistrian identity is heavily Russian influenced.

The theme of "politicised ethnicities" referred to by Marandici (2020), which may place too much emphasis on ethnicity itself rather than, for instance, different peoples, can be seen in the context of Dembinska and Iglesias' claim to identify:

Two periods in which the Transnistrian authorities have put forward different strategies to legitimize separation: first, an emphasis on 'Moldovan nationhood,' called 'Moldovanism,' in the 1990s; second, especially since 2001, an emphasis on civic 'Transnistrian nationhood.' It is shown that the transition from the first to the second was a direct response to nation-building policies in the Republic of Moldova. (2013:2)

---

* See SubSect.3.5.2 for an account of the lackadaisical approach holders of that office have taken to many issues.

The changes in 2001 they rely on flowed from the accession to the presidency of Moldova of the communist Vladimir Voronin. Under him, the Moldovan elite emphasised the existence of the Moldovan nation and "prolonged the Soviet process of differentiating Moldovans from neighbouring Romanians" (2013:6). It should be borne in mind that Moldova itself is an artificial state (Cojocaru 2006:262). Although emphasising Moldova's separateness from Romania is similar to emphasising Transnistria's own separateness from Moldova, the Transnistrian approach would require a different nuance. Otherwise, the difference between the approach of the territories' respective elites would be in danger of converging in a way that would undermine the separateness of Transnistrian nationhood. The way in which the Transnistrian regime has done that is explored next.

The management of ethnic perceptions

Nostalgic memory regime, identified by Marandici (2020), can be seen in terms of history, as Dembinska and Iglesias describe:

> Most people [in Transnistria] consider the history of the region to have begun in 1792 and stress the fact that Transnistria has never been part of Bessarabia, that the regions were united only in 1940 when the Moldavian Soviet Socialist Republic was established, comprising present-day Transnistria and Moldova and that, until then, the territory belonged to Russia or Ukraine. (2013:11)

This indeed is the emphasis the Transnistrian elite places on the territory's history (Ignatiev 2018). The teaching of history has become a plank of the development of the identity, and hence politicised. Anna Volkova, a close adviser to President Smirnov, established the sub-faculty* of Transnistrian history and edited a historical atlas of Transnistria in 2005 (Dembinska and Iglesias 2013:6). At the same time, the established academic Nikolai Babilunga, who had himself come to Tiraspol uncomfortable with the pan-Romanian nationalism expounded in Chisinau in 1991 (Matsuzato 2008:115), had his pro-Moldovan sub-faculty 'History of the Fatherland' closed. Musteaja alleges:

> The younger generations in the territories under control of separatist authorities have been educated by history textbooks written in a spirit of hatred and mistrust of the Chisinau authorities and the population that identify themselves as Romanians. (2019:97)

He points to school history syllabuses from 2004, which have a heavy emphasis, particularly for older pupils, on Russian and then Transnistrian history and far less on Moldovan (Musteaja 2019:93).

---

*   This may translate better as 'department'.

Marandici pinpoints seemingly petty matters to support his theory as to the mechanism of establishing a Russian-leaning Transnistrian identity, such as adding 12 June as a Russia Day holiday in 2017. He observes of the 2018 celebrations:

> There was no trace of political loyalty toward Moldova in the public speeches held on that occasion. On the contrary, unconditional displays of allegiance to the external patron abounded. On June 12, the key parastate institutions hoisted the Russian flag and a large crowd including participants dressed in Moldovan and Ukrainian folk costumes carried an immense Russian tricolor on the main avenue of Tiraspol. (2020:20–21)

The holiday theme is also developed by Ala Șveț. Her analysis has "a theoretical framework consistent with a constructivist view of elite manipulation of public opinion during the nation-building process" (2012:1). She points to October Revolution Day, May Day and Victory Day, which are all "key Soviet holidays which are still celebrated in Transnistria, mostly by the older generation and members of the Communist Party" (2012:4).

In contrast to the positive view of Russian identity encouraged by the regime, Marandici talks of "folklorising" the Moldovan identity (2020:17), which, although he does not use the word, really amounts to trivialising it. He says "Folkloric traditions feature as the stereotypical cultural filling of this ethnic group" (Marandici 2020:18). Moldovan-language television programmes encourage this stereotyping. He goes so far as to argue that disloyal statements in Moldovan are left unedited as the naïve utterances of "Transnistria's 'hillbillies'" (Marandici 2020:18).

However, while the nationalities may be politicised, it seems they are recognised, and even respected, by the authorities. Bobick cites his 2008–09 interviews (2017:163), epitomised by a woman who told him, as she produced her Transnistrian passport which showed her as being Ukrainian, "I am a Ukrainian and recognised as one here. We have no dominant nationality and three different languages." This is the same multi-lingual theme that was emphasised by Smirnov when I interviewed him in May 2019 (Appendix B). Indeed, Transnistrian passports continued to distinguish between different nationalities long after other former Soviet states, including Russia and Moldova, had ceased the practice (Bobick 2014:9).

This analysis is consistent with Marandici's (2020) theme of politicising ethnicities. A Russian identity celebrated on a formally allocated day under that country's flag, which even those of other nationalities choose to participate in, unifies the Russian-centric nature of the Transnistrian identity, without totally eradicating the other nationalities. This is underlined when considering Shevchuk was an ethnic Ukrainian but still emphasised the role of the Russian language in unifying Transnistrian society (Marandici 2020:32). Transnistrian elites have never proclaimed it the 'rainbow nation', in the manner of the modern South African leadership, but one can see parallels.

On the theme of history and education as part of the Transnistrian identity, Wim van Meurs, from a perspective of unequivocal hostility to the Transnistrian regime, says:

Although historgraphical (sic) traditions of Transnistrian regionalism were paper-thin, a historical synthesis was constructed and textbooks were written…the very epitome of a cynical regime lusting for power and profits actually bothered to seek national legitimacy. (2015:205)

This perspective in substance, if not emphasis, is little different from that advanced by Marandici (2020). The political marginalisation of Moldovans is harder to square with a genuine multi-ethnic state. The percentage of ethnic Moldovans in parliament has ranged between 18% and 26% (Dembinska and Iglesias 2013:8; Protsyk 2008*). The effects of the heavy promotion of education in the Russian language, or at least not in what the Transnistrian elite regard as Romanian, is also a feature of Russification. When that language is written with Cyrillic letters, as it was in Soviet times, it is recognised as 'Moldovan'; written in Latin letters, as the schools saga (SubSect.4.1.2) shows, it is vilified. However, the Cyrillic-lettered language becomes even less than a minority language, having virtually no users outside Transnistria – Latin script for it is universal in Romania and Moldova – and too small a group use it with Cyrillic letters for written materials to be economically produced, resulting in a chronic shortage of such materials (Marandici 2020:14–15). A newspaper, *Adevărul Nistrean*, is produced, but as of November 2017, it had a circulation of just 1,500 (2020:15). Even artists are left with little choice but to express themselves in Russian if they are to have an audience (Dembinska 2013:9).

The constructivist approach to nationhood and 'imagined communities'

Şveţ's analysis is expressly said to be consistent with a constructivist perspective (2012:1). She draws on the work of Anthony Smith (2002:15), citing his argument that:

Without myths, memories and symbols by which to mark off group members from 'strangers,' and without the cultural elites to interpret and elaborate them, there can be no real ethnie.** Myths gave meaning and purpose to cultural entities, and a sense of attachment and belonging to mobilized populations. (2012:7)

Constructivist theory is generally regarded as an opposite to the more conservative view of the nation. Finkel contrasts the "proto-jingoist conservatism of the 'primordial nation' of the German nationalist school of thought" with:

The 'imagined community' of Benedict Anderson and the 'congruence principle' of Ernest Gellner to the militant anti-nationalism of Thongchai Winichakul's notion of the artificed 'geo-body' and the Marxist 'bottom-up' nation of Eric Hobsbawm. (2016:1)

---

*   Presumably updated as 2010 figures are referred to in this version.

**   This, according to Smith, himself is what combines with the pure congruence of state to create the nation state (1985:127).

The clearest expression of this argument is Anderson's contention (1991) that as people within a nation will not know most of their compatriots, any community on which the nation is based can only be imagined. Gellner (1983) sees nationalism as coming from the fabrication of recognition and at odds with the primordial idea that nations existed before their tangible manifestations. Indeed, they are formed primarily out of necessity. There is no other way for a modern and industrialised society to exist. Hobsbawm's view, which Finkel describes as Marxist (2016:1),* is encapsulated by the claim, or at least "initial working assumption" that "any sufficiently large body of people whose members regard themselves as members of a 'nation' will be treated as such" (Hobsbawm 2012:8).

The opposing primordial theory may largely have been consigned to history. Even those insisting it has some life in it do so tongue in cheek, particularly Ronald Suny: "Like the monster in slasher movies, just when you think that view is dead and buried, it springs up once more" (2004:22).**

Analysing the work of those who still do argue primordial theory is plausible, Coakley (2017) treats Steven Grosby as its best-known proponent. He bases his position on the link between humans and what they believe is their territory (Grosby 1995, cited by Coakley 2017:11). Indeed, Grosby (1994) cites Israel as an example representing an attachment between people and land going back to the ancient world. The Middle Eastern situation, though, is far from the norm, and while the Holy Land, to adopt a neutral term, undoubtedly has an immense pull for Jews and Palestinians, the relatively recent founding of Israel and the influx of immigrants as it was founded is far from the Germanic primordial concepts. Indeed, there are links between this form of nationalism and Nazism (Smith 1991), and Weaver (2011) specifically considers the doctrine in the light of Hitler's rantings in *Mein Kampf*.

The constructivist theories, particularly of Anderson (1990) and Gellner (1983), may provide a theoretical context for the development of a state such as Transnistria, where a nation can exist because it is what its inhabitants imagine and because there is some recognition, at least in *de facto* terms, of its existence. The debate among academics has moved from a constructivist versus primordial discussion to the nuances of constructivism. Even without the perhaps cheap shot of dismissing primordial theory as a creature of the far right, it is hard to see how in the modern world, where few countries are based on any attachment to a particular land, the nation is more than a pragmatic entity. There is, understandably, little discussion of the development of the Transnistrian identity in the context of these theories. Marandici (2020:4) explicitly adopts Anderson's (1990) definition of the nation as an "imagined political community" but does not explore it further. There is no good reason why Transnistria cannot be so regarded, but it is whether the elite has been successful in creating that image in the minds of the inhabitants that ultimately determines whether a Transnistrian nation has been built.

---

* Though much of Hobsbawm's work was undoubtedly influenced by Marxism, it is not immediately obvious why the arguments flowing from this assertion are.

** John Coakley (2017:1) identifies this striking quote.

1.2.3 HAS THE NATION-BUILDING SUCCEEDED?

Osipov and Vasilevich return to the topic of Transnistrian identity in a paper which focuses more than their previous work on the evaluation of nation-building, which they judge has been a "success story" (2019:13). They reassert concisely their 2017 conclusion that "the Transnistrian diversity policy can be described as predominantly symbolic production [sic]". However, they also recognise that "the system does not create an institutional basis for the construction and articulation of separate ethnic interests and demands" (Osipov and Vasilevich 2019:12), pointing to three senior non-Russian politicians.

A strong case that Transnistrian nation-building has been successful was made by Blakkisrud and Kolstø:

> Consequently, we would argue that both the time factor and the quest for recognition have contributed to pushing Transnistria away from being a 'black hole' and 'racketeer state,' and toward developing something akin to full-fledged statehood (minus official recognition). (2013:182)

In support of their premise, they point to both the creation of economic viability and the institutions of a state as well as national identity. The perceived identity represents "a supra-ethnic community spanning the ethnic divides" (Blakkisrud and Kolstø 2013:196).

In 2007, the then Transnistrian deputy foreign minister, Sergey Simonenko, claimed when interviewed by Blakkisrud (2013:198) that the civic nation-building, which he implicitly recognised had taken place, had been successful and that the post-USSR generation already identified itself as Transnistrian. There were echoes of that in my own interview on 29 May 2019 of former Foreign Minister Vladimir Yastrebchak in Tiraspol who told me, unsolicited and at the outset, his own identity was as a third-generation Transnistrian whose grandparents were buried there.

Dembinska and Iglesias' interviews indicate that Transnistrian Moldovans, as they describe the territory's inhabitants, were "responsive to this additional supra-ethnic identification" (2013:11). This is in keeping with my own discussions at Tiraspol's main university (SubSect.1.3.1).

Superficially, Marandici is a doubter of the existence of a Transnistrian nation, arguing:

> The repeated claim that a Transnistrian nation has already been born expresses the aspiration of the local elites to construct an impermanent, regional identity, which would legitimize the provisional functioning of the parastate until its expected annexation by the patron-state. (2020:33)

This analysis is over-theoretical. Even if the premise that nation-building expresses little more than elite aspirations is correct, that does not detract from the reality, which can be based on the evidence Marandici cites, that the process has taken place.

Even those who remain unequivocally condemnatory of Transnistria show a grudging willingness to accept that the process has succeeded. Wim van Meurs (2015:200) states: "The puzzling question is why the regime bothered with nation-building at all." Once stripped of its rhetorical hostility to the Tiraspol regime, van Meurs' question virtually answers itself. If that regime wanted a lasting power, it could only achieve it with a degree of consensus. The Russian army's presence could not create that. The nation-building exercise gives a degree of legitimisation to the exercise of power. Without that legitimacy, the step from autonomy to statehood would be unthinkable.

While there is force in the arguments of Marandici (2020) and van Meurs (2015), the fact that the nation-building has been initiated by the elite does not detract from the success identified by Osipov and Vasilevich (2019) and Blakkisrud and Kolstø (2013) and in my own discussions. Returning to Guibernau's (1996) test, the common culture component of nationhood, which derives from identity, has been met, and that stepping stone to statehood is securely in place.

1.3 WHAT DO TRANSNISTRIANS (AND MOLDOVANS) THINK TODAY?

Against the background of a history and identity considered in the previous sections, the next issue to consider in relation to the existence of a Transnistrian nation and the path to statehood is what the population actually wants, or whether, as Guibernau (1996) puts it, there is a common project for the future. The regime's aims, which presumably reflect its aspirations, are apparent from its actions, including the nation-building projects, as well as its expressions epitomised by Foreign Minister Vitaly Ignatiev's compendium of arguments for independence (2018). It is just as important to consider the views of non-elite Transnistrians in this context as their perceptions largely reflect the success or otherwise of the nation-building. As the remainder of Moldova will be affected by any changes in status, some regard has also to be had to opinion on the Right-Bank of the Dniestr.

This section will consider the opinion of Transnistrians, not just on questions directly relating to nationhood and independence but also on a broader range of issues with a view to establishing both what they want for the future and how they perceive their nation at the moment.

1.3.1 MY OWN ETHNOGRAPHIC RESEARCH

Discussions at the university (May 2016)

In May 2016, the Tiraspol Shevchenko University's department of social science kindly arranged for me to have a discussion with a group of twelve teaching and support staff. All but one were female, most were under about 35 and only one, who I found out later was a secretary, was able or confident enough to address me directly in English. I tried initially to create a dialogue about Transnistrian life rather than political issues, asking, "What makes you happy about life in Transnistria?" A lack of pollution was cited first, and then, more interestingly, a woman of about 30 said they could bring up their children – she had two – without fear of the state taking them away, which she believed happened routinely in Western Europe.* I tested this belief with others in the room, particularly one who said she taught social work. It did turn out that there were cases in Transnistria where children were taken from parents but only in extreme circumstances. I gently suggested that that was also the case in Britain and probably most of Europe, but this was met with scepticism.

Turning the conversation to what they did not like about their lives, the immediate response was that there were many things they could not do because of the frozen conflict. Travel was more difficult than they would like it to be, and several participants, without any prompting from me, expressed the view that this problem would ease if Transnistria had independence. The question of whether a union with Russia was desirable was not raised by any of the interviewees, nor me. There were no complaints about health services or education or even availability of goods. The conversation was then dominated by an older woman who seemed intent on giving me a favourable impression of the country and discouraging anyone else from doing otherwise. I thought it unlikely that anyone was giving these answers out of fear. People were able to drift in and out of the discussion as they wanted. No one, other than me, was taking notes. I suspected I was being given a 'rosy' picture of the country but that the motive was patriotism rather than anything more sinister.

Discussions at a youth club (May 2019)

Club 19 is a youth club which meets most nights in central Tiraspol. It was established as an alternative platform for youth in 2012. It is attended by teenagers and those a little older who drink tea, practise languages, play games (including solving imaginary murder mysteries), strum guitars and sing on a karaoke machine (Johnson 2017 and personal observation).

In May 2019, I arranged with Alexandra Telpis, one of the club's organisers, to visit the club for a Tuesday evening session, when news is discussed. I went with my interpreter. We decided merely to observe and not attempt to ask questions or join in, fearing doing so might affect the behaviours of those we were observing. We were not introduced, and if the kids were surprised at the presence of a middle-aged foreigner and his younger, but still definitely not teenaged, interpreter, they were too polite to show it.

About a dozen attendees read out cuttings in a dimly lit but freely accessible basement.

---

* There had been recent reports of Norwegian social workers taking five children from a Romanian immigrant mother because she had used mild corporal punishment. I could not establish if these were the source of this belief. See http://www.bbc.co.uk/news/magazine-36026458 (29 June 19).

There was little sign of subversion; the sharpest comment in response to an article on the growth of churches in Russia was, "Soon Russia will be one big church and we will be one big Sheriff." Someone did remark in response, "Are we allowed to say things like that?" but it seemed to be in jest and there were no furtive glances at me. Although a lot of the kids had tattoos and after 45 minutes there was a cigarette break, they generally seemed better behaved and less inclined to any form of rebellion than a similar-aged group in England would be. This reflected my view of Transnistria having a somewhat conformist society, where political outlooks fall within quite a narrow compass. Of course, I could not say with complete confidence whether a fear of the authorities was preventing robust criticisms being made, but I was inclined to think that there was genuinely little urge to criticise.

Discussions at the university (October 2019)

In October 2019, the foreign language faculty at the university arranged a focus group of students for me to question. It was unfortunately not a representative sample of the population. Strikingly, all fourteen participants were female – I was told that hardly any boys study modern languages – young, probably 18 to 22, well educated and primarily Russian-speaking, although I had asked for Romanian speakers to be included. Only three had been brought up in Tiraspol. In response to my question, "Do you think your country should be independent, part of Russia or part of Moldova?" the positions got seven, five and one vote respectively. This result was close to that of other research, though it may be that if I had interviewed more Romanian speakers, the last figure would have risen. Fortunately, the reunification supporter* was one of the more confident participants and explained her view: "Moving closer to Europe would give us more opportunities and a better way of life." The most vociferous independence-supporting girl said, "I want my country to be part of the world. Putin has strange internal policies, but he does make it easier for us to study in Russia." One favouring union with Russia said, "We are closer to Russian traditional ways."

I raised other topics in an unstructured manner. I was handicapped by the shyness of most of the group, the dialogue being dominated by the three confident young women who articulated opinions on the future of the territory. On human trafficking, no one had any experience, however indirect, and tellingly one girl did remark, "It might have been a problem in the 1990s but isn't now." There was a general feeling that the police were susceptible to bribery, and one girl talked of her father having to pay money to the police when he had problems with his car. Driving test examiners would pass poor drivers who would pay bribes of US$50 or US$75 – the discussion focused more on the amount rather than the fact of bribery. When I raised the subject of why there were so many prisoners, the sole example I got of someone being imprisoned was from the girl who had spoken up for independence who said her brother's classmate's father had

---

*   I don't give even first names here for reasons discussed below.

received a ten-year sentence for something he had done while in a senior position in the customs service.

1.3.2 OTHER EVIDENCE OF WHAT TRANSNISTRIANS WANT

The starting point in ascertaining Transnistrians' opinion on the territory's future is the 17 September 2006 referendum, where 97.1% voted for independence. The results were consistent throughout the territory, with 98.2% in favour in almost entirely Russian-speaking Tiraspol and the lowest support (94.7%) in Dubasari, where more Moldovan is spoken (Kireev 2007). In a December 1991 referendum, 98% had voted for independence (Schwirtz 2006).

The results of these referendums have largely been mirrored in other research, including my own, as discussed above. A February 2011 survey showed that the support for independence remained overwhelming, if a little short of the referendum figures: 89.8% said they would vote for independence, "If a referendum under UN auspices on granting sovereignty and independence to the republic were held in Transnistria next Sunday" (*Dniester* 2011). In response to a separate question, 8% favoured unification with Moldova and 4.5% with Ukraine. There was considerable division on whether Transnistria should in both the short and the long term aim for independence or unification with Russia: 45.3% thought in ten years it should be independent and 42.9% a part of Russia (*Dniester* 2011).

In June 2016, the Russian Public Opinion Research Centre* polled 1,200 respondents** on political matters, including the upcoming presidential election, about which its answers were largely reflected in the outcome. The poll asked about wishes for the future of the territory. In line with all other research, there was a vast majority against reuniting with Moldova, which just 2% supported, with 86% in favour of becoming part of the Russian Federation (*Sputnik Mundo* 2016).

Research into other aspects of Transnistrian opinion

Research at Shevchenko University was conducted by Natalia Cojocaru (2006) in February 2002. She, facing a similar demographic and linguistic distortion to mine, conducted 35 in-depth interviews with students at the university aged 20 to 25.

The purpose of Cojocaru's interviews was to establish how interviewees perceived the 1992 conflict and its aftermath. There is no statistical presentation of answers. A series of quotes from younger students suggests a strong feeling that the Transnistrian purpose in that conflict was justified. A majority agreed with the statement that "Transnistria is a multinational republic, regardless if it is not recognised" (Cojocaru

---

* The centre appears to have official approval in Transnistria, conducting the sole exit poll during the 2016 election.

** This is an astonishingly high number in a population of less than 500,000.

2002:268). The main theme which can be extracted from Cojocaru's work is a feeling of nationalism concerning Transnistria that seems to be shared by most of its inhabitants.

In 2010, O'Loughlin, Toal and Chamberlain-Creangă (2013) interviewed 912 subjects in Transnistria and 1,102 in Moldova. In both territories there was a belief that the Soviet system was the best. This was particularly so among older people, with 72% in Transnistria and 57% in Moldova so answering (O'Loughlin, Toal and Chamberlain-Creangă 2013:54). The overall figures across all ages were 51% and 41%, respectively, but these were considerably higher than for those favouring any other system. Even among the younger group, only 40% and 45% preferred Western democracy. Furthermore, 7% and 12% thought the current systems in the respective countries – notionally, and largely in reality, democracies – were best. Around half in Moldova and 70% in Transnistria thought the collapse of the USSR was a bad thing, with the greatest agreement coming from those in the worst economic circumstances (O'Loughlin, Toal and Chamberlain-Creangă 2013:55). Generally, Transnistrians gave more positive answers to questions about economic situations: 64% of Moldovans said they only had enough money to buy food, as opposed to durables, and 23% not even enough for that; the comparable figures in Transnistria were 27% and 7% (O'Loughlin, Toal and Chamberlain-Creangă 2013:47).

Tatiana Cojocari, in extensive opinion research which avoided direct political questions, ascertained that when asked to identify themselves personally, irrespective of ethnic origin, 37.3% said they were Transnistrian, 35.7% Russian and only 14% Moldovan (2019:48). The proportion who answered Transnistrian seemed surprisingly low in view of the intensity of the nation-building project, but this is explained by the *Russkii Mir* elements of that project. As the regime identifies so strongly with Russia, it is likely to regard the creation of split Transnistrian-Russian identities as a success.

Marta Melnykevych (2014) conducted survey research on 190 student subjects at the Tiraspol College of Business and Service on topics mostly to do with Transnistrian identity. The outcome of her research led her to state:

> Based on my sample, I argue that people do not respond positively to the state's nation-building policies, as Transnistrians are not encouraged via education, media, tokens of banal nationalism, and political elite to cultivate their own identity. (2014:82)

This view is inconsistent with any other commentators' and with the other research findings. The statement that Transnistrians are not encouraged by those factors, particularly the political elite, suggests a virtual blindness to a well-documented process, and this blindness forms the basis for an unsustainable argument.

O'Loughlin, Toal and Kolossov (2015) did similar work across Transnistria and South Ossetia and Abkhazia. One theme that emerged across the three *de facto* states was the feeling that the collapse of the USSR was to be regretted: 75% of respondents took that view in South Ossetia and around 70% in Transnistria. The fundamental question of "What is your preferred political option to the final status of your republic?" led to contrasting responses: 81% of South Ossetians preferred integration with Russia, while 59% of Abkhazians preferred independence.*

1.3.3 RESEARCH IN MOLDOVA

Moldovan attitudes towards Transnistria were thoroughly surveyed in 2012, with 1,097 respondents and answers broken down by age, sex, language, class, residence and education (Survey Based Research 2012). 85% said Moldova needed Transnistria in its composition (Survey Based Research 2012:41); this figure fell to 78% for Russian speakers, but there were no other significant demographic-based variants. There seemed little interest in the 5+2 negotiations, with 37% not having heard of them (Survey Based Research 2012:5). About 80% considered resolving the Transnistrian issue important, and 44% said the failure to do so affected the well-being of their family (Survey Based Research 2012:44).

A total of 1,551 Moldovans were polled by Gallup and Baltic Surveys funded by the US Agency for International Development (Alisauskiene 2013:2) and were asked, "What do you think the future of Transnistria should be?" 64% responded that it should be a part of Moldova with no special status, and 21% answered that it should be an autonomous entity within Moldova (2013:53). Only 7% thought it should be independent and 2% part of Russia. The pollsters compared this with nineteen similar surveys dating back to April 2006. Except for the first poll, where 80% had said there should be no special status for Transnistria, the results had been stable over the years (Alisauskiene 2013:53).

1.3.4 THE EFFICACY OF OPINION RESEARCH

It is natural for anyone facing research that shows others' opinions do not accord with their own outlook to question the veracity of that research. That was the reaction of the deputy director of the Moldovan Bureau for Reintegration when I put to him in a 2019 interview (SubSect.5.2.2 and Appendix D) that the overwhelming majority of Transnistrians did not want to be governed from Chisinau. Even before I referred to the 2006 referendum, he dismissed it as "so-called" and made clear that he attached little weight to other research. When conducting opinion research in Abkhazia in 2010, O'Loughlin, Kolossov and Toal (2011) received a similar, if more measured, reaction from Temuri Yakobashvili, the then Georgian reintegration minister:

> Opinion polls in these kinds of areas are very tricky not only because of the informa-tion environment. Who will be asking the questions? And how will these questions be formulated, in a society where you have fear? I mean if you conducted an opinion poll

---

* The results included 'don't knows' and refusals to answer as free-standing percentages, so the figures given for specific answers are in a sense an understatement.

in the Soviet Union, you would get very funny results. People are not really expressing themselves freely, and they will be very much scared to answer the question properly if they are not sure that nothing is going to happen to them if their answer will not fit some kind of official policy. Official policy is that we don't need anybody else. We are fine with Russians. (2011:5)

With perhaps such considerations in mind, O'Loughlin, Kolossov and Toal (2011) accepted there were "legitimate concerns about trust and professionalism", leading them to employ a "highly reputable" Russian public opinion company, the Levada Centre, to conduct the survey in Abkhazia. It hired and trained eight local people to do the questioning in Sukhumi (O'Loughlin et al. 2011:10). A further eighteen interviewers, mainly school teachers with knowledge of the relevant local languages, were used in areas away from the capital. O'Loughlin et al. (2011) believed their status would be such that respondents would feel secure that no harm would come to them as a consequence of answering questions.

In relation to her research, Cojocaru observes, "Carrying out surveys in Transnistria represents a challenge. The governing elite…tends to be authoritarian" (2006:237). Ten of the first group she approached for interviews refused, but she ultimately found sufficient willing participants and does not specify whether it was fear of authorities or just lack of interest that appeared to spark the refusals.

O'Loughlin, Toal and Chamberlain-Creangă (2013:44) asked their interviewers to assess how open the interviewees seemed to have been. In Transnistria, 89% were judged as very open or rather open, compared with 86% in Moldova.

Melnykevych explains how she dealt with this in her research:

A lot of people, when asked directly, usually claim that everything is normal and fair in matters concerning inter-ethnic affairs. However, then during the flow of the conversation they open up and tell more stories with some details of their inter-ethnic coexistence. (2014:38)

A reluctance to discuss difficult matters with a stranger is a normal feature of human nature and not necessarily the result of official interference. There was a contrast between my 2019 discussions, where I was frustrated by a lack of dynamic dialogue, to those in 2016, where most participants were anxious to say something. That contrast was probably the consequence of an older, more confident group having been gathered on the earlier occasion, rather than any attempt at official influence. In 2019 when I asked for names, no one hesitated to provide them. I was, however, told by the university's visiting Fulbright Scholar from Los Angeles, who had attended and contributed to the session, that I should not use participants' names as it could cause trouble for them. While that did not accord with my own perception, nor I assume that of the participants, I have veered on the side of caution and have omitted names.

The concern that there could be adverse consequences for speaking to researchers is probably stronger in Right-Bank Moldova. This was seen in the O'Loughlin, Toal and Chamberlain-Creangă research (2013) and in the 2018 poll there. In answer to the question, "Are people in Moldova afraid or not to openly express their political views?" only 18% of respondents said that nobody was afraid (Alisauskiene 2013:21). That figure had risen over the years, being around 14% until 2010 and consistently higher ever since. Curiously, the possible fear seems to have increased since the end of the rule of President Voronin (SubSect.1.1.3), who was often regarded in the West as oppressive, because, although democratically elected, he had been a member of the Communist Party hierarchy in the Soviet Union (Alisauskiene 2013:41).

1.3.5 THE EFFECT OF OPINION ON THE PRESENT SITUATION

However much the Chisinau government sees itself as the champion of the Transnistrian people (SubSect.5.2.1), multiple referendums, formal surveys and my discussions and observations show that only a small minority of those people want Moldovan involvement in the territory.

The other inferences that can be drawn from opinion research in the territory are of a reasonably harmonious relationship between people and government. I did not hear any serious criticisms of the government in the discussions described in this chapter or with any other Transnistrian, except the human rights lawyer Stepan Popovskiy (SubSect.3.3.1).

The relative consistency of outlook in Transnistria, Abkhazia and South Ossetia point towards similar aspirations in all three territories. However, the economic conditions, particularly in desperately poor South Ossetia (SubSect.5.2.3), and the fact that relations between those other states and Tbilisi are more hostile than between Transnistria and Chisinau are significant distinguishing factors in the context of potential independence. The tendency towards regret about the Soviet Union's demise is consistent with support for unification with Russia. An essential feature of the Soviet Union was, of course, rule from Moscow, and the nationalistic urges in the territories do not seem to lead their inhabitants to have disdain for such rule.

Conversely, the fundamental difference between Moldovan and Transnistrian attitudes does not bode well for a consensual settlement. For Transnistrians, though, the desire for independence is politically all-consuming, while in Moldova it is of less concern, as shown by the survey research and my own discussions. Moldovan opinion is of less importance to the resolution of the Transnistrian situation than that in Transnistria, as Moldova's inhabitants are less affected; even those who claimed it would harm their families' welfare probably had national pride in mind rather than any personal consequences.

The clear desire for separation from Moldovan is consistent with the attempts at nation-building by the Transnistrian elite, discussed in the previous section, having succeeded. Without such a desire, there could be no case for separation. While desiring to secede from a state does not, outside the abstract analysis of primary right theorists

(SubSect.5.1.4), of itself give any right to do so, the existence of such desire is an essential stepping stone on the route to such an outcome.

1.4 CONCLUSION: IS THERE A TRANSNISTRIAN NATION?

The three previous sections provide support for the contention that a Transnistrian nation now exists. The tenuous and intermittent historical ties with the rest of Moldova are a basis on which it can be fairly asserted the two territories do not form a natural fit. Moldovan history has been tied on many occasions to that of Romania, and that is reflected in the primacy of the Romanian language there. Conversely, Transnistria has been far more closely linked to Russia and Ukraine. The inclusion of Transnistria in 1940 in the Moldovan SSR was not a reflection of any natural link other than geographic proximity and was a consequence of the short-lived Molotov-Ribbentrop Pact.

A war of independence in 1992, in which around 1,000 Transnistrians died, showed that an identity existed then; otherwise, there would have been no motive to fight. Nearly three decades of *de facto* independence has underlined that separation. A fully fledged government and electoral system, over which Chisinau has no influence, has continued throughout that time. Transnistria has enjoyed more stable government than Moldova. In ways that have been indicated in this chapter, and are more fully developed in the next, it has been at least as successful as Moldova economically. There is little reason why, with that background, Transnistrians would wish to be part of Moldova.

While the history alone may lead to the often-cited observation of Mitrofanova (2015:203) that there is a certainty among Transnistrians that they are not from the Right-Bank of the Dniestr, the evidence is strong that the government's nation-building efforts have been successful in creating a positive identity. This is not an identity based on ethnicity, a term that itself is far from clear. Bowring's argument (2014:24) that the Transnistrians may constitute a people is a pragmatic way of considering where the population have arrived at. However, as his reasons for their being a people flows from their identity, the argument in this context becomes circular. Better, and more pragmatic still, is to accept the evidence of a common identity, without consideration of ethnicity in any guise, as being enough to lead to nationhood.

The primacy given to Russian language, history and culture is part of that identity: clearly there is some Moscow-driven influence, and Cojocari's (2019) findings show that many Transnistrians identify as Russian. The military, political and, as will be seen, economic support from Russia has helped, perhaps enabled, the creation of Transnistria in its present form. The nation-building effort, however, has been locally led and is consistent with an elite that wants to have the privileges and prestige of running a country presiding over a largely supportive population.

The preponderance of opinion favouring the severing of ties with Chisinau, as seen in referendums, my own discussions and others' survey research, is consistent with the nation-building having succeeded in achieving a population with that outlook. There are many Transnistrians who see the most desirable long-term aim as union with Russia. That does not detract from the existence now of a separate, closely identified Transnistrian nation. That position may be inconvenient for those who argue for the reunification of Moldova. However, Transnistria is a territory which has had complete autonomy for thirty years and whose population regard themselves as being of that territory, not Moldova. Arguments that a Transnistrian nation does not exist have no basis in reality, and the existence of that nation provides a stepping stone towards full independence.

CHAPTER TWO

TRANSNISTRIA AS AN ECONOMICALLY VIABLE NATION

In considering the potential for a territory to become independent, regard must be had to the viability of that territory's economy. While in international law surprisingly little weight is given to this topic, it is of little benefit to a population to govern themselves if there are not sufficient resources available to create a standard of living at least commensurate with that of other states in similar geographical positions. The disaster of South Sudan, granted independence in 2011 and now far poorer than even impoverished Sudan (*IndexMundi* 2020), from which it broke away, is a prime example of how independence in the wrong circumstances can be economically disadvantageous to the vast majority of the population. Also significant in this context is the very strong correlation, particularly if the oil-rich but generally oppressively governed Arab Gulf states are disregarded, between a country's economic strength and the freedoms its people enjoy (Balakrishnan and Heintz 2018).

This chapter considers the economic challenges Transnistria faces now and would as an independent state and explores its viability. A full study of the Transnistrian economy would be a thesis in itself, so the chapter focuses on the issues that are most important and distinctive in establishing whether the independence of the territory is economically viable. Historical context is provided by considering how it has separated economically from the rest of Moldova. A dependence on remittances from émigrés and on Russia clearly undermines any claim to self-sufficiency, if not viability, and these are explored along with the internal workings of the economy. Although the industrial base is of some significance, more attention is paid to the politically influential Sheriff conglomerate There is an examination of the government's handling of the economy and controls on banking and the possibility of money laundering, which is of particular importance in the context of a territory that has suffered allegations that it is a centre of criminality, and the management of resources as well as their existence is an important factor in the success of an economy. Currency and money supply, including a possible excursion into cryptocurrencies, fall within this category. The territory's diminishing population impacts on the economy, even if bringing the arguably questionable benefit of remittances. These strands, when pulled together, provide evidence to enable consideration of whether Transnistria is economically viable; to conclude that it is; and to examine the further advantageous effects independence and a reduction in international isolation would have on that viability.

Economic viability is not a precise term. Gertrude Schroeder treats it as meaning "the capability to exist and develop as a separate state in a world of highly economically interdependent states" (1992:549). This she contrasted with it wrongly "often being taken to mean potential economic self-sufficiency based on near self-sufficiency in supplies of energy and other natural resources". The point about self-sufficiency not being a basis for viability is obvious, illustrated by reference to Liechtenstein and China (Schroeder 1992:550), neither of which have that quality. All countries are dependent on trade, and Schroeder oversimplifies the position she sees as opposing hers. Indeed, Isachenko and Schlichte (2007:23) state that Transnistria is "not self-sufficient but viable". Schroeder did not, for instance, attempt to build on the definitions given in studies on the economic viability of Palestine, culminating in Elias Tuma's (1978:102) statement that, in an economic context, a society is considered viable "if its economic characteristics permit it to experience sustained growth and rising welfare per capita" (partially cited by Bull 1976:143). Milica Bookman (1992:145), considering the issue in the context of secession, adopts what she describes as a "simple working definition" that the "viability of a region implies the ability to sustain growth in the aftermath of secession at the pre-independence levels", which in the case of seceding nations should include an "ability to sustain growth in the aftermath of secession at the pre-independence levels" (Bookman 1992:2).

These definitions are not easy to reconcile but have the common feature of growth or development. Bookman's has the attractions of putting the levels required to achieve viability into the context of a particular secession, rather than just against a vague global standard. I adapt that slightly to treat it as meaning a country which is organised so that the population can enjoy a standard of living not significantly worse than that which can be expected in the region in which the country is located; and this is close to a test not only for viability but also, as posited at the beginning of this part, for whether independence would benefit the populace. A narrower comparison with only the previously dominant state would militate against many potential independencies where the new state is economically weaker than the existing one, most obviously Palestine itself but also, for instance, Northern Cyprus or even Quebec, one of Canada's poorest provinces (Van Praet 2012).

The reality is that many countries are not remotely economically self-sufficient, notably Israel, which would not be able to survive, let alone enable most of its inhabitants to have virtually a Western European standard of living (World Bank 2020a), without US economic backing. Micro-state countries such as Monaco, San Marino and Schroeder's (1992) example Liechtenstein, have economies almost entirely dependent on the benevolence of a relatively large and rich neighbour and are viable without being self-sufficient. Without a combination of Australian, New Zealand and Chinese aid, most of the sovereign Pacific island nations would not be viable (Dziedzic 2018). This is in contrast to 'failed states', a term which has entered the vocabulary of international relations in the last few decades although 'fragile states', which admits of degrees of failure, has largely replaced it. These have become almost terms of art. Those that attract the label, perhaps most obviously South Sudan, Somalia and Yemen (Fund for Peace 2020), have little in the way of a centralised economy. It is these countries, although fully recognised in international law, which are not viable in that the state does nothing to provide any meaningful physical or economic security for the vast majority of the populace. World Bank figures (2020a) rank Moldova's economy as one of the most fragile in Europe, only marginally ahead of Serbia and Russia; Ukraine is not assessed.

The practical manifestations of a state's viability may be in the provision of basic human needs, such as housing, healthcare and education, as well as a police force with some effectiveness and a judicial system that can uphold the rule of law. 'Fragile states'* have a common feature of not providing these things for their populace, at least in part because of the devastating weakness of their economies, invariably combined with bad governance. The discussion in this chapter should be considered in the context not just of whether Transnistria's economy has risen above the level of these unfortunate countries, but, as will be considered in Chapter 4, whether it has succeeded in meeting basic human needs in its present status. The case for independence is strengthened if the economy is strong enough to enable it to continue doing so should that status change.

Irena Sabor considers the question of Transnistrian viability in depth, concluding:

Juxtaposition of the vulnerability scores and resilience assessments show the low potential of economic viability in the Transnistrian economy. As comes from the research, the economy is generally non-viable but made subsistent by efforts of its patron state – Russian Federation, as well as by virtue of income from heavy industry, exports, remittances and shadow economy. (2012:5)

Sabor was most influenced by Bookman's (1993) definition of viability. Although her approach distinguishes subsistent from viable, it can be argued that what she identifies as making an economy subsistent in fact makes it viable as well. It is only on the basis of little-adopted definitions of self-sufficiency being an element of economic viability that Transnistrian dependence on Russia defeats the case for viability.

---

*   See the discussion and examples at Global Policy Forum (2013).

2.1 THE DEVELOPMENT OF THE TRANSNISTRIAN ECONOMY

2.1.1 THE DIVERGENCE AND INTERACTION OF THE ECONOMY WITH MOLDOVA'S

During Soviet times, the bulk of Moldovan heavy industry was in Transnistria and the territory remains more industrialised than the rest of Moldova, where agriculture plays a greater role (World Bank 1995). Shortly before the USSR broke up, consideration was given to ascribing free economic zone status to Tiraspol and Bender (Kolstø and Edemsky 1995:157), perhaps along similar lines to Kaliningrad. This might have resulted in a more self-sufficient Transnistrian economy. Even Moldova initially agreed to exempt Transnistrian trade from taxation. The hostilities between the two parts of Moldova made the agreement of formalised privilege for Transnistria impractical, and the economies drifted apart.

Economically, the independent Moldova had a disastrous start. Its first president, Mircea Snegur, renounced communism (Shafir 1998) and attempted to rapidly move Moldova to a market economy. This led to an ongoing economic crisis that left much of the country in poverty (CSSR 1998). The denationalisation of land was particularly counterproductive. While two million landowners may have emerged, only those who had experience of collective farming were able to successfully adapt to this status (Shafir 1998:117). There was a fall of 21% in the GDP and a 2,200% increase in prices (World Bank 1994:11). By 2000, the average monthly wage in Moldova was US$32 (Quinlan 2002) and the per capita GDP (World Bank 2020a) was US$440. By 2019, the latter had increased to US$4,498 (World Bank 2020a).

The lack of coordination between the Chisinau and Tiraspol economies, which could have complemented each other, has probably prevented each fulfilling its potential. Other than Gazprom, discussed below, few businesses conspicuously operate in both territories, the exceptions being Andy's Pizza chain and its slightly more upmarket sister brand *La Placinte* and some mobile phone companies. Nadja Douglas and Stefan Wolff (2018) considered the relationship between the two economies. They argue in essence that the 40 years in which the territories were treated as a single entity within the USSR should have provided a "natural basis for rapprochement, which might have resulted in healthier economies for both" (2018:7). That, however, did not occur, with Transnistria quickly and forcefully "decoupling" its economy by establishing its own central bank, currency and customs controls along the Dniestr. They argue the consequence was that "During the 1990s and early 2000s, much of the trade there was unregulated, and the region was a place for unrecorded foreign trade, tax evasion, and smuggling" (Douglas and Woolf 2018:7).

Despite their differences with Tiraspol, Moldovan authorities have generally not sought to obstruct Transnistrian trade. On Moldova's entry to the World Trade Organization in 2001, its parliament adopted Government Decision 1001 – "On the declaration of goods by economic operators from the eastern districts of the Republic Moldova" (UNECE 2017:72) – to create a workable legal framework for Transnistria to export and import goods. This was to keep the policies in line with Moldova's "international obligations for controlling and keeping evidence for external economic transactions". The WTO (2000: para 43) in its report considering Moldovan membership had noted:

> As regards issues related to foreign trade commitments, Moldova succeeded in finding common ground with the Transnistrian authorities. The representative of Moldova stated that Moldova had signed a special protocol on customs cooperation with the Transnistria region that foresaw mutual elaboration of customs policy, exchange of statistics and facilitation of border measures.

This has provided a largely workable framework. The Transnistrians were given a waiver from paying customs charges (Vahl and Emerson 2004:13). In 2003, the Moldovan government attempted to introduce a tax on Transnistrian exports to Ukraine: in practice, the lack of control Chisinau exerts over Transnistria made such a tax unenforceable (Borsi 2007:47). In August 2005, the Chisinau government introduced 'C-type' certificates to facilitate Transnistrian exports to Ukraine (Gudim 2006:3). The politics of these positions were opaque, but it is likely that imposing customs duties on Transnistrian goods entering Moldova would be seen as an implicit recognition of the separation of the territories, whereas those leaving Transnistria for Ukraine are – on Chisinau's position – crossing Moldova's international border. Milakovsky points out that the lack of industrial exports from Moldova means it does not have businesses to which Transnistria presents meaningful competition, and hence there is a "limited economic lobby against integrating Transnistrian firms into the Moldovan customs space" (2019:5).

The UN's European Economic Commission in its report on barriers to Moldovan trade (UNECE 2017:71) states that Transnistrian businesses show a strong preference for transporting goods by road. This could be either through Moldova and Romania or Ukraine and often in combination with rail for goods destined for Belarus, Russia or Turkey. More difficulties were actually identified in respect of using Ukraine's Odessa port (UNECE 2017:72, 80) and on arrival in Russia (UNECE 2017:79) than in passing through Moldova. This is in the absence of any viable airport in Transnistria, and no reference was made to air-freighting through Chisinau or any other airport.[*]

Goods exported from Transnistria do require Moldovan documentation, which has been issued by the Chisinau authorities since 1996 (Vahl and Emerson 2004:13), even before Moldova's accession to the WTO. However, the UN report (UNECE 2017) says there was an increase in delays and losses at Russian customs, who may make no distinction between Transnistrian and other Moldovan goods, after the 2014 association agreement between Moldova and the EU. Wait times for goods destined for the EU were typically 3–5 days, less than half of those for other destinations but still meriting an assessment by business as

---

[*]   There is a daily cargo flight from Chisinau to Bucharest (Spotterguide 2020).

"rather difficult" (UNECE 2017:76). The report refers to what it euphemistically describes as "informal payments" being required at several stages of the process. This is not with reference to Transnistria, though, and it is largely Moldovan customs officers who "are prepared to revise their assessment upon the provision" of such payments (UNECE 2017:49).

This divergence of the economies is important to the Transnistrian case for independence, and the limited interaction does nothing to detract from that case. While Transnistria is not self-sufficient, the lack of dependence on Chisinau is important. The cooperation over customs documentation would become an irrelevance upon independence, as Transnistria could then deal with this without outside help. There is trade between the territories, particularly of energy provided by the Transnistrian Moldavskaya power plant, as discussed below. Both sides have recognised the desirability of this trade despite the political tensions: there is no reason for it not to continue were Transnistria no longer legally a part of Moldova.

2.1.2 THE STATE OF THE ECONOMY

Since the end of the presidency of Igor Smirnov, there has been a tightening of controls on internal corruption and foreign money laundering (SubSect.1.3.3). While welcome improvements, these have not given tangible economic benefits to the territory's inhabitants. Emigration (SubSect.2.4.2) remains a significant problem, and the economy subsists on Russian subsidies and remittances from émigrés. The Transnistrian rouble fell by around 40% between 2015 and 2018, largely as a result of deliberate actions by the Pridnestrovian Republican Bank (PRB) (Ernst 2017).

Statistical information about the state of the Transnistrian economy comes in the form of bulletins from the PRB. There is no consistent pattern to the figures released, which can make identifying trends difficult. In the later years of the Shevchuk government, which ended in 2016, there was a distinct decline. GDP fell from US$1,048 million in 2013 to US$1,005 million in 2015, equating to a per capita figure of around US$2,200. During that time, though, there was an increase in industrial production from US$738 to US$795 million (Lupusor *et al*. 2015:4).* Some of the fall in GDP may be accounted for by depopulation, but the average monthly wage also fell from US$336.50 to US$300, which is still significantly more than the rest of Moldova and indeed Ukraine.

The rouble was devalued in June 2017 from about 11 to the US$ to 16.1 (see SubSect.2.2.2). The PRB claims this benefited the economy in helping expand exports and removing the nascent dual currency system caused by keeping the rouble at an artificial high (PRB 2018). Inflation was then running at about 5%. The bank's bulletins consistently express the view that the economy is improving: it is impossible to say whether that is the result of political pressure. It is to be borne in mind that any guarantee of independence of the bank or its governor is a noticeable omission from the constitution (Sect.3.1.1), which calls into question the credibility of the figures its bulletins contain.

---

* Directly comparable figures for subsequent years are not available.

Industry and privatisations

Leaving aside the ubiquitous Sheriff group, discussed in Sect.2.3, Transnistria has four major industrial resources: the MSW Ribnita steelworks, Tirotex textiles, itself partially owned by Sheriff, the Ribnita cement plant and the Moldavskaya GRES power plant (Całus 2013:1), all dating from the Soviet era. In proportion to the size and population of the country, this a large amount of heavy industry, and these companies reach a variety of international markets. Tirotex exported around US$163 million – 70% of its total output – in 2011, largely to Italy, Russia and Ukraine (Tirotex 2020). I was assured by former Foreign Minister Vladimir Yastrebchak in an interview in Tiraspol on 27 May 2019 that it operates tighter quality controls and produces better products than any factory in Moldova. The steelworks exports primarily to the US, Germany and Italy (Całus 2013:2). The cement plant's main market was in Russia. It was reported in the international cement manufacturing press in 2015 to be upgrading its working plant (CW Group 2015). The power plant, in which a controlling stake is held by the Russian nationalised company Metalloinvest, supplied around 50% of Right-Bank Moldovan power as well as most of Transnistria's (Całus 2013:2).

According to the PRB, in 2017, the electricity industry accounted for 30.8% of Transnistrian industrial output, ferrous metals 29.3%, and food 13.3%. Forestry, despite the potential for developing this, was less than 0.1%. Textiles were not specifically identified but probably made up a significant amount of the 13.3% ascribed to other light industry. The total industrial production from January to November 2017* was worth 9,972 million roubles or just over 11 billion annually, around US$683 million (PRB 2018: Table 1.2). This figure for industry of about US$1,250 per capita is similar to Georgia and Armenia's, though falls short of that for most of Europe.**

These are export-orientated businesses. While it has been argued (Całus 2016:1) that this makes Transnistria particularly sensitive to any changes in the economic situation of its main trading partners, the demand for the products these industries creates may be relatively inelastic compared with, say, that for luxury goods. There will always be a need for steel, power and clothes, even if that for cement may depend on the construction trade, which in turn will depend on the strength of the economy of the purchasing country. The fact that wages are among the lowest in Europe and the long-established nature of the physical structure with little rent or land acquisition cost may together make Transnistria potentially very competitive in these fields.

All these entities became state assets after Transnistria's acquisition of *de facto* independence. In the early 2000s, perhaps following similar events in Russia, there was a privatisation programme which resulted in all of them being sold off between 2003 and 2005

---

* It seems to be a Transnistrian quirk to produce statistics before a year is complete.

** Comparisons can be extrapolated with some difficulty from NationMaster (n.d.), where only total figures dating back to around 2011 are given for each country. The overall figures for both Armenia and Georgia are, without making any allowance for inflation, similar to Transnistria's, but they have populations about nine and six times as large, respectively.

(Borsi 2007:46), often to Russian entrepreneurs (Munteanu 2018). These were generally popular with the Transnistrian population. For example, Rebecca Chamberlain-Creangă, who spent considerable time in industrial areas around Ribnita, contended, "This Russian private take-over was seen by locals not as a capitalist intrusion, benefiting a small clan of Kremlin cronies, but as beneficial to the break-away region's livelihood" (2011:74).

Privatisations usually resulted in sales to Russian companies, though this was not done at the massive and inherently corrupt undervalues which were particularly notorious during Boris Yeltsin's presidency. Indeed, Borsi (2007:47) alleges, not entirely coherently, that shortly after the sale of Transnistria's gas debt to Alisher Usmanov,* Transnistrian President Smirnov announced that there was no actual debt to Gazprom, presumably depriving Usmanov of any benefit he might have hoped to obtain from the transaction. Igor Munteanu, a Moldovan MP, alleges in an 'opinion' piece for *Emerging Europe* (2018) that Usmanov was pressured by the Kremlin to buy the steelworks as a means of preventing Transnistria's economy collapsing. When I interviewed Smirnov in his Tiraspol office in May 2019 (Appendix B), he insisted that the money from the privatisations had been used primarily for pensions and other necessities, with some shares distributed to workers in the entities. He was critical of the Shevchuk government having forced Usmanov from the territory.

Others do not see the picture as being so rosy. Margarita Balmaceda goes so far as to allege (2013:451) that the steelworks exports "were subject to an illegal export tax accruing directly to Smirnov's family". This, she says, caused resentment among other elements of the Transnistrian "elites", including the Sheriff group and the Russian government (2013:450), thus creating the climate in which Smirnov lost the 2011 election. Balmaceda sees this in the context of a falling-out between Smirnov and Usmanov, which does not lie comfortably with Smirnov's own support of Usmanov. While it is unlikely the entire privatisation process was conducted without some corruption by Smirnov, there is little to support any contention that the damage to the territory's economy was significant. Indeed, the manoeuvrings over the gas debt, discussed below, may have brought considerable benefit to Transnistria and demonstrates why Smirnov felt no ill-will towards his former adversary.

Unemployment

Unemployment has not been a significant problem in Transnistria. Fomenko (2017:44) provides figures published by the Unitary Social Security Fund of Transnistria of just 2,684 or 2.7% of the potential working population: 46.7% of these were women despite women making up over 54% of the territory's population. Over half of these, with a higher proportion of men, were aged over 41. Although there may be a converse problem

---

*   Usmanov, who is best known in the UK for his partial ownership of Arsenal Football Club, is said to be the 83rd richest person in the world (Forbes 2020) and has been imprisoned for corruption in his native Uzbekistan – a conviction the British ambassador to Uzbekistan contended was wholly justified.

of a depleted workforce (see SubSect2.4.1), the lack of unemployment is one of the healthy features of the Transnistrian economy.

This discussion of the economy, while no more than outline, show is the existence of the features that create a functioning economy, including industry, with public and private involvement and employment. These can be taken to be part of the theme of economic viability, which ultimately contributes to the case for independence.

2.2 ECONOMIC GOVERNANCE

There are some aspects of an economy that are a direct preserve of government, most obviously taxation, financial regulation and, in many countries, control of the currency. Banking, although often a matter of private enterprise, invariably has government over-sight, and in respect of Transnistria, this is particularly significant in relation to money-laundering controls, implemented through its central bank. This section explores how some of these aspects currently work in Transnistria and how that might transplant to an independent state.

2.2.1 TAXATION

Transnistrian income tax has been charged at a flat rate since 2001; it began at 30% but reduced to 10% with an annual exemption for the first US$1,200 in July 2006 (Rabushka 2007), then increased to 13% in August 2015 (PSTRC 2015). This figure has been combined with a social insurance tax of 24% since 2005. Since 2000, there has also been a uniform sales tax, which absorbed value-added tax, a tax on profits, a road tax, a property tax on legal entities, and a fuel tax. Sales tax was set at 18% for most goods in 2015, in line with Russian rates, with reduced rates for food and other 'socially important goods', and, as with most sales tax regimes, a complete exemption for exports (Suvorov 2015).

Transnistrian tax rates are slightly higher than Moldovan, although that is structured differently (KPMG 2019). This analysis is similar to that in an article by Transnistria's then deputy minister for economic affairs, Natalia Sokolova (2015). She said the overall tax burden in Transnistria is around 33% of GDP, in line with Moldova's 32% and Russia's 34% (Ukraine's is 38%).

The taxation and tariff levels do not provide the Transnistrian treasury with the full sum it needs; in 2013, for instance, it obtained only 60%, leaving a shortfall that can only be filled by Russian aid. It operates on what can be regarded as a "survival budget", providing basic health and education, government employees' salaries and some social benefits but not being able to fund infrastructure projects. Official government bulletins suggest that the Krasnoselsky government is continuing with these priorities (PRB 2018).

2.2.2 CURRENCY

The Transnistrian currency – the rouble – was created in September 1994, the territory previously having used over-stamped old Russian rouble notes (Atlas of Transnistria 2000:32). The new notes were issued at the rate of one to a thousand old roubles. Initially, these were colloquially known as *suvorykys,* as on each note there was a portrait of national hero Aleksander Suvorov (Melnykevych 2014:44). However, rampant inflation soon rendered most of the new notes virtually worthless, with a 500,000-rouble note in production from 1997. By 1999, the rouble had fallen to 1.1 million to the US$. In 2000, a replacement currency was issued, which has maintained a reasonable degree of stability until today (Blakkisrud and Kolstø 2013:189). It is said that the reason for the introduction of the currency was Russia's decision in 2000 to disband the rouble zone (2013:189). While that may have been a catalyst, it would have been possible for Transnistria to have continued using the rouble in the way; for instance, Kosovo and Montenegro now use the euro and Zimbabwe and Ecuador use the US dollar.*

The exchange rate is controlled by the PRB and is pegged to the US dollar, without regard for the dollar's value against other currencies. In 2002, it was 8.07 to the dollar; there were constant fluctuations until February 2009, when it fell suddenly from 8.50 to 9.00 and remained frozen until March 2010 (Blakkisrud and Kolstø 2013:189). It fell in regular, and probably managed, amounts to 11.3 in January 2017 (PRB 2017) until its June 2017 devaluation to 16.1.

There are notes from 1 to 500 roubles. Kopeks remain, but few of the metal coins representing these are used in everyday business. In August 2014, the country became the first in the world to produce plastic coins: in denominations of 1, 3,** 5 and 10 roubles. These are brightly coloured, aesthetically pleasing, and round, square, pentagonal and hexagonal, respectively (*World Coin News* 2014 and personal observation). By 2019, they were virtually out of circulation, and former Foreign Minister Vladimir Yastrebchak, who had been involved in their introduction, told me on 27 May 2019 in Tiraspol that they had been intended mainly as novelties.

Initially, the production of coins was contracted to the Polish mint. This led to protests by the Chisinau government to their Warsaw counterparts. The Poles responded by saying that there was no political significance to this production: ingeniously, it was argued that what was being produced was not actual coins and was merely part of the mint's subsidiary business of making small metallic mementos. In December 2004, a truckload of coins, worth around 8 million roubles, was seized in Ukraine en route to Tiraspol, and the Ukrainian authorities passed it on the Chisinau authorities. At this point, the Polish government put pressure on the mint to stop working with Transnistria, leading the Tiraspol government to open its own mint (Moldova.org 2005).

Although not remarked upon in the analyses of Transnistria's nation-building

---

*   See Muller (1999) for a discussion of the phenomenon of 'currency substitution'.
**   This, along with the Cuban 3-peso note and the Kyrgyzstani 3-som coin, appears to be one of the only three-denomination notes or coins in circulation in the world (c.f. the old US expression, "As queer as a $3 bill").

(SubSect.1.2.2), the desire of the regime to have its own currency and go to considerable lengths to mint it may be an instance of the nation-building process. Obviously, a currency is a feature of an independent state and the sort of thing that could be expected to make the inhabitants think of themselves as Transnistrian. The only person other than Suvorov* who appears on the currency is Taras Shevchenko, the Ukrainian poet who also gives his name to the territory's main university.** The other pseudo-states do not have their own currencies. Postage stamps have also been produced, possibly with a similar effect in mind. However, these are only valid within Transnistria and when I wanted to send a postcard home in 2016, the Tiraspol central post office happily sold me Moldovan stamps.

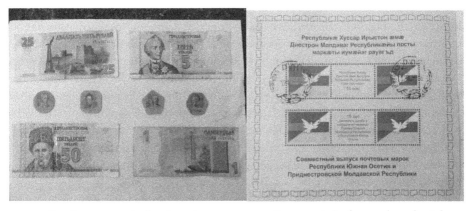

2: Banknotes and plastic coins   3: Stamps jointly produced with
South Ossetia***

The falling exchange rate is partially contributed to by moderate 'quantitative easing' on the part of the PRB (*Infotag* 2014). It was reported in November 2014 that the total money supply was 5,991 million roubles (then US$539.7 million) and had been increased by 0.8% in the previous few months. At the same time, foreign currency reserves had fallen from US$43.27 million to US$37.1million.

2.2.3 CRYPTOCURRENCY AND MINING

There have been suggestions that the Transnistrian government has been considering introducing cryptocurrency as its main form of money (*EurAsia Daily* 2018). Sergei

---

*   He can be seen on the 5-rouble note and Shevchenko can be seen on the 50-rouble note; the others in the photo show the flip side.

**   Shevchenko in fact has no personal connection to Transnistria but is eulogised in many cities in the former USSR. The university, then combined with the same institution in Kiev, was named after him in 1939 (The Times 2020).

***   See SubSect.5.2.4.

Russov, the deputy head of the PRB, said in October 2016 this would be, "A perfect means to both store value and tackle money laundering and fighting terrorism financing" (*ForkLog* 2016). It is not obvious how that would work, as such currencies are hard to control and trace, and is used disproportionately for sanction-busting activities. Adgur Ardzinba, the minister for economy of Abkhazia, about where there is more evidence of the likely use of cryptocurrency, has admitted this purpose motivates his territory, saying on its official website (cited by Owen 2017):

> The advantage of the cryptocurrency market has to do with the fact that any citizen in the entire world can invest in our economy, not fearing sanctions or other awkward limitations placed on us by the international community.

Related to this may be Transnistria's recently expressed desire, encapsulated in legislation, to attract Bitcoin 'mining', a process resulting in the creation or discovery* of Bitcoins by running numerous computers requiring vast amounts of electricity, which the territory can, by reason of the Russian gas subsidies (SubSect.2.6.1), provide cheaply. This is done with the aim of boosting investment, rather than for the government to become involved in the mining process or even tax its fruits. It has the approval of the Transnistrian Soviet and President Krasnoselsky, who claimed to have organised discussions with people well versed in the technology and its legal implications before asking the Soviet to pass the relevant legislation. The Kuchurgan electricity plant is now used primarily for this purpose (Smith 2020).

Cryptocurrency mining is identified as a something of a common endeavour in poorer parts of the European former USSR (Smith 2020), but Abkhazia's experience has not been successful. In 2018, the drain on the territory's energy resources proved so great that the government banned it (Hess 2020). However, later in the year the process is still continuing. It was described by John Daly (2020) as "a manifestation of a get-rich-quick mindset in an area plagued by a lack of economic opportunity". While it may be that a few people will succeed in enriching themselves from the mining process, it is fantastical to imagine any national economy, even one as small as Transnistria's, could be built upon it.

As there are few economic sanctions against Transnistria, it is hard to see why the territory should need an alternative currency for that purpose, and introducing one will draw suspicions that money launderers are being given tacit encouragement to transact through the territory. Confidence in the integrity of the process is not supported by the seeming involvement of Igor Chaika, son of Russian attorney general Yuri Chaika (Necsutu 2018). Father and son and other family members have faced numerous corruption allegations and indeed are the subject of the mocking Pussy Riot song, *Chaika* (Kramer 2016).

---

* The technical and philosophical question of whether these are created or discovered is, of course, outside the scope of this thesis.

2.2.4 BANKING AND MONEY LAUNDERING

The PRB controls banking in Transnistria. It is a state institution and, unlike many central banks, not constitutionally guaranteed independence (Sect.1.1.1). Five financial institutions, Agroprombank, Ipotecinii, Pridnestrovskii, Sberbank and Eximbank hold approximately 90% of the banking market in Transnistria. There are many bank branches in Tiraspol and a few in other major towns. The country's population seems to be adapting to modern banking, albeit at a slower rate than most of Europe, with 44% using bank cards* as well as cash in October 2018 (*Novosti Pridnestrovie* 2018).

The PRB claims considerable efforts to prevent money laundering. Article 12 of the 2009 Law No. 704-3-IV On Counteracting Legalization (Laundering) Proceeds from Crime and Financing of Terrorism gives the bank powers and responsibilities in this area. On the face of its reports, at least, it takes these seriously, particularly ensuring ongoing foreign exchange operations, including those of Transnistrians returning from living abroad, comply with that law. In the first eleven months of 2017, it identified 109 violations, leading to 52 decisions to impose administrative fines, amounting in total to US$374,700 (PRB 2018b:34). Seven cases were investigated because there were suspicions of criminal money laundering, two of which were referred to the prosecuting authorities (2018b:35).

The Transnistrian authorities' reporting of money laundering is, of course, not definitive on whether or not it represents a problem in the territory. There is little doubt the regime of Igor Smirnov was corrupt and that his sons used positions Smirnov had appointed them to make illicit private profits (Sect.1.3.1). Whether this amounted to the very specific act of 'money laundering' – by which, according to the International Compliance Association (n.d.), criminals disguise the original ownership and control of the proceeds of criminal conduct by making such proceeds appear to have derived from a legitimate source** – is less clear. It is likely that things immediately improved on Shevchuk's election in 2011.

Chisinau, which has its own obvious financial mismanagement problems, is at the forefront of those inclined to make allegations of financial misfeasance against Tiraspol. For instance, in October 2012, the deputy director of the Moldovan Information and Security Service, Vadim Vrabie, alleged, probably with approval of the Chisinau government (*Infotag* 2012), that:

> Local and foreign groups that commit financial crimes are using the Transnistrian banking system for tax-dodging and money-laundering illegal schemes. Thus, the banking separatism on the left bank of the Dniester River undermines Moldova's economic safety.

---

* These cards are restricted to Transnistria, though, which generally does not link to international credit card processing systems.

** The definition in s327 of the English Proceeds of Crime Act 2002 is too convoluted to be of help here.

When Nina Shtanski, then foreign minister, demanded Vrabie produce proof of this allegation, she was met with a significant silence. Not only was there no proof, but there was a striking lack of particularity, and Chisinau has not repeated this.

The United States State Department in its 2015 International Narcotics Control Strategy Report (USSD 2015) alleged:

> The breakaway region of Transnistria is highly susceptible to money-laundering schemes. Due to the Moldova government's inability to enforce the laws on this territory Transnistrian banking and financial laws and regulations are not in compliance with any accepted international [anti money-laundering] norms.

It is not clear if the report's author had regard to the 2009 law and enforcement proceedings set out above. The allegations lack both specifics and supporting evidence, and seem to be based on an inference that controls cannot be effective because they are not under the supervision of an internationally recognised government. My experiences, described in Appendix E, suggest a stolidity to Transnistrian banking that would make money laundering hard. Whether checks on me would have been more or less vigorous had I been seeking to deposit, say, 3 million rather than 300 dollars is a matter for speculation. The actual evidence for Transnistria as a centre of money laundering is extremely flimsy.

The allegations against Transnistria pale into insignificance compared with the disappearance of around US$1 billion from three Moldovan banks in 2014 (Monahov and Jobert 2017). This amounted to about 12% of the nation's assets. There was a 'carousel' scheme, by which banks were constantly making loans to each other with no commercial purpose. Foreign banks, particularly those in Latvia, were said to be complicit in laundering the proceeds. The former prime minister, Vlad Filat, received nine years' imprisonment in June 2016 for his part, though he was released prematurely in December 2019 (Necsutu 2019), and many other politicians and judges have been subject to criminal proceedings.

The Moldovan economy has recovered well from the crisis and has thrived since 2014, more so than Russia's, Ukraine's or Transnistria's (*The Economist* 2016). The prosecutions and economic revival may go some way towards restoring confidence in the political class. However, in terms of proportions of a nation's assets being stolen, this may be the world's, and certainly modern Europe's, worst financial misfeasance. It makes any argument against Transnistrian independence *from Moldova* based on the territory having a lack of financial probity seem ludicrous.

2.2.5 THE EFFECT OF INTERNATIONAL ISOLATION

The lack of the trappings of statehood have made economic stability, let alone prosperity, harder for Transnistria to achieve. Not being a universally recognised state makes it impossible to join or even associate with international organisations which typically lend expertise to countries with smaller, weaker economies. World Bank membership would assist greatly with access to attractive rate loans for social projects and to high-level advice on relieving poverty. The International Monetary Fund loans, although perhaps a mixed blessing, would assist with stabilising the currency exchange rate without artificial pegging. Many UN agencies, such as the International Labour Organization and the Food and Agricultural Organization, would bring obvious assistance in important fields. The World Trade Organization, outside UN auspices, has a membership of 164 countries with around twenty more seeking to join (WTO 2020). Although non-membership may not have been a barrier to Transnistrian international trade, partly because of the arrangements made on Moldovan accession (Gudim 2016), its future as an independent nation would naturally fall within that organisation and its rules.

The plausibility of a stronger economy because of the specific trappings of statehood can be seen as supporting a contention that independence is viable economically. An economy which has survived without these can only become stronger as part of an international community, and independence should be seen in the context not just of present viability but in the context of that potential.

2.3 THE SHERIFF GROUP

The Sheriff group is a major part of the economic matrix of present-day Transnistria, though the attention it attracts in most analyses of the country may be more the result of its political than economic influence. Its 12,000 employees (Całus 2016) constitute around 4% of the working population, a proportion which makes it the territory's largest private employer, as it would in most countries in the world, but of itself hardly amounts to domination of the economy. Its ties with government mean, however, that it could have a role in any determination of the territory's future, even though it has expressed no public views on the topic.

2.3.1 SHERIFF AS A BUSINESS

Although on some analysis, Sheriff is only the second largest company in Transnistria (Thorik, Petrusevici and Veliciko 2016), it has an economic and political influence far beyond any other commercial entity. It does not publish accounts or lists of shareholders the way substantial corporations in most Western countries are required to. Buttin alleges (2007:23) that its annual turnover was US$4 billion, amounting to US$8,000 per inhabitant. This figure – or even a tenth of it – is highly implausible.

To visitors, Sheriff's omnipresence is obvious. Its branded petrol stations and supermarkets are visible throughout Transnistria and it owns the Kvint cognac factory. Most strikingly, FC Sheriff's stadium, one of the best in Eastern Europe, is conspicuously placed, alongside its Mercedes showroom, on the main road into Tiraspol from Chisinau. The Sheriff group also owns a television station, a bank, the territory's largest mobile phone company and a substantial part of European's second-largest textile producer, Tirotex (Lungu 2016).

Founded in around 1998* by Viktor Gushan and Ilya Kazmaly (Całus 2016), it was likely that one of President Smirnov's sons, Vladimir (*The Washington Times* 2004), was among the company's first leaders. It is inconceivable that the business would have grown and flourished to the extent it has without considerable active government backing. However, the family involvement did not prevent the company falling out with Smirnov. From 2006, its support for Yevgeny Shevchuk, a former executive of the company turned politician who was to become president in 2011, was a matter of internal and external comment (e.g. Botan 2006).

Many of Sheriff supermarkets' goods are sourced from Ukraine, a process that has continued despite the tightening of border controls. Indeed, ROSHEN, the family chocolate company of Ukraine's president until 2019, Petro Poroshenko – who was virulently anti-Russian and imposed an embargo on the Ribnita steelworks in May 2018 (Munteanu 2018) – sold US$55,000 worth of chocolate to the territory in July 2017 (Vlas 2018). Vlas estimates that since the start of the Ukrainian war in 2014, about 300 Ukrainian companies have traded with Sheriff in transactions amounting to more than US$100 million (Vlas 2018). This is likely to be the primary source of many Western goods, including Coca-Cola and Nestle products, on sale in the supermarkets. Even if not all the legally required custom duties are paid to the Tiraspol government, this still provides a significant source of taxation revenue.

4: *The Sheriff stadium complex*   5: *Strikingly well-stocked shelves in a Sheriff store*

The government has been helpful to Sheriff in the provision of land. Michael Bobick's paper traces Sheriff's success to a contract it made, in its embryonic form,

---

* The official site (Sheriff 2021) claims June 1993, but most reports say it was later than that.

in 1996 (2012:8) with the Transnistrian government on "mutual cooperation". This involved the state leasing its existing large food stores to Sheriff. These had previously been run along USSR-style lines with dull, locally produced food and the bureaucratic, sometimes mildly confrontational, service which typified that regime. Sheriff quickly converted these into Western-style supermarkets, which these days are better stocked and run than, for instance, Muswell Hill Sainsburys.* While the terms of this contract were not published, Bobick (2012) says Sheriff was "rumoured" to have paid US$500,000 initially, with ongoing monthly payments of hundreds of thousands of dollars.

Bobick is sceptical about Sheriff's success, saying, "Sheriff's monopoly was not built upon ingenuity or hard work, but upon connections, that most valuable commodity in the former Soviet Union" (2012:8). This, though, is to disregard the organisational skills that have gone into making Sheriff one of the most successful commercial enterprises in that territory. Nothing in Moldova or Ukraine begins to compare.

Bobick recognises that Sheriff has had a substantial role in reducing crime and corruption, and even seems inclined to accept its 7% deduction in supermarkets for pensioners in off-peak hours as charitable rather than a Western-style marketing ploy. His summary of the impact of Sheriff's benevolence is:

> While other corrupt individuals steal and consume luxury goods, the notion of Sheriff giving back to the community is reinforced every time one passes its stadium, shops in one of its supermarkets, or receives a discount in one of its stores. (2012:13)

A similar view is taken by Piotr Olesky (2015). He argues that Transnistrians are not under the illusion that Sheriff is a "clean business" but recognise the benefits it brings in terms of swimming pools and football clubs, selling goods at relatively low prices, and being a good employer which, unlike the state, has not cut salaries by 30%.

Bobick also manages to portray the political influence of Sheriff in a way few Western or even Russian commentators have. He talks of Sheriff having political *parties,* including but not restricted to Obnovlenie. The 2011 presidential election run-off, after the elimination of the incumbent Igor Smirnov in the first round, he characterises as being between Shevchuk, a protégé of Sheriff's political machine, and Anatoliy Kaminski, head of Sheriff's Obnovlenie or Renewal party (2012:17). Locals, however, identify certain politicians as being 'Sheriff' rather than of a particular party. Those politicians are given access to Sheriff warehouses so they can, on occasion, make goods available to their constituents (2012:15). There seems to be little consensus on whether this is genuine benevolence or a crude bribe. Most people Bobick spoke to seemed grateful for it, but

---

*   Dr Bobick, clearly no admirer of Sheriff supermarkets, claims they tend to stock food past its expiry date and sell counterfeit Western goods, including Old Spice deodorant which gave him a rash (2012:10). That has not been my own experience. They sell German pepper brie – a delicacy impossible to find in London and frequently not available even in Germany.

he also cites some dissent, including an elderly man who saved all his Sheriff 'holiday cards' (it was not made clear what they were) as evidence that Sheriff had purchased the electorate.*

2.3.2 SHERIFF AS A POLITICAL FORCE

Sheriff's political influence can be traced back to at least the 2006 presidential election, (Sect.1.1.3) when Shevchuk, at the company's behest, withdrew his proposed candidacy against President Smirnov in consideration for legislation transferring control of Russian subsidies from the president to the Soviet. Russia then expressed support both for Smirnov's re-election and for 2007 legislation which, as promised, did transfer that control (Bobick 2012). The motivation behind this was there being more advantage to Sheriff, whose relationship with Smirnov was increasingly difficult, in having a formalised, if indirect, control of this money through its many Soviet representatives than in being dependent on the vagaries of a president who might not always serve its interests.

In the 2011 election, it was Shevchuk who enjoyed Sheriff's backing. This was despite him having started falling out with the company and its party Obnovlenie (Całus 2016). On taking office, he clamped down on the customs privileges that Sheriff had under Smirnov, formally cancelling them by presidential decrees on 29 December 2012. This required the company to pay customs duty for foreign currency exports or to use the services of the PRB, paying 25% commission (Całus 2016:3). While the 2012 election may have shown that Sheriff was not so powerful that a politician's aspirations would be destroyed by not pleasing it, Shevchuk's presidency was hampered by battles with the company. Shevchuk accused Sheriff of trying to create an oligarchic system, with unhealthy amounts of power vested in the senior officers of the company, and of removing significant sums to tax havens. In response, Obnovlenie deputies blamed Shevchuk for the territory's increasing economic problems and launched vociferous attacks on his competence and efficiency (Całus 2016a), contributing to the heavy defeats his supporters and he respectively suffered in the 2015 Soviet and 2016 presidential elections.

By 2015, the Moldovan press could identify several Sheriff employees who were also Soviet deputies, including Oleg Baev, the director of Kvint brandy makers, Dmitrii Oghirciuk, Sheriff's general manager, and Vladislav Tidva, president of Sheriff's Agroprombank. Less convincingly, other papers have alleged one third of the deputies have been conducting Sheriff-related business while in office (*Mold Street* 2016). While it is not strictly illegal for deputies to have other employment – Shevchuk's attempts in his last years in office to pass legislation preventing this came to nothing (*Mold Street* 2016) – the obvious scope for conflicts of interest makes a large commercial bloc in any legislature undesirable and damaging to the territory's credibility. The dual involvement

---

*   There was no suggestion that Bobick or his informants suffered, or even feared, any intimidation for making criticisms of Sheriff.

in politics and business of Evgenhy Gushan, the parliamentary deputy son of Sheriff founder Viktor Gushan, is particularly striking. He and a fellow deputy, Porfiri Skiliniuk, own the Moldovizalit factory, probably ultimately under the Sheriff umbrella, which was in receipt of US$2 million tax incentives between 2014 and mid 2016. Although these incentives were supposed to be linked to preserving employment, the plant allegedly dismissed 150 employees during the relevant period, without any sanction (Anghel 2016).

The enthusiasm of the Moldovan press for highlighting this issue illustrates the embarrassment it could cause Transnistria if the West were ever to seriously consider its case for independence.

By the 2016 presidential election campaign, relations between Sheriff and Shevchuk had deteriorated to an extent that it clearly would not back him. It used TSV, a private TV channel associated with the company, to broadcast allegations that Shevchuk had implemented elaborate financial schemes to enrich himself (Lesanu 2016). Conversely, the state channel, Pervyj Pridnestrovskij, tried to undermine Krasnoselsky's claims to be independent by portraying him as Sheriff's stooge, a description colourfully translated by Alexandru Lesanu (2016:) as: "A marionette figure of Transnistria's largest commercial enterprise." The Chisinau press was in no doubt that Krasnoselsky was the candidate of Sheriff and that Obnovlenie was the Sheriff party (e.g. Vasiliu 2016).

Government officials with whom I worked when observing the 2016 presidential election (see Appendix A) also believed that Sheriff was firmly backing Krasnoselsky. As a result, one of the electoral rules they wanted enforced was the prohibition on photographing ballot papers, believing, probably fancifully, that Sheriff was requiring its employees to produce evidence that they had voted for Krasnoselsky. When I conducted discussions with language students at Shevchenko University in October 2019 (Sect.1.3.1), the comment "Our president is under Sheriff" was met with general assent, and a similar comment I heard about Sheriff in May 2019 at the Club 19 youth club also met with approval (SubSect.3.6.5).

Even more alarming than Sheriff's involvement in the election may have been its treatment of Shevchuk after his defeat. Promo-LEX (2017) reported a June 2017 interview with Shevchuk indicating that his relationship with Sheriff had deteriorated spectacularly, Shevchuk supposedly saying:

> The management of Sheriff company would have been involved in contract killing in the region. He also said that he knows who was the one who took the advantage of murdering business people and who could contract their killing.

The interview it referenced for this did not actually make such serious allegations, though Shevchuk claims his car was followed in an intimidating way from Tiraspol to Ribnita and that Gushan had commissioned his murder (Agora.md 2017). This happened the day before Shevchuk fled the territory. He may have been using it as justification for fleeing, perhaps trying to refute the perception that he was escaping prosecution. Shevchuk does not appear to have repeated the allegation, and it has gained little traction even in the Moldovan media.

It is implausible that Sheriff would wish to kill a senior politician in circumstances that would inevitably lead to a thorough investigation, probably with foreign involvement. Such an investigation would be far more damaging to Sheriff than anything Shevchuk could say about it. The theory that Shevchuk was laying the ground for a credible exit from the territory before he could be prosecuted, and that Promo-LEX, as it is prone to, has not only unquestioningly accepted implausible allegations against the Transnistrian elite but has exaggerated them, is more likely.

Conversely, the deference to Sheriff on the part of Transnistrian politicians was apparent from the minister of internal affairs, Ruslan Mova, when I interviewed him on 6 December 2018 at the ministry. He had no doubt about the misappropriation of substantial amounts of money by Shevchuk during his presidency and the desirability of bringing him to justice in Transnistria. Sheriff indeed had been very generous to Shevchuk, but Mova said, seemingly without irony, that it had done so, "hoping it would make Shevchuk do good for Transnistria". Sheriff, the minister went on to assure me, "plays by the rules; you can see this by examining them on the internet".

Sheriff is reported to pay approximately US$30 million taxes annually, almost 30% of those paid by Transnistrian businesses and 17% of the total state income (Thorik, Petrusevici and Veliciko 2016). In October 2016, Shevchuk persuaded the Soviet to endorse legislation requiring Sheriff to pay US$250 million, this being about a quarter of the benefits it had supposedly received from the lax controls on it during the Smirnov years (Ernst 2016). This was a considerable political feat considering the influence that Sheriff has in the Soviet. Outright tax avoidance has not in recent years seemed a particular goal of the company, which may accept that contributing to state coffers is a legitimate price to pay for its privileged commercial position.

In July 2019, after considerable political upheaval in Moldova, William Hill and David Kramer (2019) suggested that Sheriff has contributed to:

> Practical progress in dealing with Transnistria as a result of improved relations between oligarchs: [Vladimir] Plahotniuc…Viktor Gushan and former Ukrainian President Petro Poroshenko.

The proposition is questionable and uncorroborated but identifies a possibility that it could ultimately be commercial negotiations through the Sheriff group, rather than political ones, that determine the Transnistrian question. More generally, the involvement of Sheriff in politics, particularly if it behaves in ways that are unlawful, is likely to undermine any case that may be made for independence. For a commercial organisation to have such influence over a government will not be seen as healthy in either Western Europe or Russia and may be advanced as an argument that the government is not itself independent enough to govern an independent country. However, that is to be balanced against the economic success of the group and the economic benefits that brings to Transnistria.

2.3.3 FC SHERIFF TIRASPOL

One of the benefits that Sheriff may bring to Transnistria is its eponymous football team. Sheriff Tiraspol football club is the highest profile and most glamorous, if not lucrative, part of the Sheriff empire. Its current president is Viktor Gushan (Sheriff 2021). The club was founded in 1997* and is the most successful in all of Moldova, having won eighteen league titles since 2000 (Soccerway 2020). Its 12,746-seater stadium – one of the best, though not the biggest, in Eastern Europe – supposedly cost US$200 million.** At the start of the 2019/20 season, its squad included two Brazilians. As Misha Glenny put it (2009:112), "As the Moldovan/Transnistrian equivalent of Chelsea, it can buy better players than all the other teams put together." To UEFA, it remains part of Moldova, and its relative strength gains it regular access to the European club competition.

A reflection on the strange interaction between the Chisinau and Tiraspol establishments is that not only does Sheriff play in the Moldovan league but Moldova's international games are also occasionally played at its stadium. It is larger and in better condition than Chisinau's ageing national Zimbru Stadium (Rainbow 2013), but the political situation makes many international teams reluctant to travel to Transnistria, and all Moldova's qualifying games for the 2018 World Cup were played in Chisinau. The Transnistrian authorities have been keen to gain prestige by having such games held in Tiraspol, even accepting UEFA's conditions, such as ticket pricing in Moldovan lei and playing the Moldovan national anthem. Moldovan government ministers were generally not allowed to attend, seemingly a matter outside UEFA's remit, until 2010 when the then prime minister, Vlad Filat, was invited to a game between Sheriff and Switzerland's FC Basel and reportedly cheered on Sheriff. He met President Igor Smirnov at the game, and it is said that the reintroduction of the passenger railway between Chisinau and Tiraspol was a consequence of that meeting (Eberhardt 2016:17).

The club is a considerable draw on Sheriff's resources. There are, predictably, no published accounts. Tickets cost from around US$2 for ordinary league games and the capacity of the stadium, of around 13,000, is rarely reached, meaning there is little money to pay for rights in Moldovan and Transnistrian television – indeed, Sheriff owns the main broadcaster of football in the territory – and sponsorship is restricted to Sheriff

---

*   A date which, unlike that of the founding of the main company, seems to be universally accepted.

**   A figure which leads to it being described cuttingly by David McArdle (2013) as having a 'Ceausescuian quality', although the Romanian dictator's hideous palace in Bucharest cost at least fifteen times more.

companies. The club's income won't be sufficient to even pay the wages bill of the foreign players. If it is purely a vanity project for the rich owners of the conglomerate, it would hardly be alone among football clubs at all levels. The obvious suggestion is that it is a money-laundering front, as noted by Rory MacLean, who reports a supporter pointing out on a visit to the stadium that he believes the oligarchs who own Chelsea and Monaco football clubs do so for such reasons (MacLean 2015:39). Glenny speculates that the club is funded by sales of Russian arms and "two or three" factories in Transnistria that continue to produce weapons without any apparent supervision, regarding this as a more plausible source of funding than supermarkets (2009:112).

A more benign conclusion about the club's purpose is drawn by Melissa McDonald in her thesis on the use of football clubs by Eastern European oligarchs. She argues:

> Gushan's ability to make FC Sheriff a successful champion of the region promotes ideals of the power structure. By promoting Russian superiority over the Moldovan region while still including and respecting the under-represented Moldovans/Transnistrians in the process, Gushan also justifies the structure of elite control. (2014:59)

Further, she sees the ostensibly apolitical Gushan using the club for leverage over politicians. The on-field success gives prestige to the territory beyond Moldova's borders, and politicians of all hues like to be associated with success, sporting and otherwise (McDonald 2014:52). One of its 'homegrown' players told *Euronews* (2014) that the club's ambition was to join the Russian league, though whether this was anything more significant than him expressing his footballing ambitions was not clear. The potency of football teams in relation to national identity may have been recognised by Russia when it transferred some Crimean teams to its leagues, despite UEFA objections, when it annexed that territory in 2014 (Walker 2018). In the short term, the Sheriff team will not be able to play anywhere other than the Moldovan league, and it would face an embarrassing lack of meaningful opposition on independence.

In practical terms, though, the benefit of the club to Transnistria is negligible. It is hardly going to put the territory on the tourist map or even generate significant revenue when major games are played there.* Occasional qualification for international tournaments and an 'above its weight' ranking in the perplexing UEFA table** have not made the club's name or location instantly recognisable to many fans. The whole complex has an air of abandon, with virtually empty car parks whenever I have passed it on weekdays. The reality is that the club is no more than a white elephant.

In the absence of convincing evidence of its use for money laundering, or even an

---

* When Tottenham Hotspur played there in 2013, they stayed the night in Chisinau and made virtually no use of local facilities.

** Its 2016/17 triumph in the Moldovan league brought it to 68th, slightly above Bordeaux, French cup winners as recently as 2013; Torino, then the billet of England goalkeeper Joe Hart; and, even more surprisingly, Valencia – six times winners of La Liga and arguably Spain's third biggest club. It had fallen to 112th by 2020 (UEFA 2020).

explanation of how that could be achieved, FC Sheriff might be best regarded as the somewhat lame vanity project of a skilled but immensely privileged businessman. In terms of playing ability, stadium size and revenues, it is at best at the level of an English third-tier side. However, as McDonald (2014:59) suggests, its promotion of Russian superiority over the Moldovan region may contribute to the concept of nationhood and the nation-building project (SubSect.1.2.2). This is all the more so as Transnistria has been given little opportunity to participate in international sporting competitions,* leaving the relatively successful Sheriff club the only meaningful focus of a national sporting identity. A similar process is observed by Steve Menary (2019:8) in other pseudo-states, where successful Soviet clubs Spartak Tskhinvali of South Ossetia and Qarabagh Agdam of Nagorno-Karabakh "are nurtured and kept alive in the Georgian and Azeri sporting spheres by businesses sympathetic to the political administrations". In a subtle way, the football club may be making a contribution to the independence claim via a form of nation-building.

2.3.4 SHERIFF AND INDEPENDENCE

For the Sheriff group, or at least its owners, the status quo of Transnistrian autonomy and relative economic isolation has attractions, and it has never been an active voice for independence. It is not known to have any direct business interests outside the territory, despite Gushan and Kazmaly's own links. Human rights lawyer Stepan Popovskiy alleged to me in an interview in his Tiraspol office on 28 May 2019 that Sheriff owns a telecoms company in Ukraine and has interests in hypermarkets in Bulgaria and Germany, but I could find no evidence to corroborate this. It may be that the, broadly well-run, organisation could expand into the rest of Moldova and Ukraine, but it is doubtful that a wider international supermarket chain, never mind Sheriff's other more complex businesses, could be run on a larger scale without outside investment and expertise.

It is unlikely that the Sheriff management could, even if they were so minded, assert sufficient influence over the government to be a block on independence or union with Russia, were either to become plausible. There is no machinery by which it could compel a government not to follow a course of action so overwhelmingly popular among the populace, and it has the imperative of any consumer-orientated business of retaining its popularity among its customers. However, the existence of Sheriff in its present form could be helpful to the territory in meeting the many challenges independence would present. It is a significant part of the economy, is largely not dependent on state aid, and would probably adapt relatively rapidly to the challenges – not always foreseeable – that would be presented by a change in national status.

---

*　It has not even made it to the non-FIFA international tournaments where it might compete with the likes of Northern Cyprus, Tibet and Zanzibar (Menary 2007).

2.4 DEMOGRAPHY AND THE ECONOMY

Transnistria has a declining and ageing population – the consequence of considerable net outward migration, particularly by young people. Many émigrés send remittances which boost the economic circumstances of those who remain. This section considers the relative benefits and detrimental to the territory of the migration itself and the economic return it yields through those remittances.

2.4.1 THE POPULATION OF TRANSNISTRIA

In rough terms, Transnistria has a little under half a million inhabitants; if it were a country, it would probably be ranked 173rd largest in the world in terms of population, between Cape Verde and Brunei (CIA 2019). Its area of 4,163 square kilometres would rank it 165th in the world's countries in terms of size (CIA 2019). This is a slightly lower population density than Moldova as a whole, which ranks 131st for population and 135th for area (CIA 2019). The relative similarity of the two ranks shows that both have population densities close to the world average. While there are undoubtedly challenges in being a small country, there are many economically and socially successful countries with smaller areas and populations than Transnistria, including Luxembourg, Barbados and Malta.

The Transnistrian census, scheduled for 2014, didn't take place until October 2015, the Soviet having decided the estimated cost of US$500,000 was to be used for more urgent things, despite explicit recognition that it should adhere to the "international standard" of one every ten years (*Infotag* 2015). The population then was found to be 475,300, which represented a fall of over 14% from the 2004 figure of 555,347 (Crivenco 2018:5). There was a perhaps problematic gender imbalance, with 54.6% of the population being female, up from 54% in 2004. Nearly 70% of the population lived in urban areas at the time of the census (2018:6).

That gender and age imbalance is apparent in Transnistria, particularly Tiraspol. While the university is relatively thriving, there are noticeably few young people on the streets, on public transport or in bars and cafes. Almost all students and teachers who have attended my lectures and seminars there have been female.* Most voters I observed during the 2016 election were old or middle-aged. The reason for the university teachers being mainly female was explained to me on 5 December 2015 by Natalia Shchukina, the head of business and labour law at the Shevchenko University, as being due to poor pay. She thought women were more willing to tolerate this, but could not really provide any instances of well-paid jobs done by men.

There is a clear pattern of net emigration from Transnistria, but this is a relatively recent phenomenon. Indeed, on the break-up of the USSR, it had more immigration than emigration, perhaps because people were attracted to jobs in its substantial manufacturing

---

* On one occasion, I asked about this and was told that the boys had to go on military training that day.

industry (Fomenko 2017:5). An interesting feature of the Transnistrian migration is the wide range of destinations it extends to. According to information provided by the PRB for Fomenko's IOM commissioned report, remittances were received in Transnistria from 131 different countries (2017:4).

2.4.2 MIGRATION

The incentives to emigrate

The agreement with Chisinau that had the effect of giving international recognition to Transnistrian university degrees, reached under OSCE auspices in 2018 (SubSect. 5.2.4), may make studying at universities in the territory more attractive and increase the number of young people. It will not, however, solve the problem of a lack of good quality jobs for them once they graduate. The reasons that Transnistrians emigrate are analysed in detail by Ostavnaia (2017), but the relatively weak state of the territory's economy and the ease with which Transnistrians can travel have created an environment in which emigration has become commonplace.

The falling population and gender imbalance are both consequences of economic migration. The situation has been worsening since April 2014 when the EU granted visa-free travel to Moldovans, though not the right to live or work. It was reported eighteen months later that 74,000 Transnistrians had applied for Moldovan citizenship (Braw 2016), the assumption being that most of them were motivated by the travel prospects this offered.

Since 2007, it has been Romanian policy to grant passports to most Moldovans, with which comes the right to live and work anywhere in the EU. The Romanian government has deprived inhabitants of Transnistria of this possibility (*Publika* 2018), a position probably susceptible to challenge both in the European Court of Justice and the ECHR. There is a trade in forged papers, which will secure a passport, available in Chisinau for as little as €300 (Mogos and Călugăreanu 2012), which is cheaper and more certain than any application to international courts! Conversely, the lawful acquisition of such a passport by Moldovans is expensive and slow (Knott 2015), despite occasional reports in, largely right-wing, Western European newspapers prophesying an influx of Moldovans to the EU (e.g. Quinn and Murray 2013). Around 27,000 Transnistrians applied for Moldovan passports in the first year of visa-free travel to the EU (Jaroszewicz and Całus 2012), but there are no published figures for how many of those went on to seek Romanian passports.

Russia's willingness to offer passports to Transnistrians also encourages emigration. The Transnistrian Ministry of Foreign Affairs has stated that about 150,000 have Russian passports and 100,000 Ukrainian (Moldova.org 2009). The Ukrainian passport also now allows visa-free EU travel without the right to live or work. The Russian passport is of little assistance to those who wish to work in Europe, except in Belorussia, Serbia, Montenegro and Macedonia, none of which is likely to be economically attractive to migrants.

Crivenco (2018:6) notes that for pensioners Transnistria may be a more attractive place to live than Moldova and identifies a little migration to the territory. The main spur to this is lower-priced housing and lower tariffs for utilities. Such migration may be a sign of a relatively healthy economy and may even boost it a little if those who come for such reasons are not a drain on public resources.

The effect of depopulation

The detail of the demographics would present challenges to any government administering Transnistria as an independent country. The extent to which a falling population is harmful to a country is a matter of considerable debate among economists. John Maynard Keynes argued (1937:5) that, "A stationary or slowly declining population, may if we exercise the necessary strength and wisdom, enable us to raise the standard of life to what it should be."* This feature of Keynesian economic theory came to be known as 'stagnation theory'. More intuitive may be the argument of Alvin Hansen (1939) that low population growth produces a situation of persistently inadequate output growth.

The economic argument has concentrated on decline due to birth and mortality rates, both of which tend to fall in more or less directly inverse proportions to a country's prosperity. Transnistria's birth rate is relatively low – reportedly -0.4% (Całus 2016:4) – but clearly most of the population loss is due to emigration, offset now by very little immigration. Although the arguments about how migration, particularly immigration, affects a country have become highly politicised, a country which loses large proportions of its young people and workforce will, certainly on the basis of the Hansen (1939) reasoning, suffer adverse economic and demographic consequences. In a March 2016 address, UN Assistant Secretary-General for Human Rights Ivan Simonovic talked of a Moldovan "brain drain" and the country losing its human capital (UNHRO 2016). Similarly, the EU-sponsored Österreichische Gesellschaft für Europapolitik also talked in a short 2016 paper of this "brain drain" turning Transnistria into "a republic of pensioners and children" (Harzl 2016: 2).

Fomenko (2017) asked Transnistrians about attitudes to migration. Although it was generally approved of, or at least understood, an average of over 5% of respondents when asked in different years agreed with the position of "I am absolutely against [economic emigration], I think this is high treason" (2017:46), suggesting some Transnistrians recognise and resent the damage it may be doing to the economy.

Research

The most important research into Transnistrian emigration is for the International Organization for Migration (Ostavnaia 2017), which was based on structured interviews with 320 Transnistrian migrants.

---

* Strikingly, this appeared in the Eugenics Review.

Slightly more women than men were interviewed. Around 20% were over 50. Most respondents had a first degree and nearly half a postgraduate qualification (Ostavnaia 2017:161). The high level of education among the migrants shows both that Transnistria is a well-educated society and that it is well-educated people who can and do leave.

Of those emigrating to Russia, 88% either were already or became citizens there. The proportion in other countries was vastly lower. The report identifies various motivations for, and indeed types of, migration, including political, educational, economic and family motivations (Ostavnaia 2017:59).*

The seeking of political migration, or refugee status, continued long after the cessation of 1992 hostilities and any meaningful physical risk (Ostavnaia 2017:21–22). After the 2011 and 2016 elections, both of which brought substantial governmental change, many officials and political activists who didn't agree with or have a place in the new regime also departed, generally to Russia (Ostavnaia 2017:21–22). The report cannot say how many left for such reasons, but concludes, "Nevertheless, due to the public status of some individuals, we can see cases of this type of migration" (Ostavnaia 2017:24).**

Educational migration occurs as it is easy for Transnistrians to obtain free places at Russian universities. Russia has a quota system for former Soviet countries and allows as many Transnistrians citizens as other Moldovans (Ostavnaia 2017:29–30). Although no precise figures are cited for educational migration, the impression is given that it is a relatively small factor in the exodus from Transnistria.

Sham marriages for the purpose of obtaining Russian citizenship may have occurred around 2000, but since then the practice has stopped. The report suggests, though no empirical evidence is cited, that such marriages now take place largely with a view to gaining Romanian citizenship (Ostavnaia 2017:41).

Far more significant for Transnistria is economic migration. In 1996, "economically active and inactive people", presumably meaning adults, within the territory amounted to 232,900 and 103,400 respectively, but by 2016, those figures were 136,600 and 145,600 (Ostavnaia 2017:25). This means the working population fell by around 40% in twenty years while the non-working population increased commensurately, with the inevitable result that the remaining population lives increasingly on remittances from those who have left.

The author points out that return migration, particularly of skilled people, would be desirable and feasible if economic conditions and salary levels improved. Effectively, though, were there to be a substantial return now, it would lead to a lowering of salaries and a deprivation of the territory in terms of the remittance income on which it currently depends (Ostavnaia 2017:128–129). That understandable gloominess about the consequences if a substantial number of emigrants did return, as might happen were

---

* See Costin (2012:10) for a distinction between 'push' and 'pull' factored migration: most Transnistrian emigration can be characterised as push.

** It is to be borne in mind that after losing the 2016 election, former President Shevchuk and his wife were widely thought to have gone to either Chisinau or the south of France, though she now lives openly in Russia (SubSect.3.5.2).

independence attained and émigrés felt a patriotic pull back, is a substantial concern. The obvious problem of depopulation merges into one of over-dependence on remittances, and were there to be that sudden mass return, the damage caused by the drying up of remittance support to the territory could be devastating. While this should not bear directly on Transnistria's entitlement to independence, it is something the leadership should have in mind and have a plan to deal with.

Whether the population currently in Transnistria and Moldova intends to remain was first researched by Natalia Costin. She interviewed 266 students in the four universities she described as the best in the territories (2012:6), including Shevchenko University in Tiraspol (Costin 2012:22). She does not differentiate in her results between the territories but gives the impression there were no significant differences. Of all the respondents, 27% of men and 40% of women told her there was a more than 50% chance they would emigrate on graduating, and only 9% of each said there was no chance (Costin 2012:26). These figures were doubtless motivated by salary expectations, with just 4% expecting to earn more than €1,000 a month if they remained, whereas 40% expected that much if they emigrated, with the average for those who would remain expecting being around €325 (Costin 2012:27).

Similar research specifically on Transnistrians was included in Tatiana Cojocari's study with 499 respondents (2019). 10.4% of respondents, slightly more men than women, including 22.4% of those aged 18–29, said they planned within the next one to two years to leave forever, with a further 11.8% (20% of the younger group) saying they would leave for a limited time. Russia was the preferred destination for 65.9% of respondents (Cojocari 2019:34).

Refugees

Transnistria has neither offered nor been asked to take any of the refugees fleeing to Europe from conflict and poverty, particularly that in Syria, in recent years. The Chisinau government has been sympathetic to the relatively few who have sought to settle in the country that way (Gonța 2014), and there would seem no reason why Transnistria should not do likewise. Indeed, accepting refugees and asylum seekers would seem an obvious way of relieving many of the demographic-based problems the territory faces. Refugees tend to be young, predominantly male, and often highly skilled or educated (Pew Research Center 2016); they would be likely to make a considerable contribution to Transnistria economically and socially.

Comparative migration figures

Although the figure of emigration from Transnistria, and indeed Moldova, is worryingly high, there are other countries which have lost a considerably higher proportion of their population. According to UN figures (UNDESA 2015), the highest in Europe was

Serbia's 43.3%, followed by Albania's 38.8%. Portugal's 22.3% was strikingly similar to Moldova's 21.8%. No percentage figure is given for Transnistria, but it is probably around the same as Moldova's.

This is significant for putting in context what appears a worrying trend identified in the research and other discussions above. It is clear that economies can remain highly viable despite levels of migration of the sort Transnistria is experiencing, and ultimately the present levels should not bear adversely on the claim for independence, particularly if taking refugees were to reverse the trend of net emigration. Further, independence might lead to some citizens returning, excited by helping to build a new country.

2.5 REMITTANCES TO TRANSNISTRIA

A consequence of emigration from a country is that a considerable amount of money will be sent to it by those who find employment in other, usually wealthier, countries, and a feature of the Transnistrian economy, like that of many other former Soviet states and most poor countries, is the voluntary sending home of money by émigrés. Any analysis of that economy has to have regard to the extent and effect of such remittances.

By 2019, remittances were on course to overtake direct foreign investment as the largest source of foreign financing to emerging market economies, having reached US$689 billion in 2018 (*Financial Times* 2019). The effect of remittances on an economy is a matter of some debate, but they are not usually regarded as entirely beneficial. In a web post for the World Economic Forum (2015), Connel Fullenkamp argues that "there is no example of a country for which remittances have clearly driven its economic development". This is on the premise that the remittances are likely to be greater the worse the economic situation is in the recipients' country, providing an "incentive to work and invest less" (Fullenkamp 2015). A UN report accepted the limitations of remittances while recognising theirs benefits, particularly in areas recovering from conflict (UNDP 2008:xxi):

> Microfinance and remittances play crucial reinforcing roles in economic recovery. Microfinance can fund self-employment and ease the financial constraints on poorer households; but its limited potential to generate jobs means it cannot be the anchor for economic recovery overall.

Fullenkamp's argument (2015) is not an easy one to accept in relation to Transnistria or anywhere else. It is premised on a wish by those who receive remittances to be living on the benevolence of those who send them. This is a very cynical view of human nature, particularly as most senders will be close relatives and often poor themselves. There is nothing to suggest Transnistrian residents work any the less hard because of such payments. The UN view is more plausible. Large enterprises, which will generate significant employment, inevitably need more formal funding; however, providing enough money to enable a person to set up a business as, for instance, a craftsman or shop owner, is of value not only to that person but to the community in which that business is situated. The remittances should be seen as contributing to the economic viability of the territory. While events like the current global pandemic can and have caused a dramatic short-term fall in such payments (World Bank 2020), they are still a more secure source of income than support from a foreign sponsor, which can be entirely withdrawn on a whim. Even if not ideal, Transnistria's dependence on remittances is not a serious bar to its economic viability.

The December 2017 report *Extended Migration Profile of Transnistria*, also for the International Organization for Migration (IOM) (Fomenko 2017), explores the extent of Transnistria's dependence on remittances from people living abroad. In 2012, these amounted to 18.3% of GDP – the world's ninth highest if it were for a recognised state. Moldova's comparable figure was 23% (2017:53). Two other former Soviet countries, Tajikistan with 46.9% and Kyrgyzstan 29.1%, were ranked highest (2017:39). Around 160,000 Transnistrians are involved in labour migration, compared with the 136,400 people employed there as of January 2016, though many of the 160,000 may only work abroad seasonally (2017:38).

The quoted figures for remittances, provided by what the report refers to as the Transnistrian Bank, presumably the PRB, had fluctuated wildly on an annual basis from US$211 million in 2013 to US$45.5 million in 2016 and back to US$91 million in 2017 (PRB 2018a). This was partly attributed to the fall in the Russian rouble in 2014 and to a decline in the economy of Ukraine, from where remittances fell ten-fold (2018a), although that had never been a particularly significant source. The report's authors also suggest that a shortage of foreign currency in Transnistria's banks may have led some to send their remittances to Moldova or Ukraine instead (2017:41), which would partially explain the bank's figures. However, it is unlikely that these factors would cause the nearly 500% dip in remittances reflected in the figures, and as emigration itself has remained fairly stable, much of it is probably attributable to poorly produced statistics. While the precision of these figures may be questionable, the dependence on remittances is beyond dispute. The same bank (2018a) provided data that 70.8% of the remittances came from Russia and just 2% from Moldova. The other main sources in 2017, according to that data, were Israel (4.9%), Turkey (2.5%) and Italy (2.5%), but overall they came from 131 different countries (2017:40).

A less formal indicator of the extent of remittances is that in Tiraspol there are 37 Western Union outlets and throughout the country there are around 100 (Western Union 2020), which is a convenient indicator of the territory's dependence on remittances from overseas workers.* Most personal exchanges are done at small bureaux, which are mainly free-standing but occasionally incorporated into other businesses. These invariably offer to sell other currencies but often have none available. There is typically a spread of about

---

* By contrast, Grimsby, which is the British town with a population closest to Tiraspol's 135,000, has 11. However, Plovdiv in Bulgaria, whose EU accession has made it easier for its citizens to work abroad, with a population of 126,000 has round 90. Balti in Moldova, which has a slightly larger population than Tiraspol, also has around 37 (Western Union 2020).

1% on the US dollar and 4–5% on the euro; this is greater on Russian, Moldovan and Ukrainian currencies, as shown by the author's photos below.

6 and 7. Exchange rates offered in Tiraspol in November 2015
and October 2019

The importance and effect on the Transnistrian economy of remittances from migrants is also considered by Ostavnaia (2017). Most Transnistrian migrants send remittances, ranging from 90% of those in Portugal to 46% in Israel averaging around 60% globally (Ostavnaia 2017:133). This is mainly done through bank transfers. The remittances are sent almost entirely for family support with, worryingly, well over half saying they have been at least in part spent on food. Slightly more had sent money for "health", followed by house construction and education. Negligible numbers said they sent money to invest in either agriculture or industry (Ostavnaia 2017:134).

Ostavnaia argues (2017:139) that there is a need to divert remittances into investment:

It is necessary to differentiate migrants as a group of potential entrepreneurs, to motivate and build perspectives for entrepreneurship activity, and to include returned migrants in training programmes on entrepreneurship activity.

These sage words may point to a more general problem in Transnistria: a lack of investment generally, other than by the Sheriff group. The Russian involvement has not led to it taking a significant direct financial stake in the country except for the purchasing of privatised industries (SubSect.2.1.2).

The extent of remittances, like the levels of migration, does present problems for the Transnistrian economy. Nevertheless, there are fully independent countries with viable economies that have a greater dependence on remittances, just as there are those with higher emigration rates. These factors do not prevent the economy of those countries being viable and their functioning as independent states, and there is no reason why these issues should have such an impact on Transnistria.

2.6 TRANSNISTRIAN ECONOMIC DEPENDENCE ON RUSSIA

It has been suggested that Russia provides up to 70% of Transnistria's finances (Puiu 2015), and recent weakening of the Transnistrian economy has been a consequence of Russia's economic problems and fall in its rouble. This is clearly another vulnerability in the economy, even more so than remittances, as it is possible, in theory at least, for a single source of funding to be suddenly and totally withdrawn in a way that could never happen with disparately sourced remittances.

The Warsaw-based Centre for Eastern Studies argued in 2013 that Russia deliberately boosts the Transnistrian economy to make it seem desirable to Right-Bank Moldovans, particularly the low energy and gas prices and the complex welfare system (Całus 2016:7). Thus, Transnistria would become a form of "propaganda bait", showing the Moldovans the advantages of closer cooperation with Russia, presumably in distinction to the consequences of looking to the EU. Even before the Ukrainian crisis, this reasoning was a little far-fetched, as life in the countries west of Chisinau was more comfortable than those to the east. However, it cannot be completely dismissed as a factor in the pro-Russian Dodon's victory in the 2016 Moldovan presidential elections, with many electors perhaps hoping his approach would bring Russian largesse to Chisinau.

2.6.1 GAS SUBSIDIES

A further and more significant source of income is 'gas subsidies'. Gas is supplied by the Moldovan company MoldovaGaz, which receives it from the Russian Gazprom, to Tiraspoltransgaz-Pridnestrovie. The Transnistrian company, however, does not pay for it. It sells it to Transnistrian consumers and businesses for around US$85 and US$163 per thousand cubic metres, respectively, in contrast to the US$391 that Gazprom charges the Moldovans.* The situation is summed up by Brian Milakovsky (2019):

---

*   In Britain, the same amount of gas would typically be around £170 or US$230.

Moscow provides Transnistria with free gas and presents the bill to Chisinau, which understandably refuses to pay. The Russian gas continues nonetheless, keeping down both utility costs and local discontent, and allowing Tiraspol to sell electricity at artificially low prices to industrial customers.

The reason for this indulgence is that MoldovaGaz is owned by Gazprom and there is seemingly a political decision not to enforce the debt, which was estimated in 2013 to have reached US$3.7 billion (Całus 2016:4) and by 2017 around US$5.8 billion as well as £700 million from Moldova (Necsutu 2018a). By allowing the debt to mount, Russia is able to use the threat of enforcement to exercise influence in both Moldova and Transnistria (Całus 2016:5). It has been argued that in the early days of Transnistrian *de facto* independence, Chisinau was reluctant to let Tiraspol take responsibility for any of the debt on the basis that doing so would be a recognition of Transnistrian sovereignty (Napieralska 2012:62 citing Quinlan 2002:88).

The matter is further complicated by the partial ownership of MoldovaGaz and its transmission system subsidiary Moldovatransgaz by Gazprom (Sabadus 2020). This may now have access to Romanian gas through the construction of a pipe from Ungheni in Romania to Chisinau, which may be completed by 2023. While Gazprom has not ostensibly opposed this development, Sabadus (2020) reports MoldovaGaz president Vadim Ceban as saying that the debt to Gazprom, now assessed at US$7 billion, presents a substantial obstacle to the project, as would the status of Transnistria's transmission company Tiraspoltransgaz. Ceban's tone suggests a degree of personal independence from Gazprom but along with a recognition that the companies are intertwined by the debt in a way which means Moldova, and particularly Transnistria, can have very little autonomy on energy matters.

The current legal status of Transnistria makes the recovery of any debts owed in respect of gas, or indeed anything else, complex. Victor Parlicov, Tudor Şoitu and Sergiu Tofilat make the startling assertion (2017:3) that "legally, claims against [*Tiraspoltransgaz-Pridnestrovie*] are equivalent to claims against an entity registered only by the self-proclaimed authorities of the Islamic State". Even leaving aside the clear governmental differences between Transnistria and Islamic State, the claim is misplaced as, in practice, organisations in pariah states do not wish to acquire a reputation for not paying debts, for obvious commercial reasons. In the Turkish Republic of Cyprus, numerous businesses, including banks and solicitors' firms with roots in the UK, flourish. Iran, for all its revolutionary fervour since 1979, has participated in the international court system (e.g. *Islamic Republic of Iran v. United States of America* 1996) and satisfied judgements against it. Indeed, it is states whose political credibility is seen as doubtful who have the most incentive to show their creditworthiness and not face ostracisation from international trade for economic or political reasons. There have been no allegations of debt default against Transnistria. The Sheriff group imports and resells numerous consumer goods and foods as well as petrol and even luxury cars. This requires access to credit.

Were there ever to be a serious attempt to enforce the Gazprom debt, Transnistria would be forced into a form of international bankruptcy and perhaps left at the mercy of the distressed debt funds which have preyed on defaulting nations, particularly in Latin America.* Were Russia to retain control of the indebtedness that would enable it to continue exercising political leverage in the territory, though Parlicov *et al.*'s argument (2017) could be adapted to maintain that the government of an independent Transnistria bore no liability for debts incurred before independence. It has even been suggested that the Chisinau government could be liable for the debt (Najarian 2017). While the legal basis would be tenuous indeed, the possibility of cutting off future supplies would be a potent threat. As Najarian (2017) points out, Moldova is one of the most energy-vulnerable countries in the world. Chisinau can take some comfort from the fact that cutting off supplies would also lose Gazprom revenue 'downstream' as supplies to other countries pass through Moldova. There appears to be a finely balanced interdependence between Russia, Moldova and Transnistria, which it would be in the interests of none to disturb.

2.6.2 THE SIGNIFICANCE OF RUSSIAN SUPPORT

Agnieszka Miarka argues (2020:63) that "Russian financial support is still so significant that it is an important factor in strengthening the pro-Russian society and the elite of Transnistria". She goes so far as to state that the dependence prevents Transnistrian "political decision makers from creating a fully independent political line" (2020:66). The argument may not fully address the nuances of the present situation particularly that Russia has been unable to, at least in electoral terms (SubSect.1.1.3), fully impose its will on Transnistria. While there are few Transnistrian political decisions that have not allied with Russia, there is no evidence that this is a result of economic pressure rather than a genuine and consensual alignment between Tiraspol and Moscow.

The popular wisdom of dependency is partially questioned by Madalin Necsutu (2019a) because Transnistria is benefiting from being able to export to the EU. She was told by Moldovan economist Iurie Morcotilo that, "Transnistria is applying the same model as Russia – 'we trade with the west, but we promote our own politics and interests.'" Ultimately, the interest in preserving the subsidies may be even greater than the advantages of the trade with the EU. Indeed, perhaps with an eye on the customs issues discussed in SubSect.2.1.1, a Ukrainian political scientist Ruslan Kermach (2017, cited by Milakovsky 2019: footnote 5) argues that, "The Republic of Moldova itself, despite its official non-recognition of Transnistria, actually serves as one of the sponsors of its economic sustainability, along with Russia."

---

* The international abhorrence for these funds, often called vulture funds, was expressed in a 2014 UN motion which supported a new form of bankruptcy for sovereign nations; however, this was vetoed by the US (Charbonneau 2015).

2.7 CONCLUSION: IS TRANSNISTRIA ECONOMICALLY VIABLE?

An economy's viability does not depend on self-sufficiency (Schroder 1992). In practice, there is little difference between the "subsistent" label Transnistria was given by Sabor (2012) and viability, meaning the most plausible position is that of Isachenko and Schlichte (2012): that the territory is viable without being self-sufficient.

The Soviet industrial heritage, particularly the Tirotex factory, brings a stability to the economy and has enabled Transnistria to access foreign currency. It has to be accepted that this industry is not as great a contribution to the economy as would be ideal, and that Russian support and remittances each play at least as large a role, without generating the employment an economy needs to thrive.

The Transnistrian government, despite not being dealt the best of hands economically, has performed the functions of fiscal and economic control reasonably satisfactorily. A strong central bank operates with some autonomy, if not full political independence.* The development of Transnistrian currency has been a success in that it is used for the vast majority of transactions within the territory and has contributed to the establishment of the national identity. The fact that since 2017 the currency has floated freely is a promising sign. A currency that cannot be freely traded is anathema in modern-day Europe, and the removal of controls then greatly reduces the risk of rapid devaluations of the sort that have recently plagued Ukraine, Turkey and Russia. The remaining functions of banking are performed adequately, even with a degree of competitiveness, at the moment. There are relatively low unemployment rates within the territory.

Trivial though it is, becoming the first place in the world to introduce plastic coins showed a degree of boldness on the part of the government, which could be applied in more important fields. The flirtation with cryptocurrencies may be seen as another manifestation of this boldness. Whether this, particularly in league with dubious foreign businessmen, such as Igor Chaika, is the best place to take an innovative spirit is questionable. The sophisticated laws to prevent money laundering, which deserve more international plaudits than they receive, may be undermined if Transnistria goes far down that road. Even if short-term gains can be made from Bitcoin mining or similar activities, they are cancelled out by the devastating effect of sanctions that would probably follow if Transnistria was shown to genuinely have become a centre for money laundering.

There is evidence that the Sheriff group has influence over the government in a way that can be regarded as politically undesirable. However, that cannot detract from Sheriff's economic success, and the territory has benefited from it. The balanced views of Bobick (2012) and Olesky (2015), that it is generally both a beneficial force within the territory and perceived as such by the population, are in accordance with my own perceptions. The fact that it has made substantial contributions in tax is obviously good for the economy, as well as showing it does not have complete political leverage.

---

* For an argument that no central bank can be truly independent, see e.g. Redwood (2018).

Even if a largely a vanity project, its successful football team can be seen as contributing to the national identity.

The depopulation is a challenge to the Transnistrian economy. Economic theory (e.g. Hansen 1939) largely supports the view that this tends to be bad for a country, despite Keynes' (1937) slightly contrary stagnation theory. The present degree of viability has been obtained despite that challenge. The research of Ostavnaia (2017) and Fomenko (2017) show a reluctance on the part of émigrés to return, but there might be some reversal of that trend were Transnistria to become an independent state. Remittances are a corollary of that migration, and while they may not stimulate the economy directly in the way investment would, they ensure money circulates in a way that benefits more than only their immediate recipients.

Russian assistance, which goes wider than the complexities of the gas credits, is another important feature of the economy. In crude terms, Russia injects money into Transnistria by subsidies and otherwise, and the economy benefits from that. It provides a market for Transnistria's exports. The Russian support for Transnistria has created the viability which is part of the route to independence. On the basis of Schroeder's (1992) position that viability depends on an ability to exist and develop separately among economically interdependent states, the support from Russian is not a barrier to economic viability and hence independence.

The separation of the economy from that of Moldova since 1992 is a feature of Transnistria as an independent nation. The assistance with documentation and facilitation of the international transport of goods that Moldova has provided does not undermine that. An independent Transnistria providing the documentation for itself would not present any meaningful challenge. The ability to trade with both Russia and the EU would remain and both would have reason to compete for favour within the territory hoping it would be within their sphere of influence.

For all the difficulties, in the regional context Transnistria is no worse off than its obvious comparators, Moldova and Ukraine. If the test I posit for viability, close to Bookman's (1992) – of its economy enjoying a standard of living not significantly worse than that which can be expected in the region it is located – is applied, Transnistria clears the bar comfortably. This is in the context of a government which has been able to introduce a nuanced tax system and, as will be seen in Chapter 4, which has moved towards providing adequate services for its population.

Moving to the definitions of Tuma (1978) and Bookman (1992) that involve a potential for growth, the case may be even stronger. Independence would bring a right to associate with other countries formally through membership of organisations such as the UN and the WTO. It may be that a surge of patriotism would reduce the damaging trend towards emigration and the resulting depopulation.

A strong case can thus be made that, by most criteria, Transnistria does have a viable economy. At the very least, it can be said that a lack of economic viability would not stand in the way of Transnistrian independence, but it can plausibly be argued that the economy, unfettered by Chisinau, has already contributed to the building of the Transnistrian nation. Looking to the future, should it become an independent nation, the ability to join and be supported by international organisations will improve its economic position and increase that viability further.

CHAPTER THREE

TRANSNISTRIA AS A FREE, DEMOCRATIC NATION, SUBJECT TO THE RULE OF LAW

This chapter considers the nature of Transnistrian government. The first section focuses on the constitution, which sets out the aspirations of the Transnistrian regime, and the following sections on how the governance actually works. Those following sections consider specific topics which fall under or are related to the heading of the chapters and how Transnistria performs in relation to them. Once the constitution itself is explored, six different aspects of the topics or "outcomes", as Massimo Tommasoli describes them (2012), are examined. Electoral democracy itself is the first of these, as there is little chance of a society which respects other freedoms developing if the electoral process is completely flawed. The rule of law is an essential restraint on how political leaders can exercise their powers and underpins the freedom of a society. How human rights have been respected in the light of the democratic and legal processes is examined in detail. Imprisonment, the high rate of which is one of the most distinctive features of Transnistrian governance, has a section (3.4) of its own. The freedom of the media and other forms of communication is another important facet of a successful democratic and legal system within a country. Religion, because of its repression under the USSR, is a significant issue in post-Soviet societies and also merits a separate section (3.7). The thrust of the chapter is to consider whether the flaws in governance in relation to all these matters is sufficient to significantly undermine Transnistria's case for independence.

3.1 THE TRANSNISTRIAN CONSTITUTION AND FUNDAMENTAL LAWS

Like nearly all countries,* Transnistria has a written constitution. Predictably, it is full of worthy aims on matters such as education, healthcare and housing, as well as democracy and free speech, and prescribes a system of government. Its protection of free speech is

---

* The UK is the main exception.

not as unequivocal as might be hoped. It is against the aims of that constitution that the evaluations of how the features of a democratic society work in practice should be judged.

3.1.1 THE CONSTITUTION

The Constitution of Pridnestrovskaia Moldavskaia Respublica (2011), to give its full title, begins in a familiar tone with, "We the multinational people…" Originally adopted in December 1995 after being approved in a referendum (Haynes 2020:166), it was last amended in June 2011, when the post of vice president was scrapped and replaced with a prime minister. It is very similar to the Constitution of the Republic of Moldova (2016). Both have similarities to the Constitution of the Russian Federation (1993). Many of the features could also have been taken from the US constitution, such is the common outlook both in terms of ideals and creation of state institutions of drafters of most presidential constitutions: virtually all aim to separate executive, legislative and judicial power. These are the fundamentals of a free society and their adoption by Transnistria is the first step towards creating that outcome.

The Transnistrian version is in itself an admirable document, containing exhortations such as:

> No one can assume power in [Transnistria]. Seizure of power and appropriation of powers of authority are the gravest crime against the people (Article 1);
> The state, its organs and officials act in the conditions of democratic diversity of political institutions and opinions (Article 8);
> Basic human rights and freedoms are inalienable and belong to everybody from birth (Article 16);
> The media is not subject to censorship (Article 28); and
> No one should be forced to pay taxes and other obligatory payments not established by law, or calculation and collection of which are not carried out according to law, or in another order than provided by law (Article 98).

The constitution is premised on Transnistria being an independent country and capable of forming conventional relationships with other countries (Article 10). There is little in its content, except perhaps the qualification on free speech in Article 27 discussed below, that would be ineffective or undesirable were Transnistria to be granted independence.

It provides for a secular state (Article 9), the establishment of armed forces subject to the law (Article 11), and for 'Moldovan',* Russian and Ukrainian (listed presumably in alphabetical order**) to be the official languages (Article 12). There is a mix of capitalist and socialist ideals. The right to conduct private business (Article 36) and to own

---

* While Moldavian with a Cyrillic script is acceptable to the Transnistrian authorities, its use with Latin script is frowned upon in practice.
** The order is the same in Cyrillic letters.

property (Article 37) is guaranteed. So is the right to social security for the disabled and in an (undefined) "old age" (Article 38) and to universal free healthcare (Article 39). Free and compulsory education up to secondary school level is provided for. That right extends on a "completive [*sic*] basis" to higher education (Article 41). Everyone has a right to housing and there is specific provision that the state is to provide it for poor people for free or for "reasonable pay" (Article 42).

Freedom of speech, virtually the lynchpin of the US and many other constitutions, is not given prominence, only appearing in Article 27 and then with a worrying qualification:

> Everyone has the right to the freedom of thought, speech and opinion. Everyone has the right in any legal way to seek, receive and spread any information, except for the one* directed against [the] existing constitutional system.

"Spreading information" against the existing constitutional system, which it might be argued could apply to something as anodyne as saying that medical care should be privatised or that the state should not fund university education – positions that prevail in much of the world – could be prevented. It is not difficult for politicians to argue that attacks on them are attacks on the constitution: a situation that becomes particularly dangerous if there is not a strong independent judiciary. The right to freedom of speech is one that may be suspended during a state of emergency (Article 54), as can the right of the media not to be censored. The penal code, despite the constitution, has been amended to make criticising the role of Russian peacekeeping troops on the border with Moldova a crime carrying up to three years' imprisonment (Vlas 2016).

There are provisions restricting the imposition of arrest and punishment except in accordance with legal process (Articles 18–25). That a person is presumed innocent of crime until the contrary is proved (Article 22) is also enshrined in the constitution. Capital punishment, "unless it is abolished", can only be used for grave crimes against life (Article 19). Theoretically, the death penalty remains in the criminal code, but there have been no executions since a moratorium was decreed by President Smirnov in 1999 (CoE 2006).

Compulsory universal military service is provided for (Article 48) in armed forces, the role of which is prescribed later in the constitution (Articles 93–95). Some, like the charming "Everybody must take care of the environment", are meaningless (Article 50). Less attractively, there is provision for states of emergency during which some rights can be determined (Article 54).

Section III provides for the system of government, a presidential republic with a standard separation of powers provision.** The president, who must be over 35 and have been a citizen of Transnistria for ten years, is elected by universal suffrage every

---

* A better translation of the last clause is "with the exception of information directed against the existing constitutional order".

** Articles 55 and 60 provide that the president, judges and public servants cannot be deputies to the Supreme Soviet.

five years (Article 68). There is provision for a 43-member Supreme Soviet, effectively a parliament, also elected every five years (Article 59). National legislative power (Article 63), including levying taxes, is reserved to the Soviet, though the president has a right to initiate legislation and veto laws passed except for constitutional ones (Article 65). The Soviet can remove the president or other senior officials but only after a Supreme Court determination that there has been a relevant dereliction of duty by that official (Article 67).

A subsidiary law-making power is given, in vague terms, to the president (Article 72):

> Decrees and enactments of the President of [Transnistria] shall be legal acts of sub-law character, which must not be inconsistent with the Constitution and the laws of [Transnistria].

There is provision for the president to form a cabinet. The president and cabinet members are restricted from taking up other occupations, including sitting on boards of commercial organisations, with a few exceptions. An unusual stipulation is that neither president nor cabinet can remain as members of any political party (Article 74).

Local government is provided for in the constitution, and elections to a single tier of local soviets are prescribed, but nothing is said about the actual powers of local authorities (Articles 77–79).

The constitution recognises the desirability of judicial independence, though, perhaps paradoxically, charges the president with securing that independence. Crucially, there is explicit provision for the process generally known as judicial review in common law systems, such as the English and the US's (Article 81):

> A court, having revealed during consideration of a case an inconsistency between a normative act of a state organ or another organ and the Constitution or law, shall take a decision according to the Constitution and law.

The term "judicial review" is expressly used in connection with detention and arrest, creating a remedy not dissimilar, at least in theory, with the common law's *habeas corpus* (Article 20). There is protection against self-incrimination, again a feature important in most common law jurisdictions (Article 23).

The president is responsible for appointing most judges. There is proper provision in place to fix judges' terms and prevent arbitrary removal (Article 83), and judges are given the personal immunity (Article 84) generally reckoned to be an essential feature of judicial independence (UNODC 2019).

There is a separate Constitutional Court, to which the president, the Soviet and the congress of judges each appoint two judges for seven-year terms (Article 86). It is given wide-ranging power over government and constitutional matters. It has a concurrent jurisdiction with the Supreme Court, which governs civil, including family and divorce, criminal and administrative matters (Article 89), and the Court of Arbitration (Article 90), which has a role broadly similar to the Commercial Court of the English High Court.

There is provision for the appointment and role of a prosecutor, akin to the attorney general in the US or UK, by the president (Article 91). The prosecution system is centralised, with all those working as prosecutors answerable to the prosecutor, who in turn is answerable to the president (Article 92) and the Soviet.

The financial and budgetary system is more closely regulated than in most constitutions. There is a constitutional imperative to maintain a reserve fund to meet potential budgetary deficits (Article 96). There is provision for a state central bank, the Pridnestrovian Republican Bank (PRB), which issues currency within limits set by the Soviet (Article 100), but there is no specific provision guaranteeing the independence of the PRB or its governor.

The constitution is entrenched, though not irreversibly. The "Rights Freedom and Duties" section (Articles 16–42) can only be changed by a referendum (Article 102). The remainder can be changed by three votes of the Supreme Soviet over at least a three-month period. A two-thirds majority of the Soviet is required to either make such amendments or call a referendum to do so (Article 104).

Russian law

A draft law exists which in principle would introduce all Russian laws to Transnistria. This was approved by the Supreme Soviet at a first reading in December 2013 (Ivan 2014:3) but was not actually implemented (Kolstø 2014). Promo-LEX (2018:9) has reported that Shevchuk, who was voted out of office in 2016, issued a presidential decree in September 2017 (sic) that would adjust Transnistrian law in line with Russian. Such a decree would have no effect under the constitution and has not been reported elsewhere.

The position is summed up in the *Russian Law Journal* by Tolstykh, Grigoryan and Kovalenko:

> In practice, [the non-recognised states] tend to borrow main Russian codes and laws adapting them to their local circumstances. For example, [Transnistria] grants a legal entity status not only to organizations (as Russia does), but to administrative-territorial entities as well (Art. 49(4) of the Transnistrian Civil Code). (2019:84)

They cite (2019:85) Fedyakina (2013), who points out the processes which would have had to be gone through for such a law to be introduced and the hurdles it faced. They also point to a September 2016 decree by Shevchuk, possibly what Promo-LEX (2018) had in mind, saying Transnistrian policy was *aimed* at bringing its law into line with Russia (2019:84). The matter has not been taken forward under the Krasnoselsky regime. Such a law has in fact been introduced in South Ossetia (2019:85).

Had the law been implemented, it would have been a substantial surrender of autonomy by Transnistria. Technically, sovereignty would not have been given up so long as it remained possible for Transnistria to unilaterally repeal the legislation. Kolstø (2014) likened it to the way EU law has direct effect and supremacy in member states. Such surrendered sovereignty can only be reclaimed by withdrawal from the union. From a legal perspective, there may now be little significance to this proposed law; however, the fact that it was seriously considered may reinforce the views of those who contend that aspirations for Transnistrian independence are merely a stepping stone to an ultimate ambition of union with Russia.* That, of course, is a separate issue to whether independence from Chisinau is viable before that supposed ambition is fulfilled.

International conventions

As Transnistria is not internationally recognised, it does not have the legal capacity to enter into treaties. However, in September 1992, shortly after *de facto* independence, Resolution 226 of the Supreme Soviet decreed that the terms of the International Covenant on Civil and Political Rights, the European Convention on Human Rights**, the International Covenant on Economic, Social and Cultural Rights, and the Convention for the Prevention and Punishment of the Crime of Genocide all have effect in Transnistria (FIDH 2012).

3.1.2 OTHER FUNDAMENTAL LAWS

Criminal law is set out in single codifying document (Criminal Code of Transnistria 2019). This covers the whole range of crime, including, for instance, prostitution (only illegal if someone is forced into it) (2019 Article 38), bribery (2019 Articles 286-87), theft (2019 Articles 154-58) with burglary and robbery, that are similar to crimes identified by English law, and waging war and genocide (2019 Articles 349-56). While the code is nothing like as detailed as the criminal law of Western European countries or the US, there is little in it that could be regarded as objectionable. It outlaws most conduct that would be criminal in any civilised society. Except for the provision about not criticising Russian troops (SubSect.3.1.1), it contains little restraint on recognised freedoms and generally provides for sentences less than those the English courts could impose.*** Contrary to some reports, including one from the UK Home Office (2017), consensual adult homosexuality is not illegal. The penal code also contains procedural safeguards,

---

*   On independence, many former British colonies passed 'reception statutes' incorporating existing English law. These however did not extend to future laws.

**   It is to be noted that this Convention expressly prohibits capital punishment and is thus incompatible with Transnistria's retention at least nominally of such punishment (2010 Articles 6 and 13).

***   For instance, for burglary there is a sentence of up to six years, compared with fourteen or ten years in England, depending on whether or not it is in a dwelling (s9(3) Theft Act 1968).

such as new crimes not having retrospective effect (2019 Article 9) and the provision of defences such as self-defence, necessity and coercion (2019 Articles 36-39).

There is a Civil Code (2018 Articles 452–455), which is a longer and more sophisticated document than the Criminal Code, dealing with virtually all aspects of civil law, including corporations, powers of attorney, property transactions and state enterprises. Much of it is alien to a common lawyer, though the fundamental rule about contracts being made by offer and acceptance is stipulated.

Family law is not codified in the same way, but Professor Irena Lemeshva, head of the Shevchenko University family law department, summarised it to me at the university on 27 May 2019. Children are occasionally taken away from their parents, but only by a court and after other agencies, including the police, have tried to solve things. It is always possible to get a divorce within three months. The courts consider property matters, but they will usually let whichever parent the children will live with keep the house. It sounds like, and perhaps is more efficiently operated than, the English system.

3.1.3 THE APPLICATION OF THE CONSTITUTION

It is against the commendable ideals of this constitution that political and indeed much of general life in Transnistria must be judged. Of course, mere aspirations say little about the way a territory is actually governed. As Massimo Tommasoli, writing for the *United Nations Chronicle*, puts it:

> A common feature of both democracy and the rule of law is that a purely institutional approach does not say anything about actual outcomes of processes and procedures, even if the latter are formally correct. (2012)

The following sections consider the successes, failures and uncertainties of the application of the constitution in light of the institutional approach that would be taken from purely looking at the constitution. This is examined in relation to the ideals of the democratic process, the rule of law and the various forms of freedom discussed at the start of this section as enunciated in the constitution. Chapter 4 will look at it in terms of whether the government does achieve the aims of providing for the population's 'positive rights' to things like education, housing and social security in accordance with the constitution discussed in SubSect.3.1.1.

3.2 ELECTORAL DEMOCRACY

Electoral democracy, in the sense of there being free elections, is now the norm in much of the world: Belarus is the only country in Europe not to be predominantly democratic – a view taken even before the outrages following the August 2020 elections (Pew Research

Center 2020).* The Transnistrian constitution (2011), particularly Section III, is inherently democratic, and independence would not mean handing power to an unelected clique. This section explores how electoral democracy has developed in the years since *de facto* independence.

Elections in the post-Soviet world are viewed with a degree of scepticism by many observers. Sofie Bedford and Ryhor Nizhnikau reflect on this in detail in their introductory paper for an edition of *The Journal of Post-Soviet Democratization*, considering several post-Soviet 2016 elections, including briefly Transnistria's. None of these elections, they concluded, contributed to change: "Rather, for good or ill, they reinforced the political *status quo*" (2017:359). The core of that argument was expressed earlier:

> The political parties are dominated by oligarchs, or are only a vehicle for promoting narrow interests. The society is limited in its rights and is also incentivized to 'invest' in the incumbent authority or systemic opposition and restrained in its ability to engage in collective action. The whole system generates preferences and behavior from the state and society embedded in the dominant political culture. (2017:352)

The argument is a simplistic, almost circular, one. An 'oligarch' according to the Cambridge English Dictionary (2020) is "one of a small group of powerful people who control a country or an industry". Political and industrial leaders throughout the world make their way into that oligarchy, and generally the president or prime minister emerges from within it.

There are exceptions both within and outside the former Soviet space. A striking example is Ukraine's Volodymyr Zelensky, who went straight from being a comic actor playing the role of the president to the actual presidency in 2019. The Armenian prime minister since 2018, Nikol Pashinyan, was a radical newspaper editor who came from outside the ruling elite, and had indeed been imprisoned for his opposition activities. It might be said that Donald Trump came from outside a traditional political oligarchy to be elected US president in 2016, but this was very much an exception in a country which has a long history of electing former vice presidents, congressmen and governors, who all form part of an oligarchy, to that office.

Even if Bedford and Nizhnikau (2017) intended "oligarch" to refer to those who prospered financially from the opportunities the break-up of the USSR gave, they cannot point to a consistent pattern of such persons achieving electoral office throughout the region. They may be right in their perceived veneration of the "dominant political culture" in the electoral process, but what they fail to show is it being more significant in the countries they consider than more established democracies. While in the Transnistrian context it may be argued that all three presidents have come from firmly within an

---

* This is not the place to debate whether Putin's domination of Russia is sufficient to undermine democracy, and some commentators argue that Britain and other monarchies are not truly democratic.

existing political class, it does not follow that that is an inherent feature of the system. The likelihood is that in due course a young democracy will mutate, as the Ukrainian and Armenian examples show. There is no formal process in place that would prevent a maverick contender emerging from outside the political elite, and the fact that it has not happened yet does not undermine the electoral process. The more fundamental issue, considered in the rest of this section, is whether the elections between members of that political elite have been conducted fairly.

3.2.1 THE EVOLUTION OF DEMOCRACY

It is arguable that in the early days of Transnistria's independence there was little genuine democracy. Popescu contends (2006:2):

> In Transnistria there is no credible opposition, no active civil society…and it is policed by a strong repressive apparatus guided by the ministry of state security. The economy is highly concentrated and even if big businesses are dissatisfied with the current political leadership they do not dare to challenge the authoritarian leader who has held power for a decade and a half.

Popescu was not alone in his criticisms. A more nuanced critique of Transnistrian democracy was made by Oleh Protsyk (2008:2), who wrote:

> Given the level of harassment that Transnistrian opposition leaders face, the scope of restrictions on open democratic contestation, and the degree of penetration of the regime's security services into civil society, it is difficult to qualify any election or plebiscite held in Transnistria as free and fair.

These views, even if justifiable when written, did not portend the future. Indeed, the influence of "big businesses", which in effect both then and now refers to the Sheriff group, has become one of the most striking aspects of Transnistrian democracy, contributing to the removal of incumbent presidents in 2011 and 2016. The emergence of the Obnovlenie (SubSect.2.3.2) party, largely associated with Sheriff, shortly after Popescu's comments were written has meant that there has been meaningful opposition in Transnistria for well over a decade, albeit not based on policy or the left–right differences that generally prevail in Western democracies. The president has not been able to control the outcome of elections to the Soviet (Kosienkowski 2012:13). In 2007, the Social Democratic Party was formed by Alexandr Radchenko, advocating reunification with Moldova (Blakkisrud and Kolstø 2013:202). He had been permitted by a Constitutional Court decision to run in the 2001 presidential election, where he obtained 5% of the vote (Ryan 2007). The party never attracted significant popular support and had become defunct by Radchenko's death in 2014 (*NewsMaker* 2013).

Smirnov's election victories

The constitution was amended in 2000 to remove the prohibition on a president standing for more than two terms (Isachenko and Schlichte 2007:86), enabling Smirnov to seek his third term in November 2001. This amendment, unlike the 1995 constitution itself, was not approved by a referendum. The defeated candidate in the 2001 election, former mayor of Bender Tom Zenovich, who advocated confederation with Moldova, claimed to have been severely harassed (Freedom House 2002) and, peculiarly as he was not Jewish, to have been subject to anti-Semitic propaganda (Isachenko and Schlichte 2007:85). It is surprising that Smirnov would have done this, as he might be expected to have welcomed an obviously weak opposition candidate.

Smirnov's re-election seemed little more than a formality until 2011. In 2006, he captured 82% of the votes, almost identical to the 2001 figure. That election was, according to the Transnistrian Central Election Committee, monitored by 40 external observers, all from former Soviet countries, and there were exit polls, which indicated a smaller, but still substantial, margin of victory for Smirnov (*Infotag* 2006). Despite the startlingly high vote Smirnov received, there was no evidence, or indeed specific allegation, to suggest that the votes themselves in his successful elections were rigged: his support was such that they did not need to be.

Smirnov's 2011 defeat

In 2011, Moscow made it clear that it favoured Anatoliy Kaminski, the Soviet's speaker, in the presidential election (Kosienkowski 2012:13). It had discreetly suggested to Smirnov that he should not stand again (RFE 2011a), but when this was ignored provided Kaminski with technical and financial support and abundant photo opportunities with Putin. Three days before the election, a Russian-ordained television programme, 'Transnistria: The Deadline for the President', accusing Smirnov of embezzlement of Russian aid, was shown in the territory. Smirnov ran using the slogan "The homeland is not for sale" (Bobick 2012:17), but without Russian support and with a poorly performing economy, his campaign was doomed, and he obtained just 24% of the vote in the first round against Kaminski's 26% and Shevchuk's 38% (Protsyk 2012:181). Russian interest in the election subsided after Smirnov's elimination and Shevchuk won the run-off against Kaminski, obtaining 74% of the vote.

A key factor in Smirnov's defeat was the poor economy (Devyatkov and Kosienkowski 2013:317). The government's figures showed the population had shrunk from 750,000 in 1989 to 514,000 in 2011, largely as a consequence of the emigration of the working-age population, resulting in pensioners outnumbering workers, with a consequent reduction in living standards (SubSect.2.4.1). More than any other factor, it is the economy that tends to influence democratic elections throughout the world, and that (Devyatkov and Kosienkowski 2013) analysis is likely to be both correct and a sign of a genuine democratic process having taken place.

3.2.2 THE 2016 ELECTION

My observations of the 2016 presidential election, described in Appendix A, left me in no doubt that there was a free and fair, indeed pedantically supervised, process. Although no Western government would officially sanction observers, there were many, some of whom were highly experienced in election observing, from various EU nations including Germany. There was a rivalry between the Ministry of Foreign Affairs, my host, which was broadly speaking supportive of the incumbent Shevchuk, and the Soviet-controlled Central Election Committee (CEC), which favoured Krasnoselsky. Both had invited observers, the CEC's mainly from Russia. I was able to randomly select polling stations at short notice to visit, with the assistance of a government guide and driver – I had insisted on my own interpreter.

Nowhere did I see anything to suggest that there was sharp practice going on. All the election officials I met were polite, some were much more welcoming and informative than others. All insisted on checking my paperwork before admitting me to the polling station. The candidates themselves had observers in the polling stations. Some voters were prepared to talk to me and answer my questions, strictly outside the remit of an observer, as to why they had voted a certain way. Answers, if anodyne, were given freely and with a tilt towards the eventual winner Krasnoselsky, which could have formed the basis for a primitive exit poll. There was a prohibition on photographing ballot papers, which I was told was for fear that some voters might otherwise have been put under pressure to vote a certain way – a sign that some proper thought had gone into ensuring a fair election.

The count I attended that evening in central Tiraspol was meticulously done. It took nearly six hours just to tally up and verify the votes – around 4,000 were counted there – before the counting of votes for individual candidates took place. Again, the process was observed closely by nominees of all the candidates and no allegations of misfeasance were made.

OpenDemocracy, an organisation which in other ways is highly critical of Transnistrian government (e.g. Okrest 2018), had specifically said of the 2015 parliamentary elections, "Unlike Russia, Transnistria is hosting a real election for parliamentary seats, and not just imitating one", and expressed no adverse opinion on the 2011 election (Litoy 2015). There had been no suggestion by unsuccessful candidates at any of these elections that their defeats were anything other than legitimate.

While it is possible for an election itself to be fair as it is conducted, with other factors negating that fairness, there is no evidence of that in Transnistria. During the 2016 election campaign, new laws to secure the propriety of elections were promulgated by President Shevchuk and passed by the Soviet. These made specific offences of coercing someone into voting for a particular candidate, trying to check voting results by photographing ballot papers, and obstructing election commissioners (*Infotag* 2016). While rigorous laws against establishment interest can be passed purely for show, the involvement of both the president and the Soviet, which was generally opposed to Shevchuk, as was the laws' uncritical reporting by the Moldovan press, suggest these were passed in good faith. My own experience at the election left me in no doubt that they were being respected and enforced. Some criticisms of the process were made by more experienced observers, but these were of occasional lapses by election workers, such as failing to display running turn-out figures as they were required to do, and not anything that was conceivably politically motivated or likely to bear on the outcome.

3.2.3 THE SUCCESS OF ELECTORAL DEMOCRACY

In the fundamentals of democracy – the electoral process – Transnistria now performs well. Whether in the early days of independence the same could be said is harder to tell but that does not bear on the present state of democracy, except in as much as an improvement would underline the democratic intentions of the present regime. The paramount factor is that in the last decade two incumbents have been forced out of office electorally and have accepted their defeats. That gives the Transnistrian government a continuing legitimacy which makes a sound basis for it to lead the territory to and in any independence that it may attain.

3.3 THE RULE OF LAW AND THE JUSTICE SYSTEM

Whether the rule of law is applied robustly anywhere is harder to judge than the electoral process. Elections, which take place over a short time, can be closely monitored. The day-to-day interactions between a state and its subjects, which should be regulated by the rule of law, are virtually impossible to scrutinise except in an occasional and random way, as will be illustrated by the tentativeness of the UN observer's conclusions on Transnistria (Hammarberg 2013).

   In almost all democracies, the power of the executive is subject to judicial control* and in many the legislature is too.** The Transnistrian constitution (2011: Section III) specifically provides for a separation of the powers between the executive, the Soviet and the judiciary, and powers to strike down acts of government are reserved to the judiciary (2011: Article 89). This is the framework for the rule of law to be applied, and this section explores the extent to which that happens. This involves considering judicial independence, based largely on my interviews of judges; the possibility of submitting to a supra-national court; the position of lawyers who represent those who have offended the authorities; the ombudsman charged with protecting human rights; and how the regime deals with NGOs, particularly those who act on human rights issues.

---

*   In England, the Administrative Court, formerly the Divisional Court of the Queen's Bench Division, has exercised that power for centuries.

**   Most obviously the US, whose Supreme Court has power to strike down Acts of Congress that it deems not compatible with its constitution; see Zirin (2016) for full discussion.

3.3.1 THE JUDICIARY

The World Justice Project (n.d.) defines the judicial element of the rule of law as requiring that:

> Justice is delivered timely by competent, ethical, and independent representatives and neutrals who are accessible, have adequate resources, and reflect the makeup of the communities they serve.

Constitutionally, the most important stipulation in that definition is that the judges, to which this definition refers, be independent, without which the executive effectively has absolute power. This creates what is colloquially known as a police state: "a system of repressive government control where law is derived from executive power, with widespread state surveillance and suppression of free speech" (McDonald 2013).

While only a small proportion of non-criminal cases are between the individual and the state, the fair, independent determination of those cases is crucial to maintaining a proper relationship between a government and its subjects.* Conversely, most criminal cases are between state and subject, and for any criminal justice to be considered fair, judges must be able to determine cases without fear of any punishment or hope of reward by the state.

I have seen signs of judicial independence in Transnistria. I certainly felt the court that was quickly convened on the evening before the December 2016 election was acting independently in determining, after several hours' argument, a point of electoral procedure against the incumbent president (Appendix A). This was underlined by the court excluding a government minister who the judges felt was adopting a disrespectful demeanour.

Ruslan Mova, the minister of internal affairs, gave me a less obvious indication of that independence in an interview at his offices on 6 December 2018, talking of the large property Shevchuk had built for himself, allegedly with corruptly obtained money. I asked if the government intended to confiscate it, and he replied that they would like to but did not know if a court would make the necessary order. My view of Mova, who was speaking through an interpreter, was that he lacked the sophistication to instantly tailor an answer to impress an interviewer who might be thought concerned about judicial independence and the rule of law. My impression was that he was admitting to a sign of weakness in not being able to simply take property he thought should become the state's.

Bowring visited the territory in 2004 and met judges of the Constitutional Court. He says that it has, "but not often", decided cases against the authorities (Bowring 2014:17). He didn't cite examples or statistics, but any willingness of the judiciary to defy the executive is an indication of a healthy existence of the rule of law. It should be borne in

---

* The Polish government has attracted opprobrium for trying to lower the usual retiring age for judges while reserving the power to extend the terms of those it favours. This was ruled unlawful by the European Court of Justice in June 2019 (Rankin 2019).

mind that even in advanced democracies findings of unconstitutionality against a government are rare.* Judges who exercise their power to rule government actions unlawful are in theory and practice exercising a restraint on executive power. That does mean the rule of law is upheld, which ensures the accountability of that executive and stops it arbitrarily imposing its will on the populace. Any minister who knows he or she may be held to account in this way will have an incentive to have regard to the actual powers they have rather than just follow their own whims.

My discussions with judges (May 2019)

I met the presidents of both the Supreme Court and the Constitutional Court on 29 May 2019 at their respective courts. Vladimir Sezquevich Rimar of the Supreme Court gave a particularly good impression, understated and thoughtful in his manner and always answering questions directly. There are twenty judges in that court and 57 in all the Transnistrian courts. Twenty appellate judges in a population of around 500,000 is proportionately about fifteen times the amount of High Court, Court of Appeal and Supreme Court judges in England – and that disregards the eight judges in the Transnistrian Constitutional Court. Rimar and his fellow judges regularly hold open meetings with citizens. It was such meetings that had led to the dismissal, about a month before my interview, of a local judge in Ribnita who had been the subject of many complaints. Rimar, in answer to my questions, was emphatic that the process by which he was removed was wholly judicial, with no political input at any stage, and that the president and the Soviet could not dismiss judges.

I asked Rimar about the involvement of lawyers and was told that about 50% of parties in civil cases are represented and, somewhat bafflingly, "In criminal cases the majority have lawyers. There is no state funding for lawyers. If a person can't afford a lawyer the government pays the bill."

The positive impression Rimar gave was undone a little when he took me into the criminal chamber of the Supreme Court. One side of it was taken up with a hideous-looking cage about 1.5 metres high, in which defendants would be made to sit. Although Rimar told me it was necessary "for security", the justification for such a barbaric contraption, let alone its routine use, was hard to see.

Oleg Kabaloev, president of the Constitutional Court since 2010, was keen to tell me at some length about the history and composition of the court, largely contained in the constitution, but was prepared to answer questions too. Like Rimar, he had come to the court having first been a lower court judge. In the last years of Shevchuk's regime, the court had been called upon to resolve many disputes between the Soviet and president, usually finding in favour of the Soviet, but its present workload had retracted to about twenty petitions a year from citizens, of which it allowed "many".

---

* In England, only about 1% of applications for judicial review, the process by which the law-fulness of an executive decision is challenged, actually succeed (Ministry of Justice 2015:5).

He had no statistics on this. I expressed surprise that if, as he said, anybody could petition the court over any constitutional matter there were only twenty such petitions a year. Unprompted, though he may have seen where my questions were going, Kabaloev said:

> The Constitutional Court is the really independent court of Transnistria. The court itself and the judges are not trying to please higher institutions. In all the years [I have been sitting on the court] no head of government, none of the three Presidents tried to influence the court.

Law reports were published and formatted like English reports: from 2002 to 2010 they had been translated into English, French and German. In recent years, the judges of the court, usually eight, had always reached unanimous decisions, but there is provision for dissenting judgements.

Although Kabaloev gave no examples of decisions his court had made, one was cited in its official press release in February 2019. This concerned the constitutionality of a law requiring those claiming unemployment benefit to take part in "socially beneficial" activities for four days a month. On a narrow point of detail, not clearly expressed in the release, the Constitutional Court concluded that, "The contested norm does not comply with the constitution of the PMR" (President 2019).*

I did not find Kabaloev's protestations of judicial independence convincing in themselves, even bolstered by a specific recent example of deciding against the government. Taken with Rimar's evidence about judges' security of tenure; the undoubted history of some decisions against the government, dating at least back to Bowring's 2004 visit (2014:17), including that in relation to opposition politician Radchenko in 2001 (2014:53); and my 2016 observations of the electoral court (Appendix A), they become plausible. The Constitutional Court's role in holding the ring between the president and the Soviet would give it leeway in playing one off against the other and might put it beyond the control of either, giving credence to the argument that not only is there a strong judiciary but also a genuine separation of powers between all three branches of government.

A petty detail which impressed me was that both judges were wearing suits that could, if a little unkindly, be characterised as 'Soviet style'. Even if they had been more expensively dressed, it would not have been evidence of any nefarious enrichment from their positions; but in view of the allegations of Stepan Popovskiy, discussed below, that judicial corruption occurs, this obvious non-manifestation of it was encouraging.

Visiting the criminal court in central Tiraspol incognito on 1 October 2019 proved more difficult. The security officer said there was a policy that people not connected to a case would only be admitted if permission was obtained from a judge. This seemingly spectacular

---

* The fact that the Constitutional Court's messages are hosted by the president's site is not ideal in the eyes of a lawyer well versed in the theory of separation of powers, but this may be a bit pedantic when one considers the limited resources of the territory.

violation of the principle of open justice was disavowed to me the next day by former Foreign Minister Vladimir Yastrebchak, himself a former prosecutor, who assured me the courts were meant to be open. My interpreter and I were admitted after the court staff discreetly relayed my request to the judge, who grudgingly said we could come in. We saw the prosecution of a man and woman for attacking a female neighbour. The procedure followed was inquisitorial and alien to a common lawyer* – disputed facts could be evidenced simply by the prosecutor reading them out – and the defendants were questioned at length by the judge, not the prosecutor. Other aspects, like the obviously competent, if grumpy, judge; the defendants not being required to sit in the cage, which was like the one I had seen in the Supreme Court; and meticulous note-taking by all involved, were suggestive of a fair trial.

Is there an independent judiciary?

The latest Freedom House (2020) report gave 0/4 to Transnistria in considering the question "Is there an independent judiciary?" However, it is doubtful much consideration, or updating, goes into these annual assessments or even into the original score (SubSect.3.5.2). While the Transnistrian authorities should be concerned about any international organisation seeing it in that light, the better evidence is of a reasonably strong independent judiciary. The greater concern is the number of conflicts between the state and individuals which are effectively determined by the police or the executive without involving the judiciary. That trials may not be routinely open to the public is superficially a concern, though the difficulties I faced getting into one were probably merely administrative in nature – court staff are simply not used to people wanting to observe – and not a sinister attempt to make the process secret.

3.3.2 THE CASE FOR A SUPRA-NATIONAL COURT

Concerns about judicial independence had led Stepan Popovskiy of Apriori, probably the most active 'human rights' lawyer within Transnistria, to call for a court overseeing those in the territory to consist of judges from several countries, including Moldova, in an interview at his offices on 28 May 2019. This would make justice more accessible for Transnistrians, particularly those in dispute with the government, without the need to take cases to the European Court of Human Rights (ECHR). He claimed the idea had met with approval by the US ambassador in Chisinau and the Ukrainian government, but the Moldovan authorities had effectively vetoed it.

Although Popovskiy did not dwell on the point, the ECHR is an unsatisfactory tribunal for many reasons. Its resources mean it has to be highly selective in the cases it takes. Its procedures require highly specialist lawyers to present cases. It is also extremely slow,

---

*   Common law is used in distinction to civil law. The former system, used in most anglophile countries, is accusatorial in that the prosecution bears the burden of proving nearly all aspects of a criminal case. In the latter, the court itself has a major role in investigating the facts. Few would argue that either system is inherently fairer or more efficient than the other.

exemplified by the case of Stefan Mangir and four other Moldovan policemen illegally detained in Transnistria in 2006, which was only finally determined, in their favour, in July 2018 (*Infotag* 2018).

Popovskiy was reluctant to accept the reasoning, which would have been apparent to most lawyers and must have been put to him before in similar discussions, that the Chisinau government could not acquiesce in a court making decisions over what it continued to regard as its land without, in effect, surrendering sovereignty. Not surprisingly, the idea found no favour with Ion Manole of Chisinau-based Promo-LEX when I interviewed him at his offices on 30 May 2019. Although Manole is, if anything, an even more vociferous critic of the Transnistrian authorities than Popovskiy, many of his arguments are premised on the territory's lack of recognition in international law (Sect.5.1).

There seems little basis, therefore, on which such a court should be established, even if Transnistria were to acquire independence.* Its actions are currently susceptible to the jurisdiction of the ECHR, albeit with the fiction of making Russia or Moldova the defendant, and after any independence would inevitably submit to the jurisdiction being itself a defendant.

3.3.3 CONCERNS ABOUT THE JUSTICE SYSTEM

Attacks on lawyers

Closely related to an independent judiciary is the ability of lawyers, particularly those who are known for acting in claims against the authorities, to work without fear of official oppression or interference. Indeed, a government that operates by oppressing its population will often do so by making life difficult for the lawyers that represent those of whom that government does not approve: a virtually invariable indication of the breakdown of the rule of law. There is little doubt that this currently happens in China (Kuo 2019), Iran (Qiblawi *et al.* 2019) and Saudi Arabia (*France 24* 2018) among others. There are suggestions that Transnistria may be going down this route. The inability of Promo-LEX's Ion Manole and Alexandru Zubko to enter Transnistria (SubSect.3.5.2) is a manifestation of this.

Popovskiy told me he had been subject to police and KGB harassment and the leader of the latter had required him to attend a private meeting. His home had been searched, and he had been subject to a peculiar-sounding prosecution on the basis that he "used his power too much", in which Thomas Hammarberg had given him some help.

Even more serious are the allegations that a lawyer who had been critical of the Shevchuk government, Vladimir Maimust, had an explosive device attached to his car in September 2013. The only primary source of this is the Transnistrian press, and it

---

* The Eastern Caribbean Supreme Court, which was formed largely to take over the residual judicial powers of the UK's Privy Council, is probably the closest example of what Popovskiy is arguing for. However, the relationship between the subscribing islands is very different to that between Transnistria, Moldova, Ukraine and other neighbouring countries.

seems that the country's security forces were instrumental in neutralising the device after it had been spotted (TIRAS 2013). There are also reports that Maimust was previously beaten up by four policemen, who subsequently opened a conspiracy case against him (Thoolen 2013). Although this potentially carried twelve years' imprisonment, it was not pursued and Maimust remains at liberty, again suggesting that the Transnistrian authorities usually do not behave as oppressively as is reported.

The human rights ombudsman

The Transnistrian authorities appointed Vassily Kalko as human rights ombudsman on 3 November 2006, and he remained in the post until his death in September 2017 (Ombudsman of PMR 2020). He was succeeded by Vyacheslav Kosinsky. Kalko was undoubtedly an 'establishment' man, his career having started in a Soviet militia; he then worked in the criminal investigation department, heading it from 2002 to 2006 (Ombudsman of PMR 2020).

Ombudsmen fulfil a quasi-judicial role, although their tasks and powers will vary from country to country. Thomas Hammarberg, then as commissioner for human rights of the Council of Europe, wrote of that role well before his specific involvement with Transnistria:

[Ombudsmen's] constitutional or statutory authority places them in a unique position for promoting human rights. Ombudsmen are part of the 'checks and balances' of a democratic society based on the rule of law. They have been officially mandated to speak out for human rights and to defend those whose human rights have been violated. (2009:1)

The role has been recognised at least since the adoption by the UN General Assembly in December 1965 of the International Convention on the Elimination of All Forms of Racial Discrimination (Newman 1967). As this involves ombudsmen challenging and criticising government policy and actions, their independence from that government is as essential as it is for judges.

Both Transnistrian ombudsmen have closely chronicled their activities on the organisation's website. There are few entries critical of Tiraspol authorities, though robust comment is made when Chisinau appears to be violating Transnistrians' rights (e.g. Ombudsman of PMR 2014). There are occasional reports of interventions on matters such as pension payments (Ombudsman of PMR 2014a) and providing holidays for servicemen's children (Ombudsman of PMR 2017, though far fewer than one would expect from a robust organisation monitoring a government over nearly thirteen years. While Hammarberg made no explicit criticism of Kalko in his report (2013), he did not seem impressed by his work, talking of a lack of references to him from civil society organisations and an overlap with his and the prosecutor's work, concluding:

For the monitoring of the human rights situation the office of the Ombudsman is crucial and should be given all possibilities for an effective and independent work, including the necessary budgetary resources and constructive responses on demarches to the various authorities. (2013:48)

The International Federation for Human Rights (FIDH 2012), in a joint report with Promo-LEX, seemed concerned at the ombudsman's somewhat lackadaisical attitude not only to prisoners' rights (FIDH 2012:76) but to torture, which he said was "a subjective notion" (FIDH 2012:36).

Shortly after assuming office in November 2017, Kosinsky informed President Krasnoselsky there had been about 500 applications to the ombudsman's office in the previous nine months, of which 63 had been found justified (Ombudsman of PMR 2017). Krasnoselsky's response was ostensibly supportive of the ombudsman:

Man and his rights are the highest value. Meet people more often. Only they can tell the whole truth about the existing problems to which the state can respond quickly, avoiding their systemic nature. If necessary, the law should be amended. (President 2017)

The ombudsman's office has not yet attained anything like the degree of independence and vigour it would need to effectively challenge acts of government that were specifically implemented at the highest levels, and is not therefore a significant restraint on executive power. While it might be argued that ombudsmen rarely exercise such powers, there is a reasonable expectation that they will use what they have to robustly challenge governments, and particularly the executive. My reservations about Kosinsky were enhanced when he appeared to go to considerable lengths to avoid meeting me in October 2019. Rather than simply say he was too busy, he gave Vladimir Yastrebchak, who had passed on the request, a convoluted story about various officials whose approval he claimed to need before meeting me – itself a worrying fetter on his independence. This in Yastrebchak's view was nonsense. Yastrebchak, himself part of the Transnistrian elite, told me at Seven Fridays Restaurant, Tiraspol, on 2 October 2019 that Kosinsky is reluctant to be interviewed by anyone and regards himself as just a "postman for complaints".

The Ministry of State Security

In January 2017, shortly after assuming office, President Krasnoselsky transferred the powers of the State Security Committee, usually known by its Cyrillic initials KGB, to those of the Ministry of State Security (Livadari 2019). The new ministry's powers include regional security, fighting terrorism, border controls and overseeing other internal security organisations. The Moldovan report of that move suggests this was done to enable Krasnoselsky to extend his powers over security so as to bypass the Supreme Soviet (Livadari 2019).

The KGB had been involved in attempting to prosecute Promo-LEX in 2015, alleging it had been "planning actions aimed at destabilizing the region in order to block the negotiations in the 5+2 format" (Promo-LEX 2015:1). As Promo-LEX representatives are not permitted in Transnistria, and Tiraspol would have no way of extraditing them, the move was fairly pointless, but corroborates concerns that the Transnistrian regime seeks to intimidate lawyers who it sees as persistently acting against its interests.

Although the KGB was at the forefront of posturing against Promo-LEX, and the Ministry of State Security's position seems to be the same, it does not seem to be a notably invidious or powerful force in the territory. Its encounters with Stepan Popovskiy and, particularly, Karolina Dutka (SubSect.3.6.4) suggest that, in practice, it can do little more than try to persuade Transnistrians to do as it would prefer. It has probably been involved in closing a few websites, but these have not had a significant impact on civil liberties.

The position of NGOs in Transnistria

The difficulties caused by the pressure Transnistrian authorities may put local lawyers under is compounded by the outlawing of foreign involvement in legal proceedings. There are severe restrictions on foreign NGOs operating within the territory. This was a complaint of both Alexandra Telpis and Stepan Popovskiy of Apriori in separate interviews on 11 April 2019 in Chisinau and 28 May 2019 in Tiraspol, respectively. A prohibition on receiving foreign funding was severely hampering their organisation's work.* The NGO law, the current form of which came into force in May 2018, criminalises NGOs which engage in "political activities", an inadequately defined term, and receive financial donations from abroad. Preventing organisations which may challenge human rights abuses from operating in a territory is akin to oppressing lawyers who do that kind of work, though it can be argued that any state, especially one which is insecure in its existence, has a right to stop foreign interference.**

This 2018 law strengthens one passed in 2014, which in turn re-enacted a similar provision in force since at least 2006, supposedly replicating Russian and Belorussian laws (Moldova.org 2006). There was credible evidence that this law had been used oppressively. Anna Rurka, president of the Council of Europe's Conference of INGOs, suggested that the Transnistrian authorities were going even further than this law in exerting "undue pressure" on human rights defenders (CoE 2015). Attempts by the Chisinau government to introduce a similar law were abandoned in September 2017 (Amnesty International 2018).

It may be that international charities, even those with no possible political purpose, are reluctant to become embroiled in a territory where their presence may amount to implicit recognition of a regime that is generally regarded as illegal, and may even

---

* See People in Need (2019) for further discussion about this.
** For a comparative account of how various countries, including the UK, legislate for NGOs, see Kelly (2019).

explain Amnesty's failure to report on the territory (SubSect.3.5.2). While that is an issue beyond the Transnistrian authorities' immediate control, preventing external involvement, whether directly or by funding, particularly of human rights organisations, reflects poorly on the regime. This raises to the outside observer greater concerns than open discussion of alleged human rights violations is likely to.

In so far as the regime fails to exploit all the advantages for its inhabitants that foreign charitable involvement might bring, it is a serious concern. While there are credible arguments that in some cases NGOs may do more harm than good (e.g. Barber and Bowie 2008), a blanket ban on external help in dealing with the challenges that the territory faces is counterproductive. If the leaders are actively discouraging such benefits, that is a breach of the inhabitants' rights and lends credence to arguments which may otherwise have little to support them, namely that it is run for the benefit of an elite.

Other expressions of concern about the justice system

Hammarberg expressed concerns about the judicial system in guarded terms (2013:18):

> The Expert was confronted with many and fairly consistent complaints against the functioning of the justice system. One was that the accusations in a number of cases were 'fabricated'; that procedures were used to intimidate persons; that the defence lawyers were passive; that people with money or contacts had an upper-hand compared to ordinary people; and that witnesses changed their statements because of threats or bribery – and that such tendencies sabotaged the proceedings.

> It is very difficult for an outsider to assess the basis for such accusations but some factors made the Expert reluctant to ignore them. They were strikingly frequent and even alluded to by a few high-level actors in the system.

This accords with Stepan Popovskiy telling me on 28 May 2019:

> Of course, there are problems with bribing judges here. In high court,* there are one or two lawyers who can solve cases by paying money. Nobody knows how much it costs. I remember a case about a house. Was asked 15% of the money, which was a total of about US$30,000 for the lawyer and the judge. Would have to arrange it in both courts.

Garbled though it was, this account had a ring of truth to it, as specific allegations tend to. Similarly, in his Promo-LEX offices in Chisinau on 11 April 2019, Ion Manole told me in general terms that he thought the Transnistrian situation was corrupt, and he cited the case of Boris Mozer (SubSect.3.5.2) as an example.

---

* 'High court' appears to be a generic term for the Supreme Court, Constitutional Court and Arbitration Court.

3.3.4 THE QUALITY OF THE JUSTICE SYSTEM

While I did not receive allegations outside those specifically related by Popovskiy and Manole,* I certainly share Hammarberg's reluctance (2013:18) to dismiss these concerns. The supine approach of the ombudsman to serious breaches is a relatively minor matter. The fact that there are credible allegations of state interference with lawyers and the refusal to allow any foreign involvement in the justice system are much more important.

Doubts about the standards of the judiciary may be a regional more than a specifically Transnistrian problem. I have been given first-hand accounts of judicial corruption in Ukraine and Kosovo in circumstances which made them completely credible, and others in Moldova and Russia which seemed plausible. The then English Lord Chief Justice remarked in a speech:

> I am fortunate in coming from a jurisdiction where it is inconceivable that a litigant should even attempt to bribe a judge. I have told this to visiting judges from some of the new Central and Eastern European democracies and it was quite obvious that they simply did not believe me. (Phillips 2007)

It would be naïve to assume that Transnistria would have standards significantly different from those which prevail in its locality.

Even in that regional climate, jurists of the obvious calibre of Rimar and Kabaloev are unlikely to be doing anything other than their honest best to determine cases fairly, and the dismissal by senior judiciary of a failing judge was a very encouraging sign. There may be inherent judicial biases, including some in favour of a state which most judges will feel loyal to. That sort of bias, very different from consciously favouring one party let alone acting corruptly, is hardly unique to Transnistria or even Eastern Europe. In many supposedly enlightened democracies, most strikingly the US,** judges are appointed precisely because they do have certain biases that appeal to politicians or electors appointing them. That, however, is no reason to dismiss concerns about the extent to which the rule of law and justice flounders in other ways in Transnistria. Taken together with the instances of lawyers being intimidated by the regime's apparatus, occasional breaches of police powers (Sect.4.5), the supine ombudsman, and the lack of any external court having direct powers, it is clear Transnistria has been far less successful here than it has been in relation to electoral democracy.

However, while there are some lapses in the administration of justice, these are not sufficient to suggest to a reasonable observer that they should be a barrier to Transnistria being given *de jure* independence. Gross violations of human rights do not take place,

---

* Popovskiy was prone to improbable undocumented claims, such as that Transnistria's population had fallen to 300,000. Despite that, evidence of matters within his own knowledge seemed to be convincingly and sincerely expressed.

** Appointments to the Supreme Court, particularly that of Brett Kavanagh in October 2018, attract international attention, but the US president has the right to appoint judges to around 800 federal court posts (Zirin 2016).

nor is it a police state that relies upon repression in order to survive. Recognition of its sovereignty should lead to it relaxing its restrictive laws on the activity of human rights NGOs and improve its performance in this regard. In this way, the recognition of independence would represent an advance for the territory's people.

3.4 IMPRISONMENT

Transnistria's prison population is high, and its government has faced credible allegations of detaining people in unsatisfactory conditions. The function of imprisonment is an inevitable manifestation of statehood. The fact that the Transnistrian government runs a prison system is a further indication of *de facto* statehood. How it exercises that power is relevant to the question of whether it can be regarded as a free democracy.

While high rates of imprisonment instinctively seem to indicate an oppressive state, there appears to be no obvious correlation between conventional freedoms and low prison rates, according to the comparative table provided by Prison Policy (Wagner and Sawyer 2018:1). Guinea-Bissau and the Central African Republic have the world's lowest rates, with Zimbabwe ranking just below Spain and China lower still. Countries often perceived as liberal, such as New Zealand, Uruguay and Costa Rica, come high up the table. Perhaps in an attempt to explain such anomalies, Marc Mauer, director of the US *Sentencing Project*, argues:

> …while it might be assumed that if a given nation has a rate of incarceration 20% higher than another's, it is more punitive. But what if it has a rate of violent crime that is 30% higher? In that case, the policies and practices in that system have combined to impose less punishment on persons convicted of crime. (2017:4)

That be may logical, but does not detract from the likelihood of a pattern linking rates of incarceration with a punitive regime, even if there are some which will be out of line because of unusual rates of serious crime. A more specific attempt to explain discrepancies in national rates was provided by Christopher Hartney, writing for the National Council on Crime and Delinquency (2006:3), who argues that US rates, the highest in the world, are in large driven by disproportionate minority incarceration. That again is plausible but not a full explanation. The countries just below the US in the table relied upon by Hartney (2006:2) – Russia, Cuba and Ukraine – were relatively racially homogenous, while much more mixed countries like Canada, France and the UK were further down the table.

A change in prisoner levels may be a better indicator of the punitive nature of a government than the underlying figure. Often right-wing populist governments use prison more freely than has been the previous norm. Turkey* and Philippines**

---

*   Up from 200,000 in 2016 to 260,000 in 2018 (WPB 2019).
**   Up from 142,000 in 2016 to 188,000 in 2018 (WPB 2019).

illustrate this, in the former mainly because of Erdogan's clamping down on all forms of opposition after the attempted July 2016 coup, and in the latter because of Duterte's 'war on drugs'. Conversely, but less dramatically, the election of a liberal government will often reduce the prison population, as happened under Greece's radical prime minister, Alexis Tsipras,* and slightly under centre-left French president, Emmanuel Macron.** Whatever the force of the explanations of Mauer (2017) and Hartney (2006), any regime which uses prison oppressively, whether by gaoling people unnecessarily or by making conditions unnecessarily harsh, even if popular with much of the population, is misusing its power in a way which is incompatible with a free democracy.

Transnistria's prison population

It is difficult to obtain reliable statistics in respect of Transnistria's prison population, but those that exist suggest it is high. The USSD reported (2013:6) there were 2,819 detainees in Transnistria, including 671 awaiting trial, 83 minors and 165 women. These figures are largely corroborated by a report of the Institute for Criminal Policy Research which says there were 2,814 prisoners in 2014, and Thomas Hammarberg (2013:20) was told while conducting his research in 2012 that there were 2,854 prisoners. Ion Manole of Promo-LEX, who had not cited a high prison population among the many human rights concerns he told me of when interviewed on 11 April 2019 at his Chisinau office, showed me on request a graphic suggesting 0.475% of the Transnistrian population, around 2,400 people, was imprisoned in 2016.

Hammarberg (2013:43) noted a fall in prisoner numbers of around 250 by the time he reported and said further changes were expected as a consequence of laws introduced by recently elected President Shevchuk. Yuriy Mamatuk, professor of criminal procedure at Shevchenko University and a former prosecutor, told me at the university on 27 May 2019 he thought the then figure was around 1,800. I asked if he could provide any explanation for the relatively high prison figure, and he could only answer, "Maybe a lot of them are for tax offences." After a little discussion, we agreed this was implausible.

When, on 28 May 2019, I asked for these numbers from the head of the Tiraspol police, Sergy Kirman, he told me, smiling but possibly not jokingly, this was classified information. However, Sergy Vasilievich, the governor of Tiraspol women's prison, on the same day said unhesitatingly there were 102 inmates in his prison (Appendix C), the only women's prison in the territory, and this figure was borne out by a quick count of the beds in the dormitories. Assuming that the USSD (2013) has the correct proportion of women as total prisoners (5.8%), Mamatuk's estimate would be reasonably accurate.

Even if the USSD (2013) figure is treated as exaggerated or historical, the prison population figure is still large for a country where there is relatively little manifestation

---

*   Down from 12,700 in 2014 to 10,000 in 2019 (WPB 2019).
**   Down from 74,000 in 2018 to 70,100 in 2019 (WPB 2019).

of either crime or law enforcement. The territory's population is around 500,000. That would mean on the probable 2019 figure, 0.36% of the population was imprisoned (0.56% on the USSD figure).

The world's highest rate is the US's 0.70%, with the probable exception of North Korea for which there are no figures. El Salvador's, the next highest, is 0.51%. Only seven other countries exceed even the lower Transnistrian figure (Wagner and Sawyer 2018). The UK's rate is 0.14% and Moldova's 0.21%, with a total of 7,643 (WPB 2019) based on a prison population that includes Transnistria's.

I have not been able to obtain a satisfactory answer as to why the Transnistrian regime imprisons so many people. My own discussions with women prisoners (Appendix C), to whom I was afforded access outside the hearing of the prison staff, was revealing. I had three conversations: two gave accounts of sentences that were significantly longer than those likely to be have been passed by English, and probably other Western European, courts, and one whose 'crime' – failing to financially maintain a child who was not living with her – should not be prosecuted in a humane society. This is reinforced by the only such discussion with a female prisoner cited in the Hammarberg report (2013:22) – a Roma woman sentenced to twelve years for a vaguely defined crime associated with fortune telling.

Transnistrian prison conditions

FIDH (2012), a highly respected organisation which has a consultative status before the UN, UNESCO and the Council of Europe, reported several instances of torture in Transnistrian prisons and police stations. The Transnistrian ombudsman's response, seemingly plausible, was that the small size of the territory and close community ties mean such instances would not go unheard of (FIDH 2012:37), but this was contrary to the testimony taken by FIDH.

The USSD report (2013) also catalogues serious deficiencies in prison conditions. It says 70 prisoners were infected with tuberculosis, among whom there was a "high" but unspecified mortality rate. The doctor in charge of prisoners' welfare at Tiraspol police station, who would only give her name as Alina, told me in discussions there on 28 May 2019 that 30% of those detained have tuberculosis. I queried this, astonishingly high, figure several times through my interpreter, but she was adamant it was right.

Promo-LEX is also vociferous in its condemnation of prison conditions. Its Nikoleta Khriplivy told openDemocracy (Okrest 2018) that, "The PMR has its own prisons, but conditions there are terrible – much as in Moldova until recently. The conditions could almost be equated with torture."

My observations of the women's prison gave the impression that there was unlikely to be any deliberate mistreatment. None of the women I spoke to made any complaints, and one who was uninhibited in expressing bitterness about her conviction was full of gratitude for the medical treatment given to her baby, who had been born in prison. The conditions were overcrowded in that women were sleeping in (very large) dormitories of about 50 beds. However, there was a pleasant mother and baby unit, women were encouraged but not compelled to work, the food looked palatable, and there seemed to be a reasonably happy atmosphere.

I was not given access to a men's prison by the Ministry of Internal Affairs, but that may have been because it was logistically easier to grant my request to visit a prison by taking me to the women's one.* As the visit was arranged on little more than twelve hours' notice, it is inconceivable that there was a significant sprucing up to give a favourable impression. Indeed, our escort from the ministry was not admitted herself as she had forgotten to bring her identification papers.

Although I did not visit a men's prison, I was shown the far less impressive cells at the Tiraspol central police station, where detainees could be held for up to ten days while investigations were carried out. These took a variety of shapes, including one where there was a common sleeping platform for up to about ten prisoners. They were uniformly unpleasant, but only marginally more so than many of the London cells I visited as a young lawyer in the late 1980s. There were only four prisoners there at the time. This was in contrast with Thomas Hammarberg's visit to the smaller Bender police station in 2012, when he found ten prisoners in the cells there and was told that was only about a third of the typical number the previous year (2013:15).

In an interview with a then partially EU-funded journal, *Foreign Policy Association of Moldova* (2013), journalist Nicolae Buceaţki said that prisoners in Transnistria were kept in inhumane conditions and subject to torture, including the application of electric shocks to their genitals and suspension by their arms. He alleged, "Several human rights defenders operating in Transnistria are subject to daily threats of harassment and ongoing persecution." Although Stepan Popovskiy told me in an interview on 29 May 2019 of incidents in which he had understandably felt harassed, they were not of the horrific nature of those recounted by Buceaţki and were all the more credible for being expressed moderately.

In his report, among 38 recommendations, Thomas Hammarberg (2013:13) calls on the Transnistrian authorities to reduce the prison population and end inhumane practices in the prisons. There is praise for the access given to Hammarberg and the UN high commissioner for human rights, Navi Pillay, on their visits. Hammarberg's report was mentioned in several discussions I had, and was brought up by the governor of the women's prison, who told me on 29 May 2019 that ongoing efforts were being made to implement it.

In 2012, the then human rights ombudsman, Vassily Kalko, told FIDH that each prisoner costs 70 roubles (US$6·50 then) per day (FIDH 2012:37). That would amount to nearly US$16 million per year based on the USSD (2013) figure: 1.6% of the country's estimated US$1billion GDP (Caluş 2013:1). The US spends US$74 billion on prisons (Kincade 2018) out of its US$17.4 trillion GDP (World Bank 2019): 0.43%. Kalko was

---

* In preparing its report, FIDH (2012:45) was told by a former inmate that the Sizo (men's) prison was the one normally used to "impres" foreign delegates.

not unduly sympathetic to prisoners, telling FIDH that pensioners and sick children were a greater priority and pointing out in a report:

> I agree that the conditions of detention should be humane, but this does not mean prisoners need more care than children. In current socio-economic situation, not all the pensioners or patients can allow themselves to buy meat or milk, while prisoners are provided with these products. (2014:37)

While many would applaud the priorities expressed, one would not expect an ombudsman, appointed to protect a particular class, to be downplaying the importance of doing that, and this lackadaisical attitude to prisoners is a concern.

Steps to reduce the prison population

In December 2011, just after Shevchuk's election, laws were passed with a view to reducing the prison population, providing fines for more offences and making the detention of juveniles rarer (FIDH 2012). In April 2014, Shevchuk said that his government had approved a plan for the implementation of Hammarberg's recommendations (*Infotag* 2014a). While there has to be some scepticism about the accuracy of the prison statistics, the seeming fall in prisoners between the 2012 and 2019 figures cited or extrapolated above suggest Shevchuk and perhaps his successor have managed to partially implement these reforms.

Every two months, the ombudsman chairs a meeting to decide which prisoners should be granted pardons and sends a report to the president (Ombudsman 2020). This results in some releases of prisoners, including high-profile ones. The details of such meetings are not published.

The significance of imprisonment to independence

Ultimately, the onus is on the government, and particularly President Krasnoselsky, to consider carefully whether the present level of prisoners benefits anyone. Every time the state uses its powers to take away a person's freedom in the way imprisonment does, it should be able to show clear justification for that course. Where there is no real justification, the desirability of bestowing more powers on those who run that state becomes more questionable. The Transnistrian combination of high imprisonment, a society with little ostensible crime (Sect.4.5) and a racially homogenous population suggests little justification on the basis of the analysis discussed at the beginning of this section. A high proportion, especially of women prisoners, could be released while presenting no threat to the public, and that would not unduly reduce the deterrent factor resulting from sentences. The state would free up resources for greater needs, and the depleted working population would be increased a little. While it could not be maintained that a high prison population is in itself a barrier to independence, it is a factor that weighs against it in determining whether it is a free enough society to merit international recognition.

3.5 HUMAN RIGHTS AND FREEDOMS

The actual extent of political and individual freedoms in Transnistria, against which the constitutional aspirations discussed in Sect.3.1, the manifestations of democracy (3.2) and the rule of law (3.3) are to be judged, is the subject of this section. Those relating specifically to freedom of speech are considered in Sect.3.6. Consistent serious violations, especially if they have continued through successive governments, could weigh against independence, and a belief that there are such violations leads Cornet (2016), among others, to argue that the territory should not be given statehood (Sect.5.1).

3.5.1 THE RELEVANCE OF HUMAN RIGHTS TO INDEPENDENCE

There is much discussion by philosophers and academic lawyers about when a right to secession arises in international law. Many argue that the right should apply only, or predominantly, when the dominant state is violating the human rights of the inhabitants of the subservient territory. As Lina Laurinavičiūtė and Laurynas Biekša put it:

> Therefore, as in the cases of South Ossetia and Abkhazia, Transdniestria and Nagorno-Karabakh also claim that they are not only entitled to self-determination, but to secession, and they base their claim on charges of discrimination and massive human rights violations committed by their parent states, which form the basis of the right to remedial secession. (2015:67)

In support of the unlikely assertion that Transnistria bases its claim for independence on "massive human rights violations" by Chisinau, they draw on Walter, van Ungern-Sternberg and Abushov (2014:73), whose conclusion is that Transnistria does not have a right to independence based on remedial right theory (SubSect.5.1.4), which may arise where there have been such violations.

The corollary of that is that the human rights prospects for the seceding nation should not be significantly worse than those of the parent state. According to Joel Day (2012:29), legitimacy breaks down "when it fails to protect and promote the rights of its inhabitants". If a government of an unrecognised state has not acted in a way that prevents that breakdown, it cannot be in a stronger position than a similarly nefarious government of a recognised state.

The human rights element of the remedial right theory gives little help to the Transnistrian case, as for the last thirty years the Moldovan government has not been in a position to violate the rights of the inhabitants of Transnistria. Indeed, in terms of access to, for instance, healthcare and passports, it has given those people considerable benefits. A case for independence can be built on much more than that aspect of that theory, but a really bad human rights record would weaken the case.

3.5.2 CONCERNS ABOUT HUMAN RIGHTS

General criticisms of the Transnistrian government

Many criticisms of Transnistria's human rights record are based on poorly sourced, uncorroborated allegations. Such criticism is often relayed by those who might be expected to know better and given more weight than it deserves. This is epitomised by the UK's Home Office's *Guidance Notes for Immigration Officers*:

> Residents of Transnistria cannot choose their leaders democratically, and Transnistrian authorities restrict political activity. Freedom of religion, association, speech and assembly are all severely restricted and independent voices against the regime are suppressed. (2017:5)

No source is given for these words, but they may derive from a US evangelical charity's, wholly unreferenced, website (Earthchildren's Mission 2017):

> In the breakaway territory of Transnistria, human rights abuses are grave. Torture, arbitrary arrests and unlawful detentions are widespread. Freedom of expression and association is tightly controlled and independent voices against the regime are suppressed.

That a major government department in Britain is able to relay such information is not just an indication of how slackly such reports are produced but also of the carelessness that government, and perhaps many others, have put into evaluating Transnistria.

Sections of the international media have had little hesitation in roundly condemning Transnistrian rule of law and respect for human rights, often on virtually no evidence. A Channel 4 (UK) (Wickens and Mason 2014) report concludes, "Transnistria is a land of complete lawlessness and chronic corruption, where those in power can grab resources as and when they want to. It is a mafia state." It cites, by first name only, instances of two men, one a former policeman, who had been given long prison sentences and had their property informally, but permanently, confiscated. There are reports of random imprisonment of Moldovans by Transnistrian militias for ransom, with families required to pay fees to ensure they are treated humanely, including a €40 (surprising, as dollars are invariably used for non-rouble prices) fee if they are to be allowed to hug them (*DW* 2015).

Academics too have been willing to make strident criticisms of the territory. As late as 2009, a commentator from the Washington-based Centre for International Relations asserted that Smirnov maintained a virtually dictatorial control over Transnistria (Sanchez 2009). Bahar Çamözü (2016:5), a Belgian academic, called it "Stalinist".

Amnesty International (2019) has published a report critical of Moldova. Its only direct comment on Transnistria* is a brief report referring to Valentin Besleag, who had been detained in Dubasari, after entering the territory with electoral materials, as a "possible prisoner of conscience" (Amnesty International 2007:2)

Freedom House

A very low ranking is given to Transnistria by the Freedom House (2018) organisation – in its report the territory was given 6/7 (7 being the lowest) for all freedom, civil liberties and political rights. It has reached those scores every year since its reporting started in 1998, and since 2016, there has annually been a more finely divided "aggregate score" of 24% (down to 22% in 2020). Moldova itself gets creditable 3/7s and 60% (Freedom House 2020). There is little evidence cited by the organisation in its reports, which embrace every country in the world. It said of the Transnistrian 2016 presidential election (Freedom House 2018):

> Shevchuk was defeated even as his campaign draw [sic] significantly on public resources, including the state media, which heavily favoured him and sought to portray Krasnoselsky as a crony of Sheriff Enterprises, the powerful business conglomerate that dominates the economy and backs the Renewal Party; Krasnoselsky had previously served as the company's security chief. Given Transnistria's political status, established election monitors did not send missions to oversee the contest.

The factual premise, that the state media favoured Shevchuk, is questionable (Subs.3.2.2) and disregards the context of Sheriff having as much control over the media as the state: the 'mark' of 1 out of 4 given for fairness of an election in which a challenger resoundingly beat someone supposedly favoured by state media is extraordinary. For my observations of that election – the scrupulousness, to the point of tedium, with which it was conducted; the presence of many highly experienced foreign monitors; and the freedom and facilities given to all observers – see Appendix A. The absurdity of the Freedom House (2018) mark undermines the figures it gives in areas where the evidence is less clear.

The organisation giving a top rating of 1/7 for civil liberties in the US, well after the Trump administration had, for instance, placed restrictions on travellers from many Muslim countries, indicates a tendency to commend the US and its allies. Israel's overall 79% might also cause a few eyebrows to rise, as will Nigeria, anecdotally the most corrupt country of all, getting 50%. Some of Australia's recent immigration policies

---

*   Amnesty Moldova was one of 38 mostly Chisinau-based NGOs to sign an open letter calling on Transnistria to let Promo-LEX operate in the territory (LRCM 2015).

might have made a bigger dent in its gold-plated 98% rating. Turkey, despite the mass imprisonment of journalists, academics and judges after the 2016 coup attempt, managed a semi-respectable 32%. Russia, which for all its faults is arguably still a democracy, got only 20% and 0/12 for its electoral process. The ranking that most undermines the damning 22% given to Transnistria, whose leaders have certainly never been accused of genocide, is Myanmar's 30% (Freedom House 2020).

It is doubtful that much detailed research goes into the Freedom House annual reports, particularly on the more obscure territories, and most scores remain constant from year to year. Its observations cannot be dismissed out of hand, though there is undoubtedly a bias towards countries perceived as friendly to the US. For a blistering, if dated, critique of Freedom House – "a flak machine" – see Herman and Chomsky (1988:15). Steiner (2016) made more moderate criticism and suggested it was then less biased against countries opposed to US interests than it had been previously, but that it still reflected political prejudices. What Freedom House, which is the source of much criticism of Transnistria, says on the territory's human rights and democracies merits very little credence.

Promo-LEX cases

While many of the allegations against the Transnistrian regime are hyperbolic if not fanciful, there are specific cases that cause concern; for example, the case of Alexandr Lipovcenco, a young Ukrainian, has been reported by several news outlets (e.g. Ciurcă 2016). He was said to have been imprisoned in March 2016 for three years for "extremism" because he had written in a notebook that only the presence of UN troops would solve the Transnistrian situation. He was tried and sentenced in absence because the judge said otherwise he would have spoken too much. The source of these allegations seems to invariably be his mother and are passed on through Promo-LEX. They were adopted in the USSD (2016) report seemingly without any independent corroboration. My interpreter and I could find no reference to this case on any Russian or Ukrainian website and it seems surprising that the crudely unjustified imprisonment of a Ukrainian would not have become a *cause celebre* in his own country.

Like the Lipovcenco case, most of the allegations of human rights abuses, and indeed lawlessness, originate with Promo-LEX, a Moldovan human rights organisation. Its director, Ion Manole, told me in an interview in his offices on 11 April 2019 that it had brought 75 cases involving Transnistria to the ECHR. He thought about another 25 had been brought outside the auspices of his organisation. In fact, there are 21 individual case entries, which with duplicate entries gives a total of 45,* recorded on the European Court of Human Rights (ECHR) website (2020) as of September 2020.

The most notorious case is that of Boris Mozer (*Mozer v. Russia and Moldova* 2016), a petition determined in the ECHR by a claimant represented by Promo-LEX. This was

---

* This should be seen in the context of there being 4,865 entries recorded concerning Moldova (ECHR 2020). The UK has 10,272.

the first case Manole brought up. Mozer had been accused of economic crime, causing the Transnistrian state a substantial loss. His arrest was in 2008 and trial in 2010. He was a severe asthmatic and required an inhaler to have any quality of life and possibly even to survive. According to Manole, the authorities withheld this from him unless his family agreed to pay "compensation" of €40,000, which was followed by a demand for a further €40,000. The report of the case does not refer to this demand but makes the less damning finding that he was kept in conditions that exacerbated his asthma and that his "mother was told by the prison staff that she had to bring her son the medication he required since there was none available in the prison" (*Mozer* 2016: para 38). The damages were awarded against Russia alone,* although the claim had also been brought against Moldova. Transnistria, as an unrecognised state, is not susceptible to the ECHR's jurisdiction.

In January 2020, Ilie Cazac, represented by Promo-LEX lawyers, was awarded €35,000 damages by the ECHR arising from a 2010 detention and 2011 conviction, in a closed trial, for spying for Moldova (*Cazac v. Moldova* 2020).

Not surprisingly, Transnistrian authorities claim that Promo-LEX has ties with Romania's secret services and that its investigations into Transnistria are intended to be subversive (*Novosti Pridnestrovya* 2015). Manole told me that it was unthinkable that the Transnistrian authorities would admit him to the territory. Another Promo-LEX employee, Alexandru Zubko, has been explicitly banned. He was responsible for making, in the Moldovan- and English-language press, allegations that Transnistria forces young men to engage in paramilitary groups against their will.

Promo-LEX does receive funds from the US and several other Western governments (Promo-LEX n.d.). I was told, off the record in London in 2019, by one of the leading academic commentators on Transnistria that Promo-LEX was a front for the Romanian government, though Romania is not one of the governmental donors listed by that organisation (n.d.). Shevchuk said in a May 2015 television interview that there were clear links between it and Romanian intelligence services (*Novosti Pridnestrovya* 2015). However, Natalie Shchukina, a Shevchenko University law professor generally supportive of the Transnistrian regime, told me at the university on 6 December 2018 that she thought it was a well-respected organisation which carried out very thorough research. The Swedish International Development Agency (Sida) ceased providing funds to Promo-LEX in 2016 alleging it, "Hampers the dialogue and undermines the conflict resolution process in Transnistria." Promo-LEX (2016), however, alleges that Sida did so after receiving death threats from the Transnistrian KGB, a position strongly disputed by Sida itself (Resare 2016).

My view after interviewing Manole was that he, and hence probably the organisation, was sincere and well motivated in his criticisms of Transnistrian human rights. The organisation

---

* The Russian judge Dmitry Dedov was the only dissenter on the 16-person court, expressing, "regret that the Court's judgement…will lead to an escalation of tension between the Russian Federation and the Council of Europe" (2016: para 16).

certainly could not be dismissed as a stooge of the US in the way Freedom House can. He was nuanced in his criticisms of Transnistria, focusing mainly on abuses of police powers and a somewhat opaque power structure. Some of his arguments are founded on the principle of anything an unrecognised state does being inherently illegal. For that reason, he would, for instance, regard the extradition of any criminal to Transnistria a breach of that person's human rights, however clearly non-political the crime and however strong the evidence. His sincerity does not mean Promo-LEX could not be funded, or even to an extent controlled, by political forces opposed to the territory in a more general way than just being concerned by human rights abuses. I did feel that Manole preached at me a bit, and that my questions were not always answered: outside the reference to ECHR cases, he produced little specific information.* He seemed keen to make criticisms of the Chisinau government in a way that might be expected to give him an image of impartiality. Nonetheless, there was a consistency and objectivity to what he said that seemed credible. He was obviously a skilled lawyer, capable of handling the demanding written and oral presentation required by the ECHR, and a shrewd media operator, shown by the prominence he achieves for Promo-LEX reports. It is difficult to see any reason why he would be working for such an organisation if he did not genuinely believe in its aims, and I was persuaded by talking to him that there are real human rights abuses occurring in Transnistria.

The criminal proceedings against Shevchuk and his associates

After the 2016 presidential election, Shevchuk and his wife, Nina Shtanski, came under investigation for corruption. On 27 June 2017, they left Transnistria and the next day the Soviet voted to strip Shevchuk of immunity (Ernst 2017a). They probably lived in secret in Chisinau for a while, where Shevchuk may have provided information on the new leaders to the authorities (Tabachnik 2017a), before Shtanski publicly surfaced in St. Petersburg, where she maintains a Facebook (2018) page,** largely discussing her work as a university teacher.

The allegations against Shevchuk were explained to me by the new minister of internal affairs, Ruslan Mova, in December 2018. It appeared that around US$5 million from government funds was unaccounted for, to which only Shevchuk had access. He had built the largest private dwelling in Transnistria and retained title to it. He had commissioned the printing of many millions of roubles, ostensibly for legitimate economic purposes, but in reality, so that he could cream off a fair proportion, leaving Transnistria to face the inevitable consequences of inflation and a weakened currency.

There would seem little advantage to the present leadership in pursuing Shevchuk, the margin of whose electoral defeat probably prevents him being a significant political force for the foreseeable future. It indeed sets a precedent which could come to cause problems for Krasnoselsky or any successor. Shevchuk's provision of information to

---

*   Although his spoken English was not quite fluent, he was happy to be interviewed without an interpreter.

**   She did not respond to my requests, sent via that page, for an interview.

the Chisinau authorities may have been a price of freedom and can hardly benefit the present regime. It was a predictable consequence of the Transnistrian authorities trying to make a criminal case against him.

A report by Refworld (2018), part of the UN's Refugee Agency, says the "corruption charges were widely viewed as politically-motivated". Promo-LEX (2017) takes the view that Shevchuk may himself have a complaint against those seeking to prosecute him. It lists a long litany of his crimes, which go far wider than those Mova highlighted to me, and it is clear that the organisation thinks Shevchuk is guilty.

Mova made a persuasive case against Shevchuk, both on its merits and on the integrity of his own motivation. He had served under Shevchuk and would have no political motive for pursuing his former leader. There is no evidence that the prosecution of Shevchuk was a politically motivated violation of human rights and indeed is a healthy instance of the Transnistrian elite attempting to call one of their own to account.

Coliban: "The last political prisoner in Transnistria"

During Shevchuk's term in office, Alexandru Coliban, a 22-year-old opponent of his was, according to Promo-LEX (2013), gaoled for thirty months for, in October 2011, allegedly committing defamation arising out of posters he put up while participating in the electoral campaign (*IPN* 2013). He was released as a result of a pardon granted by Shevchuk after serving over a year in prison (*Point News* 2013). This case also does not appear to have been reported on or adopted by any organisation outside Moldova and Romania, though the OSCE (2013) issued a press release welcoming his release. Revealingly, one of the Moldovan reports on the matter referred to Coliban as, "the last political prisoner in Transnistria" (Moldova.org 2013).

Horjan

A more recent worrying prosecution was of the leader of Transnistria's Communist Party, Oleg Horjan. Chisinau news reports have attributed the prosecution to Horjan's demands for a fuller enquiry after a fifteen-year-old girl was killed in a collision with a "luxurious car" in October 2017 (*Infotag* 2017). He was imprisoned for four and a half years in June 2018 at a trial which Ms Alex Mayer, then a British Labour MEP, said took place shortly after his parliamentary immunity was removed and involved "intimidation by judges" who refused to allow him to call witnesses (European Parliament 2018). The charges were related to organising a protest rally in Tiraspol (RFE 2018), where allegedly violence occurred followed by a scuffle in Tiraspol police station (*Infotag* 2019). Horjan is described as a close friend of Shevchuk.

It is scarcely credible that a middle-aged parliamentarian, with no reputation for inappropriate behaviour, would conduct himself so as to cause violence justifying a long prison sentence, particularly as there were no reports of injuries at that rally. If the motive of the prosecution has been to silence Horjan, that has proved unsuccessful as he has been able to make wide, even if only locally circulated, attacks on the government from prison, writing on 3 June 2019 that his aim was "to liberate the republic from those who have robbed it for almost 30 years" (LACT 2019).

International protection against human rights violations

As an unrecognised state, Transnistria cannot be a signatory to international treaties but has unilaterally adopted several international standards on human rights including the European Convention (Sect.3.1.2). The existence of these in Transnistrian law could add a degree of protection for those accused of crimes, but their efficacy depends on the regime and its judiciary actually respecting the laws rather than just introducing them. A country which does not in practice respect the rule of law can still have sophisticated laws protecting citizens' rights which would be of no actual help to those whom the state wished to oppress, and Tommasoli's distinction (2012) between an "institutional approach" and "outcomes and procedures" is strikingly apt in this context.

3.5.3 THE QUALITY OF RESPECT FOR HUMAN RIGHTS

There are quite obviously flaws in Transnistria's human rights record. Equally obviously, there are exaggerated and sometimes politically motivated allegations, such as those of Freedom House and the UK Home Office, which have served to give it an unjustified reputation. Similarly, Promo-LEX, even if an organisation with considerable insight into Transnistria, may tend towards a hypercritical rather than balanced approach. The unquestioned adoption of its allegations, as in the cases of Lipovcenco and of Belova and Mirovici in USSD reports (2016 and 2020 respectively) maybe gives credence to allegations which are not fully justified. The US and UK governments would be less likely to so criticise a state which was able to protest through formal diplomatic channels. The position, or at least the volume of allegations, was considerably worse in the early part of its *de facto* independence. The likelihood that once Coliban was released in 2013 there were no more political prisoners may have been a high point. The attempts to prosecute former President Shevchuk for corruption appear to be well motivated.

The imprisonment now of Horjan, particularly if there is anything in the uncorroborated report that he faces further prosecution for saying the government are "puppets", is indefensible, as would be any detention of blogging pensioners, Tatiana Belova and Serghei Mirovici (SubSect.3.4.6).

So long as Transnistria draws attention to itself by politically motivated detentions, any ensuing discussion will bring in historic cases like Cazac, Vardanean (SubSect.3.6.3) Mozer, Lipovcenco and the Romanian-language case (4.1.2). The credible argument that they were features of another time and other regimes is greatly diluted if there are current instances of the process.

That none of the cases before the ECHR relate to events since 2011 is a promising sign. However, the banning from Transnistria of lawyers like Ion Manole, who have the experience and resources to bring such claims, may mean a true picture is not painted by the figures that can be extracted from the court's records. Were the authorities to welcome outside lawyers and non-governmental organisations in the cooperative way they treated Hammarberg, and indeed myself, it would be a tremendous step forward and probably lead to an end of such ill-informed attacks as the Home Office (2017) report. Showing more common sense in the treatment of those who have offended it would contribute to that effect.

The Transnistrian case for independence cannot be made out on the basis of primary right theory as there is no basis to claim its people are oppressed by Chisinau. Human rights concerns, considered in this section, which Cornet (2016) specifically argues are a bar to Transnistrian independence and Day (2012) more generally sees as undermining any regime's legitimacy, are of relevance to a debate over independence. Even though they are not egregious enough to destroy the claim for independence, the present Transnistrian regime should reflect carefully on whether they are doing unnecessary damage to their own cause.

3.6 MEDIA AND CENSORSHIP

An abundant, diversely owned media which has the freedom to criticise elites is a feature of most successful societies. This section considers the nature of Transnistrian media and then examines to what extent it is subject to censorship. While the focus is primarily on questions of freedom, that is best considered in the light of an examination of what media actually exists.

3.6.1 THE MEANING OF MEDIA AND PRESS FREEDOM

Michael Abramowitz (2017), writing for Freedom House, defines a free press as:

> A media environment where coverage of political news is robust, the safety of journalists is guaranteed, state intrusion in media affairs is minimal, and the press is not subject to onerous legal or economic pressures.

Jenifer Whitten-Woodring and Daniel Van Belle (2015:2) define media freedom slightly different, citing McQuail (2000:146–147) and describing "the right to publish without any prior censorship or license and without incurring penalties, within the limits of other legal obligations". They, the former also drawing on her 2009 work, then divide countries into three categories (2015): those where the government exercises complete control which are not free (including Mexico and Armenia*); those where there are some pressures but the media remain capable of criticising elites, described as imperfectly free (e.g. Italy and India); and those where the media is generally free to engage in "watchdog reporting" (e.g. Uruguay and Australia). It is against these tests that the relative freedom of Transnistrian media and expression is considered.

There are laws governing the media in all European countries (Koltay:56) and most of the world (Whitten-Woodring and Van Belle 2015). No country, though, allows complete freedom of the media. András Koltay argues for only restricted powers of the state to intervene, particularly in respect of the internet:

> But the desire for regulation should be carefully kept within the appropriate limits… the legal solution is by no means a panacea but, at best, merely a useful prop for achieving the objectives of public interest. (2015:85)

While Abramowitz's (2017) and McQuail's (2000) definitions have similarities, the latter's acceptance of a qualification of "other legal obligations" does not lie comfortably with Koltay's (2015) approach and may be relied upon to justify constraints, some more controversial than others. National security is a legitimate, if easily abused, exception. Laws of privacy, even defamation, reflect rights of individuals which counter those of a completely free press.

Further constraints are harder to justify. Some societies hold that certain people and ideas should be beyond criticism. Many Islamic countries make any attack on Mohammed severely punishable, by death in a few cases. Some Christian countries have blasphemy laws.** In Thailand, any 'insult' to the king, queen or heir is punishable with three to fifteen years' imprisonment. This *lese-majeste* law, itself a crude restriction of free speech, may be used more widely to clamp down on opposition to the executive and the military (BBC 2017).

More invidious still are laws that criminalise insulting the president or other political leader. These have been used to considerable effect in Erdogan's Turkey, where Article 299 of the penal code makes it an offence carrying one to four years' imprisonment (Venice Commission 2016:4,13). By May 2016, almost 2,000 had been prosecuted under that law since Erdogan assumed the presidency earlier that year. It technically remains an offence in a number of Western European countries, including Germany and France (Venice Commission 2016:14). In Poland a protester has recently been charged with such a crime (Tilles 2020) for holding up a banner saying, "We have an idiot for

---

* The Mexican example is specifically ascribed to the conduct of drugs cartels rather than the government, which is acknowledged to be democratic. Armenia may also not be a good example since the election there in 2018 of a former newspaper editor, Nikol Pashinyan, as president.

** The common law offences of blasphemy and blasphemous libel, which only applied to Christianity, were not abolished in England until 2008.

president".* There is no follow up to this report, and it is likely judicial common sense intervened at an early stage. The episode was damaging both by showing the world the intolerance of the Polish authorities and drawing infinitely more attention to the sign than a small demonstration in a provincial town ever could.

Conversely, in the US it has long been a frustration for conservatives that the constitution's first amendment means they cannot prosecute those who commit, in their eyes, the ultimate sacrilege of burning or desecrating the national flag. The repeated failure of attempts to change this law, largely by virtue of Supreme Court decisions, *Texas v. Johnson* (1989) and *United States v. Eichman* (1990), is a sign that whatever the US's other human rights concerns, free speech is robustly protected. Similarly, there is a healthy failure of presidents – from Washington to Trump according to *Time* magazine (Battistella 2020) – despite their frustration about it, to be able to do more than complain about, and in the latter case return, such insults.

Clooney and Webb (2017) in the *Columbia Human Rights Law Review* argue specifically for a right to insult to be recognised in international law. They acknowledge the clash this causes with the requirement of Article 4 of the Convention on the Elimination of Racial Discrimination (CERD), which requires the criminalisation of, among other things, racial insults (Clooney and Webb 2017:18). They conclude by devising eight principles, drawing on US practice under its first amendment (Clooney and Webb 2017: 51-54), arguing for a repeal of Article 4 of CERD (Clooney and Webb 2017:53). While some of their proposals, including effectively legalising Holocaust denial and going further than even the view advanced by Koltay (2012), may seem extreme, they do have the benefit of making for a clearer right to freedom of speech than many European countries allow.

3.6.2 THE MEDIA

There is no definitive list of Transnistrian newspapers. The BBC (2015) identifies seven, but my own observations at newsstands suggest there are more than that. There is one each in Moldovan and Ukrainian. Unusually for practically anywhere in the world, there is no English-language paper. The oldest newspaper is the *Dnestrovskaya Pravda*,** founded in 1941 and now published weekly (*Dnestrovskaya Pravda* 1998 and see Hill 1977). It is partially dependent on donations for its funding, but has an income from sales and advertising. It does not admit to any government funding.

Several newspapers have been characterised as "opposition" or perhaps more precisely as independent of the government, including Ribnita-based weekly *Dobry Den*, *Chelovek i ego prava*, a local version of Alexander Lebedev's Moscow-based *Novaya Gazeta*, Russian *Proriv*, *Profsoyuznye Vesti* and *Glas Naroda*.

---

* A more ingenious Pole was given a suspended prison sentence in 2008 for causing the president's name to appear at the top of search engine rankings when anyone searched for what Tilles (2016) describes as "a slang word for penis".

** Pravda literally translates as 'truth'.

There are no published circulation figures for these papers. The lack of Western-style newsagents* and the seeming absence of any news home delivery means circulation is likely to be very low, with the vast majority of reading done online, making that medium more important in political and practical terms. Television broadcasting is also inevitably far more widely received than the print media.

The state-owned broadcaster *Pervy Pridnestrovski* was noted to have seamlessly switched from whole-hearted backing of then President Shevchuk in the run up to the 2016 election to unconditional praise of his successor Krasnoselsky shortly afterwards. In a similar vein, the news agency *Novosti Pridnestrovya*, also state-owned, removed most of the material that could be seen as supportive of Shevchuk from its website even before Krasnoselsky was inaugurated (Comai 2018).

The Sheriff group distributes cable television packages, which consist largely of Russian state channels and its own Tiraspol TSV channel, which tends to be fairly apolitical and indeed quite dull.** Other packages include Moldovan, Romanian and Ukrainian channels.

Foreign, largely Russian, television is also widely watched, a fact that may be of political significance. The three most widely watched channels, according to Tatiana Cojocari's research, were all Russian (2019:42). A paper authored by a former UK ambassador to Moldova and Stefan Wolff argues:

…most of the Transnistrian population remains firmly oriented towards Russia and suspicious of the EU. This is due to the fact that most Transnistrian residents (as most residents on the right bank) watch Russian TV, and there has been little movement by the Moldovan government to project EU or Moldovan TV or radio into Transnistria. (Beyer and Woolf 2016:342).

Andis Kudors had, in effect, the reverse view:

In regards to the reasons for the credibility and popularity of Russian television, radio, and newspapers in Moldova, we believe that this situation can be explained by nostalgia and some form of dependence of a large portion of the population. (2010:239).

In other words, Kudors' position is that the sympathy to Russia draws Transnistrians to that country's broadcasts, more than the broadcast inducing the sympathy. While television could influence Transnistrians' views on Russia, Beyer and Woolf may be exaggerating the effect, and the more plausible and intuitive view is that expressed by Kudors of people turning to television that accords with their existing perceptions.

There are around six radio stations based in Tiraspol, largely broadcasting light entertainment, and dozens of Russian and Moldovan ones are available. Several can easily

---

*   There are probably about a dozen kiosks selling newspapers and magazines along with other goods in Tiraspol, and a greater density in Bender. They never appear very busy.
**   How to Make a Woven Bag with your Own Hands featured prominently in its listed page links on 5 August 2018 when first checked (TSV 2020).

be listened to online (Radiomap.eu 2020). Reasonably good wi-fi is widely available in hotels and restaurants. Nearly all Transnistrian organisations have websites, some basic and not kept up to date; many, especially official ones, have passable English translations.

3.6.3 RESTRAINTS ON MEDIA FREEDOM

There is little reported censorship in Transnistria. The evidence it occurs is generally of isolated incidents, rather than anything that could be regarded as systematic. Luiza Dorosenco, who has herself been cited as a victim of minor attacks by the government (FIDH 2014), complained in the Moldovan *Media-Azi* newspaper that:

Journalists from independent media complain about difficulties regarding access to information...officially there is no censorship. However, the journalists get verbal instruction about the angle they need to take when reporting certain topics, some people known for their habit of criticizing the Transnistrian leadership would be denied space in newspapers, access to radio and TV broadcasts. (Dorosenco 2015)

Her measured summary of the situation may indicate a considerable degree of self-censorship among Transnistrian journalists, who refrain from publishing serious criticism of the government.

There is no independent organisation specifically on press freedom which assesses Transnistria. Moldova is ranked 91st (out of 180 countries) on the Press Freedom Index (Reporters Without Borders 2020). It is not stated whether this included Transnistrian media. Its main criticism was the hardly unique one that, "The editorial line of the leading media outlets correlates closely with the political and business interests of their owners." Reporters Without Borders commented, in 2010 and 2011, extensively on Ernest Vardanean's imprisonment, discussed below, but has made no specific criticisms of Transnistria since his 2011 release (*c.f.* Reporters Without Borders 2020).

Restrictions on websites

Ghenadie Cornitel, who created a successful website about Transnistria on Russian media, felt the need to self-censor, having three moderators to remove comments, "Such as ones that criticise the regime or call for demonstrations" (Beurq 2017). This was written around the time of handover from Shevchuk to Krasnoselsky.

A more politically significant site, dniester.ru, was closed down in July 2012 during the Shevchuk regime by use of technical interference, which prevented it operating without any judicial process, on the basis it had been identified as an "opposition site" (TIRAS 2012). Shevchuk relented and in 2013 allowed it to register (*Publika* 2013) with a consequent restoration of service. A Freedom House report said the owner, Roman Konoplev, had received, unspecified, threats:

Presidential Decree No. 241, issued on 5 August 2014, purportedly aimed at preventing extremist activity, was used to clear the Transnistrian region of potential critics of Shevchuk's regime. (Litra 2015:448)

On first checking in 2017, dniestr.ru could be accessed from the UK, Chisinau and Tiraspol, but by May 2019 it was wholly inaccessible from anywhere. Allegations were made that in 2016 the KGB had ordered the closure of some sites relying on the 2014 presidential decree (USSD 2017). Since the election of Krasnoselsky at the end of 2016, there have been no reports of the censoring of any websites or other media by the Transnistrian authorities, other than dneistr.ru and the 'disappearance' of Shevchuk's personal website. Iulia Rotarescu (2014a:7) pointed to the "oppression" of another web-site, *Novai Reghion*, because the Tiraspol authorities did not like how it had reported events in Ukraine.

The imprisonment of Ernest Vardanean

The most serious assault on press freedom was the April 2010 arrest of Ernest Vardanean, a reporter for the Tiraspol-based Russian news agency *Novy Region*. In 2009, he also started to work for the Chisinau newspaper *Puls* and contributed to Radio Free Europe (RFE), producing material critical of the Transnistrian regime. It was alleged that he was spying for the Chisinau government (RFE 2011). After the arrest, he gave a televised confession (*Timpul* 2010), and then in October 2010, he was subject to a closed trial – both perhaps the stock-in-trade of totalitarian regimes – convicted and sentenced to fifteen years in prison. This led to protests from the US Embassy in Chisinau, the OSCE, whose representatives were refused access to the trial (RFE 2010), and international NGOs, all denouncing the case as violating due process and basic rights. The Moldovan government alleged it was an attempt by Transnistria's politicians to undermine efforts to build trust and confidence between Chisinau and Tiraspol. Vardanean was pardoned by President Smirnov, bowing to international pressure, in May 2011 (*Mediafax* 2011), but his initial imprisonment has never been fully explained, let alone justified, by the Tiraspol authorities.

3.6.4 OTHER RESTRAINTS ON FREEDOM OF SPEECH

Horjan and others criticising the Transnistrian government

The imprisonment of Communist Party leader Oleg Horjan (SubSect.3.5.2) is the biggest individual human rights concern in Transnistria as of December 2020. This concern is compounded by a report in August 2020 (RFE 2020) that he was to face further charges for "insulting the president" as a result of having alleged in a newspaper article that the Transnistrian regime are "puppets". The report is from a source which is generally opposed to the Transnistrian regime, is uncorroborated, and adopted by Promo-LEX (2020).

The same source (Wheat and Ursul, writing for RFE, 2020) also reports three other recent cases of people being accused of "extremism", including Larisa Kalik, a 22-year-old writer who fled Moldova as well as Transnistria after creating a website in 2020 about conditions in the Transnistrian army. Although reference is made to veiled threats over the phone from the Transnistrian authorities, no indication is given as to why Kalik would need to flee Moldova too.

There were reports in the Moldovan press in 2019, repeated in a US State Department report (USSD 2020), that a pensioner couple, Tatiana Belova and Serghei Mirovici, had been arrested and imprisoned for insulting President Krasnoselsky in a blog. The reports have not been confirmed, and Promo-LEX has said the couple refused legal assistance from that organisation.

If correct, these stories would have the proverbially 'chilling'* effect on any perception of freedom of expression in Transnistria. No government in the world is beyond criticism or gains the uncritical support of all those it governs. Attempting to prevent such criticism is usually far more harmful to the society than the criticism itself, and mature democratic governments rarely attempt to do so. The cases of Vardanean and Kalik are to an extent explicable because of governmental insecurity about the status of the territory. Spying and challenges to military service may represent an existential threat to the territory in a way they would not to an established state. The allegations against Horjan and Belova and Mirovici are routine criticisms of government, and there can be no more excuse for invoking the penal apparatus of the state there than anywhere else.

Sexual freedom and Karolina Dutka

Homosexuality is little discussed in Transnistria, though there is no evidence of actual oppression by the authorities. In October 2016, Karolina Dutka, then a medical student at Shevchenko University, tried to put on an exhibition of photos about the LGBT community in Transnistria, discussed below, at Club 19 in Tiraspol. She told the Ukrainian *Pravda* (2017):

> Everybody pretends that LGBT doesn't exist. But with the help of word of mouth I was able to talk to over 150 people. Among them there were not only students, but also adults, those who work, for example, in state institutions, teachers. Only sixteen people out of those 150 agreed to participate in the project, still they wouldn't disclose their faces.

---

* The word is used virtually as a term of art in connection with the US constitution, particularly its first amendment, and means the inhibition of the exercise of a legal right, like that to free speech, by the threat of legal sanction.

The day after she published plans for the exhibition, she was summonsed to a meeting with a representative of the "security service", probably the KGB, who told her, in a conversation she covertly recorded and published (Dutka 2017), it had to be cancelled as it would "contradict the ideology of the state". The person she was speaking to asked her to sign an undertaking not to disclose the conversation, but she refused. The thrust of the pressure put on her was not directly homophobic, but that she was defaming Transnistria by suggesting there was a problem of homophobia there.

Dutka stood her ground at first, although she faced threats of problems with her studies and her parents' work, and eventually converted her work into an online exhibition (Dutka n.d.), which she claimed attracted over 15,000 visitors. The photos were subsequently exhibited in Odessa and then Chisinau, at the US Embassy's resource centre (Myachina 2018).

Although Dutka was not harmed beyond receiving large amounts of abusive email, she says the director of Club 19 was forced to emigrate when thugs beat her son up – Dutka does not say why – and mentioned his parents in the process. Dutka left Transnistria to live in Moscow, without completing her medical studies, though this was largely for family reasons, I was told by Alexandra Telpis, a friend of hers, on 11 April 2019.

Dutka's story, while not showing Transnistria's authorities in a good light, may indicate the relative powerlessness of the KGB, now the Ministry of State Security (SubSect.3.3.3), at least compared with that which operated in Soviet times. It was not clear what they would have been able to do to her or her parents. Even though the university is far more subject to political control than those in most of Europe or the US, the security services are in no position to dictate directly to it. The economy is not centralised enough for most employment to be dependent on state, let alone KGB, approval. The fact that Dutka and her parents remained unscathed despite her partial defiance of the edict bodes well for the society.

3.6.5 OTHER EXPRESSIONS OF DISSENT

Street protest

A response to the concerns raised in the RFE articles (2020) could come in the form of YouTube videos of senior Transnistrians interacting with protesters. In one (YouTube 2020), the minister of internal affairs, Ruslan Mova, converses for over two hours, sometimes heatedly but never threateningly, with those protesting against COVID-19 restrictions over access to the bridge to Moldova in Ribnita. He has no visible security protection and holds nothing other than a water bottle. Both he and the protesters are happy for the exchange to be filmed. The protesters are too many, disparate and vociferous for the event to be staged.* Whatever the merits and whether or not the protesters

---

*   I found them by searching online – nothing was done by anyone in Transnistria to draw my attention to them.

changed their policy, it was a superb example of informal democracy in action which would credit any country. My own view that Mova is not particularly sophisticated in understanding the ways those from more traditionally liberal countries might see such issues (Subs.3.5.2) underlines the likelihood that he sincerely wants to interact with the territory's populace and sees dissent as legitimate, just as does any Western politician. Another video (YouTube 2020a) underlines this, showing a crowd remonstrating in similar, obviously unafraid terms, with a reasonably good-natured senior police officer charged with enforcing the block over the bridge.

Similarly, an earlier YouTube post (2015) entitled 'Pensioners went to an Unauthorised Rally' shows the protesters being invited into a government hall to listen to the head of the organisation they were protesting about give a defence of the policy.

Club 19

Club 19 (see SubSect.13.1) itself has the features of a well-run youth club, while purportedly being mildly subversive. While not overtly political, many of the discussions have a political element, including criticism of what is seen as Transnistria's elite. There is little interference by the authorities, but Alexandra Telpis, an organiser, told me (interview 11 April 2019 and written clarification) of an incident which concerned her:

> We hoped to invite for discussion in Club 19 the Moldovan journalist Natalia Morai who was one of the leaders who campaigned for people to go to the rally, she was accused by the Moldovan authorities as organiser of violent demonstrations when President Voronin was re-elected in 2009. We called the KGB and they said there will be problems with her entering the country, for sure. So she decided it was best she did not even try to come.

Morai had previously interviewed Shevchuk in Tiraspol; had never been charged with any crime in Moldova; and is a respected journalist, so her possible exclusion was surprising and worrying.

3.6.6 THE PROSPECTS FOR FREEDOM OF MEDIA AND SPEECH

The variety of newspapers, news websites, and television and radio stations in Transnistria makes direct state control a little harder to exercise. Most are in Russian, and while there are suggestions that this is the consequence of the governmental identification with Russia, which might be part of the nation-building discussed in Sect.1.2, the more mundane explanation by Kudors *et al.* (2010) – that it is what people prefer – is plausible. There is a good base on which abundant and free media which would benefit the society could be built.

As for that freedom, in the absence of objective monitoring and based on limited anecdotal evidence, the most that can be said is that one is left, through the hotchpotch of examples discussed above, with a suspicion that the media is not currently as free as it could be in Transnistria. Rotarescu argues that:

> The media institutions and the journalists carrying out their activity in Transnistria… face many problems when it comes to independent broadcasting and publication from the regime in Tiraspol. (2014a:9).

However, the instances she cites are not of serious oppression, and her main point is that only 10–15% of the media is independent of the government and of large companies such as Sheriff (Rotarescu 2014a:7).

The Vardanean incident aside, media restrictions flow more from perceptions induced in those who might be inclined to criticise the authorities and occasionally financial influence being used by businesses, particularly Sheriff, than crude government interference. That climate of trepidation of, largely unspecified, consequences can inhibit reporting and might lead to a lower ranking for Transnistria on scales like the Press Freedom Index than Moldova. This I found echoed in the reluctance of people at universities to talk to me without obtaining official approval: which approval was paradoxically, so far as I was aware, never withheld.

There is no experience of a free Western-style media in Transnistria. The state was the successor to the Soviet Union, and its isolation since 1992 has made it harder than in other former Soviet territories to adapt to different norms. International monitoring can be an effective counterbalance to control of the media. The obvious willingness of the Transnistrian authorities to seek and respond to election observers (Appendix A) and engage with the Hammarberg report (2013) bodes well on this. International monitoring of media freedom could be expected to achieve the same.

Returning to Whitten-Woodring and Van Belle's (2015) categories, discussed at the start of Sect. 3.6, it is clear that there are too many impediments to watchdog reporting for the media to be classed as *free*. Conversely, it cannot be said that the government operates total control over the media such as to make it *not free*, leaving it within the *imperfectly free* class. Although Rotarescu does not explicitly address these categories, she does conclude (2014a:9), "The freedom of information and the freedom of expression are only partially observed." To put such a conclusion in context, it should be noted that Freedom House (Abramowitz 2017) reported that only 13% of the world's population live in a society where the media can be classed as free.

While present restrictions on media freedom may undermine the concept of Transnistria as a free democracy, they are not of such an extensive nature that they should be an impediment to Transnistrian independence. Statehood should make the Transnistrian leadership more secure and less likely to perceive criticism or even spying as representing such a threat to the territory: present restrictions may flow from such insecurity. Similarly, pressure from international organisations, whose access is likely to quickly follow any independence, is likely to mean a free press tainted by nothing more sinister than the commercial interests of its owners will probably ensue.

3.7 RELIGION AND RELIGIOUS FREEDOM

Religious freedom is potentially a major concern in Transnistria because restrictions on religion in Soviet times were notorious and received much, and sometimes highly emotive, worldwide attention (Phillips 2016). It is against that background that the practice of religion in Transnistria should now be evaluated. This section will consider the degree of freedom accorded to both the, at least informally, established Orthodox Church and minority religions and how the latter are treated.

3.7.1 RELIGION IN THE USSR AND RUSSIA

Although never formally outlawed in the USSR, religion existed in the context of an ideological objective that it should be eliminated (Library of Congress 2016). The Russian Orthodox Church was targeted, except for a brief revival in 1941 by Stalin, who believed it could be a patriotic focal point for resistance to Nazi Germany. Otherwise, it faced a continual campaign to close its churches, carried on as virulently by Khrushchev and Brezhnev as Stalin. By 1985, only 7,000 churches remained active, out of around 50,000 that had existed before the USSR was formed. Nearly all Catholic churches were closed (Library of Congress 2016). The practice of Judaism became virtually impossible, despite Stalin's bizarre experiment creating the Autonomous Jewish Oblast in Siberia (Walker 2017). Muslims were oppressed, often by force in the Central Asian republics (Erikson 2017); although they too were granted greater tolerance after the 1941 Nazi invasion. King (2000:125) points to admissions of previous religious intolerance in the guidelines that led to the implementation of *perestroika* in the Moldovan SSR. The last years of the USSR under Gorbachev saw a virtual end to state oppression of religion, and in September 1990, a law was passed by the Moscow supreme soviet that meaningfully guaranteed religious freedom (Ramet 1992).

The post-USSR Orthodox resurgence means the church now claims around 150 million members and 40,000 churches (Stroop 2018), numbers that are growing rapidly (*Orthodox Christianity* 2017). Its hierarchy, particularly the Patriarch Kirill, enjoys a mutually supportive relationship with Vladimir Putin, who has photographs of himself performing religious rites regularly published.*

3.7.2 RELIGION SINCE DE FACTO INDEPENDENCE

Transnistria too has, since attaining *de facto* independence, developed as a predominantly Orthodox country, with some 91% of the population at least nominally subscribing to

---

* For further discussion on this topic, see McCrum and Mrachek (2019).

that religion, usually through the Moldovan Orthodox Church (USSD 2014), which is subordinate to the Russian Orthodox Church. O'Loughlin and Toal recorded 82.3% (2013: Table 3) of Transnistrians giving their religion as Orthodox. Although Matsuzato (2009: Abstract) says that the "competition between the Russian and Romanian Orthodox Churches over Moldova inevitably affects Transnistria", the Church's own information suggests the position in Transnistria is settled in favour of the Russian Church (Tiraspol Diocese 2009). The UN (Refworld 2013) lists Roman Catholics, followers of Old-Rite Orthodoxy, Baptists, Seventh-day Adventists, evangelical and charismatic Christians, Jews, Lutherans, and Jehovah's Witnesses as practising in Transnistria.

The Transnistrian constitution (2011) guarantees freedom of conscience (Article 30) and separation of church and state (Article 9), although there were not dissimilar provisions in the USSR constitution. The aesthetically pleasing but unremarkable main Nativity Cathedral just outside the centre of Tiraspol has, I have observed, well-attended Sunday morning services. Despite its classic Orthodox look, it was only completed in 1999. It is the chief church for the diocese of Tiraspol and Dubasari, which covers all of Transnistria. The diocese (Tiraspol Diocese 2009) was established in 1998 as a symbol of the Moscow church's support for the independence of the territory.

There have been complaints of persecution by members of the Church of Jesus Christ the Saviour, the main protestant church in Tiraspol, reported by the conservative Christian Broadcasting Network (Lane 2007). These complaints seemed more directed against bribes demanded by officials than any ideological oppression. The USSD states (2014), with no substantiation, "In the separatist Transnistria region, authorities restricted the activities of minority religious groups, which were reluctant to report problems." This may have been a reference to the complaints of Jehovah's Witnesses, discussed below, but there is no reason for not giving a more specific basis.

Religious groups of more than ten may, but are not legally required to, register with the government. However, without registration it would not be possible for an organisation to rent property and the holding of public meetings and distributing literature would be illegal. There were 49 such groups registered in 2012 (Refworld 2013).

There seems little point in the requirement of registration and it was questioned in the Hammarberg report (2013:9) which said it, if "deemed necessary – should be swift, not unduly bureaucratic, and not discriminatory". Members of religious groups can avoid military service on the basis of conscientious objection but have to perform civilian service instead (JCW 2014). In practice, this is a concession to Transnistria's Jehovah's Witness community of about 2,500. Prior to the passing of this law, Witnesses had complained of their Transnistrian members being punished for refusing to serve (Baran 2011:13), but stated the punishment of one year's imprisonment had always been served on probation and fines of US$450 had been imposed (JCW 2006).

It was, during the Smirnov presidency, the Jehovah's Witnesses who suffered the most active oppression of any religious group from the Transnistrian state. This was largely at the hands of Petr Aleksandrovich Zalozhkov, who was appointed commissioner of religious and cultural affairs in 1997 despite having no practical or academic experience in theological matters (Baran 2011:441. In a state school textbook, Zalozhkov (2001:441-442) wrote of the Witnesses that they are "totalitarian and a pyramid scheme out to fleece converts of their money". He claimed that, although ostensibly being registered, the Witnesses were not a recognised religious group; prevented them building a Kingdom Hall, as their places of worship are known, in Tiraspol; and caused difficulties in operating the hall in Ribnita, including arresting eighteen people carrying out maintenance on it (Baran 2011:437). Meetings of Witnesses in private homes were occasionally broken up by police. In March 2008, a group, some wearing Cossack uniforms and holding whips, led by an Orthodox priest gathered outside a house in Parcani where such a service was due to be held. There was no actual violence, but police watched without making any attempt to prevent the harassment of would-be worshippers (2009:18).

There were many successful court challenges by Witnesses to Zalozhkov's activities, the resulting orders not always being fully respected. In 2008, the Soviet passed a religious law abolishing his post, upon which President Smirnov appointed him as an unofficial special adviser on religious affairs (2009:19). I attempted to raise this episode when interviewing Smirnov in May 2019, but three times he evaded the questions (see Appendix B).

Despite the influence of the Orthodox Church in post-Soviet Russia, the Putin regime passed laws in 2016 prohibiting any form of evangelism or religious activities anywhere but recognised church buildings (Shellnutt 2016). While such laws would have been adopted in Transnistria had the proposed 2013 law bringing the territory's laws into line with Russia been passed (Sect.3.1), there is no similar prohibition there. Foreigners do not count as church members for registration purposes, and the involvement of foreign organisations in religious groups is a reason to refuse registration (JCW 2006). Missionary activity in Transnistria is virtually unknown, other than some door-to-door proselytising by Jehovah's Witnesses, which led to small fines in 2001 (Baran 2009:439). It is impossible to predict what the government would do if North American or European evangelists took an interest in the territory.

Non-Christian religions

There are small Jewish communities in Tiraspol and Ribnita numbering perhaps 1,000–1,500* and 10,000 in Moldova (CLM 2020), the bulk of the Jewish population having been destroyed by Romania's Nazi-collaborating Antonescu regime during World War II (SubSect.1.1.1). There was a 2001 pipe-bomb attack on the Tiraspol synagogue, possibly timed to coincide with Hitler's birthday, and a Molotov cocktail thrown at the

---

* A figure of 4,500 is cited in the Hammarberg report (2013:39), but that is almost certainly too high where the community has little visible presence. In my interview with her, discussed below, Anna Kondrashchenko could give me no overall figure but said there were 235 under 18. The United States Commission for the Preservation of America's Heritage Abroad (2010:4) said there were 40,000 in Moldova in 1998.

synagogue and vandalism of Jewish graves in 2004 (USCPAHA 2010:7). There is no basis on which to assume state involvement or sympathy for these outrages.

I interviewed Anna Kondrashchenko director of the thriving, largely US-funded Hesed, a Jewish welfare centre, at its offices in Tiraspol on 2 October 2019. There is an 80-seat synagogue – built in 1998 – in Tiraspol, which had been full on the high holy day just before I visited. It has no rabbi, and *bar mitzvah* and *bat mitzvah** training is usually undergone in Chisinau. Kondrashchenko assured me the Jewish community enjoys good relations with the Orthodox Church and other public organisations.

There is no registered Islamic organisation and little evidence of existence of such communities in Tiraspol. When discussing religion with me, Smirnov said there were no Muslims in Transnistria (Appendix B). There are said by the Islamic League to be about twenty Muslims, largely elderly and of Tartar and Azeri origin, who communally study the Koran in Bender and who were in 2013 subject to some state interference (Nielsen 2015:419). Hijab-wearing women are never seen in Transnistria, though are in Chisinau.

The Hindupedia website (Bhatt n.d.) claims there is a Hindu temple in Tiraspol but provides no address and regards the city as being in Ukraine. There is no other evidence of such a temple online or in my viewing of Tiraspol.

3.7.3 THE EXTENT OF RELIGIOUS FREEDOM

There is no oppression now of the Orthodox community in Transnistria. The requirement for registration of religious organisations and the discouragement of foreign members seems pointless and even undesirable. This is more about the government's level of control over the population, particularly where there may be foreign involvement, than an attempt to target religion specifically.

Probably the last vestiges of state anti-religiosity went at the end of Smirnov's presidency in 2011, and the leadership passed to a generation who had little political experience of Soviet times. There are no recent complaints of oppression and it is hard to see any advantage to the present regime in using its powers to restrict religious freedoms, at least of its own citizens, so long as minority religions present no security threat. Refworld (2013) observes that "there were no reports of abuses of religious freedom", though was critical of the government for failing "to prevent and prosecute instances of societal discrimination against [religious minorities]". Other than concerns about Jehovah's Witnesses, the only specific complaint it identified was that the "Lutheran Church was unable to reclaim property seized during the Soviet era". The claims of oppression by non-Orthodox religions are trivial compared with the real restrictions on any freedom to worship imposed in the USSR (Library of Congress 2016) and are not an adverse factor in evaluating Transnistria as a country that respects freedoms.

---

* This less familiar term is the ceremony for girls, now universal in all but ultra-orthodox communities.

3.8 CONCLUSION: IS TRANSNISTRIA A FREE, DEMOCRATIC NATION, SUBJECT TO THE RULE OF LAW?

It will be clear if there is a weak link in the conditions Transnistria might be expected to fulfil before being thought ready for statehood, it is its human rights record. This chapter has considered six different aspects of what can broadly be called democracy and freedoms. These have a theoretical underpinning from the constitution (2011), which, although generally robust, does contain a worrying qualification on the right to free speech and involves the president in the appointment of judiciary so as to undermine the separation of powers, even if less so than in the US. Accepting Tommasoli's (2012) reasoning set out at the start of this chapter, this of itself says little, if anything, about how far rights are respected.

There is strong evidence to support the contention that Transnistria has succeeded in creating a genuine electoral democracy, after two successive elections with defeated incumbents who properly and promptly left office. Similarly, an area where there are no major criticisms of the Transnistrian government is in relation to religious toleration. There are concerns over the requirement for religious groups to register and why that persists, even after Hammarberg's powerful recommendation (2013) to modify it, is a mystery. Other concerns in that area are either minor, to do with church property rights, or concern the historic treatment of Jehovah's Witnesses during the Smirnov regime. This is all the more laudable when compared with the climate of non-toleration of religions that pervaded right up until the last few years of the USSR.

An independent judiciary with a power, and occasional willingness, to find against the government has emerged. There are flaws, though, in how the justice system works, which may compromise the rule of law. Attacks on lawyers championing causes unpopular with the government, even if rare, strike at the heart of the system. Ideally, judges should be appointed by a commission independent of the president or any direct political control, something which would require constitutional amendment.

The high prison population is a concern, even if academic writing and comparative analysis does not suggest there is generally a strong correlation between high levels of imprisonment and other forms of state oppression. However, in a country peaceful and law abiding enough for, for instance, the interior minister to argue with irate demonstrators with no protection (YouTube 2020), there seems little explanation other than an unnecessarily heavy-handed use of state machinery.

There are significant question marks over both human rights and freedoms of expression through the media and otherwise. Most of the high-profile cases of mistreatment of those who have offended the regime date back to the Smirnov years pre-2011. Certainly, under Shevchuk the regime was moving in the right direction. The Lipovcenco case may be illusory and is impossible to verify. The observation that Alexandru Coliban, released in 2013, was the last political prisoner in the territory was immensely encouraging, though also impossible to verify.

However, recent developments may have undone optimism that could be gleaned from Coliban's release. The alleged detention of Tatiana Belova and Serghei Mirovici for insulting the president online, if true, is a crude instance of political imprisonment. The continued detention of Oleg Horjan is verifiable and deplorable. Although there may have been scuffles following on from his arrest, itself an act hard to justify, no one was injured, and in civilised countries long prison sentences are not imposed for minor disorder in police stations or elsewhere. It is impossible to escape the conclusion that his imprisonment is an act of political oppression. Were it to be proved true that he is to be further charged with insulting the president or a similar expression-based crime, the matter would be compounded.

If there is a saving grace in Horjan's detention it is that it was subject to proper judicial process, unlike the police holding of Mozer that led to the 2016 ECHR judgement. The lack of direct susceptibility to an external court is beyond Transnistria's control. That Russia, and even Moldova, may be liable for Transnistrian actions in that court is an uncomfortable legal fiction. While it enables some victims to obtain redress, the court's giving judgement against other countries does not properly hold the territory to account. Stepan Popovskiy's suggestion for an international court may not work in the form he advances it, but some form of external accountability would improve the present situation.

The media is not as free as would be ideal. There is not a robust opposition press. There is evidence that the climate in the territory is such that journalists feel the need to self-censor. In that climate, it is not surprising that there is little need for active state censorship and that the instances that can be identified of such censorship are not egregious. That the Vardanean case stands out even ten years after his conviction may lead one to the conclusion that imprisonment of journalists is a thing of the past. If, however, an opposition leader, as Horjan is, is charged with insulting the president, Transnistria will have slipped back a decade.

It is unlikely that Transnistria will move to being a properly free state without a greater degree of external advice as well as accountability. The Hammarberg report (2013) was a welcome assessment and there were signs that some of the recommendations were being followed. Another external assessment is overdue: the UN or EU should make its willingness to accommodate this known.

Internally, there also needs to be more scrutiny. While the present judiciary does assert a degree of independence, the ombudsman system is not working in respect of matters where state power is potentially exercised in a coercive way. The role would be much better performed or overseen by someone experienced in human rights law from outside the Transnistrian elite.

The theoretical analyses considered at the start of this chapter, Habermas (1995) and particularly Raz (1977 cited by Waldron 2016), allow for some distinction between the attainment of the rule of law and democracy and human rights and social justice, despite Waldron's own (2016) reservations. This is borne out by the situation in

Transnistria, where "outcomes", as Tommasoli (2012) describes them, vary considerably across the range of topics considered. Taken as a whole, the level of democracies and freedoms in Transnistria is neither ideal nor deplorable. Events unfolding in Belarus as this section is written, where there has been an election whose results have been internationally questioned, with protesters being attacked by police and imprisoned by a compliant judiciary, show that even in Europe there are countries in a much worse state. Conversely, it falls short of the parts of Europe where there is almost complete freedom to criticise governments, imprisonment for political activities is unthinkable, there are vastly lower prison populations, and there is no attempt to control religious groups.

Transnistria improved from its Soviet legacy even during Smirnov's regime: the fact that he listened to international pressure and released Vardanean was a sign of this. The territory is to be given credit for having come a good deal further under the presidents who have followed him and progressing as much as it has despite its isolation. This progress would continue, and probably hasten, as a meaningful part of an international community. While there are concerns on human rights issues and there is much to improve, that does not create an argument that Transnistria should not be independent. Even leaving aside that there are many countries currently far worthier of terms such as 'pariah' because of human rights records, which do not have their right to independence questioned, the flaws which mean there cannot be an unequivocal 'yes' to the question posed by this section should not be bars to Transnistrian independence.

CHAPTER FOUR

TRANSNISTRIA AS A FUNCTIONING SOCIETY

While the previous chapter explored the extent to which the Transnistrian government respects the rights of inhabitants to enjoy democracy and freedoms, this chapter is concerned with the way that those people and the government have produced a society that deals with the matters that are of concern in everyday life. There is a widely recognised distinction between the *positive* rights, largely of the sort discussed in this chapter, and the *negative* ones in the previous chapter. As the *Encyclopaedia of Global Justice* (Chatterjee 2011) puts it:

> A positive right is an obligation by others to provide some benefit to the rights holder. A right is a correlative of a wrong, so if one has a right to something it means that it is wrong or unlawful for others to negate that right or to not provide some benefit. In contrast, a negative right is an obligation by others to avoid negating some actions and properties of the rights holders.

Both types of rights are recognised in the Transnistrian constitution. Despite that distinction, there is a considerable degree of overlap between what can be explored under the category 'society' and what is examined in relation to other features about Transnistria. There has to be a society for the nation-building, considered in Chapter 1, to be of any effect. The economy, considered in Chapter 2, into which inhabitants will contribute and draw from, is itself a feature of a society and indeed enables the tangible matters considered in this chapter to be funded. Democracy and freedoms, considered in Chapter 3, are again an integral part of any society, as they bear on how people can live their lives. When looking at education in Sect.4.1, it will be seen that in Transnistria aspects of it became for a time highly politicised, to the extent that the government was actively impinging on inhabitants' negative rights, rather than just not advancing their positive ones. However, this chapter will focus primarily on whether these positive rights have been provided successfully in the context of Transnistria's resources.

For most of the time and most of the population, the most important feature of government is how it provides for that population – that is meets what may be regarded as positive rights. The most obvious ways are by the provision of education, health services and a financial safety net. Therefore, each of these is explored in this chapter. They are lumped together by David Crook in his short, but seminal, paper "Education, Health and Social Welfare":

> Enlightenment thinking from the mid eighteenth century signalled the birth of modernity and was a catalyst for ideas and developments in the fields of science, medicine, health promotion and education including compulsory schooling in the West. (2007:651)

It is meeting these needs that, as Crook goes on to explore, has remained at the forefront of what governments can be expected to do for their populaces. These are the core needs of a society, but there are others which regard should be had to in the Transnistrian context. This chapter also explores housing, partly provided by most states, particularly so in communist and former communist countries, including Transnistria. The present, and largely satisfactory, provision of housing is considered in the historical context of rapid building of homes throughout the USSR, particularly during Khrushchev's rule.

Communal, as well as individual, needs are also regarded as the preserve of the modern state. Increasingly important is protection of the environment, where Transnistria has had for decades legislation of remarkable sophistication. Policing is vital in any society. Discussion of policing often focuses on the abuse of the function, which can be a crude breach of the rights discussed in the previous chapter. However, it has, of course, a positive side in keeping people safe, and this aspect of policing is explored in this chapter along with the related question of crime levels. The focus is on the areas where serious allegations have been made against the territory, particularly human trafficking, along with corruption and smuggling, though more routine matters, including traffic policing, are also considered.

Transport, while outside the core government function, is of importance for most people, and in practice involves some governmental intervention. The vast majority of roads and railways worldwide are government run, as is urban public transport, particularly in developed countries. So fundamental is this area, it can be credibly argued that it bears on human happiness. As Duarte *et al.* argue, "Governments should adopt measures in order to support transport solutions with which individuals feel happier" (2009:30). An important, if low-profile, government function is keeping transport, largely that on the roads, safe. That has presented problems in Transnistria at least as serious as those in the rest of the region, which the government could take basic steps to remedy.

Numerous other topics are considered by sociologists in the evaluation of societies. The structure of the population itself in terms of numbers, genders and ages is an essential feature of society, considered in relation to the economy in Sect.2.4. Governments do interfere with this, but it is rarely successful. China's one-child policy is regarded by many as having been disastrous (e.g. Yu 2015; Kuo and Wang 2019) and Ceausescu's attempts to prevent the use of contraception is totally discredited (Kligman 1992). Religion, in which it can be argued a government should have little part, is another important feature of many societies. The historic interference by the USSR, and the re-emergence of the Orthodox Church post-communism, has been considered in Sect.3.7. The media is also of significance – mass media and society has spawned a significant literature of its own* – and in the Transnistrian context this is dealt with in Sect.3.6.

The question of whether Transnistria is a functioning society needs to be considered, which the remainder of this chapter does in the light of all these factors.

4.1 EDUCATION

This section considers how education is now provided in Transnistria and thus how the government is meeting the relevant constitutional obligations (SubSect.3.1.1). It then focuses on the controversial, if historic, treatment of the Romanian-language schools.

4.1.1 EDUCATIONAL PROVISION

Schools

According to the Agency for Regional Development in Transnistria, in 2016 there were 192 secondary schools with a total of 92,532 students (ARDT 2020).** Of these, 182 were public. Around 4,500 pupils attended the other ten schools. There were 176 "pre-school educational institutions", attended by 21,359 children. Russian was the language of instruction in 135 secondary schools; Moldovan with Cyrillic script in 33; Russian and Moldovan jointly in sixteen; Romanian, which is how Moldovan written in Latin script is described by the Transnistrian authorities, in six; and Ukrainian in two (ARDT 2020).

Separate literacy figures are not published for Transnistria, but its rate appears to be encompassed within, and probably in line with, the 99.5% attributed to Moldova by UNESCO, with 99.81% for those aged 15 to 24 (UNESCO 2020). The tiny minority who are not literate may mainly be among the Roma population (Hammarberg 2018).

The openDemocracy analysis (Pashentseva 2018) suggests an enviably low average class size of nineteen throughout the school system but says that cutbacks meant this could rise to 35 in some advanced secondary schools and is otherwise 25. It points to only two new schools having been commissioned, one still under construction, since the end of the Soviet era, perhaps as a consequence of the diminishing population. Many schools, and it cites the specific example of Plot School near Ribnita, are at least partially dependent

---

*   For example, Curran (2010) and the journal Mass Communication and Society (1998–2020).
**   The figure is a surprisingly high one and would suggest that around one sixth of the population fell into the 11–18 age bracket. A better figure may be that given by openDemocracy of 44,547 in 160 schools (Pashentseva 2018).

on voluntary contributions from parents to boost increasingly meagre state funding. Since 2011, there has been an obligatory unified state university entrance exam, with Russian methodology adopted with very little variation (Pashentseva 2018).

Education in Transnistria is overseen by a ministry divided into twelve boards, each dealing with a different aspect of education, with deputy ministers each presiding over several boards. The ministry expresses worthy objectives starting with, "Ensuring and protection of rights of citizens of the Pridnestrovian Moldavian Republic to education, creative and cultural activities" (President n.d.-a). That to an extent conceals what has become the most controversial issue in Transnistrian education: language, particularly the use of Moldovan with Latin script, discussed later in this section.

Universities

Transnistria's university is the Taras Shevchenko State University based largely in Tiraspol,* with its two main teaching buildings straddling the country's major road roundabout along with the national theatre. Its prominent position may be symbolic of the importance attached to higher education in Transnistria. It claims around 13,000 students, nearly all of whom are Transnistrian, and 1,000 staff. In contrast, there are 2.34 million university students in the UK, of whom 1.88 million are British (Universities UK 2019), meaning virtually the same proportion of Transnistrians receive a home-based university education as do Britons. The willingness of Russia to receive Transnistrian students may mean a higher proportion of the territory's population receive a tertiary education than Britain's.

The university was founded in 1930 as the Moldovan Institute of Public Education and was the first higher education institute in Moldova, subsequently under Soviet rule moving some faculties to Chisinau and Balti. It is a member of a consortium of sixteen Russian universities, including the prestigious Moscow State Law University and the Moscow First State Medical University (Consortium 2020). There is a branch of the university in Ribnita, which city also hosts outposts of the St Petersburg North-West University, and a 'consultation centre' of the Moscow Academy of Economics and Law (President n.d.).

The ability of the Transnistrian regime to educate its population at all levels, including the training of doctors discussed in Sect.4.2, benefits its case for independence in two ways. Firstly, it shows an area in which the government itself has been successful and would doubtless continue to be in independence, and secondly, the educated population that has resulted is an asset to the territory in more general terms.

One matter of concern, which flows into the discussion in the next subsection on the Romanian-language issue, arises from the university's introductory webpage written by the then rector – effectively vice-chancellor – Professor Stepan Beril:**

---

*   Not to be confused with the Tiraspol State University, based in Chisinau and run by Moldova, which also claims to be the successor of the original institution in Tiraspol (Tiraspol State University 2020).

**   A Bulgarian.

As in all of Transnistria, equally in high school has three official languages: Moldovan, Ukrainian and Russian. Moreover, the Moldovan language we keep studying and prepodaom [sic] in its native Cyrillic script.

This failure to adopt Moldovan or Romanian with Latin letters in the territory's leading educational institution could continue fuelling the dispute which has largely manifested itself in secondary schools.

4.1.2 THE ROMANIAN-LANGUAGE SCHOOLS

There are now six schools which teach in the Moldovan language using Latin letters. Their existence is an indication of the post-Smirnov liberalisation of much of Transnistrian society. Steven Roper (2005:503) considered the closing of many such schools in 2004, explaining that the motivation was resentment at the use of the Latin alphabet, rather than disgruntlement with the language itself. The disdain for Latin letters was apparent in my May 2019 interview with Smirnov (Appendix B). Roper adopts the view of the OSCE high commissioner on national minorities, Rolf Ekeus, that this amounted to "linguistic cleansing" (Roper 2005:503).

However, the historical context admitted by Roper is that prior to 1991, nearly all education in Moldova, including Transnistria, had been conducted in Russian. The Romanian language was introduced after the break-up of the USSR. Chisinau gave Moldovan government officials until 1994 to learn both languages, though in practice the deadline was not enforced (Roper 2005:505). Gradually, Romanian began to predominate in government, while Russian remained the language of business and private commerce. The 2004 census indicated that Romanian was the first language of 75% of the Right-Bank Moldovan population (Clyne 2015). The figure has remained fairly constant, the 2014 census showing that 78.7% spoke primarily Romanian or Moldovan, with respondents divided roughly equally as to how they labelled that language, but does not reflect the Transnistrian alphabet-based distinction, as Cyrillic-Romanian is virtually unknown in Moldova. Only 13.2% then spoke Russian (NBS 2014). Fifteen years after Roper wrote, Romanian has begun to dominate more, even in commerce; for instance, Romanian-Russian bilingual menus are the exception rather than the rule.

Probably the rapid government-led growth of the Romanian language in Moldova in the early days of independence made the Transnistrian government wary of it within their territory. This led to the decree of 18 August 1994 where the Transnistrian authorities forbade the use of the Latin script in schools. This was widely ignored, as was a further decree in May 1999 requiring the registration of all schools, with registration only being allowed to those which used the Cyrillic script. Unwisely, school closures were mandated by the Soviet on 28 January 2004 (Roper 2005:510), though even then there was a several-month lag before any action was taken. The seven targeted schools used Moldovan syllabuses and had express approval from the Chisinau government. The

Transnistrian authorities regarded these schools as Trojan horses* (Roper 2005:511). Chisinau countered the justification for the closures by pointing out that the schools had all existed in that format in Soviet times and could hardly have been founded as a way for its government to undermine Transnistria's autonomy (Roper 2005:511).

Ultimately, the closure attempts, although unpleasant, showed little more than that the Transnistrian government is not very effective at being oppressive. The first occurred in July 2004 on the basis that the school in question had not been properly registered. In August, the remaining schools were closed on the same grounds, with six teachers arrested trying to resist in Ribnita. There was international criticism of the actions. The US declared a travel ban on ten officials deemed responsible and Russia stated "in principle" that Transnistria should re-open the schools (Roper 2005:511); Ekeus made his hyperbolic "linguistic cleansing" pronouncement; and a minor trade war broke out between Moldova and Transnistria.

Sensibly, the Ministry of Education backed down. There were soon government suggestions that the schools could obtain registration as "foreign institutes of learning". By October 2004, the schools had done this. Some could not re-open immediately because of physical damage caused in skirmishes while closures had been implemented, leaving many pupils temporarily attending Russian-language schools or being bussed over the border to Moldovan schools (Roper 2005). A few weeks later, all seemed to be back in action much as they had been before the ill-advised and cack-handed attempts at closure.

Subsequently, however, the situation deteriorated and, such was the outrage, a suspended travel ban was imposed on most of the Transnistrian leadership by the EU (European Council 2010). The ban remained on Smirnov after he left office, finally being repealed in September 2012 (European Council 2012). In 2014, bans on those directly involved were extended to October 2015 (European Council 2014) but then lapsed.

Although the schools had been allowed to function after 2004, there were constant complaints of harassment by parents and pupils. Attendances at the schools dropped substantially, in some cases by over 50% (*Catan v. Moldova and Russia* 2012: para 172).

In 2012, the European Court of Human Rights formed a fifteen-judge panel to consider the lead case of *Catan*** (2012), brought by eighteen pupils and thirteen parents at the Romanian-language school in Ribnita against Moldova and Russia. This was consolidated with similar claims in respect of schools in Bender and Grigoriopol. The court decided unanimously that despite Moldova's lack of *de facto* control over Transnistria, that country was susceptible to jurisdiction in respect of the complaint (*Catan* 2012: para 102) and, with one dissent, that Russia was too (*Catan* 2012: para 123).

The substantive allegation in each case (*Catan* 2012: para 124) was a breach of Article 2 of Protocol No.1 to the 2010 European Convention on Human Rights, which provides,

---

*   My phrase, not Roper's nor the Transnistrian government's.
**   The lead claimant Alexei Catan was head of the Ribnita Lyceum and an outspoken critic of the Transnistrian government. For an enlightening, if not wholly objective, analysis of Moldovan–Transnistrian relations, see his lecture at Georgetown University, Washington, DC (Moldova.org 2017).

"No person shall be denied the right to education." The court recognised that this was a qualified, not an absolute, right which could be interfered with by a contracting state where it was proportionate (para 140).

The court found the evidence supported the allegations that the authorities were deliberately making it difficult for students to attend those schools, attaching much weight to the falling roll numbers and the accepted fact that many children were crossing the border to Right-Bank Moldova each day (*Catan* 2012: para 142). It trenchantly concluded there had been a clear breach of the protocol:

> There is no evidence before the Court to suggest that the measures taken by the [Transnistrian] authorities in respect of these schools pursued a legitimate aim. Indeed, it appears that [Transnistria]'s language policy, as applied to these schools, was intended to enforce the Russification of the language and culture of the Moldovan community living in [Transnistria] in accordance with [Transnistria's] overall political objectives of uniting with Russia and separating from Moldova. Given the fundamental importance of primary and secondary education for each child's personal development and future success, it was impermissible to interrupt these children's schooling and force them and their parents to make such difficult choices with the sole purpose of entrenching the separatist ideology (Catan 2012: para 144).

Moldova was found not to be liable for the breach, perhaps not surprisingly as it had been largely supportive of the claims and had done much financially and practically to assist the schools (para 147). Russia was liable because of its "continued military, economic and political support for [Transnistria], which could not otherwise survive" (para 150). The court awarded damages of €6,000 (para 166) to each of the 170 named applicants and €50,000 for their combined legal costs (para 170).

An OSCE report shortly after the *Catan* decision suggests a considerable improvement in the treatment of the Romanian-language schools on a day-to-day basis, particularly after Smirnov left office. Long-term issues in respect of the nearly completed, but unused, school building in Ribnita continued, and schools formerly in Grigoriopol and Dubasari remained displaced in Dorotcaia and Cocieri (OSCE 2012:2).

A strongly worded anti-Transnistrian motion was tabled in the European Parliament in February 2014, condemning the human rights situation there and calling on Russia to implement the European Court of Human Rights decision (European Parliament 2014). It was adopted by the political group sponsoring it, the Verts/ALE group (Green MEPs), but no one else.

A further case was lodged in 2014 by the Moldovan Promo-LEX organisation (SubSect.3.5.2), asserting that individuals involved in teaching in Romanian in Transnistria had been harassed by being accused of smuggling currency when taking money intended for teachers' salaries across the border with Moldova. On 20 October 2015, the ECHR indicated that it was willing to determine the case, which was decided in favour of the claimants against Russia in September 2019 (*Iovec v. Moldova and Russia* 2019).

Even though there may be little active discrimination against Romanian speakers now, in practice they are at a disadvantage in a country where Russian predominates. Those at the biggest disadvantage may be the ones who use Moldovan with Cyrillic script, supposedly taught in 13.5% of schools (Dembinska and Iglesias 2013:9). It is a language unique to a small proportion of a small territory and hence virtually no books or magazines are published in it now, and there are few left that date back to Soviet times, when that script would have prevailed in all of Moldova. Conversely, the 3.8% of schools which use Moldovan with Latin letters, now with little interference by the authorities, have access to a vastly wider range of publications from Moldova and Romania.

The actions taken against the Romanian speakers may have been part of the Russian identity promoted as part of the nation-building project discussed in SubSect.1.2.2. The success of the nation-building (SubSect.1.2.3) has contributed to the national identity, which is a necessary block on which to build a case for independence. As the nation has matured, the oppression of schools has ended, showing a development in government which also contributes to the case that the territory's governance is compatible with independence.

4.2 HEALTHCARE

While the constitution of Transnistria provides for universal free healthcare (2011: Article 39), a lack of resources has made this somewhat limited. According to information provided to Thomas Hammarberg, the life expectancy in the territory is 73 for women and 64 for men (Hammarberg 2013:25), an average of 69.5. This is lower than anywhere else in Europe, significantly below North Korea (72.1), similar to Indonesia, and only just above India (69.1). Moldova (71.4) and Russia (72.3) are the lowest in Europe. The UK figure is 81.9. The male figure is particularly low, on a par with Burma and Ethiopia and behind many other impoverished African states (World Population Review 2020).

A report by Galina Selari and Elena Bobkova, directors of health institutions in Chisinau and Tiraspol respectively, sums up the stark reality which may contribute to these worrying figures:

In the opinion of Transnistrian experts, in order to provide necessary medical assistance to the population, to equip healthcare institutions with necessary equipment, medicines, in order to repair medical treatment facilities and to provide for at least minimal increase of salaries for medical workers it is necessary to have around US$135 million. In reality, based on the results of 2012, the sector received only US$40.8 million (31% of the necessary amount). Meanwhile, in the total amount of funded expenses labor remuneration comprises 72.8%. In 2012, actual financing of acquisition of medicines comprised US$5.2million, out of a needed US$23.3million, or 22% of the necessary amount. The indicators attest to the fact that funding satisfied the needs only of one out of five in need and entitled to get free medicines. (2013:11)

There is little evidence of improvement since: indeed, the worsening Transnistrian economy may have commensurately worsened healthcare. When written, this report identified and approved of political attempts in Transnistria to introduce compulsory health insurance. Such insurance was intended to be in force by 2018 (Selari and Bobkova 2013:12), but that has not happened either.

The problem is more one of lack of equipment than lack of doctors. Around 60 doctors graduate yearly from the Transnistria State University and two medical colleges in Tiraspol and Bender (de Colombani 2013): well over ten per 100,000 population, similar to the UK's 12.8 and the 34 OECD countries' 12.1 (OECD 2017). The training of doctors was aided by the opening of a teaching building at Tiraspol's Republican Clinical Hospital, largely funded by ANO Eurasian Integration, a Russian organisation founded by a Putin-supporting Duma member (*Novosti Pridnestrovya* 2015a). The hospital itself appears from the outside and grounds similar in terms of size and quality of buildings, and amount of construction work going on, to what one might expect in a similar-sized British town. When I visited the hospital on 2 October 2019, the grounds were well landscaped considering the unpromising flat setting in central Tiraspol. The hospital's schematic diagram was clearly laid out and indicated a large number of different departments. This can be seen in the (author's) photographs below.

8: The grounds of the Republican   9: The diagrammatic map of
            Hospital   the hospital

An International Organization for Migration report (Ostavnaia 2017:50) states there were 376 doctors and 821 other medical "specialists" per 100,000 inhabitants. The figure for doctors is higher than in the UK where it is 280 (Moberly 2017). There were five times as many doctors proportionally available in the cities and towns as in rural areas. The discrepancy was said to be the consequence of a pay gap between the two types of area. If this is correct, there seems to be little government action to redress it.

The World Health Organization has an established presence in Moldova and, since 2013, has tried to provide assistance, largely by way of training, in Transnistria. This has particularly been in the areas of mother and child health, tuberculosis and HIV, as well as public health matters such as health financing, non-communicable diseases management and (perhaps surprisingly) public relations (WHO 2016).

There are occasional encouraging signs, like a full renovation of the Ribnita District Hospital in 2013 with the help of the UN Development Programme and the EU. However, the sums involved were paltry in the context of healthcare: €163,000 was spent on renovating and refurnishing buildings and €118,800 on modern medical equipment (UNDP 2015), making the effusive praise of the project given by the head of the EU delegation to Moldova on that UNDP webpage seem disproportionate.

Vaccination of children seems to be conducted successfully, if not comprehensively, under international auspices (WHO 2014). As long ago as 2011, vaccination levels were reported at over 90% (WHO 2015), with the BCG, for tuberculosis, at 98.6% in 2009. Although the figures seem high, they are generally short of the WHO's 95% target. It is difficult to square this report with the high levels of tuberculosis reported in Transnistrian prisons.*

President Krasnoselsky, according to the official Transnistrian news website, has taken personal control of healthcare issues as of June 2019, saying, "The provision of a network of medical institutions of the country with highly qualified specialists is no less important than the restoration of the medical infrastructure" (*Novosti Pridnestrovya* 2019). While presidential interest is to be welcomed, ultimately the ability to improve will depend upon greater funding, internal and external, being made available.

The Council of Europe has provided some help to Transnistrian, as well as Moldovan, healthcare under the auspices of its Confidence-Building Measures in Post-Conflict Areas Programme. This has been directed particularly towards dealing with the perennial problems in prisons (CoE 2016 and Sect.3.4).

The problems are compounded by the at best ambivalent attitude of the Transnistrian authorities to foreign NGOs. The law which criminalises 'political' activities or funding (SubSect.3.3.3) seems to act as a deterrent even to obviously non-political organisations. There is little sign of NGO activity in Transnistria, although some Swedish organisations may have made inroads in humanitarian spheres (SubSect.5.3.2). An EU paper sums up the position:

A large number of NGOs registered in Transnistria exist on paper or else are Soviet style organisations dealing with trade union activities, pensioners, etc, and those

---

* See SubSect.4.5.1 for the almost certainly unreliable figure of 30% given to me by the doctor at Tiraspol police station.

organisations which do exist have poor resources and limited capacities. (Action Fiche for Moldova 2007:19).

One of the few instances of an active non-Russian charity in Transnistria is Speranta Terrei, which under the auspices of GlobalGiving gives medical and social help to tuberculosis sufferers in the community (Rodiucova 2018). Based in Balti in northern Moldova, it does not appear to have been recently obstructed by the Transnistrian authorities, although a 2007 report suggests it and others working against tuberculosis in Transnistria had to "overcome political obstacles" (AIHA 2007:5). Even if Speranta Terrei is now accepted by the authorities, not enough has changed in respect of NGO or charity involvement in Transnistria. There should be far more signs of such activity in the territory.

The practical application of healthcare in Transnistria was described to me by Professor Natalia Shchukina at Shevchenko University on 5 December 2018:

> On the whole, it is free. There is some good research into rare diseases. If they can, they will treat you for these, but those who have Moldovan citizenship will often use medical help in Chisinau. Russian NGOs will sometimes fund sick children going to Russia for treatment.

Healthcare in Chisinau, if not the rest of Moldova, is generally superior to that in Transnistria, and many Transnistrians travel for treatment, including for instance a television journalist I met in 2015 who was undergoing IVF treatment at very little cost there. However, the view of former Foreign Minister Vladimir Yastrebchak expressed to me in the 7 Fridays restaurant in Tiraspol on 27 May 2019 was that the Chisinau authorities use the healthcare services for propaganda purposes and it provides little benefit to most Transnistrians. There are no official statistics on the use Transnistrians make of Moldovan services, but Cojocari's research (2019:43) suggests nearly 50% of Transnistrians had visited Moldova for healthcare in the last five years. Yastrebchak's view on this may be motivated by the Transnistrian elite's disdain for the Chisinau government rather than an evaluation of the actual value of those services to Transnistrians.

That healthcare is inferior to that in Moldova is a weakness in the Transnistrian independence case. However, to say that it undermines the whole case would be disproportionate. There is a functioning system and a reasonable-quality hospital; the president is committed to improvement and Russian support in dealing with the most complex cases provides some safety net. The ability to use Moldovan facilities has not dampened the Transnistrian people's desire for independence.

4.3 SOCIAL SECURITY AND PROTECTION FOR WORKERS

4.3.1 SOCIAL SECURITY AND PENSIONS

The basis of Transnistrian social security payments was described by the minister of labour and social protection, Elena Kulichenko, in January 2017 (*PRN* 2017).* Many features of the pension and social security system have parallels with benefits that are provided in Britain. Pensions are insurance-based. The minimum monthly pension provided by the Transnistrian government as of 2017 was 616 roubles (about US$38), set to increase to 755 roubles by 2020, although this figure may not keep pace with inflation. Those who participated in the 1992 war get at least a 25% enhancement. There are generous gas allowances, up to 377 cubic metres per month in winter, for the disabled and pensioners living alone. The retiring age is 60 for men and at most 55 for women, lowered for those who have more than two children (Surchician 2016).

Unemployment benefit is a minimum 252 roubles, rising to 504 roubles for those who had previously worked for over twenty years and with considerably enhanced payments to 1992 war veterans. Payments of childcare allowance had increased to 776 roubles per month for non-working parents, with a 339-rouble supplement for disabled children (Surchician 2016).

There are around 145,000 people eligible for a pension, roughly the same number as work. Pensioners who are Russian citizens receive a supplement to the Transnistrian figures, discussed by Kulichenko (*PRN* 2017), of around 230 roubles per month (Comai 2016a). In July 2018, Russia's own problems led to cessation of its 'humanitarian aid', which funds those pensions. Payments were resumed and backdated in October (Carnegie Europe 2018), but the withdrawal, even temporarily, will inevitably have caused a hardship for many pensioners that does not lie comfortably with Transnistria's constitutional obligation (Constitution 2011: Article 38) to provide security in old age.

Virtually no Transnistrian inhabitants receive a pension from the Chisinau government: just twenty, according to Moldova.org (Surchician 2017). Promo-LEX says this is an illegal withholding of benefits to what are technically its own citizens, while recognising that the Russian-subsidised pensions paid in Transnistria are inevitably higher than those paid in Moldova (Zubko 2012).

These figures are strikingly low, even by the standards of poor countries: having to survive on little more than US$1 per day, as some Transnistrian pensioners do, in present-day Europe seems unthinkable to those in at least the western part of the continent. This is about one thirtieth of the UK pension, often regarded as one of the meanest in Western Europe (House of Commons Library 2021). Prices, particularly of housing and energy, less so food, are of course lower in Transnistria but not by anything like that factor.

---

*   This report in Russian is of a question-and-answer session at the offices of the newspaper, which has close government links (SubSect.3.6.2), and is as full an account as appears to have been published.

Despite the low levels of social security payments, there is no evidence of dire poverty and begging is rarely seen on the streets. The Transnistrian regime can be seen as being relatively successful in this, which may enhance the case that it could function as an independent state.

4.3.2 MINIMUM WAGE AND WORKERS' RIGHTS

In 2017, the hourly minimum wage was set at 9.7 roubles, which remained unchanged in August 2020 despite the rouble's fall in the intervening period. I was told this by Professor Natalia Shchukina at Shevchenko University on 5 December 2018. She also pointed out that by then the wage had been falling to effectively US$100 per month, which was then around 1,650 roubles. In practice, although this was expressed as an hourly rate, it was usually considered as a monthly sum, for about 160 hours' work. She believed the government would start regularly increasing it "every three or four months", particularly if the rouble fell further or prices rose substantially.

Shchukina also described a system of collective agreements between employers and different trade unions acting ultimately under the auspices of the Federation of Trade Unions of Transnistria. The unions were focused on employees in professional sectors, such as teachers, university lecturers – she was one of the 80% of staff at the Shevchenko University who had joined the union – doctors and even the self-employed. They had a lesser role in manufacturing, largely because of the decline of these industries. Union dues were set at a uniform 1% of salary. She, rather surprisingly, claimed not to know if there were any unions for Sheriff group employees, and I could find no evidence of any.

There is a Labour Code, governing relations between employers and employees. This was largely adapted from Russian law into Transnistrian, but English law also had some influence, particularly in respect of trade unions such as these, so Shchukina took the view it had originated in Britain.

Again, there can be seen, particularly in respect of the minimum wage, sensible protections put in place by the Transnistrian regime to protect the more vulnerable in society, which is consistent with an argument that that regime could govern an independent state.

4.4 HOUSING

The centres of Tiraspol, Ribnita and Dubasari consist mainly of bleak-looking apartment blocks, typically of around five storeys,* which can fairly be styled 'Soviet era'. On the outskirts of Tiraspol are a few older detached houses. A little historical context is necessary to understand the reasons for, and perhaps acceptability of, this unglamorous mass housing in Transnistria and most other parts of the USSR.

These blocks are *khrushchyovkas*. Although there are many regional and other differences,

---

*   In contrast to Chisinau, where tower blocks prevail.

they are all three- to five-storey blocks, typically containing 40 to 50 small flats, with kitchens, basic bathrooms and often balconies. They hardly ever have lifts. The ceilings are low, and two-room flats are around 33–45 square metres. The blocks were often prefabricated and assembled on-site. They are aptly described by Kuba Snobek (2017), an urban planner and architectural commentator, as the "Kalashnikov of mass housing".

Despite the tendency to call the excesses of anything Soviet 'Stalinist', these buildings date from the period after Stalin's death. Nikita Khrushchev, on assuming the leadership of the USSR in September 1953, faced a terrible housing shortage, this, like many aspects of social policy, having been neglected by Stalin. Millions were living in wooden barracks or barely covered dugouts. Building in Stalin's time was typically grandiose: richly decorated apartment blocks lining wide Haussmannesque boulevards, with resources diverted into sky-scraping luxury hotels or grace-and-favour flats for artists and bureaucrats (Hatherley 2015). Some residential blocks known, probably retrospectively, as *Stalinikas* were built for 'Soviet workers' in the same style but with much smaller dimensions than those intended for the elite (Andrianova 2014:7).

In December 1954, Khrushchev made a speech, effectively a government decree, ordering the full industrialisation of construction, harnessing heavy industry to work on housing and to quickly end the crisis. For around fifteen years, the production of these units, which inevitably and semi-officially bear his name,* was a priority for Soviet industry. The first was erected in Moscow in 1957. The Soviet state during the second 'five-year plan' (1933–37) built just 26.9 million square metres of housing, but this rose to 152.2 million in 1956–60. Around 1.3 billion square metres of living space was created by 1975 (Luhn 2017), something that was and will remain, possibly aside from Chinese development, the biggest housing project in history. Production continued, albeit at a slower pace, until the USSR broke up. However aesthetically hideous these may seem, the post-Stalin approach to the housing crisis was a great humanitarian achievement, for which the leaders of the USSR are rarely praised. After Brezhnev succeeded Khrushchev in 1964, architects were given more freedom to depart from the standard design, and apartments generally became larger than *khrushchyovkas* but not so large as *Stalinikas* (Andrianova 2014: 21).

These architectural, humanitarian and economic paradoxes and achievements of Soviet housing are summed up by architectural historian Owen Hatherley on the CNN website:

> It is ironic that these 'inhuman' structures, barely even recognizable as 'architecture', are usually the result of what was one of the Soviet empire's most humane policies – the provision of decent housing at such a subsidy that it was virtually free – rents for this housing was usually pegged at between three and five per cent of income. (Hatherley 2015a)

---

* Not official at all is the term kruschobi, which plays on the Russian word for slum (Raspopina 2017).

In many parts of the USSR, these structures were laid out in *microrayons,** glorified housing estates, which became the basic unit of Soviet city planning. Sizes were variable: the largest, in Moscow, was 200 acres; some were only around 30. Most contained basic services, the larger ones schools and cinemas. In Moscow and wealthier parts of the former USSR, *khrushchyovkas* and indeed whole *microrayons* are now facing demolition, often in the face of resistance by residents, who fear property developers will profit while they are sent to less desirable housing (Luhn 2017).

Slightly higgledy-piggledy *khrushchyovkas* abound in the centre of Tiraspol, laid out more in a US-block style than as *microrayons,* with slightly smarter ones next to the hairpin bend in the Dniestr. They are usually scruffy but far from dilapidated**. It is clear that residents have differing levels of pride in their properties, just as would be the case in a Western housing block. Schools and other services all seem to lie outside a specific estate, more in Western style.

The housing stock inherited from the USSR has been managed successfully by successive Transnistrian regimes. As the (author's) pictures below show, it is generally well maintained, the block on the right being built after *de facto* independence. In October 2019, construction of apartments far smarter than *khrushchyovkas* was apparent, particularly on Tiraspol's central Strada Karl Liebknecht. There is no sign of homelessness, and it is not mentioned in official reports. When passing a dilapidated building with a guide on the way to visit Noul Neamț Monastery in November 2014, my enquiry as to whether anyone lived there was met with incredulity: not for decades, I was assured, would Transnistrians be expected to live somewhere like that.

10 and 11: Typical housing in Tiraspol – an older khrushchyovka and more modern block

---

* Russian for 'micro-district'.
** I have rented one for a couple of nights. It was warm, clean and reasonably comfortable.

Conversely, there is, perhaps commendably, little evidence of opulent housing in Tiraspol, either when exploring it directly or by perusing Google Maps.* The only strikingly large dwelling is close to FC Sheriff's ground on Negruzzi Street and itself has a curtilage about the size of a football pitch. There are a few hundred good-sized detached dwellings, largely in the Zaprepostanya Slobodka area south of the main road into the town from Bender; around two dozen have outdoor swimming pools visible from the air.** There is no comparable area of even that much affluence in Bender, Ribnita (sometimes said to be the territory's most affluent town) or Dubasari. The only exception, it was alleged to me by the minister of internal affairs in December 2018, is an enormous villa built by Shevchuk near Ribnita during his presidency (SubSect.3.5.2).

When I asked a group of students at Shevchenko University in October 2019 about their housing conditions, they generally spoke positively, all saying the conditions were good: about half lived in modern – probably post-*khrushchyovka* – housing.

If there were really as much corruption in Transnistria as is sometimes alleged in the Western media, it is surprising that those who benefited from it have not built themselves more impressive homes within the territory. There is scarcely enough semi-luxurious housing to accommodate the foreign footballers there, let alone the supposed hordes of nefariously enriched officials.

The Transnistrian regime had the advantage of inheriting an adequate housing stock built up in Soviet times, but has continued to manage it successfully with the emphasis on ensuring the population is properly housed rather than creating an environment where there is substantial building of housing for the wealthy or the political elite. This is another area in which the Transnistrian regime has shown it would be capable of successfully governing an independent state.

4.5 POLICING AND CRIME

An effective police force is necessary to maintain order in any society. Policing can be carried out by many organs of the state. SubSect.2.1.2 discusses the powers exercised by the Transnistrian central bank in respect of financial matters and SubSect.4.6.2 the policing of motorists. Despite its high prison population (Sect.3.4), Transnistria appears to have relatively little crime: indeed, it might be argued that high prison population is a reason for there being little crime. I never received any warnings from well-meaning locals about not being on the streets at night or visiting certain poorer areas that are

---

*   The settings used for this check on 30 December 2020 were: https://www.google.co.uk/maps/place/Tiraspol,+Moldova/@46.8452144,29.6082228,8188m/data=!3m1!1e3!4m5!3m4!1s0x40c902e8fd3f4cbf:0xffffe2ce60be34818!8m2!3d46.848185!4d29.596805.

** The settings used for this check on the same date were: https://www.google.co.uk/maps/place/Zakrepostnaya+Slobodka,+Tiraspol,+Moldova/@46.8332177,29.5730628,1021m/data=!3m1!1e3!4m13!1m7!3m6!1s0x40c902e8fd3f4cbf:0xffffe2ce60be34818!2sTiraspol,+Moldova!3b1!8m2!3d46.848185!4d29.596805!3m4!1s0x40c903aff476bfa1:0x37df05a9da04c130!8m2!3d46.8336385!4d29.5780438.

offered in many countries. In none of my discussions with Transnistrians was a fear of crime mentioned. The US government warning to travellers sets out nothing more alarming than, "Travelers to Transnistria should adhere to all posted traffic signs and follow verbal orders of security personnel posted there" (OSAC 2020).

4.5.1 POLICING

This section sets out my own discussions with the Tiraspol police. I go on to consider whether the allegations of human trafficking made about the territory, and which would indicate a very serious failure of policing, are made out.*

Police powers and my discussions with police officers (May 2019)

Between the platitudes of the Transnistrian constitution (2011) (SubSect.3.1.1) and the vehement allegations of Promo-LEX (SubSect.3.5.2), Freedom House and others intractably hostile to Transnistria's proposed governance, there is little assessment of how the police actually operate there.

My request to the Ministry of Internal Affairs to visit the police station in central Tiraspol in May 2019 was granted on less than 24 hours' notice, and the chief officer, Sergei Kirman, was happy to answer most of my questions. The building itself, constructed in 1986, was a little dilapidated. It had a gymnasium for officers and their families that the minister had been particularly keen for me to see when I interviewed him in December 2018, which did not contain particularly modern equipment. Kirman's own offices were opulent, more so than the minister's, with an attached shower suite.

I met eight officers of various ranks, seemingly the full complement in the station at the time. All were polite and pleasant, some a little shy, none spoke English. One of Hammarberg's recommendations had been to ensure police recruitment procedures which excluded unsuitable applicants (2013:5). Superficial though my analysis of course was, I saw nothing to make me think anyone remotely unsuitable was working for the Tiraspol police force. Kirman himself was as confident as one would expect a senior police officer to be but unintimidating in manner and appearance.

I was told of procedures in place to ensure punishments are imposed properly: the police have a power to impose fixed administrative fines of between 150 and 368 roubles but if disputed, the matter goes to court. There is a protocol for imposing, collecting and recording these. The police are generally armed with pistols. The senior police officers were proud that the crime rate had been improving and was at its lowest for at least ten years.** There were on average about five murders a year, mostly domestic, with currently none unsolved.

---

* Other allegations of government involvement in serious crime, particularly in relation to weapons, are discussed and dismissed in the introduction.

** See INR (2018) for a news report showing very low levels of recent crime.

Frustration was expressed that they could no longer go to Chisinau to arrest and return fleeing criminals. I had been told by Promo-LEX's Ion Manole on 11 April 2019 that the arrangement which allowed the police forces in the two territories to help each other apprehend fugitives had been stopped some years before. There seemed nothing sinister in either position: Manole's that the arrangement was a breach of international law as Chisinau could not cooperate in the prosecution by an unrecognised state, or Kirman's more practical one that criminals should be arrested and tried.

Although rarely called upon to exercise powers to extradite fugitives to other countries, the Transnistrian police cooperated in the December 2017 arrest of Minneapolis fugitive Igor Vorotinov, who had been living in the territory for two years after faking his own death in an insurance scam (Walsh 2018). It is difficult to see how such an arrest could have been effected in accordance with the same interpretation of international law that prohibits the Chisinau authorities from extraditing Transnistrian suspects as it would have needed Transnistrian authorities to exercise the coercive powers of a state.

At odds with the impression the officers I met gave were my discussions with students at Shevchenko University in October 2019, which showed resignation to low-level police corruption (SubSect.1.3.1). It would be unrealistic to pretend it has been eliminated completely, any more than it has in Russia and most other parts of the former Soviet Union.*

While there may be imperfections in policing and the existence of some corruption by officialdom, the evidence is that it is far from widespread enough to suggest a systemically corrupt society of the sort that might undermine the case for independence.

4.5.2 CRIME

Human trafficking

The most serious allegation against Transnistria is that people, usually young women, are taken from the country against their will to be used as prostitutes or cheap labour and that the government acquiesces in this. While many claims about this have been made, there is little hard, or even anecdotal, evidence to support the allegations, particularly in recent times.

The Moldovan EU-funded NGO, one of the few active in Transnistria, Vzaimodeistvie, which assists in numerous social projects in Transnistria, reported on aiding more than 250 actual and potential victims of trafficking between around 2004 and 2009, though it doesn't make clear whether those are Transnistrian or Moldovan (SALTO n.d.). In 2003, the International Programme on the Elimination of Child Labour, part of the ILO, reported that 5,000 girls were trafficked out of Moldova, predominantly Transnistria, every year (IPECL 2003). A report by the USSD (2006) alleges that Transnistria is "a significant source and transit area" for people trafficking but cites no evidence, examples or even numbers.

---

* I have rather half-heartedly been asked for a bribe by Right-Bank Moldovan police officers when – justifiably I am afraid – I was stopped for speeding close to Gagauzia in November 2014, but never in Transnistria.

Felix Buttin (2017) alleges, "Crime networks acting internationally are actually sky-rocketing and the leaky border between PMR and Ukraine obviously facilitates transfers of trafficked human beings." It is not clear whether this was based on any better or more up-to-date evidence than the 2006 USSD report he cites, but it seems to go further than that report.

Stefan Wolff (2012:16) writes of "reliable estimates" of 25,000 being affected by this annually in Moldova and Transnistria. This figure, though, leads back to a report by the US Embassy in Moldova (2009), which is no longer accessible but which relied on International Labour Organization figures which in turn drew figures from the Chisinau government's Bureau of Statistics. Subsequently, that bureau (2010) reported there were 410 trafficked persons in 2008: 86.8% were women and 83% of the cases related to prostitution (2010:19).* It is hard to see how the Moldovan government could make such a precise estimate as to the extent of the problem within its own borders, let alone Transnistria's, but the figures seem vastly more plausible than the 25,000. A thorough summary of reports on human trafficking in Moldova and Transnistria was compiled by Martin Patt (2017). Other than completely unparticularised allegations by Freedom House and the USSD, there has been no report of this since 2010, and most of the earlier ones are from Moldova rather than Transnistria. Predictably, Shevchuk emphatically denied such allegations when interviewed by *Euronews* (2014a), saying:

> I must officially declare the Transnistrian state is not involved in these kinds of smuggling activities. Such rumours are spread with the aim of generating fear inside EU countries to push them to intervene in Transnistria to solve this smuggling problem.

I made a point of asking young Transnistrians about this, and whether they knew of anyone who mysteriously disappeared. While in about 25 such conversations, some with groups and some with individuals, there has not been a single answer suggesting any knowledge of trafficking. However, those I have talked to have tended to be the more highly educated, who are probably less vulnerable. While there is little evidence of this now occurring, it would be naïve to say it could not happen.

The unreliability of many allegations about human trafficking is corroborated by similarly exaggerated allegations in respect of weapons smuggling. Investigations in 2005 by the EU and OSCE failed to find a single instance, causing the EU's external relations commissioner, Benita Ferrero-Waldner, to hastily rewrite a speech in Chisinau into which had already been inserted such allegations (Lobjakas 2005).

Organised crime

Wolff also reports wider allegations of organised crime in the territory:

---

* Transnistria is not (by any of its names) referred to in the report.

Organised crime has been variously highlighted as a serious issue for both Moldova and the Transnistrian region, and is linked to serious structural reform deficits and corruption, including the manifold links between political and economic elites, the general lack of an independent judiciary and the fact that widespread poverty creates conditions in which transnational organised crime can flourish. (2012:15)

This draws on other secondary research, including that of Bobick (2011) and Owen (2009). Bobick's (2012:14) own take on the situation, particularly in his later paper *There's a New "Sheriff" in Town*, was that there is considerable corruption in the territory and this is "accepted as a fact of life there". In his 2011 writing, he had asserted that Sheriff substituted consumerism and charitable works for corruption and was thus in this regard an improvement on what Transnistrians were resigned to. Indeed, the policing-type name of the conglomerate was one of its attractions to consumers.

Even by 2012, the case in respect of organised crime being prevalent was not great. Wolff, Bobick and Owen do not point to specific examples. Subsequently, that case has become even less convincing. As Robert O'Connor puts it in the heading of article in *Foreign Policy* (2019), "Transnistria Isn't the Smuggler's Paradise It Used to Be". This he largely attributes to the post-Crimean war tightening of the border with Ukraine. It was the Ukrainian foreign minister and OSCE representative Leonid Kozhara who told *El Pais* (Bonet 2013) that no evidence of arms smuggling had ever been found in Transnistria.

A peaceful society

Transnistria is a relatively peaceful society, something which is desirable and bodes well for independence. The allegations that it was a hot bed of serious criminality and human trafficking are historic, dating back to perceptions in the Smirnov era and exaggerated even then. There is nothing to undermine the superficial impression of it being a safe place, as described at the beginning of this section. The fact that even the sale of sleeping tablets is tightly controlled, as I identify in Appendix E, suggests a government aware of the need to control drugs of all sorts. Similarly identified in the same appendix, that phone SIM cards can only be bought on producing proof of identity shows the government has identified an essential tool of drug dealers and many other criminals, and has taken some steps – more than in most Western European countries – to prevent it. There is anecdotal evidence of some police corruption, but not so much that it strikes at the heart of the relationship between police and public. The outlook of the police seems no more aggressive than in Western Europe. The racially homogenous nature of the Transnistrian society means that allegations of individual and systemic racism that have highlighted the aims of the 'Black Lives Matter' movement in 2020 have not arisen.

One exception to the perception of Transnistria as a peaceful society may be in respect of domestic violence, a crime that is uniquely hard to detect and record as so many victims do not feel able to report it. Partly in the light of recommendations in the Hammarberg (2013) report, the authorities combined with a Swedish government agency in opening a centre for such victims in 2015. In its first year, it received 95 women and children fleeing violence (Sida 2016). By way of comparison, the 2018/19 figure reported for Women's Aid (2019) in the UK showed that 11,489 women were supported by refuge services in England. Bearing in mind the population of England is slightly more than 100 times that of Transnistria (SubSect.2.4.1), the proportions are similar, though the English figure does not include children. A concern is that the laws of Transnistria do not currently specifically address domestic violence (Hammarberg 2013), which may make it harder for victims to flee their abusers.

While there are issues, such as low-level corruption, domestic violence and the high prison population, which are problematic, for the most part in creating a peaceful, well-policed and law-abiding society the Transnistrian government, particularly recent regimes, has been successful and would continue to be if the territory were granted independence.

4.6 THE TRANSNISTRIAN ENVIRONMENT AND TRANSPORT

All governments have a remit in matters that can loosely be described as the environment. These are sufficiently important to bear on the viability of a Transnistrian state, particularly in central matters – environmental control and transport and its safety – which this section explores. This is not an exhaustive list of what could fall within a section of this heading. Agriculture, forestry, food standards and other matters are within the remit, for instance, of the UK's Department for Environment, Food and Rural Affairs. Public spaces, such as parks, and monumental architecture are of importance to many and their management is a responsibility of the state. However, for the purpose of evaluating the success of the Transnistrian regime in the environmental area, the matters analysed in this section can be regarded as the core topics that concern people most, and by which that regime can fairly be judged.

4.6.1 PROTECTING THE ENVIRONMENT

The Transnistrian constitution exhorts that, "Everybody must take care of the environment" (2011: Article 50), which is developed a little by proclamations that, "Exercising the right of property should not damage the environment" (Article 37) and a requirement of government of, "Creating and preserving a favourable environment" (Article 56). These statements put Transnistria among the forerunners for making environmental protection a specific constitutional issue. Sweden started the trend in 1974 but by 1994, when these Transnistrian provisions were enacted, only five other countries had done so (Oury 2017).

The environmental aims of the constitution are supplemented by a 1994 document, "On a Concept of Environmental Safety of the Pridnestrovian Moldavian Republic",* which sets out basic laws of environmental protection and ownership of natural resources. In an astonishingly detailed and under-publicised report, Ivan Ignatiev (2006), president of the Bender-based Ecospectrum Research and Production Association,** identifies both the body of legislation then protecting the Transnistrian environment and the practical problems it faces. Ignatiev points to eight laws in relation to the environment:

On the Animal World (1998);
On the Hydrometeorological Activities (1998);
The Water Code (1999);
On the Subsoil (2000);
The Forestry Code (2000);
On Fees for Environmental Pollution and Use of Natural Resources (2000);
The Land Code (2002); and
On the Nature Reserve Stock (2006).

The problem Ignatiev considers most is water pollution. The Dniestr, the source of drinking water for most of the population, is regarded as having class three pollution on a scale out of five, which significantly compromises the water's quality. Air pollution, waste disposal, and degradation of lands and forests all present serious ongoing challenges for the territory but are capable of resolution (Ignatiev 2006:6).

In 2012, concerns were expressed about potassium salts from Ukraine's Dombrov mine contaminating the Dniestr (*OOSKAnews* 2012a). Superficially, there appear to be no major environmental issues on visiting Transnistria. Ignatiev continues to run Ecospectrum. There are no warnings against, or apparent adverse consequences from, drinking tap water, though Ignatiev alleged to the same water trade site (*OOSKAnews* 2012) that one third of the wells in the territory were of poor quality. The atmosphere does not appear polluted, in contrast to Chisinau where it clearly is.***

That comprehensive range of topics being addressed by a poorly resourced territory's legislation is impressive, and a positive indicator of the viability of statehood.

4.6.2 TRANSPORT

The trolley bus service in Transnistria dates from 1967 and the Soviet Union.**** On 19 June 1993, to commemorate the first anniversary of the outbreak of war, the 11km

---

* The document itself is no longer available but is extensively summarised by Ignatiev (2006).
** The organisation continues to operate with OSCE support (Aarhus Centres 2020).
*** This is mainly a consequence of the large numbers of old cars running in the Moldovan capital (Publika 2017).
**** See Ymtram (1980) for a map of early routes.

route between Tiraspol and Bender, said to be the longest trolley bus route in the world, was opened with the apposite route number 19 (Maller 2011).

Most of Tiraspol is covered by frequent government-run buses, costing 3.50 roubles (about 20 US cents). The service between Tiraspol and Bender runs about every fifteen minutes during the day; it cost 6 roubles when I first went there in 2014 and had been reduced to 3, despite the devaluation of the rouble, by 2019. The decrease suggests the Transnistrian authorities have identified the need to provide affordable public transport to its inhabitants. Local buses also run in Bender and Dubasari and other substantial towns. There are a few minor traffic jams in rush hour Tiraspol, but I have never seen or heard of any in other parts of the country. Bus services regularly run along the Tiraspol-Dubasari-Ribnita 'spine', with some going on to Camenca in the north.

The Odessa to Chisinau railway runs three times a week – until around 2016 it was daily – and stops at Tiraspol. The carriages are reasonably comfortable but old and gloomy. It is little used by Transnistrians: sometimes I have been the only passenger getting on or off in Tiraspol. Theoretically, there are buses, usually large minivans or *marshrutkas*, every twenty minutes or so to Chisinau and about hourly to the Ukrainian border, though my experience is that these are not as frequent or organised as the published timetable would suggest. There is supposedly a daily bus to Moscow and a weekly one to Berlin.

The buses and trolley buses are generally state owned, while minibuses operate privately in a regulated market. Those buses which go to Ukraine are also regulated by the Chisinau government, under the auspices of the OSCE (MTRI(M) 2010). While the size and shape of Transnistria may mean transport provision is easier than in most countries, the ability of citizens to move around, often an important factor in people's quality of life, is something many Western European countries would envy. The Transnistrian government has a significant role in this and is a small area where it can be said to have succeeded in a way that supports the viability of statehood.

Cars and road safety

Driving in Transnistria seems safe by Eastern European standards. I have witnessed few incidents of aggressive speeding or other bad driving, and traffic is relatively light. Roads, particularly in Tiraspol, are good and the main highway between Tiraspol and Ribnita is as wide and well surfaced as most Western European single carriage roads.

Rather contrary to that impression, EU research (EASST 2013) over two six-month periods in 2011 and 2012 identified in Tiraspol alone a total of 282 injuries and 27 deaths in road accidents. The 27 deaths in a population given for the city as 159,163 – a rate of one in 5,894, or seventeen per 100,000 people – is comparable to Colombia: the highest other rates in Europe are Russia's 16.4, Montenegro's 14.5 and Moldova itself with 13.6; the UK figure is 3.0 (WHO 2018). The proportion of injuries to deaths (10.4) seems low. In the UK there are around ten *serious* injuries, and around 200 injuries altogether, for every fatality (DoT 2015), suggesting the EU research was considering at least relatively serious injuries in Transnistria.

Combined with that research was a survey conducted by the Automobile Club of Transnistria, a non-governmental organisation formed primarily to improve road safety. In this, 94.5% of respondents claimed they always obey traffic regulations and 100% said they observe the speed limit, "Except when they were late" (UNDP 2012). A more useful statistic is that 87% of drivers and passengers do not usually use front seatbelts and 100% do not use rear ones. The writers of the report suggest that the low fine, then of just over US$1, combined with a culture dating back to Soviet times of traffic police not enforcing seatbelt laws was probably the reason for this.* It would seem likely that if normal patterns of seatbelt effectiveness were followed, rigorous enforcement of Transnistria's largely disregarded seatbelt law would save around twelve lives** and dozens of serious injuries each year.

In 2013, a 18.5% reduction in road accidents was reported in Transnistria by the Eastern Alliance for Safe and Sustainable Transport. Advice had been given on both sides of the Dniestr by experts from Britain and Georgia (UNDP 2012).

When I visited Tiraspol's main police station in May 2019, I was shown screens monitoring traffic as well as crime, and was told there were around 200 cameras in the city and 500 in the rest of the country. Fines for violations were 92 roubles, then about US$6 and perhaps not that different from the Automobile Club's figure, but increasing ten-fold if another offence was committed in the same year.

Air travel

There is no commercial airport in Transnistria. Chisinau airport is on the Tiraspol side of the city, just over an hour's drive away, and functions effectively as Transnistria's national airport. Odessa airport, which until the Ukrainian embargo on direct flights to Russia offered many direct flights to that country, is two hours.

Currently all Russian troop movements to Transnistria are carried out through Chisinau airport (Karamazov 2015). Since 2014, Russian planes, civilian and military, have not been permitted to overfly Ukraine, making Odessa no longer viable as a staging post.

There is a small abandoned airfield outside Tiraspol. Despite a complete lack of terminal buildings, its runway appears reasonably serviceable and sufficiently long to allow modern passenger jets to land. There were reports that Shevchuk might try to re-open it (Moldova.org 2012a) but that did not happen. It is unlikely now that the Transnistrian government would direct its inadequate resources to such a project, and

---

*   This was reflected in my own experience being driven around in a government car to observe elections in 2016, when I had to ask the driver to retrieve the seatbelt he had obligingly buried under the seat cushion to prevent passengers being inconvenienced by it.

**   I extrapolate this figure from a discussion with Dr John Searle, former chair of the BSI Committee on (Vehicle) Occupant Safety, in London on 2 December 2019. He told me that belts reduce deaths by about 50%.

there is not sufficient demand for international travel to make it attractive to private investors. Marginally more plausible would be Russian development of the airport at least for military purposes, but despite speculation before (Socor 2013), and then more credibly after, the outbreak of the Ukrainian war that that might happen, there is little to indicate Russia, with all its own economic problems, would do so.

Political control of transport

There is no specific ministry of transport in Transnistria and little sign of, or indeed need for, a Western-style integrated transport policy. The government provides information on transport matters, along with energy and housing, on its website, often descending to trivial but useful information such as roadworks and street closures. This relatively informal system of supervision allows transport to work reasonably well, though it might be thought that the enforcement of traffic laws is left too much to the whims of individual police officers.

Taken as a whole, transport – sometimes directly controlled by the government and sometimes left by the government to private enterprise – can be seen as an area where Transnistria has been successful in that there is a satisfactory and reasonably priced system. It is thus a further argument for a fully independent state.

4.7 CONCLUSION: IS TRANSNISTRIA A FUNCTIONING SOCIETY?

In facing the challenges of providing for the 'positive rights' of its population in accordance with international expectations and the aspirations of its own constitution, the Transnistrian government has in many particulars been successful. There are education and health systems that function adequately, particularly the former.

It is hard to fault the provision of education. Schools and the university fulfil their purpose and there is a literate and often highly educated population, with levels of university attendance on a par with the UK. The intolerance of the Romanian language being used in the education system has been a concern. The excesses of the Smirnov regime in trying to stop that language being used in schools are in the past and have been roundly condemned in the ECHR. However, the position of the main university on the topic – that it will only teach Romanian with Cyrillic letters – suggests full tolerance has not yet been attained. The fact that the vast majority of Romanian speakers use the Latin alphabet and the much greater range of written materials in that language would, were it not for political constraints, lead to the teaching of it with Latin letters. It may be that on independence, the national identity would be considered to have been created to an extent that made the regime more secure about such matters, and Romanian-language teaching in its more natural format would no longer be seen as undermining.

Healthcare is not as developed as would be ideal, but the existence of a hospital in the centre of Tiraspol that is not dissimilar from one which might serve a small British city is an achievement in the light of the territory's relatively small resources. That it trains an adequate numbers of doctors credits both the education and healthcare systems. Healthcare has been less of a priority than education, and it may be that, notwithstanding Vladimir Yastrebchak's view, the ease with which Transnistrians can receive treatment in Moldova contributes to this. The right to that would be unlikely to survive independence, and the adequacy of the local medical services would present concerns for the Transnistrian authorities. Even if Russia is prepared to provide treatment to Transnistrians, it will not be feasible for many sick people to make the arduous journey there. Transnistrian discouragement of foreign NGOs may have hindered the development of healthcare. Even factoring in the nation-building motivation, this cannot be justified. It is to be hoped that the government of an independent nation would be more receptive to the benefits that such organisations may bring to the populace, rather than following any perception that national identity might be undermined.

As for social security and pensions, they cannot be generous in a country where there is relatively little money with which to pay them. A system has been put in place which provides a universal safety net against destitution and hunger. Consideration should be given to whether retirement ages could be brought more in line with those in Western Europe, thus reducing the numbers eligible for a pension and bolstering the workforce. There is a minimum wage at just about an adequate level. Workers are able to unionise, and there is little to suggest exploitation of the labour force represents a problem. It is also to be borne in mind that there is little unemployment (SubSect.2.1.2).

For most Transnistrians, home may be an unprepossessing two- or three-room flat, but for a country whose economy falls vastly below the European average this represents a real achievement, and is far better than that provided in slum-ridden, but theoretically wealthier, countries such as Nicaragua and India. 'Soviet era' may sound like a term of condemnation, but the *khrushchyovkas* represented significant progress for the people of the USSR, and that minimalist approach to housing remains a benefit to Transnistria, which might otherwise face an ongoing housing shortage.

Policing has worked to the extent that Transnistria is peaceful with little sign of crime – paradoxically for a country that has been subject to many criticisms, invariably unsubstantiated, over really serious crimes including human trafficking. There is a residual problem of police and official corruption, no worse than is generally the case in the region, and not enough to cause significant disruption to the population (Sect.4.5). It is a mark of a government's success if it has created a society where people have little fear of crime, and that has been achieved in Transnistria. While there are worries that domestic violence may not be as legally constrained as would be ideal, there is no evidence that this translates into a high rate of such conduct.

On the environment, including transport, Transnistria seems to be relatively well served. Sophisticated environmental protection policies are in place, which many countries with much greater resources have baulked at introducing. Overall, it is perhaps on environmental issues above anything else that Transnistria has shown, considering its limited resources, it can perform as a state should, and it is an area where viability has been clearly established.

A functioning transport and road system means the population can get around the country, and few will suffer the detriment to happiness that it is argued flows from not having this facility (Duarte 2009). If there is a blot in this area, it is the reluctance of the Transnistrian authorities to take steps to make their roads safer, even neglecting the obvious expedient of saving dozens of lives by enforcing the seatbelt law. An international airport is virtually a defining feature of a country, which only the European micro-states Andorra, Monaco, San Marino and Liechtenstein lack. In the long term, one would doubtless be built, but so long as Transnistria's border with Moldova, and hence easy access to Chisinau's airport, remains open, this does not present an immediate problem.

The functioning society the Transnistrian regime has in most respects created is a natural stepping stone to an independent state. There may still be weaknesses in the limited acceptance of the use of Romanian with Latin script in education and the failure of any health service to increase life expectancies to a level usually found in Europe. However, these are relatively minor matters, both of which should improve upon any independence. Balanced against the successes of the regime in educating and housing almost all the population, creating a safe society, protecting the environment and having adequate roads and transport, the case that there is a well-functioning society ripe for independence is overwhelming.

CHAPTER FIVE

HOW CAN TRANSNISTRIA BECOME AN INDEPENDENT STATE?

The previous four chapters have shown the case that can be made for Transnistrian independence, on the basis that it: has become a nation; has a viable economy; is, with some reservations, a free democracy; and has a functioning society. This chapter considers the obstacles to that independence and how they might be overcome.

The position regarding Transnistrian statehood in international law is explored first, examining established definitions and how they apply to both *de facto* and *de jure* statehood. Respect for a country's territorial integrity, sometimes referred to as Westphalian sovereignty, is ostensibly paramount and a bar to changing a territory's sovereignty and hence statehood. However, once one starts scratching below the surface, it can be seen that that is a principle often diluted and sometimes wholly disregarded when it is convenient to do so, leading to the pithy label "organized hypocrisy" Stephen Krasner (1999) coined for the concept. The position of those who argue that independence should be granted when a people seek it – primary or plebiscitary right theory – provides a solid theoretical basis to the Transnistrian cause.

The second section looks at the attitudes of non-Transnistrian 'actors', including the Chisinau government, involved in the situation. With no country or significant international organisation supporting Transnistrian independence, attaining it will be a struggle, but there are chinks in the resistance. Chisinau's own opposition, although robustly expressed, is not supported by firm reasoning or economic self-interest. The Russian position is one of ambivalence which could move to support independence, particularly as a consequence of its strained relations with Ukraine, which could come to have a bearing on Transnistria's situation. The possibility of Moldova seeking union with Romania, and hence being absorbed into the EU and NATO, is considered. That would make its retention of Transnistria unacceptable to Russia. The German Meseberg Memorandum of 2010 might have provided a solution for Transnistria that fell short of independence, but was abandoned soon after its execution, without closing the route to independence.

The third section looks at comparable situations, particularly that of Kosovo, where it can be said that the territorial integrity of the Serbian state was disregarded in a way that was less in accordance with international law than international recognition of Transnistria would be. Brief comparisons are made with other territories which have similarities with Transnistria, including Northern Cyprus, Somaliland, the other-pseudo states and Gagauzia.

The actual mechanics of how independence could be attained are the subject of the fourth section, in which it is seen how South Sudan, the world's newest country, was created. Recent precedents show that once independence is agreed in principle, there is usually little practical or legal difficulty in implementing the independence. The Vienna Convention on Succession of States in respect of Treaties (1996) would govern some aspects of the separation, and a state which according to the principle of *uti possidetis juris* would have the same boundaries as Transnistria does at present could be created.

5.1 THE CASE FOR TRANSNISTRIAN STATEHOOD IN INTERNATIONAL LAW

As a prelude to considering Transnistria's case for statehood, this section first considers what statehood is, taking from the Montevideo Convention (1933), Badinter Commission (1991, cited by Fitzmaurice 2019) and Global Policy Forum (n.d.) definitions. These lead to discussion on the declaratory and the constitutive theories of statehood, which broadly coincide with *de facto* independence, which Transnistria has attained, and *de jure* independence, which it has not. The discussion of statehood flows into one of sovereignty and its dilution, which is considered in the following parts.

The desirability of preserving the integrity of the dominant state, in this case Moldova, is the basis for resisting most secessionist movements. It is the concept of sovereignty which underscores the respect for states' territorial integrity, upon which most opposition to Transnistria's independence is notionally based and which presents an obstacle to Transnistrian statehood. To fully understand those theoretical arguments, it is necessary to consider both the concept of sovereignty and how much respect there really is for it throughout the world. The history, theory and modern *actualitie* of sovereignty are evaluated in Sect.5.2, which then considers the arguments against it and looks at how in the modern world sovereignty is often disregarded in favour of political expedients. It is the latter analysis which may give Transnistria a route through the obstacles to *de jure* statehood. The arguments of primary or plebiscitary right theorists, who contend that once a majority of people want to be a separate state, they should have the right to secede – a theory supportive of the Transnistrian position – is considered in SubSect.5.4.1.

5.1.1 THE MEANING OF STATEHOOD

The primary definition of a state can be derived from the Montevideo Convention on the Rights and Duties of States (1933),* Article One of which provides:

> *The state as a person of international law should possess the following qualifications: (a) a permanent population; (b) a defined territory; (c) government; and (d) capacity to enter into relations with the other states.*

This definition leads to the acceptance that there is a state once the manifestations of statehood have been achieved. Accepting a state exists without examining how it is perceived by other states is in accordance with the declaratory theory of recognition, by which international recognition is merely a response to a state of affairs that already exists. This is in contract with the constitutive theory, which holds that without recognition, statehood cannot exist. The position is well summarised by Shruti Venkatraman:

> The two main theories of recognition are the declaratory theory, which holds that recognition is an acknowledgement of pre-existing legal capacity, and the constitutive theory, which holds that recognition is a necessary precondition for international legal personality. (2018:36)

The Montevideo definition is not posited upon actual recognition by other states (Bobick 2014:3). Indeed, Article Three (1933) makes clear that the reverse applies:

> The political existence of the state is independent of recognition by the other states. Even before recognition the state has the right to defend its integrity and independence, to provide for its conservation and prosperity, and consequently to organize itself as it sees fit, to legislate upon its interests, administer its services, and to define the jurisdiction and competence of its courts.

It has already been seen that Transnistria clearly fulfils the first three Montevideo Article One qualifications. In the remainder of this chapter, it will be seen how it has now formed some international relations, namely with Moldova (SubSect.5.2.1), Russia (5.2.2), the other pseudo-states (5.3.2) and the UK (5.2.3), and is thus a 'Montevideo' state.

The status Transnistria has reached is, however, only of *de facto* independence or statehood. While the New York report reluctantly accepted that Transnistria had attained *de facto* status as it had "effective control of territory" (2006:65), it considered that it was still illegal and that any measures beyond those required for the immediate care and security of the population under its control may be unwound by the Moldovan government (2006:66).

---

* It was signed only by Americans, largely South Americans but including the US, which ratified it with some expressed reservations.

Although the New York position may have been born of an overt hostility to the regime, Transnistria has beyond argument not achieved *de jure* independence, which is based on recognition by other countries and the United Nations. It is one of many instances where there is the latter without the former, examples considered below include Northern Cyprus, Somaliland and the other pseudo-states. The other way around is rarer and is currently restricted to insignificant examples of tiny states such as Monaco, Liechtenstein* and perhaps San Marino, whose existence, and indeed economy, is wholly dependent on the surrounding country.

The *de jure* status of a territory, which depends on the recognition given to it externally, is usually clear. Rarely is there long-term disagreement between world powers over the recognition of a state. The only significant ambiguities that now exist are those of Kosovo (SubSect.5.3.1); Palestine, which is recognised by 136 countries and has UN observer status; and Taiwan,** which is recognised by just fifteen countries (Yip 2020) but has a thriving economy and democratic institutions. The Vatican, or Holy See, also has some pretentions to statehood and has enjoyed permanent observer status at the UN since 1964.

In practice, Kosovo and Taiwan have complete autonomy over their internal affairs and an ability to form relations on all but the highest levels with other countries, including those which do not formally recognise them.*** Palestine's autonomy is limited by the real threat of military action from Israel should the fledgling state adopt too extreme a position or rhetoric. Also it has failed to create its own currency – in legal and practical terms an indicator of an independent country and achieved by Transnistria – and still relies on the Israeli shekel (al Ghoul 2015).

A simple indicator of *de jure* statehood is full UN membership, which is "open to all peace-loving States that accept the obligations contained in the UN Charter and, in the judgment of the Organization, are able to carry out these obligations" (UN n.d.). In practice, a propensity to war-like behaviour is rarely a bar to membership. Neither Iran nor Iraq had to leave in consequence of their brutal, pointless war from 1980 to 1988, even after both sides continued fighting in defiance of the 1987 Resolution 598 (UNP 1987). Similarly, and even less plausibly fitting the "peace-loving" requirement, North Korea retains its place, having been simultaneously admitted with its southern counterpart in 1991, despite its nuclear weapon programme and oppression by the government of its populace. It is ultimately UN membership that any would-be independent state, including Transnistria, aspires to.

A variation on the Montevideo definition which has gained traction among international lawyers is that of the 1991 Badinter Arbitration Committee. This was set up by the EU to adjudicate on questions arising out of the break-up of Yugoslavia and defined

---

* See Rezvani (2014:90), where these states and some of the smaller pacific islands are categorised as "partially independent".

** Its government purports to be the legitimate government of mainland China too.

*** The British Office in Taipei (n.d.) seems to perform the functions of an embassy and consulate without being dignified with those titles.

a state as "a community with a territory and a population subject to an organized political authority that is sovereign" (Fitzmaurice 2019). As that does not require the ability to enter relations with other states, it sets the bar lower than the Montevideo (1933) definition but does introduce the requirement of sovereignty, which relates to *de jure* sovereignty. The Global Policy Forum (n.d.) says:

> A state is the means of rule over a defined or 'sovereign' territory. It is comprised of an executive, a bureaucracy, courts and other institutions. But, above all, a state levies taxes and operates a military and police force. States distribute and re-distribute resources.

This definition, unlike many uses of 'state', most obviously for US states, again requires sovereignty,* yet it is only putatively sovereign states about which the question of international recognition arises. Sovereignty itself is a separate but related concept meaning that the power is not derived from or constricted by a higher level of government.**

Sovereignty, in the words of King's College, London's purportedly authoritative website on UK–EU relations, "Is the authority of a state to govern itself, and determine its own laws and policies" (2020). This neatly provides a definition encapsulating both *de jure* and *de facto* sovereignty but raises the question of where the authority flows from. While there cannot be an absolute answer to that, it is largely dependent on international recognition, which is what the following parts of this section consider.

5.1.2 WESTPHALIAN SOVEREIGNTY AND TERRITORIAL INTEGRITY

The Peace of Westphalia, as the Treaties of Munster and Osnabruck are known, in 1648 is often treated as producing the modern idea of sovereign states, which falls broadly within the definition (King's College 2020) given above. The treaties ended the Thirty Years' War (Cavendish 1998).*** An effect of the Peace was the partial abandonment of a Roman Catholic empire of Europe, headed spiritually by a Pope and temporally by an emperor, and its replacement by a series of sovereign states. The classic, if simplistic, view of the 1648 Peace is encapsulated by Daud Hassan:

> The [Peace] emphasised the separation and equality of states rather than the unity of

---

* Yet, theoretically, US federal government gets its power from states and each is free to secede from the union. See Lerner (2004) for a discussion of this.

** Arguments that British sovereignty was surrendered by accession to the EU are fallacious. Power may have been delegated to European institutions by the European Communities Act 1972, but as no Parliament can bind a successor, the power can always be reclaimed by a repeal of that Act, without which even Parliament would not have had the power to make Britain leave the EU after the 2016 referendum.

*** The Westphalian negotiations themselves lasted nearly four years and involved 194 different states.

Christendom. It rejected any idea that the Pope or Emperor had any universal authority. The Westphalia settlement established the anti-hegemonic concepts of territorial sovereignty and sovereign equality. (2006:62)

More nuanced views are taken by others, notably Derek Croxton (2001, 2013), generally regarded as the leading English-language authority on Westphalia, who sees it as a stepping stone on the way to modern sovereignty. Similarly, in thoroughly reviewing the literature about the workings of Westphalian sovereignty, Rachel Alberstadt argues that:

While the Peace of Westphalia holds significant value and relevance for the evolution of both international relations and law, it does so not from a big-bang theory but as a gradual formulation. (2012:2)

She then qualifies this, citing particularly the work of Stephane Beaulac on the development in the centuries since the Peace of the growth of sovereignty, as it being a "gradual, though by no means uniform process" (2004:189). This contrasts with the ironically labelled "big bang theory of international relations" (Krasner 1999). There is little support for the view that the world changed so dramatically as to come close to there being a big bang in 1648, and writers like Alberstadt and Beaulac may be sniping at a position no one holds. Even Hassan's view (2006) does not take there to be a dramatically changing world in 1648, more a marked step on the way to the development of the modern sovereign state.

'Westphalian sovereignty' has, for all the debate about its development, embedded itself in the lexicon of international lawyers and many academics. That does not detract from the fact that from whatever angle one approaches the concept, there will have to be qualification of the idea of this sovereignty being the basis for governance throughout the world. If arguments against recognising Transnistrian independence are to be based on a respect for Moldovan sovereignty, the force of those arguments is inevitably diluted by the manifest qualifications in the concept of sovereignty across the world. The Kosovan situation (SubSect.5.3.1) is the clearest modern example of such disregard leading to the creation of a new country, but as shall be seen below, there are many instances of lesser dilution of sovereignty. The less rigid support for respecting sovereignty is, the less of an obstacle it presents to Transnistrian statehood.

Until the latter half of the twentieth century, the concept of sovereignty may have had little practical import outside Europe and America, with most of Africa and much of Asia remaining under colonial rule. Even Australia was not formally granted independence until 1931, and despite the supposed sovereignty, in 1975 the British monarch's representative, Governor-General Sir John Kerr, was able to remove Prime Minister Gough Whitlam from office. Indeed, the Queen's role as notional head of state in many Commonwealth countries, including Australia, is hard to reconcile with pure Westphalian sovereignty, though may have parallels to the vastly weakened role the Holy Roman Empire had post-1648.

While questions over Australia's sovereignty can be dismissed as theoretical, there are many parts of the world which clearly have not achieved Westphalian sovereignty and are more than notionally governed by another country. Non-exhaustively, one might cite Dutch Aruba and Curacao; French Martinique and New Caledonia;* British Bermuda and Gibraltar; the US's American Samoa and Puerto Rico; and Danish Faroe Islands and Greenland.** These territories generally do not desire sovereignty, and conversely it is difficult to see any twenty-first century European democracy seeking to assert direct political control over a colony, particularly a non-contiguous one, without the consent of its inhabitants. It can be argued that in seeking to keep control of Transnistria against the wishes of its inhabitants, Moldova has taken a stance out of line with modern European practice, which has been – with some exceptions, most notably Catalonia – to respect the wishes of inhabitants in relation to independence. This is the practical manifestation of primary right theory (SubSect.5.1.4).

5.1.3 THE ALTERATION AND VIOLATION OF SOVEREIGNTY

Sovereignty is not necessarily undermined by the division of a country. A smooth separation may change the location of the sovereignty without challenging the integrity of the seceding state, and were the Chisinau government to consent to Transnistrian independence, its fundamental sovereignty would remain intact. Conversely, forcing it to surrender *de jure* control over Transnistria, which by definition would violate its territorial integrity, would undermine that right to assert sovereignty as external forces would have taken control of the country to the extent of compelling that.

Symmetric and asymmetric alterations of sovereignty

Separations between states can be classed as symmetric and asymmetric: the former situation posited in the paragraph above would be symmetric and the latter asymmetric. Considering this theory, Fabio Fossati cites the Czechoslovakian division as an example of the former and the creation of the independent states out of Yugoslavia, other than Slovenia, as examples of the latter (2008:2). Symmetric division derives from agreement for separate statehood between the leaders of the original units involved. There is a great deal of international resistance, flowing from the principle of respecting sovereignty, to asymmetric separation where that agreement is lacking.

Territorial integrity extends to it being enshrined in 'international law' that one state should not take action to support the changing of another's borders, whether by

---

* In a curious anomaly, French Guyana and some other French overseas territories remain integral parts of France (and the EU) rather than colonies.
** See Rezvani (2014) for a detailed analysis of the impact this status has on many of these territories.

supporting secessionist movements or by promoting border changes: in other words, asymmetric separations. This is a primary concern of the United Nations, Article 2(4) of whose Charter (1945) states:

> All Members shall refrain in their international relations from the threat or use of force against the territorial integrity or political independence of any State, or in any other manner inconsistent with the Purposes of the United Nations.

This was enshrined in 1975 Helsinki Accords signed by most Europe states. Indeed, Russia's non-recognition of Transnistria is an observance of this principle, and its recognition of Abkhazia and South Ossetia (SubSect.5.2.2) a defiance.

The expedient disregard for sovereignty: organised hypocrisy

Stuart Elden says territorial integrity has two different but basically consistent meanings:

> The first is that states should not seek to promote border changes or secessionist movements within other states, or attempt to seize territory by force. The second meaning is the standard idea that within its own borders, within its territory, a state is sovereign. (2005:2083)

The distinction is important, particularly when looking at UN actions in recent decades. Humanitarian interventions involve a temporary removal of sovereignty from national leaders who are grossly incompetent or brutal or both, and such interventions violate the second meaning Elden advances. Elden's first meaning is respect for territorial integrity rather than for the powers of present rulers. While the UN could not seek to impose a change of borders without undermining its main purpose and the US and EU do not seek to do so nor seize territory by force, they (particularly the US) have, as will be shown below, little regard for the concept that a state is sovereign inside its territory. Particularly in respect of Kosovo and Taiwan, many major countries and organisations have shown some willingness to support what in classic terms are secessionist movements.

Elden's second principle (2005:2084), which he unenthusiastically calls a "standard idea", leads straight to a dichotomy about the tension between respecting territorial integrity and intervening to prevent the worst disregard for human rights. The desirability of respecting territorial integrity in any form is far from universally accepted in the modern world.

A surprising and eloquent dissenter from the orthodoxy supporting the preservation of borders was Prince Hans-Adam of Liechtenstein, who in a January 2001 address to the International Institute for Strategic Studies argued:

> Let us accept the fact that states have lifecycles similar to those of human

beings who created them. Hardly any Member State of the United Nations has existed within its present borders for longer than five generations. The attempt to freeze human evolution has in the past been a futile responsibility and has probably brought about more violence, rather than if such a process had been controlled peacefully. Restrictions on self-determination threaten not only democracy itself but the state which seeks its legitimation in democracy. (cited by Gussen 2019:271)

Hans-Adam's argument undermines the position that any limb of Elden's meanings of sovereignty should be treated as sacrosanct. When a government fails to prevent activities within its border that threaten the integrity of another country, tension arises between the competing and conflicting integrities of the countries involved, even if no possible change of borders is involved. The response to that tends to be highly politicised, with little meaningful role for international lawyers. The perception that the Taliban government in Afghanistan had allowed, even encouraged, *al Qaeda* activity on its territory at the time of the attacks on New York's World Trade Center in 2001 was used by the US to justify the Afghan war, which began shortly afterwards.

Elden, in a later analysis (2007:836), argued that as Afghanistan had failed to exercise one of the key definitions of sovereignty – effective political control or the "monopoly of legitimate physical violence" – within its territory by not prosecuting criminals living within its borders, its sovereignty could be deemed contingent. Whether this could justify the Afghan war is highly doubtful, but the Bush regime came up with nothing better to support it (Scudder 2010). As for the second Iraq war, the evidence that Saddam Hussein had, let alone intended to use, weapons of mass destruction was unconvincing. The case for removing a brutal dictator was morally strong; the case for preserving oil supplies was economically strong; but neither provided the slightest justification in international law.

With considerable understatement, Scudder (2010) writes, in the context of the Iraq war, "In conclusion it may be of use to mention the status of international law as imperfect in its reconciliation of territorial integrity with self-determination." As she effectively observes, the US- and British-led attack on Iraq, and indeed the 2014 Russian occupation of Crimea,* are impossible to reconcile with the concept of territorial respect. The recognition of former Yugoslavian republics against Serbia's wishes led Stephen Krasner (1999) to dub the principles of sovereignty and territorial integrity as "organized hypocrisy". The point was nicely summarised in the *Washington Post*: "territorial integrity principle is a terrific principle from the US viewpoint (and from that of most states who value stability) but not necessarily from the perspective of Russia" (Voeten 2014).

That is true to the extent that the US has secure, fixed borders and virtually no

---

*   The invasion was condemned as illegal by the UN General Assembly Resolution (2014) 68/262. One hundred countries voted for the resolution. Eleven opposed and 82 abstained or were absent.

territorial aspirations,* whereas the present Russian borders are less satisfactory to the Moscow regime. The position is further complicated by the fact that the US faces no credible secessionist movements, whereas Russia does, most obviously in Chechnya. Historically, respect for territorial integrity has benefited smaller weaker nations more vulnerable to territorial encroachment from neighbouring powers. However, the US has been able to exercise tremendous control over other countries, particularly in Central America, without ever formally depriving them of sovereignty: its military and economic strength is ideally suited to such domination. Whether such involvement did less harm to the people of, say, Nicaragua and Guatemala than the USSR's domination of the 'Iron Curtain' countries is debatable, but both processes show one country can dominate another while still paying lip service to territorial integrity.

Krasner's reasoning is close to a universally accepted truth. No stalls have been set out clearly in opposition to his views. Ariel Zellman, reviewing *Organized Hypocrisy*, points out:

> The hypocrisy may travel in the opposite direction. While attempting to uphold the norm of sovereign territoriality…the international community may follow a logic of appropriateness while eschewing a logic of consequences. (Zellman n.d.)

This is developed by Amitav Acharya, whose paper, responsive to Krasner's, is entitled "State Sovereignty After 9/11: Disorganised Hypocrisy". He argues:

> Failure to distinguish principled and organised departures from Westphalian sovereignty aimed at protecting human security from unilateral breaches of sovereignty aimed at protecting national or coalitional security and fulfilling an ideology-driven foreign policy agenda, is a critical flaw in Krasner's organised hypocrisy thesis. (2007:291)

While it would be convenient to take 'organised' and 'disorganised' positions as opposing sides in the classic 'conspiracy or cock-up' conundrum, the differences between Krasner, Zellman and Acharya are largely illusory. Ultimately, the departures Acharya identifies are done with a specific purpose, even if they protect only one country, and the lack of interest in protecting global human security – rarely the concern of a single government – and their narrow purpose does not make them disorganised or even random. Similarly Zellman's distinction between appropriateness and consequences merely underlines that states will, when convenient, accept

---

* A spat showing the US has not wholly given up such aspirations did arise between it and Denmark in August 2019, when President Trump announced – to Danish hilarity – that he thought they should sell Greenland to the US.

consequences that may not be appropriate if the concept of sovereignty were rigorously applied.

Just as the US is quick to condemn other nations for not respecting territorial integrity, most obviously Russia in Ukraine and Iraq, whose invasion of Kuwait in 1990 led to war, it finds itself the subject of complaints from others about its own conduct. Among the most vociferous is Pakistan (Geo TV 2017), whose territory the US has frequently violated in its 'war on terror', most spectacularly with the assassination of Osama Bin Laden in May 2011. This was considered an act of war by the Pakistani government (Strange 2013). Inevitably, the US would take a similar view if Pakistani government forces assassinated someone on US soil, however strong the justification or expedient for doing so. The US cannot defend its actions in Pakistan on the basis of helping anyone seek self-determination. There may be legitimate reasons for attacking terrorist camps there and the US may feel that the Pakistani government's approach to preventing terrorism is, at best, ambivalent. To do so while trumpeting the need for other nations to respect territorial integrity is, of course, hypocritical.

The Russian invasion and annexation of Crimea in 2014 brought international outrage, with President Obama pronouncing, "In this century, we are long past the days when the international community will stand quietly by while one country forcibly seizes the territory of another" (Voeten 2014). In reality, the international community could do nothing beyond imposing trade sanctions on Russia. Military action by one major power against another would be disastrous. It will never be attractive to those who wish international relations to be tightly and fairly regulated for one country to be able to take or violate another's territory. However, to give complete credence to the concept of territorial integrity over and above all the other needs of humanity shows an impractical disregard for those needs.

The value of territorial integrity

Ultimately, there is no clear argument for respecting territorial integrity except that it tenuously promotes stability which, while generally desirable, should not be allowed to prevail over human needs that are better met by change. Looked at through the arguments of those who accept the hypocrisy premise, even the abstract concept analysed in SubSect.5.1.2 ceases to have much attraction, certainly not enough to use it as a brake on plausible aspirations for self-determination of a minority within a sovereign state.

Where there is a failed state or the secessionist movement has already created a wholly autonomous state, as is clearly the case in Transnistria, neither strength nor stability of the notionally sovereign country is undermined by giving independence. A weak government may indeed have more prospect of succeeding if its responsibilities cease including managing territory whose inhabitants are intractably opposed to its rule. In practice, the granting of independence to Transnistria could benefit both parts of Moldova for exactly that reason: removing a major obstacle to Moldova joining the EU and the political distraction of aiming for a so-far-elusive reintegration.

The Hans-Adam view (Gussen 2019) that the enforced retaining of borders creates more violence than allowing change to those borders should be borne in mind, even in situations which affront the US and the EU as well as those where they are supportive of the changes, such as in the former Yugoslavia. The argument resonates in that Transnistria, as was seen in Chapter 1, has evolved into a genuine nation, and restricting the self-determination of its people does not legitimise the democratic process in Moldova. On those terms, it is ripe for a peaceful transformation to independence.

5.1.4 THE 'RIGHT' TO SECEDE IN INTERNATIONAL LAW

Primary and remedial right theories

A more theoretical approach to the alteration of sovereignty is the primary or plebiscitary right theory. This in essence says that where the majority of a territory's inhabitants want independence, it should be granted. This theory, in view of the desire of most Transnistrians for independence from Moldova (Sect.1.3), is highly supportive of Transnistrian statehood. It is an argument that has been developed mainly by philosophers rather than political scientists or lawyers and can be contrasted with the more restrictive remedial right theory. Both are neatly encapsulated by Nicolás Brando and Sergi Morales-Gálvez:

> Two broad approaches exist in the literature: Remedial Right theories argue that a group's justified secession depends on the grievances and injustices that a state has imposed on the group; and Primary Right theories defend a group's right to self-determination and/or secession, regardless of the existence of injustices, provided that a majority of the group claims such a right. (2018:108)

Primary right theory's leading exponent is Harry Beran (1998) and many commentators regard it as a "liberal theory" (e.g. Newman and Visoka 2018). The practical difficulties that could flow from small groups demanding any right to secede has led others, particularly Michel Seymour (2007), to advocate that the right should be restricted to nations or people (Brando and Morales-Gálvez 2018:5). Some doubters of this theory point to possible adverse consequences for those who are of a minority ethnicity within the territory or for other reasons do not support the secession. In this context, Gauthier (1994:370) raised concerns for the welfare of the Anglophone minority that would be created by the secession of Quebec. This could have an application in respect of the Romanian speakers of Transnistria.

The contrasting remedial right theory is premised on the right to secession being dependent on there being a people who are victim of such an injustice that only secession could remedy. Within that theory there are variants. On the one hand, the position taken by Allen Buchanan (1995:54) requires grave injustices for a right to secession, and on the other, that the infringement of specific rights and lack of constitutional recognition of minorities may suffice. Buchanan (1995:53), though, distinguishes between the right to actual secession or independence and to self-determination, specifying a lower threshold for the latter. In a later work, Buchanan (2007:351–353) identifies three forms of injustice that give rise to this right: (1) large-scale and persistent violations of basic human rights; (2) unjust annexation of a legitimate state's territory; and (3) the state's persistent violations of intrastate autonomy agreements. Transnistria would not be able to rely on any of these: (1) and (3) have simply not occurred; and (2), as far as the requirement of a "legitimate state's territory" is concerned, is a circular criterion and adds nothing to the first two.

This theory has rarely been expressly discussed in the Transnistrian context, although Khazar Shirmammadov (2016) considers it* in relation to the Russian annexation of Crimea. His core consideration is distracted from by criticisms of the legitimacy of the Crimean referendum, taking the approach that as the referendum there was not "peaceable and transparent", it could not be the basis for "any plausible moral case for secession" (2016:83). He concludes that, against that background, only the remedial right theory could work as a justification for Crimean secession from Ukraine. However, in his eyes that would not be a justification as, "The Crimean people had not been exposed to violation for their ethnic difference since 1954" (2016:94).

It is, however, the principles absorbed into remedial right theory that many who have argued against Transnistria's right to secede have relied upon. Melissa Cornet (2016) opposes even a right to self-determination, arguing it cannot be justified as, in essence, the Transnistrians are not a people; their rights are not seriously violated by Moldova; and, pointing to autonomy of the sort Gagauzia has, there are potentially other legal remedies available. She follows and draws heavily on the New York (2006) report, which only reluctantly admits Transnistria's claim to even *de facto* statehood. The New York report and Cornet both have regard to the relative lack of oppression of Transnistrians by Moldova in concluding that the territory has no right to secede. The New York (2006) report maintains that the Transnistrian government is analogous to an occupying regime, and hence in most particulars is acting illegally. Its hesitancy over Transnistria's *de facto* status is because of its dependence on Russian military and financial aid, and it wholly refutes any claim

---

*   He prefers the term "choice theory".

for *de jure* status. The five New York lawyers visited the territory and interviewed several senior officials but appear to have made no attempt to gauge the feeling of the populace.[*]

Farhad Mirzayev regards matters such as Moldovan recognition of Transnistrian driving licences and protocols reached between the territories in 2001 as being "such legal instruments [that] support the claims for statehood for Transnistria" (2014:143). He concludes on Transnistria's status that "it can be argued that Transnistria should be granted the highest autonomous status within Moldova" (2014:261) but does not address, let alone support, the case for full independence.

Bill Bowring is similarly sympathetic to the Transnistrian people to the extent they should be allowed self-determination, saying:

> Perhaps the strongest point in favour of a right to self-determination is the fact of more than 20 years of separation from Moldova, during which time a strongly state-like if unrecognised social and political entity has taken root in the territory demarcated by the Dniester river, with the addition of Bender. (2014:24)

Bowring, like Mirzayev, sees that right as being exercised through autonomy or federalism. He points to Gagauzia, whose autonomy is formally enshrined in Moldovan law. He considers that as the most likely outcome, unless Moldova joined with Romania, which he says is highly unlikely but which, although not expressly stated, could lead to independence (2014:26). Dov Lynch (2004: Abstract) also considers that Transnistria, like the other pseudo-states, has – even when he was writing – achieved *de facto* statehood. He argues for a "coordinated approach, spearheaded by the EU, that balances *de facto* and *de jure* independence and sovereignty", again falling short of full independence or statehood.

Those who favour remedial right theory, explicitly or by implication, will not support the Transnistrian case in the absence of agreement from Chisinau. While primary right theorists of the Beran (1998) school would make a case for independence, that theory has not gained traction in international law.

The effect of the renunciation of the Molotov-Ribbentrop Pact

A specific argument boosting the legal case for independence flows from the 1939 Molotov-Ribbentrop Pact (SubSect.1.1.1), which was the basis for incorporating Transnistria in Moldova and was subsequently renounced. It is regarded by Mirzayev as a factor in the weakness of Moldova's position over Transnistria (2013:140). The New York report (2006:6) considers this then argues that renouncing a treaty means that treaty has no

---

[*] The mission to Transnistria was led by Mark Meyer, who appears closely allied to the Romanian government (New York 2006:13, footnote 30).

effect in determining future events but does not automatically mean a reversion to the position prior to it.

Transnistria's own scholarly work advocating statehood (Ignatiev 2018) enthusiastically adopts the Molotov-Ribbentrop argument, as did former President Smirnov when I interviewed him in Tiraspol in May 2019. It gives a credible basis on which Transnistrian secession could be approved in international law. It does not have the strength to overcome the current universal external objections to Transnistrian statehood, but were there movement towards supporting it from some of those who could influence the situation, the argument might provide a credible basis for others, particularly the Chisinau government, to acquiesce in independence.

5.2 NON-TRANSNISTRIAN ACTORS

This section focuses on those countries and organisations outside Transnistria that have taken a position on the Transnistrian situation and how they bear on the territory's ability to attain statehood. First among these must, of course, be Moldova itself and its Chisinau-based government, followed by Russia. A currently weakened Ukraine is less likely to have a significant effect. Romania, the US and some EU members' views are considered. The OSCE's 5+2 group and the EU are the most significant organisations.

5.2.1 MOLDOVA

The Chisinau government has an overarching interest in resolving the present situation, which leaves it without any control over a significant part of its *de jure* population and territory. That the main organ of that government on the Transnistrian issue is called the Bureau of *Reintegration* leaves one in no doubt as to what its ostensible aspiration is.

Relations between Chisinau and Tiraspol

Since the 1992 war, relations between Moldova and Transnistria have been strained but largely peaceful. Technically, their relationship is one of frozen conflict, but in practice, as was seen in relation to the economy in Chapter 2, the territories have an often constructive, non-confrontational relationship. This is summed up by de Waal:

> The Moldova-Transdniestria conflict is more benign than the other post-Soviet conflicts. There is a minimal threat of violence and there have been virtually no casualties

since fighting ended in 1992. In many ways this is less a conflict than an extremely contentious political dispute. (2018: Chapter 2)

The differences between Moldova and Transnistria have manifested themselves in political disputes rather than violence, the most serious of which was in June 2013 when President Shevchuk issued a decree purporting to extend Transnistrian territory to Varnita near Bender, comprising of several villages and around 4,000 people. Nicolae Timofti, then president of the Republic of Moldova, strongly criticised this act, considering it a threat to the territorial unity of Moldova (Całus 2013). Nothing came of this and Varnita remains firmly under Chisinau's control, but it represented the greatest tension between the two for several years (Tomczyk 2013).

Meetings between the leadership of Moldova and Transnistria were for a long time infrequent, with no recorded contact from 2009 until 2017, but shortly after the accession of Transnistrian President Krasnoselsky, the two leaders met in Bender in January 2017 (*PenzaNews* 2017). The talks were focused on economic, trade and logistic matters more than any political solution. This was followed by a shorter meeting in Chisinau in March, where the Romanian-language school issue (SubSect.4.1.2) was discussed in conciliatory terms, along with easing access for farmers whose land straddles the border near Dubasari. By September 2018, five of the eight aims agreed there had been implemented (OSCE n.d.), including opening the Dniestr bridge linking Gura Bicului and Bicioc. The significance is not so much the detail of what was agreed but the increasingly productive relationship between the two regimes, which may involve recognition of the Transnistrian regime by Moldova.

While the Tiraspol regime engages increasingly with Chisinau, the Transnistrian desire for independence has remained constant. Since being elected, Krasnoselsky has followed that line, emphasising in February 2017 that he sees independence not just as a goal but as the only way of guaranteeing Transnistrian security (*Sputnik News* 2017). He doubts Chisinau's commitment to a federalisation solution:

> I wonder if those speaking about federalisation are ready for it? Pridnestrovie isn't....Are Moldovan politicians ready for that? Are they ready to change the constitution, legislation, repeal certain laws; to make Russian a national language; to give a status to the Russian troops in Moldova? No, they probably aren't. (Novosti Pridnestrovya 2017).

This largely constructive relationship between the two territories gives rise to a degree of optimism about the resolution of the dispute. The contrast with the overtly hostile relations Azerbaijan had with the Nagorno-Karabakh regime and its sponsor state Armenia is marked. That situation culminated in war, killing some 5,000 at the end of 2020 (BBC 2020), but no resolution of the dispute. So long as Chisinau and Tiraspol are engaging, not only is war unlikely but the chances of the government finding a resolution are also far higher.

The Moldovan leadership's position: federalisation, autonomy or special status

Despite the Moldovan president until December 2020, Igor Dodon, being largely pro-Russian, his stance on Transnistria was hard to fathom, causing considerable frustration in Tiraspol, as summed up in the Russian *EurAsia Daily*:

> In particular, Krasnoselsky blames Dodon for his regularly changing stance on the future of Transnistria – at first, Dodon suggested federalization of Moldova, then he promised autonomy to the Russian enclave, whereas now he speaks of the 'region with a special status' like his Ukrainian friends do. (Toporov 2018)

It may be the three positions ascribed to Dodon – which could respectively represent those of California, Kurdistan and Hong Kong, for instance – were not intended to be that divergent but taken at face value they would have different consequences.

A Moldovan July 2005 law No.173 Article 3 talks of, "The autonomous territorial unit with a special legal status: Transnistria" (see Appendix D). The original Dodon federalisation suggestion was a 27-member senate, with Transnistria having ten seats and Gagauzia four, despite their being even together substantially a minority. This was considered critically by Diana Dascalu. Although she is no admirer of Transnistria, her analysis was similar to Krasnoselsky's:

> In both Moldova and Ukraine, federalization would come at a high price. This includes inheriting economic debt, corruption, democratic backwardness, Russian military presence and armament, and, most importantly, high numbers of pro-Russian voters. (2019)

Even disregarding the unevidenced assertions about corruption and democratic backwardness, the potential liabilities (particularly arising out of Russian gas credits) and Russian presence could hamper Moldova both economically and politically. These are skimmed over by those who argue for any form of reintegration: the tighter the association the more central these matters would be to the administration of Moldova.

In December 2018, Dodon told *Der Spiegel* that Transnistria "could get special status with broad powers of autonomy within the Moldovan state" (RTA 2019). Although he was not drawn on the detail of that, seemingly he was envisaging something less than the complete *de facto* independence that currently prevails, with the Chisinau government having a nominal power to legislate for the territory. It may be this would be easier to reconcile with continuing Russian presence and economic involvement than a federal or other more practically integrated solution and might be an outcome more palatable to Russia, despite its historic notional support for federalisation. It would have little attraction for Transnistrians, who have consistently rejected any form of reunification. Only if Moscow came to regard this as a best solution to be actively followed, which, in its desire for independence, would cut Transnistria adrift, is there any prospect of it being implemented.

The fact that Dodon talked of "special status" and "autonomy" conjunctively (RTA 2019) underlines the point that Chisinau sees little to distinguish between them. However, a subtle difference between the two terms is that a special status should be irrevocable in international law, which has led to criticism of India in its recent attempts to deprive Kashmir of such status (Zarifi 2019). In contrast, the Spanish government removing Catalan autonomy, however much of an affront many might see it as, would purely be a matter of Spanish internal law, governed by Article 155 of its constitution (Blakeley n.d.). Even if the Tiraspol government could be persuaded of the effectiveness and entrenchment of an internationally recognised special status, it is unlikely they would see it as more desirable than the present position. Again, it is something which in reality could not be imposed on the territory so long as it has Moscow's support for its *de facto* independence.

Another indication of ambivalence towards the retention of Transnistria by Chisinau was a suggestion by Dodon in December 2017 that it could become part of Ukraine (UAWire 2017). There may be little attraction to anyone in the idea. Transnistrians have expressed no desire for it; Russia would not be attracted by a territory it regards as within its sphere of influence becoming part of a country it is currently hostile to; and the Kiev government may have enough problems already without becoming embroiled in Transnistrian affairs. Ultimately, though, if Dodon was prepared to countenance Transnistria being seceded in that way, it may follow he would do so by it becoming independent.

The Bureau of Reintegration

The Moldovan government maintains a Bureau of Reintegration, primarily to deal with Transnistria. Its deputy director Alin Gvidiani described to me in an interview at the Chisinau central government buildings* on 1 October 2019 and follow-up email (Appendix D) the work of the bureau, which had been created in 2002 as the Ministry for Reintegration, becoming a bureau within the State Chancellery in 2009. Fifteen people work for it. He said its goals are:

> To promote co-government and sectoral policies to re-establish unique spaces in the economic fields, customs, defence information etc. In this regard, the ministry was established so concrete people** could take measures to obtain integration.

In answer to my primary query, why Chisinau resists Transnistrian independence, Gvidiani said, "Concrete persons are dependent totally on the Right-Bank", though he went on to emphasise the extent of Russian gas subsidies and pensions. He pointed out that Transnistrians can and do use all the services available on the Right-Bank. He made no reference to sovereignty issues or the strategic importance of Transnistria, though among the written material he gave me were extracts from the New York report (2006). My suggestion that, despite what he said about economic matters, most Transnistrians wanted independence was met with, "You are relying on the so-called referendum in 2006."

He was highly critical of the Transnistrian regime, insisting there were "a lot of" political prisoners and that human rights were deteriorating, claiming around 550 Transnistrians seek the help of the Chisinau authorities each year in this regard. He said that the Transnistrian population was 300,000 to 350,000.*** Even the far from uncritical Hammarberg report (2013) was questioned:

> We have reservations about the Hammarberg Report. We think he discussed the people directly but only with the head of prisons and such like. He made some concrete recommendations and it is said after five years many of his recommendations were successfully implemented. Our estimation is that the situation is getting worse. We receive more complaints.

In respect of the upcoming 5+2 talks in Bratislava, Gvidiani took a positive view. As well as the seemingly perennial discussions about car registrations and easing the ability of

---

* Although I was asked to bring an interpreter to the meeting, Gvidiani spoke almost entirely in English.

** This expression was used, in English, by several people on both sides of the Dniester. It is probably better to disregard the word 'concrete' than try to solve that linguistic mystery.

*** The census figures point to around 475,000 (SubSect.2.4.1). My observations of the 2016 presidential election made me believe that the voters' list was genuine, which would suggest the census was too.

inhabitants to cross rural borders, there should be discussions of a "special status" for Transnistria. That, however, was qualified by him saying, "Transnistria perceives this as relations between two different states. This is not the case between the banks of the Dniester." This optimism proved to be misplaced (SubSect.5.2.4)

In our discussions, Gvidiani did not mention what a solution might be, other than referring to the 2005 law discussed above, and little is said about that on the bureau's website (Guvernul n.d.). The bureau is a high-level government department, encompassing the deputy prime minister's main role. Its inability to articulate how reintegration could take place, coupled with the ostensibly contradictory pronouncements of Dodon on the point, support Krasnoselsky's view that Chisinau is not ready for federalisation, or indeed any other solution, and only full independence or maintaining the *status quo* are currently plausible. As neither side favours the *status quo*, this lack of articulation of any alternative may strengthen the case for and prospects of independence. As will be seen in the next subsection, federation would give Russia a degree of control over the Moldovan government, which would not be acceptable to the Chisinau regime. The concessions, amounting to a tacit recognition of the Tiraspol government under the auspices of OCSE, could also point a way towards independence.

How committed is Moldova to opposing Transnistrian independence?

Nicu Popescu and Leonard Litra, in a similar vein to President Krasnoselsky, question the Moldovan economic commitment to reunification:

> The Moldovan approach to Transnistria is increasingly driven by a cold-blooded cost-benefit analysis rather than by grand aspirations to territorial integrity. Moldovan society and the elite are busy thinking through not only the benefits but also the potential costs of reintegration. And for a growing number of Moldovans, it is not clear that the benefits of reintegration will outweigh the costs. (2012:3)

While the argument seems plausible, it ascribes a degree of rationality to the Moldovan government that it lacks. Dascalu's analysis (2019) portrays the laxity in thinking of that government when it chases a federal solution regardless of consequences. The present situation does not benefit the Moldovan economy and is probably more harmful than a 'clean break' would be (SubSect.2.1.1). Moldovan membership of the EU and NATO would be more realistic if the Transnistrian problem were resolved. Moldova is not currently a formal candidate for membership, unlike Albania, North Macedonia and Montenegro. Just as Serbia's relationship with Kosovo is a barrier to that country's membership, so is Moldova's with Transnistria.*

---

*   See Brzozowski (2019) for an interview with the Moldovan Foreign Minister who talks of "European integration" when asked about EU and NATO membership and is evasive on the effect the Transnistrian situation has on Moldova's position: "We'll see what will happen in the next geo-political context to appear."

The Moldovan commitment to retaining Transnistria within its territory may not be as strong as the bare words of Dodon, even if one disregards his aside about it potentially becoming part of Ukraine, and the Bureau of Reintegration suggest. Its recent engagement with the territory may even amount to a loose form of recognition. The constructive relationship between the governments points towards an eventual peaceful resolution, which undoubtedly could be achieved by independence. There is no clear plan as to how Moldova and Transnistria could be reintegrated. Dodon sets out several alternatives, the bureau none. The lack of economic advantage to Chisinau in retaining the territory may weigh heavily in eventually surrendering it, and Moldovan opposition may not be as great an obstacle to statehood as would superficially appear to be the case.

5.2.2 RUSSIA

Russia's attitude to Transnistrian status is opaque. While it may hold the key to resolving the deadlock and even securing independence, it has shown few signs of wanting to undo that lock. However, it does provide vital support militarily and economically to Transnistria, without which its present *de facto* independence from Chisinau would not be viable.

Practical Russian support for Transnistria

The presence of Russian troops makes any attempt at a forcible reintegration with Chisinau virtually inconceivable (Blakkisrud and Kolstø 2013:186). Moldova does not have the resources or will to risk a war with a military superpower. Tiraspol's *de facto* rule without the presence, and implicit threat of, Russian troops would be hard to sustain. The troops, and particularly the manoeuvres they carry out such as was reported in June 2018 (RFE 2018a), cause considerable disquiet in Chisinau. In 1999, Russia promised at OSCE talks in Istanbul to start removing the troops. Possibly because of Yeltsin's resignation and Putin's succession shortly afterwards, that has never materialised and, although occasionally referred to by Chisinau, that promise now seems meaningless (Tomiuc 2017). There was serious speculation when the crisis in Eastern Ukraine erupted and Russia effectively invaded Crimea that there would be similar action in Transnistria (e.g. Kashi 2014; Hawksley 2014), but that proved misplaced.*

Economic support, particularly gas subsidies (SubSect.2.6.1), is vital to Transnistria. Without it the economic viability of Transnistria would be doubtful. The payment of pensions by Moscow, supplementing those provided by the Tiraspol government, is particularly significant, not only for its direct economic impact but because it makes Russia particularly attractive to the territory's inhabitants. These payments are described by Kudors *et al.* (2010) as "unfriendly", particularly as they are not made to Russian citizens living in Right-Bank Moldova, and thus "supports the administration of Tiraspol and

---

* See Rogstad (2016) for a contemporaneous explanation of why such action was never likely.

implicitly endorses Transnistrian statehood", a situation which "runs counter to the official position of Russia" (2010:229).

Russia has had less impact on the local democratic politics than might be assumed, as was shown when its preferred candidate was defeated in the 2011 presidential election (SubSect.3.2.1). As Adrian Rogstad puts it:

> As long as cautious support for Tiraspol was seen as a key tool in Russia's quest for continued influence in Moldova, the Transnistrian regime was able to resist Russian pressure to a certain extent, safe in the knowledge that Russian support would not be completely cut. (2016:28)

Russia's military and economic support is vastly appreciated in Transnistria. The near-unanimous vote in the 2006 referendum for closer ties with Russia was a fair reflection of that (SubSect.1.3.2). Pictures of Putin abound in Transnistrian buildings, by the owners' choice not compulsion. Candidates in presidential elections try to outdo each other in showing ties with Russia. I have hardly heard a Transnistrian speak of Russia in anything other than unequivocally positive terms.

Russia's ostensible position

Symbolically and significantly, the 1992 ceasefire between Moldova and Transnistria was signed by Russia's President Yeltsin along with Moldovan and Transnistrian leaders.

Russia authored the 2003 Kozak Memorandum, which explicitly provided for its troops to remain in Transnistria until 2020. However, the then Moldovan president, Vladimir Voronin, did not ratify it, arguably because of pressure from the EU, OSCE and the US, leading Putin to pronounce in 2005 that the Transnistrian conflict settlement was ruined by those exerting that pressure because of their fears of Russian influence in the region (Rotarescu 2014:5).

Moscow claims its goal is to help both sides work out an acceptable solution which would preserve Moldovan territorial integrity while protecting Transnistrians' rights. Russia's official position is that the way to achieve this is through the creation of a federation uniting Moldova and Transnistria possibly with Gagauzia (Necsutu 2019b).

It has not recognised Transnistrian as an independent state, although it did so for the other pseudo-states, Abkhazia and South Ossetia, in 2008. This lack of Russian support for independence is clearly a major obstacle to *de jure* statehood, just as the practical Russian support discussed above is vital in maintaining *de facto* independence.

Russian motivation

An attraction to Russia of a federation between Transnistria and Moldova is that so long as it exercises some *de facto* control over Transnistria, it could then effectively veto decisions of the Chisinau government, particularly those leading towards greater unity with Romania and the EU. Cornet argues:

> Concerning independence, Russia is likely to block any move in the talks towards it: its goal in the region is to keep control over Moldova, as a proxy in Eastern Europe blocking Western integration. (2016:57)

Sharifzoda puts it even more bluntly, stating, "Since there is no hint that the *status quo* may change, Russia is winning this conflict", whilst arguing that Moldova and the EU are also responsible for the prolongation of that *status quo* (2017:13). Russia's refusal to formally recognise the Tiraspol government is not easily explained in terms other than the Cornet theory. The sometimes bellicose nature of Putin's foreign policy has not been seen in relation to Transnistria, there being few pronouncements from Moscow on what its status should be.

Michael Bobick provides a more nuanced analysis of Russian aspirations:

> In situations in which the Russian military intervenes in these contested territories, intervention occurs, not in order to achieve a decisive victory, but rather to keep the de jure sovereign at bay. This happened during the 1992 war between Transnistria and Moldova, when locals loyal to separatists began taking over Moldovan police stations and government buildings. (2014:7)

The Russian occupation of and annexation of Crimea – indeed a decisive victory – shortly after Bobick expounded that theory shows the theory is not of universal application, even if consistent with what has happened in Transnistria, South Ossetia and Abkhazia and, to a lesser extent, Eastern Ukraine.

Eleonora Turkia (2008:25) identifies several attempts that had come close to creating a settlement between Transnistria and Moldova but had been thwarted at the last minute, particularly the 1997 memorandum on normalisation of relations between the territories and the Kozak Memorandum. She points to the Russian "double standard" of publicly maintaining that the territorial integrity of Moldova should be preserved while in practice supporting the Tiraspol government (2008:20). She concludes there is little hope for agreement on the primary dichotomy between Moldova's aspiration to maintain territorial integrity and Transnistria's for recognition.

Likewise, Pavel Felgenhauer, a Russian defence analyst, in Moscow's *Novaya Gazeta* newspaper, draws analogies between President Putin's policy in Ukraine's eastern Donbas region and the stance Russia has taken towards Transnistria. He envisages an unofficial use of the Russian air force over that territory along with supplying weapons to rebels while ostensibly trying to broker a truce in that area:

> Keeping this kind of separatist enclave secure in Donbas, having a comprehensive ceasefire, having negotiations, it's like a Transnistria kind of ceasefire – more than 20

years of negotiations that can last until hell freezes over. And that's what basically Russia right now is trying to achieve. (cited by Schearf 2014).

The most detailed exposition of this motivation is that of Marcel Kosienkowski (2019), who sees the Russian support for Transnistria as a means of preventing Moldova joining NATO or even getting closer to the EU (2019:27). He suggests that Russia could use Transnistria as a "bargaining chip" to entice the Moldovan authorities to align with Russia, in consideration for Russia causing Transnistria to be reunited with Moldova (2019:28). He also cites the reasoning of Hensel (2006:9) that Transnistria is an "unsinkable aircraft carrier" on the Ukrainian border and speculates on its prospective military uses.

The positions of these writers overlap. The clearest theme may be the double standard enunciated by Turkia (2008). It is simply not possible to reconcile ostensible support for another country's territorial integrity with positioning troops there in the face of express opposition from that country's government. That, of course, is not a direct explanation for Russia's motivation but leads into the views of Bobick (2014) and Cornet (2016) about its strategy of reducing the control of Moldova, the *de facto* power, over the territory. That Russia wins from, and hence wishes to prolong, the *status quo*, as suggested by Sharifzoda (2017) and Felgenhauer (Schearf 2014), also coincides with that. Kosienkowski's reasoning, except perhaps in relation to the military use of the territory, is also dependent on Russia's continuing influence in Moldovan territory rather than in an independent Transnistria. In the absence of advantage to Russia in doing so, it will not currently do anything to change the *status quo* and hence move towards Transnistrian independence.

Russia and the future of Transnistria

The Kremlin may thus have calculated where annexation, as in Crimea; recognition, as in South Ossetia; and non-recognition, as in Transnistria, are respectively in its interests. Leaving Transnistria in its present limbo subject to the notional sovereignty of Chisinau, whatever problems that causes for its people, is in Russia's interests at least for the moment. Therein does lie a significant, perhaps the most significant, obstacle to Transnistrian statehood.

A glimmer of hope for Transnistria may arise as the Ukrainian government becomes more supportive of Chisinau, something which Moscow may regard as a provocation and could in turn cause Russia to move closer to Tiraspol.* Were that to result in Russian recognition of Transnistria, it could be the first, and perhaps decisive, step to independence. Całus speculated on this possibility shortly after Russia invaded Crimea,

---

* At the time of final editing, there is a build-up of Russian troops close to the Ukraine border, leading to speculation that an invasion may be imminent. Were that to occur, there would be a realignment in relations between Moscow, Kiev and Chisinau, which may impact on the position each, and particularly Russia, takes in relation to Transnistria.

arguing that recognition would "prevent Chisinau from its pro-European aspirations" (2014b:78). Recognition would follow from Russia's allies, such as Belarus and Serbia, with a possible domino effect, and, unless Chisinau received equally strong backing from the EU and US, it would be able to do little to resist. Once there was a significant division of world opinion, as there was leading to the independence of Kosovo (SubSect.5.3.1), the prospects for Transnistrian independence would greatly increase.

5.2.3 OTHER COUNTRIES

The most significant input by another country into the Transnistrian situation was through the 2010 German-Russian Meseberg Memorandum. Although not adopted by either the EU or the OSCE, it influenced the negotiations that occurred afterwards and could even have led to a reintegration, albeit with greater autonomy than Chisinau would then have wished for.

The US position can be summed up as one of uninterested hostility to Tiraspol but not to an extent that will have any practical significance. Romania has little direct interest in the situation, but the possibility of its unification with Moldova is of potential significance. Ukraine is supportive of the Chisinau position as an incident of its enmity to Russia but currently has little influence. The British position is considered in more detail below, as I was given considerable access to diplomats in Chisinau, who were able to spell out a nuanced and constructive approach.

Germany and the Meseberg Memorandum

In June 2010, Germany entered into the short Meseberg Memorandum, signed by Chancellor Angela Merkel and then Russian president, Dmitry Medvedev. Although predominantly a trade agreement, it explicitly dealt with the Transnistrian situation and offered Russian input into European security policymaking in exchange for progress in resolving the conflict (Popescu and Litra 2012). The terms Germany agreed to relating to the territory were closer to Russia's position in relation to Transnistria than that the EU takes collectively. It stopped short of agreeing with full independence, which Russia itself does not overtly proclaim, but went well beyond local autonomy within the Moldovan state, which the EU advocates. The memorandum (2010) proposed: "Representation and participation of Transnistria at the level of the unified state, in the government and the legislature." Participation of Tiraspol in Moldova's central government, along with creating a bicameral parliament in Chisinau, were typical of Russia's proposals in the previous years, including the 2003 Kozak Memorandum (Socor 2011). Although more supportive of the Transnistrian position than most pronouncements from EU countries, it still represented an obstacle to statehood. Later in 2010, Merkel and the then French president, Nicolas Sarkozy, raised the Transnistrian issue with Russian president, Dmitry Medvedev, at a pre-summit meeting in Deauville. The reference to Transnistria was, in vague terms, calling for closer cooperation, "opening the way for settling old conflicts such as that in Transnistria" (Socor 2010). Only Lugar (2011), in his report to the US Senate, attaches any significance to this, and says it was of less importance than Meseberg.

Philip Remler (2013), former head of the OSCE Mission to Moldova, has criticised the Meseberg Memorandum, alleging that Merkel signed it without consulting the EU and that the German foreign ministry were unaware of it. Remler recognises that it brought German input into an issue that was previously neglected by the Berlin government and raised the profile of the Transnistria conflict in EU–Russia talks. It was anathema to many EU states, particularly former Soviet and Eastern Bloc countries. Popescu and Litra suggest that "From Moscow's perspective the Meseberg offer was not much more than hot air" (2012:7). It was a partial forerunner of 5+2 talks hosted, at its own insistence, by Russia in 2011, but which failed to make any tangible progress. Little has been heard of the memorandum since, and the issue has ceased to have any priority for Merkel's government.

In his report for the European Parliament, Stefan Wolff (2012) takes an optimistic view of the ongoing 5+2 negotiation process, seeing the Meseberg Memorandum as having created a positive momentum, though he is doubtful whether it can be sustained (2012:21). He is particularly admiring of the agreement achieved, indeed "skilfully mediated" under Irish chairmanship in April 2012, on "Principles and Procedures", which resolved a long-standing dispute regarding the relative status of the negotiating parties (2012:17). Also created out of that process was an "Agenda" which defined three "baskets" of topics to be negotiated: socio-economic issues, legal and humanitarian issues, and a comprehensive settlement (including institutional, political and security issues). Wolff wrote this in the early days of the Shevchuk regime, when there was a genuine expectation that the then new Transnistrian president would engage more flexibly with a negotiation process than his predecessor (2012:12).

The Meseberg Memorandum and Wolff's report represent a high point of hope for the resolution of the deadlock, albeit propounding a resolution that would not lead to statehood. His approach may have failed to recognise the intractability of Transnistria's position, none of whose three presidents have given any hint it would ever surrender sovereignty anywhere other than Moscow. The Moldovan position of opposition to independence was perceived as intractable in 2012, and Wolff made no attempt to explore that solution.

Positions have changed since 2012, when the Memorandum might have been seen as propounding other solutions, the consideration of which could prove obstacles to statehood. There can be little expectation now that the Transnistrian regime will agree to reintegration. The nation-building project continues to run its course (SubSect.1.2.2), with independence as its goal. There may be chinks in Chisinau's resistance (SubSect.5.2.1).

The US

The US takes little active interest in Transnistrian status issues. Its State Department (USSD) publishes bulletins condemning what it perceives as human rights abuses there, often based on questionable information (e.g. USSD 2013, 2014, 2016). It has no permanent, and little temporary, presence in Transnistria, not even an honorary consul. A statement on the independence referendum was issued by a USSD *deputy* spokesman, making the US lack of sympathy for Transnistria clear:

> The US does not recognize the independence referendum held yesterday in the Transnistrian region of Moldova. We welcome similar statements rejecting the referendum by the EU, member states, and the Chairman-in-Office of the Organization for Security and Cooperation in Europe.
>
> As the international community has made clear, Transnistria is a part of Moldova, and yesterday's efforts by the Transnistrian regime should not be recognized as anything other than an attempt to destabilize Moldova. (2006a)

Little has changed in the US position, and the USSD "Factsheet" (2017a) merely says of Transnistria:

> [The US] supports the 5+2 negotiations to find a comprehensive settlement that will provide a special status for the separatist region of Transnistria within a territorially whole and sovereign Moldova.

This was echoed by a memo from the US Mission to the OSCE, (2018) published over two weeks after the May talks finished, adopting words similar to those of the USSD Factsheet (2017a) and the OSCE's own position. A "minority" report to the US Senate (Lugar 2011) made a number of recommendations, including for more active involvement in conflict resolution by the US, but little regard seems to have been paid to this by the State Department and it is barely cited in academic writing on the topic.

The only US citizen living there permanently told me in November 2015 that he occasionally has been approached by purported CIA operatives in Tiraspol, but they are invariably young, inexperienced and lacking any insight into the issues concerning the territory. US government officials are restricted in travelling there (USSD 2020).

Transnistria is thus far from a priority for the US, and were other factors to fall into place that led to statehood, US opposition, if expressed at all, would not be forceful enough to amount to a meaningful obstacle.

Romania

Romania has expressed little direct interest in the Transnistrian situation, yet the possibility of its own unification with Moldova could hold the key to resolving that situation. In 2009, then president, Traian Basescu, said the division of Romania and Moldova was similar to that between West and East Germany before reunification (Hill and Kramer 2009). Romanian public opinion has supported unification, and there have been political movements within Romania advocating it. In a television interview, Basescu reiterated his 2009 position, saying that if Romania were given the option of union, it would say yes without hesitation as, "We want to complete our country" (Stirile TVR 2013). However, Basescu's successor, Klaus Iohannis, has taken a more cautious approach and does not appear to favour immediate reunification (Bird and Banila 2015).

Wolff considers this possibility but is cautious in his conclusion (2012:10). He believes that if there were a union, Russia would be willing to respect Moldova's territorial integrity in consideration for it not joining NATO. Moldovan membership of NATO with, even notionally, Transnistria and its contingent of Russian troops is unthinkable (2012:4). Romania's membership of NATO (since 2004) would inevitably lead to Transnistrian secession on any union with Moldova, unless, improbably, Romania gave up that membership. Wolff also draws parallels with the 1991 resolution of Cambodia's status after its war with Vietnam (2012:20), which was heavily dependent on international guarantees of the sort any resolution of the Transnistrian situation would require. This parallel might result in an arrangement under which, "Moldova would gain a Russian commitment to its sovereignty and territorial integrity in exchange for agreeing not to join NATO" (2012:17). However, the preservation of Moldovan territorial integrity is virtually a synonym for preserving the frozen conflict.

There is little public support for unification with Romania in Moldova, despite the view expressed to me by the British Ambassador, discussed below, that it was mainly the political elite, wary of losing their privileges, who opposed it. The question has frequently been asked by polling companies in Right-Bank Moldova; the last poll was in June 2020, where 33% supported and 55% opposed unification – a figure largely in line with earlier polls (*Deschide.md* 2020).

It is inconceivable that there could be any unification without the full support of the Moldovan people, and the Moldovan constitution would require approval by referendum, in which intriguingly Transnistrians would have the theoretical right to vote. The outcome of any union would almost certainly be the seceding of Transnistria and a resulting statehood.

Ukraine

Ukraine, despite its geographic proximity, including a 453km border (EU:EE 2016) and membership of the 5+2 group, had until the Russian invasion of Crimea in 2014 taken a supine approach to the Transnistrian question. The resulting state of enmity between the countries has led it to support Chisinau. In 2015, Ukraine cancelled the agreement which had allowed Russian troops to reach Transnistria over its territory.

In May 2017, Ukraine officially discontinued trading with Transnistria (ZIKUA 2017) and, in July 2017, announced the setting up of border posts on Ukrainian territory where there was an existing border crossing to Transnistria (*Euromaidan Press* 2017). This may have been precipitated by a deal in April 2017 that Moldova would buy electricity from the Ukrainian DTEK, trading at prices considerably lower than the Kuchurgan power plant in southern Transnistria, which previously supplied 80% of Moldova's electricity. The switch is reported to have cost the Transnistrian economy about US$100 million per year (Popşoi 2017).

While these steps make clear Ukraine's hostility to the Transnistrian regime, it is simply not in a position to be any obstacle to Transnistrian independence. Faced with Russian annexation of Crimea and losing *de facto* control of much of the eastern part of its territory, its hostility to a regime which it perceives as aligned to Russia is inevitable but little more than symbolic.

The British position

I interviewed then British ambassador, Philip Batson, on 7 April 2016 at the embassy in Chisinau. He insisted the UK's position, like that of the EU generally, was that Transnistria should "have a special status within the territorial integrity of Moldova". He maintained good relations with the Transnistrian government, visiting the territory every six to eight weeks. He talked of regular meetings with the Transnistrian foreign minister, invariably inserting a stilted "*de facto*" before referring to the post. Except for Romania, he considered that Britain was the EU country with the most active involvement in the Moldovan–Transnistrian issue.* The British involvement he talked of, though, was more educational and benevolent than political, including the sponsoring of joint camps for 24 young people identified as likely future leaders on both sides of the Dniestr. There is a cross-governmental fund controlled by Whitehall specifically for such projects in connection with frozen conflicts.**

While British support for Transnistria stops far short of recommending independence, its position is not blinkered or mired in dogmatic support for the Moldovan position. Batson was prepared to speculate on the possibility of Moldova seeking union with Romania, which he believed Moldovan opinion had swung towards in the previous nine months. He said the banking crisis that led around US$8billion – 15% of Moldova's GDP – to "disappear" during that time (SubSect.2.1.1) was causing a substantial loss of credibility of the Chisinau government. Inevitably many of the people, particularly younger, better-educated ones, would welcome the possibilities

---

*   Sixteen EU countries, predominantly from Eastern Europe, are among the 29 who maintain embassies in Chisinau. The only other country whose involvement Batson specifically commented on was Sweden.

**   Batson did not say, and I did not ask, how much that fund was.

for study and work abroad that a union might bring. The political class in Moldova – who would, in Batson's words, find themselves being little more than "an outpost like a regional council" – are resistant to the possible change. He identified an increasing disillusionment of the Moldovan population, particularly in the light of the banking crisis. However, he would not go so far as to say that such union either would or should result in Transnistrian independence.

Chrystele Todd, a political secretary at the Chisinau embassy, suggested little had changed when I interviewed her at Tucano's café in Chisinau on 7 December 2018. Despite the then seeming imminence of Brexit, she thought the UK would continue to work closely with the EU and the OSCE in trying to resolve the Transnistrian situation. Her carefully enunciated statement of the UK position was that it is:

…committed to supporting a comprehensive peaceful settlement on Transnistria's unresolved conflict based on sovereignty and the integrity of the Republic of Moldova with special status for Transnistria.

When pushed on the reasons for this, and the implicit objection to Transnistrian independence, she could not advance anything beyond the need to support the internationally recognised OSCE 5+2 process and the desirability of respecting territorial integrity. She pointed to Georgia and the precedent that would be set there, presumably for the breakaway territories of Abkhazia and South Ossetia. She pointed out that not all Transnistrians support independence.

Todd talked enthusiastically of advances from the recent OCSE Vienna discussions, such as codifying car registration plates and recognising Transnistrian university degrees. Progress was also being made on cross-border criminal investigations and emergency services. She thought that the Transnistrian authorities were no longer interfering with the Romanian-language schools. There was meaningful dialogue between Chisinau and Tiraspol on many matters, but the reluctance of the Transnistrian authorities to let senior Moldovan officials visit the territory remained a problem.

She said that recently the emphasis of British involvement had switched from "confidence building", which was perhaps the motive for the projects that Batson had spoken of, to more practical measures, identifying, for instance, providing old fire engines, which was greatly appreciated by both the Transnistrian minister of internal affairs and former President Smirnov when I interviewed them.

However, Todd, like Batson, was advancing a position that has no regard to, or perhaps even engagement with, what the vast majority of people in Transnistria want. The referendums there (SubSect.1.3.2), the unanimity among candidates for high political office, and the responses to my queries all show that *virtually* all Transnistrians want to break away from Chisinau.

While Batson and Todd could represent a balanced position on behalf of the UK Foreign Office, a Home Office (2017) policy document directed at those making decisions on asylum applications takes a negative, probably ill-considered, view of the territory internally. It draws heavily on USSD and Promo-LEX material. Some of the assertions made are simply wrong, for instance, "Transnistria held its 'presidential elections' in 2016 without the presence of international observers" (2017:40), and others are over-simplifications: "Consensual same-sex activity is illegal within Transnistria" (2017:7). It echoes the unsubstantiated USSD allegations (2017:84) about human trafficking. A major Western government permitting the publication of such poor quality material shows a lack of influence on the part of Transnistria. Were such governments to perceive it as a potential state, more care might be taken over official allegations made against it.

There is no published material suggesting any change in the British position post-Brexit. Were a solution to be found that led to Transnistrian statehood, there is no basis on which Britain would prove an obstacle.

Other European nations

Sweden has actively supported the Human Rights Joint Action Programme in Moldova and Transnistria from 2016 to 2018. This has been primarily directed at HIV testing, prisoners' rights and fighting domestic violence (Swedish Embassy 2018). The most tangible manifestation has been support for "women's economic self-determination". Seven businesses employing 38 people have been launched in Transnistria as a result.

Other countries have mainly become involved through the OSCE's rotating chairmanship, including the 2018 Italian chair Franco Frattini, said by Socor (2018) to be – like his colleague the former Italian prime minister, Silvio Berlusconi – "outspokenly Kremlin-friendly". There are few ties with Europe's other leading nations such as France, Spain and Poland. Despite a contingent of ethnic Bulgarians living in Transnistria, the Sofia government has expressed no views on the situation.

5.2.4 ORGANISATIONS

The most explicitly involved non-national 'actor' in the Moldovan–Transnistrian situation is the Organization for Security and Co-operation in Europe (OSCE). The European Union inevitably takes a position on any potential conflict within its broad sphere of influence and has been consistently supportive of the Chisinau government and opposed to any independence for Transnistria, preferring reintegration with Moldova with, at most, a degree of autonomy. The Community for Democracy and Rights of Nations (CDRN), which consists of Transnistria and the other pseudo-states, is supportive of statehood for its members but has little actual influence.

OSCE and the 5+2 group

The OSCE comprises 57 participating states: largely European, and former USSR countries, the US and Canada. It has a 'Mission to Moldova', the top priority of which is "the settlement of the Transnistrian conflict". The mission has thirteen international and 29 local staff and an annual budget of €2,292,000. It describes itself as a "mediator in the multilateral settlement process" (CoE n.d.).

It is under the OSCE's auspices that the 5+2 group operates. This consists of Transnistria, Moldova, Ukraine, Russia and the OSCE itself, with the US and EU as observers. Romania has also intermittently been involved. This group has only minor specific achievements, yet conversely it could be argued that it is a cause for the relatively civilised, peaceful relations between Transnistria and Moldova, who are theoretically still at war.

The group has adopted a position rejecting Transnistrian independence, as summarised in a press statement:

> The goal of the 5+2 talks is to work out the parameters of a comprehensive settlement based on the sovereignty and territorial integrity of the Republic of Moldova within its internationally recognized borders with a special status for Transdniestria, as reconfirmed by all 57 participating States in the Ministerial Council Statement in Vienna in 2017. (OSCE 2018).

The fundamental difficulty it faces is summed up by Samuel Goda:

> For the OSCE, finding a way to engage both sides to settle the conflict will be very complicated if Chisinau continues to talk about reintegration, and Tiraspol about independence or integration with Russia. (2016:209).

A series of talks between 2012 and 2019 led to some progress in some aspects. These included resuming the rail freight traffic; agreements on environment, social security and justice; vehicle registration numbers; access to agricultural land straddling the border; and the situation of Transnistrian Romanian-language schools (Necsutu 2017). Those talks, perhaps because of the arguably partisan position of the OSCE itself cited above as well as the obvious differences between the parties, have made no progress on the fundamental issue of Transnistria's status (Ivan 2014:1).

Vladimir Socor attaches a political significance to the provision allowing Transnistrian vehicle registrations and driving licences international recognition. He says these "negate Moldova's sovereignty and mark a small start toward international codification of Transnistria's separateness from Moldova" (2018a). His argument continues that Moldova's agreement to pay the Transnistrian authorities a rent for the five remaining Latin-script schools in Transnistria imply Transnistria's separateness from Moldova.

These points, oblique though they may be, are significant in identifying tacit recognition by the Chisinau authorities of the Tiraspol government and are perhaps further evidence of the equivocation in Moldova's position (SubSect.5.2.1).

Talks in Bratislava in October 2019 were anticipated more enthusiastically in Chisinau than Tiraspol. Alin Gvidiani of the Moldovan Bureau for Reintegration had told me in the central government buildings in Chisinau on 1 October 2019 that he thought progress would be made. Vladimir Yastrebchak, who had a major role in the Transnistrian delegation, told me the next day in Tiraspol that he expected, "There will just be time to shake hands." Yastrebchak was proved right, nothing was signed (OSCE 2018a) but Gvidiani remained optimistic that negotiations would continue (see Appendix D).

The 5+2 group may be a useful means of facilitating communication between Transnistria and Moldova on relatively low-level matters. However, there is nothing in its involvement so far which suggests that it is likely to have a significant role in overall resolution of the situation.

The EU

The EU's line is largely similar to the OSCE's, though lacking the clear enunciation which the OSCE gives its position.

Moldova and the EU entered an association agreement in July 2014, creating the Deep and Comprehensive Free Trade Area, but this falls well short of making it a short-term candidate for membership. Paradoxically, the reforms required of Moldova as a condition of that agreement also have to be implemented by Transnistria,* which seems in principle prepared to cooperate (Całus 2016a).

The EU's motivation, argues Kamil Całus (2014), "Is mainly because the existence of such a lawless entity virtually at the borders of the Union represents a source of instability for the entire area." He cites no evidence of the lawlessness, nor does he explain why the EU would see a territory which has been stable for nearly 30 years as a likely source of instability.

In 2013, Beyer and Wolff saw the EU as somewhat removed from Transnistria, saying, "While the right-bank has clearly moved closer to the EU, and would be susceptible to EU leverage for a settlement of the conflict, there has been no similarly strong increase of EU leverage and linkage on the left-bank" (2013:344). They rely on Moldovan citizens now having the right of visa-free travel in Schengen countries, which "has been a key prize for Moldovan political elites" (2013:341). This is in contrast with the Transnistrians only having "ample scope to travel to Russia" (2013:343).

While Całus (2014) may over-estimate the perception of potential instability in the region motivating the EU, the suggestion that it does not assert "leverage and

---

* No such stricture in relation to Northern Cyprus was imposed on the Republic of Cyprus when it was admitted to the EU in 2004.

linkage", meaning influence, in Transnistria is also questionable. A certain disdain for the organisation may be indicated by former President Smirnov's belief, sincere though unfounded, that Transnistria pays it US$60 million annually (Appendix B). Other Transnistrians, particularly academics who have worked in EU countries, regard it as of importance and generally talk positively of it. When interviewed in Tiraspol on 26 May 2019, former foreign minister and current government adviser Vladimir Yastrebchak described how dealing with the EU was a crucial part of his and the Ministry of Foreign Affairs' work.

The EU view was expressed more formally in the Transnistria section of its strangely titled report *Programming in the Republic of Moldova until 2020*:

> The reintegration of the Republic of Moldova should contribute immensely to economic development and the population's living standards by facilitating private sector activity and by upgrading the social services and infrastructure. (European Joint Analysis 2016:99)

Leaving aside the questionable economics of this – Transnistria is probably wealthier than the rest of Moldova, despite the concerns about the need to facilitate private sector activity – it is unrealistic for the EU to assume a surrender of *de facto* sovereignty by the Tiraspol government. The lack of talks, and presumably the resulting pressure on participants to comply with existing agreements, has been identified by Transnistrian Foreign Minister Vitaly Ignatiev (2018)* as enabling Moldova to avoid implementing even ratified agreements.

EU trade deals with Transnistria have been brokered through the Chisinau Chamber of Commerce with government support: a magnanimous approach as all the resulting tax and duty revenues go exclusively to the Tiraspol government (de Waal 2016).

Florian Kuchler (2010) considers the role of the EU in the region in his report *The Role of the EU in Moldova's Transnistria Conflict*, pointing out that the EU has had relatively little involvement in attempting to resolve the issues between Moldova and Transnistria or indeed in international relations with Moldova. He argues that it is becoming increasingly important for the EU to be involved, but much will depend on the area's relations with Russia and the US. The EU has indeed become much more closely involved with Moldova, mainly in the form of trade deals, which could be a precursor to Moldova joining the EU. However, it has taken a less active part in trying to broker any peace deal either directly or through the 5+2 group.

The EU's formal relationship with Moldova means that it has little choice but to ostensibly support the Chisinau position. However, it has not been a prime mover in opposing Transnistrian statehood, and were circumstances to change, including moves

---

* Ignatiev was originally appointed by Shevchuk and retained by Krasnoselsky. I met him briefly during the December 2016 election. He spoke fluent English, had an urbane, friendly manner and gave, in so far as my brief encounter allowed, the impression that he could be a valuable asset to the territory.

towards Moldovan accession to the union, there is no reason why it would present an active obstacle to statehood.

The Community for Democracy and Rights of Nations

In 2001, Abkhazia, South Ossetia, Transnistria and Nagorno-Karabakh agreed to form the CDRN, but this was not realised until 2006 (Cullen and Wheatley 2013). Mutual recognition was part of the accord. Besides issuing proclamations in 2007 and 2009, the organisation seems to have had virtually no meetings let alone practical purpose and is unlikely to play a significant role in resolving its member states' problems. It may be that upon receiving Russian recognition in 2008, South Ossetia and Abkhazia simply saw no further useful purpose in the organisation (Kosienkowski 2012:50).

Despite the ineffectuality of the organisation, relations between the quasi-states remain productive, with rudimentary missions being maintained in each other's capitals. In practice, I was told in Tiraspol on 29 May 2019, by Yastrebchak, who did not regard the organisation as particularly significant, that the representatives in each such mission are local people nominated by the host territory but formally appointed and funded by the territory they represent. Some five months later, with pride, he showed me postage stamps he had been instrumental in jointly producing with South Ossetia under the organisation's auspices.

A different view of the efficacy of relations between these states, if not the organisation itself, was taken by Kosienkowski (2012). In 2012, he regarded the cooperation between them as a major plank of Transnistria's foreign policy, citing Nina Shtanski's, Yastrebchak successor's, description of them as "fraternal people…who share our purposes and problems and difficulties" (2012:47). Even if that was justified then, the lack of activity by the organisation and coordinated actions by the pseudo-states since, stamps aside, makes it implausible now.

Other organisations

The United Nations has had little role in the Transnistrian situation. It admitted Moldova in February 1992 with no reference to Transnistria (UN 1992), and the General Assembly passed a resolution without debate calling for the "Complete and unconditional withdrawal of foreign military forces from the territory of the Republic of Moldova" (UN 2017). In September 2017, Transnistria sought observer status, a request which was interpreted by the Chisinau government as being only to undermine Moldova's role in the organisation (Vlas 2017). It is inconceivable that such a request would be granted at the moment, and even Russia would be unlikely to support it.

The Council of Europe is responsible for the application of the European Convention on Human Rights, mainly through the European Court of Human Rights in

Strasbourg.* The Council also publishes reports and discussion papers on human rights issues. The Council and its court have no direct role in determining the status of any territory, but rule on cases brought, through a tightly controlled gateway,** by individuals or groups concerning allegations that their rights have not been respected by states. Transnistria, not being a recognised state, is not susceptible to the court's jurisdiction, but claims have been brought against Moldova and Russia in respect of acts of its government (SubSect.3.5.2). There is no reason why, if granted independence, Transnistria would not voluntarily submit to the court's jurisdiction as has every European country.

NATO has, as the organisation puts it, no direct role in the conflict-resolution process in the region of Transnistria (NATO 2020). As Moldova is not a member, NATO would not be obliged, and probably not legally entitled to, intervene in any conflict there. That coupled with the sheer implausibility of major military action by Russia or anyone else means the Transnistrian situation is a virtual irrelevance to NATO.

5.2.5 THE OVERALL SIGNIFICANCE OF EXTERNAL ACTORS

Although many countries and organisations have had input into the Transnistrian situation, it is doubtful that any other than the Moscow and Chisinau governments will have a significant role in resolving it. As the main participants in the 5+2 process are Transnistria, Russia and Moldova, that organisation really provides no more than a facility for those countries to discuss matters. A currently emasculated Ukraine, the other national participant, is given little regard by any of the other three. The hostility between Russian and Ukraine, its military manifestations, and the willingness of the former to grant passports to the latter's population all contribute to an instability in the region, which could result in a shift in Russia's position to more ostensible support for Transnistrian independence. The OSCE itself, the fifth participant, may bring experienced diplomats and negotiators to the table, but they can only make headway if there is a willingness among the central protagonists to compromise.

Neither Moldovan nor Russian attitudes are entirely clear. The Moldovan government, particularly its president from December 2016 to December 2020, Igor Dodon, has proposed numerous solutions, even a suggestion of secession to Ukraine. It has taken steps which could be seen as recognition of the Tiraspol regiment. Were EU membership to become realistic, it may regard that as a greater prize than retaining Transnistria. Similarly, further weakening of Moldova's government, which could reduce the entire viability of that state, making, as it does, a natural fit with Romania, would plausibly lead to more active attempts to conclusively determine Transnistria's status.

---

*   See Sect.3.5 for the plethora of cases brought to that court on the bases of Transnistrian actions, mostly at the behest of Promo-LEX.

**   As a practising lawyer, I encounter many unsuccessful litigants who announce they are taking their case to the ECHR, usually on the slightly problematic grounds that their rights have been violated by a judge not believing them!

Russia, for all its practical support, may represent a bigger obstacle to statehood than Moldova if, as most commentators believe, it has decided the *status quo* is in its interests. The situation is fluid, particularly in the light of the hostility between Russia and Ukraine, which has come to support the Chisinau position. Recognition by Russia would strengthen Transnistria's hand, and that could be a consequence of Kiev's move to closer ties with Chisinau.

Other actors, most significantly the US and EU, are generally supportive of Chisinau, creating an international consensus which makes ending the current situation harder. The Meseberg Memorandum (2012), which once represented a plausible solution for the Transnistrian situation without statehood, can now be regarded as little more than an historic diversion.

5.3 SITUATIONS TO COMPARE WITH TRANSNISTRIA'S

Transnistria is, of course, not the only territory contending for statehood. The starting point for comparison is Kosovo, whose 2008 proclamation of independence from Serbia has achieved widespread, though not universal, recognition and is seen by the Transnistrian regime as a precedent for the territory's independence.* Some, like Scotland, Catalonia, Quebec and Bougainville, make the case from a position far from full autonomy and can only succeed in their aspiration with the cooperation of the Westminster, Madrid, Ottawa or Port Moresby governments, only the last of which appears to be willing to accede in the short term to independence. Others, like Northern Cyprus and Somaliland, have already achieved a high degree of autonomy, against the wishes of the Nicosia and Mogadishu governments.

The other post-Soviet pseudo-states of Abkhazia, South Ossetia – which are both Russian-controlled but legally part of Georgia – and Nagorno-Karabakh – legally Azerbaijani but partly controlled by Armenia – have some similarities with Transnistria. Abkhazia and South Ossetia are recognised by Russia, but neither Russia nor the international community have taken further steps that might lead to a *de jure* independence for them.

Relatively few territories gain independence, suggesting that despite the dilution of Westphalian sovereignty and limited respect for territorial integrity and the primary right arguments explored in the previous sections, the *status quo* ultimately tends to prevail in international law. The last country to achieve universally recognised independence was South Sudan in 2011 (SubSect.5.4.1).

---

* Russia's membership of the UN security council provides a veto on Kosovan UN membership. Kosovo claims recognition by 117 UN members (Kosovo Thanks You 2020), though the World Population Review (2020) puts it at just 97.

5.3.1 KOSOVO

The comparator of most importance to Transnistria is Kosovo, which proclaimed its independence in February 2008. This was declared illegal by Serbia and Russia and has still not been fully resolved, though Kosovo's clearly has *de facto* independence. The International Court of Justice was requested by the UN General Assembly to provide an advisory opinion on whether "the unilateral declaration of independence by the Provisional Institutions of Self-Government of Kosovo is in accordance with international law". In its 2010 opinion, the court concluded it did not violate international law. This was in the specific context of 1999 UN Resolution 1244, which provided a temporary legal regime in Serbia. While no such UN resolution exists in respect of Transnistria, an argument that the Transnistrian case for independence in international law is thus weaker is circular. The resolution itself was inconsistent with Serbian sovereignty, placing, as Enrico Milano put it, "Kosovo, a province within the Federal Republic of Yugoslavia, under joint administration of the UN and NATO" (2003:1000). The UN had taken upon itself the mantle of dismantling states. The humanitarian case was overwhelming, in a way that the Transnistrians could never claim parallels theirs. The precedent, however, had been set and it is only a matter of degree that distinguishes between the Kosovan and Transnistrian peoples' entitlements to a resolution of that sort. Were it to become expedient for Russia or the EU to support Transnistrian independence, those powers would point to the similarities rather than the differences between the two situations.

Whether there is still a frozen conflict between Serbia and Kosovo is debatable. Sanja Kljajic argues (2018) that it is only the EU membership that both countries aspire to that is restraining war. Serbian President Aleksandar Vucic in an interview with *Foreign Policy* (Mackinnon and Gramer 2020) said he did not favour a state of frozen conflict with Kosovo though thought most Serbians did. Regardless of the label, there are some similarities with the Transnistrian *de facto* situation. Belgrade has no more influence over Kosovo than Chisinau has over Transnistria. There are marked patrolled borders, state mechanisms and a separate currency: Kosovo has, without European Central Bank agreement, unilaterally adopted the euro.

Transnistria indeed relies on Kosovo as a precedent. In 2007, then President Igor Smirnov, claimed that "historically Transnistria has a better claim to independence than Kosovo" (Bowring 2014:1). Cornet (2016:55), though, argues this is not something Transnistrians could rely on, proclaiming, questionably, that Kosovars are a more distinctive people than Transnistrians and, obviously correctly, the atrocities committed against them by Serbia in the Balkan Wars were far worse than any Transnistrians have faced. Kosovo's own proclamation of independence explicitly stated that it was "a special case and not a precedent for any other situation". International political expression of the uniqueness of Kosovo's position came from former US Secretary of State Condoleezza Rice:

The unusual combination of factors found in the Kosovo situation – including the context of Yugoslavia's breakup, the history of ethnic cleansing and crimes against civilians in Kosovo and the extended period of UN administration – are not found elsewhere and therefore make Kosovo a special case. Kosovo cannot be seen as a precedent for any other situation in the world today. (cited by Fabry 2012:666).

Before there was widespread recognition of Kosovo, President Putin argued that once self-determination of a nation was taken to be more important than territorial integrity, the principle would have to be followed "all around the world" (Moldova. org 2007a). Putin had regard to the situations "in Georgia, Moldova and Azerbaijan" when he spoke. It may indeed be, as Fabry (2012:661) argues, that US recognition of Kosovo precipitated Russian recognition of Abkhazia and South Georgia six months later. The assertion that it would not be cited as a precedent was said by Ted Gallen Carpenter (2007), writing less than a week after the proclamation, to be "extraordinarily naïve".

The Kosovan situation has not however, as Rice maintained, provided a meaningful precedent for any other independence-seeking nation, and even Russian recognition has proved of little advantage to those territories. Rice's assertion and indeed reliance on the UN resolution (1999) reflect international law as it was created to deal with the Serbian problem, rather than follow the established principles discussed in SubSect.5.1.2. Smirnov's argument (Bowring 2014:1) has not been tested, and has not been subject even to much academic consideration. The distinctions between the two situations are matters of degree not fundamental principle. Were international opinion to move towards Transnistrian independence, the example of Kosovo would take on considerable importance in justifying it by recognising it even in the face of Moldovan opposition.

5.3.2 OTHER UNRECOGNISED TERRITORIES

This section focuses on the other unrecognised territories whose situations have most in common with Transnistria's. While the existence of such precedents may appear an obstacle to Transnistrian aspirations, there are distinguishing factors with these situations, particularly the most commented upon: the Turkish Republic of Northern Cyprus (TRNC).

Northern Cyprus

The TRNC has enjoyed a *de facto* independence from its Greek southern counterpart since the war of 1974, considerably longer than Transnistria's, also commonly being labelled a frozen conflict (Severin 2013). Inevitably, commentators have drawn parallels between the two situations.

Unlike the Moldovan divide, it has an ethnic and religious component. Reunification there would be attractive to most EU members and geographically convenient, and the possibility attracts more world political and media attention than that of Transnistria and the other pseudo-states. A modern unified Cypriot government is likely to be far removed from the oppressively *enosis**-leaning Makarios regime that perhaps provoked the 1974 Turkish invasion. In Cyprus, the resistance to reunification actually comes from the Greek state, the north having voted in April 2004 in favour of it, an effective reversal of the Transnistrian situation (Kosienkowski 2011:26).**

Daria Isachenko (2013) compared Transnistria with Cyprus in 2013, concluding each is more than a puppet of Russia and Turkey respectively, instead being active participants in international politics. Bahar Çamözü (2016:8) argues, plausibly, that Turkey's willingness to allow reunification there in a way Russia would not with Moldova creates a fundamental difference between the Cyprus and Transnistrian situations. This and the TRNC's own willingness to reunify may mean the dynamics are separate to an extent that the longevity of the Cypriot division is not as ominous a precedent for Transnistria as might at first be thought.

Somaliland

Less frequently compared with Transnistria, but significant in that it is a *de facto* independent state that has attracted some support for full independence, is Somaliland, as articulated by Bridget Coggins (2014). Although *de jure* still a part of Somalia, the territory is in practice independent and in many ways similar to Transnistria. It has its own currency, borders and democratic state institutions (Mahmood 2019). After the collapse of military dictator Siad Barre's Mogadishu government in 1991, it proclaimed its unrecognised independence. The position of the UN and the African Union is that once Somalia is peaceful and has a fully functioning government, the two territories should be reunited (Voice of America 2019). Academics, such as Coggins (2014), have argued for full independence, and there seems little reason why it should not be granted.

Coggins puts her position in context:

> Unfortunately, crisis and disorder draw the world's attention and resources. Somaliland is certainly not perfectly governed, few places are, but its relative stability and legitimate internal authority make it easy for those outside to ignore. (cited by Ismail 2017)

What she says could equally be applied to Transnistria. More dramatically, Peter Pham (2016), an academic and diplomat who was to become the US envoy for the Sahel region in the last months of the Trump presidency, points to why Somaliland should not be forced to join with Somalia:

---

*   The union of Cyprus and Greece.
**   The current president Ersin Tatar, elected in October 2000, does in fact support a two-state solution, effectively of independence for Northern Cyprus.

A reconstituted Somalia would require reconnecting Somaliland with what may be the world's most spectacularly failed state. Where Somaliland has a fledgling coast guard, Somalia has flourishing pirates, and where Hargeisa has a form of democracy, Mogadishu has howling anarchy punctuated by fits of sharia law. Yet this is the alternative urged by nearly everyone.

While Pham's argument cannot be applied directly to Transnistria as Somalian government has broken down in a way Moldova's has not, that someone was entrusted with high office by the US government after expressing such views shows that the US, and perhaps other world powers, will move towards support for valid independence claims.

The other pseudo-states

Also relevant to the Transnistrian situation are the other pseudo-states, particularly Abkhazia and South Ossetia, which have come into existence since the break-up of the USSR. Both are *de facto* independent, Russian-speaking and Russian-supporting but legally part of Georgia. Many commentators treat them as having at least overlapping issues, if not constituting a common problem (e.g. Kunze and Bohnet 2007; Fischer *et al.* 2016). Nagorno-Karabakh is legally part of Azerbaijan but maintains a notional independence with Armenian support. After a war in late 2020, much of the territory was reintegrated in Azerbaijan.

Economically, Abkhazia has more in common with Transnistria, having a population of around 244,000 people (President of Abkhazia 2017) and a relatively successful agricultural economy including citrus fruit, tobacco, tea and timber. There are coal mines and a hydro-electric plant. The last GDP figures that are available are for 2016 (President of Abkhazia 2017), which give it a per-capita figure of 124,180 Russian roubles (US$1,947).

South Ossetia is far poorer. Its population is well under 100,000 (Andersen and Partskhaladze n.d.). There are no reliable recent GDP estimates, but there is nothing to suggest that the 2002 figure of US$250 per capita has grown significantly in real terms (Crisis Group 2004). Its total economic dependence on Russia, limited agriculture, depleted industry and lack of tourist potential mean that absent foreign aid of some form, its population would literally not be able to survive.

There is a degree of ambivalence in the relationship each of them has with Russia, just as there is in Transnistria. South Ossetia has moved towards closer links with Russia, offering to surrender attributes of *de facto* statehood, such as the army, police, courts and all border controls (Lomsadze 2014). However, Russia exerts similarly limited political control in South Ossetia as it does in Transnistria. Leonid Tibilov, president from 2012 to 2017, was particularly identified by Western commentators as acting independently despite the territory's dependence on Russia for finance and security (Dzutsev 2014). In October 2015, Tibilov announced a referendum on unification with Russia. When the referendum occurred in April 2017, the question was restricted to the less heated one of whether the territory should change its name to "The Republic of South Ossetia-Alania", which was approved by 79.5% (Shevelev 2017). It is unclear if this was done at the behest of the Kremlin or whether Russia would accept unification (Beard 2015).

The Russian position in relation to the 1992 Abkhazian war of independence, which claimed between 15,000 and 20,000 lives with over 200,000 ethnic Georgians permanently driven from Abkhazia (Crisis Group 2007), was far from clear (Danilov 1999:48). It was generally thought to support the Abkhazis but armed both sides and was involved in the negotiations that ended the war. In December 1993, a ceasefire was agreed between Georgian and Abkhazi leaders. In response to Abkhazia's proclamation of independence in November 1994, Russian imposed an economic blockade, lifted in 1997, while at the same time continuing to provide aid. Russia has moved closer to Abkhazia since taking control of its border with Georgia in 2009. In 2014, Russia formed a 'strategic partnership' with Abkhazia, which the Tbilisi government denounced as an annexation (BBC 2015a).

Relations between these two territories and Russia are fundamentally different to those the superpower has with Transnistria in several ways. Both of them border Russia and could easily be absorbed into it. Both use Russian currency. Russia formally recognised both in 2008 (Carnegie Europe 2018), which was described by Sabine Fischer *et al.*, along with the annexation of Crimea, as "the most extreme form of Russian revisionism to date" (2016:12). Moscow's relationship with Tbilisi is more hostile than that Transnistria has with Chisinau, largely as a consequence of the support it has given those territories. Superficially, these factors may make Abkhazia* and South Ossetia more plausible candidates for a formal break with Georgia than Transnistria is with Moldova, but South Ossetia's case for independence if not absorption into Russia would flounder on its economic weakness. Abkhazia's current position is closer to Transnistria. Were the two territories to make common cause more vociferously, their respective claims might attach more international attention. The supine** Community for Democracy and Rights of Nations which the pseudo-states have formed (SubSect.5.2.4) could be and might yet become an effective advocate for their separation.

5.3.3 GAGAUZIA

Gagauzia, Moldova's other autonomous territory, comprises 1,832 square kilometres split into four non-contiguous areas*** in southern Moldova. The Gagauz people are ethnically Turkish, and the official Gagauz language is a Turkish dialect. However, that language is little used, particularly in schools, almost all of which teach in Russian

---

*   For Abkhazia's own arguments as to why its case is better than Kosovo's see Abkhaz World (2011).

**   It did not even pronounce on the war in Nagorno-Karabakh in November 2020.

***   The discontiguousness is a consequence of the territory being able to vote area by area in the 1994 referendum on autonomy and some parts which might have made a natural geographical fit with Comrat choosing to remain governed by Chisinau; see Schlegel (2018:9).

(Spinner 2003). The Ankara government provides some support to the region (Schlegel 2018:9). The inhabitants of Gagauzia are vehemently pro-Russian, with 98% voting in a February 2014 referendum against Moldova moving to closer ties with the EU and in favour of such ties with the CIS states (Rinna 2014).

It declared itself independent on 19 August 1991, some months before Transnistria. The Moldovan government took little notice: there was no history of a separate Gagauz land, and the Gagauzia People's Movement had been founded as late as 1988 (Bonnett 2017:244). In December 1994, Gagauzia was granted autonomous status within Moldova, with indications that independence would follow if Moldova united with Romania (Calus 2014a). Its legal status vis-a-vis Chisinau is more clearly formalised than Transnistria's.

In legal theory, much autonomy is granted to Gagauzia, though unlike Transnistria it has no border controls, uses Moldovan currency, and has no meaningful international relations (Gagauzia.md 2015); it is credibly regarded by Siegfried Wöber (2013:3) as having only "a symbolic autonomy". Around 50% of the area's income in fact comes from grants from Chisinau, with further support from Russia and Turkey (Calus 2014a). Unlike Transnistria, it is not economically viable without Moldovan support.

Gagauzia's size, discontiguousness and economy make independence inconceivable. It is sometimes cited as part of a possible joint federalisation solution along with Transnistria (e.g. Dascalu 2009; Necsutu 2019b; and see Sect.5.1). That is a distraction from the more plausible Transnistrian cause. Wöber (2013) points out that a greater autonomy for Transnistria could lead to similar demands from Gagauzia. While that may be true and a fear of those demands could be an obstacle to Transnistrian independence, it does not follow that the demands would be given any weight by Chisinau. So long as Gagauzia is economically dependent on Chisinau, any such demands can be shrugged off. The non-Russian ethnicity of the territory's inhabitants means that country does not have a role or interest there similar to that in Transnistria. Ultimately, Gagauzia would have no way of avoiding following whatever course the Moldovan government determined, including EU membership and union with Romania – a stark contrast with the effective stance against those that Transnistria (with Russia's support) could and would take. Gagauzia does not represent a meaningful obstacle to Transnistrian statehood.

5.4 HOW A TRANSNISTRIAN STATE COULD BE CREATED

Should Transnistria overcome the current challenges to its statehood, a multifaceted process involving external parties, particularly the UN as well as obviously Chisinau and, in practice, Moscow governments, would have to be gone through to implement that statehood. This section draws from examples of modern independences, particularly those which have resulted from countries dividing, to consider how a Transnistrian independence might legally and practically be implemented.

5.4.1 RECENT DIVISIONS OF COUNTRIES

Many separations are more complex than one between Moldova and Transnistria, where there is already a clearly demarcated *de facto* independence, would be. Some have been catastrophic, like the partition of British India and the subsequent separation of West and East Pakistan, in which at least 300,000 were estimated to have died (Dummett 2011).

Since the break-up of the Soviet Union in late 1991, there have been four significant creations of new nations out of Czechoslovakia, Sudan, Indonesia, where East Timor was created in 1999, and Yugoslavia, and the first two provide particular indications as to how an independent Transnistria could be created. Of these actual break-ups, only the Czechoslovakian experience was wholly peaceful and that provides the most desirable precedent for division of Transnistria, particularly a symmetric one.

The division of Czechoslovakia

The Czech–Slovak split in 1992 – the 'Velvet Divorce' – was, as Transnistria's probably would be, relatively simple. It was agreed to divide assets on a 2:1 ratio in favour of the wealthier and more populous Czechs. This was generally regarded as a successful separation and was cited as a precedent by advocates of Scottish independence in the run up to the 2014 referendum (Williams 2013). The process was helped by Czechoslovakian citizenship having ceased to exist in 1969, when the population became either Czech or Slovak citizens (Embassy of the Czech Republic 2012). In distinction to the position in the other modern breaks-ups, there was no specific successor state and both the Czech Republic and Slovakia had to seek UN membership, unlike Serbia, Sudan, Indonesia and Russia, which all retained it when parts of their territories were shed.

The creation of South Sudan out of Sudan

South Sudan came into being in July 2011 after over 98% of its population voted in a referendum that January for independence from the Khartoum government. Despite very substantial oil reserves, it remains one of the world's poorest countries – lacking stable, and sometimes even meaningful, government – and is wracked by civil war (World Bank 2012). Structurally, though, its separation from Sudan would have much in common with any formal granting of independence to Transnistria, with the Chisinau government, like that in Khartoum, maintaining its primacy despite seceding territory. The south of Sudan had had autonomy since January 2005, when what may have been optimistically described as a Comprehensive Peace Agreement was signed in Nairobi (*Sudan Tribune* 2005). The interim Constitution of South Sudan (2005) was unilaterally drafted by the south and became the governing document for the new country. The 2005 documents effectively governed the split, with little in the way of formalities or even clarification being undertaken in 2011. The autonomy and indeed the existence of the constitution aided at least the legal side of the separation and would similarly bear on any Transnistrian independence.

The multilateral break-ups of Yugoslavia and the USSR

The divisions into multiple countries are less significant as a precedent for what could happen in Transnistria than are bilateral divisions, but they still provide evidence of how even the most complex and heated situations can be successfully managed. Despite the ferocity of the Balkan Wars, a managed process was largely achieved in granting independence to the former Yugoslav republics. In 2001, a Yugoslav Succession Treaty was signed in Vienna by Serbia, which was still termed Yugoslavia, Croatia, Slovenia, Bosnia-Herzegovina and Macedonia.* Financial assets were divided by population and wealth, giving Serbia 36.5% and Macedonia just 5.4% (UN 2001).

The break-up of the USSR was achieved first through the Belavezha Accords on 8 December 1991, which were signed by the leaders of Russia, Belarus and Ukraine, who had until then been meeting relatively informally (BBC 2016a). These were followed on 21 December by the Alma-Ata Protocol (*The New York Times* 1991), in which eleven** of the twelve remaining Soviet republics, the Baltic states having already seceded, agreed to join the Commonwealth of Independent States*** (NTI 2011). This also ratified Russia as the successor state to the USSR, enabling it to retain its UN Security Council seat. Gorbachev resigned as Soviet leader on 25 December 1991, but by then his power had effectively ceased. Russia appropriated most of the assets of the Soviet Union (Nichol 1995:60), including the military forces and equipment (*The New York Times* 1991).

The Chisinau government would doubtless put itself in the position of the Belgrade and Moscow governments and retain nearly all the state assets. While there could be a Transnistrian argument in respect of some assets from Soviet times, the development of separate economies over some thirty years would mean that it would be hard to make a case for releasing any of what is now held by Chisinau to Tiraspol.

5.4.2 INTERNATIONAL LAW ON IMPLEMENTING INDEPENDENCE

The Vienna Convention on Succession of States in respect of Treaties (1996) is the main provision specifying the framework of independence. Much consideration has been given, particularly at the UN, to Kosovo's claim to be independent from Serbia, but the mechanics of that independence, including the unilateral adoption of the euro by Kosovo without European Central Bank approval, have emerged

---

*   Montenegro and Kosovo then remained parts of Serbia.

**   Georgia did not agree at this stage.

***   This theoretically continues to exist as an intergovernmental organisation but has been virtually dormant since around 2007.

outside any established legal framework except for the UN resolution discussed in SubSect.5.3.1.

The Vienna Convention represents an attempt to set out the treaty obligations of newly independent countries. It distinguishes between those new countries: those that do not inherit the treaty rights and obligations of the former state, which will often be a colonial ruler, and others which do. It has limited force, being ratified by just 15 countries and signed by 22, not including any major world powers.* Significantly to the Transnistrian question, Moldova is a party. Although the UK is not a signatory, this treaty was cited in the discussion of the legal nature of Scottish independence if the 2014 referendum had supported it (Murphy 2013). The preponderance of opinion was that Scotland, but not the rest of the UK, would take on the mantle of a newly independent state. Scotland would therefore have had to apply for EU membership, rather than having automatic membership under the UK's accession to the Treaty of Rome. Transnistria would find itself in the position posited for Scotland.

The boundaries of a Transnistrian state

The principle of *uti possidetis juris*,** which provides that newly formed sovereign states should have the same borders as those of the dependent area that they previously comprised, was largely applied in the break-up of the Soviet Union. This principle is enshrined in international law (*Burkina Faso v. Mali* 1986: para 25). In English legal terms, it is a presumption, rebuttable where there is clear evidence or other indications to the contrary, not an absolute rule. The doctrine's applicability depends on the express definition of borders within the previously sovereign state (Shaw 1997). In Transnistrian terms, it may mean that small areas around Bender, which are subject to a separate dispute to the main one about Transnistria's status, could, on any granting of independence, be returned to Chisinau on the grounds they were not part of the Transnistrian autonomous territory under the USSR.

How Moldovan law would implement Transnistrian independence

The Constitution of the Republic of Moldova (2016) refers to Transnistria as the Left-Bank of the Dniestr. It is mentioned only in the constitution in Article 110(2), which provides, "Places on the Left-Bank of the Dniester River*** may be assigned special forms and conditions of autonomy, according to the special statutory provisions adopted by organic law." Much greater detail is given to the status of Gagauzia in the following article.

The Chisinau parliament is given full legislative power (Article 72) and there is provision for referendums (Article 75). There is no reason why a simple act of the parliament could

---

* Egypt is the most significant to have ratified it; Brazil and Pakistan have signed but not ratified.
** Latin for "as you possess under law".
*** Part of Transnistrian territory, particularly most of Bender, is on the Right-Bank. It is not clear if the reference to Left-Bank is a deliberate attempt to assert a different claim over the small area of Transnistrian-controlled Right-Bank.

not, despite the entrenchment of the constitution, alter the country's borders so as to exclude Transnistria from them, at the same time recognising it as an independent state. In that case, international recognition would inevitably follow. It is, of course, possible for a state to achieve such recognition without the consent of the former dominant nation, though that is less likely to lead to an orderly and peaceful transformation. The ongoing Kosovo uncertainty is an illustration of a disorderly transformation, which, in recent years at least, has not had significant adverse humanitarian consequence. The relatively benign nature of the governments of Moldova and Transnistria, as well as the overwhelming external pressures to maintain peace in Europe, makes further armed conflict virtually inconceivable for the moment.

5.4.3 THE LIKELY MANNER OF INDEPENDENCE

In a consensual break between Chisinau and Tiraspol there would be relatively little to negotiate, most of the issues that have clouded other national separations having been *de facto* resolved during the 25 years of effective Transnistrian independence. The borders are fairly clear. While Moldova might assert that only land east of the Dniestr should form part of Transnistria, it is more likely that Bender's hinterland, east of the current *de facto* border, although on the other side of the river, should also be in Transnistria. It is unlikely that Tiraspol would lay claim to any Moldovan assets, such as embassies. The respective economies, in private and public sectors, have so much diverged that there are few areas where there could be any dispute over who would get what. More vexed might be the question of whether Transnistrians could retain Moldovan citizenship. Most Transnistrians, regardless of whether they also have a Russian, Ukrainian or any other passport, exercise their entitlement to a Moldovan one. As soon as Transnistria attained universal recognition, the political imperative to allow citizenship for Transnistrians would disappear and Moldova would have no motive to allow those with no connection to the country to retain its passports and citizenship. A more important issue for many Transnistrians might be losing access to Moldovan healthcare.

While there could be unforeseen and serious difficulties in managing a Transnistrian independence, the probability is that the transition would largely be a smooth one on the lines of the Czechoslovakian example, there being no factors present likely to prevent this. The legal similarities with the Sudanese divide would be a useful precedent, particularly the adoption of a unilaterally drafted constitution just as South Sudan had. Assets have already been divided between Transnistria and Moldova just as they had in practice been between Indonesia and East Timor, albeit in a far less equitable way there. It may be that some assistance could be gleaned from the more complex Yugoslav and USSR divides. The Chisinau government would emerge as the main successor state in the way Serbia and Russia did.

Moldova would retain its UN seat, but there is no reason why Transnistria would not be offered one as soon as statehood was achieved. Many of the external actors discussed in Sect.5.2, particularly Russia and EU, would be actively involved in a negotiation, whether under the OSCE or directly. Sabre-rattling from these superpowers could be an unwelcome distraction, but the practical and legal challenges would almost certainly be overcome with little difficulty, the process being greatly eased by the countries' *de facto* separation.

5.5 HOW STRONG ARE THE BARRIERS TO TRANSNISTRIA FULFILLING ITS POTENTIAL FOR STATEHOOD?

On the premise of Transnistria having developed a national identity, a viable economy, a democratic regime and a functioning society, there is a strong case for statehood. The present situation of *de facto* independence gives the inhabitants self-determination, which is a step below full statehood and often a forerunner to it. International recognition is the key to taking the necessary step up, and attaining this continues to represent the real obstacle to Transnistrian statehood. The situation with Moldova, which remains technically a frozen conflict, calls for a resolution, of which Transnistrian independence would be one.

The Moldovan government remains steadfastly opposed to independence for Transnistria, though the arguments advanced through the Bureau of Reintegration, and otherwise, are not convincing. Moldova's position is supported by the EU and its members as well as the US. The union of Romania and Moldova remains a remote possibility but would make Transnistrian statehood far more plausible. Currently, creating a country which would align with and perhaps even become part of Russia is understandably anathema to powers opposed to Russia, such as the EU and Ukraine, though Germany and Britain have taken slightly more nuanced positions, which still fall well short of supporting outright independence. Russia itself will give no ostensible support to Transnistrian independence, refusing even recognition, despite providing substantial military and economic support.

A conventional analysis of the rights of sovereign nations to have their territorial integrity respected is incompatible with foisting Transnistrian independence on Moldova without its agreement. Respect for such rights is enshrined in international law and the UN Charter, but there are many exceptions to it both by the conduct of other nations and organisations and by the willingness of countries to depart from it when it is expedient to do so. Kosovo remains the most compelling precedent in international law, and the distinctions between it and Transnistria are based as much on expediency as on principle.

While Transnistria would qualify for statehood on virtually any application of primary or plebiscitary right theory, those have gained no traction in international law or politics and in the 'real world' even the principles of remedial right theory, which posits a much more restrictive right to secession based on oppression by the sovereign state, are rarely applied. Marginally more plausible as a form of real-world leverage would be to point to the renunciation of the Molotov-Ribbentrop Pact and the position before it was made.

The fact that a frozen conflict and related *de facto* independence can last even longer than Transnistria's has may not bode well for a short-term determination of the situation. Northern Cyprus has survived in a limbo not dissimilar to Transnistria's since 1974, but the dynamics there, particularly the fact that that territory is willing to accept reintegration, are entirely different. Somaliland has enjoyed an unrecognised independence for as long as Transnistria, also with little sign of resolution. That independent states such as East Timor and South Sudan do sometimes emerge may give some cause for optimism, but their situations are remoter from Transnistria's.

The Russian domination of parts of Ukraine as well as South Ossetia and Abkhazia are instances where conflicts have lasted less time than that of Transnistria but, except in Crimea where there has been actual annexation, there is no obvious route by which the conflict will be ended. More encouraging is the Kosovo precedent: its *de facto* independence is beyond argument, and it enjoys widespread recognition backed by an ICJ decision. That decision was based on a specific UN resolution, and while there are arguments that without such underpinning cannot be convincingly applied to the Transnistrian situation, the reasoning behind the UN resolution could be. Kosovo certainly sets a precedent which has to be taken into account in any consideration of Transnistrian independence.

Should there be a Moldovan willingness to allow Transnistria statehood, then there is likely to be little difficulty under Moldovan or international law in implementing that. While there would be some matters needing negotiation, the long-standing separation of the two territories would make that a relatively simple and uncontroversial task.

In the short term, the barriers to statehood for Transnistria may seem insurmountable, but there are many factors which could give it some hope:

Its satisfaction of the qualifications of Article One of the Montevideo Convention (1933);

An international tendency to disregard sovereignty when expedient to do so;

The fact that national sovereignty is already diluted by many factors;

The arguments of Hans-Adam (2001) that states have limited "life cycles";

The development of primary right theory;

Moldova's flirtation with union with Romania;

The paucity of Moldova's own case to retain Transnistria;

The ambiguities in former Moldovan President Dodon's positions;

Russia's military and soft-power disregard for Ukrainian sovereignty, which suggests it would do likewise for Moldova if the circumstances were right;

A large degree of recognition for Kosovo, whose situation may not be entirely distinguishable;

Russia's recognition of Abkhazia and South Ossetia, which may lead it to similarly recognise Transnistria;

Arguments based on the effect of the revocation of the Molotov-Ribbentrop Pact; and

The possibility of Russian recognition as Russian–Ukrainian relations become more strained.

The examples of South Sudan and East Timor, as well as Kosovo, show that independence can eventually arise from circumstances where initially there appeared to be very many obstacles; therefore, there may be ways in which Transnistria can become an independent state.

CONCLUSION

IS TRANSNISTRIAN STATEHOOD THE SOLUTION TO THE PRESENT SITUATION?

The journey this thesis has taken through various aspects of Transnistria has shown that the territory is ripe for full statehood. It already satisfies the definition of a state given in the Montevideo Convention (1933) (SubSect.5.1.1), which holds that statehood is declaratory and is dependent on meeting the conditions of having population, territory, government and a capacity to enter into relations with other states. While full *de jure* statehood, and indeed statehood itself on the constitutive theory, depends on international recognition, no compelling reason has been found for not granting that.

The desire of the Transnistrian people to not be part of Moldova is clear (Sect.1.3). This is a theme that has emerged from referendums, opinion polls (SubSect.1.3.2) and my own research (SubSect.1.3.1). Whether in the long term Transnistria would gravitate to Russia is not clear, and, I would suggest, unimportant in considering independence, which would enable the Transnistrian people to decide what happens afterwards. Opinion on that question is divided evenly in the territory: it is not known whether Russia would agree to a union and if so on what terms. A Kaliningrad-style exclave would be plausible, and that *oblast* could be a model for Transnistria's role. Equally, a close friendly relationship, like Russia has with Belarus might be the long-term outcome Transnistrians prefer.

That desire to separate from Moldova is a reflection of Transnistria having become a nation and is the subject of Chapter 1. There is a clear lack of a common history with Moldova: only on the Molotov-Ribbentrop Pact in 1939 were they lumped together (SubSect.1.1.1). The argument that on the renunciation of that treaty its consequences should be undone may be questionable in international law (SubSect.5.1.4) but adds weight to the case made by the territory's leadership (e.g. Ignatiev 2018) that there is no historic basis for it being part of Moldova. A separate identity clearly existed by the time the USSR broke up, as shown by around 1,000 Transnistrians dying while fighting for the territory's independence in the 1992 war (SubSect.1.1.2). Since the end of that war and *de facto* independence, the territories have developed separately governmentally, with long periods of no contact between the respective leaderships (SubSect.1.1.3).

From the separate development to Moldova flows a separate identity. There is much debate over whether that makes Transnistrians a 'people', refuted by the New York report (2006) but tentatively accepted by Bowring (2014) (SubSect.1.2.1.). What is clearer and more important is that there is a Transnistrian identity. Even if the argument of Mitrofanova (2015) that that identity amounts to no more than a distinctiveness from Right-Bank Moldovans is correct, that would not deprive the identity of validity. That identity has been taken further by a conscious nation-building project embarked upon by the territory's leadership since *de facto* independence (SubSect.1.2.2). The identity has been created in many, and often seemingly trivial, ways, such as the teaching of history, the designation of public holidays and the emphatic rejection of Latin-lettered Moldovan language (SubSect.3.1.2). The success of this nation-building is recognised and underlined by the empirical research of Dembinska and Iglesias (2013) (SubSect.1.2.3) and is corroborated by my own research (SubSect.1.3.1). While, in contrast, research in Moldova suggests most people there oppose Transnistrian independence (SubSect.1.3.3), that has little bearing on the Transnistrian case. The opinion research I cite can generally be seen to be reliable in that the researchers take steps to ensure the subjects can give answers free from any fear of reprisal (1.3.4). While unlikely to be a major factor in determining Transnistria's future, the clear wishes of the Transnistrian people strengthen its case for independence when the primary right theory (SubSect.5.1.4) is considered (SubSect.3.1.5).

The Transnistrian nation sets a basis for moving to an independent state, and it is seen in Chapters 2–4 that the major facets of statehood, an economy, governance and a society have been created. The existence of a viable economy is demonstrated in Chapter 2. Like practically every country, it is not self-sufficient, but that is not a condition of viability. Its separate development from Moldova since 1992 means that it only has economic dependence on that country for the provision of matters where a recognised government is required, such as customs documentation (SubSect.2.1.1). On independence, it would have these facilities for itself like any other country (SubSect.2.2.5). The Transnistrian government has raised taxes (SubSect.2.2.1) and controlled the economy in a relatively conventional way since *de facto* independence. State assets have been sold off in a manner similar to those in Russia but with less obvious corruption. A central state bank has controlled its currency, which is now permitted to flow freely (SubSect.2.1.2). There are several banks offering facilities to the population; furthermore, the government, in conjunction with the central bank, has brought in proper controls to prevent money laundering (SubSect.2.2.4). Unemployment is low.

While those central aspects of the economy are unremarkable, there are many striking features. The government's flirtation with cryptocurrency mining is fraught with danger, but Abkhazia's disastrous experiences with that may deter Transnistria from going further (SubSect.2.2.3). The omnipresent Sheriff group is a dominant force in that economy (SubSect.2.3.1) and has its own political party which has influence over government (SubSect.2.3.2) and contributed to the downfall of Presidents Smirnov and Shevchuk (SubSect.1.1.3). Its success has helped the territory economically and it is largely perceived positively by the population. It and particularly its football team FC Sheriff, which, unlike Transnistria itself, can compete in international competition, have contributed to the establishment of the national identity (SubSect.2.3.3). Sheriff might benefit from independence but has not been active in calling for it (SubSect.2.3.4).

A significant depopulation since independence (SubSect.2.4.1), largely caused by economic migration (SubSect.2.4.2), may have prevented the economy from reaching its potential. That, though, is a problem it has in common with Moldova and many other countries in the region. Independence could reverse that trend, with many wishing to play an active part in a new country (SubSect.2.4.3).

The economy is supported by remittances from migrant workers (Sect.2.5) but even more so by Russia (Sect.2.6). The gas credits Russia provides are a source of revenue as well as of cheap fuel for the inhabitants (SubSect.2.6.1). So long as Russian support continues, the territory's economy should improve materially on independence (SubSect.2.6.2) when international markets would be more readily open (SubSect.2.2.5). The possibility of entering into trade agreements with other countries and blocs would help it, and the Sheriff group would benefit from the ability to expand internationally (SubSect.2.3.4). The constraints on banks linking with international financial organisations and the non-recognition of the currency are both factors that have impeded Transnistrian trade and which independence would quickly see reversed.

There is nothing in Transnistria's economic situation that can be regarded as a barrier to independence. Viability would not stand in the way of Transnistrian independence, but it can plausibly be argued that the economy, unfettered by Chisinau, has already contributed to the building of the Transnistrian nation. Looking to the future, should it become an independent nation, the ability to join and be supported by international organisations will improve its economic position and increase that viability further (Sect.2.7).

The most compelling justification for denying Transnistria independence may be aspects of its human rights record. Chapter 3 considers this, including the bearing it may have on the independence claim (SubSect.3.5.1). There is a constitution expressing commendable ideals (SubSect.3.1.1), supplemented by other well-expressed laws (SubSect.3.1.2). The evidence of it being a genuine electoral democracy is overwhelming (SubSect.3.2.1). Even during the Smirnov years and his four electoral victories (Subsect.3.2.2), there were fairly conducted, if predictable, elections. The obvious fairness of the 2016 presidential election (SubSect.3.2.3), which I witnessed, and the approval by openDemocracy, normally hostile to Transnistria, of the 2015 Soviet election makes that clear and is supported by two successive presidents being voted out and leaving office peacefully. The rule of law is established, with a Supreme Court having the power to overturn government decisions, exercised rarely, but not more so than proportionately in, for example, England (SubSect.3.3.1). An interesting case was made out for Transnistria to submit to a supranational court before independence, but it is impossible to see how this could work in practice (SubSect.3.3.2). Religion is now officially tolerated (SubSect.3.7.2) – a contrast with how it was treated in the Soviet Union (SubSect.3.7.1) – and with a few largely historic instances of unwarranted actions against Jehovah's Witnesses, there is little to criticise there (SubSect.3.7.3).

The bigger concerns are the level of imprisonment (Sect.3.4), the mistreatment of those who oppose the government (Sect.3.5) and the restrictions on the media (Sect.3.6), particularly the continued detention of Oleg Horjan, an opposition politician, on a sentence vastly disproportionate to any crime alleged against him (SubSect.3.5.1). Unfortunately, the release of Alexandru Coliban in 2013, credibly then described as the last political prisoner in Transnistria, has not been the end of such detentions. Plausible if uncorroborated reports suggest an elderly couple have been imprisoned for blog posts critical of the government. A young woman felt the need to flee the territory after publishing a book alleging mistreatment of conscripts; another came under pressure from the state security services not to put on an exhibition about homosexuality in Transnistria (SubSect.3.6.4). The territory's leading human rights lawyer claims, convincingly, to have been harassed by the authorities. Lawyers in Moldova who would be effective advocates for causes opposed to the government are not admitted to the territory, and foreign NGOs are allowed no role in legal processes (SubSect.3.3.3). The rate of imprisonment, the vast majority not for political crimes, is the highest in Europe, with no apparent reason as the territory is relatively free of both serious and petty crime. The government has been involved in closing down at least one opposition website. Transnistrian media on the basis of an informal but helpful classification system (SubSect.3.6.1) can on an assessment of relatively minor, at least in recent years, state interference (SubSect.3.6.3) be fairly classed as imperfectly free (SubSect.3.6.6).

The matters listed in the previous paragraph are not attractive, but it should be remembered that it is virtually an exhaustive list of the government's current failings in that area. Cases such as those of Vardanean (SubSect.3.6.3) and Mozer (SubSect.3.5.2), both inappropriately treated but released prematurely by then President Smirnov, are little evidence of the present situation. Conversely, the minister of internal affairs, probably the third highest-ranking in the government, was prepared to spend two hours on the streets arguing heatedly but unthreateningly with people protesting against COVID-related restrictions he had introduced in an impressive display of informal participatory democracy (SubSect.3.6.5).

While the questions posited at the end of Chapters 1, 2 and 4 can all be answered positively with a little equivocation, there are far more reservations about whether Transnistria is a free, democratic nation subject to the rule of law (Sect.3.8). The concerns discussed above are ones that need to be addressed by the Transnistrian leadership. That leadership should, however, be given credit for allowing and preserving freedom at a level unthinkable in Soviet times. International isolation may have made it harder for the leadership to appreciate what is generally considered unacceptable in modern Europe. The failings identified, particularly those in the justice system, are no worse than in some other countries in Eastern Europe (SubSect.3.3.4.). With that comparison in mind, these failings cannot credibly be said to be an obstacle to Transnistrian independence.

The final aspect of Transnistria that is evaluated, in Chapter 4, is its success as a society. In most areas it has been successful. It educates its population to around the same extent as the UK does (SubSect.4.1.1). Its greatest failure in education has been in obstructing teaching in Latin-script Moldovan (SubSect.4.1.2). Although the schools which so teach have been tolerated since around 2005, opposition to this language still seems to be a plank of Transnistrian nation-building: laws requiring the use of languages other than Russian are often disregarded (SubSect.1.2.2) and the main university in Tiraspol does not allow it (SubSect.4.1.1). Healthcare, particularly in rural areas, is still limited and may be supplemented by access to the Moldovan system (Sect.4.2).

Social security and pensions are, with Russian assistance (SubSect.2.6.2), just about adequate (SubSect.4.3.1). There is legislation to guarantee a minimum wage (SubSect.4.3.2) and little unemployment (SubSect.2.1.2). As a result, there is no extreme poverty in Transnistria, despite it being a poor country by European standards. A system of low-quality and ugly-but-functional, low-rent mass housing inherited from the Soviet Union is another manifestation of the Transnistrian people being adequately provided for (Sect.4.4).

Transnistria's lurid reputation as a hotbed of human trafficking, weapons smuggling, money laundering and other serious crime (e.g. Buttin 2017; Wolff 2012) means the policing of the territory is a particular concern. However, it was clear from my own observations that policing was carried out in a relatively innocuous and efficient manner (SubSect.4.5.1). It is not possible to say that there are no instances of corruption or oppression, but there is nothing to suggest that those are any more prevalent than elsewhere in the region. Similarly, evidence of any serious crime with international effects emanating from Transnistria is very weak (SubSect.4.5.2). As long ago as 2005, OSCE and EU investigations failed to find a single instance of human trafficking, and no tangible evidence has emerged of it since. Transnistria can fairly be described as a peaceful society, although one which still has some problems, including some low-level official corruption (SubSect.1.3.1) and a tendency towards excessive imprisonment (Sect.3.4).

Quality of life is also enhanced by extensive environmental protection laws, which the Transnistrian government was one of the first in the world to introduce (SubSect.4.6.1), and the provision of at least adequate public transport systems and roads (SubSect.4.6.2), though a failing of the government is to address a needlessly high traffic accident death rate. There is acceptably wide-ranging and accessible media (SubSect.3.6.2).

While there are some concerns identified in the discussion above, they do not result in any less of a functioning society than is present in many countries that have full independence. In most particulars, the Transnistrian government has succeeded in producing a successful society that supports its claim to independence (Sect.4.7).

Looking back at the consideration of Transnistrian matters enables one to identify many areas where the government could effect improvements. In perhaps descending order of importance, these are:

Release Horjan and any other political prisoners (SubSect.3.5.2);

Reduce prison numbers both by releasing existing prisoners and ensuring fewer are incarcerated in future (Sect.3.4);

Allow critical organisations such as Promo-LEX access to the territory and its courts (SubSect.3.3.3);

Curtail the state security service's powers in relation to publications and websites critical of the government (SubSect.3.6.2);

Encourage, and certainly do not deter, foreign NGOs and charities from working in the territory (SubSect.3.3.3);

Cease trying to exercise control over internet sites, public exhibitions or any other form of media (SubSect.3.6.4);

Remove the requirement for religious groups to register with state authorities (SubSect.3.7.2);

End any official flirtation with cryptocurrencies, with all the damage they could cause to Transnistria's reputation (Sect.2.2);

Ensure citizens' rights are protected by a robust, independent 'watchdog' not drawn from the territory's elite and perhaps not from the territory at all (SubSect.3.3.3);

Allow use of the Latin alphabet without any inhibition in schools, universities and elsewhere (SubSect.4.1.2);

Raise the retirement and state pension ages to those that usually apply in Western Europe (SubSect.4.3.1);

Put in place robust systems to detect and punish police and other public officials, particularly it seems driving examiners, who demand or accept bribes (SubSects1.3.1 and .4.5.1);

Investigate ways of discouraging emigration by young people and encouraging existing emigrants to return (SubSect.2.4.2);

Allow at least a small number of refugees, particularly skilled ones, into the territory with a view to addressing the age and gender balance (SubSect.2.4.2);

Better enforce road traffic laws, particularly in relation to seatbelts, which would save many lives (SubSect.4.6.2);

Ensure the courts are, bar exceptional circumstances, unquestioningly open to the public (SubSect.3.3.3).

Statehood cannot be awarded just as a reward for good governance, but such reforms would strengthen the case still further and weaken the hand of those opposed to independence, underlining that the objections flow from no more than political expediency, as discussed in Chapter 5.

Taking what has been seen in relation to the economy, freedoms and the creation of a society, the case can be made that the Transnistrian nation would function well as an independent state. That case for independence can be made in international law, citing the revocation of the Molotov-Ribbentrop Pact (SubSect.5.1.4) and the precedent of Kosovo, where the US and most EU countries in 2008 backed its claim for independence from Serbia in circumstances with many similarities to Transnistria's (SubSect.5.3.1). A credible body of academic thought argues that independence should be given to a people who want it (SubSect.5.1.4). Established concepts of Westphalian sovereignty weigh heavily against the pushing for Transnistrian independence in the face of Chisinau's opposition, even though that opposition is not expressed in convincing terms (SubSect.5.1.2). However, the hypocritical way in which respect for sovereignty can be disregarded when expedient has been laid bare by Krasner (1999) and Acharya (2007). Even the Prince of Lichtenstein has argued that the "attempt to freeze human evolution" (Gussen 2019:271) by preserving borders is futile and has brought about more violence than controlled changes would (SubSect.5.2.2).

It is expediency, not international law, that is frustrating Transnistrian national aspirations (SubSect.5.2.5). Its independence is not currently in the interests of Russia, which can use its presence in Transnistria that the present situation allows to assert a degree of control over the Chisinau government (SubSect.5.2.2). Nor is independence favoured by the EU, which provides support for the Moldovan position (SubSect.5.2.4). Those other countries that have taken an active interest, including Germany, the US and the UK, have largely supported the EU position, despite Germany entering the Meseburg Memorandum, which would have led to a slightly different approach (SubSect.5.2.3).

The Kosovo precedent (SubSect.5.3.1) is the situation most relevant to Transnistria's. Brief comparison was made with other territories whose situation has some similarity (SubSect.5.3.2), including Cyprus's, ominously frozen for 18 years longer than Transnistria's; Somaliland, which has some academic support for independence; and Abkhazia and South Ossetia, which have, unlike Transnistria, achieved formal Russian recognition. While the status of Gagauzia, Moldova's other autonomous territory, may superficially complicate Transnistria's claims, on close examination that territory's autonomy is weak and independence would not be viable economically or otherwise; it therefore has no bearing on whether Transnistria should be granted independence (SubSect.5.3.3).

Were there to be an agreement that Transnistria should be independent, then the mechanics of implementing it would present a few relatively minor challenges (SubSect.5.4.3). There are many recent precedents for this being done successfully (SubSect.5.4.1), and international and Moldovan law would allow for its implementation following Transnistria's present borders (SubSect.5.4.2).

While there may be no independence or other resolution of the situation in the short term, the longer and the more Transnistria thrives as a *de facto* independent nation, the more compelling the case for independence will seem to the international community, including the Chisinau and Moscow governments. Ultimately, that may cause the pendulum to swing from protecting the vested interests now opposed to it to allowing the Transnistrian people the status to which they aspire.

APPENDICES

APPENDIX A: ELECTION OBSERVING (DECEMBER 2016)

My overwhelming impression of the 2016 presidential election was that it was conducted with the utmost meticulousness. With various parts of the Transnistrian establishment, broadly aligned to the two main candidates, a crude but petty conflict arose between them, into which international observers were involuntarily drawn.

That Transnistria is a proverbial prisoner of its geography was illustrated by the difficulties, perhaps perceived more than actual, observers might have in getting to the territory. My invitation exhorted to me to fly to Odessa, over two hours from Tiraspol and with no direct flights from London, rather than Chisinau whose airport is served by Wizzair and Air Moldova and is about an hour away. This stemmed from a fear that the Moldovan authorities would try to exclude anyone associated with the election. I was a little sceptical of this concern, a view reinforced when I got through immigration and customs at Chisinau's small and surprisingly efficient airport in three minutes with no questions. The Transnistrian concern was such that we were not driven through the main border point at Bender but took a circuitous route through Dubasari, made all the more circuitous by our official driver getting thoroughly lost. The caution may have been justified as we were told next day that two members of a Serbian delegation had been picked up by the Moldovans and deported. The other geographical hurdle was the ban on flights between Ukraine and Russia, making it difficult for Russians to get to Odessa as well, funnelling most Russian observers to Chisinau too. It may have been the Serbians were softer targets for the Moldovans if they wished to make a point by deportations than Western European or Russian observers.

My invitation came from the Ministry of Foreign Affairs (MFA) which was under the control of President Shevchuk. This claimed to have asked around 40 foreign observers. Other international observers were asked by the Central Election Commission (CEC) mostly appointed by the Soviet and favouring its Speaker, Krasnoselsky. This had asked around fifteen observers of its own, and was seemingly resentful of the MFA involvement of what it felt was its province.

This tension manifested itself in a petty battle over the registration of delegates invited by the MFA. Passport details that had been emailed through in advance were 'lost' and had to be reprinted by our escort, Anastasia. The reception when we were taken to the CEC was by far the least friendly we had in Transnistria. After being kept in a draughty hallway for fifteen minutes, we were told that the Chief Commissioner, who had to sign the accreditation card, was too busy for the next hour and a half as there was a press conference. Eventually Anastasia was able to get the cards while we ate dinner.

We were then informed the MFA would like us to travel through the north of the territory the next day, visiting polling stations and preferably attend a count in Camenca in the far north. It seemed to me that this was completely at odds with the promised freedom to go where we wanted. Anastasia said this was because the MFA believed that any dubious practices would be conducted away from Tiraspol where Krasnoselsky's supporters held the greatest sway. A highly experienced German observer, slightly to my surprise, said he was prepared to accept that request, as he believed it reflected the realities of the situation. I stuck my ground, taking the line that although my invitation was from the MFA, I had to retain complete independence from either side. The matter was resolved amicably with the German, who along with Anastasia had been going to accompany me, retaining her and the driver already allocated to me, and another young civil servant, Demitry, and driver pressed into service for me.

About 10pm the night before the poll a court case began to determine whether or not police should be positioned near the polling stations to check identities, as the MFA believed was necessary to stop voter fraud. The CEC had rejected this idea because that presence would be intimidating to many voters. The court comprised three female judges from the Tiraspol city court. The Minister of Foreign Affairs was in attendance at the court, along with his deputy who was to argue what was in effect Shevchuk's case. The CEC case was presented by a senior commissioner, lawyers surprisingly having no role in this process. The hearing was thorough, perhaps tedious, in the extreme, the judges analysing scrupulously each argument put before them. A junior Minister was excluded from the proceedings for continually talking loudly- a splendid example of judicial independence. By 430am the judges retired to make their decision, ruling against the MFA at around 6am. An immediate attempt to appeal to the Supreme Court was unsuccessful.

Our election day started with several visits to polling stations in Tiraspol along with other observers as we were taken around stations for our guide and drivers to vote. Most were in schools. All had loud music playing, which Demitry explained was a throwback to Soviet times when election day was regarded as something of a celebration rather than a serious attempt to choose between credible contestants. There seemed a high proportion of old people, particularly *babushkas*, among the voters. A substantial majority of the polling station staff were women. Cheap and generally unappetising food was on sale. The ballot boxes were made of a clear plastic.

There was complete freedom to visit wherever I wanted. In the second city, Ribnita, it was most practical to follow my plan of random selection at very short notice. I asked to stop at a village called Jura, near the road between Tiraspol and Ribnita. At most of these polling stations we were greeted politely but unenthusiastically by the registration officer, who would make a note of my name from the official badge.

At Jura, where seemingly no other foreign observer called- getting there involved some skilful navigation by my driver over a farm track- there was a little more enthusiasm, and a group of cheerful middle-aged women polling clerks, asked lots of predictable, but friendly questions about what I was doing. There Moldovan was being spoken and (with Cyrillic letters) used for many of the written notices, both about the election and those that were there anyway for the school, though the ladies happily and fluently talked to me, through my interpreter, in Russian.

The Jura school was a station for voters from Moldova, who could vote on production of a Transnistrian identity document even if they had not previously been registered. Only about 30 out of 200 or so eligible voters had appeared, significantly lower than the remaining turn-out. It seemed there was a theoretical risk that that could allow ineligible people to vote, and unregistered voters' ballots were put in a separate box in case any challenge was made.

At the polls there were local observers: each candidate was allowed two in every station. Shevchuk and Krasnoselsky managed to find enough supporters to fill that quota in nearly all we visited: the other candidates usually managing only one, if any. The observers had to register and wore discreet badges showing which candidate they represented. All those I saw behaved impeccably. I asked a few questions of observers as to why they were supporting a particular candidate. Answers were invariably bland: "I want him [Shevchuk] to serve a second term and do his work"; "I like this person [Krasnoselsky] more; I trust him more; and occasionally, despite the best efforts of my interpreter, incomprehensible: "Krasnoselsky's programme is much earlier than Shevchuk's'". My few attempts to ask about policy differences between Shevchuk and Krasnoselsky drew blank responses, which Dimity said were probably a consequence of a fear of discussing politics in the polling station, which was prohibited.

It seemed to me the presence of the local, as much as the international, observers provided a very meaningful safeguard against any form of cheating by a candidate. Interestingly, the German observer said he regarded them as possibly intimidatory, no visible party presence being allowed near polling booths in Germany. I could take a less critical view of this as British practice, of course, allows party tellers to wait outside polling stations asking voters to identify themselves so they can be crossed off the list for canvassing purposes. While allowing them inside the polling station might give a theoretical risk of intimidation I did not see the slightest evidence of that happening.

There was an express prohibition in place on the photographing of ballot papers, with signs in the curtained-off voting booth in every polling stations making this clear. These signs were not uniform, some simply consisting of a camera with a red cross through it, and others having variously worded prohibitions. This was to preserve the complete secrecy of the ballot as there was a fear, whether founded or not, that employers, particularly the Sheriff Group might otherwise require its staff to produce a picture of a 'correctly' completed ballot paper.

There was a requirement that a notice be displayed in each polling-station showing the turnout at various times of the day. I was a little perturbed that each of the four stations I visited after 5pm a figure amounting to just between 50 and 52% of that station's registered voters had in fact voted. In one the notice was not on display but was quickly produced when this was pointed out.

There had been a press conference at midday in Tiraspol chaired by the head of the CEC. There a Russian deputy sent to observe had made public criticisms of technical aspects of the election, including that TV reporters had been illegally asking people who they voted for, to the visible annoyance of the head of the electoral commission.

The 'count' which began at 8pm with a strict lock-in at the cultural-centre in Tiraspol was conducted officiously by a middle-aged woman, who, despite her twelve helpers, insisted on doing nearly everything herself. Numerous forms needed to be filled in; unused ballot papers had to be accounted for; an explanation had to be given why each unregistered voter had been permitted to cast a vote. The upshot was that the ballot boxes were not opened until after 1am. Then the total number of votes needed to be counted and recounted. It was 1-45am before the votes for each candidate started to be counted. This was being done under the watchful eyes of local observers including a deputy minister, none of whom, except perhaps that minister, seemed to share our boredom with the process. I am afraid at this time I decided I could give the fairness, if not the efficiency, of the election a clean bill of health, and I asked my interpreter to feign illness, a tactic adopted by another international observer a couple of hours before, to get us released.

It turned out that we had drawn the short straw with counts, others we were told when comparing notes with observers the next morning had finished by around 11pm. One felt that the input of the electoral registration officer from Sunderland South, who typically manages to ensure the counting of 70,000 votes in under an hour, would have met a greater need of the Transnistrians than sharp-eyed foreign observers looking forlornly for sharp practices.

The results had still not been announced when I left for Chisinau airport the next morning again with an official guide and driver. This time it was decided no risk was being taken by going the most direct route, though Anastasia asked me to send her a message once I had got through immigration, which I did again with no hold up at all.

Only once I arrived in London did I receive a message from her telling me that Krasnoselsky had triumphed with 62% of the vote against Shevchuk's 27%. The results echoed those in an exit poll, published only in Russia, my interpreter had found the previous evening. The turnout had been a little over 59%. Despite the margin of victory, and its perhaps predictability, those who had been involved in the election had shown a real dedication to the process, with far less 'corner cutting' than one might see in a more established democracy.

12: The CEC press conference

APPENDIX B: PRESIDENT SMIRNOV (30 MAY 2019)

Meeting former President Igor Smirnov proved quite easy, secured by a simple request to the ever-helpful former foreign minister Vladimir Yastrebchak, who asked me to meet him the next morning outside the office still provided to Smirnov by the government, next to the Ministry of Health. Smirnov's arrival a few minutes later was striking, a casually dressed, muscular man with prominent facial hair jumped out of the passenger door of a large, but far from new, sports utility vehicle. Both my interpreter and I at first assumed he was part of the security detail, something of a compliment to a man pushing 80. Even Yastrebchak seemed a little nonplussed, though he had correctly assured me that Smirnov would arrive on time.

A few minutes later, after no security checks but all of us, former minister included, being required to leave phones, though not my camera, in an outer room, we were ushered into his large office.

My hopes of a structured interview, starting with his views as to Transnistria's future and working back through his presidency and perhaps its more ignominious features were soon dashed: it was president's territory and president's rules. He started with a brief and half-heartedly flirtatious interrogation of my interpreter in Ukrainian- like most inhabitants of Odessa, Russian is her first language- presumably to establish his linguistic credentials. The fact that Russian, Romanian and Ukrainian are all official languages of Transnistria was a theme he returned to several times.

He took amusement in my being a lawyer, a profession for which he appeared to have little regard, but restricted any disdain to a mild, "two lawyers, three opinions". He might have enjoyed my jokes about a lawyer not being eaten when encountering a shark out of professional courtesy, and of the difficulty St Peter would have in finding a lawyer for an action against the devil, but this was a presidential performance with no place for audience participation. Several times he pointed out that he was an engineer, borne out by his dirty finger nails and slightly gnarled hands.

I tried questions on the treatment of Jehovah's Witnesses, a couple of times, steering the conversation back to religion on some aspects of which he was happy to wax lyrical, but there was no engagement at all on the alleged oppression of Witnesses. He was proud that the number of churches in the territory had increased from four to 96 since independence. There were at least two synagogues* in Tiraspol, but "we have no Muslims". Asking about the imprisonment of Vardanean or the founding of Sheriff, let alone the monies embezzled by his sons, would have been a waste of breath.

---

* There is actually only one (SubsSect.3.7.2).

The nearest I got to any response to what I regarded as a significant question was about his relationship with Alexander Lebed, when the latter was the Russian commander and a member of the Transnistrian Soviet in the early days of the republic. He said the country was grateful to Alexander Rutskoy, the Russian vice-President who had given the order to Lebed to intervene to protect Transnistria from Moldovan forces in June 1992.

Although it was not a topic I initiated discussion on, he was anxious to defend the privatisation of Transnistrian industries. He told me all who worked in those industries got shares. All the other money received went towards "pensions and other needs". He spoke highly of a series of Russian investors, and was critical of the Shevchuk government for forcing one to leave Transnistria, which Yastrebchak, who had insisted on being the primary interpreter for the interview, did not translate for me. My interpreter told me afterwards, confirming my suspicion, that the reference was to Usmanov (Sect.2.2). If there was a moment of introspection it was referring to the 2006 referendum, where 97% voted for independence, saying, "We forget to ask the Russian Federation whether they wanted us".

Aside from that, he was uniformly positive about the territory. As well as his pleasure in the growth of churches, he claimed it had a higher per-capita GDP than Russia. He ventured to the argument about the effect of the renunciation of the Molotov-Ribbentrop Pact justifying Transnistria's independence from Moldova. He listed achievements, such as four higher-educational institutions, 164 schools and, in the next breath, digital television. He claimed that, "We are independent in the sphere of the economy", qualified, perhaps in the light of my sceptical look, by, "There are no truly economically independent countries".

There was nostalgia for the USSR, he talked of "betrayal" by Gorbachev and Yeltsin. When he alleged that Gorbachev had allowed the break-up to further his own career, I was allowed a little riposte on the lines that Gorbachev had actually destroyed his career in consequence of the break, which seemed to be accepted. He told me, "It is very sad when a great state collapses. The Soviet state used to protect people. No-one could shout at the USSR", but quickly, and not entirely consistently, added, "Next year we will celebrate 30 years of independence from the USSR". As for the US, "We are just a freckle on the white skin, too small for the great state to notice". He claimed, bewilderingly, Transnistria, "Pays about US$60 million to work with the EU".

The most he would say on the future of the country was, "I am not a fortune teller, I am absolutely sure that the state remains in good hands", followed by telling me again, for no apparent reason that, "We have three official languages", to which he said could possibly be added, "Bulgarian and even the Jewish language".

He showed interest in Britain. He asked what I thought about the resignation of Theresa May, which had been the previous week, but moved on without giving me a chance to respond. He wanted to show his knowledge of English history, which extended to a king who had executed three wives, but whom he couldn't name, and likening the Woolsack to the straw cushion used in the Russian *duma*. He made frequent references to the current queen. There was an incoherent anecdote about what had happened when he tried to get served in a pub in London. I was allowed to answer the question of what was the national food of Britain, but my answer- a hesitant endorsement of fish and chips- was overruled, as he believed it was "beef steak": something may have got lost in the translation. On his visit to England he had formed the impression that we were a very racially mixed nation, he had kept coming across Malaysians. He expressed the same gratitude as the Minister for Internal Affairs had to me previously for the second-hand fire engines that Britain had provided.

I tried asking about whether he shopped in Sheriff supermarkets in the hope of leading to some discussion about the formation of the group. He told that he preferred to go to the hypermarket near the Sheriff stadium as there were rarely queues there, and that he was struck by how potatoes imported from Pakistan were cheaper than the locally grown ones. He seemed to be making a semi-serious economic point in the manner many pensioners do. I think though he lacked the subtlety to also be making the point that he had to queue up in supermarkets like everyone else.

While the interview was not the mine of revelation I was hoping for, it did underline my impression of Transnistria as far from a sinister place. Smirnov came over as an eccentric, amiable and even charismatic man, no doubt still enjoying the confidence which holding high-office for a long time must give. Virtually nothing in my conversation with him gave any insight into the questions of corruption, abuse of police powers and religious and linguistic oppression which may have tainted the period in which he governed. It could be that the proceeds of privatisation, which was the only controversial topic on which there was any substantial conversation, is where he feels most vulnerable to criticism. However, I thought it revealing that he was prepared to draw attention to this area and even criticise his successor for having a different approach. That his official interpreter didn't want me to get this, actually added I thought to Smirnov's own credibility.

13: My interpreter and me with President Smirnov

APPENDIX C: PRISON VISIT
(29 MAY 2019)

After my emailed requests to visit a prison had been ignored for some weeks, a telephone call from Tiraspol by my interpreter to the Minister for Internal Affair's assistant resulted in access being granted the next day and even a police car provided to transport us.

For reasons that were never explained to me, I was taken only to the women's prison on the outskirts of Tiraspol. There I was met by the governor, Sergy Vasilievich, wearing military uniform probably in his sixties, and his younger, also uniformed and male, assistant. All the other warders we saw were female. Without hesitation, he told me the number of inmates there was 102, and that this represented the totality of female prisoners in Transnistria. I was asked if there was anything in particular I wished to see, but I preferred him to just guide me around.

We were first taken to the dormitories, large rooms each containing about 50 closely packed single beds. The few women in the room stood to attention as we walked in, which we were told was a prison rule. As I questioned Vasilievich they gradually seemed to lose attention and reverted to whatever they were doing before, probably in breach of prison rules, but without any seeming fear of sanction.

As well as the dormitories, there was a small mother and child unit for women whose children were under three. There were just four mothers in the unit, sharing two large airy rooms equipped with beds and cots. Once the children turned three they had to leave and live with family members, or failing that go to an orphanage.

At the mother and child unit was a woman who looked and sounded more like a senior administrator than a prisoner, and who made it clear she wished to speak to us. Olga had a two-year old son who had been born with a heart defect, and was grateful for the medical treatment he had been provided with while she was in prison. She had been sentenced to ten and a half years for her part in an alleged fraud involving 8 million roubles (now around £400,000). She had been five months pregnant when arrested. She wanted to appeal against her conviction, but expressed no outrage at the length of her sentence. She told me she had to pay fees to apply to the court which she was not sure if she would be able to raise the money for.

After visiting that unit, Vasilievich told me that it is a principle of the system that no child suffers from its mother being in prison. He could point with some pride to the reasonable selection of toys and nicely decorated rooms in which the kids lived with their mothers. A lunch of appetising looking chicken pieces was on display. A modern looking television was displaying cartoons.

The inmates were generally quite young, probably a majority under 30. There was no uniform, except each had a lanyard with their name on, and almost all wore jeans. It was made clear that I could talk to whichever prisoners I wished. Fairly randomly, I choose two women, both called Tatiana, one of whose body language suggested she wished to be interviewed and one of whose didn't, but who politely acquiesced.

The younger more open one told me she was in prison for killing her boyfriend. She spoke a little English, which Vasilievich later told me, again with justifiable pride, she had learned in the prison. It was clear that she had been the subject of an abusive relationship, which no doubt reflected in her sentence of eight years, reduced by Presidential decree to six years and four months. She had no complaints about medical treatment or food in prison and was well prepared to return to her parents on her release in eleven months.

The older Tatiana told an even sadder story. Her child was in an orphanage, for reasons it would not have been right to probe about, and she failed to pay the prescribed amount of maintenance for the child because she had been sick and in hospital. This had resulted in a one-year sentence, of which she had ten more weeks to serve. The arrears had been 7,000 roubles. Of course, she and the others may not have been telling me the full story*, but I was left with a disturbing feeling that all three women I had spoken to would be unlikely to still be serving sentences in most European systems.

We were shown a prayer-hall, television room, small library and two lecture-rooms, one of which had photos on the walls of prisoners in smart dresses performing a concert. On first being questioned about medical facilities Vasilievich said there was a first aid kit, but on further questioning he told me that a doctor visited and that in the event of serious illness a "special car" would take women to hospital.

There was a scheme to train the prisoners in landscape-gardening and a workshop in the prison where about thirty women could be engaged in making shoes. A representative of the factory for whom the work was done was stationed permanently there. The women were paid for the work on a piece-rate basis. We talked briefly to the representative, who said the quality of the workmanship from the prison "could be difficult". She showed us children's and adults' shoes in various stages of production, which to my untrained eye looked to be well-made. I asked about the rates of pay and the answers were opaque "five roubles per stage", but I could not ascertain what a stage was.

The prison's seemingly pleasant atmosphere may have been enhanced by our visit being on a sunny day, with most of the women outside in the yard. There was however, sufficient indoor space, both in and out of the dormitories, for it probably not to be oppressive when the weather did not allow for that. There was an isolation facility but it was rarely used.

The prison itself presented, at least superficially, few concerns, and even if a Soviet-trained military man is not the obvious person to be running a woman's prison, Vasilievich

---

*   Quite extensive internet searches failed to uncover any reports of the story of the woman who killed her boyfriend, which in a country that only has around five murders a year (SubSect.4.5.1) would inevitably have attracted media interest.

presented himself as a humane, even enlightened, governor. More worrying was that all of my talks with prisoners had revealed that their sentences may have been excessive, and underlines the suspicion that the Transnistria courts send far too many people to prison. Also Olga's aside that in effect financial constraints could stop a prisoner pursuing an appeal, points to there being others among the prison population who could and should be released on a proper consideration of their case.

APPENDIX D: EMAIL FROM THE MOLDOVAN BUREAU OF REINTEGRATION (10 OCTOBER 2019)*

Hello Mr. Colbey!

We're glad of your interest in Transnistrian issue.

We arrived from Bratislava without a signed protocol of the 5+2 round, but in one month we'll continue negotiations in Bavaria, at conference on confidence building measures.

Regarding aspects mentioned in your previous mail the situation it's the following:

1. A specialized structure on promoting governmental policy on country reintegration was created at the end of 2002 as Ministry of reintegration (first negotiator from Chisinau - Mr. Sova Vasilii), then reorganized in 2009 as Bureau for reintegration within State Chancellery of the Republic of Moldova. Main mission of bureau is to provide assistance to Deputy Prime Minister for reintegration, implement governmental goal on territorial reintegration of the country, re-establish national unique spaces and to facilitate organization of negotiation process on Transnistrian settlement. In order to be promoted efficient sectoral policies in each ministry we're designated responsible experts on country reintegration policies (economy, social protection, transport, telecommunication and so on).

2. So-called Transnistrian independence it's a propagandistic approach promoted by a small team of concrete persons with huge economic interests in the situation of an uncontrolled region where they earn huge revenues from illegal economic schemes, no payment of gas resources from Gazprom (about $400 million each year) and fiscal/customs taxes to constitutional authorities, permanent confrontation with right bank of Moldova on various geopolitical elements. Transnistrian leaders every time pretend that in 2006 was organized a referendum where 96 % of the inhabitants from region opted for so-called independence and pro-Russia, but in the reality it's a fake and provocation because all the situation it's controlled by politic militia (KGB), lack of any freedom of opinion, no democratic elections, all results are presented as will of the people but in concrete designed by a concrete team of propagandists. If Moldova will refuse to pay

---

*   I have reproduced this virtually verbatim only correcting a few spellings and clarifying abbreviations.

to Tiraspol for electricity and will insist in relation to Transnistrian leaders respect fully MD legislation and pay legal taxes and if Ukraine will impose an economic blockade Transnistria will survive independently not more than one or two months, but Moldova always think about its citizens from there (96% have MD citizenship) and always promote measures to protect their fundamental rights.

3. The real population of the region is between 300-350,000 inhabitants (333,000 documented with MD ID's, 2620 economic agents from region are registered in MD). Situation of HR protection is very bad, many cases of political persecution, thousands of people refuged on right bank, entrepreneurs terrorized by Sheriff company to cede the business, no freedom of movement, access to effective justice, right of property, right of education in mother tongue and so on. Each year Bureau for reintegration receive not less than 500 complaints from the region about the abuses of the regime and with the request to be protected. We're very sceptical about conclusions made in the Report of Hammarberg regarding the situation of human rights (HR) in the region because most of them reflect the ideas and proposals of Tiraspol, references on so-called regional legislation which is declarative and reality is totally different (ghetto territory). We want more objective and neutral reports on HR situation from the region which will not be criticized in the society and will be based not on declarations of propagandists but on proofs and testimonies of victims and HR defenders.

In case of any other clarifications we remain at your disposal.

Good luck and all the best.

Best regards,

Alin Gvidiani

APPENDIX E: BANKING, MOBILE PHONES AND NON-PRESCRIPTION DRUGS

My own experiences in Transnistria of venturing into areas which are often regulated by government have reinforced a view of a society not so unlike those of western Europe. While at some levels corruption may be pervasive, I have not encountered it and my ordinary business dealings in the territory have been boringly like those at home. The nearest to dishonesty I have encountered in Transnistria is being charged an extra five roubles for having chocolate added to my cappuccino at the inaptly named Love Café.

Banking

Opening bank accounts in November 2015 at the central Tiraspol headquarters of the Ipoteka Bank was not unlike doing so at English bank branch, taking about 45 minutes and being interviewed by a civil but humourless clerk in a private room. As there were no other customers there was, in perhaps the most striking departure from the British experience, no queuing time. Identity documentation was required and closely inspected. Numerous forms had to be completed. Although I hoped to open an account in US dollars, not being convinced of the stability of the rouble, this, for reasons I did not entirely understand, was not permitted, and my dollars, around 270 of them, were converted to 3,000 Roubles. I was promised an interest rate of 7%, at a time when one would be lucky to get 1% on a savings account in Britain or the US, if the money was left there for three years.

I was also able to open a cash card account in which I placed a meagre 100 roubles. The cards that come with such accounts are the only widely-accepted means of payment, other than cash, in Transnistria*. I used it once as a trial to withdraw twenty roubles cash, but never got around to trying it for a purchase.

On successfully opening the accounts I was told I would be entered into a draw the prize of which was a new car. I completed that in the name of my interpreter, who was much more optimistic about the chances of winning than I was. She got a note a few months later telling her she had not won.

Visiting the branch, a little over three years later to collect my money first led to the

---

* By my final visit in October 2019 a few tourist-oriented businesses, but not ATM's, were accepting international cards, with which I bought coffees in the new Bastion Hotel by Bender Fortress. The transaction was processed in Russian roubles.

disconcerting news from the man guarding the door of the building, which no longer had any bank sign on it, that the bank had closed. Despite the efficiency with which my interpreter had been told of her lack of success in the draw for the car, the bank had failed to notify me of this rather more fundamental fact. However, a few questions elicited that it had been taken over by the Exim Bank, which had a branch 200 metres away. Like the Ipoteka Bank had been, it was virtually deserted of customers. My passport and bank document had to be shown but there were no forms to fill in. I did ask about making a partial withdrawal, but that was not allowed. I could only open a new savings account on depositing US$300. A card account would not require so much but would involve a lot of forms and probably time, so I decided to draw my personal relationship with Transnistrian banks to a close. I was handed 3,660 roubles, which suggested interest had been added as promised. This, at the prevailing rate of 16.1, gave me the equivalent of US$223.60, apparently representing the proceeds of both accounts but not being apportioned.

Changing the bulk of the 3,660 roubles to dollars in the bank was simple and required no further formality, suggesting that the rouble had been allowed to fall to a real market-rate, rather than being pegged artificially high, which would lead to foreign currency scarcity and a black market. Such a scarcity had been apparent on previous visits, though I was never invited to change money illicitly and the Hotel Russia actually insisted on being paid in roubles despite quoting prices in dollars. My request for a few of the attractive plastic coins Transnistrian issued could only be met with a single five rouble coin. The cashier tried forlornly to persuade me that the newly-issued metal one rouble coin was more interesting.

A consolation for the US$55 fall from the deposited US$270 and US$8 card account balance, was that in British terms it was nearly cancelled by the fall in the Pound from its pre-Brexit referendum figure of US$1.51 to US1.27. This meant that my loss was merely about £8, a small price to pay for having been able to participate in perhaps the world's most obscure banking system.

Mobile phones

If Transnistrian bureaucracy, and quality of communication, by banks is similar to what one is familiar with, for mobile phones it is far worse. While there are several shops on Tiraspol's main street, displaying second-hand phones for about the same as a similar British shop would charge, buying a SIM card proved impossible, on the two occasions-in 2015 and 2017 when I tried. I was told that simply none were available, and that in any case they would only be sold to those who had Transnistrian identity documents. Cards, some of which do work in Transnistria, can be easily purchased in Chisinau, and sometimes are handed out free at the airport.

Non-prescription drugs

With deference to the fact that attempting to acquire Class C drugs is not an approved method of academic research, I tried to buy sleeping tablets, containing alprazolam, usually marketed as *Xanax* in Europe and the US. These are sold cheaply over the counter in Ukraine, though not Moldova. In two pharmacies in Tiraspol, I was told firmly, and I think comfortingly, that these were only available on prescription, as would be the case pretty well everywhere else in Europe. For the avoidance of doubt, I did not seek and was not offered any other form of drug, and although illegal drugs are present in the territory, I saw no evidence of their consumption, and they were not mentioned to me as a problem by judges or prison or police officers.

BIBLIOGRAPHY

A. REFERENCE LIST

Aarhus Centres. 2020. Public Environmental Centre Bender. https://aarhus.osce.org/moldova/bender.

Abkhaz World. 2011. Kosovo or Abkhazia: Contrasts and Comparisons. 15 August. https://abkhazworld.com/aw/analysis/1009-kosovo-or-abkhazia-contrasts-and-comparisons

Abramowitz, Michael. 2017. Press Freedom's Dark Horizon. *Freedom of the Press 2017*. Freedom House. https://freedomhouse.org/report/freedom-press/2017/press-freedoms-dark-horizon.

Acharya, Amitav. 2007. State Sovereignty After 9/11: Disorganised Hypocrisy. *Political Studies* 55: 274–296.. DOI: 10.1111/j.1467-9248.2007.00664.

Action Fiche for Moldova. 2007. *Support to Civil Society in Moldova* https://ec.europa.eu/neighbourhood-enlargement/sites/near/files/enpi_2007_c2007_6294_annual_action_programme_for_moldova_civilsocietytransnistria.pdf.

Agency for Regional Development of Transnistria (ARDT). 2020. *About Transnistria* http://www.ngo-ardt.com/en/about-transnistria.html.

Agora.md. 2017. *Evgheni Şevciuk Says He Was Being Prepared for a Custom-made Murder: I Was Being Chased by Black Jeeps from the Sheriff.* 29 June. https://agora.md/stiri/34123/evgheni-sevciuk-spune-ca-i-se-pregatea-un-omor-la-comanda-ma-urmareau-jeep-uri-negre-de-la-sheriff.

Alberstadt, Rachel. 2012. *Is Westphalia Relevant to the Evolution of International Law?* MA/LLM Dissertation, Leiden University. https://www.academia.edu/6266119/is_westphalia_relevant_to_the_evolution_of_international_law.

al-Ghoul, Asmaa. 2015. Will Palestine Get Its Own Currency? *Al-Monitor*, 23 October. https://www.al-monitor.com/originals/2015/10/palestine-currency-shekel-israel-economy.html.

Alisauskiene, Rasa. 2013. *Public Opinion Survey: Residents of Moldova*. Center for Insights into Field Research. http://www.iri.org/sites/default/files/2018-3-29_moldova_poll_presentation.pdf.

American International Health Alliance (AIHA). 2007,.*Strengthening Tuberculosis Control in Moldova.* https://www.aiha.com/wp-content/uploads/2015/07/StrengtheningTuberculosisControlinMoldovaProject-FINALREPORT.pdf.

Amnesty International. 2007. *Possible Prisoner of Conscience/ Health Concern/ Legal Concern*. https://www.amnesty.org/download/Documents/64000/eur590012007en.pdf.

Amnesty International. 2018. *Moldova*. https://www.amnesty.org/en/countries/europe-and-central-asia/moldova/report-moldova/.

Andersen, Andrew. n.d. *The Conflict in Transnistria: National Consensus is a Long Way Off*. Centre for Military and Strategic Studies, Victoria BC, Canada. Accessed 19/10/20. http://www.conflicts.rem33.com/images/moldova/nistru_konflikt.htm.

Andersen, Andrew and Partskhaladze, George. n.d. *Ethnic Make Up of the Area*. Centre for Military and Strategic Studies. Accessed 4/1/21. http://www.conflicts.rem33.com/images/Georgia/Tskhinvali_Soss_ethn.htm.

Anderson, Benedict. 1991. *Imagined Communities: Reflections on the Origin and Spread of Nationalism*. Verso, London.

Andrianova, Ganna. 2014. *Architecture of Soviet Housing and Main Soviet Urban Planning Concepts*. Xi'an Jiaotong, Liverpool University. DOI 10.13140/RG.2.1.5147.5366.

Anghel, Dan. 2016. Transnistrian Companies Have "Pumped" 200 Million Dollars from the Budget. *Rise.md*, 10 November. https://adevarul.ro/moldova/actualitate/rise-moldovaintreprinderile-transnistrene-pompat-buget-200-milioane-dolari-1_584ba07a5ab650cb8496d86/index.html.

Atlas of Transnistria. 2000. Tiraspol. https://www.academia.edu/37217951/Atlas_of_Transnistria_pdf.

Balakrishnan, Radhika and Heintz, James. 2015. How Inequality Threatens All Human Rights. *Open Global Rights*, 29 October. https://www.openglobalrights.org/how-inequality-threatens-all-humans-rights/.

Balmaceda, Margarita. 2013. Privatization and Elite Defection in *De Facto* States: The Case of Transnistria, 1991–2012. *Communist and Post-Communist Studies* 46(4): 445–454. https://daneshyari.com/article/preview/1046412.pdf.

Baran, Emily. 2011. Jehovah's Witnesses and Post-Soviet Religious Policy in Moldova and the Transnistrian Moldovan Republic. *Journal of Church and State,* 53(3): 421–441. http://www.academia.edu/9008689/jehovahs_witnesses_and_post-soviet_religious_policy_in_moldova_and_the_transnistrian_moldovan_republic.

Barber, Martin and Bowie, Cameron. 2008. How International NGOs Could Do Less Harm and More Good. *Development in Practice*. 18(6): 748–754. https://doi.org/10.1080/09614520802386520.

Battistella, Edwin. 2020. How US Presidents Have Tried to Use Legal Action to Stop People from Insulting Them. *Time,* 1 April. https://time.com/5813215/presidential-insult-history.

BBC. 2015. *Trans-Dneister Profile*. 7 March. https://www.bbc.co.uk/news/world-europe-18286271.

BBC. 2015a. *Abkhazia Profile*. 27 August. https://www.bbc.co.uk/news/world-europe-18175394.

BBC. 2016. *How Three Men Signed the USSR's Death Warrant.* 24 December. https://www.bbc.co.uk/news/magazine-38416657.

BBC. 2017. *Lese-Majeste Explained: How Thailand Forbids Insult of its Royalty.* 6 October. https://www.bbc.co.uk/news/world-asia-29628191.

BBC. 2020. *Nagorno-Karabakh Conflict Killed 5,000 Soldiers.* 3 December. https://www.bbc.co.uk/news/world-europe-55174211.

Beard, Nadia. 2015. South Ossetia: Separatist Leader Leonid Tibilov Plans Referendum on 'Reunification' with Russia. *The Independent,* 20 October. https://www.independent.co.uk/news/world/europe/south-ossetia-separatist-leader-leonid-tibilov-plans-referendum-reunification-russia-a6701121.html.

Beaulac, Stephane. 2004. The Westphalian Model in Defining International Law: Challenging the Myth. *Australian Journal of Legal History* 8: 181–213. https://papers.ssrn.com/sol3/papers.cfm?abstract_id=672241.

Bedford, Sofie and Nizhnikau, Ryhor. 2017. The Same But Different: "Re-Understanding" Elections in Contemporary Post-Soviet Space. *The Journal of Post-Soviet Democratization* 25(4): 337–359. https://www.academia.edu/35065383/.

Beran, Harry. 1998. A Democratic Theory of Political Self-Determination for a New World Order. In *Theories of Secession*, edited by Percy B. Lehning: 33–60. Routledge, London.

Beurq, Julia. 2017. Being 20 in Transnistria. *Equal Times,* 5 January. https://www.equaltimes.org/avoir-20-ans-en-transnistrie?lang=en#.XovsTdNKjAy.

Beyer, John and Wolff, Stefan. 2016. Linkage and Leverage Effects on Moldova's Transnistria Problem. *Eastern European Politics* 32(3): 335–354. https://doi.org/10.1080/21599165.2015.1124092.

Bhatt, Himanshu. n.d. Hindu Temples in Europe. *Hindupedia.* Accessed 31/8/20. http://www.hindupedia.com/en/Hindu_Temples_in_Europe.

Bhopal, Raj. 2004. Glossary of Terms Relating to Ethnicity and Race: For Reflection and Debate. *Journal of Epidemiology & Community Health* 58: 441–445. DOI: 10.1136/jech.2003.013466.

Bird, Michael and Banila, Nicoleta. 2015. How Realistic is a Union Between Romania and Moldova? *The Black Sea,* 27 March. https://theblacksea.eu/stories/how-realistic-is-a-union-between-romania-and-moldova/.

Blakely, Georgina. n.d. *Catalonia Declares Independence.* The Open University. Accessed 21/1/21. http://www.open.ac.uk/research/news/catalonia-declares-independence.

Blakkisrud, Helge and Kolstø, Pål. 2013. From Secessionist Conflict Towards a Functioning State: Process of State-Building and Nation-Building in Transnistria. *Post-Soviet Affairs* 27(2): 178–210. DOI:10.2747/1060-586X.27.2.178.

Bobick, Michael. 2011. Profits of Disorder: Images of the Transnistrian Moldovan Republic. *Global Crime* 12(4): 239–265. https://www.ojp.gov/library/abstracts/profits-disorder-images-transnistrian-moldovan-republic.

Bobick, Michael. 2012. *There's a New "Sheriff" in Town: Corruption and Captive*

Markets in Transnistria. Havinghurst Centre. http://www.miamioh.edu/cas/_files/documents/havighurst/2012/bobick.pdf.

Bobick, Michael. 2014. Separatism *Redux*: Crimea, Transnistria, and Eurasia's *De Facto States*. *Anthropology Today* 30(3): 3–8. https://www.offiziere.ch/wp-content/uploads/anth12108.pdf.

Bobick, Michael. 2017. Sovereignty and the Vicissitudes of Recognition: Peoplehood and Performance in a De Facto State. *PoLar* 40: 158–170. https://www.offiziere.ch/wp-content/uploads/anth12108.pdf.

Bonet, Pilar. 2013. We Want Free Trade Zones Both to the East and to the West. *El Pais*, 4 June. https://elpais.com/internacional/2013/06/04/actualidad/1370334170_344660.html.

Bonnett, Alistair. 2017. *Beyond the Map: Unruly Enclaves, Ghostly Places, Emerging Lands and Our Search for New Utopias*. London: Aurum Press.

Bookman, Milica. 1993. *The Economics of Secession*. St. Martin's Press, New York.

Borsi, Mihály. 2007. Transnistria – An Unrecognised Country Within Moldova. *South-East Europe Review* 10(4): 45–50. https://www.nomos-elibrary.de/10.5771/1435-2869-2007-4-45/transnistria-an-unrecognised-country-within-moldova-jahrgang-10-2007-heft-4.

Botan, Igor. 2006. Elections in Transnistria and the Context in Which They Took Place. *E-democracy*, 15 January. http://www.e-democracy.md/en/monitoring/politics/comments/200601171/.

Bowring, Bill. 2014. Transnistria. In *Self-Determination and Secession in International Law*, edited by Christian Walter, Antje von Ungern-Sternberg and Kavus Abushov: Chapter 8. Oxford University Press. DOI:10.1093/acprof:oso/9780198702375.003.0008.

Brando, Nicolás and Morales-Gálvez, Sergi. 2018. The Right to Secession: Remedial or Primary? *Ethnopolitics* 18(2): 107–118. http://www.sergimorales.cat/wp-content/uploads/2018/07/The-Right-to-Secession.pdf.

Braw, Elizabeth. 2016. Rush for Moldovan Citizenship. *World Affairs Journal.*, 21 May. http://www.worldaffairsjournal.org/blog/elisabeth-braw/rush-moldovan-citizenship.

British Office Taipei. n.d. Accessed 30/12/20. https://www.gov.uk/world/organisations/british-office-taipei.

Brzozowski, Alexandra. 2019. Moldova FM: We Want to Move as Quickly as Possible on EU Accession. *Euractiv*. 17 July. https://www.euractiv.com/section/europe-s-east/news/moldova-fm-we-want-to-move-as-quickly-as-possible-on-eu-accession/.

Buchanan, Allen. 1995. Federalism, Secession, and the Morality of Inclusion. *Arizona Law Review* 37: 53–64. https://heinonline.org/HOL/LandingPage?handle=hein.journals/arz37&div=17&id=&page=.

Buchanan, Allen. 2007. *Justice, Legitimacy, and Self-Determination: Moral Foundations for International Law*. Oxford University Press.

Bugajski, Janusz. 2000. *Cold Peace: Russia's New Imperialism*. Praeger, Connecticut.

Bureau of Statistics. 2010. *Criminality in the Republic of Moldova*. Moldovan Government. https://statistica.gov.md/public/files/publicatii_electronice/Infractionalitatea/Criminalitatea_editia_2010.pdf.

Burkina Faso v. Mali. 1986. International Court of Justice. https://www.icj-cij.org/public/files/case-related/69/069-19861222-JUD-01-00-EN.pdf.

Buttin, Felix. 2007. A Human Security Perspective on Transnistria Reassessing the Situation Within the Black Hole of Europe. *Human Security Journal* 3: 13–28. http://www.operationspaix. net/data/document/5385~v~a_human_security_perspective_on_transnistria___reassessing_the_situation_within_the_black_hole_of_europe.pdf.

Călugăreanu, Vitalie. 2018. Igor Dodon, Disconnected for the Fourth Time From the Position of President. *DW Bucharest*, 24 September. https://www.dw.com/ro/igor-dodon-deconectat-a-patra-oar%c4%83-din-func%c8%9bia-de-pre%c8%99edinte/a-45616376.

Całus, Kamil. 2013. *An Aided Economy. The Characteristics of the Transnistrian Economic Model*. Centre for Eastern Studies, Warsaw, 14 May. https://www.osw.waw.pl/sites/default/files/commentary_108.pdf.

Całus, Kamil. 2013a. *Tensions Between Moldova and Transnistria Pose a Threat to the Vilnius Summit*. Centre for Eastern European Studies, 10 July. https://www.osw.waw.pl/en/publikacje/analyses/2013-07-10/tensions-between-moldova-and-transnistria-pose-a-threat-to-vilnius.

Całus, Kamil. 2014. *Power Politics on the Outskirts of the EU: Why Transnistria Matters*. London School of Economics. https://blogs.lse.ac.uk/lsee/2014/06/19/transnistria-power-politics/.

Całus, Kamil. 2014a. *Gagauzia: Growing Separatism in Moldova?* Centre for Eastern European Studies, 10 March. https://www.osw.waw.pl/en/publikacje/osw-commentary/2014-03-10/gagauzia-growing-separatism-moldova.

Całus, Kamil. 2014b. The Ukrainian Crisis: A New Context for a Transnistrian Settlement. DFCTA in Transnistria: Who Gains? *Turkish Policy Quarterly* 13(3): 71–78. http://turkishpolicy.com/article/709/the-ukrainian-crisis-a-new-context-for-a-transnistrian-settlement-fall-2014.

Całus, Kamil. 2016. Transnistrian "House of Cards". *New Eastern Europe*, 7 June. http://new-easterneurope.eu/old_site/articles-and-commentary/2019-transnistrian-house-of-cards.

Całus Kamil. 2016a. The DFCTA in Transnistria: Who Gains? *New Eastern Europe*, 15 January. http://neweasterneurope.eu/old_site/articles-and-commentary/1861-the-dcfta-in-transnistria-who-gains.

Cambridge English Dictionary. 2020. Cambridge University Press.

Çamözü, Bahar. 2016. *The Road to the Reintegration of Transnistria Within the Republic of Moldova*. Political Center of the Former States of the Soviet Union. https://www.academia.edu/25768527/.

Carnegie Europe. 2018. *Transdniestria: "My Head Is in Russia, My Legs Walk to Europe"*. 3 December. https://carnegieeurope.eu/2018/12/03/transdniestria-my-head-is-in-russia-my-legs-walk-to-europe-pub-77843

Cassese, Antonio. 1985. *Self-Determination of Peoples: A Legal Reappraisal*. Cambridge University Press.

Casu, Igor. 2018. Down with Revisionism and Irredentism: Soviet Moldavia and the Prague Spring, 1968–72. In *Eastern Europe in 1968: Responses to the Prague Spring and Warsaw Pact* Invasion, edited by Kevin McDermott and Matthew Stibbe: Chapter 13. Palgrave Macmillan, Sheffield. https://www.academia.edu/36800041/_down_with_revisionism_and_irredentism_soviet_moldavia_and_the_prague_spring_1968_72?auto=download&campaign=weekly_digest.

Catan and others v. Moldova and Russia. 2012. European Court of Human Rights, 19 October. https://hudoc.echr.coe.int/fre#{%22itemid%22:[%22001-114082%22]}.

Cavendish, Richard. 1998. The Treaty of Westphalia. *History Today* 48(10). http://www.historytoday.com/richard-cavendish/treaty-westphalia.

Cazac and Surchician v. Moldova and Russia. 2020. European Court of Human Rights, 7 January. https://laweuro.com/?p=11948.

Centre for Strategic Studies and Reforms (CSSR). 1998. *Moldova in Transition Economic Survey* 2. https://core.ac.uk/download/pdf/11867387.pdf.

Central Intelligence Agency (CIA). 2019. *The World Fact Book.* https://www.cia.gov/library/publications/the-world-factbook/docs/rankorderguide.html.

Chabad Lubavitch Moldova (CLM). 2020. *Tiraspol Jewish Community.* https://kishinev.org/community/tiraspol-jewish-community/.

Chamberlain-Creangă, Rebecca. 2006. The 'Transnistrian People': Citizenship and Imaginings of the 'The State' in an Unrecognised Country. *Ab Imperio* 4: 371-399. 10.1353/imp.2006.0096

Chamberlain-Creangă, Rebecca. 2011. *Cementing Modernisation: Transnational Markets, Language and Labour Tension in a Post-Soviet Factory in Moldova.* PhD Thesis, London School of Economics. http://etheses.lse.ac.uk/274/1/Chamberlain-Creanga_Cementing%20Organisation.pdf.

Chapman, Jack. 2011. Kagame – A Benign Dictator? *Think Africa Press*, 9 June. http://thinkafricapress.com/rwanda/kagame-benigndictato.

Charbonneau, Louis. 2015. *UN Nations Approve Principles for Sovereign Debt Restructuring.* Reuters, 10 September 2015. https://www.reuters.com/article/us-un-sovereign-debt/u-n-nations-approve-principles-for-sovereign-debt-restructuring-iduskcnora2ks20150910.

Ciurcă, Aliona. 2016. The Lipovcenco Case: Torture and Inhumane Conditions for a Paper Mention. *Ziarul de Garda*, 21 April. https://www.zdg.md/stiri/stiri-sociale/cazul-lipovcenco-tortura-si-conditii-inumane-pentru-o-mentiune-pe-hartie/.

Civil Code of Transnistria. 2018. http://ukpmr.net/?deistvie_zakona.

Clark, Charles Upson. 1927. *Bessarabia, Russia and Roumania on the Black Sea .* Dodd, Mead & Co., New York. http://ukpmr.net/?deistvie_zakona.

Clyne, Conor. 2015. Moldova – Polyglot's Paradise? *Tsar Experience*, 9 April. http://tsarexperience.com/bilingualism-in-moldova/.

Clooney, Amal and Webb, Philippa. 2017. The Right to Insult in International Law. *Columbia Human Rights Law Review* 48(2): 1–55. Corpus ID: 152131527.

Coakley, John. 2017. 'Primordialism' in Nationalism Studies: Theory or Ideology? *Nations and Nationalism* 24(2): 327–347. https://doi.org/10.1111/nana.12349.

Coggins, Bridget. 2014. *Power Politics and State Recognition in the Twentieth Century: The Dynamics of Recognition.* Cambridge University Press.

Cojocari, Tatiana. 2019. *Perceptions, Attitudes and Values of the Population From the Left Bank of Dniester River.* Black Sea University Foundation. https://www.academia.edu/39083801/.

Cojocaru, Natalia. 2006. Nationalism and Identity in Transnistria. *Innovation* 19: 261–272. DOI:10.1080/13511610601029813.

Comai, Giorgio. 2016. The Upcoming Presidential Election in Transnistria. *Presidential Power*, Washington, DC. https://presidential-power.net/?page_id=11.

Comai, Giorgio. 2016a. *Russia and Pensions in Post-Soviet De Facto States.* https://giorgiocomai.eu/post/russia-and-pensions-in-post-soviet-de-facto-states/.

Comai, Giorgio. 2018. After a New President Came to Power What Happened to Transnistria's Media? *Osservatorio Balacani e Caucaso*, 18 June. https://www.balcanicaucaso.org/eng/Areas/Transnistria/Transnistria-journalism-beyond-the-Nistru-189247.

Consortium of Universities ("Consortium"). 2020. http://spsu.ru/international/konsortsium-vuzov.

Constitution of Pridnestrovskaia Moldavskaia Respublica ("Constitution"). 2011. http://mfa-pmr.org/en/bht.

Constitution of South Sudan. 2005. http://www.gurtong.net/LinkClick.aspx?fileticket=1OqRv9hqgv8%3D&.

Constitution of the Republic of Moldova. 2016. http://www.presedinte.md/eng/constitution.

Constitution of the Russian Federation. 1993. http://www.constitution.ru/en/10003000-01.htm.

Consulate of Moldova. n.d. *History and Ethnic Relations: Republic of Moldova.* http://www.consulateofmoldova.in/contact.html.

Cornet, Mélissa. 2016. *Pridnestrovian Moldovian Republic: What Legal Framework under International Law for Unrecognized Entities.* Fordham Law School. https://www.academia.edu/35804052/

Costin, Natalia. 2012. *Rethinking Brain Drain in Moldova: Migrant Youth Development.* Central University, Budapest. http://www.etd.ceu.hu/2012/costin_natalia.pdf.

Council of Europe (CoE). 2006. *Position Paper of the Parliamentary Assembly as Regards the Council of Europe Member and Observer States Which Have Not Abolished the Death Penalty.* Doc 10911: 34. http://assembly.coe.int/nw/xml/xref/x2h-xref-viewhtml.asp?fileid=11376&lang=en.

Council of Europe (CoE). 2015. *Visit by the Conference of INGOs of the Council of Europe to Chisinau.* 9 November 2015. https://rm.coe.int/1680594197.

Council of Europe (CoE). n.d. *The Council of Europe's Relations with the OSCE.* Accessed 30/12/20. https://www.coe.int/en/web/der/osce.

Cox, Patrick. 2014. *Transnistria is a Slice of Cold War Real Estate – And Even Its Name is in Dispute*. Public Radio International, 24 March. http://www.pri.org/stories/2014-03-24/transnistria-slice-cold-war-real-estate-and-even-its-name-dispute.

Criminal Code of Transnistria. 2019. http://ukpmr.net/?ugolovnyi_kodeks_pridnestrovmzya.

Crisis Group. 2004. *Georgia: Avoiding War in South Ossetia*. Report 159. https://www.crisisgroup.org/europe-central-asia/caucasus/georgia/georgia-avoiding-war-south-ossetia.

Crisis Group 2007 *Abkhazia: Ways Forward*. Report 179. https://www.crisisgroup.org/europe-central-asia/caucasus/abkhazia-georgia/abkhazia-ways-forward.

Crivenco, Andrei. 2018. *Demographic Development of Moldova Based on the Latest Censuses Conducted in 2014 and 2015 (in Transnistria)*. Hungarian Academy of Sciences. https://www.academia.edu/36567851/.

Crook, David. 2007. Education, Health and Social Welfare. *History of Education* 36(6): 651–657. https://doi.org/10.1080/00467600701619630.

Croxton, Derek. 2013. *Westphalia: The Last Christian Peace*. Palgrave Macmillan US, New York.

Croxton, Derek and Tischer, Anuschka. 2001. *The Peace of Westphalia: A Historical Dictionary*. Greenwood Press, Westport, Connecticut.

Cullen, Anthony and Wheatley, Steven. 2013. The Human Rights of Individuals in *De Facto* Regimes Under the European Convention on Human Rights 2013. *Human Rights Law Review* 13(4): 691–728. https://www.corteidh.or.cr/tablas/r32259.pdf.

CW Group. 2015. *Moldova's Ribnita Cement Plant Undergoes Upgrade*. 16 May 2015. Hartford, Connecticut.

Dailey, Erika, Laber, Jeri and Whitman, Lois. 1993. *Human Rights in Moldova: The Turbulent Dniester*. Human Rights Watch, Vienna.

Daly, John. 2020. Despite Illegality, Crypto-Currency Mining Flourishes in Abkhazia. *Eurasian Monitor* 17(121) 14 August. https://jamestown.org/program/despite-illegality-crypto-currency-mining-flourishes-in-abkhazia/.

Danilov, Dmitrii. 1999. A Question of Sovereignty: The Georgia Abkhazia Peace Process – Russia's Role. *Accord Conciliation Resources* 7: 42–49. https://www.c-r.org/accord/georgia%E2%80%93abkhazia/russias-role.

Dascalu, Diana. 2019. Frozen Conflicts and Federalization: Russian Policy in Transnistria and Donbass. *Journal of International Affairs,* Columbia University, New York, May 22. https://jia.sipa.columbia.edu/online-articles/frozen-conflicts-and-federalization-russian-policy-transnistria-and-donbass

Day, Joel. 2012. The Remedial Right of Secession in International Law. *Potentia* 4(1): 19–33. https://doi.org/10.18192/potentia.v4i0.4393.

de Colombani, Pierpaolo. 2013. *Review of the National Tuberculosis Programme in the Republic of Moldova*. World Health Organization. https://blogs.elpais.com/files/2.secession_day.pdf.

Dembinska, Magdalena. 2018. Carving Out the Nation with the Enemy's Kin: Double Strategy of Boundary-Making in Transnistria and Abkhazia. *Nations and Nationalism* 25(1): 298–317. https://onlinelibrary.wiley.com/doi/pdf/10.1111/nana.12386.

Dembinska, Magdalena and Iglesias, Julien. 2013. The Making of an Empty Moldovan Category within a Multi-Ethnic Transnistrian Nation. *Eastern European Politics and Society* 27(3): 413–428. DOI: 10.1177/0888325413484174

Department for Transport (UK) (DoT). 2015. *Reported Road Casualties Great Britain.* https://assets.publishing.service.gov.uk/government/uploads/system/uploads/attachment_data/file/467465/rrcgb-2014.pdf.

Deschide.md. 2020. Fop Survey: Over 30% of the Citizens of the Republic of Moldova Would Vote for the Union with Romania. https://deschide.md/ro/stiri/social/67226/SONDAJ-FOP--Peste-30-din-cet%C4%83%C8%9Benii-R-Moldova-ar-vota-pentru-Unirea-cu-Rom%C3%A2nia.htm.

Devyatkov, Andrey and Kosienkowski, Marcin. 2013. Testing Pluralism: Transnistria in the Light of 2011 Presidential Elections. In *Spotkania polsko-mołdawskie*, edited by Marcin Kosienkowski: 303–328, Episteme, Lublin. https://ssrn.com/abstract=2132164.

de Waal, Thomas. 2016. An Eastern European Frozen Conflict the EU Got Right. *Politico*, 16 February. https://www.politico.eu/article/transnistria-an-eastern-european-frozen-conflict-the-eu-got-right-moldova-russia-ukraine/.

de Waal, Thomas. 2018. *Uncertain Ground: Engaging with Europe's De Facto States and Breakaway Territories.* Carnegie Europe, Brussels. https://carnegieeurope.eu/2018/12/03/transdniestria-my-head-is-in-russia-my-legs-walk-to-europe-pub-77843.

Dumitru, Diana. 2018. Genocide for 'Sanitary Purposes'? The Bogdanovka Murder in Light of Postwar Trial Documents. *Journal of Genocide Research* 21(2): 157–177. https://doi.org/10.1080/14623528.2018.1534662.

Dnestrovskaya Pravda. 1998. https://tiraspol.tripod.com/.

Dniester. 2011. Geopolitical Course of Transnistria Through the Eyes of Sociologists. http://dniester.ru/content/geopoliticheskii-kurs-pridnestrovya-glazami-sotsiologov.

Dodge, Justin. 2011. *Conditions Allowing Organized Crime in Transnistria.* Baskerville Press, Milwaukee.

Dorosenco, Luiza. 2015. Although We Have No Censorship Officially, the Freedom of Journalists is Limited. *Media Azi,* 6 May. http://www.media-azi.md/en/stiri/although-we-have-no-censorship-officially-freedom-journalists-limited.

Douglas, Nadja and Wolff, Stefan. 2018. *Economic Confidence Building Measures and Conflict Settlement: The Case of Transdniestria.* Centre of Eastern European and International Studies, Berlin 2018. https://www.zois-berlin.de/fileadmin/media/dateien/work-in-progress/work_in_progress_1b_2018.pdf.

Duarte, André, Garcia, Camila. Giannarakis, Grigoris, Limão, Susana, Polydoropoulou, Amalia and Litinas, Nikolaos. 2009. New Approaches in Transportation Planning: Happiness and Transport Economics. *Netnomics* 11: 5–32. DOI 10.1007/s11066-009-9037-2.

Dummett, Mark. 2011. *Bangladesh War: The Article That Changed History.* BBC. http://www.bbc.co.uk/news/world-asia-16207201.

Dutka, Karolina. 2017. *Representative of the KGB: I Am Not Putting a Gun to Your Temple Now.* Apriori. http://apriori-center.org/en/no_silence_kgb/.

Dutka, Karolina. n.d. *No Silence.* Accessed 16/1/21. http://nosilence.tilda.ws/.

DW. 2015. Transnistria: Secret Police vs. NGOs. 19 May. https://www.dw.com/en/transnistria-secret-police-vs-ngos/a-18461829.

Dziedzic, Stephen. 2018. *Which Country Gives the Most Aid to Pacific Islands Nations.* Australian Broadcasting Corporation, 9 August.

https://www.abc.net.au/news/2018-08-09/aid-to-pacific-island-nations/10082702?nw=0.

Dzutsev, Valeriy. 2014. Russia's Dilemma in South Ossetia. *The Central Asia-Caucus Analyst*, 23 April. http://www.cacianalyst.org/publications/analytical-articles/item/12959-russias-dilemma-in-south-ossetia.html.

Earth Children's Mission. n.d.. *Human Rights in Moldova.* Massillon. Accessed 16/1/21 http://www.earthchildrensmission.org/international-development.html#:~:text=In%20the%20breakaway%20territory%20of,and%20unlawful%20detentions%20are%20widespread.&text=Moldovan%20legislation%20prohibits%20torture%20and,forms%20of%20treatment%20or%20punishment.

Eastern Alliance for Safe and Sustainable Transport (EASST). 2013. *Development of Casualty Reduction Partnerships in Chisinau and Tiraspol.* https://www.easst.co.uk/development-of-casualty-reduction-partnerships-in-chisinau-and-tiraspol/.

Eberhardt, Adam. 2011. *The Paradoxes of Moldovan Sports: An insight Into the Nature of the Transnistrian Conflict.* Punkt Widzenia: Points of View, Warsaw.

https://www.osw.waw.pl/sites/default/files/punkt_widzenia_26_en.pdf.

The Economist. 2016. How Moldova Escaped the Effects of a Giant Banking Crisis. 16 February. https://www.economist.com/europe/2017/02/16/how-moldova-escaped-the-effects-of-a-giant-banking-crisis.

Elden, Stuart. 2005. Territorial Integrity and the War on Terror. *Environment and Planning* 37(2): 2083–2104.

Elden, Stuart. 2007. Terror and Territory. *Antipode* 39(5): 821–845.

https://www.researchgate.net/publication/227522242_terror_and_territory.

Embassy of the Czech Republic. 2012. *Who is Citizen? Guide to Czech Citizenship in 1969–1992.* https://www.mzv.cz/telaviv/en/visa_and_consular_services/citizenship/who_is_citizen_guide_to_czech_2.html.

Encyclopedia of Ukraine. n.d. *Moldavians.* Accessed 25/5/21.

http://www.encyclopediaofukraine.com/display.asp?linkpath=pages%5CM%5CO%5CMoldavians.htm.

Ernst, Iulian. 2016. Sheriff Forced to Pay $250mn "Donation" to Transnistria's Budget. *Intellinews*, 14 October. https://www.intellinews.com/sheriff-forced-to-pay-250mn-donation-to-transnistria-s-budget-108096/.

Ernst, Iulian. 2017. Transnistria Devaluates [*sic*] Currency by 25%. *Intellinews*, 20 June. https://www.intellinews.com/transnistria-devaluates-currency-by-25-123825/.

Ernst, Iulian. 2017a. Ex-President Flees Transnistria as Parliament Strips

Him of Immunity. *Intellinews*, 29 June. https://www.intellinews.com/ex-president-flees-transnistria-as-parliament-strips-him-of-immunity-124401/.

EurAsia Daily. 2018. Transnistria legalizes cryptocurrency and waiting for investors. 2 February. https://eadaily.com/en/news/2018/02/02/transnistria-legalizes-cryptocurrency-and-waiting-for-investors.

Euronews. 2014. To Russia With Love: Transnistria's Yearning for 'The Motherland'. 3 June. https://www.timpul.md/en/articol/(EURONEWS)-To-Russia-with-love-Transnistrias-yearning-for-%E2%80%98the-Motherland-59816.html.

Euronews. 2014a. Transnistrian Leader Shevchuk Says He Wants a "Civilised Divorce" With Moldova." 7 June. https://www.euronews.com/2014/06/07/interview-transnistran-president-shevchuk-says-he-wants-a-civilised-divorce-.

Euro Maidan Press 2017. Ukraine helps Moldova regain control over border in Transnistrian region. 21 July. http://euromaidanpress.com/2017/07/21/ukraine-helps-moldova-regain-control-over-border-in-transnistria-region/

European Convention on Human Rights. 2010. https://www.echr.coe.int/documents/convention_eng.pdf

European Council. 2010. Decision 2010/573/CFSP, *Concerning Restrictive Measures Against the Leadership of the Transnistrian Region of the Republic of Moldova*. https://eur-lex.europa.eu/legal-content/EN/TXT/?qid=1478020811856&uri=CELEX:32010D0573.

European Council. 2012. Decision 2012/527/CFSP, *Amending Decision 2010/573/CFSP Concerning Restrictive Measures Against the Leadership of the Transnistrian Region of the Republic of Moldova*. https://eur-lex.europa.eu/legal-content/EN/TXT/?qid=1406805602453&uri=CELEX:32012D0527.

European Council. 2014. Decision 2014/751/CFSP, *Amending Decision 2010/573/CFSP Concerning Restrictive Measures Against the Leadership of the Transnistrian Region of the Republic of Moldova*. https://eur-lex.europa.eu/legal-content/EN/TXT/?uri=uriserv:OJ.L_.2014.311.01.0054.01.ENG.

European Court of Human Rights (ECHR). 2020. Court Register https://hudoc.echr.coe.int/fre#{%22fulltext%22:[%22transnistria%22],%22documentcollectionid2%22:[%22GRANDCHAMBER%22,%22CHAMBER%22]}.

European Joint Analysis (EJA). 2016. *Programming in the Republic of Moldova until 2020*. https://eeas.europa.eu/sites/eeas/files/joint_analysis_0.pdf.

European Union: External Action (EU:EE). 2016. *Where We Work*. http://eubam.org/where-we-work/.

European Union: *Official Journal (EUOJ)*. 2014. Association Agreement Between the European Union and the European Atomic Energy Community and their Member States and Moldova. 57: 4–738.

European Parliament. 2014. *Resolution on Transnistria*. 2014/2552, 6 February. https://www.europarl.europa.eu/sides/getDoc.do?type=TA&language=EN&reference=P7-TA-2014-0108.

European Parliament. 2018. Question for Written Answer E-005640-18 to the Commission Rule 130. *Parliamentary Questions,* 7 November. https://www.europarl.europa.eu/doceo/document/E-8-2018-005640_EN.html.

Fabry, Mikulas. 2012. The Contemporary Practice of State Recognition: Kosovo, South Ossetia, Abkhazia, and Their Aftermath. *Nationalities Papers* 40(5): 661–676. https://www.academia.edu/19202235/.

Facebook. 2018. *Page of Nina Shtanski.* https://www.facebook.com/nina.shtanski.

Fedyakina, Anna. 2013. Transnistria Will Heal According to Russian Laws. *Rossiyskaya Gazeta*, No. 292 (6268). https://rg.ru/2013/12/25/pridnestrovie-site.html.

International Federation for Human Rights (FIDH). 2012. *Torture and Ill-Treatment in Moldova, Including Transnistria: Shared Problems, Evaded Responsibility.* https://www.fidh.org/img/pdf/moldova_transnistria_report.pdf.

International Federation for Human Rights (FIDH). 2014. *Transnistria: Concern on the Situation of Human Rights Defenders.* https://www.fidh.org/en/region/europe-central-asia/moldova/16642-transnistria-concern-on-the-situation-of-human-rights-defenders.

The Financial Times. 2019. Record High Remittances Are Not Without Risks. 2 September 2019. https://www.ft.com/content/1538de3c-c99c-11e9-a1f4-3669401ba76f.

Fischer, Sabine, Buscher, Klemens, Smolnik, Franziska and Halbach, Uwe. 2016. *Not Frozen! The Unresolved Conflicts over Transnistria, Abkhazia, South Ossetia and Nagorno-Karabakh in Light of the Crisis over Ukraine.* German Institute for International and Security Affairs. https://www.swp-berlin.org/fileadmin/contents/products/research_papers/2016RP09_fhs.pdf.

Fitzmaurice, Malgosia. 2019. Badinter Commission (for the former Yugoslavia). Oxford Public International Law. https://opil.ouplaw.com/view/10.1093/law:epil/9780199231690/law-9780199231690-e13.

Florescu, Radu. 2004. Bucharest, Treaty of. in *Encyclopaedia of Russian History*, edited by James Millar: 176–177. Macmillan US, New York.

Fomenko, Vladimir. 2017. *Extended Migration Profile of Transnistria.* International Organization for Migration Mission to Moldova. https://www.iom.md/sites/default/files/publications/docs/extended%20migration%20profile%20of%20transnistria.pdf.

Forbes. 2020. Alisher Usmanov. https://www.forbes.com/profile/alisher-usmanov/.

Foreign and Commonwealth Office (UK) (FCO). 2015. *Somalia Background Briefing.* https://assets.publishing.service.gov.uk/government/uploads/system/uploads/attachment_data/file/626249/FOI_0328-17_documents.pdf.

Foreign Policy Association of Moldova. 2013. Interview with Nicolae Buceaţki. 3 December. https://assets.publishing.service.gov.uk/government/uploads/system/uploads/attachment_data/file/626249/FOI_0328-17_documents.pdf.

ForkLog. 2016. Moldova's Breakaway Region of Transnistria Considers Creating Its Own Cryptocurrency. 7 October. https://forklog.media/moldovas-breakaway-region-of-transnistria-considers-creating-its-own-cryptocurrency/.

France 24. 2018. Detained Saudi Human Rights Lawyer Freed: Campaigners. 24 December.

https://www.france24.com/en/20181224-detained-saudi-human-rights-lawyer-freed-campaigners.

Freedom House. 2018. *Freedom in the World*. https://www.refworld.org/docid/5bcdce18c.html.

Freedom House. 2020. *Freedom in the World*. https://freedomhouse.org/countries/freedom-world/scores.

Fruntaşu, Iulian. 2002. *O istorie etnopolitică a Basarabiei. 1812–2002*. Chisinau: Cartier.

Fullenkamp, Connel. 2015. *Do Remittances Drive Economic Growth?* World Economic Forum, 10 February. https://www.weforum.org/agenda/2015/02/do-remittances-drive-economic-growth/.

Fund for Peace. 2020. *Fragile States Index*. https://www.weforum.org/agenda/2015/02/do-remittances-drive-economic-growth/.

Gallen Carpenter, Ted. 2008. Kosovo Independence Grenade. *Middle Eastern Times*, 22 February. http://www.cato.org/pub_display.php?pub_id=9238.

Gauthier, David. 1994. Breaking Up: An Essay on Secession. *Canadian Journal of Philosophy* 24(3): 357–372. https://doi.org/10.1080/00455091.1994.10717374.

Gagauzia.md. 2015. http://www.gagauzia.md/pageview.php?l=ru&idc=363.

Gellner, Ernest. 1983. *Nations and Nationalism*. Cornell University Press, Ithaca, New York.

Geo TV. 2017. *Pakistan Tells US to Respect Territorial Integrity*. 7 September. https://www.geo.tv/latest/157020-foreign-minister-addresses-press-conference-after-envoys-moot.

Glenny, Misha. 2009. *McMafia: Seriously Organised Crime*. Vintage, London.

Global Policy Forum. 2013. *Failed States*. https://www.globalpolicy.org/nations-a-states/failed-states.html.

Global Policy Forum. n.d. What is a "State"? Accessed 27/6/19. https://archive.globalpolicy.org/nations/statindex.htm.

Goda, Samuel. 2016. The Current and Future Challenges for the OSCE Mission to Moldova. *OSCE Yearbook 2015*, Baden-Baden, 205–213. https://doi.org/10.5771/9783845273655-205.

Gonţa Valeriu. 2014. *Refugees Find Hope in Moldova*. Moldova.org, 20 June. https://www.moldova.org/en/refugees-find-hope-in-moldova/.

Google Maps. 2021. https://www.google.co.uk/maps/.

Graham, Malborne. 1944. The Legal Status of the Bukovina and Bessarabia 1944. *The American Journal of International Law* 38(4): 667–673. https://doi.org/10.2307/2192802.

Grau, Lina. 2016. *Explainer: An Unpredictable Election Unfolds In Moldova's Breakaway Transdniester*. Radio Free Europe, 11 December. https://www.rferl.org/a/moldova-transdniester-election-russia-explainer/28169591.html.

Grosby, Steven. 1995. Territoriality: The Transcendental, Primordial Feature of Modern Societies. *Nations and Nationalism* 1 (2): 143–162. https://doi.org/10.1111/j.1354-5078.1995.00143.x

Gudim, Anatol. 2016. *Transnistria: Conflicts and Pragmatism of the Economy*. Centre for Strategic Studies and Reforms. https://core.ac.uk/download/pdf/11870249.pdf.

Guibernau, Monserrat. 1996. *Nationalisms: The Nation-State and Nationalism in the Twentieth Century*. Polity Press, Cambridge.

Gussen, Benjamin. 2019. *Axial Shift: City Subsidiarity and the World System in the 21st Century*. Palgrave Macmillan, Singapore.

Guvernul. n.d. *Moldovan Government*. Accessed 27/4/21. https://gov.md/ro/advanced-page-type/I-de-presa.

Hale, Henry. 2004. Explaining Ethnicity. *Comparative Political Studies* 37(4): 458–485. DOI: 10.1177/0010414003262906

Hammarberg, Thomas. 2009. *Ombudsmen Need Independence to Speak Out for Human Rights*. Stockholm Human Rights Conference, 1 June. http://www.theioi.org/downloads/42ga1/stockholm%20conference_10.%20workshop%201_thomas%20hammarberg.pdf.

Hammarberg, Thomas. 2013. *Report on Human Rights in the Transnistrian Region of the Republic of Moldova*. United Nations. https://www.undp.org/content/dam/unct/moldova/docs/pub/senior_expert_hammarberg_report_tn_human_rights.pdf.

Hammarberg, Thomas. 2018. *Follow-up Report on Human Rights in the Transnistrian Region*. United Nations. https://www.undp.org/content/dam/unct/moldova/docs/Follow-up_Report_TH_2018.pdf.

Hansen, Alvin. 1939. Economic Progress and Declining Population Growth. *The American Economic Review* 29(1): 1–15. https://www.jstor.org/stable/1806983.

Hartney, Christopher. 2006. *US Rates of Incarceration: A Global Perspective*. National Council on Crime and Delinquency, Madison, Wisconsin.

Harzl, Benedikt. 2016. *Keeping the Transnistrian Conflict on the Radar of the EU*. Österreichische Gesellschaft für Europapolitik. https://oegfe.at/2016/10/keeping-the-transnistrian-conflict-on-the-radar-of-the-eu/#6b.

Hassan, Daud. 2006. The Rise of the Territorial State and the Treaty of Westphalia. *Yearbook of New Zealand Jurisprudence* 9: 62–70. https://opus.lib.uts.edu.au/bitstream/10453/3289/1/2006006060.pdf.

Hatherley, Owen. 2015. Moscow's Suburbs May Look Monolithic, but the Stories They Tell Are Not. *The Guardian,* 12 June. https://www.theguardian.com/cities/2015/jun/12/moscows-suburbs-may-look-monolithic-but-the-stories-they-tell-are-not.

Hatherley, Owen. 2015a. *How the Soviet Union's Utopian Ideals Turned Into an Architectural Nightmare*. CNN, 27 August. https://edition.cnn.com/style/article/communist-architecture-ussr-soviet-union/index.html.

Hawksley, Humphrey. 2014. Ukraine Crisis: Could Trans-Dniester Be Next? BBC News, March 20. www.bbc.co.uk/news/world-europe-26662721.

Haynes, Rebecca. 2020. *Moldova: A History*. Bloomsbury Publishing, London.

Hensel, Stuart. 2006. *Moldova Strategic Conflict Assessment*. UK Global Conflict Prevention Pool, London.

Herman, Edward and Chomsky, Noam. 1988. *Manufacturing Consent*. Pantheon Books, New York. https://msuweb.montclair.edu/~furrg/hj/chomskyhermanpropmodel.pdf.

Hess, Maximillian. 2020. What Abkhazia's Crypto Dalliance Teaches Us About Monetary Sovereignty. *Business Telegraph*. 20 January. https://www.businesstelegraph.co.uk/what-abkhazias-crypto-dalliance-teaches-us-about-monetary-sovereignty/.

Hill, Ronald J. 1977. *Soviet Political Elites: The Case of Tiraspol*. St. Martin's Press, New York.

Hill, William. 2013. *Russia, the Near Abroad, and the West: Lessons from the Moldova-Transdniestria Conflict*. Woodrow Wilson Center Press, Washington DC.

Hill, William H. and Kramer, David. 2019. *The Fight for the Poorest Country in Europe*. The American Interest, 2 July. https://www.the-american-interest.com/2019/07/02/the-fight-for-the-poorest-country-in-europe/.

Hobsbawn, Eric. 2012. *Nations and Nationalism Since 1780: Programme, Myth, Reality*. Cambridge University Press.

Home Office (UK). 2017. *Country Policy and Information Note Moldova: Human Rights in Transnistria*. Guidance Notes for Immigration Officers. https://assets.publishing.service.gov.uk/government/uploads/system/uploads/attachment_data/file/619539/moldova_-_transnistria_-_cpin_-_v1.0__june_2017_.pdf.

House of Commons Library. 2021. *Pensions: International Comparisons*. 21 April. https://commonslibrary.parliament.uk/research-briefings/sn00290/#:~:text=According%20to%20an%20OECD%20analysis,EU%20average%20of%2063.5%25).

Ignatiev, Ivan. 2006. *Identification and Review of Key Environmental and Security Problems in the Transnistrian Region, Republic of Moldova*. Ecospectrum Research and Production Association. http://www.envsec.org/publications/identification%20and%20review%20of%20key%20environmental%20and%20security%20problems%20in%20the%20transnistrian%20region,%20republic%20of%20moldova_eng.pdf.

Ignatiev, Vitaly (ed.). 2018. *Political and Legal Framework for International Recognition of Independence of the Pridnestrovian Moldavian Republic*. Transnistrian Government Publications, Tiraspol.

Ilascu v. Moldova and Russia. 2004. European Court of Human Rights. 8 July. https://www.refworld.org/cases,ECHR,414d9df64.html.

Index Mundi. 2020. *Countries*. https://www.indexmundi.com/south_sudan/gdp_per_capita_(ppp).html

Information and News Resource of the PMR (INR). 2018. *Territory Without Crime*. http://newspmr.com/novosti-pmr/vesti-s-mest/5034.

Infotag. 2006. *Igor Smirnov Traditionally Wins Presidential Election in Transnistria*. 11 December. https://www.moldova.org/en/igor-smirnov-traditionally-wins-presidential-election-in-transnistria-21256-eng/.

Infotag. 2012. *ISS Deputy Head Says Transnistrian Banks Are Sued for Illicit Financial Operations*. 10 October. http://www.infotag.md/news-en/597564/.

Infotag. 2014. *Total Amount of Money Supply in Transnistria Grew by US$5.5m Equivalent in October*. 11 November. http://www.infotag.md/rebelion-en/195567/.

Infotag. 2014a. *Tiraspol Leader Complains to United Nations About Restrictions by Neighbor Countries*. 11 April. http://www.infotag.md/rebelion-en/187155/.

Infotag. 2015. *Transnistrian Parliament Adjourns Census for One More Year*. 5 February. http://www.infotag.md/rebelion-en/199035/.

Infotag. 2016. *Transnistria Introduces Criminal Responsibility for Election Rigging*. 28 November. http://www.infotag.md/rebelion-en/235640/.

Infotag. 2017. *TCP Party Reports Prevented Assassination of its Leader Oleg Horjan*. 16 October. http://www.infotag.md/rebelion-en/253543/.

Infotag. 2018. *ECHR Orders Russia to Pay Compensation to Five Moldovan Policemen Illegally Detained in Transnistria*. 19 July. http://www.infotag.md/reports-en/777099/.

Infotag. 2019. *PMR Communist Leader Called on Compatriots Not to be Afraid or Keep Silence*. 3 June. http://www.infotag.md/rebelion-en/276205/.

International Compliance Association (ICA). n.d. *What is Anti Money Laundering?* Accessed 25/1/21. https://www.int-comp.org/careers/your-career-in-aml/what-is-money-laundering/.

International Labor Organization. 2008. *Action Against Trafficking Human Beings*. https://www.ilo.org/wcmsp5/groups/public/@ed_norm/@declaration/documents/publication/wcms_090356.pdf.

International Programme on the Elimination of Child Labour (IPECL). 2003. *Rapid Assessment of Trafficking in Children for Labour and Sexual Exploitation in Moldova*.

Iovec and others v. Moldova and Russia. 2019. European Court of Human Rights. https://hudoc.echr.coe.int/eng#{%22languageisocode%22:[%22FRE%22],%22appno%22:[%2240942/14%22],%22documentcollectionid2%22:[%22COMMITTEE%22],%22itemid%22:[%22001-195845%22]}.

IPN. 2013. *Alexandru Coliban's Family Protests in Front of Foreign Ministry*. 21 January. https://www.ipn.md/en/alexandru-colibans-family-protests-in-front-of-foreign-minis-try-7967_1002866.html#ixzz6WtwLLKPm.

Isachenko, Daria. 2012. *The Making of Informal States: State Building in Transnistria and Northern Cyprus*. Palgrave Macmillan, London.

Isachenko, Daria and Schlichte, Klaus. 2007. *The Crooked Ways of State-Building: How Uganda and Transnistria Muddle Through the International System*. Junior Research Group, Humboldt University. http://www2.hu-berlin.de/mikropolitik/workingpapers.

Islamic Republic of Iran v. United States of America. 1996. International Court of Justice. https://www.icj-cij.org/en/case/90/judgments.

Ismail, Nimo. 2017. Somaliland: A Stable And Independent State, But No Recognition. *World Policy*, 21 February. http://worldpolicy.org/2017/02/21/somaliland-a-stable-and-independent-state-but-no-recognition/.

Ivan, Paul. 2014. *Transnistria - Where To?* European Policy Centre. http://aei.pitt.edu/56457/.

Jaroszewicz, Marta and Całus, Kamil. 2015. *Moldova: A Year After the Introduction of the Visa-Free Regime*. Centre for Eastern Studies, 6 May. https://www.osw.waw.pl/en/publikacje/analyses/2015-05-06/moldova-a-year-after-introduction-visa-free-regime.

Jehovah's Christian Witnesses (JCW). 2006. *Transnistria Religious Persecution Continues – Jehovah's Witnesses Face Ban.* JCW Office of the General Counsel. http://www.osce.org/odihr/21490?download=true.

Jehovah's Christian Witnesses (JCW). 2014. *Information on Conscientious Objection to Military Service involving Jehovah's Witnesses.* JCW Office of the General Counsel. https://www.ohchr.org/Documents/Issues/RuleOfLaw/ConscientiousObjection/JehovahsWitnesses.pdf.

Johnson, Glen. 2017. Freedom Bubbles Away Underground in Transnistria. *Balkan Insight,* 16 November. https://balkaninsight.com/2017/11/16/freedom-bubbles-away-under-ground-in-transnistria-11-15-2017/.

Junker, Nikki. 2014. *The Role of Cossacks in the Moldovan-Transnistrian Conflict.* Graduate dissertation La Salle University. 29 April. https://www.academia.edu/7384148/The_Role_of_Cossacks_in_the_Moldovan-Transnistrian_Conflict?auto=download

Kalik, Larisa. 2020. *Year of Youth.* http://transnistrianarmy.com/.

Karamazov, Anton. 2015. Putin Will Simply Withdraw the Peacekeepers From Transnistria, He Has No Choice. *Niqnaq,* 26 May 2015. https://niqnaq.wordpress.com/2015/05/26/putin-will-simply-withdraw-the-russian-peacekeepers-from-transnistria-he-has-no-choice/.

Kashi, David. 2014. Could Moldova Be The Next Crimea? Ethnic Russians in Transnistria Call On Moscow For Accession. *International Business Times,* 18 March.

https://www.ibtimes.com/could-moldova-be-next-crimea-ethnic-russians-transnistria-call-moscow-accession-1562140.

Kelly, Luke. 2019. *Legislation on Non-Governmental Organisations (NGOs) in Tanzania, Kenya, Uganda, Ethiopia, Rwanda and England and Wales.* UK Department of International Development. https://assets.publishing.service.gov.uk/media/5d9b558ded915d354c1afoff/656_NGO_Legislation_East_Africa.pdf.

Kermach, Ruslan. 2017. The Sources of Stability of the Transnistrian *De Facto* State. *Ukraine Analytica* 3(9): 14-22. https://dif.org.ua/en/article/the-sources-of-sustainability-of-the-transnistrian-de-facto-state.

Keynes, John Maynard. 1937. Some Economic Consequences of a Declining Population. *The Eugenics Review* 29(1): 13–17. https://www.ncbi.nlm.nih.gov/pmc/articles/pmc2985686/?page=5.

Kincade, Brian. 2018. The Economics of the American Prison System. *Smart Asset,* 21 May. https://smartasset.com/mortgage/the-economics-of-the-american-prison-system.

King, Charles. 2000. *The Moldovans: Romania, Russia, and the Politics of Culture.* Hoover Institution Press, Stanford. https://archive.org/details/moldovansromaniaooking_o/page/n1/mode/2up?q=petro.

King's College. 2020. *What is Sovereignty?* https://ukandeu.ac.uk/the-facts/what-is-sovereignty/.

Kireev, Alex. 2007. Transnistria. Independence Referendum 2006. *Electoral Geography.* https://www.electoralgeography.com/new/en/countries/t/transnistria/transnistria-independence-referendum-2006.html.

Kiwanuka, Richard. 1988. The Meaning of "People" in the African Charter on Human and People's Rights. *American Journal of International Law* 82(1): 80–101. Doi:10.1017/S0002930000074170.

Kligman, Gail. 1992. *When Abortion is Banned: The Politics of Reproduction in Ceausescu's Romania and After.* National Council for Soviet and East European Research. https://www.ucis.pitt.edu/nceeer/1992-805-14-Kligman.pdf.

Kljajic, Sanja. 2018. Scenarios to End Kosovo and Serbia's Frozen Conflict. *DW*, 13 April. https://www.dw.com/en/scenarios-to-end-kosovo-and-serbias-frozen-conflict/a-43345269.

Knott, Eleanor. 2015. As a Moldovan, It's Not So Easy to Get Romanian Citizenship (and a Romanian/EU Passport). *Wordpress*, 21 December. https://eleanorknott.wordpress.com/2015/12/21/as-a-moldovan-its-not-so-easy-to-get-romanian-citizenship-and-a-romanianeu-passport/.

Kolstø Pål, Edemsky, Andrei and Kalashnikova, Natalya. 1993. The Dniester Conflict: Between Irredentism and Separatism. *Europe-Asia Studies* 45(6): 973–1000. https://doi.org/10.1080/09668139308412137.

Kolstø, Pål and Edemsky, Andrei. 1995. *Russians in the Former Soviet.* Indiana University Press, Bloomington. https://www.academia.edu/5499030/russians_in_the_former_soviet_republics.

Kolstø Pål. 2014. *Transnistria Is a Bridge Too Far for Russia.* openDemocracy, 11 June. https://www.opendemocracy.net/en/odr/transnistria-is-bridge-too-far-for-russia/.

Koltay, András. 2015. What Is Press Freedom Now? New Media, Gatekeepers, and the Old Principles of the Law. *Journal of Media Law* 7(1): 36–64. http://real.mtak.hu/id/eprint/98830.

Kosienkowski, Marcin. 2011. The Alliance for European Integration and the Transnistrian Conflict Settlement. *Sprawy Narodowościowe – Nationalities Affairs* 38: 23–32. https://papers.ssrn.com/sol3/papers.cfm?abstract_id=2136112.

Kosienkowski, Marcin. 2012. *Continuity and Change in Transnistria's Foreign Policy After the 2011 Presidential Elections.* The Catholic University of Lublin Publishing House. https://papers.ssrn.com/sol3/papers.cfm?abstract_id=2143330.

Kosienkowski, Marcin. 2019. The Patron–Client Relationship Between Russia and Transnistria. In *De Facto States in Eurasia*, edited by Tomáš Hoch and Vincenc Kopeček: 183–207. Routledge, Abingdon. DOI:10.4324/9780429244049-14.

Kosovo Thanks You. 2020. https://www.kosovothanksyou.com/.

Kozak Memorandum. 2003. https://www.stefanwolff.com/files/Kozak-Memorandum.pdf.

KPMG. 2020. *Moldova – Income Tax.* 31 January. https://home.kpmg/xx/en/home/insights/2017/03/moldova-income-tax.html.

Kramer, Andrew. 2016. Pussy Riot Video Mocks Russian Prosecutor Accused of Corruption. *The New York Times*, 2 February. https://www.nytimes.com/2016/02/04/world/europe/russia-pussy-riot-yuri-chaika.html.

Krasner, Stephen. 1999. *Sovereignty: Organized Hypocrisy.* Princeton University Press.

Kuchler, Florian. 2010. *The Role of the EU in Moldova's Transnistria Conflict*. Forum für osteuropäische Ideen – und Zeitgeschichte, Stuttgart and Hannover.

Kudors, Andis, Maliukevičius, Nerjus, Pelnens, Gatis and Pkhaladze, Tengiz. 2010. *The 'Humanitarian Dimension' of Russian Foreign Policy Toward* [sic] *Georgia, Moldova, Ukraine, and the Baltic States*. Centre for Eastern European Studies.

Kunze, Thomas and Bohnet, Henri. 2007. *Between Europe and Russia: On the Situation of the Renegade Republics of Transnistria, Abkhazia, and South Ossetia*. JSTOR, 7 February. https://www.jstor.org/stable/resrep10019?seq=1#metadata_info_tab_contents.

Kuo, Lily. 2019. Wang Quanzhang: China Sentences Human Rights Lawyer to Four Years in Prison. *The Guardian*, 28 January. https://www.theguardian.com/world/2019/jan/28/wang-quanzhang-china-sentences-human-rights-lawyer-to-four-years-in-prison.

Kuo, Lily and Wang, Xueying. 2019. Can China Recover From Its Disastrous One-Child Policy? *The Guardian*, 2 March. https://www.theguardian.com/world/2019/mar/02/china-population-control-two-child-policy.

Laboratory for Transnistrian Conflict Analysis. (LACT). 2019. *The Leader of the Transnistrian Communists Urges The Concetanators* [sic] *"Not to be Afraid and Not to be Silent"*. 3 June. https://lact.ro/infotag-md-liderul-comunistilor-transnistreni-indeamna-concetatenii-sa-nu-se-teama-si-sa-nu-taca/.

Lane, Gary. 2007. *Christians Face Abuse from Corrupt Regime*. Christian Broadcasting Network, 6 April. https://web.archive.org/web/20090418150950/http://www.cbn.com/cbnnews/133101.aspx.

Laruelle, Marlene. 2016. *The Russian World: Russia's Soft Power and Geopolitical Imagination*. Center on Global Interests. https://globalinterests.org/wp-content/uploads/2015/05/final-cgi_russian-world_marlene-laruelle.pdf.

Laurinavičiūtė, Lina and Biekša, Laurynas. 2015. The Relevance of Remedial Secession in the Post-Soviet "Frozen Conflicts". *International Comparative Jurisprudence* 1(1): 66–75. https://doi.org/10.1016/j.icj.2015.10.008.

Law and Order. 2016. *Laws of Transnistria*. http://pravopmr.ru/view.aspx?id=jp%2ft7xlxaejdr30y8nds1a%3d%3d.

Legal Resources Centre of Moldova (LRCM). 2015. Civil Society Organizations Condemn the So-Called Criminal Prosecution Against an Organization That is Defending and Promoting Human Rights. 27 April. https://crjm.org/en/38-de-ong-uri-cer-protejarea-ong-urilor-ce-activeaza-in-stanga-nistrului/.

Lerner, Craig. 2004. Saving the Constitution: Lincoln, Secession, and the Price of Union. *Michigan Law Review* 102(6): 1263–1294. https://repository.law.umich.edu/cgi/viewcontent.cgi?article=1750&context=mlr.

Lesanu, Alexandru. 2015. *Sweet History in Bitter Times: Refining Sugar in the Transnistrian Borderlands (1898–2001)*. PhD Dissertation, George Mason University. https://pdfs.semanticscholar.org/7826/9dafeddbcc1c3df50068b958e42749688a8d.pdf.

Lesanu, Alexandru. 2016. *Transnistria's Presidential Election: A Hard-Fought Contest With No Punches Pulled, As Russia Diverts Its Attention From the Unrecognised*

State. London School of Economics. https://blogs.lse.ac.uk/europpblog/2016/12/23/transnistrias-presidential-election.

Levin, Dov and Lavi, Theodore. 2014. *The Jews of Bessarabia: The Holocaust Period*. Yizkor Book Project, New York.

Library of Congress. 2016. *Anti-Religious Campaigns: Revelations from the Russian Archives*. https://www.loc.gov/exhibits/archives/anti.html.

Litoy, Alexandr. 2015. Between Real and Imitation Democracy: Elections in Transnistria. openDemocracy, 29 October. https://www.opendemocracy.net/en/odr/between-real-and-imitation-democracy-elections-in-transnistria/.

Litra, Leonard. 2015. *Moldova*. Freedom House. https://freedomhouse.org/sites/default/files/NIT2015_Moldova_0.pdf.

Livadari, Arina. 2019. *The General Prosecutor's Office of the Russian Federation Claims That Transnistria is a "Sovereign State"*. Moldova.org, 5 June. https://www.moldova.org/en/general-prosecutors-office-russian-federation-claims-transnistria-sovereign-state/.

Lobjakas, Ahto. 2005. *Moldova: Western Diplomats Say Reports of Smuggling From Transdniester Likely Exaggerated*. Radio Free Europe, 11 October. https://www.rferl.org/a/1062030.html.

Lof, Rick. 2016. *Russia's Diaspora Politics and the Transnistrian Conflict*. University of Amsterdam. https://www.academia.edu/29444978.

Lomsadze, Giorgi. 2014. More Post-Soviet Revolutions: Enter Abkhazia. *Eurasianet*, 28 May. https://eurasianet.org/more-post-soviet-revolutions-enter-abkhazia.

Lugar, Richard. 2011. *Will Russia End Eastern Europe's Last Frozen Conflict?* Report to the Committee on Foreign Relations of the US Senate, 8 February. https://www.govinfo.gov/content/pkg/CPRT-112SPRT63345/html/CPRT-112SPRT63345.htm.

Luhn, Alex. 2017. Moscow's Big Move: Is this the Biggest Urban Demolition Project Ever? *The Guardian*, 31 March. https://www.theguardian.com/cities/2017/mar/31/moscow-biggest-urban-demolition-project-khrushchevka-flats.

Lungu, Karina. 2016. *Transnistria: From Entropy to Exodus*. European Council on Foreign Relations, 1 September. https://www.ecfr.eu/article/essay_transnistria_from_entropy_to_exodus.

Lupusor, Adrian, Fala, Alexandra, Morcotylo, Iurie and Prohnitch, Valeriu. 2015. Transnistrian Economy at the Crossroads. *Regional Economic Review* 3: 3–27. https://www.undp.org/content/dam/moldova/docs/publications/regional_economic_review_december_2015.pdf.

Lynch, Dov. 2004. *Engaging Eurasia's Separatist States*. United States Institute of Peace, Washington, DC.

McDonald, Glenn. 2013. 10 Signs You're Living in a Police State. *The Seeker*, 12 June. https://www.seeker.com/10-signs-youre-living-in-a-police-state-1767589446.html.

McDonald, Melissa. 2014. *How Regimes Dictate Oligarchs & their Football Clubs: Case Studies Comparison of Oligarch Football Club Ownership in Dagestan, Romania & Transnistria from 1990–2014*. Master's Thesis, University of South Carolina. https://doi.org/10.17615/njxc-3883.

Mackinnon, Amy and Gramer, Robbie. 2020. Vucic: Most Serbs Prefer a 'Frozen Conflict' with Kosovo. *Foreign Policy Insider Access*, 4 March. https://foreignpolicy.com/2020/03/04/serbian-president-aleksandar-vucic-interview-frozen-conflict-kosovo/.

MacLean, Rory. 2015. *Transnistria: Back in the USSR*. Unbound, London.

McQuail, Denis. 2000. *McQuail's Mass Communication Theory*, 6th edition. Sage Publishing, London.

Maller, Yuri. 2011. *Tiraspol Trolleybus Network: Facts*. Ymtram. http://ymtram.mashke.org/moldova/tiraspol/descr_tb_en.html.

Mandla v. Dowell-Lee. 1982. House of Lords (UK). https://www.bailii.org/uk/cases/UKHL/1982/7.html.

Marandici, Ion. 2020. Multiethnic Parastates and Nation-Building: The Case of the Transnistrian Imagined Community. *Nationalities Papers* 48(1): 61–82. DOI:10.1017/nps.2019.69.

Matsuzato, Kimitaka. 2009. Inter-Orthodox Relations and Transborder Nationalities in and Around Unrecognised Abkhazia and Transnistria. *Religion, State and Society* 37(3): 239–262. https://doi.org/10.1080/09637490903056476.

Mauer, Marc. 2017. Incarceration Rates in an International Perspective. In *Oxford Encyclopaedia of Criminology and Criminal Justice*, edited by Henry Pontell. 26 April. https://doi.org/10.1093/acrefore/9780190264079.013.233

Mediafax. 2011. Moldovan Journalist Ernest Varadanean Pardoned by Transnistrian Leader Igor Smirnov. 5 May. https://www.mediafax.ro/externe/jurnalistul-moldovean-ernest-vardanean-gratiat-de-liderul-transnistrean-igor-smirnov-presa-9595243.

Melnykevych, Marta. 2014. *From the Separatist Movement to a New Identity Group – People of Transnistria: Declarations Countered by Reality*. Master's Thesis, Norwegian University of Life Sciences, Oslo. https://nmbu.brage.unit.no/nmbu-xmlui/handle/11250/283305.

Memorial. 2019. *Hotpoints*. http://www.memo.ru/hr/hotpoints/moldavia/benderye.htm.

Menary, Steve. 2007. *Outcasts! The Lands That FIFA Forgot*. Know the Score, Studley.

Menary, Steve. 2019. *Football's New Cold War: Soft Power in Post-Soviet Conflict States*. 6 May. https://www.researchgate.net/publication/332878453_football's_new_cold_war_soft_power_in_post-soviet_conflict_states.

Meseburg Memorandum. 2010. https://russiaeu.ru/sites/default/files/user/files/2010-06-05-meseberg-memorandum.pdf.

Miarka, Agnieszka. 2020. Transnistria as an Instrument of Influence of the Russian Federation on the Security of Moldova in the Second Decade of the 21st Century – Selected Aspects. *Communist and Post-Communist Studies* 53(2): 61–75. https://doi.org/10.1525/cpcs.2020.53.2.61.

Milano, Enrico. 2003. Security Council Action in the Balkans: Reviewing the Legality of Kosovo's Territorial Status. *European Journal of International Law* 14(5): 999–1022. http://www.ejil.org/pdfs/14/5/455.pdf.

Milakovsky, Brian. 2019. *Trade or Blockade? Economic Relations with Uncontrolled Territories in Moldova and Ukraine.* Kennan Cable no.48, Wilson Center. https://www.wilsoncenter.org/publication/kennan-cable-no-48-trade-or-blockade-economic-relations-uncontrolled-territories.

Ministry of Justice (UK). 2015. *Civil Justice Statistics Quarterly, England and Wales.* https://assets.publishing.service.gov.uk/government/uploads/system/uploads/attachment_data/file/409386/civil-justice-statistics-october-december-2014.pdf.

Ministry of Transport and Road Infrastructure (Moldova) (MTRI(M)). 2010. *Facilitating International Transport in the OSCE Area Through More Effective Regional Co-operation.* OSCE. https://www.osce.org/files/f/documents/9/9/41449.pdf.

Mirzayev, Farhad. 2014. *Uti Possidetis v Self-Determination: The Lessons of the Post-Soviet Practice.* PhD Thesis, Leicester University. https://leicester.figshare.com/articles/thesis/Uti_possidetis_v_self-determination_the_lessons_of_the_Post-Soviet_practice/10146536/1.

Mitrofanova, Anastasia. 2015. Transnistrian Conflict in the Context of Post-Soviet Nation-Building. *Sociological Studies* 9(2): 191–216. DOI: 10.1558/sols.v9i2.26392.

Moberly, Tom. 2017. UK Has Fewer Doctors Per Person than Most Other OECD Countries. *British Medical Journal*, 20 June. https://www.bmj.com/content/357/bmj.j2940.

Mogos, Adrian and Călugăreanu, Vitalie. 2012. How to Buy EU Citizenship. *EU Observer*, 14 September. https://euobserver.com/justice/117551.

Mold Street. 2016. *The Sheriff Empire at the Head of the Separatist Region.* 6 December. https://www.mold-street.com/?go=news&n=5370.

Moldova Foundation. 2014. *Prospects for Unfreezing Moldova's Frozen Conflict in Transnistria.* http://moldovafoundation.org/prospects-for-unfreezing-moldovas-frozen-conflict-in-transnistria/.

Moldova.org. 2005. *Poland Refuses to Mint Coins for Transnistria.* 20 April. https://www.moldova.org/en/poland-refuses-to-mint-coins-for-transnistria-1928-eng.

Moldova.org. 2006. *Transnistria Bans Funding of NGO's From Abroad.* 9 March. https://www.moldova.org/en/transnistria-bans-funding-of-ngos-from-abroad-10367-eng.

Moldova.org. 2007a. *Vladimir Putin Referring to the Kosovo Precedent as Regards Transnistria.* 11 June. https://www.moldova.org/en/vladimir-putin-referring-to-the-kosovo-precedent-as-regards-transnistria-52168-eng/.

Moldova.org. 2009. *Russian Passport Holders in Moldova's Transnistria on the Rise.* 3 November. https://www.moldova.org/en/russian-passport-holders-in-moldovas-transnistria-on-the-rise-204295-eng/.

Moldova.org. 2012. *Shevchuk, The Wind of Change in Transnistria?* 7 January. https://www.moldova.org/en/shevchuk-the-wind-of-change-in-transnistria-227620-eng/.

Moldova.org. 2012a. *Transnistria: Tiraspol Develops its Own Airport.* 30 October. https://www.moldova.org/en/transnistria-tiraspol-develops-its-own-airport-233686-eng/.

Moldova.org. 2013. *Alexandru Coliban, The Last Political Prisoner in Tiraspol.* 18 February.

https://www.moldova.org/en/alexandru-coliban-the-last-political-prisoner-in-tiraspol-video-report-235394-eng/.

Moldova.org. 2017. *Chisinau and Tiraspol Sign Protocols to Solve Issues of Latin Script Schools, Telecommunication, Diploma Recognition and Land Ownership.* https://www.moldova.org/en/chisinau-tiraspol-sign-protocols-solve-issues-latin-script-schools-telecommunication-diploma-recognition-land-ownership/.

Monahov, Alexandru and Jobert, Thomas. 2017. *Case Study of the Moldovan Bank Fraud: Is Early Intervention the Best Central Bank Strategy to Avoid Financial Crises?* GREDEG Working Papers Series. http://www.gredeg.cnrs.fr/working-papers/gredeg-wp-2017-07.pdf.

Montevideo Convention on the Rights and Duties of States. 1933. https://www.ilsa.org/Jessup/Jessup15/Montevideo%20Convention.pdf.

Mozer v. Russia and Moldova. 2016. European Court of Human Rights. https://www.bailii.org/eu/cases/ECHR/2016/213.html.

Muller, Henrik. 1999. From Dollarisation to Euroisation: The Future of the Euro as an International Substitution Currency. *Intereconomist* 34(6): 286–296. https://www.intereconomics.eu/pdf-download/year/1999/number/6/article/from-dollarisation-to-euroisation-the-future-of-the-euro-as-an-international-substitution-currency.html.

Munteanu, Igor. 2016. Hostile Narratives in the Moldovan Solitary Courtyard. *Der Donauraum* 53: 83–13. http://www.viitorul.org/files/Narratives_IM.pdf.

Munteanu, Igor. 2018. Ukraine Puts a Dent in Transnistria's Separatist Steel Industry Web. *Emerging Europe*, 31 May. https://emerging-europe.com/voices/ukraine-puts-a-dent-in-transnistrias-separatist-steel-industry/.

Murphy, Ciara. 2013. Scottish Independence: A Question of International Law or of the EU's "New Legal Order"? *European Law Blog*, 15 February. https://europeanlawblog.eu/2013/02/15/scottish-independence-a-question-of-international-law-or-of-the-eus-new-legal-order-part-i/.

Musteață, Sergiu. 2020. History Education and the Construction of Identity in a Conflict Region: The Case of Transnistria, the Republic of Moldova. *Dossiers Georg Eckert Institute for International Textbook Research* 6: 84–101. https://www.researchgate.net/publication/338660339.

Myachina, Katya. 2018. I Got Called in by the KGB. They Said There Were No LGBT People in Transnistria. openDemocracy, 24 January. https://www.opendemocracy.net/en/odr/they-said-there-were-no-lgbt-people-in-transnistria/.

Najarian, Mark. 2017. *Moldova's Reliance On Russia, Transdniester For Energy Seen As Risky.* Radio Free Europe, 14 July. https://www.rferl.org/a/moldova-heavy-reliance-russian-transdniester-energy-seen-risky-allin-baker-hughes/28615600.html.

Napieralska, Anna. 2012. *Russian-Moldovan Relations After the Collapse of the Soviet Union.* Graduate Thesis, West Virginia University. https://researchrepository.wvu.edu/cgi/viewcontent.cgi?article=1260&context=etd.

National Bureau of Statistics of the Republic of Moldova (NBS). 2014. *Population and Housing Census in the Republic of Moldova.* https://statistica.gov.md/pageview. php?l=en&idc=479.

NationMaster. n.d. *Industry Manufacturing Output: Countries Compared.* Accessed 25/11/20. https://www.nationmaster.com/country-info/stats/industry/manufacturing-output.

Necsutu, Madalin. 2017. OSCE Claims Some Progress in Transnistria Talks. *Balkan Insight,* 29 November. https://balkaninsight.com/2017/11/29/ osce-claims-some-progress-in-transnistria-talks-11-28-2017/.

Necsutu, Madalin. 2018. Russian Oligarch Eyes Bitcoin Farms in Breakaway Transnistria. *Balkan Insight,* 24 May. http://www.balkaninsight.com/en/article/ russian-investors-attracted-with-transnistria-s-minefarms-for-bitcoin-05-24-2018.

Necsutu, Madalin. 2018a. Russia Pledges More Financial Aid to Transnistria. *Balkan Insight,* 22 January. https://balkaninsight.com/2018/01/22/ russia-to-give-financial-aid-to-transnistria-01-22-2018/.

Necsutu, Madalin. 2019. Moldovan Ex-PM Vladimir Filat Released From Jail. *Balkan Insight,* 3 December. https://balkaninsight.com/2019/12/03/ moldovan-ex-pm-vladimir-filat-released-from-jail/.

Necsutu, Madalin. 2019a. Moldovan BIRN Fact-Check: Is Transnistria Really Economically Dependent on Russia? *Balkan Insight,* 23 December. https://balkaninsight.com/2019/12/23/ birn-fact-check-is-transnistria-really-economically-dependent-on-russia/.

Necsutu, Madalin. 2019b. Russia Pulls Transnistria Strings, With Eye on Ukraine. *Balkan Insight,* 26 September. https://balkaninsight.com/2019/09/26/ russia-pulls-transnistria-strings-with-eye-on-ukraine/.

Necsutu, Madalin. 2021. BIRN Fact-Check: What Must be Done for Russian Forces to Leave Transnistria? *Balkan Insight,* 22 January. https://balkaninsight.com/2021/01/22/ birn-fact-check-what-must-be-done-for-russian-forces-to-leave-transnistria/.

Nielsen, Jørgen. 2015. *Yearbook of Muslims in Europe.* Brill, Leiden.

New Europe. 2012. Russian Police Raid Transdnestr Banks. 8 April. https://www.new-europe.eu/article/russian-police-raid-transdnestr-banks/.

New York City Bar Association ("New York"). 2006. *Thawing a Frozen Conflict: Legal Aspects of the Separatist Crisis in Moldova.* https://papers.ssrn.com/sol3/papers. cfm?abstract_id=920151.

The New York Times. 1991. Text of Accords by Former Soviet Republics Setting Up a Commonwealth. 23 December. https://www.nytimes.com/1991/12/23/world/ end-soviet-union-text-accords-former-soviet-republics-setting-up-commonwealth. html?pagewanted=all&mcubz=1.

Newman, Edward and Visoka, Gezim. 2018. The Foreign Policy of State Recognition: Kosovo's Diplomatic Strategy to Join International Society. *Foreign Policy Analysis* 14: 367–387. DOI: 10.1093/fpa/orw042.

Newman, Frank. 1967. Ombudsmen and Human Rights: The New UN Treaty Proposals. *University of Chicago Law Review* 34(4): 951–962. https://www.jstor.org/stable/i272105.

NewsMaker. 2014. Politician and Human Rights Activist Alexander Radchenko Dies in Transnistria. 13 November. https://novostipmr.com/ru/news/14-06-16/platit-nalogi-po-novomu.

Nichol, James. 1995. *Diplomacy in the Former Soviet Republics*. Praeger, Westport, Connecticut.

North Atlantic Treaty Organization (NATO). 2020. *Relations with the Republic of Moldova*. https://www.nato.int/cps/en/natohq/topics_49727.htm.

Novosti Pridnestrovya. 2015. NGO Promo-Lex Might Have Carried Out Subversive Activity Against Pridnestrovie. *News of Pridnestrovie*. 22 April. https://novostipmr.com/en/news/15-04-22/ngo-promo-lex-might-have-carried-out-subversive-activity-against.

Novosti Pridnestrovya. 2015a. New Building of University Medical Department Inaugurated in Tiraspol. 1 September. https://novostipmr.com/en/news/15-09-01/new-building-university-medical-department-inaugurated-tiraspol.

Novosti Pridnestrovie. 2016. Pay Taxes in a New Way. 16 June. https://novostipmr.com/ru/news/14-06-16/platit-nalogi-po-novomu

Novosti Pridnestrovya. 2017. Vadim Krasnoselsky: Is Moldova Ready for Federalisation? 23 May. https://novostipmr.com/en/news/17-05-23/vadim-krasnoselsky-moldova-ready-federalisation.

Novosti Pridnestrovya. 2018. Bank Cards. 9 October. https://novostipmr.com/en/news/17-05-23/vadim-krasnoselsky-moldova-ready-federalisation.

Novosti Pridnestrovya. 2019. Deferment of Military Service for Medical Students. 6 June. https://novostipmr.com/en/news/19-06-06/measure-aimed-improving-personnel-situation-health-care-system-was.

Novosti Pridnestrovya. 2019a. Pridnestrovie, Not Transnistria. Bendery Deputies Want to Appeal to UN. 29 May. https://novostipmr.com/en/news/19-05-29/pridnestrovie-not-transnistria-bendery-deputies-want-appeal-un.

Nuclear Threat Initiative (NTI). 2011. *Commonwealth of Independent States*. 26 October. https://www.nti.org/learn/treaties-and-regimes/commonwealth-independent-states-cis/.

O'Connor, Robert. 2019. Transnistria Isn't the Smuggler's Paradise It Used to Be. *Foreign Policy*, 5 June. https://foreignpolicy.com/2019/06/05/transnistria-isnt-the-smugglers-paradise-it-used-to-be-sheriff-moldova-ukraine-tiraspol/.

OECD. 2017. *Health at a Glance: OECD Indicators*. https://read.oecd-ilibrary.org/social-issues-migration-health/health-at-a-glance-2017/medical-graduates-2015-or-nearest-year_health_glance-2017-graph135-en#page1.

Okrest, Dmitry. 2018. *Fighting Impunity in Moldova and Transnistria*. openDemocracy, 11 January. https://www.opendemocracy.net/en/odr/fighting-impunity-in-moldova-and-transnistria/.

Olesky, Piotr. 2015. Transnistria: It Is More Complicated than You Think. *New Eastern Europe*, 9 December. http://neweasterneurope.eu/old_site/articles-and-commentary/1821-transnistria-it-is-more-complicated-than-you-think.

O'Loughlin, John, Kolossov, Vladimir and Toal, Gerard. 2011. Inside Abkhazia: Survey of Attitudes in a *De Facto* State. *Post-Soviet Affairs* 27(1): 1–36. http://www.abkhaz-world.com/aw/pdf/inside_abkhazia_survey.pdf.

O'Loughlin, John, Toal, Gerard and Chamberlain-Creangă, Rebecca. 2013. Divided Space, Divided Attitudes? Comparing the Republics of Moldova and Pridnestrovie (Transnistria) Using Simultaneous Surveys. *Eurasian Geography and Economics* 54(2): 1–59. https://openknowledge.worldbank.org/bitstream/handle/10986/16188/rege-10.108015387216.2013.816619.pdf?sequence=1.

O'Loughlin, John, Kolossov, Vladimir and Toal, Gerard. 2015. Inside the Post-Soviet De Facto States: A Comparison of Attitudes in Abkhazia, Nagorny Karabakh, South Ossetia, and Transnistria. *Eurasian Geography and Economics* 55(5): 423–456. https://doi.org/10.1080/15387216.2015.1012644.

Ombudsman of PMR. 2014. *Statement in Connection with Violation of the Rights of Citizens in the Village of Dorotskoe.* http://www.ombudsmanpmr.org/p0476.htm.

Ombudsman of PMR. 2014a.*Press Release* http://www.ombudsmanpmr.org/p0496.htm.

Ombudsman of PMR. 2017 *Latest Events* . http://www.ombudsmanpmr.org/p0588.htm.

Ombudsman of PMR. 2020. *Introductory page.* http://www.ombudsmanpmr.org/.

OOSKAnews. 2012. *One-Third of Well Water in Transnistria Is of Poor Quality.* 24 August. https://www.ooskanews.com/daily-water-briefing/one-third-well-water-transnistria-poor-quality_24033.

OOSKAnews. 2012a. *Transnistrians Concerned Over Dniester Chemical Pollution From Ukraine.* 5 November. https://www.ooskanews.com/story/2012/11/transnistrians-concerned-over-dniester-chemical-pollution-ukraine_153295.

Orthodox Christianity. 2018. *Number of Churches in Russia Could Double.* 25 December. http://orthochristian.com/109491.html.

OSCE. 1994. *Transnistrian Conflict.* https://www.osce.org/files/f/documents/4/3/42308.pdf.

OSCE. 2012. The *Moldovan-Administered Latin-Script Schools in Transdniestria: Background, Current Situation, Analysis and Recommendations.* https://www.osce.org/moldova/99058?download=true.

OSCE. 2013. *OSCE Mission to Moldova Welcomes Release of Alexandru Coliban from Transdniestrian Prison.* 28 June. https://www.osce.org/moldova/103191.

OCSE. 2018. *OSCE Announces a 5+2 Meeting in Rome, Following Continued Progress on Reaching Agreements Within the Transdniestrian Settlement Process.* 11 May. https://www.osce.org/chairmanship/380935.

Osipov, Alexander and Vasilevich, Hanna. 2017. *The Phenomenon of Transnistria as a Model of Post-Soviet Diversity Policy.* European Centre for Minority Issues. Working Paper No.96. DOI: 10.13140/RG.2.2.31294.48960.

Osipov, Alexander and Vasilevich, Hanna. 2019. Transnistrian Nation-Building: A Case of Effective Diversity Policies? *Nationalities Papers* 47(6): 983–999. DOI:10.1017/nps.2018.26.

Ostavnaia, Alia. 2017. *Mapping Migration from Transnistria.* International Organization for Migration. http://xn--h1aauh.xn--p1ai/wp-content/uploads/2019/06/Mapping-Migration-from-Transnistria_0.pdf.

Oury, Jean-Paul. 2018. What Place Should the Environment Have in the Constitution? *European Scientist*, 9 July. https://www.europeanscientist.com/en/editors-corner/what-place-should-the-environment-have-in-the-constitution/.

Overseas Security Advisory Council (OSAC). 2020. *Moldova Crime & Safety Report*. USSD. https://www.osac.gov/Country/Moldova/Content/Detail/Report/a2a73c77-8c6a-4df7-9b2f-18b0ea65cfbc.

Owen, Elizabeth. 2017. *Abkhazia: Counting on a Cryptocurrency. Eurasianet*, 5 December. https://eurasianet.org/abkhazia-counting-on-a-cryptocurrency.

Owen, Jeffrey. 2009. *Neopatrimonialism and Regime Endurance in Transnistria*. Master's Thesis, Virginia Polytechnic Institute and State University. https://vtechworks.lib.vt.edu/bitstream/handle/10919/35153/Owen_JD_T_2009.pdf?sequence=1&isAllowed=y.

Parlicov Victor, Soitu, Tudor and Tofilat, Sergiu. 2017. *Energy and Politics: The Price for Impunity in Moldova*. The Institute for Development and Social Initiatives. http://www.viitorul.org/files/policy%20paper%202017%20-%20impunitate%20si%20%20intelelegeri%20rentiere%20sectorul%20energetic%20eng%20ii.pdf.

Pashentseva, Victoria. 2018. *Tough Lessons in Transnistria*. openDemocracy, 8 January. https://www.opendemocracy.net/en/odr/tough-lessons-in-transnistria/.

Patt, Martin. 2017. *Human Trafficking & Modern-Day Slavery*. http://gvnet.com/humantrafficking/Moldova.htm.

PenzaNews. 2017. Improving Relations Between Chisinau and Tiraspol to Create Conditions for Stability Growth and Reforms. 21 January. https://penzanews.ru/en/analysis/63437-2017.

People in Need. 2019. *Transnistria Discussion as a Crime?* 3 January. https://www.clovekvtisni.cz/en/transnistria-discussion-as-a-crime-5561gp.

Peoples, James and Bailey, Garrick. 2010. *Humanity: An Introduction to Cultural Anthropology*, 9th edition. Wadsworth Cengage Learning, Boston.

Peterka-Benton, Daniela. 2012. Arms Trafficking in Transnistria: A European Security Threat? *Journal of Applied Security Research* 7(1): 71–92. DOI 10.1080/19361610.2012.631407.

Pew Research Center. 2016. *Asylum Seeking Demography: Young and Male*. 2 August. https://www.pewresearch.org/global/2016/08/02/4-asylum-seeker-demography-young-and-male/.

Pew Research Center. 2019. *Democracy has Grown Across the World over the Past Four Decades*. 13 May. https://www.pewresearch.org/fact-tank/2019/05/14/more-than-half-of-countries-are-democratic/ft_19-05-02_democracyupdate_map/.

Pham, Peter. 2016. *Somalia: Where a State Isn't a State*. The Fletcher Institute of World Affairs. http://www.fletcherforum.org/home/2016/9/6/somalia-where-a-state-isnt-a-state?rq=Somalia.

Philips, Francis. 2016. Christians Suffered Unspeakably in the Soviet Union. It is a Hard

Subject to Read About. *Catholic Herald*, 14 July. https://catholicherald.co.uk/christians-suffered-unspeakably-in-the-soviet-union-it-is-a-hard-subject-to-read-about/.

Phillips, Lord Nicholas. 2007. *Judicial Independence*. Commonwealth Law Conference. 12 September.

Point News. 2013. Coliban's First Statement After Release. 28 June. https://point.md/ru/novosti/obschestvo/primele-declaraii-ale-lui-coliban-dupa-eliberare.

Polianskii, Mikhail and Wagner, Rebecca. 2021. Breaking the Vicious Circle: Can the New Moldovan President Sandu Succeed in Balancing Relations with the EU and Russia? *Prif Blog,* 28 January. https://blog.prif.org/2021/01/28/.

Popescu, Nicu. 2006. *Democracy in Secessionism: Transnistria and Abkhazia's Domestic Policies*. CPS International Policy Fellowship. https://core.ac.uk/download/pdf/11871437.pdf.

Popescu, Nicu & Litra, Leonard. 2012. *Transnistria, a Bottom-Up Solution*. European Council on Foreign Relations, Policy Brief no. 63. https://ecfr.eu/publication/transnistria_a_bottom_up_solution/.

Popșoi, Mihai. 2017. Moldova-Ukraine Energy Deal Upsets Russia by Cutting Transnistria Out. *Eurasia Daily Monitor,* 14(45). 3 April. https://jamestown.org/program/moldova-ukraine-energy-deal-upsets-russia-cutting-transnistria/

President of Abkhazia. 2017. *Economy.* http://presidentofabkhazia.org/en/respublika_abkhazia/economy/.

President of the PMR (President). 2017. *Ombudsman.* http://en.president.gospmr.org/

President of the PMR (President). 2019. *Results of 2018 Were Summed Up in the Constitutional Court of the PMR.* 21 February. http://en.president.gospmr.org/press-sluzhba/novosti/kollegiya-konstruktor-sud.

President of the PMR ("President"). n.d. *Local Administration of the Town of Rybnitsa and Rybnitsa District.* Accessed 2/5/21. http://president-pmr.org/category/74.html.

President of the PMR ("President"). n.d.-a *The Ministry of Education of the Pridnestrovian Moldavian Republic.* Accessed 2/5/21. http://president-pmr.org/material/62.html.

Pridnestrovian Republican Bank (PRB). 2017. *Indicators of the Currency Market.* 30 January. http://www.cbpmr.net/kurs_val.php?lang=en.

Pridnestrovian Republican Bank (PRB). 2018. *About the Main Directions of the Unified State Monetary Policy for 2018.* 11 January. https://www.cbpmr.net/index.php?id=2224.

Pridnestrovian Republican Bank (PRB). 2018a. *Dynamics of Money Transfers to/from PMR in 2017.* 12 February. http://cbpmr.net/data/ddp_12_02_18.pdf.

Pridnestrovian Republican Bank (PRB). 2018b. *Analytical Information Publication.* Bulletin 3:226. 11 January. https://www.cbpmr.net/data/prbvd226.pdf.

Pridnestrovian Republican Newspaper (PRN). 2017. About Retirement and More. http://pridnestrovie-daily.net/archives/17318.

Pridnestrovian State Television and Radio Company (PSTRC). 2015. *New Tax Code of the PMR.* 27 August. https://tv.pgtrk.ru/ru/news/20150827/35196.

Promo-LEX. 2013. *Evgheni Sevciuc – Becoming President Takes Revenge. Alexander*

Coliban – the Next Prisoner in Tiraspol for the Next 2.6 Years. 14 January. https://promolex.md/7907-ajuns-presedinte-evgheni-sevciuc-se-razbuna-alexandru-coliban-urmatorul-detinut-la-tiraspol-pentru-26-ani/?lang=en.

Promo-LEX. 2015. *KGB vs Promo-LEX Retrospective.* https://promolex.md/wp-content/uploads/2017/06/nr101_1433501179en_.pdf.

Promo-LEX. 2016. *Sida has Ceased to Provide Assistance After Threats From the KGB.* 22 September. https://promolex.md/3456-sida-a-incetat-sa-ofere-asistenta-dupa-amenintarile-parvenite-din-partea-kgb/?lang=en.

Promo-LEX. 2017. *The Former Transnistrian Leader, Evghenii Sevciuc, Could be Held Liable for Committing at Least 3 Crimes.* https://promolex.md/9909-fostul-lider-de-la-tiraspol-evghenii-sevciuc-poate-fi-tras-la-raspundere-penala-pentru-comiterea-a-cel-putin-3-infractiuni/?print=print&lang=en#_ftn14.

Promo-LEX. 2018. *Alternative Report on the Sixth Periodic Report of the Russian Federation under the Convention Against Torture and Other Cruel, Inhuman or Degrading Treatment or Punishment.* https://tbinternet.ohchr.org/Treaties/CAT/Shared%20Documents/RUS/INT_CAT_CSS_RUS_31607_E.pdf.

Promo-LEX. 2020. *Horjan Oleg Was Convicted by the "Courts" of the "Self-Proclaimed MRI" Who Illegally Assumed Justice Duties In The Transnistrian Region.* 27 July. https://promolex.md/18297-curtea-suprema-de-justitie-a-constatat-ca-presedintele-partidului-comunist-din-regiunea-transnistreana-oleg-horjan-nu-a-beneficiat-de-un-proces-echitabil-in-stanga-nistrului/?lang=en.

Promo-LEX. n.d. *Donors.* Accessed 2/5/21. https://promolex.md/donatori/?lang=en.

Protsyk, Oleh. 2007. "Nation Building in Moldova: Nation-Building in Moldova." In *Nation and Nationalism: Political and Historical Studies*, edited by Andrzej Suszycki and Pawel Karolewski: 1-19. http://www.policy.hu/protsyk/publications/nationalisminmoldova.pdf.

Protsyk, Oleh. 2008. *Representation and Democracy in Eurasia's Unrecognized States: The Case of Transnistria.* European Centre for Minority Issues, Working Paper 40. https://www.files.ethz.ch/isn/57184/working_paper_40.pdf.

Protsyk. Oleh. 2012. Secession and Hybrid Regime Politics in Transnistria. *Communist and Post-Communist Studies* 45(1–2): 175–182. https://doi.org/10.1016/j.postcomstud.2012.03.003.

Publika. 2013. Evgeny Shevchuk Suggests Blocked Sites Register as Media. 15 May. https://ru.publika.md/link_890051.html.

Publika. 2017. Road Traffic Makes Chisinau's Air Most Polluted in Moldova. https://en.publika.md/road-traffic-makes-chisinaus-air-most-polluted-in-moldova_2637967.html#ixzz6aUJNWRkR.

Publika. 2018. Around 1 Million Moldovans Acquire Romanian Citizenship in Past Years. 27 March. https://en.publika.md/around-1-million-moldovans-acquire-romanian-citizenship-in-past-years-_2647124.html.

Puiu, Victoria. 2015. Can Russia Afford Transnistria? *Eurasianet*, 18 February. https://eurasianet.org/can-russia-afford-transnistria.

Qiblawi, Tamara, Altaher, Nada and El Sirgany, Sarah. 2019. *Iranian Human Rights Lawyer Sentenced to 38 Years in Prison, Her Family Says*. CNN, 12 March 2019. https://edition.cnn.com/2019/03/12/middleeast/iran-sotoudeh-prison-intl/index.html.

Quinlan, Paul. 2002. Moldova under Lucinschi. *Demokratizatsiya* 10(1): 83–102. https://demokratizatsiya.pub/archives/10-1_Quinlan.PDF.

Quinn, Katheryn and Murray, James. 2013. Romanian 'Granny' Loophole Will Allow Moldovan Migrants to Work in UK. *Daily Express*, 17 March. https://www.express.co.uk/news/uk/384881/Romanian-granny-loophole-will-allow-Moldovan-migrants-to-work-in-UK.

Rabushka, Alvin. 2017. *A Low Flat Tax Has Been Adopted in Pridnestrovie*. Flat-taxes, 17 August. https://flattaxes.blogspot.com/2008/11/low-flat-tax-has-been-adopted-in.html.

Radio Free Europe (RFE). 2010. *OSCE Reps Barred From Moldovan Journalist's Trial*. 4 November. https://www.rferl.org/a/OSCE_Reps_Barred_From_Moldovan_Journalists_Trial/2210869.html.

Radio Free Europe (RFE). 2011. *RFE Contributor Released From Prison In Transdniester*. 6 May. https://pressroom.rferl.org/a/press_release_vardanean_released/24093937.html.

Radio Free Europe (RFE). 2011a. *Smirnov Encouraged by Russia Not to Stand*. 14 October https://www.refworld.org/docid/4eaaa7fec.html

Radio Free Europe (RFE). 2018. *Oleg Horjan, Leader of the Transnistrian Communist Party, Was Sentenced to 4 Years and 6 Months in Prison*. 3 November. https://moldova.europalibera.org/a/29580375.html.

Radio Free Europe (RFE). 2018a. *Moldova Concerned Over Russian Troop Movements In Breakaway Region*. 18 June. https://www.rferl.org/a/moldova-russian-troops-movement-transdniester-breakaway-region/29294739.html.

Radio Free Europe (RFE). 2020. *A New Case Against Communist Leader Oleg Horjan is Being Prepared in Tiraspol*. 24 August. https://moldova.europalibera.org/a/la-tiraspol-se-pregăteşte-un-nou-dosar-împotriva-liderului-comunist-oleg-horjan/30799617.html.

Radiomap.eu. 2020. *Radio Stations in Tiraspol*. http://radiomap.eu/pmr/tiraspol.

Ramet, Sabrina. 1992. *Religious Policy in the Soviet Union*. Cambridge University Press.

Ranadive, Ameet. 2015. *How Romania Punched Above Its Weight at the Treaty of Versailles*. 16 March. https://medium.com/@ameet/how-romania-got-its-way-at-the-treaty-of-versailles-e5e1dbc5da23.

Rainbow, Jamie. 2013. Sheriff Tiraspol, The Club at the Heart of Europe's Forgotten Conflict. *World Soccer*, 30 November. https://www.worldsoccer.com/blogs/sheriff-tiraspol-343898.

Raspopina, Sasha. 2017. Attack the Block: What Will the Upcoming Khrushchevki Demolitions Mean for Moscow? *The Calvert Journal*, 7 April. https://www.theguardian.com/world/2019/jun/24/eu-court-rules-polands-lowering-of-judges-retirement-age-unlawful.

Redwood, John. 2018. There's No Such Thing as an Independent Central Bank. *The Financial Times*, 4 September. https://www.ft.com/content/cdf8dd6e-af6c-11e8-87e0-d84e0d934341.

Refworld. 2004. *Chronology for Slavs in Moldova*. https://www.refworld.org/docid/469f38be17.html.

Refworld. 2005. *Moldova: Popular Front Political Party, Including Number of Elected Officials, Party Platform, Treatment of Members and Supporters, Availability of State Protection for Members and Supporters*. https://www.refworld.org/docid/5bcdce18c.html.

Refworld. 2013. *Report on International Religious Freedom – Moldova*. https://www.refworld.org/docid/519dd4a859.html.

Refworld. 2018. *Freedom in the World 2018 – Transnistria*. https://www.refworld.org/docid/45f147fd2f.html.

Regional Trends Analytics (RTA). 2018. *Dodon Reveals the Details of the Meeting with Krasnoselsky*. 26 December. https://regtrends.com/en/2018/12/26/dodon-reveals-the-details-of-the-meeting-with-krasnoselsky/.

Regional Trends Analytics (RTA). 2019. *Dodon: Transnistria May be a Part of Moldova with Broad Powers of Autonomy*. 5 September. https://regtrends.com/en/2019/09/05/dodon-transnistria-may-be-a-part-of-moldova-with-broad-powers-of-autonomy.

Remler, Philip. 2013. *Negotiation Gone Bad: Russia, Germany, and Crossed Communications*. Carnegie Europe, 21 August. https://carnegieeurope.eu/2013/08/21/negotiation-gone-bad-russia-germany-and-crossed-communications-pub-52712.

Reporters Without Borders. 2020. *Moldova Media as Weapons*. https://rsf.org/en/moldova.

Resare, Nils. 2016. Sida has Ceased to Provide Assistance After Threats From the KGB. *Aftonbladet*, 10 September. https://www.aftonbladet.se/nyheter/a/21yzdl/sida-stoppade-bistand-efter-hot-fran-kgb.

Rezvani, David. 2014. *Surpassing the Sovereign State The Wealth, Self Rule and Security Advantages of Partially Independent Territories*. Oxford University Press.

Rinna, Tony. 2014. Moldova, the EU and the Gagauzia Issue. *New Eastern Europe*, 14 February. https://neweasterneurope.eu/2014/02/14/moldova-the-eu-and-the-gagauzia-issue/.

Rodiucova, Feodora. 2018. *Persistence Against Tuberculosis*. Global Giving. https://www.globalgiving.org/donate/5666/speranta-terrei/reports/?page=3.

Rogstad, Adrian. 2016. *The Next Crimea? Getting Russia's Transnistria Policy Right*. Problems of Post-Communism. LSE Research Online. DOI: 10.1080/10758216.2016.1237855.

Roper, Steven. 2003. Moldova. In *Eastern Europe, Russia and Central Asia*, edited by Imogen Bell: 262–288. Taylor & Francis, London.

Roper, Steven. 2005. The Politicization of Education: Identity Formation in Moldova and Transnistria. *Communist and Post-Communist Societies* 38: 501–514. DOI:10.1016/j.postcomstud.2005.09.003.

Rotarescu, Iulia. 2014. *The Relevance of the Transnistrian Situation to Russian-Moldovan Relations: Some Considerations*. Universitatea Lucian Blaga din Sibiu. https://www.

academia.edu/6866185/the_relevance_of_the_transnistrian_conflict_to_moldova_russia_relations_some_considerations?email_work_card=view-paper.

Rotarescu, Iulia. 2014a. *Mass Media Transnistreană*. Facultatea de Stiint e Socio-Umane Universitatea Lucian Blaga din Sibiu. https://www.academia.edu/6866199/The_mass_media_in_Transnistria_Eurasian_tipology?email_work_card=view-paper.

Rudolph, Joseph. 2008. *Hot Spot: North America and Europe*. Greenwood Press, Westport Connecticut.

Russell, Shawn. 2012. The Benevolent Dictatorship in Rwanda: Negative Government, Positive Outcomes? *The Applied Anthropologist* 32(1): 12–22. https://hpsfaa.wildapricot.org/Resources/Documents/AppliedAnthropologist-2012/No.%201/Russell_2012_32(1)_12-22.pdf.

Russian Public Opinion Research Centre. 2016. *Residents of Transnistria About the Future of the Republic*. 7 September.

Russians Today. 2018. Krasnoselsky: Transnistria is Not a Fragment of the USSR. https://russianstoday.ru/krasnoselskij-pridnestrove-jeto-ne-oskolok-sssr/.

Ryan, Karen. 2007. Transnistria: New Social Democratic Party Wants Union With Moldova. *The Tiraspol Times*, 6 February. http://www.tiraspoltimes.com/node/557.

Sabadus, Aura. 2020. *Moldova in Regional Gas Role, Sector Overhaul Bid After Russian Transit Loss*. Independent Community Intelligence Services, 20 January. https://www.icis.com/explore/resources/news/2020/01/20/10460441/moldova-in-regional-gas-role-sector-overhaul-bid-after-russian-transit-loss.

Sabor, Iryna. 2012. *Economic Viability Under Frozen Conflict: "The Island of Transnistria"*. Master's Thesis, University of Oslo. https://www.duo.uio.no/bitstream/handle/10852/13411/sabor-master.pdf%3fsequence%3d2.

Support, Advanced Learning and Training Opportunities for Youth (SALTO). n.d. *NGO Interaction*. Accessed 20/9/20. https://www.salto-youth.net/tools/otlas-partner-finding/organisation/ngo-interaction-vzaimodeistvie.1017/.

Sanchez, Alejandro. 2009. The "Frozen" Southeast: How the Moldova-Transnistria Question has Become a European Geo-Security Issue. *The Journal of Slavic Military Studies* 22(2): 153–176. https://doi.org/10.1080/13518040902917917.

Sanchez, Alejandro. 2013. Moldova and NATO: Expansion Stops at the Dniester River? *E-International Relations*. https://www.e-ir.info/2013/01/09/moldova-and-nato-expansion-stops-at-the-dniester-river/.

Sato, Keiji. 2010. The Molotov-Ribbentrop Commission and Claims of Post-Soviet Secessionist Territories to Sovereignty. *Demokratizatsiya: The Journal of Post-Soviet Democratization* 18(2): 148–160. DOI:10.3200/DEMO.18.2.148-159.

Schearf, Daniel. 2014. *Analysts: Putin Wants 'Frozen Conflict' in Eastern Ukraine*. Voice of America, 16 July. https://www.voanews.com/europe/analysts-putin-wants-frozen-conflict-eastern-ukraine.

Schlegel, Simon. 2018. How Could the Gagauz Achieve Autonomy and What Has it Achieved for Them? A Comparison Among Neighbours on the Moldova-Ukrainian

Border. *Journal on Ethnopolitics and Minority Issues in Europe* 17(1): 1–23. https://www.ecmi.de/fileadmin/downloads/publications/JEMIE/2018/Schlegel.pdf.

Schroeder, Gertrude. 1992. On the Economic Viability of New Nation-States. *Journal of International Affairs* 45(2): 549–574.

Schwirtz, Michael. 2006. Transnistria Votes on Independence. *The New York Times*, 18 September. https://www.nytimes.com/2006/09/18/world/europe/18RUSSIASUMM.html.

Scudder, Jamie. 2010. Territorial Integrity: Modern States and the International System. *Exploring Geopolitics.* https://exploringgeopolitics.org/publication_scudder_jamie_territorial_integrity_modern_states_international_political_system_jurisdiction_peace_westphalia_lebanon_somalia/.

Selari, Galina and Bobkova, Elena, 2013. *Social Policies of the Republic of Moldova and Transnistria and Possibilities for their Synchronization.* CMI Project Supporting the Transnistrian Settlement Process, Tiraspol. http://www.cisr-md.org/pdf/health%20text_en_%20cisr.pdf.

Severin, Irina. 2013. Challenges to Reunification in Moldova and Cyprus: Between the EU's Soft Power and Russia's Soft Force. In *Managing Intractable Conflicts: Lessons from Moldova and Cyprus Global Political Trends Centre*, edited by Mensur Akgün: 63–76. https://www.files.ethz.ch/isn/163428/LessonsFromMDandCY_APR13.pdf.

Seymour, Michel. 2007. Secession as a Remedial Right. *Inquiry* 50(4): 393–423. https://doi.org/10.1080/00201740701491191.

Shafir, Michael. 1998. *Moldova: The Right Faces The Center In Electoral Contest.* Radio Free Europe, 9 March. https://www.rferl.org/a/1088175.html.

Sharifzoda, Khamza. 2017. *Revisiting Transnistrian Conflict.* Georgetown University. https://www.academia.edu/37024855/Revisiting_Transnistrian_Conflict?email_work_card=thumbnail.

Shaw, Malcolm. 1997. Peoples, Territorialism and Boundaries. *European Journal of International Law* 8(3): 478–507. https://doi.org/10.1093/oxfordjournals.ejil.a015594.

Shellnutt, Kate. 2016. Russia's Newest Law: No Evangelizing Outside of Church. *Christianity Today*, 8 July. https://www.christianitytoday.com/news/2016/june/no-evangelizing-outside-of-church-russia-proposes.html.

Sheriff. 2021. *The History of the Company.* https://sheriff.md/en/company/history/.

Shirmammadov, Khazar. 2016. How Does the International Community Reconcile the Principles of Territorial Integrity and Self-Determination? The Case of Crimea. *Russian Law Journal* 4(1): 61–97. https://doi.org/10.17589/2309-8678-2016-4-1-61-97.

Simonsen, Sven. 1995. Going His Own Way: A Profile of General Aleksandr Lebed. *Journal of Slavic Military Studies* 8(3): 528–546. https://doi.org/10.1080/13518049508430202.

Smith, Anthony. 1985. Ethnie and Nation in the Modern World. *Millennium Journal of International Studies* 14(2): 127–142. https://doi.org/10.1177/03058298850140020301.

Smith, Anthony. 1991. *National Identity.* Penguin Books, London.

Smith, Anthony. 2002. *Myths and Memories of the Nation.* Oxford University Press.

Smith, Hannah Lucinda. 2020. The Shady Cryptocurrency Boom on the Post-Soviet Frontier. *Wired*. https://www.wired.com/story/cryptocurrency-boom-post-soviet-frontier/.

Snobek, Kuba. 2017. Why Moscow's Massacre of Mass Housing Is a Huge Mistake. *ArchDaily*, 12 April. https://gerhard.rssing.com/chan-1468464/all_p1412.html.

Soccerway. 2020. *FK Sheriff Tiraspol*. https://uk.soccerway.com/teams/moldova/fc-sheriff-tiraspol/1498/trophie.

Socor, Vladimir. 2010. Medvedev Deflects Merkel-Sarkozy Proposal on Transnistria at Deauville Summit. *Eurasia Daily Monitor*, 7:191. https://jamestown.org/program/medvedev-deflects-merkel-sarkozy-proposal-on-transnistria-at-deauville-summit/.

Socor, Vladimir. 2011. German Diplomacy Tilts Toward Russia On Transnistria Negotiations. *Eurasia Daily Monitor*, 8:108. https://jamestown.org/program/german-diplomacy-tilts-toward-russia-on-transnistria-negotiations/.

Socor, Vladimir. 2013. Moldova, Ukraine Bar Russian Military Flights and Arms Transit to Tiraspol. *Eurasia Daily Monitor*, 10:145. https://jamestown.org/program/moldova-ukraine-bar-russian-military-flights-and-arms-transit-to-tiraspol/.

Socor, Vladimir. 2018. De-Sovereignization: Testing a Conflict-Resolution Model at Moldova's Expense in Transnistria (Part One). *Eurasia Daily Monitor*, 15:132. https://jamestown.org/program/de-sovereignization-testing-a-conflict-resolution-model-at-moldovas-expense-in-transnistria-part-one/.

Socor, Vladimir. 2018a. De-Sovereignization: Testing a Conflict-Resolution Model at Moldova's Expense in Transnistria (Part Two). *Eurasia Daily Monitor*, 15:135. https://jamestown.org/program/de-sovereignization-testing-a-conflict-resolution-model-at-moldovas-expense-in-transnistria-part-two/).

Sokolova, Natalia. 2015. *The Need for Tax Reform*. http://tiraspol.ru/wp-content/uploads/2016/06/sokolova.doc.

Solovyov, Dmitry. 2009. *Moldova's President Voronin*. Reuters, 7 April. https://www.reuters.com/article/us-moldova-election-voronin-sb/factbox-moldovas-president-voronin-idustre5366hc20090407.

Soviet History. 2008. *Seventeen Moments in Soviet History: Moldovan Independence*. Michigan University. http://soviethistory.msu.edu/1991-2/eltsin-and-russian-sovereignty/eltsin-and-russian-sovereignty-texts/moldovan-independence/.

Spinner, Maximilian. 2003. *Civil War and Ethnic Conflict in Post-Soviet Moldova: The Cases of Gagauzia and Transnistria Compared*. CEU – GRIN, Budapest.

Spotterguide. 2020. https://www.spotterguide.net/.

Sputnik Mundo. 2016. More than 85% of the Transnistrian People Want Integration With Russia. 17 June. https://mundo.sputniknews.com/rusia/201606171060863573-encuesta-integracion/.

Sputnik News. 2017. Transnistrian Leader Calls Independence a Guarantee of Security. 4 February. https://sptnkne.ws/d29A.

Steiner, Nils. 2016. Comparing Freedom House Democracy Scores to Alternative Indices and Testing for Political Bias: Are US Allies Rated as More Democratic by Freedom

House? *Journal of Comparative Policy Analysis: Research and Practice* 18(4): 329–349. https://doi.org/10.1080/13876988.2013.877676.

Stirile TVR. 2013. *Interview with Traian Basescu.* http://stiri.tvr.ro/traian-basescu-la-tvr--urmatorul-proiect-pentru-romania-trebuie-sa-fie-vrem-sa-ne-intregim-tara-_37653.html#view.

Stoetzel, Jean. 2006. Sociology and Demography. *Population* 61(1–2): 19–28. https://www.cairn-int.info/article-E_POPU_601_0017--sociology-and-demography.htm.

Strange, Hannah. 2013. US Raid that Killed Bin Laden Was an Act of War says Pakistani Report. *Daily Telegraph*, 9 July. https://www.telegraph.co.uk/news/worldnews/asia/pakistan/10169655/US-raid-that-killed-bin-Laden-was-an-act-of-war-says-Pakistani-report.html.

Stroop, Chrissy. 2018. Putin Wants God (or at Least the Church) on His Side. *Foreign Policy*, 10 September. https://foreignpolicy.com/2018/09/10/putin-wants-god-or-at-least-the-church-on-his-side/.

Sudan Tribune. 2005. Quotes from Sudan Peace Treaty Signing Ceremony. https://sudantribune.com/Quotes-from-Sudan-peace-treaty,7450.

Suny, Ronald. 2004. *Why We Hate You: The Passions of National Identity and Ethnic Violence.* Berkeley Program in Soviet and Post-Soviet Studies Working Paper Series.

Surchician, Oleg. 2015. *The Republic of Moldova Pays Pension Only to 20 Persons From Transnistrian Region.* Moldova.org, 18 March. https://www.moldova.org/en/the-republic-of-moldova-pays-pension-only-to-20-persons-from-transnistrian-region/.

Survey Based Research. 2012. *National Survey on the Transnistrian Reintegration Prospects*: *Public Perceptions.* https://documents.pub/document/national-survey-on-the-transnistrian-reintegration-1-national-survey-on-the.html

Suvorov, Ivan. 2015. *PMR Changes the Tax System.* NewsPRM, 4 September. http://newspmr.com/novosti-pmr/ekonomika/13631.

Şveţ, Ala. 2012. Staging the Transnistrian Identity: A Deconstruction of the Official Holidays. *History and Anthropology* 24(1): 98–116. https://doi.org/10.1080/02757206.2012.759326.

Tabachnik, Alexander. 2017a. *The Transnistrian Challenge: Why Tensions are Escalating Between Russia and Moldova.* London School of Economics, 22 August. https://blogs.lse.ac.uk/europpblog/2017/08/22/the-transnistrian-challenge-why-tensions-are-escalating-between-russia-and-moldova/.

Tanas, Alexander. 2016. *Moldovan Court Jails ex-PM for Nine Years for Abuse of Power.* Reuters, 27 June. https://www.reuters.com/article/us-moldova-filat-court/moldovan-court-jails-ex-pm-for-nine-years-for-abuse-of-power-iduskcnozd1xm.

Tejada, Gabriela, Varzari, Vitalie and Porcescu, Sergiu. 2013. Scientific Diasporas, Transnationalism and Home-Country Development: Evidence from a Study of Skilled Moldovans Abroad. *Southeastern European and Black Seas Studies* 13(2): 157–173. https://doi.org/10.1080/14683857.2013.789674.

Texas v. Johnson. 1989. 491 US 397 US Supreme Court.

Thoolen, Hans. 2013. *Threats Against Human Rights Defenders in Transnistria/Moldova*. Civil Rights Defenders, 1 February. https://humanrightsdefenders.blog/2013/02/01/threats-against-human-rights-defenders-in-transnistria-moldova/.

Thorik, Vladimir, Petrusevici, Natalia and Veliciko, Liubovi. 2016. Sheriff Republic. *Rise Moldova*, 30 June. https://www.rise.md/articol/republica-sheriff-3/.

Tice, Beatrice and Nelson, Jason. 2004. A Commentary to Montserrat Guibernau Nations Without States: Political Communities in the Global Age. *Michigan Journal of International Law* 24(4): 1293–1297. https://core.ac.uk/download/pdf/232700326.pdf.

Tilles, Daniel. 2020. Protester Charged for Crime of Insulting President Over Banner Calling Duda "Idiot". *Notes From Poland*, 20 February. https://notesfrompoland.com/2020/02/20/protester-charged-for-crime-of-insulting-president-over-banner-calling-duda-idiot/.

Timpul. 2010. *Journalist Ernest Vardanean Admitted to Collaborating with SIS*. 12 May.

TIRAS. 2012. *Transnistrian Authorities Hinder the Dissemination of Information*. 6 July. https://tiras.ru/jeksperty/35117-roman-konoplev-vlasti-pridnestrovya-prepyatstvuyut-rasprostraneniyu-informacii.html.

TIRAS. 2013. *Tried to Blow Up an Independent Lawyer in Transnistria*. https://tiras.ru/kriminalnoe-chtivo/38471-v-pridnestrove-pytalis-vzorvat-nezavisimogo-advokata.html.

Tiraspol Diocese. 2009. *Diocese*. 15 July. http://www.diocese-tiras.org/page.php?id=3.

Tiraspol State University. 2020. *University of Tiraspol in Chisinau*. https://sites.google.com/site/ustrmeng/contact-us.

Tirotex. 2021. *About Tirotex*. http://www.tirotex.com/?lang=en.

Tolstykh, Vladislav, Grigoryan, Mariam and Kovalenko, Tatiana. 2019. Legal Systems of the Post-Soviet Non-Recognized States: Structural Problems. *Russian Law Journal* 7(2): 81–100. https://doi.org/10.17589/2309-8678-2019-7-2-81-100.

Tomiuc, Eugen. 2017. *Russia Objects to Moldovan Call for Removing Troops From Transdniester*. Radio Free Europe, 23 August. https://www.rferl.org/a/moldova-calls-on-united-nations-russian-troops-transdniester/28693178.html.

Tommasoli, Massimo. 2012. *UN Chronicle*. https://www.un.org/en/chronicle/article/rule-law-and-democracy-addressing-gap-between-policies-and-practices.

Toporov, Alexey. 2018. Is it worthy ceding Transnistria to "neutral" Moldova? *EurAsia Daily*. 5 April. https://eadaily.com/en/news/2018/04/05/is-it-worthy-ceding-transnistria-to-neutral-moldova

Troebst, Stefan. 2003. 'We are Transnistrians!' Post-Soviet Identity Management in the Dniestr Valley. *Ab Imperio* 1(4): 437–466. DOI:10.1353/imp.2003.0056.

TSV. 2020. *Sheriff Group's Television Channel*. https://tsv.md/category/novosti/.

Tuma, Elias. 1978. The Economic Viability of a Palestine State. *Journal of Palestine Studies* 7(3): 102–124. https://doi.org/10.2307/2536203.

Turkia, Eleonora. 2008. *Resolving Frozen Conflicts: The Cases of Transdniestra, South Ossetia and Abkhazia*. MA Thesis, Central European University. http://www.etd.ceu.hu/2008/turkia_eleonora.pdf.

UAWire. 2017. *Moldovan President: Transnistria May Become Part of Ukraine.* 15 November. http://www.uawire.org/moldovan-president-transdniestria-may-become-part-of-ukraine.

UEFA. 2020. *Club Coefficients.* https://www.uefa.com/memberassociations/uefarankings/club/#/yr/2020.

United Nations Charter. 1945. https://www.un.org/en/about-us/un-charter.

United Nations (UN). 2001. *Agreement on Succession Issues.* https://treaties.un.org/pages/ViewDetails.aspx?src=TREATY&mtdsg_no=XXIX-1&chapter=29&clang=_en.

United Nations (UN). n.d. *About UN Membership.* Accessed 3/1/16. https://www.un.org/en/about-us/about-un-membership#:~:text=Membership%20in%20the%20Organization%2C%20in,to%20carry%20out%20these%20obligations%E2%80%9D.

United Nations Department of Economic and Social Affairs (UNDESA). 2015. *International Migrant Stock.* https://www.un.org/en/development/desa/population/migration/index.asp.

United Nations Development Programme (UNDP). 2008. *Crisis Prevention and Recovery Report.* https://reliefweb.int/report/world/crisis-prevention-and-recovery-report-2008-post-conflict-economic-recovery-enabling.

United Nations Development Programme (UNDP). 2012. *Joint Report on Statistical Data and Public Attitudes towards Road Safety in Chisinau and Tiraspol.* https://www.easst.co.uk/wp-content/uploads/2017/10/Raport-en-DTP.pdf.

United Nations Development Programme (UNDP). 2015. *Moldova: A hospital Where Patients Get Well Faster.* https://www.eurasia.undp.org/content/rbec/en/home/presscenter/articles/2015/04/01/moldova-a-hospital-where-patients-get-well-faster-.html.

United Nations Economic Commission for Europe (UNECE). 2017. *Regulatory and Procedural Barriers to Trade in the Republic of Moldova: Needs Assessment* (United Nations Publication, Geneva). https://www.unece.org/fileadmin/dam/trade/publications/ece_trade_433e.pdf.

United Nations Economic Social and Cultural Organization (UNESCO). 2020. *Republic of Moldova.* http://uis.unesco.org/en/country/md.

United Nations General Assembly (UN). 1992. Resolution 46/223, *Admission of the Republic of Moldova to Membership in the United Nations.* https://digitallibrary.un.org/record/147693?ln=en.

United Nations General Assembly (UN). 2014. Resolution 68/262. *Calling Upon States Not to Recognize Changes in Status of Crimea Region.* https://www.un.org/press/en/2014/ga11493.doc.htm.

United Nations General Assembly (UN). 2017. Resolution 72/282, *Complete and Unconditional Withdrawal of Foreign Military Forces from the Territory of the Republic of Moldova.* https://www.un.org/en/ga/search/view_doc.asp?symbol=A/RES/72/282.

United Nations Human Rights Office of the High Commissioner (UNHRO). 2016. *Moldova: A Time of Challenges and Opportunities, Says Senior Human Rights*

Official. 31 March. https://www.ohchr.org/en/newsevents/pages/displaynews. aspx?newsid=18550&langi).

United Nations Peacemaker (UNP). 1987. Security Council Resolution 698: Iraq-Islamic Republic of Iran. 20 July. https://peacemaker.un.org/iraqiran-resolution598.

United Nations Security Council. 1999. Resolution 1244 on the Situation Relating to Kosovo. https://peacekeeping.un.org/en/mission/unmik.

United States v. Eichman. 1990. 496 US 310. US Supreme Court.

United States Commission for the Preservation of America's Heritage Abroad (USCPAHA). 2010. *Jewish Heritage Sites and Monuments in Moldova.* https:// kehilalinks.jewishgen.org/Camenca/Kamenka_files/JDCHeritageSitesInMoldova.pdf.

United States State Department (USSD). 2006. *Trafficking in Persons Report 2006.* https://2009-2017.state.gov/j/tip/rls/tiprpt/2006/index.htm.

United States State Department (USSD). 2006a. *Rejecting the Independence Referendum in Moldova's Transnistria Region.* 18 September. https://2001-2009.state.gov/r/pa/prs/ps/2006/72413.htm.

United States State Department (USSD). 2013. *Country Reports on Human Rights Practices – Moldova 2012.* 19 April. https://www.refworld.org/docid/517e6e0518.html.

United States State Department (USSD). 2014. *Report on International Religious Freedom.* https://www.ecoi.net/en/document/1430313.html.

United States State Department (USSD). 2015. *International Narcotics Control Strategy Report.* https://2009-2017.state.gov/j/inl/rls/nrcrpt/2015/index.htm

United States State Department (USSD). 2016. *Country Reports on Human Rights Practices: Moldova.* https://www.state.gov/reports/2016-country-reports-on-human-rights-practices/moldova/.

United States State Department (USSD). 2017. *Country Report on Human Rights Practices 2017 – Moldova.* 20 April. https://www.ecoi.net/en/document/1430313.html.

United States State Department (USSD). 2017a. *Factsheet.* https://crsreports.congress.gov/product/pdf/IF/IF10894/12

United States State Department (USSD). 2020. *Country Reports on Human Rights Practices 2019 – Moldova.* 11 March. https://www.ecoi.net/en/document/2026359.html.

United States Embassy in Moldova. 2009. *Trafficking in Persons Report.* https://www.refworld.org/docid/4a4214a22d.html.

United States Mission to the OSCE. 2018. *Statement on the 5+2 Transnistrian Settlement Process.* 18 June. https://www.osce.org/files/f/documents/8/f/385191.pdf.

Universities UK. 2019. *Higher Education in Numbers.* https://www.universitiesuk.ac.uk/facts-and-stats/Pages/higher-education-data.aspx.

Vahl, Marius and Emerson, Michael. 2004. Moldova and the Transnistrian Conflict. *Journal on Ethnopolitics and Minority Issues in Europe* 1: 1–29. https://nbn-resolving.org/urn:nbn:de:0168-ssoar-61961.

van Meurs, Wim. 2015. Moldova: Nested Cases of Belated Nation-Building. *Revue d'études comparatives Est-Ouest* 46(1): 185–209. https://doi.org/10.4074/S0338059915001084.

Van Praet, Nicolas. 2012. Quebec on Pace to Become Canada's Poorest Province. *National Post*, 8 February. https://nationalpost.com/news/canada/quebec-on-pace-to-become-canadas-poorest-province.

Vasiliu, Vadim. 2016. Elections in Transnistria // Vadim Krasnoselsky, New Leader in Tiraspol. *Deschide*, 12 December. https://deschide.md/en/news/political/4292/elections%e2%80%9d-in-transnistria--vadim-krasnoselsky-new-leader-in-tiraspol.htm.

Venice Commission, 2016. *Draft Opinion on Articles 216, 299, 301 and 314 of The Penal Code Of Turkey*. Council of Europe, 25 February. https://www.venice.coe.int/webforms/documents/default.aspx?pdffile=CDL(2016)007-e.

Venkatraman, Shruti. 2018. Can the Contrasting Standards for Statehood Put Forth by the Declaratory and Constitutive Theories of Recognition be Reconciled? An Examination of Kosovo's Disputed Statehood. *Edinburgh Student Law Review* 3(3): 36–39. https://www.eslr.ed.ac.uk/wp-content/uploads/sites/30/2018/06/Edinburgh-Student-Law-Review-June-2018.pdf.

Vienna Convention on Succession of States in Respect of Treaties. 1996. https://legal.un.org/ilc/texts/instruments/english/conventions/3_2_1978.pdf.

Vlas, Cristi. 2016. *Transnistria Introduces Penal Liability for Denying the Positive Role of Russian Peace-Keepers*. Molodova.org, 16 June. https://www.moldova.org/en/transnistria-introduces-penal-liability-denying-positive-role-russian-peace-keepers/.

Vlas, Cristi. 2017. *Transnistria to Ask for Observer Status at the United Nations*. Molodova.org, 7 September. https://www.moldova.org/en/transnistria-ask-observer-status-united-nations/.

Voeten, Erik. 2014. What is so Great About 'Territorial Integrity' Anyway? *Washington Post*, 17 March. https://www.washingtonpost.com/news/monkey-cage/wp/2014/03/17/what-is-so-great-about-territorial-integrity-anyway/.

Voice of America. 2019. *Somaliland Celebrates Independence Despite Lack of International Recognition*. 17 May. https://www.voanews.com/africa/somaliland-celebrates-independence-despite-lack-international-recognition.

Wagemakers, Joris. 2015. National Identity in Transnistria: A Global Historical Perspective on the Formation and Evolution of a 'Resistance Ideology'. *Journal of Eurasian Affairs* 2(1): 50–55. https://www.geopolitica.ru/sites/default/files/ea-2.pdf.

Wagner, Peter and Sawyer, Wendy. 2018. *States of Incarceration: The Global Context*. Prison Policy. https://www.prisonpolicy.org/global/2018.html.

Wagstyl, Stefan. 2009. Voronin Viewed as Obstacle to Change. *Financial Times*. 8 April. https://www.ft.com/content/b051816e-2469-11de-9a01-00144feabdc0.

Walker, Shaun. 2017. Revival of a Soviet Zion: Birobidzhan Celebrates its Jewish Heritage. *The Guardian*, 27 September. https://www.theguardian.com/world/2017/sep/27/revival-of-a-soviet-zion-birobidzhan-celebrates-its-jewish-heritage.

Walsh, Paul. 2018. Twin Cities Man Faked Death in $2M Scheme by Putting his Clothes, ID on Body. *The Minneapolis Star Tribune*, 29 November. https://www.startribune.

com/court-filing-twin-cities-man-faked-death-in-2m-scheme-by-putting-his-clothes-id-on-body/501573151/.

Walter, Christian, von Ungern-Sternberg, Antje and Abushov, Kavus. 2014. *Self Determination and Secession in International Law*. Oxford University Press.

The Washington Times. 2004. Hotbed of Weapons Deals. 18 January https://www.washingtontimes.com/news/2004/jan/18/20040118-103519-5374r/.

Weaver, John Cai Benjamin. 2011. *Adolf Hitler's account of the 'Nation' and 'Nationalism'*. E-International Relations. https://www.e-ir.info/2011/05/16/adolf-hitlers-account-of-the-%e2%80%98nation%e2%80%99-and-%e2%80%98nationalism%e2%80%99/.

Western Union. 2020. *Find Locations*. https://location.westernunion.com/.

Wheat, Lina and Ursul, Serghie. 2020. *Ghenadi Ciorba, the Organizer of the Protest in Râbnița, was Accused of Extremism and a Criminal Case was Opened Against Him*. Radio Free Europe, 12 July 2020. https://moldova.europalibera.org/p/30722216.html.

Whitten-Woodring, Jenifer. 2009. Watchdog or Lapdog? Media Freedom, Regime Type, and Government Respect for Human Rights. *International Studies Quarterly* 53(3): 595–625. http://www.jstor.org/stable/27735113.

Whitten-Woodring, Jenifer and Van Belle, Douglas. 2015. The Correlates of Media Freedom: An Introduction of the Global Media Freedom Dataset. *Political Science Research and Method* 5(1): 179–188. https://doi.org/10.1017/psrm.2015.68.

Wickens, Jim and Mason, Paul. 2014. *Fear, Football and Torture – Undercover in Transnistria* Report for Channel Four, 1 April.

Wikipedia. 2020. *List of European Countries by Average Wage*. https://en.wikipedia.org/wiki/List_of_European_countries_by_average_wage#cite_note-109.

Williams, Kieran. 2013. The Break-up of Czechoslovakia and Scottish Independence. *History & Policy*, 26 November. http://www.historyandpolicy.org/policy-papers/papers/the-break-up-of-czechoslovakia-and-scottish-independence.

Wilson, Andrew. 2012. Beauty Contests on the Nistru. *New Eastern Europe,* 25 February. https://neweasterneurope.eu/2012/02/25/beauty-contests-on-the-nistru/.

Wöber, Siegfried. 2013. *Making or Breaking the Republic of Moldova? The Autonomy of Gagauzia*. European Diversity and Autonomy Papers. http://aei.pitt.edu/41131/1/2013_edap02.pdf.

Wolff, Stefan. 2011. A Resolvable Frozen Conflict? The Domestic and International Politics of Self-Determination in Moldova and Transnistria. *Nationalities Papers* 39(6): 863–870. DOI:10.1080/00905992.2011.617363.

Wolff, Stefan. 2012. *The Transnistrian Issue: Moving Beyond the Status-Quo*. Directorate-General for External Policies, European Parliament. https://www.gov.uk/government/uploads/system/uploads/attachment_data/file/224472/evidence-stefan-wolff-the-transnistrian-issue.pdf.

World Bank. 1994. *Moldova Moving to a Market Economy*. http://documents.worldbank.org/curated/en/920601468773757733/pdf/multiopage.pdf.

World Bank. 1995. *Moldova Agricultural Sector Review.* https://documents.worldbank. org/en/publication/documents-reports/documentdetail/551981468774295374.

World Bank. 2012. *In South Sudan.* https://www.worldbank.org/en/country/southsudan/ overview.

World Bank. 2019. *World Bank National Accounts Data, and OECD National Accounts Data Files.* https://data.worldbank.org/indicator/NY.GDP.MKTP.CD.

World Bank. 2020. *World Bank Predicts Sharpest Decline of Remittances in Recent History.* 22 April. https://www.worldbank.org/en/news/press-release/2020/04/22/ world-bank-predicts-sharpest-decline-of-remittances-in-recent-history.

World Bank. 2020a. *GDP Per Capita (current US$) Estonia. Kazakhstan, Russian Federation, Romania, Belarus, Georgia, Ukraine, Moldova.* https://data.worldbank. org/indicator/ny.gdp.pcap.cd?locations=ee-kz-ru-ro-by-ge-ua-md.

World Coin News. 2014. Transnistria 2014 – New Coin Family in Synthetic Material. 20 August. https://worldcoinnews.blogspot.com/2014/08/transnistria-2014-new-coin-family-in.html.

World Health Organization (WHO). 2014. *Immunization Programme Review in Transnistria Region.* https://www.euro.who.int/en/countries/republic-of-moldova/ news/news/2014/05/immunization-programme-review-in-transnistria-region.

World Health Organization (WHO). 2015. *Country Planning Cycle Database.* http:// www.nationalplanningcycles.org/sites/default/files/country_docs/Moldova/moldova-comprehensive_multi-year_plan_for_2011-2015_-_year_2011.pdf.

World Health Organization (WHO). 2016. *Training and Professional Development on Health Authorities' Agenda in Transnistria Region.* 12 February. https://www.euro.who. int/en/countries/republic-of-moldova/news/news/2016/02/training-and-professional-development-on-health-authorities-agenda-in-transnistria-region.

World Health Organization (WHO). 2018. Road Safety Figures.

World Justice Project. n.d. *What is the Rule of Law?* Accessed 29/12/20. https://world-justiceproject.org/about-us/overview/what-rule-law.

Women's Aid. 2019. *The Domestic Abuse Report.* Women's Aid. https://www.women-said.org.uk/shop/reports/the-domestic-abuse-report/.

World Prison Brief (WPB). 2019. *World Prison Brief Data.* https://www.prisonstudies. org/world-prison-brief-data.

World Population Review. 2020. Country Rankings. https://worldpopulationreview.com/ country-rankings/poorest-countries-in-europe.

World Trade Organization (WTO). 2000. *Draft Report of the Working Party on the Accession of the Republic of Moldova.* https://docs.wto.org/dol2fe/pages/fe_search/ fe_s_s009-dp.aspx?language=e&catalogueidlist=49035,34875,15694,49045,15353,18 175,2581,36969,53959,6174&currentcatalogueidindex=7&fulltexthash=.

World Trade Organization (WTO). 2020. *Members and Observers.* https://www.wto. org/english/thewto_e/whatis_e/tif_e/org6_e.htm.

XE. 2021. Currency Converter. https://www.xe.com/.

Yip, Hilton. 2020. It's Time to Stop Pandering to Beijing over Taiwan. *Foreign Policy*, 8 May. https://foreignpolicy.com/2020/05/08/us-taiwan-china-relations-stop-pandering-coronavirus/.

YouTube. 2015. *In Ribnita, Pensioners Went to an Unauthorized Rally.* 5 March. https://www.youtube.com/watch?v=TCBJWofc-rU.

YouTube. 2020. *Ruslan Mova Met with Protesters from Ribnita.* 2 July. https://www.youtube.com/watch?v=YhoPYqtxzzo.

YouTube. 2020a. *Spontaneous Rally in Ribnita: People Protest on the Ribnita-Rezina Bridge.* 2 July. https://www.youtube.com/watch?v=WDYMWQbhr28.

Ymtram. 1980. Tiraspol Trolleybus Network. http://ymtram.mashke.org/moldova/tiraspol/maps/tiraspol_map_1977.pdf.

Yu, Verna. 2015. China's Two-Child Policy 'Too Little, Too Late' Demographers Warn. *South China Morning Post*, 31 October. https://www.scmp.com/news/china/policies-politics/article/1874320/chinas-two-child-policy-too-little-too-late.

Zalozhkov, Petr Aleksandrovich. 2001. *History of the Transnistrian Moldavian Republic Tiraspol.* RIO PSU, Tiraspol.

Zarifi, Sam. 2019. *India: Ending Autonomy of Jammu and Kashmir Fans Flames of Existing Human Rights Crisis.* International Commission of Jurists. https://www.icj.org/india-ending-autonomy-of-jammu-and-kashmir-fans-flames-of-existing-human-rights-crisis/.

Zellman, Ariel. n.d. Review: *Sovereignty* by Stephen Krasner. Accessed 30/12/20. https://arielzellman.wordpress.com/2008/02/10/review-sovereignty-by-stephen-krasner/.

ZIKUA. 2017. *Ukraine to Stop Shipments of Food to TransNistria Without Moldova Clearance.* 23 May. https://zik.ua/en/news/2017/05/23/ukraine_to_stop_shipments_of_food_to_transnistria_without_moldova_clearance_1100933.

Zirin, James. 2016. *Supremely Partisan: How Raw Politics Tip the Scales in the United States Supreme Court.* Rowman & Littlefield, Lanham, Maryland.

Zubko, Aleksander. 2012. *Right to Pension in the Context of Armed Conflict.* Norwegian Refugee Council: 27–30. https://www.nrc.no/globalassets/pdf/reports/advocacy-papers-ukraine/right-to-pension_eng_web.pdf.

B. SELECTION OF OTHER SOURCES CONSULTED

Bellamy, Richard. 2013. The Democratic Qualities Of Courts: A Critical Analysis Of Three Arguments, *Representation* 49:3: 333–346. DOI: 10.1080/00344893.2013.830485.

Berlin Economics. 2013. *The Impact of the EU-Moldova DCFTA on the Transnistrian Economy: Quantitative Assessment under Three Scenarios.* https://get-moldau.de/download/policypapers/2013/2013.06.04_dcfta%20transnistria_en.pdf.

Bodlore-Penlaez, Mikael. 2011. *Atlas of Stateless Nations in Europe.* Y Lolfa Olfa Cyf, Ceredigion, Wales.

Bonnett, Alistair. 2014. *Off the Map: Lost Spaces, Invisible Cities, Forgotten Islands, Feral Places.* Aurum Press, London.

Brett, Daniel. 2016. *Igor Dodon's Election: A Victory for Moldova's Oligarch*. London School of Economics. https://www.academia.edu/30129956/igor_dodons_election_a_victory_for_moldovas_oligarchs?auto=download.

Brownlie, Ian. 1985. The Rights of Peoples in Modern International Law. *Bull. Austl. Soc. Leg. Phil* 9: 104–119.

Brusa, Francesco. 2018. Transnistria: Journalism Beyond the Nistru. *Osservatorio Balacani e Caucaso,* 24 July. https://www.balcanicaucaso.org/eng/Areas/Transnistria/Transnistria-journalism-beyond-the-Nistru-189247.

Camp, Jordan. 2016. *Incarcerating the Crisis: Freedom Struggles and the Rise of the Neoliberal State*. University of California Press, Oakland.

Carney, Todd. 2020. Looking for a Solution Under International Law for the Moldova–Transnistria Conflict. *OpinioJuris* in association with the International Commission of Jurists, 17 March. http://opiniojuris.org/2020/03/17/looking-for-a-solution-under-international-law-for-the-moldova-transnistria-conflict/.

Caspersen, Nina and Stansfield, Gareth. 2011. *Unrecognized States: The Struggle for Sovereignty in the Modern International System*. Polity Press, Cambridge.

Chatterjee, Deen. 2011. *Encyclopaedia of Global Justice*. Springer, Dordrecht. https://doi.org/10.1007/978-1-4020-9160-5

Chiu, Jonathan and Koeppl, Thorsten. 2017. *The Economics of Cryptocurrencies – Bitcoin and Beyond*. Bank of Canada. https://www.chapman.edu/research/institutes-and-centers/economic-science-institute/_files/ifree-papers-and-photos/koeppel-april2017.pdf.

Çiftçi Irfan and Sevinç Bilal. 2015. Rising Significance of Non-State Entities in the Global System: New Actors and New Challenges. *Dumlupınar University Journal of Social Sciences* 43: 79–84. https://dergipark.org.tr/tr/download/article-file/56038.

Ciurea, Cornel. 2007. "Frozen" Conflict of Moldova and Trans-Dniester. Will the Countries Come to an Agreement? And What is the Price of this Agreement? *Geopolitiniu*. http://www.geopolitika.lt/files/%5ben%5dkonferencijos_medziaga.pdf.

Ciurea, Cornel. 2016. *The Reform of the Peacekeeping Mission in Transnistria: A Premise for Conflict Settlement*. The Black Sea Trust for Regional Cooperation. http://neweurope.org.ua/wp-content/uploads/2017/12/reform_mission_eng.pdf.

Corobov, Roman, Koeppel, Sonja, Denisov, Nikolai and Sîrodoev, Ghennadi. 2017. Assessment of Climate Change Vulnerability at the Local Level: A Case Study on the Dniester River Basin (Moldova). *The Scientific World Journal*. https://www.hindawi.com/journals/tswj/2013/173794/.

Council of Europe. 2016. *Confidence Building Measures Implemented by the Council of Europe in Post-Conflict Areas*. SG/Inf(2016)21. https://rm.coe.int/168064e4ae.

Csergo, Zsuza, Roseberry, Philipe and Wolff, Stefan. 2017. Institutional Outcomes of Territorial Contestation: Lessons from Post-Communist Europe, 1989–2012. *Publius: The Journal of Federalism* 47(4): 491–521. https://www.tandfonline.com/doi/full/10.1080/00467600701619630?scroll=top&needAccess=true.

Curran, James. 2010. *Media and Society*, 5th edition. Bloomsbury, London.

Dewdney, John. 1990. Population Change in the Soviet Union 1979–1989. *Geography* 75(3): 273–277. https://www.jstor.org/stable/40571860?read-now=1&seq=5#page_scan_tab_contents.

Dinesen, Maria and Wivel, Anders. 2014. Georgia and Moldova: Caught in the Outskirts of Europe? In *Small States and International Security: Europe and Beyond: Europe and Beyond*, edited by A. Wivel, C. Archer and A. Bailes: 149–166. Routledge, London.

Dusciac, Dorian, Baloge, Clement and Ursu, Roman. 2018. No Lands People: Identities and Attitudes of Migrants from Post-Soviet 'Frozen Conflict' Areas. *EURINT* Proceedings: 228–245. https://www.academia.edu/38008201/.

The Economist. 2014. What Defines a Frozen Conflict. 23 October. https://www.economist.com/the-economist-explains/2014/10/23/what-defines-a-frozen-conflict.

Expert-Grup. 2015. *Republic of Moldova State of Country Report*. Chisinau. https://www.expert-grup.org/en/biblioteca/item/1145-rst-2015&category=182.

Ferejohn, John and Pasquino, Pasquale. 2003. Rule of Democracy and Rule of Law. In *Democracy and the Rule of Law*, edited by J. Maravall and A. Przeworski: 242–260. Cambridge Studies in the Theory of Democracy.

International Federation for Human Rights (FIDH). 2020. *Moldova / Region of Transnistria: Arbitrary Detention of Mr. Alexandru Rjavitin*. 6 February. https://www.fidh.org/en/issues/human-rights-defenders/moldova-region-of-transnistria-arbitrary-detention-of-mr-alexandru.

Fossati, Fabio. 2008. *Beyond the End of Violence and Conflict Freezing: Looking for Conflict Resolution*. Transcend Research Institution, Trieste.

https://pdfs.semanticscholar.org/cf52/560c0ec7f3679c5ed443de2878e4e2bfa62c.pdf?_ga=2.258513546.1635765177.1564921429-590362997.1561844014.

Gehlbach, Scott and Konstantin, Sonin. 2008. *Government Control of the Media*. Frontiers of Political Economics Conference. http://citeseerx.ist.psu.edu/viewdoc/download?doi=10.1.1.594.2663&rep=rep1&type=pdf.

Gerasymchuk, Sergiy. 2016. Hybrid Maidan in Moldova: Approbation of Russian Methods of Influence. In *Panorama of Global Security Environment*, edited by Peter Bator and Robert Ondrejcsak: 161–70. https://www.academia.edu/32689505/.

Giannone, Diego. 2010. Political and Ideological Aspects in the Measurement of Democracy: The Freedom House Case. *Democratization* 17(1): 68–97.

Grzywaczewski, Tomasz and Lachowski, Tomasz. 2016. Is There a Transnistrian Identity? *New Eastern Europe* 23(5): –94-99.

Guseinova, Esmira. 2012. *The Russia Interest Behind the Involvement in Georgia–South Ossetian Conflict*. Master's dissertation, Budapest University http://www.etd.ceu.hu/2012/guseinova_esmira.pdf.

Habermas, Jürgen. 1995. On the Internal Relation Between the Rule of Law and Democracy. *European Journal of Philosophy* 3(1): 12–20. doi.org/10.1111/j.1468-0378.1995.tb00036.x.

Hanhinen, Otto. 2019. Statehood and Recognition: The Transnistrian Question. *European Security Review*, 27 January. https://europeansecurityreview.wordpress.com/2019/01/27/statehood-and-recognition-the-transnistrian-question/.

Hatherley, Owen. 2016. *Landscapes of Communism: A History Through Buildings.* Penguin, London.

International Commission of Jurists. 2014. *Moldova: The Rule of Law in 2004.* Report of the Centre for the Independence of Judges and Lawyers.

Istomin, Igor and Irina Bolgova. 2016. Transnistrian Strategy in the Context of Russian–Ukrainian Relations: The Rise and Failure of 'Dual Alignment'. *Southeast European and Black Sea Studies* 16(1): 169–94.

Johansson, Andreas. 2006. The Transnistrian Conflict After the 2005 Moldovan Parliamentary Elections. *Journal of Communist Studies and Transition Politics* 22(4): 507–516. https://doi.org/10.1080/13523270601019565.

Johnson Coale, Ansley and Hoover, Edgar M. 1958. *Population Growth and Economic Development.* Princeton University Press.

Kapitonenko, Mykola. 2009. Resolving Post-Soviet "Frozen Conflicts": Is Regional Integration Helpful? *Caucasian Review of International Affairs* 3(1): 37–47. https://go.gale.com/ps/anonymous?id=GALE%7CA219451197&sid=googleScholar&v=2.1&it=r&linkaccess=abs&issn=18656773&p=AONE&sw=w.

Klimkiewicz, Beata. 2010. *Media Freedom and Pluralism: Media Policy Challenges in the Enlarged Europe.* CEU Press, Budapest.

Koller, Arne. 2018. *The Conflict in Transnistria: Historical Roots and Perspectives for Resolution.* 3 December. https://www.academia.edu/38311322/the_conflict_in_transnistria_historical_roots_and_perspectives_for_resolution?auto=download.

Kolobychko v. The Republic Of Moldova, Russia And Ukraine. 2018. ECHR, 18 September. https://www.bailii.org/eu/cases/ECHR/2018/725.html.

Kolstø, Pål and Malgin, Andrei. 1998. The Transnistrian Republic: A Case of Politicized Regionalism. *Nationalities Papers* 26(1): 103–127. https://doi.org/10.1080/00905999808408553.

Kosienkowski, Marcin. 2012. Is Internationally Recognised Independence the Goal of Quasi-States? The Case of Transnistria. In *Moldova: In Search of Its Own Place in Europe*, edited by Natalia Cwicinskaja and Piotr Oleksy: 55–65. http://dx.doi.org/10.2139/ssrn.2132161.

Kosienkowski, Marcin. 2017. The Gagauz Republic: Internal Dynamics of De Facto Statehood. *Annales Universitatis Mariae Curie-Skłodowska.* Section K: 115–133. DOI:10.17951/k.2017.24.1.115.

Krasniqi, Gëzim. 2018. *Contested Territories, Liminal Polities, Performative Citizenship: A Comparative Analysis.* Working Paper 2018/13, European University Institute.

Lankina, Tomila, Obydenkova, Anastasia and Libman, Alexander. 2016. Autocratic and Democratic External Influences in Post-Soviet Eurasia. *Comparative Political Studies* 49(2): 1599–1629. DOI:10.1177/0010414016628270.

Larreguy, Horacio and Marshall, John. 2020. The Incentives and Effects of Independent and Government-Controlled Media in the Developing World. In *The Oxford Handbook of Electoral Behavior.* Oxford Handbooks online. https://scholar.harvard.edu/files/jmarshall/files/media_and_persuasion_chapter_-_final_0.pdf.

Matthews, Jessica. 1997. Power Shift. *Foreign Affairs,* January/February. https://www.foreignaffairs.com/articles/1997-01-01/power-shift.

Media Sustainability Index. 2017. *Moldova.* https://www.irex.org/sites/default/files/pdf/media-sustainability-index-europe-eurasia-2017-moldova.pdf.

Miarka, Agnieszka. 2020. Para-States as an Instrument for Strengthening Russia's Position – The Case of Transnistria. *Journal of Strategic Security* 13(2): 1–18. https://doi.org/10.5038/1944-0472.13.2.1750.

Minakov, Mikhail. 2018. *Radical Periphery: Post Soviet Non-Recognised States* (1989–2018). Europa Universitaet Viadrina, 6 December. https://www.academia.edu/37950039/.

Minzarari, Dumitru. 2014. Crimea Crisis Exposes Severe Deficiencies in Transnistria Negotiations Format. *Eurasia Daily Monitor* 11(67) 9 April. https://www.refworld.org/docid/5346869d4.html.

Nodia, Ghia. 2004. Europeanization and (Not) Resolving Secessionist Conflicts. *Journal on Ethnopolitics and Minority Issues in Europe* 5(1): 1–15. https://www.ecmi.de/fileadmin/downloads/publications/jemie/2004/1-2004comment01.pdf.

OCSE. 2018a. *Commitment to Finalize all the Aspects of the "Package of Eight" Makes this Year Historic for Chisinau and Tiraspol, says OSCE Special Representative.* 30 May. https://www.osce.org/chairmanship/382879.

Papoutsi, Emilia. 2014. Frozen Conflict Zones: The Case of Transnistria. International Hellenic University. https://www.academia.edu/9652843.

Petterson, Bjorn. 2015. *External Evaluation of OHCHR Project "Combating Discrimination in the Republic of Moldova, including in the Transnistrian Region".* UN Commissioner for Human Rights. https://www.ohchr.org/Documents/AboutUs/Evaluation/CombatingDiscriminationRepMoldova.pdf.

Pridnestrovian Republican Newspaper. 2020. About the Newspaper. http://pridnestrovie-daily.net/about.

Promo-LEX. 2008. *The Military Service Obligations of the Inhabitants from the Transnistrian region of Moldova.* https://promolex.md/wp-content/uploads/2017/06/eng-doc_1233076724-2.pdf.

Radulescu, Bogdan-George. 2006. *The "Transnistrian Republic" and its Illegal Arms Export – A Major Security Risk.* International Studies Association. https://www.researchgate.net/publication/339816973.

Richter, Andrei. 2016. Defining Media Freedom in International Policy Debates. *Global Dynamics* 12(2): 127–142. https://journals.sagepub.com/doi/abs/10.1177/1742766516652164.

Risse, Thomas. 2012. *Introduction and Overview Governance in Areas of Limited Statehood*. Columbia University Press, New York.

Rosenberg, Matt. 2019. *The Difference Between a Country, State, and Nation*. ThoughtCo. thoughtco.com/country-state-and-nation-1433559.

Shelley, Robert. 2007. The Discourse Concept of the Rule of Law and Democracy. *Southern Cross University Law Review* 11(1): 59–79. http://www5.austlii.edu.au/au/journals/SCULawRw/2007/2.pdf.

Shevchuk, Nina. 2016. Settlement of Identity Conflicts: The Case of Transnistria. *International Trends* 104–117. https://www.academia.edu/43189124/.

Shevlane, Robin James. 2008. *National Minorities and Theories of the Modern State*. Northern PSA Postgraduate Conference.

Siddi, Marco and Gaweda, Barbara. 2011. *Bystander in its Neighbourhood? The EU's Involvement in Protracted Conflicts in the Post-Soviet Space*. Institut fur Europäische Politik. http://www.exact.uni-koeln.de/fileadmin/home/siddim/Protracted_conflicts_paper_updated.FINAL..pdf.

Snigyr, Olena. 2018. *A Comparative Analysis of Russian Expansionism in the Transnistria Region, the Donbas Region and Crimea, in Abkhazia and South Ossetia: Similarities and Differences*. Center for International Studies. https://www.academia.edu/36562257/.

Soskovets, Lyubov, Krasilnikov, Sergei and Mymrina, Dina. 2016. *Persecution of Believers as a Systemic Feature of the Soviet Regime*. SHS Conferences. DOI: 10.1051201628010.

Swedish Embassy in Moldova. 2018. *Impressive Results for Human Rights in Transnistria!* 17 January. https://www.swedenabroad.se/en/embassies/moldova-chisinau/current/news/impressive-results-for-human-rights-in-transnistria/.

Tabachnik, Maxim. 2017. *Defining the Nation in Russia's Buffer Zone: The Politics of Birthright: Citizenship in Azerbaijan, Moldova and Georgia*. PhD Dissertation, University of California, Santa Cruz. https://escholarship.org/uc/item/6hx5podl.

Tiersky, Alex. n.d. *Territorial Integrity*. Commission on Cooperation and Security in Europe. Accessed 26/6/19. https://www.csce.gov/issue/territorial-integrity.

Tiraspol Urban Site. 2016. *Our City Architecture*. http://urbantiraspol.ru/.

Toal, Gerald and O'Loughlin, John. 2014. How People in South Ossetia, Abkhazia and Transnistria Feel about Annexation by Russia. *Washington Post*, 20 March. https://www.washingtonpost.com/news/monkey-cage/wp/2014/03/20/how-people-in-south-ossetia-abkhazia-and-transnistria-feel-about-annexation-by-russia/#comments.

Treaty of Lisbon. 2007. Eur-Lex. http://data.europa.eu/eli/treaty/lis/sign.

Troebst, Stefan. 2004. The Transnistrian Moldovan Republic: From Conflict Driven State Building to State Driven Nation Building. *European Yearbook of Minority Issues* 2(1): 530. DOI:10.1163/221161103X00021.

Tumusiime, Jamal. 2007. The Crooked Ways of State Building: How Uganda and Transnistria Muddle Through the International System. *Working Papers Micropolitics No.4*. www.academia.edu/1997374/.

Turcescu, Lucian and Stan, Lavina. 2003. Church–State Conflict in Moldova: The

Bessarabian Metropolitanate. *Communist and Post-Communist Studies* 36: 443–465. https://www.academia.edu/3577707/.

Ulleberg, Inger. 2009. *The Role and Impact of NGOs in Capacity Development.* UNESCO. https://unesdoc.unesco.org/ark:/48223/pf0000186980.

United Nations Peacemaker. 1999. *Agreement Between the Republic of Indonesia and the Portuguese Republic on the Question of East Timor.* https://peacemaker.un.org/sites/peacemaker.un.org/files/ID%20TL_990505_AgreementOnEastTimor.pdf.

United States Department of State. 2020. *Trafficking in Persons Report.* https://www.state.gov/reports/2020-trafficking-in-persons-report/.

van de Kamp, Michiel. 2017. *An Orthodox Identity. The Russian Orthodox Church as Russia's Soft Power Tool in the Post-Soviet Space: The Case of Moldova.* Bachelor Thesis, Leiden University. https://www.academia.edu/34334464/.

Vaughan, Michael. 2011. *After Westphalia, Whither the Nation State, its People and its Governmental Institutions.* International Studies Association. https://espace.library.uq.edu.au/view/UQ:266787.

Waldron, Jeremy. 2016. The Rule of Law. In *Stanford Encyclopedia of Philosophy,* edited by Edward Zalta. https://plato.stanford.edu/entries/rule-of-law/.

Waters, Timothy. 2009. "The Momentous Gravity of the State of Things Now Obtaining": Annoying Westphalian Objections to the Idea of Global Governance. *Indiana Journal of Global Legal Studies* 16(1): 25–58. https://pdfs.semanticscholar.org/58a5/5be2299 79c94e694638362b0ff548b03e161.pdf.

Weber, Max 1919 *Politics as a Vocation.* Lecture, Munich, 28 January.

Wolff, Stefan. 2011. *The Prospects of a Sustainable Conflict Settlement for Transnistria.* 9 February. http://www.stefanwolff.com/files/the%20prospects%20of%20a%20sustainable%20conflict%20settlement%20for%20transnistria.pdf.

Wolff, Stefan and Weller, Marc. 2005. *Self-Determination and Autonomy: A Conceptual Introduction to Autonomy, Self-governance and Conflict Resolution: Innovative Approaches to Institutional Design in Divided Societies.* Routledge, Milton Keynes.

Zabarah, Daeg. 2012. Opportunity Structures and Group Building Processes: An Institutional Analysis of the Secession Processes in Pridnestrovie and Gagauzia between 1989 and 1991. *Communist and Post-Communist Studies* 45(1–2): 183–192. https://www.gla.ac.uk/media/Media_517293_smxx.pdf

C: NEW REFERENCES USED FOR PREFACE

Allen, William. 2021. Champions League 2021/22: how much money can clubs earn? *AS,* 26 August. Accessed 17/5/2022. https://en.as.com/en/2021/08/24/soccer/1629815178_447606.html

Avakov, Artur. 2021. Moldova will pay with gas for Russian observers expelled from the country (in Russian). *MKRU,* 12 December. Accessed 26/6/2022. https://www.

mk.ru/politics/2021/12/12/moldaviya-poplatitsya-gazom-za-vydvorennykh-iz-strany-rossiyskikh-nablyudateley.html

Ball, Tom. 2022 *Who could replace Putin? All bets are off, but don't expect a coup* . *The Times*, 9 March 2022. Accessed 1/7/2022. https://www.thetimes.co.uk/article/who-could-replace-putin-all-bets-are-off-but-dont-expect-a-coup-xttvjsgj2

BBC 2020. *What is quantitative easing and how will it affect you?* 5 November. Accessed 23/5/2022. https://www.bbc.co.uk/news/business-15198789

BBC. 2022. *How many Ukrainian refugees are there and where have they gone?* 23 June. Accessed 25/8/2022. https://www.bbc.co.uk/news/world-60555472

BBC. 2022a. *Ukraine conflict: What is Nato and how is it changing?* 29 June. Accessed 2/7/2022. https://www.bbc.co.uk/news/world-europe-18023383

BBC. 2022b. *Ukraine war could worsen crises in Yemen and Afghanistan.* 12 April. Accessed 3/7/2022. https://www.bbc.co.uk/news/world-60995064

BBC. 2020c. *Ukraine war: Missiles hit targets across country as G7 rallies over Russia.* 26 June. Accessed 3/7/2022. https://www.bbc.co.uk/news/world-europe-61943252

Bloomberg UK. 2022 *Russia More Than Triples Current-Account Surplus to $167 Billion.* 9 August 2022. Accessed 25/8/2022. https://www.bloomberg.com/news/articles/2022-08-09/russia-more-than-triples-current-account-surplus-to-167-billion

Bradley, Lance. 2021. *Transnistrian Presidential Elections 2021: Democratic Legitimacy Strangled by the Oligarchy.* De Facto states Research Unit, December 9. Accessed 1/7/2022. https://defactostates.ut.ee/blog/transnistrian-presidential-elections-2021-democratic-legitimacy-strangled

Braw, Elizabeth. Let's all chip in and buy weapons for Ukraine 2022. *The Times,* 30 May. Accessed 2/7/2022. https://www.thetimes.co.uk/article/lets-all-chip-in-and-buy-weapons-for-ukraine-3vrw8hhqo

Chirileasa, Andrei. 2022. Moldova Secures Gas Electricity May. *Romania Insider,* 2 May. Accessed 23/5/2022.https://www.romania-insider.com/moldova-secures-gas-electricity-may-2022

Davies, Rob & Elliott, Larry. 2022. How EU energy firms plan to pay for Russian gas without breaking the law. *The Guardian,* 28 April. Accessed 23/5/2022. https://www.theguardian.com/world/2022/apr/28/why-are-eu-energy-firms-agreeing-to-pay-for-russias-gas-in-roubles

The Economist. 2022. Russia's economy is back on its feet. 7 May. Accessed 23/5/2022. https://www.economist.com/finance-and-economics/2022/05/07/russias-economy-is-back-on-its-feet

EFE. 2022 Ukraine says 10,000 soldiers killed since start of Russian invasion. 11 June. Accessed 16.6.2022. https://www.efe.com/efe/english/portada/ukraine-says-10-000-soldiers-killed-since-start-of-russian-invasion/50000260-4829435

Elliott, Larry. 2022. Russia is winning the economic war - and Putin is no closer to withdrawing troops. *The Guardian,* 2 June. Accessed 23/5/2022. https://www.theguardian.com/commentisfree/2022/jun/02/russia-economic-war-ukraine-food-fuel-price-vladimir-putin

Erizanu, Paula. 2022. 'I don't feel safe here': Transnistria fears could spark Moldova exodus. *The Guardian,* 1 May 2022. Accessed 23/5/2022. https://www.theguardian.com/world/2022/may/01/i-dont-feel-safe-here-transnistria-fears-could-spark-moldova-exodus

Euractiv. 2021. Moldova pro-Europeans win resounding Election victory. 13 July. Accessed 2/7/2022. https://www.euractiv.com/section/europe-s-east/news/moldova-pro-europeans-win-resounding-election-victory/

Euractive. 2022 Moldova's pro-Russian leader calls for snap elections over gas price. Accessed 25/8/2022. https://www.euractiv.com/section/energy/news/moldovas-pro-russian-leader-calls-for-snap-elections-over-gas-price/

Euromaidan Press. 2022. *Tiraspol Airfield getting prepared to receive aircraft.* Twitter, 6 April. Accessed 1/7/2022. https://twitter.com/EuromaidanPress/status/1511637355639283712?ref_src=twsrc%5Etfw

Freedom House. 2022. Accessed 1/7/2022. *Freedom in the World.* https://freedomhouse.org/country/transnistria/freedom-world/2022

Gavin, Gabriel. 2022. Putin's war is forcing Moldova to escape Russia's gas trap *Politico,* 3 June. Accessed 3/7/2022. https://www.politico.eu/article/putin-war-forcing-moldova-escape-russia-gas-trap/

Gibbs, Dean. 2022. Radio Station Bombed In Transnistria, Kremlin Says It Is 'Monitoring Very Closely' Developments . *LKRLT* 26 April. Accessed 1/7/2022. https://www.lkrlt.org/radio-station-bombed-in-transnistria-kremlin-says-it-is-monitoring-very-closely-developments/

Gidadhubli, RG. 2004. Expansion of NATO- Russia's dilemma. *Economic and Political Weekly* 39 (19): 1885-1887. Accessed 16/5 /2022. https://www.jstor.org/stable/4414989

Herrera, Brenton. 2022. New explosions in Transnistria – At an airport near Ukraine. *JN News,* 7 May. Accessed 1/7/2022. https://www.fourals.com/2022/05/07/new-explosions-in-transnistria-at-an-airport-near-ukraine/

Infotag. 2021. Incumbent Tiraspol Leader Registered as Presidential Candidate for December 12 Elections. 28 October. Accessed 1/7/2022. http://www.infotag.md/rebelion-en/295020/

IPN. 2022. Residents of Transnistrian region who will go to Prosecutor's Office of Moldova or ECHR will be jailed. February 21. https://www.ipn.md/en/residents-of-transnistrian-region-who-will-go-to-prosecutors-

Keating, Joshua. 2022. *How many Russian soldiers have been killed in Ukraine? What we know, how we know it and what it really means.* Grid News, 22 August 2022. Accessed 25/8/2022. https://www.reuters.com/world/europe/almost-9000-ukrainian-military-killed-war-with-russia-armed-forces-chief-2022-08-22/

Kumzin, Nikolai. 2022. Isolated Transnistria Shaken by Tremors of War in Nearby Ukraine. *Balkan Insight*, 28 June. Accessed 2/7/2022. https://balkaninsight.com/2022/06/28/isolated-transnistria-shaken-by-tremors-of-war-in-nearby-ukraine/

Millar, Colin. 2021. Real Madrid stunned by Sheriff Tiraspol as Carlo Ancelotti finds loss "hard to describe". *Daily Mirror,* 28 September. Accessed 16/5/2022. https://www.mirror.co.uk/sport/football/news/real-madrid-sheriff-champions-league-25094738

Ministry of Health (Transnistria) (MoH(T)). 2022. *Coronavirus: official information on Pridnestrovie (in Russian)* 25 August. Accessed 25/8/2022. http://minzdrav.gospmr.org/covid-19

National Security Archive. 2017. *NATO Expansion: What Gorbachev Heard.* 12 December. Accessed 3/7/2022. https://nsarchive.gwu.edu/briefing-book/russia-programs/2017-12-12/nato-expansion-what-gorbachev-heard-western-leaders-early

NATO. 2022. *Relations with Ukraine.* 1 July 2022. Accessed 1/7/2022. https://www.nato.int/cps/en/natohq/topics_37750.htm

Necşuţu, Mădălin. 2020. Apathetic Voters Snub Election in Moldova's Breakaway Transnistria *Balkan Insight,* 30 November. Accessed 1 /7/2022. https://balkaninsight.com/2020/11/30/apathetic-voters-snub-election-in-moldovas-breakaway-transnistria/

Necşuţu, Mădălin. 2021. Although operational, the Iasi-Chisinau gas pipeline seems to have a decorative role, rather than a practical one *Verdica*, 9 December. Accessed 23 /5/2022. https://www.veridica.ro/en/analyses/although-operational-the-iasi-chisinau-gas-pipeline-seems-to-have-a-decorative-role-rather-than-a-practical-one

Necşuţu, Mădălin. 2022. Moldova Makes Plans to Escape Russian Energy Dependence *Balkan Insight,* April 20. Accessed 24/5/2022. https://balkaninsight.com/2022/04/20/moldova-makes-plans-to-escape-russian-energy-dependence/

Negura, Petru. 2021. *Transnistria Needs a Multi-Party System.* Leibniz-Institut fur Ost- and und Sudost Europaforschung, 9 December. Accessed 1/7/2022. https://ostblog.hypotheses.org/2089

Novosti Pridnestrovya. 2022.PMR security decision establishing "red" alert 22 April. Accessed 24/5/2022. https://novostipmr.com/en/news/22-04-26/pmr-security-council-decision-establishing-red-alert-because

Ombudsman of PMR. 2020. *About the Commissioner for Human Rights in the Pridnestrovian Moldavian Republic.* 30 March. Accessed 2/7/2022. http://www.ombudsmanpmr.org/upolnomochenniy.htm

OSCE. 2021. *Closing Remarks 2021 OSCE Ministerial Council*, 3 December. Accessed 3/7/2022. https://osce.usmission.gov/closing-remarks-at-the-2021-osce-ministerial-council/

Pashaeva, Yana. 2022. What Relatives Of Russian Troops Killed In Ukraine Think About The 'Special Military Operation' *The Wire* 19 June. Accessed 3/7/2022. https://thewire.in/world/relatives-russian-troops-killed-ukraine

President of the PMR ("President"). 2022. Quarantine announcement - preventative measure. 12 March. Accessed 3/7/2022. https://en.president.gospmr.org/press-sluzhba/novosti/obyyavlenie-karantina-profilakticheskaya-mera.html

President of the PMR ("President"). 2022a. *The state of emergency regime ended in Pridnestrovie.* Accessed 3/7/2022. https://en.president.gospmr.org/press-sluzhba/novosti/prezident-provel-zasedanie.html

Radio Free Europe (RFE). 2021. 22 September. Accessed 24/5/2022. https://www.rferl. org/a/moldova-russian-troop-withdrawal/31473470.html

Radio Free Europe (RFE). 2022. *Moldova's Separatist Transdniester Claims 'Drones Seen, Shots Fired' Near Huge Ammo Depot* . 4 November. Accessed 1/7/2022. https://www. rferl.org/a/OSCE_Reps_Barred_From_Moldovan_Journalists_Trial/2210869.html

Reuters. 2022. *Timeline: The events leading up to Russia's invasion of Ukraine.* 1 March. Accessed 25/8/2022. https://www.reuters.com/world/europe/ events-leading-up-russias-invasion-ukraine-2022-02-28/

Reuters. 2022a. *Almost 9,000 Ukrainian military killed in war with Russia -armed forces chief.* 23 August 2022. Accessed 25/8/2022. https://www.reuters.com/world/europe/ almost-9000-ukrainian-military-killed-war-with-russia-armed-forces-chief-2022-08-22/

Sabbagh, Dan. 2022. Russia claims to have targeted western-supplied tanks in Kyiv airstrikes. *The Guardian,* 5 June. Accessed 1/7/2022. https://www.theguardian.com/ world/2022/jun/05/russia-launches-air-strikes-into-kyiv-for-first-time-in-five-weeks

Sabbagh, Dan. 2022a. Ukraine asks the west for huge rise in heavy artillery supply. *The Guardian,* 13 June. Accessed 2/7/2022. https://www.theguardian.com/world/2022/ jun/13/ukraine-asks-the-west-for-huge-rise-in-heavy-artillery-supply

Sanchezr, Wilder Alejandro. 2022. Assessing a Possible Moldova-Romania Unification. *Geopolitical Monitor*, 6 January 2022. Accessed 2/7/2022. https://www.geopolitical-monitor.com/assessing-a-possible-moldova-romania-unification/

Sheftalovich, Zoya. 2022. Zelenskyy: Macron asked Ukraine to make concessions to help Putin save face. *Politico,* 13 May. Accessed 1/7/2022. https://www.politico.eu/article/ zelenskyy-macron-asked-ukraine-concession-help-putin-save-face/

Sidorenko, Sergey. Transnistrian War Threat for Ukraine. *New Geopolitics,* April 29. Accessed 2/7/2022. https://www.newgeopolitics.org/2022/04/29/ sydorenko-transnistrian-war-threat-for-ukraine/

Speck, Anna-Katrin. 2022. Russia and the Strasbourg Court: Evidentiary Challenges Arising from Russia's Expulsion from the Council of Europe *Strasbourg Observers*, 2 June 2022. Accessed 24/6/2022. https://strasbourgobservers.com/2022/06/02/russia-and-the-strasbourg-court-evidentiary-challenges-arising-from-russias-expulsion-from-the-council-of-europe/

Tadviser. 2022. Rosenberg Alexander Nikolaevich. Accessed 1/7/2022. https://tadviser. com/index.php/Person:Rosenberg_Alexander_Nikolaevich

TASS. 2020. Transnistrian issue can be solved only by peaceful means, Moldovan president-elect says. 2 December. Accessed 24/6/2022. https://tass.com/world/1230733

TASS. 2022. Macron says he has spent at least 100 hours in past six months in phone talks with Putin. 3 June. Accessed 16/5/2022. https://tass.com/world/1460595

Telegram. 2022. 25 April. Accessed 2/7/2022. https://t.me/tsvtiraspol/24925

Turp-Balazs, Craig. 2022. Is Russia attempting to reignite a frozen conflict in Moldova's Transnistria region? *Emerging Europe,* 27 April. Accessed 2/7/2022. https://emerging-europe.com/ news/is-russia-attempting-to-reignite-a-frozen-conflict-in-moldovas-transnistria-region/

United Nations Refugees Agency (UNHCR). 2022. Accessed 25/8/2022. *Ukraine Emergency* https://www.unrefugees.org/emergencies/ukraine/

United Nations Human Rights Office of the High Commissioner (UNHRO). 2022. UN Human Rights in Moldova: Providing vital support to Ukrainian refugees. 21 April. Accessed 24/6/2022. https://www.ohchr.org/en/stories/2022/04/un-human-rights-moldova-providing-vital-support-ukrainian-refugees

United Nations Human Rights Office of the High Commissioner (UNHRO). 2022a. Ukraine: civilian casualty update 22 August 2022. Accessed 25/8/2022.

VOA. 2022. *At 100 Days, Russia-Ukraine War by the Numbers.* 3 June. Accessed 3/7/ 2022. https://www.voanews.com/a/at-100-days-russia-ukraine-war-by-the-numbers/6601899.html

Vypritskikh, Anna. 2021. Another candidate announced his participation in the elections of the head of Transnistria. Who is it? (in Russian). *Newsmaker* 28 September. Accessed 1/7/2022. https://newsmaker.md/rus/novosti/esche-odin-kandidat-zayavil-o-svoem-uchastii-v-vyborah-glavy-pridnestrovya-kto-eto/

Wikipedia. 2022. *Tiraspol Airport.* Accessed 1/7/2022. https://en.wikipedia.org/wiki/Tiraspol_Airport

Wintour, Patrick. 2022. Response to Russia's war in Ukraine dominates G7 summit. *The Guardian,* 28 June. Accessed 2/7/2022. https://www.theguardian.com/world/2022/jun/28/g7-summit-talks-russia-war-ukraine

Wolff, Stefan & Bayok, Anastasiya. 2022. Ukraine war: fears that Belarus might invade on Russia's side are growing. *The Conversation.* Accessed 3/7/2022. https://theconversation.com/ukraine-war-fears-that-belarus-might-invade-on-russias-side-are-growing-185416

Worldometers. 2022. *Coronavirus.* 25 August 2022. Accessed 25/8/2022. https://www.worldometers.info/coronavirus/

ACKNOWLEDGEMENTS

A project like this, of course, does not come to fruition without many people helping the author, and this section is an opportunity for me to thank some who have helped.

Before I started, I spoke to many academics for advice and to discuss whether I would make a good fit with their institution. Particularly enthusiastic and helpful was Pete Duncan at UCL's School of Slavonic Studies. Both Claire Gordon and Tomilla Lankina at the LSE gave me assistance in formulating what it was I was asking in the thesis and indeed understanding how academia works. Along the way I briefly met Stepan Wolff, the doyen of Transnistrian issues, who provided useful insight into what I was writing about. Michael Bobick, although no longer an academic, was happy to discuss the topic and gave me useful food for thought. Alia Ostavnaia kindly released me an early copy of her compendious and valuable research on the Transnistrian migrants, which was essential for any writing on that topic.

I have had three supervisors whose efforts I have been grateful for. Valentina Kostadinova was initially put in charge of me. Her concern for detail was a good sop to my occasional sloppiness. Some of the comments she made, on a topic which is far from central to her own considerable expertise, were breathtakingly insightful. It was an honour, as well as a pleasure to work, and share many bottles of wine, with David Armstrong nearing the end of a stellar academic career. The biggest debt though is to Stephen Wilkinson who in the last year took on the task of converting the writing skills of a lawyer who dabbled in journalism, to those which might just stand muster in the academic world. Without his inspiring teaching my original jottings would have remained just that rather than becoming an actual thesis.

Other Buckingham academics, Bill Kappis, John Drew, Stefan Hawlin and Julian Richards provided much needed encouragement along the way and John Adamson, the high-level organisation required to keep the work on track when it might have run aground.

Much help was received in Transnistria and Moldova. In the text I refer many times to Vladimir Yastrebchak, without whose involvement much of the most important research material would not have been obtained. He was as generous with his own time as he was with his contacts book- which includes anyone who is anyone in the territory. This help was freely given, and except for hinting that he would appreciate the inclusion of the multi-national stamps he had been involved in designing, never attempted to influence what I would write, let alone ask for any form of copy approval. Thanks Vladimir, and I hope to see you in an even more senior position in the territory before too long.

Other 'elite' Transnistrians who went out of their way to help were Igor Smirnov, the former President; Ruslan Mova, the Minister for Internal Affairs; Sergy Vasilievich, governor of the women's prison; Sergy Kirman, head of the Tiraspol police; Vladimir Rimar, of the Supreme Court; and Oleg Kabaloev of the Constitutional Court. They, like the civil servants with whom I liaised, were invariably charming, and amiably answered my questions. Thanks too to Anastasia and Demitry of the MFA for being such good company as well as knowledgeable guides while I was observing the election, and Ruslan Mova's assistant Eugen who used his influence to arrange access to many people.

Shevchenko University gave me encouragement and access to its staff and students that proved invaluable. Stepan Beril the rector took a polite interest in the project and assigned me 'minders', firstly Vlada Lisenco and then Natalia Shchukina, both of whom gave far more help than they could be reasonably expected to and provided important introductions. Many academics and students were willing to talk to me, particularly helpful among the former were Yuriy Mamatuk, Irena Lemeshva and Olga Leontieva. I am very grateful to all those who took the trouble to introduce themselves, and to the languages department for arranging discussion groups.

The staff of Apriori in Tiraspol, particularly Stepan Popovskiy and Alexandra Telpis, and PromoLex's Ion Manole in Chisinau, were sources of very helpful information on the human rights situation in the territory. Anna Kondrashchenko of the Tiraspol *hesed* told me about Jewish life in the territory and I am grateful to her and to Paul Anticoni of World Jewish Relief who put me in touch with her.

In Chisinau the Bureau of Reintegration went out of its way to accommodate my requests for meetings and information. As well as Alin Gvidiani, the deputy-director, whose interview and emails feature in the text, other staff, particularly Eugen Cara, assisted and I am grateful. In London the Moldovan ambassador Angela Ponomariov and Vilen Murzac the *Charge d'Affaires* were very helpful. The British embassy in Chisinau, particularly former ambassador Phil Batson, who struck me as an exceptionally committed and concerned diplomat, and current political secretary Chrystele Todd met me and helped me understand the official British perspective, and several others provided email support.

One constant and essential presence throughout the project and particularly my trips to the territory was my interpreter Kateryna (Kate) Vaishenglots. The few occasions when I had to use other interpreters showed how invaluable she was. Kate's occasional habit of lapsing into Russian conversation with interviewees and others was more than compensated for by her willingness to gossip about the fruits of those conversations afterwards, and ability to consume as much Moldovan wine as me while doing so.

Lauren Patrick proofed the text with accuracy, thoroughness and speed. Any errors that remain are likely to be a consequence of me disregarding her recommendations rather than any omission on her part.

I was lucky enough to have the work marked by emeritus Professor Ronald Hill of Trinity College, Dublin, who had himself spent a year in Tiraspol in the late 1960's and written an excellent book about his experiences. Not only was he kind enough to forgive the lazy assumption in the originally submitted text that he was Irish, like his fellow examiner, Dr Paul Graham a senior lecturer in politics at Buckingham University, he made many helpful suggestions for improvements to the texts, that have found their way into this version.

I am grateful to the University of Buckingham Press for the assistance given in getting this ready for publication and indeed in showing confidence in an "unknown" author. Christian Müller has worked with considerable effort and tolerance in turning my Word document into a presentable book, and has assisted me with devising a means of keeping the work up to date in the light particularly of the Ukraine war.

Finally, I must express gratitude to Emma and the rest of my family. While their support may have been moral rather than practical, their tolerance of my tendency to prattle on about such an obscure subject has helped me focus my thoughts and has been an important stepping stone on the way to completing the work.

INDEX

Lightning Source UK Ltd.
Milton Keynes UK
UKHW020228101022
410220UK00007B/113